HUNTER PUBLISHING, INC.
130 Campus Drive, Edison NJ 08818
(732) 225 1900, (800) 255 0343; fax (732) 417 0482

IN CANADA
Ulysses Travel Publications
4176 Saint-Denis
Montreal, Quebec H2W 2M5 Canada
(514) 843 9882, ext. 2232; fax 514 843 9448

ISBN 1-55650-902-2
Fourth Edition

Copyright © 2001 by Payot/Rivages

For complete information about the hundreds of other travel guides offered by Hunter Publishing, visit our website at **www.hunterpublishing.com**

**Bed & Breakfasts
of Character and Charm in France**
Translator: Jack Monet, and Anne Norris
Front cover photograph: Foulara (Cruis – Provence - Riviera)
Back cover: Le Jau (Pays de la Loire)

Special Sales
Hunter Travel Guides can be purchased in quantity at special discounts. For more information, contact us at the address above.

Printed in Italy by Litho Service
10 9 8 7 6 5 4 3 2 1

BED AND
BREAKFASTS
of Character and Charm
IN FRANCE

Hunter Publishing, Inc.
www.hunterpublishing.com

Important

In accordance with standard jurisprudence (Toulouse, 14.01.1887), the publisher of this guide cannot be held responsible for any errors or omissions that may have remained despite the best efforts of the writing and editing staff.

We also inform readers that we can in no case be held responsible for any litigation arising between the users of this guide and the owners of the houses.

HUNTER RIVAGES

BED AND BREAKFASTS
of Character and Charm
IN FRANCE

Project editor
Véronique De Andreis

Conceived by
Jean and Tatiana de Beaumont,
Véronique De Andreis, Anne Deren,
and Jean-Emmanuel Richomme

Hunter Publishing, Inc.
www.hunterpublishing.com

I N T R O D U C T I O N

This tenth edition of our guide has been entirely updated and presents a selection of 680 *maison d'hôtes* (bed and breakfast establishments), including 58 new addresses. This year, as in the past, we have explored the highways and byways of France to seek out new addresses or to verify old ones, in order to offer you the best possible choice.

Let yourself be tempted by these places of "charm and character." Appreciate their excellent location and lovely surroundings, their atmosphere, authenticity, and not least of all, their comfort and the quality of their amenities. The owners will be happy to accommodate you for a night, a weekend or a longer holiday stay and to share with you a moment of their lives.

Whether you're looking for independence or sociability, authentic country living or sophisticated elegance, comfort or simplicity, whatever your preference or your budget, you will find the holiday home of your dreams. Each house has its own style and personality, from old-fashioned country homes to genuine châteaux, including elegant manor houses, old family dwellings, farmhouses (some refurbished as guest houses, others on working farms), old mills or mountain chalets.

The owners of these B&Bs will help you get to know their region. They will advise you about places to see and things to do, point out good restaurants, local "fêtes," interesting itineraries in the area, and will do their utmost to make you feel at home.

The houses reflect the personality of their owners, some more outgoing and spontaneous, others cooler and more reserved. Some of them may become real friends. But keep in mind that these are privately owned homes and the services offered cannot be the same as in a hotel.

How to choose a B&B:

To guide you in your selection, each house listed is accompanied by a photo and a brief descriptive text, as well as detailed practical information.

You can refer to the table of contents in the front of the book, where the listings are by region, or the alphabetical index at the back. The listings are arranged alphabetically by region, and within each region by department, name of town or village and, lastly, by the name of the house.

At the front of this guide you will find detailed maps showing the location of all the houses. Each house is identified by a numbered flag, the number corresponding to the number of its listing in the guide. To locate the region you are looking for, refer to the general map of France that precedes the detailed sections.

How to reserve:

As the number of rooms is usually limited, it is wise to reserve well in advance. Booking conditions are set by the individual owners and vary from one house to another. As a general rule, you will be asked to send a deposit together with a written note of confirmation. You should mention what time you plan to arrive so that the owners will be there to greet you. This is especially important in the country, where houses are often guarded by dogs and it's best not to show up unexpected. Also specify whether or not you wish to have dinner the first evening. Make every effort to arrive at the stated time and telephone if you are delayed. If you arrive too late the owner has the right to rent the room to someone else. Depending on where you're coming from, you

can also ask for further directions about finding the place.

Prices:

The prices indicated in the guide are those quoted to us at the time we went to press. You should however ask for confirmation when you phone, as they may have changed in the course of the year.

In case of cancellation:

Conditions of cancellation are also variable and are set by the owners, so be sure to get all the necessary information at the time of booking.

Part or all of the deposit may be kept by the owner in case of cancellation

Rooms:

Just as the houses vary in style and decoration, so do the rooms, which range from quite simple to extremely luxurious. In general, we select only rooms with private bath or shower and toilet. There are some exceptions, which are always indicated, often, for example, an extra bedroom that can be used by children or members of the same party.

Rooms are cleaned regularly, sometimes daily. In a number of homes, however, you are expected to make your own bed, and in some cases (always specified) rooms are cleaned only on request or are left to the responsibility of the guests.

Meals:

Here too there is a good deal of variation. The *table d'hôtes* dinner, a communal evening meal, is an excellent opportunity to get to know your hosts better, to meet the other guests, chat and exchange travel experiences. If such a meal is proposed, make your reservation as soon as possible.

Most of the time, dinner is casual and family style, though in some cases it is extremely elegant. The prices vary greatly depending on style, service, and cuisine. Meals are served at fixed times.

In some houses, dinner is served at separate tables. If a particular house does not serve dinner, the owners will recommend local restaurants.

Telephone:

In most of the houses, the telephones are not equipped for billing guests individually. The most convenient solution is to purchase a *France-Télécom* phone card or to bring along your own portable.

Do not hesitate to write to us to share your experiences and to make any comments or suggestions.

If you have discovered a B&B that you think should be included in our guide, let us have the address and the name of the owner and we will be happy to consider it for selection.

All correspondence should be addressed to:

Véronique de Andreis
Editions Payot & Rivages
Bed and Breakfasts of Character and Charm in France
106, boulevard Saint-Germain
75006 Paris
France

You can also contact us on the Guides Rivages' website at:
http://www.guidesdecharme.com

Or get in touch via our US website at
http://www.hunterpublishing.com

CONTENTS

BRETAGNE (BRITTANY)

CÔTES-D'ARMOR (22)

MIDI - PYRÉNÉES

NORD (NORTH) - PAS-DE-CALAIS

NORMANDIE (NORMANDY)

PAYS DE LA LOIRE

PICARDIE

AISNE (02)

OISE (60)

SOMME (80)

POITOU - CHARENTES

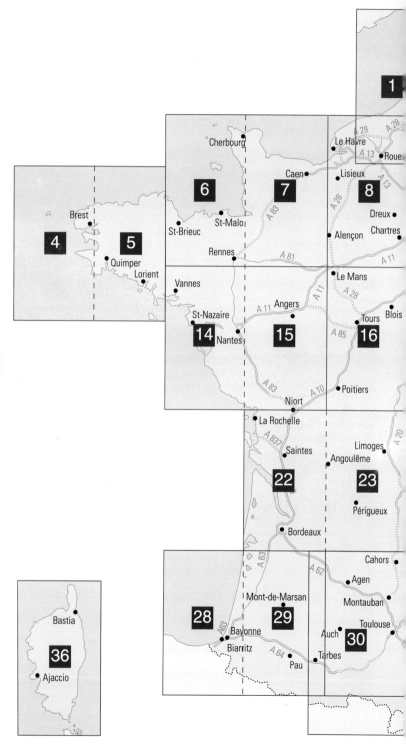

Cherbourg

Le Havre · Roue

A 29 · A 28

A 13 · Roue

1

6

7

Caen · Lisieux

A 13

8

Brest

St-Malo

Dreux ·

Chartres

4

5

St-Brieuc

Alençon

A 11

Quimper

Rennes

A 81

Lorient

A 83

Vannes

Le Mans

A 28

St-Nazaire

Angers

A 11

Blois

Tours

14

Nantes

15

A 85

16

A 83

A 10

Poitiers

Niort

La Rochelle

A 837

Limoges

A 20

Saintes

Angoulême

22

23

Périgueux

Bordeaux

A 63

Cahors

A 62

Agen

Bastia

Mont-de-Marsan

Montauban

36

28

29

Toulouse

A 63

Bayonne

Auch

30

Ajaccio

Biarritz

A 64

Tarbes

Pau

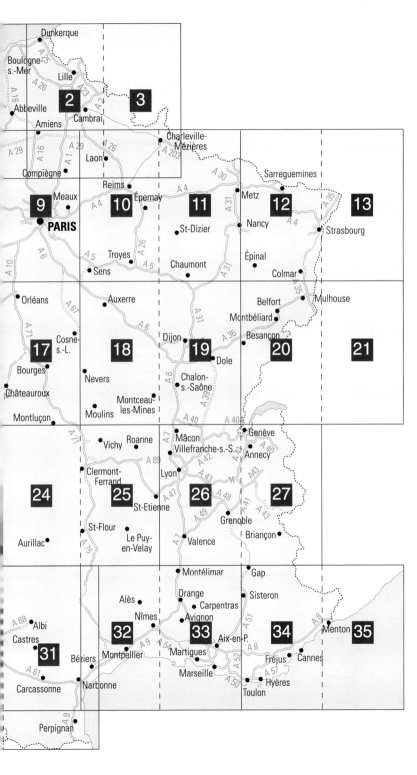

KEY TO THE MAPS

Scale : 1:1,000,000
maps 30 and 31 : scale 1:1,200,000

MOTORWAYS

A9 – L'Océane

Under construction
projected

ROADS
Highway
Dual carriageway
Four lanes road
Major road
Secondary road

TRAFFIC
National
Regional
Local

JUNCTIONS
Complete
Limited

DISTANCES IN KILOMETRES
On motorway
On other road

10

10

BOUNDARIES
National boundary
Region area
Department area

URBAIN AREA

Town
Big city
Important city
Medium city
Little city

AIRPORTS

FORESTS

PARKS
Limit
Center

Cartography

Sélection
du Reader's Digest

Created by

Editerra

4

Plouguerneau
Landéda D10
Portsall • Lannilis
Ploudalmézeau •
Porspoder • • Plouguin
• Plourin
Brélès • Bourg-B.
Gouesnou
St-Renan 13
24 **Brest**
Le Conquet

Lampaul

Ile Molène

MER

D'IROISE

Camaret-s.-Mer •
Lanvéoc
Crozon 9 Tal-a Groa
• Morgat

Baie de Douarnenez

Ile de Sein Plogoff Pont-Croix
Audierne
Plouhinec
Plozévet

Pouldreuz'

Penmarc'h

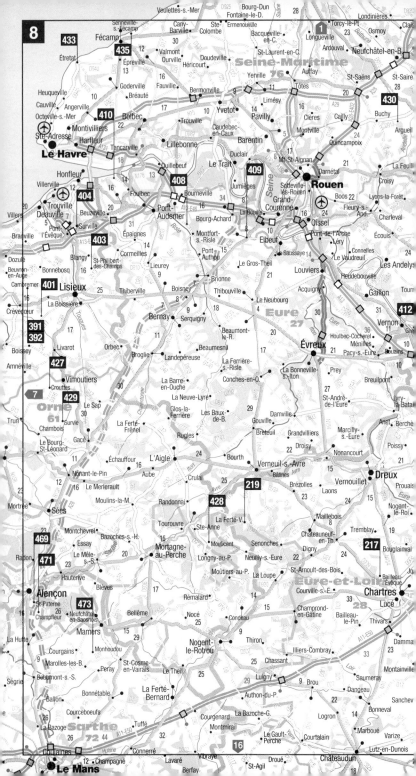

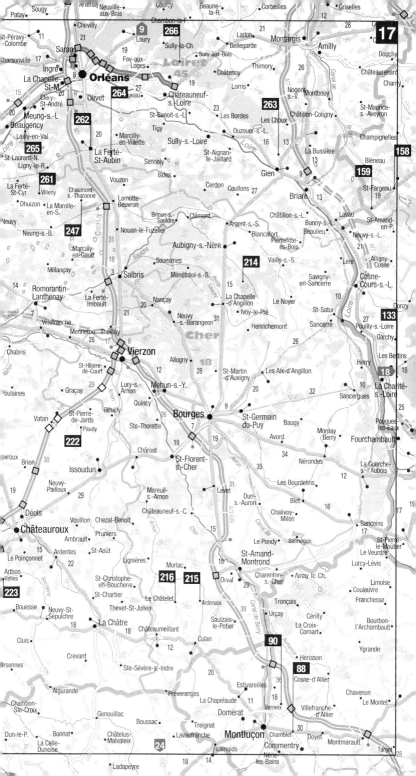

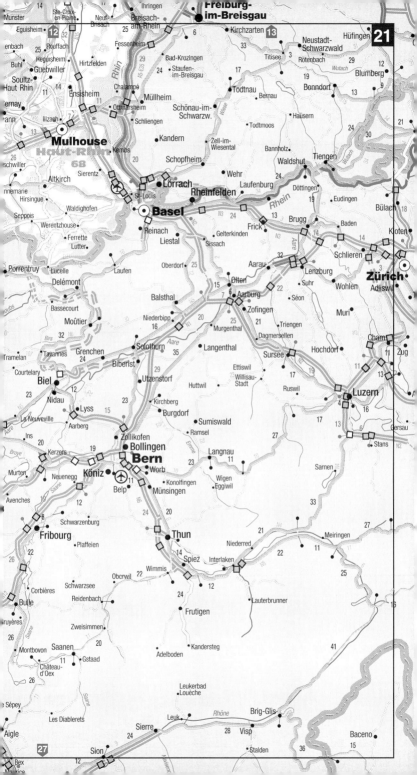

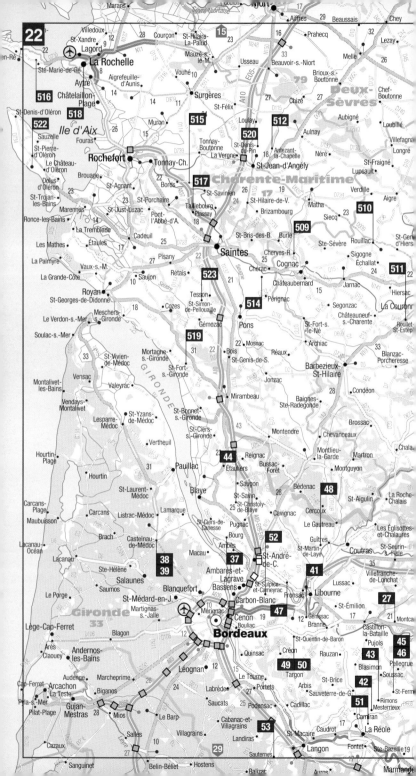

Mimizan-Plage

Contis-Plage

Lit-et-Mixe

St-Girons-Plage
St-Girons-
en-Marensin

Léon

60

Messanges
Vieux-Boucau

Soustons

St-Geours-
de-Maremne
Soorts-
Hossegor 16

Hossegor
Capbreton

St-Vincent-
de-Tyrosse
19

74

Labenne

Ondres
9

78

Tarnos
Boucau

18

17 **77**

76

Bayonne

Anglet
Biarritz

Adour Urt

86
87

24

Bidart

80

Briscous

Guéthary

Arbonne Arcangues

La Bastide-
Clairence 17

Bidasoa

St-Jean-de-Luz

Ustaritz

Hasparren

Bonloc

Hendaye

Ciboure

Cambo-
les-B.

St-Esteben

Lekeitio

Urrugne

22
Sare

St-Pée-s.-N.

Louhossoa

Ondarroa

Irun

28

Ainhoa

Espelette

Iholdy

Deba

20

A8

19

Vera-de-
Bidasoa

Dancharia

Markina
Alzola
21
6

San Sebastian

29

Lesaca

Bidarray

Calay

Zarauz

Zestoa

Usurbil

Hernani

Oyartzun

83
84
85

Elgoibar
Eibar

18

Iroulèguy

St-Jean-
le-Vieux

24

Santuario de S.
Ignacio de Loyola
10

19

Andoain

St-Étienne-
de-Baïgorry

St-Jean-
Pied-de-Port

Bergara

Azpeitia

Villabona

Baztan

Régil

Goizueta

Arrasate-
Mondragon

Irurita

Aldudes

Arnéguy

43

Villafranca-de-Ordizia

Tolosa

Santesteban

30

Eskoriatza

Beasain

Oñati

Arantzazu
21

20

28

Leiza

Zubieta

Ezcurra

Roncesvalles
Orbaiceta

Betelu

Jaunsaras

33

Eugui

Burguete

17

Alsasua

35

Echarri-
Aranaz

Lecumberri

Larasa

Ulzama

Olazagutia

Villanueva

14

Goni

Anoz

27

Zubiri
Enderiz

Erro

Arrieta

Arive

14

22

Oiza

Echauri

Villava

Egués

Itoiz

Salinas-

Pamplona

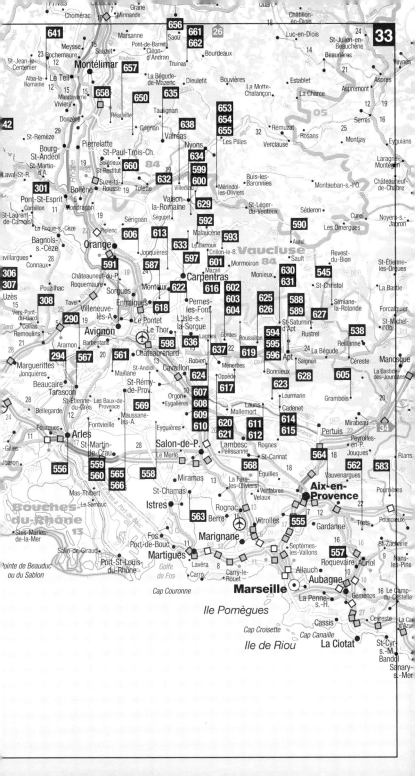

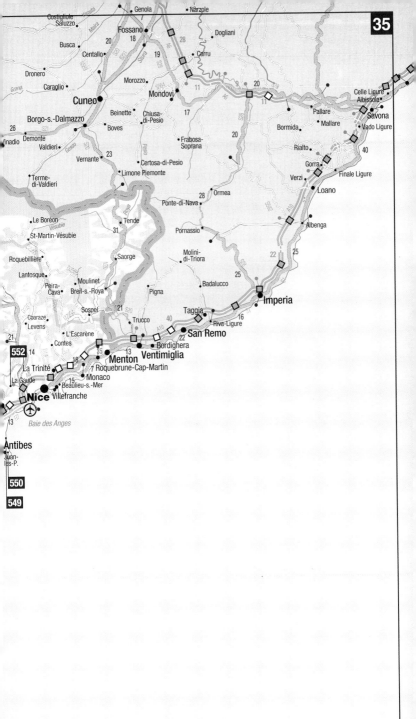

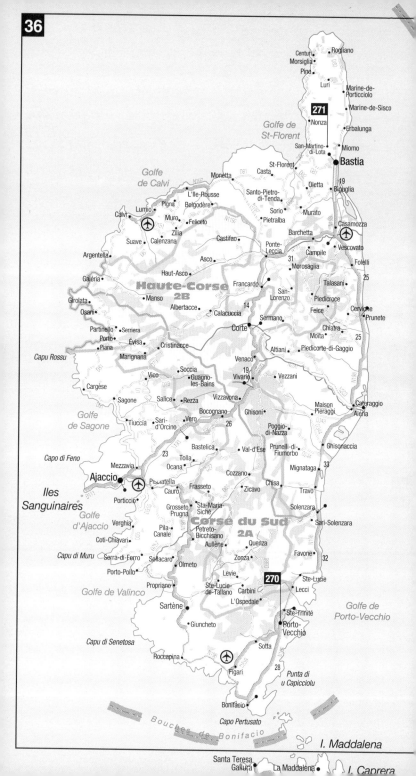

Centuri • • Rogliano
Morsiglia •
Pino •
Luri •
Marine-de-Porticciolo •
Marine-de-Sisco •

271

Nonza •
Erbalunga •

*Golfe de
St-Florent*

San-Martino-di-Lota •
Miomo •
● **Bastia**

St-Florent •
Monetta •
Casta •
Oletta •
19
Biguglia •

*Golfe
de Calvi*

Santo-Pietro-di-Tenda •
Sorio •
Pietralba •
Murato •
Barchetta •
✈ Casamozza
Vescovato •

L'Île-Rousse •
Pigna •
Belgodère •
Muro •
Feliceto •
Castifao •
Ponte-Leccia •
Campile •
Folelli •

Calvi •
Lumio •
Zilia •
Calenzana •
Asco •
31
Morosaglia •
25

Suave •
Haut-Asco •
Francardo •
San-Lorenzo •
Talasani •

Argentella •
Piedicroce •
Felce •
Cervione •
Prunete •

Galéria •
14
Calacuccia •
Sermano •
Chiatra •
Moïta •

Girolata •
Albertacce •
Haute-Corse 2B
Corte
25

Osani •
Manso •
Altiani •
Piedicorte-di-Gaggio •

Partinello • Serriera •
Porto •
Évisa •
Cristinacce •
Venaco •
Vezzani •

Piana •
Marignana •
Soccia •
19
Vivario •

Capu Rossu
Vico •
Guagno-les-Bains •

Cargèse •
Salice • Rezza •
Vizzavona •
Maison Pieraggi •
Cateraggio •
Aléria •

Sagone •
Vero •
Bocognano •
Ghisoni •

*Golfe
de Sagone*
Tiuccia •
Sari-d'Orcino •
26
Poggio-di-Nazza •

Capo di Feno
Bastelica •
Val-d'Ese •
Prunelli-di-Fiumorbo •
Ghisonaccia •

23
Tolla •
33
Mignataga •

Mezzavia •
Ocana •
Cozzano •
Chisa •
Travo •

● **Ajaccio** ✈
Pisciatella •
Cauro •
Frasseto •
Zicavo •

*Iles
Sanguinaires*
Porticcio •
Grosseto-Prugna •
Sta-Maria-Siché •
Solenzara •

*Golfe
d'Ajaccio*
Verghia •
Pila-Canale •
Corse du Sud 2A
Petreto-Bicchisano •
Sari-Solenzara •

Coti-Chiavari •
Serra-di-Ferro •
Aullène •
Quenza •

Capu di Muru
Solacaro •
Olmeto •
Zonza •
Favone •
32

Porto-Pollo •
Levie •
Ste-Lucie •

Propriano •
Ste-Lucie-de-Tallano •
Carbini •
Lecci •

270

Golfe de Valinco
Sartène •
L'Ospedale •
Ste-Trinité •
Porto-Vecchio •

*Golfe de
Porto-Vecchio*

• Giuncheto
Sotta •

Capu di Senetosa
Roccapina •
✈
28
*Punta di
u Capicciolu*

Figari •

Bonifacio •

Capo Pertusato

Bouches de Bonifacio
I. Maddalena

Santa Teresa
Gallura •
La Maddalena •
I. Caprera

A L S A C E - L O R R A I N E

1 - Château Labessière

55320 Ancemont
(Meuse)
Tel. 03 29 85 70 21
Fax 03 29 87 61 60
M. and Mme Eichenauer
E-mail: rene.eichenauer@wanadoo.fr

Rooms 3 and 1 suite with bath or shower and WC. **Price** 400F/60,98€ (2 pers.), suite 600F/91,46€ (2 pers. and 2 children), +50F/7,62€ (extra pers.). Ask for our all inclusive US pack. **Meals** Breakfast incl. Evening meals at communal table or not 125F/19,05€. Half board 325F/49,54€ (per pers., children's reductions). **Facilities** Sitting room, covered parking, swimming pool with whirlpool, tandem, airplane tour of Verdun and battlefields. **Credit card** Amex. **Spoken** English, German. **Closed** Christmas and New Year's. **How to get there** (Map 11): Strasbourg Autoroute, Verdun exit, towards Dieue, then right to Ancemont. On Paris Autoroute, exit Voie Sacrée toward Bar-le-Duc to Lemmes, then left to Senoncourt-Ancemont.

You will receive a warm welcome in this small château opposite an old wash house in the village of Ancemont. The interior has been completely refurbished, offering comfortable, well-kept bedrooms and lovely antique wardrobes. One of them, with old woodwork, faces the park. Some of the bathrooms could use a bit of improvement.The ground-floor furniture is less authentic. Breakfast and excellent dinners are served at several tables in the pleasant dining room. The garden is very pretty, despite some noise from the road.

2 - Château d'Alteville

Tarquimpol
57260 Dieuze
(Moselle)
Tel. 03 87 86 92 40
Fax 03 87 86 02 05
M. and Mme L. Barthélemy

Rooms 6 with bath, WC and tel. **Price** 500F/76,22€ (2 pers.). **Meals** Breakfast 45F/6,86€. Evening meals at communal table, by reservation 200F/30,49€ (wine not incl.). **Nearby** Restaurants, tennis, riding, fishing. **Credit cards** Not accepted. **Spoken** English, German. **Open** Apr 15 – Oct 15. **How to get there** (Map 12): 54km east of Nancy via N74 and D38 towards Dieuze, then D999 towards Gelucourt and D199F, then D199G.

This is a very charming country property close to a number of lakes. The public rooms include a billiard room/library, a drawing room with antique furniture, and a dining room festooned with hunting trophies. The bedrooms are a bit small and the decoration somewhat disappointing, particularly in view of the prices. However, the spontaneity and good humor of Monsieur and Madame Barthélemy well make up for it. Delicious table d'hôte dinners are elegantly served with fine china, crystal and silverware.

3 - La Musardière

57340 Lidrezing
(Moselle)
Tel. 03 87 86 14 05
Fax 03 87 86 40 16
Cécile and René Mathis
E-mail: musardiere.mathis@free.fr

Rooms 3 with bath or shower (incl. 1 with whirlpool, +40F/6,09€), WC, TV, minibar and tel. **Price** 310F/47,26€ (2 pers.). Special rates in low season and after 2 nights. **Meals** Breakfast incl. Evening meals at communal table, by reservation 110-150F/16,77-22,87€ (wine not incl.). Vegetarian or regional cooking. **Facilities** Sitting room, fragrance garden. **Pets** Dogs not allowed. **Nearby** Tennis, golf, riding, hiking in Lorraine Regional Park; Vic sur Seille, Marsal. **Credit cards** Not accepted. **Spoken** English, German. **Open** Easter – Nov 1. **How to get there** (Map 12): Autoroute A31 20km south of Metz direction Nancy, Saint-Avold exit. In Han-sur-Nied, D999 towards Morhange, then 10km towards Dieuze; follow signs.

This is a small, simple and unpretentious village house where you will find a warm and attentive welcome. The bedrooms are quiet and have many useful and charming objects for guests' pleasure. However, the upstairs rooms are somewhat dark, having small windows, and we therefore prefer the ones on the ground floor. Excellent dinners are served in a bright room overlooking the garden, where you will find some thirty aromatic plants and herbs.

4 - Chez M. et Mme d'Andlau

15, rue du Haut Village
Stotzheim
67140 Barr
(Bas-Rhin)
Tel. 03 88 08 90 45
Fax 03 88 08 48 06
M. and Mme Raymond d'Andlau

Rooms 2 with shower and basin and shared WC. **Price** 300F/45,73€ (2 pers.). **Meals** Breakfast incl. No communal meal. **Facilities** Sitting room. **Pets** Dogs not allowed. **Nearby** Restaurants, tennis (1km), bicycles, riding, hiking; Haut-Koenigsbourg, Unterlinden museum (Colmar), Mont Sainte-Odile, Romanesque church, "Bibliothèque humaniste" (Sélestat). **Closed** Oct 15 – Apr 15. (2 nights min.). **How to get there** (Map 12): 9km south of Obernai. From Strasbourg N422, exit Zellwiller, to Stotzheim, turn on right before the bridge, then on left.

On the route winding through the Alsatian vineyards, this 18th-century gentilhommière covered with Virginia creeper is in a quiet location, its two guest rooms decorated with old furniture and interesting engravings on the walls. Overlooking trees and shrubs, one room has a double bed, and the other twin beds. In each room, the washbasin and shower are concealed behind a floral curtain. The colorful living room with its ceramic stove and ancestral portraits offers the relaxing atmosphere of a country house.

ALSACE - LORRAINE

5 - Chez M. et Mme Krumeich

23, rue des Potiers
67660 Betschdorf
(Bas-Rhin)
Tel. 03 88 54 40 56
Fax 03 88 54 47 67
M. and Mme Christian Krumeich

Rooms 3 with shower, WC and TV. **Price** 200-290F/30,49-44,21€ (2 pers.), +80F/12,19€ (extra pers.). **Meals** Breakfast incl. No communal meal. **Restaurant** "La Table des Potiers" in Betschdorf. **Facilities** Sitting room, sheltered parking, garden sitting room, pottery courses (extra charge). **Pets** Dogs not allowed. **Nearby** Swimming pool, tennis, pottery museum, picturesque villages. **Credit card** Visa. **Spoken** English, German. **Open** All year. **How to get there** (Map 13): 15km north of Haguenau via D263 towards Wissembourg, then D243.

Betschdorf is well-known as a village of potters and the house we have selected here belongs to one of them. The rooms are of different sizes and appointed in various ways, but all are quiet and comfortable. We would particularly recommend the one that has just been installed on the ground floor. Although the breakfast room is not very exciting, it is livened up by some nice pieces of stoneware. Breakfast itself is good and the welcome is pleasant.

6 - Le Tire-Lyre

2, hameau du Tirelire
67310 Cosswiller
(Bas-Rhin)
Tel. 03 88 87 22 49
Fax 03 88 87 29 46
Mme Maud Bochart

Rooms 3 and 1 suite of 2 bedrooms (4 pers.) with bath and WC. **Price** From 2 nights 300F/45,73€ (1pers.), 400F/60,97€ (2 pers., double bed), 450F/68,60€ (2 pers., twin beds), suite 650F/99,09€ (4 pers.); +50F/7,62€ for 1 night. **Meals** Breakfast incl. No communal meal. **Restaurants** 3km away and farm/auberge in village (by reserv.: 03 88 87 04 70). **Pets** Dogs allowed in kennel. **Facilities** Sitting room. **Nearby** Tennis, riding, hiking; châteaux, Westhoffen. **Credit cards** Not accepted. **Closed** Jun, Jul, Aug and Jan. **How to get there** (Map 12): 25km west of Strasbourg. RN4 between Strasbourg and Saverne. In Wasselonne take the road towards Cosswiller in the direction of the fountain and the road to the village (800m); signposted.

You can't miss the charming Tire-Lyre and its garden which are located in a small hamlet surrounded by pastures and woodland. This is a remarkably well kept hotel, which has been lovingly decorated by Madame Bochart. With several handsome pieces of antique furniture, the owner's passion for beautiful fabrics can be seen in each comfortable bedroom, where the pretty curtains, bed canopies and eiderdowns are beautifully coordinated. There is a large, bright sitting room in which to relax, and the breakfasts, served on beautiful china, are excellent.

7 - Chez Colette

19, rue de Neuve-Église
67220 Dieffenbach-au-Val
(Bas-Rhin)
Tel. 03 88 57 60 91
Fax 03 88 85 60 48
Mme Colette Geiger

Rooms 1 studio (3 pers.) with shower and WC. Rooms cleaned every day; linens changed every 5 days. **Price** 290F/44,21€ (2 pers.), +100F/15,24€ (extra bed). **Meals** Breakfast incl. No communal meal. **Pets** Dogs not allowed. **Nearby** Restaurants, tennis, swimming pool (4km), cross-country and downhill skiing (15km); Haut-Kœnigsbourg, Riquewihr, Wine Route, Mont Sainte-Odile, swan park, eagle sanctuary. **Credit cards** Not accepted. **Spoken** German. **Open** All year. **How to get there** (Map 12): 13km northwest of Sélestat. Autoroute Exit 11 at Sélestat, then direction Villé via D424 to Saint-Maurice and D697: indications for Diffenbach-Haut-Val on left; access via private lane.

If this small house were not of fairly recent construction, it could well be Hansel and Gretel's with its colored, half-timbered walls and flowery decor. The bedroom is quite large, simply decorated and impeccably kept. Just next to it is a kitchenette which has been installed for your use. The breakfasts are excellent and are served in your room or on your balcony facing a beautiful countryside.

8 - La Maison Fleurie de Doris Engel-Geiger

19, route de Neuve-Église
67220 Dieffenbach-au-Val
(Bas-Rhin)
Tel. or fax 03 88 85 60 48
Mme Doris Engel-Geiger

Rooms 3 with shower and WC; 1 child's room (2 beds), price according to age. **Price** 250F/38,11€ (1 pers.), 265-285F/40,39-43,44€ (2 pers.). **Meals** Breakfast incl. No communal meal. **Facilities** Refrigerator at guests' disposal, sitting room. **Pets** Dogs not allowed. **Nearby** Restaurants, tennis courts, swimming pool (4km), cross-country and downhill skiing (15km); Haut-Koenigsbourg, Riquewihr, Wine Route, Mont Sainte-Odile, Obernai. **Credit cards** Not accepted. **Spoken** German, some English. **Open** All year. **How to get there** (Map 12): 13km northwest of Sélestat, Autoroute Exit 11 at Sélestat, then towards Villé via D424 to Saint-Maurice and D697. **No smoking.**

Located on a hillside in a small village, this typically Alsatian house overflows with flowers. Madame Engel-Geiger is a youthful, friendly hostess and the small bedrooms are very simple but very well kept. (In the Familiale room, the children's corner is more warmly decorated than the parents' side.) Good breakfasts are served at a large table in the dining room or outside on the terrace.

A L S A C E - L O R R A I N E

9 - La Romance

17, route de Neuve-Église
67220 Dieffenbach-au-Val
(Bas-Rhin)
Tel. 03 88 85 67 09
Fax 03 88 57 61 58
M. and Mme Serge Geiger
Web: www.la-romance.net

Rooms 2 and 2 suites (with small private sitting room) with bath or shower, WC and tel. **Price** 360-420F/54,88-64,02€ (2 pers.); 2 days min. in high season. **Meals** Breakfast incl. No communal meal. **Facilities** Sitting room (TV), refrigerator, and microwave. By reservation, use of sauna, whirlpool, jet-shower, relaxation area. **Pets** Small dogs allowed on request. **Nearby** Restaurants (in the village), cross-country and downhill skiing, tennis, swimming pool; Wine Route, Haut-Kœnigsbourg, Riquewihr, Mont Sainte-Odile, eagle and stork sanctuaries, Obernai. **Credit cards** Not accepted. **Spoken** German, some English. **Open** All year. **How to get there** (Map 12): 13km northwest of Sélestat. Autoroute Exit 17 at Colmar, then towards Villé, D424 to Saint-Maurice not enter in village and D697; indications for Diffenbach-Haut-Val on left. **No smoking.**

From the Romance, you will enjoy a panoramic view out over the luxuriant Vosges countryside. Here, the welcome is warm and the hotel is in good taste. An independent entrance leads to the bedrooms, which are comfortable with impeccable bathrooms. The rooms on the upper floor make ideal suites for families, with sitting areas that can easily be made into extra bedrooms. Tasty breakfasts of excellent quality food.

10 - Le Landhome

23, route de la Wantzenau
67720 Hoerdt
(Bas-Rhin)
Tel. 03 88 51 72 29 or 06 08 25 01 51
Fax 03 90 29 00 79
M. and Mme René Stoll

Rooms 5 and 1 studio with shower, WC and tel. **Price** 295F/44,97€ (2 pers.), +40F/6,10€ (extra bed). **Meals** Breakfast incl. No communal meal. **Facilities** Sitting room. **Pets** Dogs not allowed. **Nearby** Restaurants, fishing, riding on request and tennis (5 mn), 18-hole golf course; Strasbourg, Haguenau, Vosges Regional Park, châteaux. **Credit Cards** All major except Amex. **Open** All year. **How to get there** (Map 13): 15km northeast of Strasbourg. Aut. A4, then N363 to Lauterbourg, exit Wantzenau, then on left to Hoerdt. Near the church. **No smoking.**

The Landhome stands next to the church in this little village near Strasbourg. Inside the pale green house with geraniums in its window boxes are six guestrooms, simple, pleasant, bright and scrupulously clean (except for the studio, which we do not recommend.) They are quiet at night, though there is some noise from local traffic mornings and evenings. Nice breakfasts in the company of Monsieur and Madame Stoll feature ham, a selection of jams, and the local kugelhof as a special Sunday treat.

A L S A C E - L O R R A I N E

11 - Neufeldhof

67280 Oberhaslach
(Bas-Rhin)
Tel. 03 88 50 91 48
Family André and Biehler

Rooms 3 with basins (shared shower and WC) and 1 suite (4 pers.) of 2 bedrooms with shower and WC. **Price** 150F/22,86€ (1 pers.), 280F/42,68€ (2 pers.), suite 560F/85,37€ (4 pers.). **Meals** Breakfast incl. Evening meals at communal table, lunch on Sat, Sun, and national holidays 90F/13,72€ (wine not incl.). **Facilities** Heated swimming pool, equestrian center, sitting room. **Pets** Dogs not allowed. **Nearby** Tennis, fishing. **Credit cards** Not accepted. **Spoken** German, English. **Open** All year. **How to get there** (Map 12): 36km west of Strasbourg via A352. At Molsheim, N420 to Urmatt and D218; in the village, D75 towards Wasselonne for 2km; first dirt road on right.

Thirty horses roam the paddocks of this large and very old farm which has been transformed into an equestrian center. The periphery of the center is not terribly well kept, but this minor drawback is made up for by the rustic charm of the interior. Each bedroom has fine old furniture and an antique ceramic stove. We have been assured that this year every effort will be made to improve the amenities in the bathrooms. The communal meals are remarkable and the hospitality is simple and very friendly. There is a superb panorama over the countryside.

12 - Château de Vaudoncourt

88140 Vaudoncourt
(Vosges)
Tel. 03 29 09 11 03
or 06 08 78 57 23
Fax 03 29 09 16 62
M. and Mme Boudot

Rooms 1 and 2 suites (3-4 pers.) with shower and WC. **Price** 350-400F/53,35-60,97€ (2 pers.), 500F/76,22€ (3 pers. in suite), 600F/91,46€ (4 pers. in suite). **Meals** Breakfast incl. No communal meal. **Facilities** Tel., swimming pool, badminton. **Pets** Animals not allowed. **Nearby** Restaurants in Bulgnéville (3km), 18-hole golf course, tennis, riding, fitness equipment; Vittel. **Credit cards** Not accepted. **Spoken** English. **Open** Apr 1 – Sept 30. **How to get there** (Map 11): 12km west of Vittel via Neuchâteau. On leaving Bulgnéville, go beneath autoroute, left at first intersection. Left of the church. **No smoking** in bedrooms.

Both inside and outside of this enormous house, we were immediately impressed by the feeling of space. There are two immense, bright suites with modern baths, and a pretty bedroom overlooking the park. The decoration and antique furnishings lend them a 19th-century atmosphere, which also prevails in the large dining room and corner veranda. The large park surrounding the house is delightfully lush and quiet.

13 - Le Relais de Lavergne

Lavergne
24150 Bayac
(Dordogne)
Tel. or fax 05 53 57 83 16
Mme Pillebout and Mme Calmettes

Rooms 5 (1 for disabled persons with possibility to make 1 suite with another bedroom) with bath or shower and WC. **Price** 320F/48,78€ (2 pers.), 500F/76,22€ (suite of 2 bedrooms). **Meals** Breakfast incl. Evening meals at communal table, by reservation 110F/16,76€ (wine incl.). **Facilities** Sitting room (fireplace, TV), swimming pool. **Pets** Dogs allowed on request. **Nearby** Sarlat, Bergerac, Bastides, Wine Route, château of Biron. **Credit cards** Not accepted. **Spoken** English. **Open** All year, by reservation and deposit. **How to get there** (Map 23): 25km east of Bergerac via D660 to Bayac by Port de Couze. In Bayac, turn right D27 dir. Issigeac, then left and follow signs Lavergne.

This fine ensemble of 17th-century buildings, formerly a working farm, is located in a tiny hamlet from which there are superb views on all sides. Recently refurbished with an eye to comfort as well as style, the bedrooms are furnished with family pieces or period furniture and the bathrooms are all new and beautifully done. On the ground floor, a large, comfortable lounge is at your disposal. You can go for a dip in the swimming pool every evening if you like, before having dinner all together in the small but charming dining room.

14 - Château de Regagnac

Montferrand-du-Périgord
24440 Beaumont
(Dordogne)
Tel. 05 53 63 27 02
Fax 05 53 73 39 08
M. and Mme Pardoux

Rooms 5 with bath or shower and WC. **Price** 656F/100€ (2 pers.). **Meals** Breakfast incl. Champagne dinner by candlelight, by reservation 393,60F/60€ (all incl.). **Facilities** Tel., tennis, hunting, walks. **Nearby** Golf, equestrian center; Les Eyzies, Trémolat, Domme, Valley of the Dordogne, prehistoric sites. **Credit cards** Not accepted. **Spoken** English, Spanish. **Open** All year, only by reservation. **How to get there** (Map 23): 39km east of Bergerac via D660 to Beaumont, then D2 to Cadouin-Regagnac.

With its large roofs, its corner turret and its terrace overlooking the countryside, Regagnac is a perfect illustration of the charm and allure of a typical mansion of the Périgord region. The interior is truly cozy,with antique furniture and accessories that make it look like some eclectic sort of museum. The bedrooms are well furnished with period pieces; embroidered sheets and a full toilet kit in each bathroom. Madame Pardoux, a Cordon Bleu cook of great talent, presides over a festive table every evening. A fine and hospitable house.

15 - La Lande

24440 Beaumont
(Dordogne)
Tel. and fax 05 53 23 48 49
M. and Mme Zangerl

Rooms 2, 1 with bath, WC and 1 with private bath but outside the room, WC, sitting room. Rooms cleaned on request. House rental (4-5 pers.). **Price** 250F/38,11€ (2 pers.). **Meals** Breakfast incl. Evening meals at communal table, on request 130F/19,81€ (all incl.). **Facilities** Lounge, boules, children's games. **Pets** Dogs not allowed. **Nearby** Swimming pool, tennis, canoes, kayaks, golf; Route des Bastides. **Credit cards** Not accepted. **Spoken** English, German. **Open** All year. **How to get there** (Map 23): 27km east of Bergerac towards Lalinde. In Port-de-Couze, turn right dir. Cahors, Beaumont. Entering Beaumont, take dir. Naussannes, Issigeac for 1.9km, then left dir. Carrière for 1.6km.

This lovingly-restored little farmhouse, situated in the heart of the countryside, offers panoramas of great natural beauty. The rooms are simple, comfortable, and extremely well-kept, in a rustic style full of charm. One of the bedrooms is situated in a separate small building. The spacious sitting room has a cozy corner with a fireplace, a large table and American style cooking. It is here that the guests get to know one another as they savour Madame Zangerl's tasty dishes. An excellent choice for a family holiday.

16 - Les Métairies Hautes

La Rigeardie
24310 Bourdeilles
(Dordogne)
Tel. 05 53 03 78 90
Fax 05 53 04 56 95
M. and Mme Trickett
E-mail: langues.vives@wanadoo.fr

Rooms 5 with shower (2 shared WCs), 1 family room (3 pers.). Rooms cleaned every 2-3 days. **Price** Rooms 220F/33,55€ (1 pers.), 260F/39,64€ (2 pers.); family room 320F/48,78€. **Meals** Breakfast incl. No communal meal. **Facilities** Language courses (full-board). **Pets** Dogs allowed on request. **Nearby** Restaurants, golf, tennis, kayak, riding, hiking. **Credit cards** Not accepted. **Spoken** English, German, Italian, Spanish. **Open** All year. **How to get there** (Map 23): 27km north of Périgueux via D939 towards Angoulême; at Brantôme take D78 to Bourdeilles, then continue 4km in towards Ribérac.

A cottage gate opens into the pretty garden of this house, which stands on a small road in a hamlet, welcoming you with kindness and discretion. The bedrooms are comfortable and plainly furnished; each contains a charming old school desk and a comfortable bed. The rooms all have a view of the garden. Breakfast with excellent homemade jams is served at a long wooden table in a pretty dining room decorated with exposed stones and pale woodwork.

17 - Château de La Borie-Saulnier

24530 Champagnac-de-Belair
(Dordogne)
Tel. 05 53 54 22 99
Fax 05 53 08 53 78
M. and Mme Duseau
E-mail: chateau-la-borie-saulnier@wanadoo.fr
Web: //perso.wanadoo.fr/chateaudelaboriesaulnier

Rooms 5 (1 with TV) with bath or shower and WC. **Price** 390-490F/59,45-74,70€ (2 pers.), +130F/19,82€ (extra bed); suite 690F/105,19€. **Meals** Breakfast incl. Evening meals, some days, by reservation 180F/27,44€ (wine not incl.). **Facilities** Sitting room, possible sitting room with TV, swimming pool, Napoleon III stables (2 boxes, 3 stalls). **Pets** Dogs allowed on request. **Nearby** Restaurants, tennis (free, 800m); Brantôme, Bourdeilles. **Credit cards** Not accepted. **Spoken** Some English. **Closed** Jan (on request, from Nov 1 to Mar 30). **How to get there** (Map 23): 3km north of Brantôme towards Angoulême, before Brantôme exit, just before Total station, follow "La route de chez Ravailles" for 3.2km.

In the heart of the countryside and the immediate proximity of Brantôme, this château is undergoing progressive renovation whose magnificent results can already be seen in the bedrooms. Many are large, with refined decoration (old 19th-century furniture, coordinated fabrics and wallpapers in cheerful colors, engravings, decorative objects...) most of them have superb bathrooms. Delicious dinners are served by candlelight in a vast dining room or the interior courtyard. The owners are convivial and will do their utmost to make your stay a pleasant one.

18 - Les Pouyades

24320 Cherval
(Dordogne)
Tel. and fax 05 53 91 02 96
M. and Mme Truffaux

Rooms 3 with bath or shower and WC. **Price** 350-450F/53,35-68,60€ (2 pers.); special rates for long stays. **Meals** Breakfast incl. No communal meal. Poss. snacks available at night. **Restaurants** "Le Périgord" in Verteillac; "L'Hôtel du Vieux-Mareuil" in Vieux-Mareuil; and in Ribérac. **Pets** Dogs not allowed. **Nearby** Riding, swimming pool, tennis (5km); Romanesque church tour, châteaux of Mareuil, Villebois, Bourdeille, Brantôme Abbey, Saint-Jean-de-Côle. **Credit cards** Not accepted. **Open** All year (on request from Nov to Mar.). **How to get there** (Map 23): 40km from Angoulême via D939 towards Périgueux. In La Rochebeaucourt, take D12, then D708, towards Verteillac. Follow signs 5km before Verteillac.

This is a family house surrounded by a large park. The inviting, very pleasant bedrooms have been renovated with a great deal of taste. The antique furniture, some in fruit wood and some walnut, is very much in the regional style and the bathrooms are impeccable. Elegant breakfasts are served in the pretty dining room and include delicious homemade brioches.

19 - La Commanderie

24570 Condat-sur-Vézère
(Dordogne)
Tel. 05 53 51 26 49
Fax 05 53 51 39 38
Mme Roux

Rooms 5 with bath or shower, WC, tel. and TV. **Price** 380F/57,93€ (1 pers.), 420-450F/64,02-68,60€ (2 pers.), +50F/7,62€ (extra child's bed). **Meals** Breakfast 45F/6,86€. Dinner at separate tables 120-185F/18,29-28,20€ (depending on menu, wine incl.); half board 720F/109,76€ (2 pers.) **Facilities** Sitting room, swimming pool, trout fishing in river and trout farm on property. **Pets** Dogs allowed on request. **Nearby** Canoeing/kayaks, tennis in village; Périgord, Lascaux. **Credit cards** All major except Amex. **Closed** Jul – Aug. **How to get there** (Map 23): 25km north of Sarlat. At Le Lardin, on N89 between Périgueux and Brive, take the road to Condat-sur-Vézère; house in village.

This beautiful commanderie – a residence of the Knights Templars that dates in part from the 18th century – is in a stunning village that has many vestiges of the Templars. The immaculate private park is traversed by small canals which empty into the Vézère River bordering the property. The Commanderie is elegantly decorated inside, and the handsome stairways, vaulted ceilings, and wall recesses lend touches of character. The bedrooms are pleasant and bright, and are furnished with antiques. This is a lovely place to stay, with the atmosphere of an old family home.

20 - Château de Cazenac

24220 Le Coux-et-Bigaroque
(Dordogne)
Tel. 05 53 31 69 31
Fax 05 53 28 91 43
Philippe and Armelle Constant

Rooms 4 with bath, WC and tel. **Price** 900-1200F/137,20-182,93€ (2 pers.), +100F/15,24€ (extra bed). **Meals** Breakfast 80F/12,19€. Evening meals at communal tables, by reservation 300F/45,73€ (all incl.). **Facilities** Sitting room, swimming pool, tennis, cooking lessons and other courses. **Pets** Dogs allowed on request. **Nearby** Golf courses, fishing, hunting, riding; Dordogne (châteaux, sites). **Credit cards** Not accepted. **Spoken** English, Italian. **Open** All year. Rented only weekly in Jul, Aug. **How to get there** (Map 23): 25km west of Sarlat. In Périgueux, towards Brive, then D110 towards Fumel. In Le Bugue, take D51 to Le Buisson, then Le Coux-et-Bigaroque. Sign before village on left.

Overlooking the valley of the Dordogne, this pretty château enjoys a most beautiful view. Well appointed and tastefully decorated by a charming and hospitable young couple, it offers a wonderful setting for anyone who wants to explore this lovely region or simply to relax. The bedrooms are harmonious and comfortable with bathrooms that are sometimes well-integrated into the room. A world of beauty and refinement where one can feel truly at peace.

A Q U I T A I N E

21 - La Daille

24250 Florimont-Gaumiers
(Dordogne)
Tel. 05 53 28 40 71
M. and Mme Derek Vaughan Brown

Rooms 3 with bath, WC and terrace. **Price** 650F/99,09€ (2 pers.), 3 nights min. **Meals** Breakfast incl. No communal meal. Tea room in the garden from Fri to Mon and public holidays (Service 4:00PM-6:30PM; 40F/6,09€). **Pets** Dogs not allowed. **Nearby** Restaurants, 9-hole golf; Sarlat, L'Abbaye-Nouvelle. **Credit cards** Not accepted. **Open** May 1 – Sept 30, only by reservation. **How to get there** (Map 23): 25km south of Sarlat via D46 (Cenac/Saint-Martial). 3km after Saint-Martial go right on D52, then in 500m. turn left, towards Gaumiers; after bridge go left, towards Péchembert and La Daille.

Set in the midst of wild and rolling country, this quiet old farmhouse is surrounded by one of the most beautiful gardens imaginable. The comfortable bedrooms are very well decorated with English furniture. All have large bathrooms and private terraces overlooking the flowers and the hills. The reception is cool but correct and the peace and quiet is total.

22 - L'Enclos
Pragelier
24390 Hautefort
(Dordogne)
Tel. 05 53 51 11 40
Fax 05 53 50 37 21
Dana and Robert Ornsteen
E-mail: rornsteen@yahoo.com
Web: www.lenclos.hypermart.net

Rooms 3 and 1 studio (kitchenette) and 1 suite (2-3 pers., sitting room and kitchen) with bath or shower and WC. **Price** 350-450F/53,36-68,60€ (2 pers.); studio 600F/91,47€ (2 pers.), +50F/7,62€ (extra bed); suite 800F/121,95€ (2 pers.) +50F/7,62€ for 1 night. **Meals** Breakfast 50F/7,62€ (served at 9:00AM in the house), 60F/9,14€ (served 8:00AM-10:00AM in bedrooms and terrace). Evening meals at communal table, by reservation 150F/22,87€ (all incl.). **Facilities** Sitting room, swimming pool. **Pets** Small dogs allowed on request. **Spoken** English, Spanish, Italian. **Credit cards** Not accepted. **Closed** Sept 30 – Apr 30, by reservation. **How to get there** (Map 23): 10km northwest of Hautefort. In Périgueux, take D5 towards Tourtoirac. In Tourtoirac, turn on left towards Saint Raphael on D67; 1.6km on left. Pragelier is 100m farther.

L'Enclos has the appearance of an old hamlet of traditional houses, superbly renovated and connected to one another by an attractive garden. The rooms are comfortable and elegant, each one with its own style. The table d'hôte dinners are delicious and cosmopolitan and the breakfast is excellent despite the fact that it is served a bit early for some tastes. A nice place to stay if you like to feel completely independent. The reception is courteous and the hosts are English-speaking.

A Q U I T A I N E

23 - Rouach - Hautefort

Rue Bertrand-de-Borne
24390 Hautefort
(Dordogne)
Tel. 05 53 50 41 59
(from 7:30PM)
Mme Rouach

Rooms 2 with private bath and shared WC. 1 suite (4 pers.) with bath, WC and kitchen. **Price** 350F/53,35€ (2 pers.), suite 500F/76,22€. **Meals** Breakfast 30F/4,57€. No communal meal. **Restaurants** "Auberge du Parc" in Hautefort, "Les Rocailles" in Les Broussilloux and "Les Tilleuls" in Badfol d'Ans. **Facilities** Sitting room. **Pets** Dogs not allowed. **Nearby** Swimming pool, lake, tennis courts in village; Château de Hautefort, Brantôme, Saint-Jean-de-Côle, Dordogne Valley, concerts in Jul-Aug. **Credit cards** Not accepted. **Closed** Oct 15 – May 1. **How to get there** (Map 23): 50km northeast of Périgueux via N89 towards Brives, then after Thenon, go left on D704. House in center of village.

Built on the flank of the magnificent village of Hautefort, this beautiful residence enjoys a breathtaking panorama over the countryside. The garden follows the configuration of the hill, with rare flowers cascading down the slope. Inside, Rouach is decorated with traditional old furniture and it has all the charm of a family home. The pretty bedrooms have modern amenities and immaculate bathrooms. Breakfasts are served on the terrace and the hospitality is both refined and very warm. This is a dream place for discovering the Dordogne.

24 - Le Petit Pey

Monmarvès
24560 Issigeac
(Dordogne)
Tel. 05 53 58 70 61
Mme Annie de Bosredon

Rooms 3 with shower and WC, 1 with bath and WC and 3 with single beds for teenagers in the dovecote. **Price** 300F/45,75€ (2 pers.), +50F/7,62€ (extra pers.). 1 night free for 6 nights **Meals** Breakfast incl. No communal meal. **Facilities** Sitting room. **Pets** Dogs allowed (+15F/2,29€). **Nearby** Golf (18km), sailing, fishing, riding. **Credit cards** Not accepted. **Spoken** English. **Open** Easter – Oct 15. **How to get there** (Map 23): 2km south of Issigeac towards Castillonnès, then follow the signs.

This elegant 17th- and 18th-century house has 3 guest rooms. The most attractive and the "youngest" is all in pink and occupies the upper floor, under the eaves. The other two rooms share a bath on the same landing and are recommended for families. Outside, the old converted dovecote has 3 single beds and is suitable for teenagers. A lovely salon is available for guests. The beautiful park is a perfect place for a picnic. The welcome is lively and cordial.

A Q U I T A I N E

25 - Château de Lanquais

24150 Lanquais
(Dordogne)
Tel. 05 53 61 24 24
Fax 05 53 73 20 72
Mme Magnan and M. Vivier

Rooms 2 with bath or shower and WC. **Price** 500-700F/76,22-106,71€ (1-2 pers.). **Meals** Breakfast 45F/6,86€. No communal meal. **Facilities** Sitting room, tel. **Pets** Dogs allowed on request. **Nearby** Restaurants (800m), lake (100m), fishing and swimming, 9-hole golf course (6km); Monbazillac, Bergerac, Sarlat (50km), Périgord (châteaux and sites). **Credit cards** Not accepted. **Spoken** English. **Closed** Nov 15 – Mar 1. **How to get there** (Map 23): 15km east of Bergerac and 50km west of Sarlat. 500m of Lanquais.

Lanquais is one of the loveliest châteaux in all of Périgord. Its wonderful Renaissance fireplaces, vast rooms and antique furniture, as well as the wealth of fascinating information possessed by Gilles Vivier will enchant all history lovers. On the other hand, the austerity of the place and the rather spartan sanitary facilities will not satisfy those who need their creature comforts or seek a particularly cozy atmosphere. Still, this is a rare jewel that ought to be seen, particularly in fine weather.

26 - Saint-Hubert

24520 Liorac-sur-Louyre
(Dordogne)
Tel. and fax 05 53 63 07 92
Muriel and Patrice Hennion

Rooms 4 with bath or shower and WC. **Price** 300-350F/45,73-53,35€ (2 pers.). **Meals** Breakfast incl. Dinner at communal table 100F/15,24€ (drinks incl.). **Facilities** Sitting room, swimming pool and hiking in forest on property. **Pets** Dogs not allowed. **Nearby** 9-hole golf course, bicycle rentals, riding, tennis; Périgord châteaux, old villages and bastides, Bergerac vineyards. **Credit cards** Not accepted. **Spoken** English. **Open** All year. **How to get there** (Map 23): 14km northeast of Bergerac. In Bergerac, take D32 towards Sainte-Alvère, Centre hospitalier road; 14km on right, 0.8km before Liorac.

This pretty house where "the living is easy" (especially in summertime) stands at the edge of a forest and has a beautifully kept park and a swimming pool. Inside it resembles a real country house, comfortable and carefully appointed. The nicest bedroom, decorated in various shades of green, is on the ground floor and opens onto an inviting living room reserved for the guests. Upstairs, the attic room with its blue and white checks and sloping ceiling is also very pleasant. The two remaining rooms are small but well kept. The table d'hôte dinners are good and convivial. The owners' dogs keep watch over the property; telephone before coming to announce your arrival.

27 - Fonroque

24230 Montcaret
(Dordogne)
Tel. 05 53 58 65 83
Brigitte Fried

Rooms 5 with bath or shower and WC. Rooms cleaned twice weekly. **Price** 310F/47,25€ (1 pers.), 350F/53,35€ (2 pers.), 465F/70,88€ (3 pers.). **Children** Under 2 (free). Child under 12 in parents' room 1/2 price. **Meals** Breakfast incl. Dinner at communal table 110F/16,76€. Half-board 395F/60,21€ (1 pers.), 520F/79,27€ (2 pers.), 720F/109,76€ (3 pers.). 20% off for 2 days and more Oct 1 - Apr 30. **Facilities** Sitting room. **Pets** Dogs allowed on request. **Credit cards** Not accepted. **Spoken** English. **Closed** Dec 1 – Feb 15. **How to get there** (Map 22): 8km east of Castillon-la-Bataille, on D936 between Bergerac and Libourne; in Montcaret, go to the Gallo-Roman ruins, then follow signs for Fonroque.

On this small winegrowing estate, near the place where Montaigne wrote his Essais, the guest rooms are pleasantly decorated with sponge-painted walls, curtains in soft, luminous colors, and a scattering of old furniture. Each has a private bath. At the table d'hôte dinner, you can enjoy family cooking served in a charming room. The park is lush with trees and foliage, and you will find a beautiful swimming pool there, installed in the former greenhouse. Fonroque is popular with families in summer.

28 - Le Bastit

Saint-Médard-de-Mussidan
24400 Mussidan
(Dordogne)
Tel. 05 53 81 32 33
Fax 05 53 81 32 33
M. Kenneth and Mme Wendy Burt

Rooms 6 with bath and WC. **Price** 320F/48,78€ (1 pers.), 380F/57,93€ (2 pers.), +100F/15,24€ (extra bed). 3 nights min. in Jul-Aug. **Meals** Breakfast incl. No communal meal. **Facilities** Sitting room, fishing on the Isle River (boat), bicycle. **Pets** Dogs not allowed. **Nearby** Restaurants, 18-hole golf course (30km); Périgord vert, Bergerac, hiking. **Credit cards** Not accepted. **Spoken** English, Spanish, Italian. **Open** All year, by reservation and deposit. **How to get there** (Map 23): 35km west of Bordeaux. N89 to Mussidan. Continue on N89 dir. Bordeaux (1km), then on right Saint-Médard-de-Mussidan. On right just before the church. **No smoking.**

This lovely house built in 1837 stands in a cool and verdant garden along the Isle River. It recently changed hands and the new owners have created six new bedrooms, each with a spanking new bathroom. What has been lost in charm is made up in comfort. For the rest, the house remains as before, a delightful haven of peace and the joy of nature. Kenneth and Wendy Burt will offer you a warm welcome.

29 - Le Cèdre de Floyrac

Floyrac
24140 Queyssac
(Dordogne)
Tel. 05 53 61 78 17
Fax 05 53 74 51 31
M. and Mme Christian Bleu

Rooms 2 suites and 3 apartments (poss. kitchen) with bath, WC, TV, private terrace on a level with the park and tel. in apartments. **Price** 650F/99,10€ (2 pers.), +100F/15,24€ (extra pers.). **Meals** Breakfast (brunch) 60F/9,15€. Communal meals on request 190F/28,96€ (all incl.). **Facilities** Sitting room, billiards, swimming pool, tennis, riding (for good riders), lake fishing (children), mountain bikes. **Pets** Animals not allowed. **Nearby** Restaurants, 18-hole golf course (20km), Equestrian center (5min.). **Spoken** English. **Open** All year. **How to get there** (Map 23): 8km north of Bergerac via N21, towards Périgueux. At first intersection after Lembras (Périgord pottery), turn left towards Queyssac, go in front of Mairie. At first intersection, towards Villambard 30m on right.

Very close to Bergerac, this beautiful 18th-century manor house is surrounded by a superb park with trees and offers comfortable bedrooms, suites and apartments, which are colorfully decorated with Provençal cottons. The swimming pool, tennis courts, mountain bikes and the sitting room with billiards all make for wonderful relaxation. Very pleasant breakfasts are served beneath the trees. The owners are attentive and cordial, the atmosphere quiet and peaceful.

30 - Les Granges Hautes

24590 Saint-Crépin-Carlucet
(Dordogne)
Tel. 05 53 29 35 60
Fax 05 53 28 81 17
Nicole and Jean Querre
E-mail: jquerre@aol.com
Web: www.les-granges-hautes.fr

Rooms 3 with shower, WC and 2 with bath and WC. **Price** 350F/53,35€ (1 pers.), 390F/59,45€ (2 pers.) +100F/15,24€ (extra pers.). **Meals** Breakfast 45F/6,86€. No communal meal. **Facilities** Lounge, telephone (card), salt-water swimming pool, park. **Pets** Dogs allowed on request. **Credit cards** All major. **Nearby** Restaurants, hiking, tennis, riding, golf. **Spoken** English. **Open** Easter – Oct 1. **How to get there** (Map 23): 11km from Sarlat on Brive road. On Paris-Toulouse N20, exit Brive towards Périgueux, Sarlat.

Near Sarlat and the Eyrignac Gardens, the Granges Hautes is a typical, old, Périgord house that stands in a lovely park with a sumptuous lawn. In authentic Périgord style, the interior decoration is imaginative and elegant, with each bedroom different and personalized. The Toscane room even opens onto a small Italian garden! There are beautiful bathrooms and showers. Hearty breakfasts, with homemade preserves and other specialties of the house are served in a large, elegant sitting room or in the garden. This charming place is very quiet and warmly inviting.

31 - Château d'Argentonesse

Castels
24220 Saint-Cyprien-en-Périgord
(Dordogne)
Tel. 05 53 29 35 08
Fax 05 53 29 46 58
Dr. and Mme Walsh

Rooms 3 and 2 suites (2 pers.) with bath or shower and WC; 1 small house with lounge and kitchen (4 pers.). **Price** Rooms 500F/76,22€ (2 pers.); suites 700F/106,71€ (2 pers.). Small house 5000F/762,24€/week **Meals** Breakfast incl. (only in rooms). No communal meal. **Credit cards** All major. **Facilities** Restaurant, lounge, parking, swimming pool, jacuzzi, sauna. **Pets** Dogs not allowed. **Nearby** 18-hole golf course; Proumeysac Caverns, châteaux of Beynac and Castelnaux, Les Eyzies (15 min.). **Closed** End Sept – Easter. **How to get there** (Map 23): 54km southeast of Périgueux via N89 and D710 to Le Bugue, then D703 and D35 to Saint-Cyprien. 1km east of Saint-Cyprien.

This is a splendid, gracefully proportioned 17th-century residence which has been beautifully restored by an Australian couple. The interior is luxuriously appointed with period furniture, deep sofas.... Similar attention has been given to the bedrooms and their baths with modern amenities. Built on barrel vaults, the terrace overlooks the park and enjoys a beautiful view. The château is majestic, yet the owners are informal and hospitable.

32 - Doumarias

24800 Saint-Pierre-de-Côle
(Dordogne)
Tel. and fax 05 53 62 34 37
Anita and François Fargeot

Rooms 6 with bath or shower and WC. Rooms cleaned on request. **Price** 280F/42,68€ (2 pers.) +40F/6,09€ (extra pers.). **Meals** Breakfast 25F/3,81€, half board 460F/70,12€ per day (2 pers. in double room, 4 days min.). Evening meals at communal table 85F/12,95€ (wine incl.). **Facilities** Swimming pool, fishing in the river. **Pets** Dogs not allowed. **Nearby** Tennis, riding, golf; caves and château at Villars, Brantôme, Bourdeilles. **Credit cards** Not accepted. **Open** Apr 1 – Sept 30, by reservation. **How to get there** (Map 23): 12km southeast of Brantôme via D78 towards Thiviers; 1.5km after Saint-Pierre-de-Côle.

Doumarias stands beneath an old ruined château not far from the lovely village of Saint-Jean-de-Côle. The bedrooms are charming, with beautiful antique furniture, curios and small paintings. They are comfortable and quiet. Breakfast and dinner are served in a pretty dining room overlooking the garden and the cuisine is excellent. You will receive a very friendly welcome.

33 - Le Moulin Neuf

Paunat
24510 Sainte-Alvère
(Dordogne)
Tel. 05 53 63 30 18
Fax 05 53 73 33 91
Robert Chappell and Stuart Shippey
E-mail: moulin-neuf@usa.net
Web: www.francedirect.net/moulin.htm

Rooms 6 with bath or shower and WC. **Price** 304F/46,35€ (2 pers.), +100F/15,24€ (extra bed). **Meals** Breakfast 45F/6,86€. No communal meal. **Facilities** Sitting room; swimming in lake on property. **Pets** Small dogs allowed on request. **Nearby** Restaurants (3km), fishing in river, canoes, kayaks, yacht basin, tennis; the Périgord Noir (caves, châteaux), La Roque-Gageac. **Credit cards** Not accepted. **Spoken** English, German. **Open** All year, in winter by reservation (3 days min.). **How to get there** (Map 23): 8km southwest of Le Bugue via D703, towards Sainte-Alvère, then D31 towards Limeuil. After the Cingle de Limeuil, on D31, go downhill, then D2, towards Sainte-Alvère, 2km down, left at the small crossroads. **No smoking**.

This beautiful estate consists of two houses, one of which is entirely reserved for the guests. The garden is an enchantment: always in bloom, it is flanked by a delightful stream and a small lake. The front room of the guest house is a comfortable lounge with some old English furniture, two bottle-green settees with yellow cushions and skirted tables where excellent breakfasts are served with thoughtful kindness. The bedrooms are small, sober, cozy and impeccably clean, as are the bathrooms.

34 - Château de Puymartin

24200 Sarlat-la-Canéda
(Dordogne)
Tel. 05 53 59 29 97
Fax 05 53 29 87 52
Comte and Comtesse
Henri de Montbron
E-mail: ch.puymartin@lemel.fr
Web: www.best-of-dordogne.tm.fr

Rooms 2 with bath and WC. **Price** 750F/114,33€ (2 pers.) +150F/22,86€ (child). **Meals** Breakfast incl. No communal meal. **Restaurants** "La Métairie" (4km) or in Sarlat and in Eyzies (8km). **Facilities** Sitting room, private tours of the château. **Pets** Dogs allowed on request. **Nearby** Swimming pool, tennis, golf, riding. **Credit cards** Not accepted. **Open** Apr – Nov 1. By reservation for weekends Nov 2 – Mar 31. **How to get there** (Map 23): About 60km southeast of Périgueux towards Sarlat, then on D47 dir. Les Eyzies. 11km after Les Eyzies on left, follow signs. Airports in Périgueux (60km) or in Bordeaux (180km).

The evocative, crenellated silhouette of the Château de Puymartin looms over a landscape of hills and forests. The welcome is simple and kind. One of the bedrooms is furnished in medieval style and has two splendid canopied beds. The other is arranged like a sitting room with a collection of mostly Louis XVI marquetry furniture. Both rooms are very large and comfortable and contain some charming objects.

A   Q   U   I   T   A   I   N   E

35 - La Métairie Haute

Lasserre
24200 Sarlat-la-Canéda
(Dordogne)
Tel. 05 53 30 31 17
Fax 05 53 59 62 66
Martine and Michel Pinard-Legry
Web: www.abscise.com/perigord/plegry/
plegryO.html

Rooms 5 and 1 suite (4 pers.) with bath or shower and WC. **Price** 400-500F/60,98-76,23€ (2 pers.) +150F/22,87€ (extra bed). **Meals** Breakfast incl. No communal meal. **Facilities** Sitting room, pond on property. **Pets** Small dogs allowed on request. **Nearby** Restaurants, tennis, swimming pool, riding, canoeing/kayaking, 9-hole golf course; Les Eyzies, Dordogne Valley, Lascaux. **Credit cards** Not accepted. **Spoken** English, Spanish. **Open** All year. **How to get there** (Map 23): 5km southwest of Sarlat via D25 dir. Le Bugue. After 4km, turn on right towards La Métairie Haute. After 800m on right and on right at 400m (sign posted).

This old family mansion stands in the middle of a vast park overlooking a peaceful, verdant landscape. It has been renovated with outstanding taste and the interior decoration is both classic and elegant. The bedrooms rival one another for beauty and comfort, with assorted fabrics, lovely period furniture or genuine antiques, old engraving on the walls. All of them have exposed beams and wonderful modern bathrooms. The breakfasts are excellent, the welcome full of warmth and refinement. An ideal spot from which to explore the region of Sarlat and the Vallée de l'Homme.

36 - Château d'Arbieu

33430 Bazas
(Gironde)
Tel. 05 56 25 11 18
Fax 05 56 25 90 52
Comte and Comtesse
Philippe de Chénerilles
E-mail: arbieu@wanadoo.fr

Rooms 4 and 1 suite (4 pers.) with bath or shower, WC and tel. **Price** 450 and 500F/68,60 and 76,22€ (2 pers.); suite 570F/86,90€ (2 pers.), 770F/117,38€ (4 pers.); +100F/15,24€ (extra pers.) Special rates for long stays on request. **Meals** Breakfast incl. Half board 2 days min. Evening meals at communal table, by reservation 160F/24,39€ (all incl.). **Facilities** Sitting room, swimming pool. **Credit cards** Amex, Visa, Diners, JCB. **Spoken** English. **Closed** Feb. **How to get there** (Map 29): 60km southeast of Bordeaux via A62, exit Langon, then D932 to Bazas, then on right at Bazas exit D655, towards Casteljaloux.

Set in a park overlooking the Bazas countryside, the Château d'Arbieu belongs to a very hospitable family. Its bedrooms are large and bright and have a very authentic look thanks to vintage furniture, sometimes of high quality (like the "Empire suite") and some antique pieces, paintings and engravings. They are all pleasant, though Number 5 is a bit drab for our taste. Nice bathrooms recently renovated, large, elegantly furnished salons and a pleasant dining room for delicious and convivial dinners.

37 - Château de la Grave

33710 Bourg-en-Gironde
(Gironde)
Tel. 05 57 68 41 49
Fax 05 57 68 49 26
M. and Mme Bassereau

Rooms 3 with shower and WC. **Price** 260F/39,63€ (1 pers.), 300F/45,73€ (2 pers.) +100F/15,24€ (extra bed) **Meals** Breakfast incl. No communal meal. **Facilities** Sitting room, wine tasting and store. **Pets** Dogs allowed on request. **Nearby** Mountainbiking, hiking, Wine Route, scenic route along the estuary. **Credit cards** Not accepted. **Spoken** English, Spanish. **Closed** Aug 15 – Sept 1, by reservation and deposit. **How to get there** (Map 22): 35km northwest of Bordeaux. Autoroute A10, exit Saint-André-de-Cubzac, towards Bourg. At the village exit, on right towards Berson, then 2nd on right (sign posted).

Perched on a hillside, this wine-producing château offers three fine bedrooms renovated with old-fashioned charm, each with its own small shower room. The old family mansion stands amid the gentle curves of the surrounding vineyards. Breakfast is served in a lovely old dining room or, in summer, under an awning that recalls an ancient tented hall. The reception is unpretentious and dynamic.

38 - Château du Foulon

Le Foulon
33480 Castelnau-de-Médoc
(Gironde)
Tel. 05 56 58 20 18
Fax 05 56 58 23 43
Vicomte and Vicomtesse
Jean de Baritault du Carpia

Rooms 3, 1 studio (2-3 pers.) and 1 suite (4 pers.) with bath and WC. **Price** Rooms 400F/60,97€ (1 pers.), 450F/68,60€ (2 pers.); suite or studio 500-600F/76,22-91,47€ (2 pers.), +150F/22,86€ (extra pers.). **Meals** Breakfast incl. No communal meal. **Restaurants** "Le Savoye" in Margaux, "Le Lion d'Or" in Arcins. **Facilities** Sitting room, tel. **Pets** Dogs not allowed. **Nearby** Tennis, equestrian center, 36-hole golf course; châteaux of Médoc. **Credit cards** Not accepted. **Spoken** English. **Open** All year. **How to get there** (Map 22): 28km northwest of Bordeaux via D1.

Some distance out of the village, the Château du Foulon, built in 1840, is a small paradise where you will feel completely at ease. The comfortable bedrooms are handsomely decorated with beautiful antique furniture, and all have views of the park. A studio and a suite for long stays have been added. Before setting out for the great Médoc vineyards, you will enjoy a delicious breakfast served in a lovely dining room. This is a welcoming, especially elegant place to stay.

39 - Domaine de Carrat

Route de Sainte-Hélène
33480 Castelnau-de-Médoc
(Gironde)
Tel. 05 56 58 24 80
M. and Mme Péry

Rooms 3 with bath and WC. **Price** 260-270F/39,63-41,16€ (1 pers.), 290-340F/44,21-51,83€ (2 pers.); suite 500F/76,22€ (4 pers.). **Meals** Breakfast incl. No communal meal. Equipped kitchen at guests' disposal. **Facilities** Sitting room, swimming in the stream (safe for children). **Pets** Dogs allowed on request (15F/2,28€/day). **Nearby** Restaurants, tennis, 18-hole golf course, equestrian center, lakes; châteaux of Médoc. **Credit cards** Not accepted. **Spoken** English, German. **Closed** Christmas. **How to get there** (Map 22): 28km northwest of Bordeaux via D1; at the 2nd set of traffic lights in Castelnau towards Sainte-Hélène on N215; turn right 200m after leaving Castelnau.

This lovely house stands in a park in the midst of a forest. Monsieur and Madame Péry have tastefully transformed the spacious old stables into comfortable guest rooms with family furniture; some can be made into suites, and all look out on the peaceful countryside. (In summer, the ground-floor room is the loveliest.) Good breakfasts are served in the attractive dining room, and the people are very friendly.

40 - Cabirol

33430 Gajac-de-Bazas
(Gironde)
Tel. and fax 05 56 25 15 29
M. and Mme Xavier Dionis du Séjour

Rooms 2 and 1 suite (4 pers.) with bath, shower, WC and 1 room with shower and WC. **Price** 240F/36,58€ (1 pers.), 280F/42,68€ (2 pers.); suite 460F/70,12€ (4 pers.). **Meals** Breakfast incl. 10% reduction after 4 days. No communal meal. **Facilities** Sitting room, ping-pong, visit to farm (geese, ducks, cows). **Pets** Dogs not allowed. **Nearby** Restaurants, boats, fishing, bird observatory (500m), swimming pool, tennis, riding, lakes, 18-hole golf course; Old Bazas, vineyards, Ostrich farm. **Credit cards** Not accepted. **Spoken** English. **Open** All year. Only by reservation Nov 15 – Feb 15. **How to get there** (Map 29): 4km northeast of Bazas. In Bazas dir. A62, follow signs "autoroute Toulouse". The house is 4km on D9 (sign posted).

You will be received very graciously in this beautiful house where one part is entirely reserved for guests. There you will find pleasant, very comfortable bedrooms, brightened with pretty fabrics; their bathrooms are lovely. Fine breakfasts are served at the large dining table in the salon-library (which is at your disposal) or in summer, they are served outside where you can gaze at the peaceful countryside. A most pleasant halt in your journey.

A Q U I T A I N E

41 - Domaine de Guillaumat

33420 Génissac
(Gironde)
Tel. 05 57 24 49 14
and 05 57 51 18 99
Fax 05 57 51 90 69
M. and Mme Fulchi

Rooms 3 and 1 small suite (bedroom, with kitchenette and dining area) with bath or shower and WC. **Price** 250F/38,11€ (1 pers.), 300F/45,73€ (2 pers.); suite 350F/53,35€ (1 pers.), 400F/60,97€ (2 pers.); +70F/10,67€ (extra bed). **Meals** Breakfast incl. No communal meal. **Facilities** Sitting room, swimming pool, riding. **Pets** Small dogs allowed. **Nearby** Restaurants; Wine Route, Saint-Émilion, Bordeaux. **Credit cards** Not accepted. **Spoken** English, Spanish. **Open** All year. **How to get there** (Map 22): 28km southeast of Bordeaux. On RN89 (4-lane highway Bordeaux-Libourne). About 28km, exit Génissac. In Génissac, at the traffic circle, towards Arveyres. About 1km, 2nd road on left, then follow signs.

At the edge of a plateau overlooking the vineyards of Entre-Deux-Mers, this wine estate has a small house reserved for guests. The bedrooms, all on the ground floor, resemble the guest rooms of a private country home: white walls, terra cotta floors, some nice old furniture... They all face east, thus receiving the morning sun. Excellent breakfasts, which you can have, depending on your mood, either in the kitchen or beside the pool. A perfect spot on fine weather days for all those seeking quiet and privacy.

42 - Le Moulin de Mesterrieux

33540 Mesterrieux
(Gironde)
Tel. 05 56 71 32 90
Fax 05 56 71 33 90
M. and Mme Reydi

Rooms 3 with bath or shower and WC; TV and tel. (on request). **Price** 350-450F/53,35-68,60€ (2 pers). **Meals** Breakfast incl. Evening meals at communal table, by reservation 125F/19,05€ (all incl.). Equipped kitchen at guests' disposal. **Pets** Dogs allowed on request. **Facilities** River fishing, bikes. **Spoken** English. **Open** Easter – Nov 1 (in winter on request). **How to get there** (Map 22): 9km north of La Réole, towards Libourne D670. On leaving La Réole, at intersection take dir. Saint-Sève/Loubens via D21 (about 6km). After the bridge over the Dropt River, first right, go in front of the coopérative, then 1st road on right; in 50m, at the cross on right (D15); at the cross on right (sign posted).

Don't be intimidated by the iron gates and the hard cobblestones: the building where guests stay, overlooking a large park traversed by the Dropt River, is extremely pleasant. You will find a salon/breakfast room, two large bedrooms with spacious baths and a third room, for summer, which opens onto the garden and has a marvelous round shower room installed in the former bread oven. The kitchen, which has a clothes washer, will delight guests who are here for a long stay.

43 - Le Grand Boucaud

33580 Rimons
(Gironde)
Tel. and Fax 05 56 71 88 57
M. and Mme Lévy

Rooms 3 with bath and WC. **Price** 330F/50,30€ (2 pers.), 390F/59,45€ (3 pers.). **Meals** Breakfast incl. Evening meals at independent tables 120-200F/18,29-30,48€ (Wine not incl., wine list). Poss. vegetarian meals. **Pets** Dogs not allowed. **Facilities** Swimming pool, cooking lessons. **Spoken** English, German. **Closed** Oct 15 – Dec. **How to get there** (Map 22): 28km northeast of Langon. Autoroute A62, exit Langon, then N133 dir. Agen, exit Saint-Macaire; then D672 to Sauveterrre-en-Guyenne; take D670 dir. La Réole for 2km, turn left on D230, go past Rimons and take 1st road on left after the sawmill.

Guests come to Madame Levy's above all for her outstanding traditional cuisine of Bordeaux and Alsace, and her wine selections. Her large, late-18th-century house offers two bedrooms located beneath the eaves and equipped with modern amenities. The latest addition, the Yellow Room, has visible beams and a mezzanine for the children. A small, shady garden, a swimming pool with a pergola, and the surrounding vineyards are three more pleasures that guests can enjoy in this simple, friendly place.

44 - La Bergerie

Les Trias
33920 Saint-Christoly-de-Blaye
(Gironde)
Tel. 05 57 42 50 80
M. and Mme de Poncheville

Rooms 2 houses for 3-6 pers. with sitting room, kitchen, bath and WC. **Price** 400F/60,98€ (2 pers.) +150F/22,86€ (extra pers.). Special rates for long stays in low season. **Meals** Breakfast 25F/3,81€. No communal meal. **Facilities** Swimming pool, riding on request, boating on the lake. **Pets** Dogs allowed on request **Nearby** Restaurants, 18-hole golf course, lake (Bordeaux), tennis; Wine Route, Saint-Emilion, châteaux and places of historic interest, Médoc via the Blaye Ferry. **Credit cards** Not accepted. **Open** All year. **How to get there** (Map 22): 35km northeast of Bordeaux via A10 exit 40B, dir. Blaye via N137. In Pugnac, D23 towards Saint-Savin. In Saint-Urbain, D137 towards Saint-Christoly-de-Blaye. About 3km, on right follow signs "Les Trias". From Paris, A10 exit 38, dir. Reignac, Saint-Savin, Pugnac.

In a magnificent park with a lake, La Bergerie comprises two well-renovated old houses. They have been converted into guest houses with a living room and fireplace, a kitchen, and one to three bedrooms. The handsome terra cotta floors, beautiful antique furniture and elegant fabrics all create a lovely ensemble. You will be offered several breakfast menus. The owners are charming people.

45 - Château du Parc

Le Parc
33580 Saint-Ferme
(Gironde)
Tel. 05 56 61 69 18
Fax 05 56 61 69 23
M. and Mme Lalande

Rooms 5 and 2 suites with bath or shower, WC and tel. **Price** 700-850F/106,71-129,58€ (2 pers.); suite 990F/150,92€ (2 pers.); +200F/30,48€ (extra bed). **Meals** Breakfast 75F/11,43€. Evening meals at separate tables, by reservation 250F/38,11€ (wine incl.). **Facilities** Sitting room, swimming pool. **Pets** Dogs allowed on request. **Nearby** Fishing, tennis, bicycle rentals, golf; Saint-Émilion, Wine Route, wine and historic castles. **Credit cards** All major. **Spoken** English. **Open** All year. **How to get there** (Map 22): 62km southeast of Bordeaux to Créon/Sauveterre-de-Guyenne (N671), then to La Réole, then on left D14 Saint-Ferme, then D139 to Saint-Ferme/Château du Parc.

This 18th-century château has a brand new formal garden in front and rolling vineyards all around. Inside it has been beautifully renovated, with delicate patinas often highlighted by stenciled borders. Furnished with an artistic eye in warm colors, with unusual objects, engravings, a charming blend of antique furniture with a hint of Provençal style. Beauty and comfort are found as well in the large bedrooms with their carefully chosen furniture and linens. Breakfast is served in the spacious kitchen or in the sitting room. The reception is youthful and friendly.

46 - Manoir de James

33580 Saint-Ferme
(Gironde)
Tel. 05 56 61 69 75
Fax 05 56 61 89 78
M. and Mme Dubois

Rooms 3 with bath and WC. **Price** 300F/45,73€ (1 pers.), 360F/54,88€ (2 pers.); +50F/7,62€ (extra child), +80F/12,19€ (extra pers.). -10% from beg Oct to end Apr and from 5ᵗʰ day in high season. **Meals** Breakfast incl. **Facilities** Sitting room, garage, swimming pool, ping pong, bike rentals. **Pets** Dogs allowed on request. **Nearby** Restaurants, 18-hole golf course (35km), riding, mountain bikes, tennis, lakeside sports, fishing in river; Abbaye of Saint-Ferme, Romanesque churches. **Credit cards** Not accepted. **Spoken** English, German, Spanish. **Closed** Dec 15 – Jan 15 **How to get there** (Map 22): In Libourne towards Langon La Réole via D670; in Sauveterre towards La Réole, then 2km farther follow signs to Saint-Ferme. In Saint-Ferme go towards Sainte-Colombe; the Manoir is 2km on left.

You will be courteously welcomed to this small manor house located on a hillside among the Entre-Deux-Mers vineyards. The large, quiet bedrooms are furnished with antiques. In summer, an English-style breakfast is served early around the swimming pool. Madame Dubois will be happy to tell you about the many attractions of this beautiful region near Bordeaux.

47 - Château de l'Escarderie

33240 Saint-Germain-de-la-Rivière
(Gironde)
Tel. and fax 05 57 84 46 28
Mme Claverie
E-mail: lescarderie@free.fr
Web: lescarderie.free.fr

Rooms 4 with bath or shower and WC. **Price** 260F/39,63€ (1 pers.), 280-330F/42,68-50,30€ (2 pers.), +80F/12,19€ (extra bed). **Meals** Breakfast incl. No communal meal. **Facilities** Sitting room, dining room. **Pets** Dogs not allowed. **Nearby** Restaurants, swimming pool, tennis, riding club; Wine Route, visit to wine cellars just a few steps away, Bordeaux, Le Médoc. **Credit cards** Not allowed. **Spoken** English. **Open** All year, by reservation and deposit. **How to get there** (Map 22): 35km north of Bordeaux. Autoroute A10, exit Saint-André-de-Cubzac dir. Libourne via D670. At the exit of Saint-Germain, 1st road on left after the stop and follow signs.

Escarderie, really more like an old villa than a château, is a nice place to stop along the Bordeaux Wine Road. It is set high in the hills, off the road and offers four good sized rooms, all recently renovated. Colorful hangings and well-kept bathrooms. The traditional style furniture was made by Monsieur Claverie, a skilled cabinet-maker. A very pleasant stop at reasonable prices.

48 - Gaudart

Gaudart
33910 Saint-Martin-de-Laye
(Gironde)
Tel. 05 57 49 41 37
M. and Mme Garret

Rooms 3 with bath or shower and WC, independent entrances. **Price** 200-260F/30,48-39,63€ (2 pers.), +90F/13,72€ (extra pers.). 10% reduction after 3 nights except in Jul and Aug. **Meals** Breakfast incl. Evening meals, by reservation (except Jul 10 – Aug 31) 95F/14,49€ (wine incl.). **Facilities** Sitting room, terrace. **Pets** Dogs not allowed. **Nearby** Restaurants, swimming pool, 18-hole golf course; Saint-Emilion, Guîtres Abbey, vineyards. **Credit cards** Not accepted. **Closed** Mid Apr – Oct 10. **How to get there** (Map 22): 9km northeast of Libourne via D910 towards Guîtres. In Saint-Denis-de-Pile, left on D22 for 5km, then follow signs for 1km.

A few minutes from the great vineyards of Saint-Emilion, this typical Gironde house is surrounded by quiet pastures . The vast living room, where breakfast and dinner are served, has its original old regional furniture. The bedrooms are quite large and the beds are comfortable. Two have very charming bathrooms. We preferred the one with the curtained bed, which is very well furnished. In fair weather, breakfast and dinner are served on the terrace. You will receive a very kind welcome.

49 - La Forge

33750 Saint-Quentin-de-Baron
(Gironde)
Tel. 05 57 24 18 54
Fax 05 57 24 20 63
Mme de Montrichard
E-mail: laforge@in-net.inba.fr

Rooms 1 with bath and WC, 1 studio (2-3 pers.) with shower, WC, kitchen; (baby bed possibility). **Price** 400F/60,97€ (2 pers.); studio 600F/91,46€/night. (4 nights min.). **Meals** Breakfast incl. Meals at communal tables possible on prior request 100F/15,24€ (wine not incl.). **Facilities** Sitting room. **Pets** Animals not allowed. **Nearby** Restaurants, tennis, bicycle rentals, equestrian center, 18-hole golf course (10km); châteaux, wine tasting, Saint-Émilion. **Spoken** English, German. **Open** All year. **How to get there** (Map 22): 30km east of Bordeaux via D936 to Saint-Quentin-de-Baron and first road on right after the service station.The house is on this little road in the 5rd corner. **No smoking.**

Life in this peaceful country house centers around a small interior garden full of flowers. Overlooking woods and vineyards, the bedrooms and studios are independent, with a separate entrance for guests. You can also enjoy the lovely, informal living room or the large garden at this old forge which has been rebuilt over the years. Madame de Montrichard will give you an enthusiastic account of her artistic activities as well as good advice on visiting the region.

50 - Le Prieuré

33750 Saint-Quentin-de-Baron
(Gironde)
Tel. 05 57 24 16 75
Mobile 0687 82 96 64
Fax 05 57 24 13 80
Mme de Castilho
E-mail: stay@stayfrance.net
Web: www.stayfrance.net

Suites 3 (2 pers.) with bath and shower and WC. 1 family suite of 2 bedrooms with WC. **Price** 500F/76,22€ (2 pers.), +150F/22,86€ (extra bed); family suite 200F/30,48€ (pers.). **Meals** Breakfast incl. No communal meal. **Facilities** Swimming pool, ping-pong, barbecue. **Pets** Animals not allowed. **Nearby** Restaurants, tennis, riding, bikes, golf; Saint-Emilion. **Spoken** English, Spanish, Portuguese. **Open** All Year. **How to get there** (Map 22): 25km east of Bordeaux via D936 dir. Bergerac; go through Saint-Quentin-de-Baron dir. Branne/Bergerac, go past the Carré Bleu Swimming Pool and the Shell station. Continue for exactly 1km and in front of the K25 marker, Le Prieuré sign is on right; at the end of the lane. **No smoking.**

Located in the heart of the Bordeaux vineyards, this old priory offers you all the advantages of a modern house. Several pleasant bedrooms open onto the wooded garden overlooking a magnificent countryside; others are located upstairs. Madame de Castilho has created an atmosphere of English hospitality here, and children are welcome. It is possible to have simple meals at lunch.

A Q U I T A I N E

51 - Domaine de la Charmaie

33190 Saint-Sève
(Gironde)
Tel. 05 56 61 10 72
Fax 05 56 61 27 21
M. and Mme Chaverou

Rooms 4 with bath or shower and WC. **Price** 360F/54,88€ (2 pers.) +100F/15,24€ (extra bed). **Meals** Breakfast incl. Evening meals at communal or separate tables 120F/18,29€ (wine incl.). **Facilities** Sitting room, billiard, swimming pool. **Pets** Animals not allowed. **Nearby** Equestrian center, fishing (le Dropt), 18-hole golf course (18km); bastides de Bazas, Monségur, Sauveterre. **Spoken** English, Spanish. **Open** All year. **How to get there** (Map 22): 70km southeast Bordeaux. Aut. A6 to Langon, then N113 to Agen to La Réole, then take D668 to Monségur. On the traffic circle, D21 to Saint-Sève and follow signs.

Just outside of Saint-Sève, you will come to the delightful La Charmaie, a 7 1/2-acre estate where a former decorator from Bordeaux, Madame Chaverou, has created a haven of tranquillity in a bright and elegantly decorated house. The furniture, the objects she has chosen with taste and a sense of comfort, all go beautifully with this handsome 17th-century building. Around the swimming pool in summer or by the fireside in winter, we felt as if we were in a lovely family home enjoying the art of country living. It's worth a detour.

52 - Château Lamothe

33450 Saint-Sulpice-et-Cameyrac
(Gironde)
Tel. 05 56 30 82 16
Fax 05 56 30 88 33
Luce and Jacques Bastide

Suites 3 with bath and WC. Poss. 2 bedrooms nearby. 1 large suite with bath, shower and WC. **Price** suites 1000F/152,44€ (2 pers.); rooms 300-400F/ 45,73-60,97€ (1pers.); large suite 1300F/198,18€ (2 pers.), +150F/22,86€ (extra bed). **Meals** Breakfast incl. No communal meal. **Facilities** Sitting room, swimming pool, fishing in moat, boat on property. **Nearby** Restaurants. **Credit cards** Not accepted. **Spoken** English, Spanish. **Open** Easter – Nov 1 (on request in winter). **How to get there** (Map 22): 18km east of Bordeaux via N89 (Bordeaux/Libourne); exit 5 (Beychac, Cameyrac), then D13 to Saint-Sulpice. Road to stadium on right as you enter village. Follow signs. **No smoking** in bedrooms.

The very old, beautifully restored Château Lamothe is totally surrounded by water. It has superb bedrooms with all the modern amenities, including stunningly beautiful bathrooms. All the rooms are vast, bright and decorated in the same tasteful spirit, with some traditional old furniture, white drapes, pictures of luxuriant landscapes, pretty faïences and the family's handsome decorative objects. Delicious breakfasts are served in the beautiful dining room. The owners are helpful and graciously hospitable.

53 - Domaine du Ciron

Brouquet
33210 Sauternes
(Gironde)
Tel. 05 56 76 60 17
Fax 05 56 76 61 74
M. and Mme Peringuey

Rooms 4 with bath or shower and WC. **Price** 240-250F/36,59-38,11€ (2 pers.), +70F/10,67€ (extra bed). **Meals** Breakfast incl. No communal meal. **Restaurants** "Auberge des Vignes" and "Le Saprien" in Sauternes. **Facilities** Swimming pool and patchwork initiation. **Pets** Dogs not allowed. **Nearby** Tennis, 18-hole golf course, riding (8km), canoeing (8km), Sauternes Wine Route, châteaux. **Credit cards** Not accepted. **Spoken** English. **Open** All year. **How to get there** (Maps 22 and 29): 11km of Langon. Take A62, then D8 in the direction of Villandraut. For 1km after the Sauternes crossroads; at Brousquet (1km) turn right by the water tower; follow signs.

Monsieur and Madame Peringuey are wine merchants and they have installed in their house four guest rooms which are plain but with all the necessary amenities. The rooms are very well kept and are part of the family life so that, particularly in summer, everyone quickly gets to know each other. Breakfast is served in a pleasant dining room not far from the swimming pool. This unpretentious house with its reasonable prices is a perfect place for exploring the vineyards and learning more about wine.

54 - Château de Bachen

Duhort-Bachen
40800 Aire-sur-l'Adour
(Landes)
Tel. 05 58 71 76 76
Fax 05 58 71 77 77
M. and Mme Guérard

Rooms 2 and 2 apartments with bath and WC. **Price** Rooms 800F/121,95€ (2 pers.); apart. 1200F/182,93€ (2 pers.), 3 days min. and 1 week in Jul and Aug. **Children** Under 12 note when you reserve. **Meals** Breakfast 100F/15,24€. No communal meal. **Restaurant** "Guérard" in Fugénie-les-Bains. **Facilities** Sitting room, swimming pool. **Pets** Dogs not allowed. **Nearby** Thermal waters at farm, 9-hole golf course. **Credit Card** Not accepted. **Spoken** English, Spanish. **Open** Jun 1 – Nov 1, by reservation. **How to get there** (Map 29): 4km west of Aire-sur-l'Adour, towards Eugénie-les-Bains for 2.5km, go through small forest, in about 300m turn right between two cypress trees; follow signs. **No smoking** in bedrooms and apartments.

Surrounded by the vineyard of Tursan, this building in pure 18th-century style looks down onto the plain and offers fine panoramas over the valleys of Gers. Inside the decoration is stunning: quality antiques, elegant objects, old paintings, all in richly assorted colors. The surroundings add to your enjoyment of the excellent breakfasts served in the old kitchen or in the sitting room. The bedrooms are irresistible, decorated with taste and artistry as well as with concern for comfort. The reception is both pleasant and professional.

55 - Lamolère

40090 Campet-Lamolère
(Landes)
Tel. 05 58 06 04 98
Béatrice and Philippe de Monredon

Rooms 2 with bath or shower and WC. 1 family suite with 2 bedrooms, 2 showers and shared WC. Rooms cleaned every three days or on request. **Price** 270 and 290F/41,16 and 44,21 €. Family suite 220 and 250F/33,53 and 38,11€ (for 1 bedroom, 2 pers.) **Meals** Breakfast incl. Evening meals at communal table 80F/12,19€ (wine and coffee incl.). **Facilities** 2 sitting rooms (piano, library, TV); less than half a mile away, a gîte (accommodations) for children from 5 to 10 is run by the owner's daughter; 12th-century chapel, horse stalls, fishing, bicycles. **Pets** Dogs allowed in the kennel on request. **Nearby** Golf, swimming pool (4km). **Credit cards** Not accepted. **Spoken** English, Spanish. **Open** All year. **How to get there** (Map 29): 5km northwest of Mont-de-Marsan via D38; on the Morcenx road.

A large mansion set in an 18-acre park, Lamolère has bedrooms which combine beauty and modern comfort. Most of the beds are very wide, the colors are tastefully coordinated and there are many charming decorative details. You will find some handsome pieces of antique furniture. The excellent evening meals are usually served outside on a large terrace. You will enjoy beautiful views, a warm welcome and very reasonable prices for the quality.

56 - Château de Bezincam

Chemin de l'Adour
Saubusse-les-Bains
40180 Dax
(Landes)
Tel. and fax 05 58 57 70 27
Claude and Guy Dourlet

Rooms 3 and 1 suite (3-4 pers.) with bath or shower and WC. **Price** Rooms 300-350F/45,73-53,35€ (2 pers.); suite 350F/53,35€ (2 pers.) +100F/15,24€ (extra bed). **Meals** Breakfast incl. No communal meal. **Facilities** Sitting room, river fishing. **Pets** Dogs not allowed. **Nearby** Restaurants, tennis, riding, beach, golf; Adour Valley, coasts of the Landes and the Basque country, bullfights. **Credit cards** Not accepted. **Spoken** English, Spanish. **Open** All year. **How to get there** (Map 29): 15km southwest of Dax via N10 or N124. At Saint-Geours-de-Maremne, D17 towards Saubusse. In Saubusse, on right of bridge, take small road along the Adour for 800m (last house).

From the small road that runs along the Adour River, you can occasionally catch a glimpse of superb estates built facing the river. Bezincam is one of them and the minute we set foot inside, we were reminded of vacation houses of the past. The furniture, objects, engravings and even the garden furniture seem to have been here forever. Very prettily decorated, the bedrooms are bright and pleasantly spacious. The bathrooms are charming and some are vast. The breakfasts are delicious and the owners are especially pleasant. This is a spot to be discovered.

57 - Myredé

40270 Grenade-sur-l'Adour
(Landes)
Tel. and fax 05 58 44 01 62
M. and Mme de la Forge

Rooms 2 with bath or shower and WC. **Price** 300-350F/45,73-53,35€ (2 pers.). **Meals** Breakfast incl. No communal meal. **Facilities** Sitting room (TV), bicycles, ping-pong, barbecue and garden furniture at guests' disposal. **Pets** Dogs allowed on request. **Nearby** Restaurants, swimming pool, tennis, riding, hiking, horse trekking, canoeing/kayaks, 18-hole golf course (10km); Despiau museum, bullfighting in Mont-de-Marsan (Jul). **Closed** Nov 1 – Easter. **How to get there** (Map 29): 10km south of Mont-de-Marsan via RN124 to Aire-sur-l'Adour/Grenade; on left (white fence and avenue of plane trees), at the end of the road (400m). **No smoking.**

A large old house with great charm, Myredé nestles among shrubs and immense trees, including an oak which is several hundred years old, offering lovely cool shade in the summer. You can choose one of two beautiful guest rooms overlooking the garden, one with a small adjacent office. The rooms are comfortable and have a holiday air about them, making Myredé a restful, quiet place to stay in the heart of Gascony's Landes region.

58 - Le Bos de Bise

40630 Luglon
(Landes)
Tel. 05 58 07 50 90
Fax 05 58 07 50 90
M. and Mme Congoste

Rooms 2 (1 with sitting room), with terrace, shower and WC. Rooms cleaned on request. **Price** 270F/41,16€ (2 pers./night), 250F/38,11€ (2 pers. from 3 nights), +100F/15,24€ (extra pers.). **Meals** Breakfast incl. No communal meal. **Facilities** Sitting room, lake. **Pets** Animals not allowed. **Nearby** Restaurants, riding, tennis, golf, canoeing (8km), seaside (45km); Napoleon III museum, Marquese museum. **Credit cards** Not accepted. **Open** Apr – Nov. **How to get there** (Map 29): 25km northwest of Mont-de-Marsan via N134 towards Sabres, then D14.

Surrounded completely by pine trees, Le Bos de Bise is made up of several buildings connected by a carefully tended lawn. The two bedrooms each have a private terrace and are both very comfortable and decorated in traditional style. One has an adjoining sitting room. Breakfast is served in a rustic beamed dining room. Outside, a covered kitchen for preparing light meals, a pond with ornamental animals, and a hiking path have been added for your enjoyment.

59 - Capcazal de Pachiou

40350 Mimbaste
(Landes)
Tel. and fax 05 58 55 30 54
Mme Dufourcet-Alberca

Rooms 3 with bath or shower. **Price** 260-300F/39,63-45,73€ (2 pers.), 400F/60,97€ (4 pers., with 2 canopied beds) +100F/15,24€ (extra bed). **Meals** Breakfast incl. Evening meals at communal tables 90F/13,72€ (wine incl.). **Facilities** Sitting room, Tel., pond and private lake (1km). **Pets** Dogs not allowed. **Nearby** Tennis, golf; Basque coast. **Spoken** English, Spanish. **Open** All year. **How to get there** (Map 29): 12km east of Dax. Take D947 dir. Pau, after the cross roads Mimbaste (C15) and take C16 1km after on right, then follow signs (1km).

This noble mansion, which has been in the same family ever since it was built four hundred years ago, enjoys a privileged setting in an unspoiled natural site. Inside you will be enchanted by the vestiges of past centuries (woodwork, fireplaces, flooring…), antique furniture and objects full of charm. The same authenticity permeates the bedrooms, which are comfortable and some of which have a fireplace. You will sleep on beautifully embroidered sheets. Add to this the kind and generous welcome of Madame Dufourcet-Alberca and you have a fine stopping place with reasonable prices.

60 - Le Cassouat

Magescq
40140 Soustons
(Landes)
Tel. 05 58 47 71 55
M. and Mme Gilbert Desbieys

Rooms 5 with shower and WC. **Price** 290F/44,21€ (2 pers., 1 night), 260F/39,63€ (2 pers., from 2 nights) +80F/12,19€ (extra pers.). 3 nights min. in Jul and Aug. **Meals** Breakfast incl. No communal meal. **Facilities** Sitting room, tel., lake (pedalo), bikes. **Nearby** Tennis in Magescq, 9- and 18-hole golf course (16km), mountain biking, hiking, seaside (18km), lake, swimming pool (15km), Landes regional park. **Credit cards** Not accepted. **Spoken** English, some Spanish. **Open** All year. **How to get there** (Map 28): 16km northwest of Dax. From N10 (Paris/Bayonne), take exit 10 at Majescq, then Herm road (D150).

This very modern house with triangular shapes and long roofs is set in the middle of a beautiful oak forest. The atmosphere is pleasant and the very comfortable bedrooms are decorated in contemporary style. Beyond the big bay windows, there is a lovely sheltered terrace where you can enjoy breakfast and admire the pretty countryside. And, with luck, a deer might just leap in the distance!

A Q U I T A I N E

61 - Domaine de Montfleuri

47250 Bouglon
(Lot-et-Garonne)
Tel. 05 53 20 61 30
Dominique Barron

Rooms 3 with bath or shower and WC. 2 rooms and 1 suite (3-4 pers.) with private shower and communal WC. **Price** Rooms 270-320F/41,16-48,78€ (1 pers.), 300-370F/45,73-56,41€ (2 pers.), 400F/60,97€ (3 pers.) +100F/15,24€ (extra pers.); suite 450F/68,60€ (3 pers.), 500F/76,22€ (4 pers.). **Meals** Breakfast incl. Communal meals, vegetarian cooking on request 100F/15,24€ (wine incl.) **Facilities** Sitting room, tel., swimming pool, bicycles. **Pets** Dogs not allowed. **Nearby** Restaurants. **Credit cards** Not accepted. **Spoken** English. **Open** All year. **How to get there** (Maps 29 and 30): 15km south of Marmande, towards Casteljaloux; at Le Clavier, take towards Bouglon and then towards Guérin; at about 1km on left.

Montfleuri is a beautiful, vast family house surrounded by a garden with trees and flowers growing in many colorful, fragrant nooks and crannies. It overlooks the gentle, rolling landscape of the Lot-et-Garonne département, whose environs are beautiful. The four bright bedrooms have simple amenities. In the evening dinner is served either in the kitchen in front of the fireplace or on the terrace in the shade of the large trees. Great for nature lovers and all who seek peace and quiet. Madame Barron is a true lover of gardening and a kind and attentive hostess.

62 - Chanteclair

47290 Cancon
(Lot-et-Garonne)
Tel. 05 53 01 63 34
Fax 05 53 41 13 44
Mme Larribeau

Rooms 3 and 1 suite (2-4 pers., 2 bedrooms) with bath or shower and WC. **Price** Rooms 310-340F/47,25-51,83€ (2 pers.); suite 310-460F/47,25-70,12€ (2-5 pers.). Reduced terms for 7 days +, special rates in low season Sept 15 – Jun 15. **Meals** Breakfast 30F/4,57€. No communal meal. Picnic possible in park and veranda. Barbecue and kitchenette at guests' disposal. **Facilities** Sitting room, billiards, piano, swimming pool, bicycle, pétanque. **Pets** Dogs not allowed. **Nearby** Châteaux, bastides; 27-hole golf course (7km), tennis (800m), lake fishing, river fishing, riding, mountain biking, sailing, canoeing. **Credit cards** Not accepted. **Spoken** English, Spanish. **Open** All year. **How to get there** (Maps 23 and 30): 500m west of Cancon, on D124 towards Marmande.

This large country house lies on the edge of the Périgord region. The interior decoration is elegant right down to the beautiful, comfortable guest rooms. They are furnished with prettily colored eiderdowns, lovely wallpaper and many pleasant decorative details. You might wander in the lovely garden, enjoy the swimming pool, or try the billiard table inside. You will be warmly welcomed.

63 - Manoir de Roquegautier

Beaugas
47290 Cancon
(Lot-et-Garonne)
Tel. 05 53 01 60 75
Fax 05 53 40 27 75
Brigitte and Christian Vrech
E-mail: roquegautier@free.fr
Web: //roquegautier.free.fr

Rooms 2 and 2 suites (3-4 pers.) with bath or shower and WC. Rooms cleaned on request. **Price** Rooms 320-350F/48,78-53,35€ (2 pers.); suites 485F (3 pers.)-495F (4 pers.)/73,93(3 pers.)-75,46€ (4 pers.). **Meals** Breakfast 30F/4,57€. Evening meals at communal table 105F/16€ (wine incl.), 70F/10,67€ (children). Lunch at separate tables à la carte. **Facilities** Sitting room, tel., playroom, piano, clothes-washer, swimming pool, child care facilities on the property. **Pets** Animals not allowed. **Nearby** 27-hole golf course (3km), equestrian center, tennis, lake; châteaux of Bonaguil and Biron, Monpazier, Monflanquin. **Credit cards** Not accepted. **Open** Apr – Oct. **How to get there** (Maps 23 and 30): 17km north of Villeneuve-sur-Lot via N21 towards Cancon, stay on N21.

The popularity of Roquegautier owes much to the kindness of Brigitte and Christian and to the ambiance they have created here. The bedrooms are light and very comfortable, with thick quilts on the beds and pretty pastel-colored curtains. The large bedroom under the eaves has handsome beams overhead and extends into a round tower. The dinners are excellent.

64 - La Biscornude

Fernand
47320 Clairac
(Lot-et-Garonne)
Tel. 05 53 84 01 39
Fax 05 53 79 19 72
Jérôme Quilan

Rooms 2 with shower and WC. **Price** 260F/39,63€ (2 pers.). **Meals** Breakfast incl. No communal meal. **Facilities** Sitting room **Pets** Dogs allowed on request. **Nearby** Restaurants, fishing, swimming (Lot), tennis, riding, 18-hole golf course; Romanesque architecture, frescoes, Clairac (medieval village), Prune Museum, Automaton Museum. **Open** All year. **How to get there** (Map 30): 4km east of Aiguillon. Exit "Entre-Deux-Mers" at Aiguillon then via N113 to Bordeaux. After the bridge, on right to Clairac (4km, house on right).

Isolated from a small, quiet road by a curtain of large trees, La Bicornude overlooks a marvelous garden filled with a happy, sun-dappled disorder of rose bushes, aromatic plants, bushes, and fruit trees. The simple, elegant bedrooms, which you reach via a gallery, have beautiful bathrooms. Breakfast is usually served outside or in a charming dining room filled with old furniture and interesting objects. You're certain to love La Bicornude as much as we did.

65 - Château de Lamothe

47330 Ferrensac
(Lot-et-Garonne)
Tel. and fax 05 53 36 98 02
Vicomte and Vicomtesse
Marc Dauger
E-mail: lamothe1@worldonline.fr

Rooms 4 with bath or shower and WC. 1 children's room without bath and WC. **Price** 450-600F/68,60-91,46€ (2 pers.). **Meals** Evening meals at communal tables twice weekly 200F/30,48€. **Facilities** Sitting room, tennis, billards. **Pets** Small dogs allowed on request. **Nearby** Riding, lake, swimming pool, 18-hole golf course; Wine Route. **Credit cards** Not accepted. **Closed** Dec – end Mar, by reservation in winter. **How to get there** (Map 23): 4km southeast of Castillonnes. D2 dir. Villeréal. 3.5km, on right to Ferrensac, go past the church to the Calvary, then on right towards Pompiac (v 1): sign posted (800m).

In the heart of the bastide country, this château from the 11th and 17th centuries stands on a vast property of rolling hills. It has been superbly renovated, the modern amenities added with complete respect for the traditional character. The books, objects and family heirlooms lend a distinct personality to each room. Large or small, the bedrooms are furnished with antiques, have very comfortable beds and impeccable bathrooms. A wonderful place where you will enjoy a thoughtful and refined reception.

66 - Cantelause

47420 Houeillès
(Lot-et-Garonne)
Tel. and fax 05 53 65 92 71
Nicole and François
Thollon Pommerol

Rooms 2 with bath and WC in guest house. **Price** 240F/36,58€ (2 pers.), poss. extra bed. **Meals** Breakfast 25F/3,81€. Communal evening meals 130 and 150F/19,81 and 22,86€. **Facilities** Sitting room. **Pets** Dogs not allowed. **Nearby** 18-hole golf course (Casteljaloux, 20km); riding, tennis, swimming pool, lake, bikes; Circuits of Bastides and Chapels. **Credit cards** Not accepted. **Spoken** English, Spanish. **Open** All year. **How to get there** (Maps 29 and 30): 20km south of Casteljaloux, towards Houeillès via D933; then turn left on D156 and D154 towards Durance; it's 8km east of Houeillès.

Nestling in the midst of pine groves on the edge of the Landes Forest, Cantelause is a lovely house with a rustic but elegant annex. There are two small, prettily decorated bedrooms with very modern bathrooms. Breakfasts and dinners – including homemade foie gras, bread and brioches – are served in the main house or, in summer, in the garden. A haven for golfers (package stays are possible), Cantelause is also delightful for those who love peaceful surroundings and fine food.

67 - Manoir du Soubeyrac

in Envals
47150 Le Laussou
(Lot-et-Garonne)
Tel. 05 53 36 51 34
Fax 05 53 36 35 20
Claude Rocca

Rooms 3 and 1 suite (4 pers.) with bath (whirlpool and 2 jet-showers), WC, tel. and TV. **Price** Rooms 580-680F/88,42-103,66€ (2 pers.); suite 880F/134,15€. **Meals** Breakfast incl. Evening gastronomic meals at separate tables 130F/19,81€. **Facilities** Lounge, library, piano; park, patio, a pool with artificial waves and water jets, ping pong, bicycles, forest paths, fitness facilities (whirlpool). **Pets** Dogs not allowed. **Nearby** Fishing, tennis, hiking, golf; festivals, vineyard. **Credit cards** Not accepted. **Spoken** English. **Open** All year. **How to get there** (Map 23): 20km north of Villeneuve-sur-Lot via D676. In Monflanquin towards Monpazier on D272; then after 2km left towards Envals on C3; then follow signs.

Situated amid gently rolling hills, this little 17th-century manor house has been extensively and lovingly restored and offers accommodation of the greatest comfort. Everywhere the decoration strives to create a festive atmosphere: brightly colored fabrics, lamps of colored glass, charming knickknacks, paintings and furniture of different styles. Claude Rocca is a thoughtful, sensitive host as well as an excellent cook, preparing delicious meals based on local products. An elegant and inviting place.

68 - L'Ormeraie

47150 Paulhiac
(Lot-et-Garonne)
Tel. and fax 05 53 36 45 96
M. de L'Ormeraie
Mme Sanders

Rooms 5 and 1 suite with bath or shower and WC. **Price** 400-725F/60,97-110,52€ (2 pers.); suite 725F/110,52€ (2 pers.), 130F/19,81€ (extra bed). −20% from 3rd night **Meals** Breakfast incl. (for 1 pers. on request). Communal meals three times weekly, by reservation 150F/22,87€ (wine incl.). **Facilities** Sitting room, tel., swimming pool. **Pets** Small dogs allowed on request (+15F/2,28€). **Nearby** Golf, Bonaguil, Biron, Bastides. **Credit cards** All major. **Spoken** English, Spanish. **Open** All year, by reservation and deposit. **How to get there** (Maps 23): 27km northwest of Villeneuve-s/Lot dir. Monflanquin for 17km, then dir. Monpazier for 8km. At Laussou, on right in front of the church (2km).

This handsome house and its outbuildings overlook the attractive hilly grounds with a nice swimming pool. The rooms vary in size, some open directly onto the garden and all are furnished with antique pieces of different periods. They are comfortably fitted and carefully decorated (though the shower room of the attic bedroom is really a bit cramped). The suite occupies all the space of a large atelier. Breakfast and dinner are both served outdoors in fine weather and Madame Sanders offers guests a pleasant and enthusiastic welcome.

69 - L'Air du Temps

Mounet
47140 Penne-d'Agenais
(Lot-et-Garonne)
Tel. 05 53 41 41 34
Melle Anne Cazottes

Rooms 5 with bath or shower and WC. **Price** 250-300F/38,11-45,73€ (2 pers.). **Meals** Breakfast incl. No communal meal. **Facilities** Sitting room, tel. **Nearby** Restaurants, lake and tennis (500m), yacht basin on Lot (2km), mountain bikes, equestrian center; Penne-d'Agenais, Castelnau. **Credit Cards** All major. **Spoken** English, Spanish. **Closed** 15 days in Mar and in Oct. **How to get there** (Map 30): In Agen dir. Cahors via D656. 15 km go left towardsLaroque-Timbaut, then Hautefage and Penne. Go 200 m after the lake, to the calvary.

Halfway between Port-de-Penne and the charming medieval village, you feel in a different world the moment you open the door. One of the buildings has two bedrooms that open directly onto the shaded side of the garden. Both have white walls and pale parquet floors set off by fine fabrics and colorful objects. In another building, three bedrooms opening onto a terrace are also white, with a decoration that combines eclectic objects with an air of the exotic, including mosquito netting. Breakfast is served in a large bright room with a sofa and tables or in summer under an awning facing the other garden. A pleasant spot in every way.

70 - Château de Cantet

Cantet
47250 Samazan
(Lot-et-Garonne)
Tel. 05 53 20 60 60
Fax 05 53 89 63 53
M. and Mme J.-B. de la Raitrie

Rooms 2 (1 with dressing room) with bath and WC. 1 suite (4-5 pers.) with shower and WC. Rooms cleaned twice a week on request. **Price** 280-340F/42,68-51,83€ (1 pers.), 320-380F/48,78-57,93€ (2 pers.); suite 580F/88,42€ (4 pers.) +110F/16,76€ (extra bed). **Meals** Breakfast incl. Baby's price 40F/6,09€/day. Communal meals in evening 120F/18,29€ (wine incl.), 60F/9,14€ (children under 12). **Facilities** Sitting room, covered swimming pool, 3 horse stalls, bicycles. **Pets** Dogs not allowed. **Nearby** Golf, lake; Casteljaloux, opera festival in Aug. **Credit cards** Not accepted. **Spoken** English. **Closed** Dec 15 – Jan 12, only by reservation. **How to get there** (Maps 29 and 30): 10km southwest of Marmande via D933 towards Casteljaloux, Mont-de-Marsan. After bridge above autoroute, take 2nd road on right, 2nd lane after railroad crossing.

This is a solidly built, traditional house, surrounded by tall trees and lovely flowers. The owners will greet you with great enthusiasm and informality. The bright bedrooms are tastefully decorated with antiques and look out over the gentle Gascon countryside. One room is located on the ground floor. Meals are served around the large dining table or, in summer, in the garden. For a family or a group of friends, this is an ideal place to stay.

71 - Domaine de Clavié

Soubirous
47300 Villeneuve-sur-Lot
(Lot-et-Garonne)
Tel. 05 53 41 74 30
Fax 05 53 41 77 50
M. Diserens
E-mail: domdeclavie@wanadoo.fr
Web: www.domainedeclavie.com

Rooms 4 with bath or shower and WC and 1 guest house with 2 double rooms, 2 baths, living room and kitchen. **Price** 650-850F/99,09-129,58€. Guest house 1200F/182,93€/day. **Meals** Breakfast incl. Communal meals at separate tables (except Mon and Tues), by reservation 165F/25,15€ (wine not incl.). **Facilities** Sitting rooms, tel., swimming pool. **Pets** Animals not allowed. **Credit cards** All major. **Spoken** English, Italian. **Closed** Jan 3 – Mar 1. **How to get there** (Map 30): 7km north of Villeneuve-sur-Lot via N21 towards Bergerac/Soubirous; After going downhill to intersection, go left towards Casseneuil, Sainte-Livrade, then immediately right, on a small road for 500m. Signs on a pillar on left.

The Domaine de Clavié is an elegant 17th-century mansion in the countryside near Agen. A charming stay awaits you here, where your hosts are attentive and friendly. You will find large bedrooms with pretty antique furniture; luxurious baths, and a patio where meals are served in summer. The delicate cuisine is made with fresh products from this rich farmland; meals are served at a charming table set with lovely china. In short, everything is provided for your comfort and relaxation in totally quiet surroundings.

72 - Les Huguets

47300 Villeneuve-sur-Lot
(Lot-et-Garonne)
Tel. and fax 05 53 70 49 34
Gerda and Ward Poppe-Notteboom

Rooms 5 with bath and WC. **Price** 260 and 310F/39,63 and 47,25€ (2 pers.) +60F/9,14€ (extra pers.). **Meals** Breakfast 35F/5,33€. Evening meals at communal tables 120F/18,29€ (aperitif and wine incl.). **Facilities** Sitting room, tel., swimming pool, tennis, riding, sauna (whirlpool); concerts around campfire, organized tours of region. **Pets** Dogs not allowed. **Nearby** Water skiing on the Lot, hiking, fishing, canoeing and kayaking, golf. **Credit Cards** Not accepted. **Spoken** English, German, Flemish, Spanish. **Open** All year. **How to get there** (Map 30): 4km south of Villeneuve-sur-Lot via the bypass towards Cahors, 2nd road on right and immediatly on left, then follow signs.

This large rustic house in the midst of the country has been decorated by a young Belgian couple. Equipped with all the modern amenities, the bedrooms are bright and simple, with views out over the valley or the old village. Monsieur Poppe will be delighted to take you horseback riding or touring the region. In the evening, he occasionally organizes concerts. You can also relax around the swimming pool or in in the garden. Traditional Périgord cuisine, with organic vegetables, is served in the evening. There is a happy family atmosphere at Les Huguets.

A Q U I T A I N E

73 - Moulin de Labique

Saint-Eutrope-de-Born
47210 Villeréal
(Lot-et-Garonne)
Tel. 05 53 01 63 90
Fax 05 53 01 73 17
M. and Mme Boulet-Passebon
E-mail: moulin-de-labique@wanadoo.fr
Web: www.moulin-de-labique.fr

Rooms 2 suites (4 pers.), 1 suite (sitting room and terrace) and 3 rooms with bath and/or shower and WC. **Price** 500F/76,22€ (2 pers.), suite 680-780F/103,66-118,91€. **Meals** Breakfast incl. Meals at communal or separate tables 150F/22,86€ (wine not incl.). **Facilities** Sitting room, tel., swimming pool, pond, riding, fishing (lake and river). **Credit cards** Diners, Visa, Eurocard, MasterCard. **Pets** Dogs allowed on request. **Spoken** English. **Closed** 15 days in Nov. **How to get there** (Map 23): 45km southeast of Bergerac via N21 towards Villeneuve-sur-Lot. In Cancon D124 on left towards Monflanquin. In Beauregard go on left towards Saint-Vivien to the mill on right. 1km after Saint-Vivien, then follow signs.

This lovely rustic 17th-century mansion is decorated with great charm and refinement. In one of the suites, two bedrooms share a huge bathroom and a loggia has columns reminiscent of a sort of colonial villa. The other bedrooms, comfortable, cheery and full of old-fashioned charm, are on the upper floor of an outbuilding overlooking the mill. On the ground floor is a small restaurant with a terrace for summer dining. A lovely view over flowers, a small pond and paddocks with ponies scattered over the hillside.

74 - Zubiarte

Chemin du Bosquet
64200 Arcangues
(Pyrénées-Atlantiques)
Tel. and fax 05 59 43 08 41
M. and Mme Picot

Room 1 (double bed) with bath and WC. **Price** 400F/60,97€ (2 pers.). **Meals** Breakfast 25F/3,81€. No communal meal. **Facilities** Sitting room, laundry. **Pets** Dogs not allowed. **Nearby** Restaurants, 18-hole golf course in Arcangues (600 m), beach; Spain (20km), Biarritz Musical Weeks (end Apr) and in Saint Jean-de-Luz (Sept), Latino-Americain Cinema Festival (Sept). **Spoken** English, Spanish. **Open** All year. **How to get there** (Map 28): 3km south of Biarritz. Aut. A63, exit n. 4, Biarritz-centre and Arcangues. After the motorway bridge the first on right, Chemin du Bosquet, 1.3km. After the white bridge, on left.

Sheltered by lush greenery and large trees, this refined, elegantly decorated house offers guests a pretty bedroom with a lovely bath. For reading and relaxation, you'll find a small private sitting room or you can enjoy the shady garden, welcome in the summer heat. Madame Picot, a discreet and friendly hostess, serves delicious breakfasts. Zubiarte is a beautiful place to stay for golfers and those who enjoy peaceful countryside.

75 - Sauveméa

64350 Arroses
(Pyrénées-Atlantiques)
Tel. 05 59 68 16 01
and 05 59 68 16 08
Fax 05 59 68 16 01
Annie and José Labat

Rooms 4 and 1 suite (4 pers.) with bath and WC. **Price** Rooms 240F/36,58€ (1 pers.), 280F/42,68€ (2 pers.); suite 450F/68,60€ (4 pers.). **Meals** Breakfast incl. Farm/auberge 75F/11,43€ (wine incl.). **Facilities** Sitting room, swimming pool, fishing, horse stalls, riding. **Pets** Dogs allowed in rooms. **Nearby** Vineyards of Madiran. **Credit cards** Not accepted. **Spoken** English. **Open** All year. **How to get there** (Map 29): 44km north of Tarbes via D935 towards Aire-sur-l'Adour, then D248 and D48 to Madiran, and D66 towards Arroses, then D292.

This spacious farmhouse-auberge is built around a very beautiful mansion. The bedrooms and bathrooms are all roomy, well renovated, and have attractive furniture in light wood They are comfortable and quiet. Breakfast is served in a large sitting room and the dinner menus are excellent. You can enjoy a pretty swimming pool with view sover the countryside and the lake below.

76 - Maison Marchand

Rue Notre-Dame
64240 La Bastide-Clairence
(Pyrénées-Atlantiques)
Tel. 05 59 29 18 27
Fax 05 59 29 14 97
Valérie and Gilbert Foix
E-mail: valerie.et.gilbert.foix@wanadoo.fr
Web: //perso.wanadoo.fr/maison.marchand

Rooms 5 with bath or shower and WC. **Price** 280-340F/42,68-51,83€ (2 pers.) +30F/4,57€ (in high season for 1 night) +95F/14,48€ (extra pers.). **Meals** Breakfast incl. Communal evening meals (Tue., Thurs and Sat or Sun in Jul and Aug; on request in the morning the rest of the year) 80F/12,19€ (wine not incl.), 120F/18,29€ (aperitif and wine incl.), children's menu 60F/9,14€. **Pets** Small dogs allowed on request. **Credit cards** Not accepted. **Spoken** English. **Closed** 2 weeks in Jan and 2 in Jun. **How to get there** (Map 28): 20km east of Bayonne. Autoroute A64 (Bayonne/Pau), exit 4 towards Saint-Palais and Bidache via D10. The house is in the village.

On the main street in the heart of a handsome bastide-village, this well-renovated old farmhouse has kept its fine structure of beams and all its rustic character. The simple and homey decoration go well with the relaxed atmosphere. The spacious sitting room is organized around a large dining table (very festive indeed for the memorable dinners). Pleasant bedrooms and excellent breakfasts make you feel you'd like to stay a little bit longer, especially with the warm welcome offered by Valérie and Gilbert.

77 - Maison Sainbois

Rue Notre-Dame
64240 La Bastide-Clairence
(Pyrénées-Atlantiques)
Tel. 05 59 29 54 20
Fax 05 59 29 55 42
Mme Haramboure
E-mail: sainbois@aol.com
Web: //members.aol.com/sainbois

Rooms 4 and 1 suite (4 pers.) with bath or shower and WC. **Price** 350-460F/53,35-70,12€ (2 pers., depending on room and season), suite 500-600F/76,22-91,46€ (4 pers., depending on season) **Meals** Breakfast 35-60F/5,33-9,14€. Evening meals at communal tables 140F/21,34€ (wine incl.). **Facilities** Sitting room (TV), tel., fax, answering machine, swimming pool. **Pets** Animals not allowed. **Nearby** Basque pelota, hiking, horse trekking, 18-hole golf course; Basque villages. **Credit cards** Visa (from Jun 1 to Sept 30). **Spoken** English, German. **Open** All year. **How to get there** (Map 28): 20km of Bayonne. Aut. Bayonne/Pau exit 4 dir. Urt-Bidache. In the village

Situated on the main street of a charming village, this house has undergone an impressive renovation. The interior has lost something of its age-old patina, but has gained a truly homey atmosphere. The decoration is sober, in tones of gray and white brightened by paintings or touches of colorful fabric. The bedrooms are meticulous and have all modern amenities, but one of them, "Souletine," is a bit small. Delicious breakfasts and dinners served on the terrace near the swimming pool. A house of high quality and the kindness of Madame Haramboure as a bonus.

78 - Irigoian

Avenue de Biarritz
64210 Bidart
(Pyrénées-Atlantiques)
Tel. 05 59 43 83 00
Fax 05 59 43 83 03
Philippe Etcheverry
Web: www.irigoian.com

Rooms 5 with bath, WC, TV, tel and minibar. **Price** from 450F/68,60€ (2 pers.) (2 nights min.) **Meals** Breakfast 40F/6,09€. No communal meal. **Restaurant** On beach 600m away. **Facilities** Sitting room-library, possibility of golf or thalassotherapy packages, Ilbarritz golf center just at the foot of the garden. **Pets** Dogs not allowed. **Nearby** Beach (300m), water sports, riding, Basque pelota, thalassotherapy (900m), nightclub (200m). **Spoken** English, Spanish. **Open** All year. **How to get there** (Map 28): 500m south of Biarritz on CD911. Autoroute A63, exit Biarritz, then N10, towards Bidart; first traffic light on right, CD911. 600m on your left.

Built in the 17th century, this is the oldest farmhouse on the Basque Coast. Once farmland, the area today is developed for tourism (not surprising as it is 30 meters from the ocean!). But Irigoian has been entirely restored, its beautiful interior decoration including fine materials, tinted plasters and paintings by Uria Monzon. The bedrooms are vast, with parquet floors and superb bathrooms; there is something peaceful in their uncluttered elegance (and double-glazed windows conveniently soundproof them from the street.) You will enjoy a gourmet breakfast in this superb place to stay on the Ilbarritz Gulf.

A Q U I T A I N E

79 - Trille

Chemin Labau
D 934 - Route de Rébénacq
64290 Bosdarros-Gan
(Pyrénées-Atlantiques)
Tel. 05 59 21 79 51
Fax 05 59 21 66 98 / 05 59 21 57 54
Mme Christiane Bordes
E-mail: christine.bordes@libertysurf.fr

Rooms 5 with bath or shower, WC and TV (independent entrance). **Price** 280F/42,68€ (1 pers.), 365F/55,64€ (2 pers.). **Meals** Breakfast incl. Dinner by reservation. **Restaurant** "Auberge le Tucq" (100m). **Facilities** Sitting room, tel., large terrace and interior courtyard. **Pets** Small dogs allowed. **Nearby** Golf, fishing; Lourdes. **Credit cards** Not accepted. **Spoken** English, Spanish. **Open** All year. **How to get there** (Map 29): 10km south of Pau via N134 towards Saragosse to Gan; from the 'Cave des Producteurs de Jurançon' in Gan, pass 4 sets of traffic lights, then take D934 towards Rébénacq, Arudy and Laruns, for about 3.5km. It's on the left. When you reach Auberge le Tucq, cross the bridge and take first left (some 50 m. farther on).

Trille is a Béarn house that has been completely refurbished. The comfortable, immaculately kept bedrooms look out over a beautiful panorama of high hills. Friendly and energetic, Christiane Bordes welcomes her guests with obvious pleasure. There is an inviting sitting room with a fireplace, which is reserved for guests. It opens onto the terrace where you can occasionally hear cars on the road. The breakfasts are excellent.

80 - Domaine Xixtaberri

64250 Cambo-les-Bains
(Pyrénées-Atlantiques)
Tel. 05 59 29 22 66
Fax 05 59 29 29 43
Mme Noblia

Rooms 4 with bath, WC, Tel. and TV. **Price** 370F/56,40€ (2 pers., low season) and 390-570F/59,45-86,89€ (2 pers., in Jul and Aug). **Meals** Breakfast 46F/7,01€. Farm/auberge, lunch and evening meals in summer (farm produce) 90-120F/13,72-18,29€ (Wine and coffee incl.). **Facilities** Sitting room. **Pets** Dogs allowed on request. **Nearby** Tennis, swimming pool, riding, mountain bike rentals, Basque pelota, golf; Theater Festival (Aug), concerts (summer), Edmond Rostand's house. **Credit Cards** Visa, Eurocard, MasterCard. **Spoken** English. **Open** All year. **How to get there** (Map 28): 4km east of Cambo-les-Bains.In Cambo-les-Bains, to Hasparren. In Urcuray, on right at the bakery, and follow signs (2,5km).

Standing on the slopes of Ursula Mountain, the Domaine Xixtaberri is a farmhouse-inn offering many different activities and meals made with farm-grown products. Guests will find four modern, comfortable, tastefully decorated bedrooms. Located in a converted sheepfold, they are arranged around a large, inviting living area where you can prepare your own breakfast. Each room has a small terrace or a balcony. All in all, you can enjoy a restful stay here, with good country cooking and a sumptuous natural setting.

A Q U I T A I N E

81 - La Maison Sallenave

Route de Haux
64470 Montory
(Pyrénées-Atlantiques)
Tel. 05 59 28 59 69
M. and Mme Ruata

Rooms 3 with shower and WC. **Price** 250F/38,11€ (2 pers.) +60F/9,14€ (extra bed). **Meals** Breakfast incl. Evening meals at communal tables, by reservation 85F/12,95€ (wine incl.). **Facilities** Sitting room. **Pets** Dogs allowed on request. **Nearby** Hiking, tennis, swimming (6km), fishing; gorges of the Kakouetta, crevasse of Holzarte, Iraty forest, Romanesque churches with three bell-towers. **Closed** Nov 15 – Mar 1. **How to get there** (Map 29): 22km west of Oloron via D919 to Saragosse, then Tardets. In Montory, on left, toward Haux for 2km, then turn on right and follow signs (500m).

Surrounded by the grassy slopes of the Haute Soule region, this converted farmhouse has retained its rustic charm while offering comfortable amenities. The three bedrooms with old parquet floors are sober and quiet. Breakfast and dinner are served at a communal table in an attractive dining room. Guests enjoy coming here for walking, hiking in the mountains, fishing with Jean-Piere Ruata, who knows his fish, or to discover this beautiful, unspoiled region.

82 - Le Lanot

64520 Sames
(Pyrénées-Atlantiques)
Tel. 05 59 56 01 84
Mme Liliane Mickelson

Rooms 3 with shower and WC. **Price** 285F/43,44€ (1 pers.), 345F/52,59€ (2 pers.) +75 and 150F/11,43 and 22,86€ (extra pers.). **Meals** Breakfast incl. Communal meals in evening, only by reservation 150F/22,86€. **Facilities** Conservatory. **Pets** Dogs allowed on request, **Nearby** Golf, lake, rowing, fishing, ocean and surf (35km); Saint-Jean-de-Luz, Saint-Jean-Pied-de-Port, Biarritz. **Credit cards** Not accepted. **Spoken** English, Spanish understood. **Open** All year. Reservations desirable. **How to get there** (Map 29): 6km southwest of Peyrehorade exit from A64 autoroute; follow signs beginning at Peyrehorade (on the bridge over river Adour) through Hastingues, Sames-Bourg, and small road for Bidache.

Le Lanot is an 18th-century Basque house not far from the River Adour. Very prettily furnished, it has three comfortable guest rooms which are decorated in a mixture of tasteful styles and colors. The bathrooms are beautiful and have thoughtful small touches that say much about the hostess' charming hospitality. Loquacious and original, Liliane Mickelson knows her beautiful region intimately; she has been known to regale her guests with stories about it over a hearty, delicious breakfast, which is served in the conservatory.

83 - Larochoincoborda

64310 Sare
(Pyrénées-Atlantiques)
Tel. 05 59 54 22 32
M. and Mme Berthon

Rooms 3 with bath and WC. **Price** 330-350F/50,30-53,35€. (2 nights min.) **Meals** Breakfast incl. Communal meals in evening on request 100F/15,24€ (low season). **Restaurants** In village and ventas (mountain inns) in Spain. **Pets** Dogs not allowed. **Facilities** Sitting room. **Nearby** Hiking (GR10), horse trekking, 18-hole golf course (14km), tennis, swimming pool, ocean (14km); small La Rhune train, Basque villages, Saint-Jean-de-Luz, Spain (3km). **Credit cards** Not accepted. **Spoken** English. **Open** All year, by reservation. **How to get there** (Map 28): 15km southeast of Saint-Jean-de-Luz to Ascain, then Sare; take, road to Vera (signs); house is 2.5km from village. **No smoking** in bedrooms.

You will find this beautiful house in a landmarked site off a long path that slowly ascends the breathtakingly beautiful Rhune Mountains. There are very pleasant, comfortable small bedrooms. Breakfasts are served in a large, inviting, elegantly decorated room, or outside on the terrace. You will enjoy a stunning view out over superb countryside: hills, pastures with low stone walls, beautiful vegetation and scattered Basque houses. The welcome is very friendly.

84 - Maison Dominxenea

Quartier Ihalar
64310 Sare
(Pyrénées-Atlantiques)
Tel. 05 59 54 20 46 (Hôtel Arraya: Reservation Dominxenea)
Fax 05 59 54 27 04 (Hôtel Arraya)
M. Jean-Baptiste Fagoaga

Rooms 3 with bath or shower and WC. **Price** 300-350F/45,73-53,35€ (2 pers.), 450F/68,60€ (3 pers.). **Meals** Breakfast incl. No communal meal. **Restaurants** In the Hôtel Arraya (next door), "Barachartea" (in front) and Ventas (rustic mountain auberge-restaurants) in Spain. **Facilities** Sitting room (TV), pay tel. in Hotel Arraya. **Pets** Dogs not allowed. **Nearby** Swimming pool, tennis, hiking, horse trekking, sports on Basque coast. Chantaco Golf Course (18-holes, 11km). **Credit cards** Not accepted. **Spoken** English, German, Italian, Spanish. **Closed** Nov 15 – Apr 1. **How to get there** (Map 28): 1km north of Sare, go to Hotel Arraya on the main square, and you will be taken to the Maison Dominxenea.

There is not a single house built after the 17th century in this lovely small Basque village where you will find the Maison Dominxenea. The bedrooms are very pleasant, with beautiful wallpaper, comfortable beds, and large bathrooms. In the morning, an excellent breakfast awaits you; you may enjoy it in the dining room or on the terrace, which looks out on the village and the garden. A charming house reserved entirely for the guests, it will delight all those who enjoy feeling independent.

85 - Olhabidea

64310 Sare
(Pyrénées-Atlantiques)
Tel. 05 59 54 21 85
Mme Jean Fagoaga

Rooms 4 with bath and WC. **Price** 300F/45,73€ (1 pers.), 350-380F/53,35-57,93€ (2 pers.) +60F/9,14€ (extra bed). **Meals** Breakfast incl. No communal meal. **Facilities** Sitting room, riding (tel. for info.). **Pets** Dogs not allowed. **Nearby** Restaurants, mountains, seaside, Basque villages, Spain (3km), golf (14km), swimming pool, tennis. **Credit cards** Not accepted. **Spoken** English. **Open** Mar – Nov, in winter by reservation. **How to get there** (Map 28): 14km southeast of Saint-Jean-de-Luz; from A63 take Saint-Jean-de-Luz Nord exit, then D918 to Ascain and D4 to Sare. Leave Sare in the direction of Saint-Pée-sur-Nivelle and go 2km. Turn right in front of the old chapel; follow signs.

If you do not know the Basque country here is a marvellous reason for a visit. The comfort and interior decoration of Olhabidea are as splendid as the landscape. You will find lovely embroidered sheets, old engravings, exposed beams, balustrades and bright terra cotta floors, notably in the magnificent entrance hall. Madame Fagoaga's friendly welcome lends further charm to this special place.

86 - Eskoriatza

Chemin Villa Rosa
64122 Urrugne
(Pyrénées-Atlantiques)
Tel. 05 59 47 48 37
Mme Badiola

Rooms 2 with bath or shower, WC and 1 extra bedroom that can form a suite. **Price** Rooms 330-350F/50,30-53,35€ (2 pers.) +100F/15,24€ (extra bed); suite 600F/91,46€. **Meals** Breakfast incl. No communal meal. **Facilities** Sitting room. **Pets** Dogs not allowed. **Nearby** Restaurants, sea (3km), tennis (1,5km), riding, moutain bikes, 18-hole golf course (3km); Saint-Jean-de-Luz, Spain (5km), Basque villages. **Spoken** English, Spanish. **Closed** Nov 1 – Feb holidays. 2 nights min. in summer. **How to get there** (Map 28): 3km south of Saint-Jean-de-Luz. Aut. A64, exit Saint-Jean-de-Luz-Sud, to Saint-Jean-de-Luz during 200m and first road on right (Centre Leclerc). Go above the Autoroute, then take first turn on right and first on left; house in 400m.

Eskoriatza is a modern house, built in pure Basque style and decorated with taste. A few pieces of antique furniture and colorful fabrics brighten the bedrooms. You will find a very attractive living room and a sunny garden, the quiet setting and the view of the mountains adding further charm to this house. You will be welcomed with simple, friendly hospitality.

A Q U I T A I N E

87 - Haizean

Chemin d'Achaharria Ttipy
64122 Urrugne
(Pyrénées-Atlantiques)
Tel. and fax 05 59 47 45 37
Mme Nardou

Rooms 4 with bath or shower, 2 with private WC and 2 with shared WC. **Price** 280-330F/42,68-50,30€ (2 pers.), +70F/10,67€ (extra bed). **Meals** Breakfast incl. No communal meal. **Facilities** Sitting room, bicycles. **Pets** Dogs not allowed. **Nearby** Restaurants, sea (4km), tennis, riding, 18-hole golf course (10km); Saint-Jean-de-Luz, Basque coast, small La Rhune train. **Spoken** English, Spanish. **Open** All year. **How to get there** (Map 28): 10km southwest Saint-Jean-de-Luz. Aut. A63, exit n. 2 to Urrugne. On the first traffic circle, to Col d'Ibardin during 2km. Take the road on left after the 2nd traffic circle. Go 600m, the house is after the junction on left.

Lying ten kilometers from the Atlantic Coast, this huge, modern Basque-style house stands in a country setting with a sweeping view of La Rhune Mountain, the Basque Country's most spectacular peak (in Basque: "good pastureland"). The bedrooms are comfortable and colorful, each enjoying a small terrace and a beautiful bathroom. In good weather, breakfast is served outside on a covered terrace. It's a pretty house, and Madame Nardou is a delightful hostess.

88 - Château du Plaix

03170 Chamblet
(Allier)
Tel. 04 70 07 80 56
M. and Mme Yves de Montaignac
de Chauvance

Rooms 1 room and 1 suite with bath or shower, WC, and 1 room with washroom and WC not adjacent. **Price** Room 495F/75,46€ (1 pers.), 550F/83,84€ (2 pers.); suite 860F/131,10€ (3 pers.), 950F/144,82€ (4 pers.), +140F/21,34€ (extra bed). Room with washroom 450F/68,60€ (2 pers.) **Meals** Breakfast incl. No communal meal. **Restaurants** In Commentry, Monluçon, Reugny. **Facilities** Sitting room, tel. **Pets** Dogs not allowed. **Nearby** Tennis, swimming pools, fishing, golf; Romanesque churches, châteaux, museums and forests. **Credit cards** Not accepted. **Spoken** Some English. **Open** All year, by reservation. Arrival after 4:30PM. **How to get there** (Map 17): 9km west of Monluçon. Autoroute A71, exit 10-Monluçon, then towards Commentry, Chamblet. Take direction Monluçon for 1km, signs at top of hill on left. **No smoking.**

Built in the 18th century by an ancestor of the family, this small château has just been entirely and very tastefully refurbished. All the furniture is antique and each room is harmoniously proportioned. The very comfortable bedrooms overlook a vast park with trees; they are imaginatively decorated and have new bathrooms. Breakfasts are served in a pleasant dining room with Louis XV wood paneling. Atmosphere of refinement and the owners are extremely friendly.

89 - Château de Boussac

03140 Target
(Allier)
Tel. 04 70 40 63 20
Fax 04 70 40 60 03
Marquis and Marquise de Longueil
E-mail: longueil@club-internet.fr

Rooms 4 and 2 suites with bath and WC. **Price** 600-900F/91,46-137,20€ (1-2 pers.); suites 950-1100F/144,82-167,69€ (1-3 pers.). **Meals** Breakfast 55F/8,38€. Half board 960F/146,35€ (1 pers.), 1300F/198,18€ (per pers.) in double room (5 days min.). Evening meals at communal table, by reservation 260-320F/39,63-48,78€ (all incl.). **Facilities** Sitting room. **Pets** Dogs allowed on request (+50F/7,62€ per day). **Nearby** Tennis, golf; Romanesque churches. **Credit card** Visa. **Spoken** English. **Open** Apr 1 – Nov 30. **How to get there** (Map 25): 44km east of Montluçon. From A71, exit 11 Montmarault, then D46 and D42 to Chantelle.

Boussac is a beautiful château reflecting many architectural styles, from medieval austerity to the grace of the 18th century. The rooms are magnificently furnished in the purest traditional style, and the bedrooms are comfortable and well decorated, with charming family mementos (the rooms with mansard ceilings are very handsome even if the corridor outside needs a bit of refurbishment.) The convivial evening meals are much prized by lovers of game in season. This is truly a noble and welcoming place in the heart of the countryside.

90 - Château de Fragne

03190 Verneix
(Allier)
Tel. 04 70 07 88 10
Fax 04 70 07 83 73
Comtesse Louis de Montaignac
E-mail: fragne@minitel.net

Rooms 3 with bath and WC. 1 suite of 2 small bedrooms with bath and WC. 1 suite of 2 bedrooms, 2 baths and WC. **Price** Room 400-600F/60,97-91,46€ (1-2 pers.), suite 600F and 1000F/91,46-152,44€ (3 pers.). **Meals** Breakfast 50F/7,62€. Evening meals (from Jun 1) at communal table 300F/45,73€ (wine incl.). **Facilities** Sitting room, fishing in lake; receptions, weddings. **Pets** Dogs allowed on request. **Nearby** Equestrian center, golf. **Credit cards** Not accepted. **Spoken** English. **Open** May 1 – Oct 15, or by reservation. **How to get there** (Map 17): 10km northeast of Montluçon. From A71 take Montluçon exit, then D94 towards Montluçon for 2km, then right on D39 towards Verneix; sign at the stop sign on the right.

An immense drive leads up to this château and its beautiful park. All the bedrooms have been restored and are decorated in soft colors with antique furniture, while the bathrooms have modern amenities. The sitting rooms and dining room overlook a large terrace where you may have breakfast when the weather is fine. The overall effect is lovely, recreating the elegance and simplicity of château life in the past. The owners are very hospitable.

91 - Manoir de la Mothe

03450 Vicq
(Allier)
Tel. 04 70 58 51 90
Fax 04 70 58 52 02
M. and Mme van Merris
E-mail: michelvanMerris@aol.com

Rooms 3 and 2 suites (4 pers.) with bath or shower and WC. **Price** Room 525-600F/80,03-91,46€ (2 pers.); suite 575F/87,65€ (2 pers.); +100F/15,24€ (extra bed). **Meals** Breakfast incl. Evening meals at communal table or not, on request 200F/30,48€ (all incl.). Special rates for children. **Facilities** Sitting room, swimming pool, sauna (extra charge), fishing and boat, bicycles (deposit requested), pony. **Pets** Dogs allowed on request. **Nearby** 18-hole golf course; Bourbonnais tour, Festival (classical music). **Credit cards** Visa, Eurocard, MasterCard. **Spoken** English, German. **Closed** Nov – end Mar, except by reservation. **How to get there** (Map 25): 30km west of Vichy. Aut. A 71, exit n. 12 to Ebreuil, then to Vicq. Near the church. **No smoking** in bedrooms

Surrounded by a wide moat, this small château, built in the 15th century and restructured in the 18th, has been magnificently restored by its hospitable owners. We were surprised to find such comfortable amenities in such an old edifice. The bedrooms, the largest of which is truly striking, brim with beauty and character. There is lovely antique furniture throughout. The salon, the dining room, and the kitchen with its large fireplace are also very attractive. And the small house for rent has all the conveniences of the château.

A U V E R G N E - L I M O U S I N

92 - Château du Riau

03460 Villeneuve-sur-Allier
(Allier)
Tel. 04 70 43 34 47
Fax 04 70 43 30 74
Baron and Baronne Durye

Rooms 4 with bath or shower, WC and possible suite (3-5 pers.). **Price** 650-750F/99,09-114,33€ (2 pers.), suite 1000F/152,44€ (3-4 pers.), 1250F/190,56€ (5 pers.). **Meals** Breakfast incl. Evening meals at communal table, by reservation 250F/38,11€ (all incl.). **Facilities** Sitting room. **Pets** Dogs not allowed. **Nearby** Swimming pool, tennis, riding, golf; Tronçais forest, Balaine arboretum, châteaux. **Credit cards** Not accepted. **Spoken** English. **Open** Mar 1 – Nov 30. **How to get there** (Map 18): 15km northwest of Moulins via N7 to Villeneuve-sur-Allier, then D133

This is an exceptional ensemble of buildings in typically Bourbonnais style. Having crossed the moat and passed through the postern gate, you reach the main part of the château. The bedrooms look the same as they must have to guests in past centuries; each is still decorated with beautiful 18th-century or Empire furnishings. Breakfast is served at the big table in the dining room, which, like the sitting room, is pleasant and well furnished. The hospitality is familial and elegant.

93 - Château de Bassignac

15240 Bassignac
(Cantal)
Tel. and fax 04 71 40 82 82
M. and Mme Besson

Rooms 3 with bath and WC and 1 apartment (3-4 pers.) with 2 bedrooms, bath and WC. **Price** Rooms 340-620F/51,83-94,51€ (2 pers.), apartment 820F/125€ (4 pers.). **Meals** Breakfast incl. Half board (3 days min.) 385-525F/58,69-80,03€/pers. in double room. Evening meals at communal table on request 250F/38,11€ (wine incl.). **Facilities** Sitting room, fishing, artist's studio and exhibition gallery on the property. **Pets** Dogs allowed on request. **Nearby** Golf, cross country skiing, villages, Romanesque churches, châteaux, activities, fishing and hiking (Jul-Aug). **Credit cards** Not accepted. **Spoken** English. **Open** Easter – Nov 1, by reservation in winter. **How to get there** (Map 24): 67km north of Aurillac via D922; 12km before Bort-les-Orgues take D312 towards Bassignac-église.

Bassignac is a fortified house of great character set in rolling, wooded countryside An immediately welcoming impression is given by the two ground-floor rooms. There are lovely bedrooms with 19th-century furniture, curios and charming fabrics. A log fire adds atmosphere to the excellent evening meals. The younger generation of the family runs a farmhouse-auberge at the entrance to the park.

94 - Barathe

15130 Giou-de-Mamou
(Cantal)
Tel. 04 71 64 61 72
Isabelle, Pierre and Julien Breton
E-mail: barathe2@wanadoo.fr

Rooms 5 with shower and WC. **Meals** Evening meals at communal table. Half-board 190F/28,98€/day per pers.in double room (wine incl.). Special rates for children. **Pets** Dogs not allowed. **Nearby** Riding, tennis (3km), swimming pools, 9-hole golf course (5km), cross-country and alpine skiing; village of Salers, Tournemire, Château of Anjony, Route des Crêtes, Puy Mary. **Credit cards** Not accepted. **Open** All year. **How to get there** (Map 24): 8km east of Aurillac via N122 towards Clermont-Ferrand, then in 7km turn left towards Giou-de-Mamou; follow sign.

Overlooking a beautiful countryside lulled by the tinkling of cowbells, this very old house truly revives the atmosphere of centuries past. The large dining room is stunningly typical of the region, with its old Auvergne furniture and its splendid "souillarde", an old wash tub of the Auvergne. The bedrooms are basic but comfortable, and they can easily accommodate children. The evening meal is a joyous occasion, and the cuisine, often praised in the guest book, is made with fresh products from the farm. (Nearby Salers is famous for its beef). The owners are very kind at Barathe, a rustic place ideal for families.

95 - Domaine de Courbelimagne

15800 Raulhac
(Cantal)
Tel. 04 71 49 58 25
M. and Mme Welsch

Rooms 3 and 2 suites with bath or shower, WC. **Price** Rooms 380 and 480F/57,93 and 73,17€ (1-2 pers.); suites 680F/103,66€ (3-4 pers.). **Meals** Breakfast incl. Communal meals (lunch and dinner) at separate tables 160F/24,39€ (wine not incl.). **Facilities** Sitting room, tel., ornamental pool. **Pets** Dogs allowed on request. **Nearby** Fishing in river (4km), 18-hole golf course; châteaux, Salers, Carlat, Conques. **Spoken** English, German. **Closed** Sept 30 – Easter. **How to get there** (Map 24): On D600 then D900 connects Aurillac to Mur-de-Barrez. 5km after Raulhac and 5km before Mur-de-Barrez.

This 16th-century château, which stands with its back to the hillside and facing a superb view, has come back to life thanks to the efforts of Monsieur and Madame Welsch. This warm and friendly couple have managed to restore each room without destroying the patina of centuries. The decoration is in shades of light brown, cream and old yellow and throughout the house one feels the charm of bygone days. The beds are new and very comfortable, the bathrooms well equipped. The candle-light dinners are excellent and served in a glass-walled dining room hung with samples of an herb collection dating from 1855. A wonderful place to stop in fine weather.

96 - Château d'Arnac

Nonards
19120 Beaulieu-sur-Dordogne
(Corrèze)
Tel. 05 55 91 54 13
Fax 05 55 91 52 62
Joe and Jill Webb

Rooms 4 with bath or shower and WC. **Price** 540F/82,32€ (2 pers., Jul and Aug), 440F/67,07€ (2 pers., in low season). Special rates for long stays. **Meals** English breakfast 40F/6,09€. Evening meals at communal table 200F/30,48€ (wine incl.). **Facilities** Sitting room, fishing in river, tennis-practice, swimming pool. **Pets** Dogs allowed on request. **Nearby** Riding, canoeing, golf; Collonges-la-Rouge. **Spoken** English. **Closed** Christmas. Only by reservation. **How to get there** (Map 24): 40km southwest of Brive. At the exit of Brive towards Aurillac, Beaulieu via D38. Before Beaulieu, at the cross road go turn left on D940, 500m, then left in front of cemetery.

This château has been adopted by an English couple and refurbished in the style of an English country house. Each year a few more improvements are made. The nicest bedrooms are the smallest ones, but even they are quite spacious, full of light and charm with their woodwork, fireplaces, lovely fabrics and eclectic furnishings. The bathrooms are comfortable. The decoration in the hallways is still incomplete. The large sitting room has a table at which dinner is served. English style breakfast. The prices are rather high.

97 - La Maison

11, rue de la Gendarmerie
19120 Beaulieu-sur-Dordogne
(Corrèze)
Tel. 05 55 91 24 97
Fax 05 55 91 51 27
Christine and Jean-Claude Henriet

Rooms 5 and 1 suite (2-4 pers.) with bath or shower and WC. **Price** Rooms 250-290F/38,11-44,21€ (1 pers.), 300-370F/45,73-56,40€ (2 pers.), +80F/12,19€ (extra bed); suite 550F/83,84€ (4 pers.). **Meals** Breakfast incl. No communal meal. **Facilities** Sitting room-bar, swimming pool. **Pets** Dogs not allowed. **Nearby** Canoeing, kayaks, tennis, fishing, 2 18-hole golf courses (30km), very beautiful villages: Gouffre-de-Padirac, Rocamadour, Collonges-la-Rouge. **Credit cards** Not accepted. **Spoken** Some English. **Closed** Oct – Apr 1. **How to get there** (Map 24): 40km south of Brive. Autoroute A20, exit Noailles; follow signs for Collonges-la-Rouge, then Beaulieu.

This extraordinary 19th-century house was inspired more by Mexico than by the irresistible medieval village of Beaulieu. The patio is surrounded by passageways in colored plaster which lead to the bedrooms. All the bedrooms – such as La Provençale, Les Caricatures and Les Indiens – reflect Christine and Jean-Claude Henriet's sure sense of taste and lively imagination. Excellent breakfasts are served in the 1930s decor of the Bar des Sports. This is a fabulous, very welcoming house, which you absolutely should not miss.

98 - La Raze

19500 Collonges-la-Rouge
(Corrèze)
Tel. 05 55 25 48 16
M. and Mme Tatien

Rooms 4 with shower and WC. Rooms cleaned on request. **Price** 235-270F/35,82-41,16€ (2 pers.). **Meals** Breakfast incl. No communal meal. **Facilities** Swimming pool, pond, "Jardin de peintre" (garden). **Pets** Dogs allowed on request. **Nearby** Restaurants, tennis, equestrian center; Collonges-la-Rouge, Rocamadour, Padirac. **Open** All year. **How to get there** (Map 24): 1km south of Collonges-la-Rouge. Follow signs from the village.

Just a stone's throw from quaint Collonges-la-Rouge, La Raze is a haven of tranquillity where you will find four delightful, bright bedrooms that have recently been redecorated with colorful curtains and bedspreads. They are located in a converted farmhouse which retains all its traditional charm, very near the main house where breakfast is served. The beautiful "Painter's Garden" is planted with sweet-smelling flowering trees and bordered with a stone balustrade overlooking a majestic countryside.

99 - La Chapelle Saint-Martial

23250 La Chapelle-Saint-Martial
(Creuse)
Tel. and fax 05 55 64 54 12
Alain Couturier

Rooms 4 with bath or shower, WC and TV. **Price** 260-380F/39,63-57,93€ (2 pers.), +50F/7,62€ (extra pers.). **Meals** Breakfast incl. No communal meal. **Restaurants** In 4km and 5km (gastronomic). **Facilities** Sitting room, swimming pool. **Pets** Dogs allowed on request. **Nearby** Tennis (6km), fishing in many streams and lakes, paths for long hikes: Plateaux des Millevaches; villages of Moutiers-d'Ahun; châteaux of Villemonteix, Aubusson tapestry. **Credit cards** Not accepted. **Spoken** English. **Open** All year. **How to get there** (Map 24): 22km southeast of Guéret via D940 via Limoges. Just before Pontarion, take D13 towards Ahun. In the village.

The road here runs along rolling pastureland, forests, an unspoiled lake and a few houses, one of which is the Chapelle Saint-Martial. The first surprise of this lovely house is a ravishing walled garden with a swimming pool. Inside everything is arranged with beauty and comfort in mind. The decoration of the very comfortable bedrooms is a model of taste, with brightly waxed antique furniture, elegant fabrics, soft beige carpets (except in the small room on the garden), selected paintings: everything is perfect. This is an excellent, welcoming bed and breakfast with very reasonable prices.

AUVERGNE - LIMOUSIN

100 - Le Celivier

Paulagnac
43500 Craponne-sur-Arzon
(Haute-Loire)
Tel. and fax 04 71 03 26 37
M. and Mme Champel

Rooms 5 with private shower and WC, 3 of which are outside room. **Price** 250F/38,11€ (1 pers., 1 or 2 nights) or 230F/35,06€ (1 pers. from 3 nights); 300F/45,73€ (2 pers., 1 or 2 nights) or 280F/42,68€ (2 pers., from 3 nights). **Meals** Breakfast incl. No communal meal. **Restaurants** 3km and 9km **Facilities** Sitting room. **Pets** Dogs not allowed. **Nearby** Fishing (2km), mushroom gathering, many hiking paths; country festival in village; Festival de la Chaise-Dieu, villages of Chalonçon, Old Town of Le Puy. **Credit cards** Not accepted. **Spoken** English. **Open** All year. **How to get there** (Map 25): 40km north of Le Puy. In Ambert, take D906 towards Le Puy. At Arlanc, D202 towards Craponne. At Craponne, take D498 for 3.5km and signs on left. **No smoking.**

This old house is located on a superb rolling plateau of the Livradois region. Inside, each room is delightful. Old woodwork, a vast stone fireplace, beautiful antique furniture, wood ceilings: all contribute warmth and cheer. The soft and snug bedrooms decorated in cool colors add further to the charm. The harmonious overall effect well reflects the hospitality with which you will be greeted.

101 - La Maison d'à côté

43100 Lavaudieu
(Haute-Loire)
Tel. 04 71 76 45 04
Fax 04 71 50 24 85
Marie Robert

Rooms 4 with shower and WC. **Price** 280F/42,68€ (2 pers.). **Meals** Breakfast incl. No communal meal. **Facilities** Sitting room, river (fishing, swimming) bordering the property. **Pets** Dogs not allowed. **Nearby** Restaurants, riding, fishing; Lavaudieu Abbey, château of Lafayette. **Credit cards** Not accepted. **Spoken** Some English. **Closed** Nov 1 – Easter. Arrival Mon to Fri from 6:00PM. **How to get there** (Map 25): 9km east of Brioude, dir. La Chaise-Dieu. After Pont-sur-l'Allier, 1st road on right towards Fontannes-Lavaudieu. In front of the bridge.

Lavaudieu is a little jewel of a medieval village clustered round an 11th-century abbey on the banks of the Senouire River. The house stands along the riverside facing the old bridge. Entirely renovated, its bedrooms are small but cozy, bright and cheery. Marie Robert runs the place with meticulous care and warm hospitality. Delicious breakfasts are served in a small pastel-colored sitting room that opens directly outside. There is no garden, but you can go for delightful strolls along the riverbanks.

102 - Le Moulin des Vernières

63120 Aubusson-d'Auvergne
(Puy-de-Dôme)
Tel. and fax 04 73 53 53 01
Suzette Hansen

Rooms 1 and 1 suite (4 pers.) with bath or shower and WC. **Price** 220F/33,53€ (1 pers.), 320F/48,78€ (2 pers.), +120F/18,29€ (extra bed). **Meals** Breakfast incl. Evening meals at communal table (except Wed) 90F/13,72€ (wine incl.). **Facilities** Lounge, billards, swimming pool, fishing. **Pets** Animals not allowed. **Nearby** Riding, tennis, karting, downhill and cross-country skiing, mountain bike rentals; Knife and Paper Mill Museums, Romanesque churches. **Closed** Nov 15 – Feb 15. **How to get there** (Map 25): 21km south of Thiers via N89 and D906 to Courpière, then turn left dir. Aubusson-d'Auvergne, Lac d'Aubusson D311. Go through the village. **No smoking**.

The small river tumbling down the hillside long ago drove the mill wheel, while the miller lived a little higher up in a pretty house. Then the mill was no longer, and brambles overran the slope. With the arrival of Suzette Hansen here, the terraces were again planted with flowers and the house took on a welcoming, festive air which we love. The bedrooms are very cozy, with pastel, floral-bordered wallpaper, charming "grandmother" furniture, pleasant baths; and the dinners and breakfasts are very copious.

103 - La Vigie

Rue de la Muscadière
63320 Chadeleuf
(Puy-de-Dôme)
Tel. 04 73 96 90 87
Véronique and Denis Pineau

Rooms 2 with shower and WC. **Price** 320 and 400F/48,78 and 60,97€ (2 pers.), +120F/18,29€ (extra bed). Special rates from 4 nights. **Meals** Breakfast incl. Evening meals at communal or separate tables 100F/15,24€ (wine incl.). **Facilities** Lounge, mountain bikes, swimming pool, ping-pong. **Nearby** Cross-country and downhill skiing, riding; Volcano Park, Romanesque churches. **Spoken** English, German, Italian. **Closed** Christmas. **How to get there** (Map 25): 10km northwest of Issoire. Aut. A75, exit N. 9 at Sauvagnat-Saint-Yvoire; go through Sauvagnat, then D712 towards Chadeleuf; turn right at 3rd intersection, then pink sign. 1st road on left after the mairie/école (town hall/school). **No smoking** in bedrooms.

This beautiful, 19th-century country house on the edge of the village enjoys a panoramic view of the countryside and is arranged with admirable good taste and a sense of comfort. The delightful bedrooms, in shades of blue or écru beige, are decorated with regional furniture, antique rattan, charming objects....In the evening, drinks are offered in a garden full of flowers facing the setting sun, and the delicious dinners are served in a youthful, friendly atmosphere. Excellent breakfasts are enjoyed outside in the morning sun.

104 - Chaptes ✓

8, route de la Limagne
63460 Chaptes
via Beauregard-Vendon
(Puy-de-Dôme)
Tel. 04 73 63 35 62
Mme Elisabeth Beaujard

Rooms 3 with bath or shower and WC. **Price** 300-350F/45,73-53,35€ (2 pers.), +100F/15,24€ (extra pers.). **Meals** Breakfast incl. No communal meal. **Restaurants** Many in Riom (9km) and in Chatelguyon (6km). **Facilities** Sitting room. **Pets** Dogs not allowed. **Nearby** Tennis (2km), riding (6km), swimming pool, 18-hole golf course (10km), mountain bikes, canoeing (21km), archery; Riom (for its art and history), Romanesque churches, châteaux, lakes, Volvic, Chatelguyon. **Credit cards** Not accepted. **Spoken** English. **Open** All year, but only by reservation from Nov 1 to Mar 31. **How to get there** (Map 25): 9km from Riom via N144. 2.5km after Davayat turn right on D122; follow signs.

This 18th-century family mansion made of Volvic stone is located in a small hamlet. Inside, family furniture, paintings, objects and beautiful wallpapers create a refined atmosphere. The bedrooms are charming and very pleasant: two rooms give onto the garden, and the third overlooks a small road and the countryside. On the side of the house, there are a few chairs beneath an immense barn roof where you can have drinks and enjoy the flowers in the garden. Madame Beaujard is very friendly and hospitable.

105 - Château de Collanges

63340 Collanges
(Puy-de-Dôme)
Tel. 04 73 96 47 30
M. and Mme Huillet

Rooms 6 with bath or shower, WC, tel. (TV on request). **Price** 380-450F/57,93-68,60€ (1 pers.), 380-600F/57,93-91,46€ (2 pers.), +130F/19,81€ (extra pers.). **Meals** Breakfast incl. Evening meals 200F/30,48€ (drinks incl.). **Facilities** Sitting room, billiards, piano, pond. **Pets** Dogs allowed on request. **Nearby** Tennis, riding, lake and water sports, gliding, hiking, cross-country and alpine skiing (45km); châteaux, Romanesque abbeys. **Credit cards** Not accepted. **Spoken** English. **Open** All year. **How to get there** (Map 25): 10km south of Issoire. From A75, take exit 17 to Saint-Germain-Lembron, towards Ardes, and then follow signs to Collanges and château.

Several years ago, Georges and Michelle Huillet fell in love with this château, which was built in the 12th century and then modified in the 18th. They live here with their children and now offer guests three lovely, large bedrooms with period furniture and ultra-modern bathrooms. The elegant linens, the beautiful red walls of the salons, the orange groves and the music room in the romantic private park all combine to ensure you of a pleasant stay. You will be welcomed to the Château de Collanges with enthusiasm and warmth.

106 - Brigitte Laroye

7, rue du 8 mai
63590 Cunlhat
(Puy-de-Dôme)
Tel. 04 73 72 20 87
Mme Brigitte Laroye

Rooms 4 and 1 family room (4 pers.) with bath or shower and WC. **Price** 230-250F/35,06-38,11€ (1 pers.), 280-330F/42,68-50,30€ (2 pers.), +100F/15,24€ (extra bed); family room 550F/83,84€. **Meals** Breakfast incl. Communal meals, by reservation 100F/15,24€ (wine incl.). **Facilities** Lounge, museum of the environment. **Nearby** Swimming pool with bar, tennis, riding, sailboarding; châteaux of Vollore, Auteribe, Busséol, Les Martihanches; Richard-de-Bas paper mill. **Spoken** English. **Open** All year. **How to get there** (Map 25): 51km southeast of Clermont-Ferrand via D212 to Billom, then D997 towards Ambert. 10km after Saint-Dier-d'Auvergne, on left D225 towards Cunlhat.

Just at the edge of the street as you leave the village, this house has several very pleasant guestrooms. They are furnished with antique furniture and are truly very charming; in one bedroom, you can even use the fireplace. Brigitte Laroye slips a hot-water bottle between your sheets with the first cold weather and offers you no fewer than fifteen kinds of tea for breakfast. She will delight in sharing her love of the Livardois region with you and showing you the wonderful little museum on local ecology that has been installed in the barn.

107 - Loursse

63350 Joze
(Puy-de-Dôme)
Tel. 04 73 70 20 63
M. and Mme Jehan Masson

Rooms 1 suite (3-4 pers.) with bath and WC. **Price** 300F/45,73€ (2 pers.), 480F/73,17€ (3-4 pers.). **Meals** Breakfast incl. No communal meal. **Facilities** Sitting room, tennis, fishing. **Pets** Dogs allowed in kennel. **Nearby** Restaurants, riding, mountain bike rentals, 18-hole golf course (35km), cross-country and alpine skiing; châteaux d'Auvergne, Romanesque church, Museum of Modern Art in Clermont-Ferrand. **Open** All year. **How to get there** (Map 25): 25km northeast of Clermont-Ferrand. Aut. A71, exit Riom, to Ennezat-Maringues. At 5km of Maringues to Joze on left: white posts. From Lyon, exit Thiers-ouest then towards Maringues.

This solid family house with beautiful outbuildings opens wide onto a large flower garden and countryside that stretches as far as the eye can see. Its owners offer guests a large, cheerful bedroom with antique furniture and a huge bathroom. The small communicating bedroom can be opened to form a suite for four people. A large dining room with a small sitting room corner and the lovely garden put alluring finishing touches on this beautiful place to stay.

108 - Le Chastel Montaigu

63320 Montaigut-le-Blanc
(Puy-de-Dôme)
Tel. 04 73 96 28 49
Mobile 06 81 61 52 26
Fax 04 73 96 21 60
Mme Anita Sauvadet

Rooms 3 with bath or shower and WC. **Price** 450-600F/68,60-91,46€ (1 pers.), 550-700F/83,84-106,71€ (2 pers.), +150F/22,86€ (extra bed). **Meals** Breakfast incl. No communal meal. **Facilities** Sitting room. **Pets** Dogs not allowed. **Nearby** Restaurants. **Open** All year. By reservation Nov 1 – Easter. **How to get there** (Map 24): 20km southwest Clermont-Ferrand. Aut. exit 6 (Besse/Saint-Nectaire), cross Plauzat, Champeix, Montaigut-le-Blanc; on right follow signs "village ancien" and "Chambres d'hôtes au château". **No smoking.**

Perched on high like an eagle's nest, the impressive château has been partly rebuilt and is far less austere than it seems at first glance. The living-dining room looks very medieval with its long table and Louis XIII furniture, but the bedrooms are cheerier and less formal. Their decoration, except for a few objects and some canopied beds, is more youthful, with light colors and floors painted with flowers and foliage. The bathrooms are impeccable. The welcome is simple and pleasant. Around the castle keep is a pretty terraced garden with an impressive view of the Monts de Forez and the Monts Dore range.

109 - Chez M. Gebrillat

Chemin de Siorac
63500 Perrier
(Puy-de-Dôme)
Tel. 04 73 89 15 02
Fax 04 73 55 08 85
Mireille de Saint Aubain
and Paul Gebrillat
E-mail: lequota@club-internet.fr

Rooms 2 with bath or shower and WC (1 with staircase for disabled persons). 1 suite with bath and WC. **Price** Rooms 250-280F/38,11-42,69€ (1 pers.), 280-325F/42,69-49,55€ (2 pers.) +100F/15,24€ (extra pers.); suite 560F/85,37€ (4 pers.). **Meals** Breakfast incl. No communal meal. **Facilities** Lounge with kitchenette at guests' disposal, parking. **Nearby** Restaurants, golf (40km), lakes, swimming pool, equestrian center, ski slopes and cross-country skiing, hang-gliding; volcano park, Livradois Forez park, châteaux, forests. **Credit cards** Not accepted. **Spoken** English. **Open** All year. **How to get there** (Map 25): 3km west of Issoire towards Champeix (D996); it's in the middle of the village.

In a village at the edge of the volcano country, this fine old house has three pretty guest rooms, all simply and tastefully decorated. In fine weather breakfast is served out of doors under an awning well situated to offer a splendid view of a verdant interior garden. Paul Gebrillat is an excellent host with a passion for Auvergne. He is an endless source of information about sights and facilities in the surroundings and his advice is most valuable for those who like their touring independent and off the beaten track.

110 - Château de Voissieux

Saint-Bonnet près Orcival
63210 Rochefort-Montagne
(Puy-de-Dôme)
Tel. 04 73 65 81 02
Danielle and John Phillips

Rooms 3 with bath and WC. Rooms cleaned once/week. **Price** 320F/48,78€ (2 pers.). **Meals** Breakfast incl. No communal meal. **Facilities** Sitting room, river fishing. **Pets** Dogs allowed on request. **Nearby** Restaurants, Servière Lake, fishing, hang-gliding, paragliding, mountain bikes, 9- and 18-hole golf course (20km), cross-country and alpine skiing, thermal station; Orcival's cathedral. **Spoken** English. **Closed** Nov 15 – Feb 15, except by reservation. **How to get there** (Map 24): 22km southeast of Clermont-Ferrand. To Bordeaux to "Les quatre routes de Nébouzat", then towards Orcival to Saint Bonnet then to Voissieux. Follow signs from the church.

The small Château de Voissieux, made of volcanic rock, has recently been restored and tastefully redecorated by its friendly new owners. They offer guests three bright, cheerful bedrooms, smartly furnished with antiques and decorative objects; a small salon with comfortable, deep armchairs, and a sunny terrace which serves as the breakfast area. All around the property, green hills, woods, and streams are inviting places for beautiful walks.

111 - Le Château de Savennes

63750 Savennes
(Puy-de-Dôme)
Tel. 04 73 21 40 36
M. and Mme Martin

Rooms 1 suite with bath, WC, sitting room, 1 bedroom with bath, WC and 1 extra bedroom. **Price** Suite 380F/57,93€ (2 pers.). Bedroom 350F/53,35€ (2 pers.). Extra bedroom 180F/27,44€ (2 pers.) **Meals** Breakfast incl. No communal meal. **Restaurants** in Saint-Sauves and Bourg Lastic (10mn). **Facilities** Sitting room, millpond. **Pets** Dogs not allowed. **Nearby** Fishing, hiking, mountain bike rentals, riding, 9-hole golf course, skiing; Sancy mountains. **Spoken** English, German, Italian. **Open** Apr – Oct. **How to get there** (Map 24): 20km north of Ussel. From Clermont and Ussel via N89. In Bourg Lastic, take D987 via Messeix then Savennes via D31. It's at the end of the village.

Situated at the border between Auvergne and Limousin, this large family mansion with its broad facade, many windows and two old watchtowers is a good example of the art of country living at the end of the 19th century. The period furniture, unusual objects and painting of different styles are skillfully mixed for an original look. The suite is nicely decorated and also extremely comfortable and the bedroom has a lot of charm. Breakfast is served out of doors or in a large dining-living room that opens on the garden. The reception is relaxed and unpretentious.

112 - Les Baudarts

63500 Issoire
(Puy-de-Dôme)
Tel. and fax 04 73 89 05 51
M. and Mme Verdier

Rooms 2 and 1 suite (4 pers.) with bath or shower, WC (TV in 1 room). **Price** Rooms 320-380F/48,78-57,93€ (2 pers.); suite 250F/38,11€ (1 pers.), 320F/48,78€ (2 pers.); +100F/15,24€ (extra bed). **Meals** Breakfast incl. No communal meal. **Facilities** Sitting room, swimming pool. **Pets** Small dogs allowed. **Nearby** Restaurants, riding, tennis; Romanesque churches, volcanos, lakes. **Credit cards** Not accepted. **Spoken** English. **Open** May 1 – Qept. 30. (except by special arrangement in advance). **How to get there** (Map 25): In Issoire, exit 13 autoroute towards Parentignat and on left towards Varennes/Usson. At the exit, on right towards Saint-Rémy-de-Chargnat, first driveway on right, white door.

Behind a crisp pink facade you find three old village houses, completely refurbished and reorganized, and in their midst a heated swimming pool. A vast sitting room is entirely reserved for guests with a fireplace, library, fine furniture – antique or exotic – paintings and some modern drawings. Very comfortable bedrooms in shades of cream are decorated with the same refined taste as the sitting room. Impeccable bathrooms. A truly warm welcome. All in all, a fine address to know.

113 - Château du Chambon

87370 Bersac-sur-Rivalier
(Haute-Vienne)
Tel. and Fax 05 55 71 47 04
M. and Mme Perrin des Marais
E-mail: perrin-desmarais.eric@wanadoo.fr

Rooms 4 and 1 suite with bath or shower and private WC. **Price** Rooms 300-400F/45,73-60,97€ (2 pers.), suite 650F/99,09€. **Meals** Breakfast incl. Communal meals 100F/15,24€ (wine not incl.). **Facilities** Sitting room, river fishing. **Nearby** Aubazac Mountains, Romanesque churches, Porcelain Museum in Limoges; riding (10km). **Credit cards** All major. **Spoken** English. **Open** Apr 1 – Nov 1. **How to get there** (Map 23): 35km north of Limoges. Autoroute A20, exit Bersac and Bessines; then turn right, then left; at traffic light on left, take towards Bersac, follow signs "Château du Chambon".

Built in the late 13th century and given softer lines in the Renaissance, this family château is set in a beautiful hilly location. The bedrooms are spacious, and some are vast, like the superb bedroom with a four-poster bed; the decoration and furniture are of fine quality, the bathrooms modern and well equipped. There are beautifiul 18th-century salons whose classicism is attenuated by a collection of drawings and landscapes. The mouthwatering dinners are enlivened by the delightful presence of Monsieur and Madame Perrin. The château is an excellent address at truly very reasonable prices.

114 - Domaine de Moulinard ✓

87220 Boisseuil
(Haute-Vienne)
Tel. 05 55 06 91 22
Fax 05 55 06 98 28
M. and Mme Ziegler
E-mail: philippe.ziegler@wanadoo.fr

Rooms 5 with shower and WC. **Price** 180F/27,44€ (1 pers.), 230F/35,06€ (2 pers.), 310F/47,25€ (3 pers.). **Meals** Breakfast incl. No communal meal. **Facilities** Sitting room. **Pets** Dogs allowed on request. **Nearby** Restaurants, heated swimming pool, tennis, sports center, sports track, basketball (6km), 18-hole golf course (6km); Romanesque Abbey of Solignac, Limoges (12km). **Credit cards** Not accepted. **Spoken** English. **Open** Apr – Oct. **How to get there** (Map 23): 12km south of Limoges. Exit Limoges, towards Toulouse via autoroute A20, exit Boisseul (n. 37), commercial center; follow signs from N20 or A20.

Facing the farmhouse, the big white house and its shady garden are reserved for guests. Downstairs, a very simple room is at your disposal for quiet relaxation. Upstairs, there are five bedrooms equipped with modern showers. The white bedrooms still have the atmosphere of the past with their parquet floors and authentic regional furniture. This is a lovely place to stay for relaxation in the heart of the lush Limoges countryside. The welcome is courteous.

115 - Château de Brie

87150 Champagnac-la-Rivière
(Haute-Vienne)
Tel. 05 55 78 17 52
Fax 05 55 78 14 02
Comte and Comtesse
du Manoir de Juaye
E-mail: chateaudebrie@wanadoo.fr

Rooms 4 with bath and WC. **Price** 500-600F/76,22-91,46€ (2 pers.); possible suite 800F/121,95€ (3 pers.). **Meals** Breakfast incl. Evening meals, by reservation. **Facilities** Sitting room, lake, swimming pool. **Pets** Dogs allowed on request. **Nearby** Restaurants, riding, sailing, fishing, walks, mountain biking; lake Saint-Mathieu. **Credit cards** Not accepted. **Spoken** English. **Open** Apr 1 – Nov 1, or by reservation. **How to get there** (Map 23): 45km southwest of Limoges via N21 to Châlus, then D42; it's between Châlus and Cussac.

Built in the 15th century on medieval foundations, the Château de Brie has superb views over the countryside. The bedrooms are all large and well decorated with antique pieces, each in a style of its own. Decorative styles range from 16th century to Empire; the small, impeccable bathrooms are resolutely modern. A very elegant sitting room is available and breakfasts are served in the library. You will receive a warm and natural welcome in a château which has retained all its traditional style.

AUVERGNE - LIMOUSIN

116 - La Croix du Reh

Rue Amédée-Tarrade
87130 Châteauneuf-la-Forêt
(Haute-Vienne)
Tel. 05 55 69 75 37
Fax 05 55 69 75 38
Elizabeth and Patrick Mc Laughlin

Rooms 5 with bath or shower, WC. **Price** 230-260F/35,06-39,63€ (1 pers.), 300-350F/45,73-53,35€ (2 pers.); +80F/12,19€ (extra bed), +100F/15,24€ (extra bedroom). **Meals** Breakfast incl. Evening meals at communal or separate tables 120F/18,29€ (wine not incl.). **Facilities** Sitting room, tea room in house. **Pets** Dogs allowed on request. **Nearby** 3 tennis courts in village, lake (200m), fishing; Pompadour, Uzerche, Saint-Léonard-de-Noblat. **Credit cards** Visa. **Spoken** English. **Open** All year. **How to get there** (Map 24): 36km southeast of Limoges. From A20 exit Pierre-Buffière, then to Saint-Hilaire-Bonneval and follow Châteauneuf-la-Forêt.

Lying at the foot of the picturesque Millevaches Plateau, this pretty village house was restored by a Scottish couple who will welcome you with friendly, informal hospitality. The Rose, Bleue and Familiale bedrooms are pleasantly decorated and have modern conveniences. The living room also serves as a charming tea room, where excellent Scottish pastries are served. In summer, dining tables are set out amidst the flowers and trees of the private park.

117 - Les Hauts de Boscartus

87520 Cieux
(Haute-Vienne)
Tel. 05 55 03 30 63
Paulette and Paule Hennebel

Rooms 2 with private shower and shared WC. Rooms cleaned, beds made at extra cost. **Price** 195F/30€ (1 pers.), 295F/45€ (2 pers.), 380F/58€ (3 pers.), 460F/70€ (4 pers.). **Meals** Breakfast incl. No communal meal. **Facilities** Sitting room, tel. **Pets** Dogs not allowed. **Nearby** Restaurants, tennis, lake, golf; Montemart, Monts de Blond. **Credit cards** Not accepted. **Open** All year. **How to get there** (Map 23): 30km northwest of Limoges. From Bellac D3 to Blond, then Rochers de Puychaud, Villerajouze Boscartus. **No smoking**.

Standing on a hillside, this house is surrounded by fir trees. The pleasant sitting room is arranged around a fireplace at one end and a large picture window with a view of the beautiful lake. The attractive and comfortable bedrooms have lovely views and are totally quiet. On the breakfast table you will find white cheese and excellent home produce (honey, jams, gingerbread). You will be warmly welcomed.

118 - Moulin de Marsaguet

87500 Coussac-Bonneval
(Haute-Vienne)
Tel. 05 55 75 28 29
Valérie and Renaud Gizardin

Rooms 3 with bath or shower and WC (1 outside the bedroom). **Price** 240F/36,58€ (2 pers.). **Meals** Breakfast incl. Evening meals at communal table 90F/13,72€ (wine incl.). **Facilities** Sitting room, tel., 13-acre lake, sports fishing and boat rides, hiking. **Pets** Dogs allowed on request. **Nearby** Swimming pool (10km), tennis, hiking paths; Limoges, Ségur-le-Château, Pompadour Stud Farm, Lascaux (1 hr.). **Credit cards** Not accepted. **Spoken** English. **Open** All year, by reservation in winter. **How to get there** (Map 23): 40km south of Limoges via A20; exit Pierre-Buffière; take D19 towards Saint-Yrieix to intersection with Croix-d'Hervy, then D57 towards Coussac for 5km along lake; it's on the left.

Renaud Gizardin and his young wife live on the family duck farm at the charming Moulin de Marsaguet. They both are very friendly and he will be happy to take you fishing on the immense lake at the foot of the house. The bedrooms here are simple, bright and have modern amenities. There is a large room for reading where evening meals are served in winter. In summer, breakfasts and dinners with homemade products are served beneath a beautiful linden tree.

119 - Fougeolles

87120 Eymoutiers
(Haute-Vienne)
Tel. 05 55 69 11 44
and 05 55 69 18 50
M. Jacques du Montant

Rooms 3 with bath and WC (poss. 1 extra bedroom). **Price** 250-300F/38,11-45,73€ (2 pers.), +50F/7,62€ (extra bed). **Meals** Breakfast incl. Possible communal meals, by reservation 75F/11,43€ (Wine not incl.). **Facilities** Fishing, toy train museum, pedal cars. **Pets** Dogs not allowed. **Nearby** Golf, tennis, swimming pool, marine sports, riding; plateau des Millevaches, lake Vassivière, Aubusson. **Credit cards** Not accepted. **Spoken** English. **Open** All year. **How to get there** (Map 24): 45km southeast of Limoges via D979 towards Eymoutiers; follow signs 500m before entering the village, on the left.

In the heart of a vast farm, very close to the Eymoutiers exit, this 17th-century residence has pleasant, comfortable bedrooms furnished with antiques and brightened with lovely fabrics. The rooms in the main house are vast and well renovated, while the small bedrooms in the old house are warm, delightfully old-fashioned and will appeal to those who enjoy places of genuine charm. The sitting room and dining room have their original furnishings and numerous unusual objects.

AUVERGNE - LIMOUSIN

120 - Le Val du Goth

Le Vansanaud
87440 Marval Saint-Mathieu
(Haute-Vienne)
Tel. 05 55 78 76 65
Fax 05 55 78 23 79
M. and Mme Francis Pez

Rooms 2 with bath or shower, WC and TV-video and 1 small house with kitchen, bath or shower and 2 WC. **Price** 200F/30,48€ (1 pers.), 300F/45,73€ (2 pers.); small house 1500F/228,67€ weekend, 3000-6000F/457,34-914,69€/week (6 pers.). **Meals** Breakfast 30F/4,57€/pers. Communal meals in evening 110F/16,76€ (aperitif incl.). **Facilities** Sitting room, Tel., swimming pool, pond, lake fishing, boat, mountain bikes, ping-pong. **Pets** Dogs not allowed. **Nearby** Karting, 9-hole golf course, riding, tennis, forest, châteaux. **Credit cards** Not accepted. **Spoken** English. **Open** All year. 2 nights min. **How to get there** (Map 23): 9km southeast of Saint-Mathieu, towards Marval. 1.5km after Milhaguet turn left towards Cussac for 1km; turn right onto road for Vansanaud.

Lying between the Périgord and the Limoges region, this very well-renovated farmhouse occupies a lush, green location. You will find the swimming pool at the foot of the garden and, several meters farther on, a vast lake. Inside, the rustic charm of the exposed stones is still in evidence, but the decoration is more refined: The small bedrooms have floral fabrics, gleaming bathrooms, a few pieces of antique furniture and decorative glass objects. You are sure to enjoy the delicious dinners and the pleasant ambience here.

121 - Laucournet

Glanges
87380 Saint-Germain-les-Belles
(Haute-Vienne)
Tel. and fax 05 55 00 81 27
M. and Mme Desmaison

Rooms 1 suite (up to 5 pers.) with 2 bedrooms, bath, shower and WC. Rooms cleaned once a week for long stays. **Price** 250F/38,11€ (1 pers.), 300F/45,73€ (2 pers.), +50F/7,62€ (extra pers.). **Meals** Breakfast incl. No communal meal. **Facilities** Sitting room, horse stalls. **Nearby** Restaurants, farmhouse-auberge, tennis, riding, golf; rivers, lakes. **Credit cards** Not accepted. **Spoken** English. **Open** Jun 15 – Sept 15. **How to get there** (Map 23): 36km southeast of Limoges via A20 exit 41 "Magnac-Bourg", then D82 for 1km towards Glanges. After the level crossing take D120 for 5km towards Saint-Méard road. Follow signs "Chambres d'hôtes".

Even if there are only two of you, this delightfully typical Limousin house will be reserved for you alone. On the ground floor is a living room with a corner library and fireplace and some regional furniture, a more modern bathroom and a covered terrace for breakfast. On the premier étage, two comfortable and pleasantly decorated bedrooms have lovely views over the fields. You will enjoy the quiet privacy and excellent hospitality.

122 - Le Masbareau

Royères
87400 Saint-Léonard-de-Noblat
(Haute-Vienne)
Tel. and fax 05 55 00 28 22
M. and Mme Boudet

Rooms 1 (3 pers.) with shower and WC. **Price** 240F/36,58€ (1 pers.), 265 and 285F/40,39 and 43,44€ (2 pers., double or twin bed), 315F/48,02€ (3 pers.), +75F/11,43€ (extra pers.). **Meals** Breakfast incl. Communal meals 85F/12,95€ (wine incl.). **Facilities** Sitting room, riding (+80F/12,19€), 100-acre forest (mushrooms and hiking path), fishing. **Pets** Dogs not allowed. **Nearby** golf, lake (water sports); Limoges, Saint-Léonard. **Credit cards** Not accepted. **Spoken** English, some German. **Open** All year. **How to get there** (Map 23): 18km east of Limoges via N141 towards Clermont-Ferrand. Signs on right in Fontaguly; then go 3km (or turn right at the traffic light in Royères and go 3km).

This is a real family home in an outstanding setting. The place is full of life. Monsieur Boudet and his children take care of the cows and horses. The children at the gîte provide animation without disturbing the comfort of the guests. Madame Boudet busies herself with excellent breakfasts and dinners, which are served in a cozy room with a wood fire. You will sleep in the lovely guest room with its waxed parquet floor, antique furniture, library and splendid view. The handsome living room contains some souvenirs of Indochina brought back by one of the family forebears. The whole house is full of charm.

B U R G U N D Y

123 - Château de Chorey-les-Beaune

Rue Jacques-Germain
21200 Chorey-les-Beaune
(Côte-d'Or)
Tel. 03 80 22 06 05
Fax 03 80 24 03 93
Estelle Germain
E-mail: chateau-de-chorey@wanadoo.fr

Rooms 5 and 1 family suite (2 adults and 2 children) with bath, WC and tel. **Price** Rooms 750-950F/114,33-144,82€ (2 pers.), 900-1100F/137,20-167,69€ (3 pers.); suite 1200F/182,93€. **Meals** Breakfast incl. No communal meal. **Facilities** Sitting room, wine tasting in the cellars. **Nearby** Restaurants, 18-hole golf course; Beaune, vineyard, Romanesque churches, abbeys. **Credit card** Visa. **Spoken** English, German. **Open** Easter – end Nov. **How to get there** (Map 19): 3km north of Beaune, at the entrance to the village.

The Château de Chorey-les-Beaune is very close to Beaune, in a wine-growing village. Entirely restored, it has belonged to the Germain family for several generations. The main building is 12th-century, the towers are 13th-century and the garden, encircled by a moat, breathes the Burgundian art de vivre. The bedrooms have been tastefully and simply decorated. The winery operated by the Germain family is on the same property.

124 - La Cure

21230 Foissy
par Arnay-le-Duc
(Côte-d'Or)
Tel. and fax 03 80 84 22 92
Mme Reny
Web: hote-de-france.com

Rooms 3 with bath or shower and WC. **Price** 400F/60,97€ (2 pers.), +150F/22,86€ (extra bed). **Meals** Breakfast incl. No communal meal. **Facilities** Sitting room. **Pets** Dogs not allowed. **Nearby** Restaurants, hiking, fishing (8km), tennis (7km), riding (25km), 18-hole golf course (20km); Wine Route, Beaune, Dijon (Fine Art Museum), Autun, châteaux, Cormatin, Châteauneuf-en-Auxois. **Spoken** English, Spanish. **Open** Easter – Nov 1. **How to get there** (Map 19): 25km west of Beaune via D970 to Bligny/Ouche, then towards Arnay-le-Duc (8km). Or autoroute A6 exit Pouilly/Auxois, to Arnay-le-Duc via N81, then D17 towards Beaune (7km).

The small hamlet of Foissy is proud of its 18th-century vicarage, which seems to preside over the entire lush countryside. At the back, there is the "vicar's garden" planted with shrubs and a few vegetables; in front, a terrace and a lawn invite you to relax as you listen to the church bells chime the hour. The bedrooms, located upstairs, have gleaming, all-white bathrooms; for the most attractive room, ask for the one with the blue bed.

125 - Château de Longecourt

21110 Longecourt-en-Plaine
(Côte-d'Or)
Tel. 03 80 39 88 76
Fax 03 80 39 87 44
Comtesse Bertrand de Saint Seine

Rooms 3 with bath, WC, and 2 with bath, shared WC. **Price** 750F/114,33€ (1-2 pers.), +150F/22,86€ (extra pers.). **Meals** Breakfast incl. Evening meal at communal table 270F/41,16€ (wine incl.). **Facilities** Sitting rooms, horse stalls, fishing. **Pets** Dogs allowed. **Nearby** Riding, 18-hole golf course; Wine Route. **Credit cards** Not accepted. **Spoken** English. **Open** All year. **How to get there** (Map 19): 18km southeast of Dijon via D996 and D968 towards Saint-Jean-de-Losne; it's on the Place de la Mairie in Longecourt.

Built in the 17th century, Longecourt is a jewel of a château, with rose-colored brick and stucco-work and surrounded by a broad moat. After driving up through the graveled courtyard, you enter the house, where every detail is authentic. The reception rooms are luxurious, especially the grand salon, with its stunning inlaid marble walls and its carved and gilded ceiling. The same authenticity is to be found in the bedrooms, with their antique furniture, paintings, engravings, etc. They are all comfortable, as are the bathrooms, even though some of them are not the last word in modernity. A must for lovers of history.

126 - Château de Beauregard

21390 Nan-sous-Thil
(Côte-d'Or)
Tel. 03 80 64 41 08
Fax 03 80 64 47 28
Nicole and Bernard Bonoron

Rooms 3 with bath, WC, tel., and 1 suite (4 pers.) with bath, shower, 2 WCs and tel. **Price** 620-820F/94,51-125€ (2 pers.), suite 1200F/182,93€ (4 pers.); +150F/22,86€ (extra pers.). **Meals** Breakfast incl. No communal meal. **Facilities** Sitting room, pond. **Pets** Dogs allowed on request (100F/15,24€ extra charge). **Nearby** Restaurants, tennis, riding, bicycles, lakes (water sports), golf; Abbaye of Fontenay, Semus-en-Auxois. **Credit cards** Not accepted. **Spoken** English. **Closed** Nov – Easter. In winter by reservation 3 bedrooms min. **How to get there** (Map 18): 18km north of Saulieu. Autoroute A6, exit Bierre-Les-Semur towards Saulieu for 3km, then on left towards Vitteaux for about 3km. At stop sign, turn left towards Vitteaux and immediately on right to Nan-sous-Thil; go through village.

Beauregard, "beautiful view", well deserves its name, for it looks out far over the rich valleys of Burgundy. It has just been magnificently restored by Monsieur and Madame Bonoron, who will greet you with warm hospitality. There are three comfortable, elegant bedrooms decorated with antiques and the ultra-modern bathrooms have kept the charm of the past. There is also a sumptuous suite. Excellent breakfasts are served in a bright salon.

B   U   R   G   U   N   D   Y

127 - Domaine de Loisy

28, rue Général-de-Gaulle
21700 Nuits-Saint-Georges
(Côte-d'Or)
Tel. 03 80 61 02 72
Fax 03 80 61 36 14
Comtesse Michel de Loisy
E-mail: domaine.loisy@wanadoo.fr

Rooms 3 and 2 suites (4 pers.) with bath and WC. **Price** 600-850F/91,46-129,56€ (2 pers.). **Meals** Breakfast incl. No communal meal. **Facilities** Sitting room, visit to the wine cellars and wine tasting 800F/121,95€ (2 pers.). **Pets** Dogs allowed on request. **Nearby** Restaurants; Dijon, Beaune, château of Clos-de-Vougeot. **Credit cards** Visa, MasterCard. **Spoken** English, Italian. **Open** Mar 21 – Nov 19, by reservation and deposit (50%). Arrival between 5:00PM-8:00PM. **How to get there** (Map 19): 22km south of Dijon via N74; it's on the edge of town on the Beaune road.

You will find Madame de Loisy's residence right on the Wine Route. The hostess's personality and culture are the delight of her regular guests: Madame de Loisy is, in fact, an enologist and leads wine tastings and visits to vineyards. The bedrooms and the salon of the house are furnished with antiques and have the charm of the past. Very fortunately, double-glazing provides insulation from the noise of the road, which is very busy. The rooms overlooking the courtyard are somewhat farther away but still are noisy. Breakfast is served in the large dining room. The Domaine has an enormous amount of personality.

128 - Commanderie de la Romagne

Hameau de la Romagne
21610 Saint-Maurice-sur-Vingeanne
(Côte-d'Or)
Tel. 03 80 75 90 40
M. Quenot

Rooms 2 and 1 apart. (jet-shower and whirlpool) with bath or shower and WC. Rooms cleaned on request. **Price** 400F/60,97€ (2 pers.), +80F/12,19€ (extra bed) or 60F/9,14€ (children). **Meals** Breakfast incl. No communal meal. **Facilities** Fishing, river fishing, mountain bikes. **Pets** Small dogs allowed on request. **Nearby** Restaurants, hiking; châteaux. **Credit cards** All major except Amex. **Spoken** some English, some German. **Open** All year. **How to get there** (Map 19): 35km south of Langres. Aut. A31, exit 5 Til-Chatel towards Langres via N74 to Orville, then on right to Chazeuil, Sacquenay, Courchamp and La Romagne.

Situated on an arm of the Vingeanne River, this was the residence of the Knights Templar Commander from the 12th to the 15th centuries. The drawbridge tower, totally rebuilt in the Haute Epoque style, contains one bedroom and a small salon on the premier étage; the well-equipped apartment on the top floor is more modern. Our favorite bedroom, on the ground floor, has a private terrace and a bathroom in a barrel-vaulted room with a turn-of-the-century bathtub. Breakfasts are served in a spacious room in the château.

129 - Le Presbytère

La Motte Ternant
21210 Saulieu
(Côte-d'Or)
Tel. 03 80 84 34 85
Fax 03 80 84 35 32
Marjorie and Brian Aylett

Rooms 4 with bath or shower and WC. **Price** 370F/56,40€ (1 pers.), 400F/60,97€ (2 pers.). (2 nights min). **Meals** Breakfast incl. Evening meals at communal table, by reservation 130F/19,81€ (wine incl.). **Facilities** Lounge, tel., bikes. **Nearby** Country walks and hiking in the Morvan (12km), 18-hole golf course (20km); Vézelay, Fontenay, Semur-en-Auxois, Saulieu. **Spoken** English. **Open** All year, by reservation. **How to get there** (Map 18): 10km west of Saulieu. Autoroute A6 exit at Bierre-les-Semur, then dir. Saulieu. At Saulieu via D26 to La Motte Ternant. **No smoking.**

This former presbytery stands just next to a little 11th-century church and looks out over a vast landscape of forests and hills. Around the house the lovely sloping garden is divided by ancient moss-covered walls that mark off the lawns, the flower beds and the vegetable plots. Renovated by a British couple, the interior combines the charm of the old house with nice pieces of English furniture. The result is pleasant and comfortable. The price of the rooms is a bit high but this is made up for by the dinners, which are French style and made with good fresh produce.

130 - Péniche Lady A

Port du Canal - Cidex 45
21320 Vandenesse-en-Auxois
(Côte-d'Or)
Tel. 03 80 49 26 96
Fax 03 80 49 27 00
M. and Mme Jansen-Bourne

Rooms 3 cabins (twin beds or double bed) with shower and WC. **Price** 250F/38,11€ (1 pers.), 300F/45,73€ (2 pers.). **Meals** Breakfast incl. Evening meals at communal table 130F/19,81€ (wine incl.). **Facilities** Lounge. **Pets** Animals not allowed. **Nearby** Fishing in canal, lake with water sports facilities (2km), 18-hole golf course (7km); Châteauneuf, Cormatin Château, Semur-en-Auxois, Beaune, Dijon, Great Wine Route. **Spoken** English, German, Dutch. **Closed** Dec – Jan. **How to get there** (Map 19): 7km southwest of Pouilly. Autoroute A6, exit Pouilly, then D18 towards Créancey, then Vandenesse. In the canal port. **No smoking** in cabins.

Having made its way up and down many canals, Lady A finally dropped anchor and guests are delighted. The identical cabins are small, bright, and very well designed with a big, comfortable bed and a large shower room. Guests spend a good part of their time sitting on the deck observing sheep grazing and the beautiful old Burgundian houses reflected in the peaceful waters of the canal. A very friendly hostess, Lisa, will serve you good dinners either outside or in a charming lounge.

B U R G U N D Y

131 - Bouteuille

58110 Alluy
(Nièvre)
Tel. 03 86 84 06 65 / 06 86 12 61 95
Fax 03 86 84 03 41
Colette and André Lejault

Rooms 4 with bath or shower, WC and TV (1 with extra room). **Price** 230-260F/35,06-39,63€ (1 pers.), 270-340F/41,16-51,83€ (2 pers.). **Meals** Breakfast incl. No communal meal. Kitchen for guests, barbecue and flat-stone grill in pigeon loft. **Facilities** Tel. **Pets** Dogs not allowed. **Nearby** Restaurants, barge trips on canal, mountain bikes, riding, swimming pool, fishing and hunting; Château of Châtillon, Septennat Museum and Mining Museum. **Credit cards** Not accepted. **Spoken** English. **Open** All year. **How to get there** (Map 18): 40km east of Nevers via D978 towards Château-Chinon and Autun: after Rouy, follow signs from l'Huis-Moreau. From Châtillon-en-Bazois, D978 towards Nevers (4km) (don't go to Alluy), then first road on right 600m before "Avia-Citroën" station.

This inviting 17th-century house is part of a beautiful group of farm buildings which look out over fields as far as the eye can see. The house is furnished with a number of lovely antiques and is kept immaculate. The bedrooms are quite large and comfortable and have gleaming, modern bathrooms. Madame Lejault serves delicious breakfasts in a pleasant small room in the kitchen, and the welcome at Bouteuille is very friendly.

132 - Château de Nyon

58130 Ourouër
(Nièvre)
Tel. 03 86 58 61 12
Mme Catherine Henry

Rooms 3 with bath or shower and WC. **Price** 260F/39,63€ (1 pers.), 340F/51,83€ (2 pers.), 320F/48,78€ (2 pers., from 2 nights). **Meals** Breakfast incl. No communal meal. **Facilities** Tel., lounge. **Pets** Animals not allowed. **Nearby** Restaurants, tennis and swimming pool (6 and 7km); Romanesque Church Circuit, many châteaux, Pottery Museum in Nevers, Septennat Museum. **Open** All year, by reservation and deposit (25%). **How to get there** (Map 18): 15km north of Nevers via D977 dir. Auxerre. Go 6-7km, take D958 to Montigny-aux-Amognes, then D26 towards Ourouër; signs. **No smoking** in bedrooms.

Nestling in the hollow of a small valley and surrounded by large trees, this small 18th-century château catches the eye with its beautiful architecture. Madame Henry has brought new life to the Château de Nyon, renovating it and opening rooms for guests. The bedrooms have been given priority: their original character and antique furniture have been conserved, but they have new wallpaper, elegant fabrics, and beautiful bathrooms. Further renovation will include the corridors, the elevator and certain details in the reception rooms. The good breakfasts are served in a friendly atmosphere and the prices are very reasonable.

133 - Le Bois Dieu

58400 Raveau
(Nièvre)
Tel. 03 86 69 60 02 / 06 62 36 12 78
Fax 03 86 70 23 91
Mme Mellet-Mandard
E-mail: leboisdieu@wanadoo.fr
Web: www.leboisdieu.com

Rooms 4 with bath or shower and WC. **Price** 310F/47,25€ (2 pers.), +90F/13,72€ (extra bed); Children under 2 (free). **Meals** Breakfast incl. Evening meals at communal tables, by reservation 110F/16,76€ (wine incl.). **Facilities** Sitting room, fishing, wine and gastronomy tours available (4 to 8 persons, English-speaking escort). **Pets** Animals not allowed. **Nearby** La Charité-sur-Loire, Sancerre, Nevers, vineyard, Varzy museum. **Spoken** English. **Closed** Nov 15 – Feb 15. **How to get there** (Maps 17 and 18): 6km of La Charité-sur-Loire via N7, exit Auxerre, then after 20m on right to Raveau and follow signs for 6km. **No smoking** in bedrooms.

You follow a lane that winds around several farm buildings and then stops in front of the carefully tended garden of the Bois Dieu farmhouse. We were immediately taken with the happy atmosphere that reigns throughout: the walls painted in shades of tender green, buttercup or sky blue; handsome paintings, abundant tourist information on the region....The bedrooms and their charmingly old-fashioned furniture are pleasant (especially the Philibert and Irma rooms), as are their immaculate baths. Madame Mellet-Mandard is especially hospitable, and we do recommend her table d'hôte, which is best to reserve.

134 - Château du Vieil-Azy

Le Vieil-Azy
58270 Saint-Benin-d'Azy
(Nièvre)
Tel. 03 86 58 47 93
Vicomtesse Benoist d'Azy

Rooms 5 and 1 suite (view on the lake) with bath, WC and tel. **Price** 400-450F/60,97-68,60€ (1-2 pers.); suite 800F/121,95€ (1-4 pers.). **Meals** Breakfast 40F/6,09€. Evening meals, by reservation 140F/21,34€. **Facilities** Fishing. **Nearby** Riding, swimming pool, tennis; château of the dukes of Nevers, Apremont, Septennat museum, archeologique site of Bibracte, Magny-cours circuit. **Credit cards** Not accepted. **Open** Easter – Nov 1. **How to get there** (Map 18): 16km east of Nevers via D978 towards Châlon-sur-Saône to Saint-Benin d'Azy; entrance to château on leaving the village (towards La Machine), on left of the lake. From Paris, take expressway at the exit of Dordives, dir. Nevers and Château-Chinon Autun.

The Château du Vieil Azy is set in the heart of a large park with century-old trees, facing a vast lake. An imposing stairway leads to several beautiful bedrooms appointed with authentic antique furniture (we are somewhat less fond of the two small rooms on the second étage).On the ground floor, a magnificent salon, also well-furnished, and a dining room in Haute Epoque style are at your disposal. The château is a pleasant starting point for taking many lovely walks.

135 - La Chaumière

Route de Saint-Germain-du-Plain
71370 Baudrières
(Saône-et-Loire)
Tel. 03 85 47 32 18
Mobile 06 07 49 53 46
Fax 03 85 47 41 42
Mme Vachet

Rooms 3 with bath or shower, WC and TV. Rooms cleaned on request. **Price** 320F/48,78€ (1 pers.), 350F/53,35€ (2 pers.), +100F/15,24€ (extra pers.); 450F/68,60€ (suite 2 pers.). **Meals** Breakfast incl. No communal meal. **Facilities** Sitting room, swimming pool, tennis. **Nearby** Restaurants, riding, lake, fishing, 18-hole golf course; wine cellar visits, Beaune, Cluny. **Credit cards** Not accepted. **Spoken** English, Italian. **Open** Mar – Nov (or on request). **How to get there** (Map 19): From north, exit Châlon-Sud on A6, towards Châlon. Itineraire Lyon bis for 15km via D978 to Ouroux-sur-Saône, then D933 to Nassey, and on right, signs Baudrières via D160. From south, via RN6. In Sennecy-le-Grand, D18 to Gigny, Saint-Germain-du-Plain. Go across Saône via Le Nassey and D160 to Baudrières.

This very pretty house covered in Virginia creeper is in a peaceful small village. The bedrooms, tastefully arranged, are comfortable and welcoming. The decor is equally tasteful in the sitting room, which has old regional furniture. Excellent breakfasts are served outside under a wooden canopy in good weather. You will be received with friendly hospitality.

136 - Le Moulin des Arbillons

71520 Bourgvilain
(Saône-et-Loire)
Tel. 03 85 50 82 83
Fax 03 85 50 86 32
Sylviane and Charles Dubois-Favre
E-mail: arbillon@club-internet.fr

Rooms 5 with bath or shower, WC, tel. and TV (on request). **Price** 350-450F/53,35-68,60€ (2 pers.). **Meals** Breakfast incl. No communal meal. **Facilities** Sitting room. **Pets** Dogs allowed on request. **Nearby** Restaurants, Saint-Point Lake with facilities (2.5km); Circuit Lamartine, Cluny Abbey, Wine Route. **Credit cards** Not accepted. **Open** Jul 1 – Aug 31. **How to get there** (Map 19): 24km from Mâcon. On Mâcon-Moulin highway (N79), take exit Cluny, then take D22 to Tramayes: Moulin on right of village of Bourgvilain.

We are in the country of Lamartine, in a small valley traversed by a charming river which feeds the millrace of the Moulin des Arbillons. You will be very hospitably welcomed here, where the extensively renovated (perhaps too much so) interior is comfortable and impeccably kept. So are the bedrooms, which also have luxurious bathrooms. You can have your breakfast in a little orangerie that looks out over the countryside. This is a very pleasant stopover.

137 - La Griolette

71460 Bresse-sur-Grosne
(Saône-et-Loire)
Tel. 03 85 92 62 88
Fax 03 85 92 63 47
M. and Mme Welter

Rooms 2 sets of 2 rooms (2-5 persons) each sharing a separate bathroom and WC. **Price** 270F/41,16€ (1 pers.), 300F/45,73€ (2 pers.), 370-450F/56,40-68,60€ (3 pers.), +70F/10,67€ (extra pers.). **Meals** Breakfast incl. No communal meal. **Facilities** Sitting room, swimming pool, boules equipment, swings, climbing bars and bicycles for children. **Nearby** Restaurants, tennis, riding, 18-hole golf courses (30km); Romanesque churches, Cluny, Tournus; theater and music festivals (Aug). **Spoken** English. **Open** All year. **How to get there** (Map 19): 20km west of Tournus. Aut. A6 exit Tournus, dir. Saint-Gengoux-le-National via D215 for 14km. On right, dir. Bresse. In the village.

The guest house stands at the foot of a magnificent flower garden, shaded by tall trees. It's an old house and offers two sets of two bedrooms, each sharing a meticulously kept bathroom, well-designed to accommodate the guests of both rooms. An old barn is used as a lounge in summer and delicious breakfasts are also served there. The welcome is pleasant and generous and the village is well worth a stopover.

138 - Château de Nobles

71700 La Chapelle-sous-Brançion
(Saône-et-Loire)
Tel. 03 85 51 00 55
M. and Mme de Cherisey

Rooms 2 with bath and WC. **Price** 400F/60,97€ (2 pers.), +100F/15,24€ (extra bed). **Meals** Breakfast incl. No communal meal. **Nearby** Restaurants, hiking and bicycles, riding, tennis, fishing; 18-hole golf courses (25 and 35km); Romanesque churches, Cluny, Tournus, Wine Route, Taizé, museum (Châlon-sur-Saône), château de Cormatin, Brançion. **Spoken** English. **Open** Easter – Nov 11. **How to get there** (Map 19): 14km west of Tournus. A6 exit Tournus, take to Charolles/Cluny on D14 (leave La Chapelle-sous-Brançion on the right).

The 15th-century Château de Nobles stands in the marvelous countryside around Brançion. In decorating the guest rooms, which are located in the outbuildings, the wine grower owners, Monsieur and Madame de Cherisey, have emphasized the traditional character and charm of the regional style. The two bedrooms, which you reach via a Macon-style gallery, overlook a square courtyard. Each has twin beds and a modern bath, while one room has a loft which is ideal for children. You can enjoy your breakfast in a huge salon dominated by a Renaisssance fireplace.

B U R G U N D Y

139 - Ferme-Auberge de Lavaux

Chatenay
71800 La Clayette
(Saône-et-Loire)
Tel. 03 85 28 08 48
Fax 03 85 26 80 66
M. and Mme Paul Gelin

Rooms 5 (incl. one in the tower with a dependent balcony) with bath or shower and WC. **Price** 290F/44,21€ (2 pers.), room in the tower 340F/51,83€ (2 pers.). **Meals** Breakfast incl. Meals at the farm restaurant 80-120F/12,19-18,29€ (wine not incl.). **Facilities** Fishing. **Pets** Dogs not allowed. **Nearby** Walks; Romanesque churches, Cluny, Paray-le-Monial, Dun, Saint-Cyr. **Credit cards** Not accepted. **Open** Easter – Nov 15. **How to get there** (Map 18): about 40km southeast of Paray-le-Monial via N79 towards Charolles, then D985 towards La Clayette and D987 towards Mâcon for 5km, then left on D300 towards Chatenay.

Amid a lush and rolling countryside, this lovely auberge-farm lies on a hillside in a setting rich with flowers. The bedroom in the tower is our favorite, with its terra cotta flooring and antique furniture, but the others, which have recently been attractively redone, are also very nice. The decoration of the auberge is quite rustic. Excellent meals are served at modest prices for guests and other travellers. Lavaux gets better every year and you will find a warm welcome and excellent advice for your touring.

140 - La Courtine

Pont de la Levée
71250 Cluny
(Saône-et-Loire)
Tel. and fax 03 85 59 05 10
Mme Donnadieu

Rooms 5 with bath or shower and WC. **Price** 320F/48,78€ (2 pers.), +80F/12,19€ (extra bed, children under 10). **Meals** Breakfast incl. No communal meal. **Restaurants** "Le Forum"(on the property) and others nearby. **Facilities** Sitting room. **Pets** Dogs allowed on request. **Nearby** Hiking and bicycling (Voie Verte between Cluny and Givry), fishing (Grosne), bicycle rentals (Cluny), 18-hole golf course, tennis, riding; Abbey of Cluny, Romanesque churches, Wine Route.**Open** All year. **How to get there** (Map 19): in front of La Grosne, to Azé, just after the bridge of La Levée.

On the edge of the town of Cluny and the Grosne River, this converted farmhouse, covered in wisteria, is occupied by a brocante shop selling old furniture and objects; it also offers travelers bed and breakfast in rooms beneath the eaves. The Rose room with whitewashed beams is the most spacious, with a large bathroom and a view over the garden. Views from the low windows in the other rooms overlook the famous Cluny Abbey. Breakfast, with fruit and homemade preserves, can be served in the courtyard adjacent to the Forum Restaurant in the former stables, where you can enjoy grills and salads.

141 - Manoir des Chailloux

Le Manoir des Chailloux
71390 Jully-les-Buxy
(Saône-et-Loire)
Tel. 03 85 92 13 62
Fax 03 85 92 12 62
Mme Flèche

Rooms 2 with bath, WC, tel. and TV. **Price** 550 and 700F/83,84 and 106,71€ (2 pers.), +100F/15,24€ (extra bed). **Meals** Breakfast incl. No communal meal. **Restaurants** In Buxy and in Givry. **Pets** Dogs not allowed. **Facilities** Swimming pool, tennis. **Nearby** Hiking and bicycling (Voie Verte), riding, fishing, 18-hole golf course; Romanesque churches, Cluny, Tournus, château de la Verrerie (Le Creusot), château de Cormatin, Buxy, Brançion. **Spoken** English. **Open** May 1 – Sept 15. **How to get there** (Map 19): 16km southwest of Châlon-sur-Saône. A6, exit Châlon-sud, to Le Creusot, Montçeau, turn on Buxy, then to Cluny, Saint-Boil, then 1km on left Jully-les-Buxy.

Surrounded by vineyards and pastures, this former silkworm farm overlooks a 17 1/2 acre park planted extensively with conifers. You have a choice of two bedrooms in the Manoir, each with direct telephone and television: one on the village side with twin beds and a small living room panelled in gold wood; and the spacious room on the swimming pool side (it has electric blankets), which enjoys a terrace and an immense bathroom. For breakfast, Madame Flèche serves organic milk, yogurt, and preserves.

142 - Chez M. et Mme Lamy

Anzy-le-Duc
71110 Marcigny
(Saône-et-Loire)
Tel. 03 85 25 17 21
Fax 03 85 25 44 82
M. and Mme Christian Lamy

Rooms 2 with bath and WC. Rooms cleaned every five days. **Price** 250F/38,11€ (1 pers.), 270F/41,16€ (2 pers.), +100F/15,24€ (extra bed). **Meals** Breakfast incl. No communal meal (kitchenette and washing machine available). **Facilities** Sitting room (TV). **Pets** Dogs allowed on request. **Nearby** 18-hole golf course (15km), tennis, swimming in river (500m), riding; barge trips on Canal de Bourgogne, Paray-le-Monial. **Credit cards** Not accepted. **Closed** Nov 1 – beg Apr. **How to get there** (Map 25): 25km southeast of Paray-le-Monial via D982 towards Roanne. In Montceaux-L'Etoile, towards Anzy-le-Duc. In village near church.

Monsieur and Madame Lamy have a small independent guest house – once a schoolhouse – which is in the beautiful village of Anzy-le-Duc, a veritable haven of tranquillity. The modern, comfortable bedrooms are decorated in pretty, bright colors and each has its own bath; the toilets, however, are shared. The large living room is warm and welcoming with music, games, or television. You can enjoy two lovely gardens, as well as warm hospitality, in this friendly family house.

B U R G U N D Y

143 - Les Récollets

Place du Champ-de-Foire
71110 Marcigny
(Saône-et-Loire)
Tel. 03 85 25 05 16
Fax 03 85 25 06 91
Mme Badin

Rooms 7 and 2 suites (4-6 pers. with 2 bedrooms) with bath and WC. **Price** 320F/48,78€ (1 pers.), 450F/68,60€ (2 pers.); +120F/18,29€ (extra pers. in suites). **Meals** Breakfast incl. Evening meals at separate tables, by reservation 200F/30,48€ (wine incl.). **Facilities** Sitting room. **Nearby** Golf; Romanesque art tour. **Credit cards** Amex, Visa. **Open** All year. **How to get there** (Map 25): 30km north of Roanne via D482 and D982 in the Digoin towards Marcigny.

Marcigny was once a charming village and Les Récollets was a beautiful house, with bedrooms elegantly decorated with antique furniture and floral fabrics. The house is still pleasant, but we were horrified by what has become of the view. The beautiful garden today is spoiled by two sheds which have been subsidized by the village and built at its edge. Fortunately, Madame Badin's devotion and kindness have not changed and Les Récollets has not lost its personality. It is a good place for an overnight stay.

144 - L'Orangerie

Vingelles
71390 Moroges
(Saône-et-Loire)
Tel. 03 85 47 91 94
Fax 03 85 47 98 49
M. Niels Lierow and
M. David Eades

Rooms 5 with bath or shower, WC and tel. **Price** 375-500F/57,16-76,22€ (1 pers.), 400-550F/60,97-83,84€ (2 pers.), +100F/15,24€ (extra bed), +50F/7,62€ (TV). **Meals** Breakfast incl. Communal meals 160F/24,39€ (wine incl.). **Facilities** Sitting room, swimming pool, walled park with trees. **Pets** Dogs not allowed. **Nearby** Tennis, lake, golf; Beaune, Cluny, Tournus. **Credit cards** Not accepted. **Spoken** English, German. **Closed** Nov 1 – Easter, by reservation. **How to get there** (Map 19): 15km west of Châlon-sur-Saône. N6 for 2km dir. south; N80 for 13km dir. west (Le Creusot); exit Moroges. In the village, take on left and go down for 800m. **No smoking** in bedrooms.

The charms of Victorian England have crept into this elegant Burgundy house situated in a little valley close to the village. Niels and David have furnished and decorated it in the style of their native England, and the result is most successful. The pretty living-dining room has arched windows. The bedrooms are quiet, comfortable and well-kept, but the one on the top floor is too small for the price. Excellent breakfasts served on china dishes with silver tableware. The flower-filled garden is on two levels and on the lower level there is a nice swimming pool.

145 - Maisons Vigneronnes

Château de Messey
71700 Ozenay
(Saône-et-Loire)
Tel. 03 85 51 16 11
Fax 03 85 32 57 30
Marie-Laurence and Bernard Fachon
E-mail: bf@golfenfrance.com

Rooms 4 with bath or shower and WC. **Price** 400-500F/60,97-76,22€ (2 pers.). **Meals** Breakfast incl. Evening meals at communal table, by reservation 95F/14,48€ (wine not incl.). **Facilities** Sitting room, river fishing, visit to the wine cellars and wine tasting. **Pets** Dogs not allowed. **Nearby** Riding, tennis, swimming pool, boating on the Saône, 18-hole golf course; Romanesque churches, Cluny, Tournus, Brancion, Wine Route, music in the churches. **Credit card** Visa. **Spoken** English. **Closed** Jan. By reservation: deposit or credit card number. **How to get there** (Map 19): 9km west of Tournus. Aut. A6 exit Tournus dir. Ozenay via D14.

On the banks of the Natouze (in which one can go fishing), at the foot of the pale gray walls of the château, these houses were once the homes of the wine growers. The bedrooms are comfortable. One is quite large and has its own entrance and a little plot of garden. Two others have the simple charm of a refurbished attic. There is a pleasant living-dining room where you can taste regional specialties and, under the guidance of Bernard Fachon, sample the wines produced on the estate. Your hostess is always present, yet always discreet. A good place for a friendly stopover or a longer stay.

146 - Château de Martigny

71600 Poisson
(Saône-et-Loire)
Tel. 03 85 81 53 21
Fax 03 85 81 59 40
Mme Édith Dor
E-mail: chateau.martigny@worldonline.fr

Rooms 3, 1 studio (4 pers.) and 1 suite (3 pers.) with bath, WC; 1 room with bath, shared WC, and 1 room with shared bath and WC. **Price** 350-600F/53,35-91,46€ (1-2 pers.), 500-700F/76,22-106,71€ (3 pers.), 600-750F/91,46-114,33€ (4 pers.). **Meals** Breakfast incl. Lunch and evening meal at communal table, or not as preferred 180F/27,44€ (wine incl.). **Facilities** Sitting room, swimming pool, bicycles, drama courses, dance, painting (introduction to artists). **Pets** Dogs allowed on request. **Nearby** Riding, tennis, fishing (2km), golf (25km); Romanesque churches. **Credit cards** Not accepted. **Spoken** English. **Open** Easter – Nov 1. **How to get there** (Map 18): 8km south of Paray-le-Monial via D34.

Standing in the midst of the countryside, the Château de Martigny has been very tastefully furnished and has a superb view. The beautiful, comfortable bedrooms are furnished with antiques. (Those beneath the eaves are less classic yet handsomely arranged, but the view is less beautiful.) The cuisine is excellent and artists occasionally come here for dinner or to work. An ambience of art and conviviality thanks to the kind hospitality of Edith Dor.

147 - Les Lambeys

71140 Saint-Aubin-sur-Loire
(Saône-et-Loire)
Tel. 03 85 53 92 76
M. and Mme de Bussierre

Rooms 4 with bath or shower, WC; 1 suite (3 pers.) with bath and WC. **Price** 300-350F/45,73-53,35€ (2 pers.), +80F/12,19€ (extra bed); suite 450F/68,60€ (3 pers.). **Meals** Breakfast incl. Evening meals at communal table on request 140F/21,34€ (wine incl.). **Facilities** Fishing (Loire). **Nearby** Swimming pool, tennis, riding, thermal establishing and health center (Bourbon-Lancy). **Spoken** English. **Closed** Dec 31 – Apr 1. **How to get there** (Map 18): 30km east of Moulins-sur-Allier.

A lover of old objects and art, Monsieur de Bussière enjoys collecting old sepia-colored photos with their traditional village figures: school classes, wedding parties, craftsmen, village dignitaries....Displayed in his house, they set the tone for the deliberately old-fashioned decoration of Les Lambeys. The bedrooms have yesteryear furnishings, their décor predominantly in tones of sienna; the baths are lovely. There is a soft, serene atmosphere in this special place, which overlooks a beautiful, bucolic landscape. Monsieur de Bussière is a friendly host, and he sparkles with personality.

148 - Chez M. et Mme Lyssy

Champseuil
71350 Saint-Gervais-en-Vallière
(Saône-et-Loire)
Tel. and fax 03 85 91 80 08
M. and Mme Lyssy
E-mail: martine.lyssy-chambres-dhotes@wanadoo.fr

Rooms 3 with bath and WC (1 private WC outside the room). **Price** 300F/45,73€ (2 pers.), +100F/15,24€ (extra bed). **Meals** Breakfast incl. Evening meals at communal table or not, by reservation 100F/15,24€ (wine not incl.). **Facilities** Sitting room, mountain bikes, ping-pong. **Pets** Dogs allowed on request. **Nearby** Fishing, 18-hole golf course; Beaune, Dijon, Châlon-sur-Saône Festival (Jul). **Spoken** English. **Open** Mar 1 – Nov 30. **How to get there** (Map 19): 14km southeast of Beaune. A6, exit Beaune-Chagny, then to Verdun-sur-Doubs via D970. In Saint-Loup-de-la-Salle, D183 to Saint-Martin-en-Gâtinais, then Champseuil.

In a remote hamlet of the Saône Plain, Madame Lyssey has arranged her country house as a bed and breakfast. A talented professional decorator, forever bright and cheerful, she has created a distinctive style in the small, bright bedrooms and baths, decorating them with old furniture and objects found in brocante shops around the region. Breakfast is served around her large dining table or on the terrace in summer, where you can enjoy a barbecue or a cold buffet in the evening.

149 - La Salamandre

Lieu-dit Au Bourg
71250 Salornay-sur-Guye
(Saône-et-Loire)
Tel. 03 85 59 91 56
Fax 03 85 59 91 67
M. Forestier and M. Berclaz
E-mail: info@la-salamandre.fr
Web: www.la-salamandre.fr

Rooms 4 and 1 suite with bath or shower, WC and tel. **Price** 310F/47,25€ (1 pers.), 430F/65,55€ (2 pers.), +100F/15,24€ (extra bed); suite 540F/82,32€ (2-3 pers.). **Meals** Breakfast incl. Evening meals at communal table, by reservation 120F/18,29€ (wine not incl., à la carte). **Facilities** Lounge, bikes. **Pets** Dogs allowed on request. **Nearby** Riding (Cluny Haras, Stud Farm), 18-hole golf course; Romanesque Burgundy (Tournus, Chapaize, Gourden...), Lamartine Route, prehistoric sites (Blanot, Solutré). **Credit cards** Visa, MasterCard, Eurocard. **Spoken** English, German, Italian. **Open** All year. **How to get there** (Map 19): 25km east of Tournus via Autoroute A6, exit Tournus, then D14 for Cormatin and Salorney. From Lyon, exit Mâcon-sud, then Cluny. **No smoking** in bedrooms.

Surrounded by a park, this elegant 18th-century family house has been restored with taste and refinement. All different in style, the bedrooms are spacious, bright, and handsomely decorated with antique furniture and very beautiful fabrics. The bathrooms are new. Dinner is served in the dining room or in the park beneath the linden trees. Monsieur Berclaz, a charming conversationalist, will give you interesting information on the historic places of the region.

150 - Maison Niepce

8, av. du 4 septembre 44
71240 Sennecey-le-Grand
(Saône-et-Loire)
Tel. 03 85 44 76 44
Fax 03 85 44 75 59
M. Moreau de Melen

Rooms 4 with bath, WC and 1 with shower and WC. **Price** 300-500F/45,73-76,22€ (2 pers.), +150F/22,86€ (extra bedroom). Children under 12 (free). **Meals** Breakfast 50F/7,62€. Evening meals at communal table (Regional cooking) 120F/18,29€ (wine incl., à la carte). **Credit cards** All major. **Facilities** Sitting room, swimming pool, mountain bikes. **Pets** Dogs allowed on request. **Spoken** English. **Open** All year. **How to get there** (Map 19): 14km south of Châlon-sur-Saône. A6, exit Châlon-sud., to Mâcon N6 at 14km, Sennecey-le-Grand. At the end of the village, impasse on left.

Behind the austere portal of this 17th-century townhouse lies a park and an interior that seem to have just awakened from a sleep of centuries. The rooms have remained much as they were in times gone by, like the kitchen with its antique cupboards or the sitting room, once a meeting place for the cousins of the photographer Nicéphor Niepce. But in fact each room has been discreetly renovated so as to add modern comfort to the charm of yesteryear. One feels truly comfortable in the bedrooms and bathrooms (don't look too closely at the details.) The rooms facing the avenue are also comfortable but the view is not as nice. Very good breakfasts.

151 - Château de Beaufer

Route d'Ozenay
71700 Tournus
(Saône-et-Loire)
Tel. 03 85 51 18 24
Fax 03 85 51 25 04
M. and Mme Roggen

Rooms 5 and 1 suite with bath and WC. **Price** Rooms 620-800F/94,51-121,95€ (2 pers.); suite 700F/106,71€ (3 pers.), 800F/121,95€ (4 pers.). **Meals** Breakfast 50F/7,62€. Evening meals at separate tables on request 100-350F/15,24-53,35€ (wine not incl.). **Restaurants** In Tournus. **Facilities** Sitting room (TV), swimming pool. Seminars (10 pers.), meetings (8-10 pers.). **Pets** Dogs allowed on request (+60F/9,14€). **Nearby** Golf, polo. **Credit card** Visa. **Spoken** English, Italian, German. **Open** All year. Nov 1 – Easter, by reservation (+50F/7,62€/bedroom, heating). 3 nights min. in Jul and Aug. **How to get there** (Map 19): 25km south of Châlon-sur-Saône via N6 and A6 to Tournus, then D14 towards Ozenay; signposted 3km from Tournus.

This small château backs onto a hill and faces a rural, wooded landscape. Beautifully arranged for the comfort and pleasure of its guests, it has a handsome, high-beamed sitting room that opens onto a swimming pool. The bedrooms, spread throughout several buildings, are large, well kept, and decorated with prints and pretty furniture; the beds are huge and the bathrooms superb.

152 - La Maîtresse

Le Bourg
71250 La Vineuse
(Saône-et-Loire)
Tel. 03 85 59 60 98
Fax 03 85 59 65 26
M. and Mme Serres

Rooms 3 and 2 suites with bath or shower, WC and TV. 1 studio with kitchenette, bath, WC and TV. **Price** Rooms 270F/41,16€ (1 pers.), 320-380F/48,78-57,93€ (2 pers.), suite 450F/68,60€ (2 pers.), studio 450F/68,60€ (2 pers.), +100F/15,24€ (extra bed) or 2800-3200F/426,85-487,83€/week (2-3 pers.).**Meals** Breakfast incl. No communal meal. **Facilities** Sitting room, swimming pool, ping-pong, mountain bike rentals. **Pets** Dogs allowed on request. **Credit cards** Not accepted. **Spoken** English. **Open** Easter – end Sept. **How to get there** (Map 19): 20km northwest of Mâcon. Aut. A6 exit Mâcon-sud dir. Cluny, then Montceau-les-Mines for about 3km. On left to La Vineuse. Below the church. **No smoking** in bedrooms.

This traditional old house, which was once the village inn, looks out on a lush and verdant landscape. The barn, formerly used as a ballroom, has been refurbished to provide attractive and agreeable guest rooms in cheerful colors and highlighted with some fine pieces of furniture and appealing objects. The bathrooms are all brand new. A nice place to stay at a reasonable price.

B U R G U N D Y

153 - Château de Ribourdin

89240 Chevannes
(Yonne)
Tel. and fax 03 86 41 23 16
M. and Mme Brodard

Rooms 5 with bath or shower and WC. **Price** 300F/45,73€ (1 pers.), 350-400F/53,35-60,97€ (2 pers.), +70F/10,67€ (extra bed), +100F/15,24€ (2 extra beds). **Meals** Breakfast incl. No communal meal. **Restaurants** in the village, Vaux and Auxerre. **Facilities** Sitting room, swimming pool, fishing (Yonne), mountain bike rentals. **Pets** Dog not allowed (or small in 1 room) **Nearby** Tennis, riding, 18-hole golf course; Auxerre, châteaux. **Credit cards** Not accepted. **Spoken** English. **Open** All year. **How to get there** (Map 18): 6km southeast of Auxerre. Autoroute A6 exit Auxerre-nord, dir. Auxerre via N6 and after 500m, dir. Saint-Georges/Baluche on right then Chevannes.

In the outbuildings of this rustic Renaissance château 6 kilometres from Auxerre, the owner himself has designed five guest rooms overlooking a peaceful landscape of wheat fields. They are decorated in a simple rustic style and each one bears the name of a nearby château. All face east and get the morning sun. The one called "Château Gaillard" is accessible to the disabled. In the downstairs breakfast room or in front of the fireplace you can taste the home-made cakes and preserves.

154 - Les Morillons

89250 Mont-Saint-Sulpice
(Yonne)
Tel. 03 86 56 18 87
Fax 03 86 43 05 07
Françoise and Didier Brunot

Rooms 3 with bath or shower (2 nights min.). **Price** 480F/73,17€ (2 pers.). **Meals** Breakfast incl. Communal meals 180F/27,44€ (wine incl.). **Facilities** Sitting room, fishing, horse-drawn carriage, mountain bikes. **Nearby** Tennis (1km), 18-hole golf course (26km); Wine Route (Chablis), Auxerre, Canal de Bourgogne. **Credit cards** Not accepted. **Spoken** English. **Open** All year. **How to get there** (Map 18): 22km north of Auxerre. Autoroute A6, exit Auxerre-nord towards Moneteau (D84), go through Seignelay, Hauterive, on right Mont-Saint-Sulpice: take the road in front of "Mairie", 3.5km after leaving the village. **No smoking.**

Surrounded by fields, the Morillons estate is made up of several buildings built around a vast courtyard, with a terrace overlooking the peaceful Serein River. The interior is tastefully decorated and very well kept. Nice convivial breakfasts are served outdoors in fine weather. Our favorite bedrooms are the ones upstairs. The third one is more independent but also more impersonal. Didier and Françoise Brunot adore their region and will be happy to advise you on sports, cultural and wine-tasting activities. Hospitable and friendly, they attach great importance to the quality and atmosphere of their dinners.

155 - Le Château d'Archambault

Cours
89310 Noyers-sur-Serein
(Yonne)
Tel. 03 86 82 67 55
Fax 03 86 82 67 87
M. Marie

Rooms 5 with bath or shower and WC. **Price** 350-380F/53,35-57,93€ (2 pers.), +80F/12,19€ (extra bed). **Meals** Breakfast incl. Evening meals at separate tables, by reservation 90-110F/13,72-16,76€ (wine not incl.). **Facilities** Sitting room, tel., bicycle rentals. **Pets** Dogs allowed (30F/4,57€/day) **Nearby** Restaurants, hiking, golf (15km); Noyers-sur-Serein, Vezelay, Fontenay Abbey, châteaux (Tanlay, Ancy-le-Franc). **Credit cards** All major. **Spoken** English. **Open** All year, by reservation and deposit or credit card number. **How to get there** (Map 18): 2km of Noyers-sur-Serein via D86 towards Avallon. **No smoking.**

The term château may seem a bit pompous for this large house with a slightly bohemian air, but as soon as you set foot inside you will be enchanted by the light and spaciousness of the dining and sitting rooms. The bedrooms are also very pleasant, decorated in all simplicity with cheery colors and some antique furniture items, and equipped with very handsome bathrooms. The house is surrounded with a park with large old trees and a large vegetable garden.

156 - La Coudre

La Coudre
89120 Perreux
(Yonne)
Tel. 03 86 91 61 42
and 03 86 91 62 91
M. and Mme Lusardi

Rooms 3 with bath and WC. **Price** 490-570F/74,90-86,89€ (2 pers.). **Meals** Breakfast incl. Evening meals at communal table, by reservation 180F/27,44€ (wine incl.). **Facilities** Sitting room, tel., potter's studio. **Pets** Dogs not allowed. **Nearby** 18-hole golf course, tennis, riding; château of Saint-Fargeau. **Credit cards** Not accepted. **Spoken** English, Italian. **Open** All year. **How to get there** (Map 18): From Paris, 15km from A6 Joigny exit (south, exit 18 Charny/Château-Renard), then towards Montargis, then D3 towards Toucy to Sommecaise and D57 towards Perreux; 1km before the village.

On the edge of a small country road, this is a large, handsomely restored house surrounded by a well-tended garden. We were especially impresssed with the beautiful proportions of the rooms, the materials used, and the lovely antique furniture. Similar care has been given to the bedrooms, which are especially pleasant. Very good breakfasts and dinners are beautifully served at a long table.

157 - Le Moulin de Poilly-sur-Serein

89310 Poilly-sur-Serein
(Yonne)
Tel. 03 86 75 92 46
Fax 03 86 75 95 21
Hester and Pascal Moreau

Rooms 5 with bath or shower and WC. **Price** 310F/47,25€ (1 pers.), 360-450F/54,88-68,60€ (2 pers.), 420-540F/64,02-82,32€ (3 pers.), +90F/13,72€ (extra bed). **Meals** Breakfast incl. No communal meal. **Facilities** Sitting room, fishing and swimming in river. **Pets** Dogs not allowed. **Nearby** Restaurants; visit of village of Noyers, Wine Route (Chablis). **Credit cards** Not accepted. **Spoken** German, English, Dutch, Swedish. **Closed** Nov 1 – Easter. **How to get there** (Map 18): 12km southeast of Chablis. Autoroute A6, exit Auxerre-sud, then D965 towards Tonnerre. In Chablis, D45 towards Chichée, Chemilly. 3km after Chemilly: Moulin at entrance to Poilly.

This majestic mill, restored by a friendly couple (Madame is a potter and Monsieur is a winegrower), spans the Serein River at the entrance to the village. The spaciousness and the dominant colors – the natural wood tones of the beams and pillars, white and beige – confer a beautiful harmony to the interior decoration, including that in the comfortable bedrooms. Beautiful antique furniture and decorative objects further enhance the decor. The Moulin is a refined place to stay, and is as serene as the river of that name.

158 - Dannery

89170 Saint-Fargeau
(Yonne)
Tel. 03 86 74 09 01
and 01 46 24 16 47
M. and Mme Couiteas Conemenos

Rooms 3 with bath or shower and WC. **Price** 380-420F/57,93-64,02€ (2 pers.). **Meals** Breakfast incl. No communal meal. **Facilities** Sitting room, swimming pool, fishing in the moat. **Nearby** Restaurants (4km), tennis and riding (4km), water sports (15km), Saint Fargeau Sound and Light, Chablis vineyards, Fishing Museum at the Château de la Bussière. **Credit cards** Not accepted. **Spoken** English. **Open** All year. **How to get there** (Maps 17 and 18): 7km northeast of Saint-Fargeau. Autoroute A6 exit Joigny, then towards Toucy, then dir. Saint-Fargeau; in Mezilles go 4km. Signs on right.

Nestling in a countryside of fields and forests, this elegant manor house offers you a beautiful, spacious guest room with comfortable amenities, antique furniture, and a view out over the surrounding moats. Installed in the outbuildings, the other rooms are attractive and cheerful, although somewhat sparsely furnished for their price (the smallest room has only a roof window). Good breakfasts are served in the dining room, adjacent to a salon with white rattan furniture. Dannery is a lovely place to stay where you will always be kindly received.

159 - Domaine des Beaurois

Lavau
89170 Saint-Fargeau
(Yonne)
Tel. and fax 03 86 74 16 09
Mme Anne-Marie Marty

Rooms 1 and 1 suite of 2 bedrooms with bath and WC. Rooms cleaned every 3 days or +30F/4,57€/day **Price** 280F/42,68€ (2 pers., 1 night) or 240F/36,59€ (2 pers., from 2 nights); suite 470F/71,65€ (4 pers., 1 night) or 400F/60,97€ (4 pers., from 2 nights). **Meals** Breakfast incl. No communal meal. **Facilities** Sitting room, swimming pool, bicycles. **Pets** Animals not allowed. **Nearby** Restaurants, canals, hunting, fishing. **Credit cards** Not accepted. **Spoken** English. **Closed** Christmas and New Year. Reservation by mail. **How to get there** (Maps 17 and 18): Autoroute A6 exit Dordives, then N7 to Bonny-sur-Loire, then D965 dir. Auxerre to Lavau. In Lavau, take D74 dir. Bléneau for 3km and follow signs (Make sure not to take direction Bléneau on N 7.).

This flower-decked house in the heart of a wooded countryside is owned by a family of wine growers. They offer comfortable, nicely decorated rooms for guests (including two that can form a family suite). There's a pleasant sitting room with a fireplace and a friendly dining room where breakfast is served, unless the weather is nice enough to eat in the garden. The welcome is warm and relaxed and the price are reasonable – all in all, a good address to keep in mind.

160 - Chez Mme Defrance

4, place de la Liberté
89710 Senan
(Yonne)
Tel. 03 86 91 59 89
Mme Defrance

Rooms 1 with shower, WC, and 2 sharing bath and WC. **Price** 300-420F/45,73-64,02€ (2 pers.), +140F/21,34€ (extra bed). **Meals** Breakfast incl. Evening meals at communal table, by reservation 120F/18,29€ (wine incl.). **Facilities** Sitting room. **Pets** Dogs not allowed. **Nearby** Restaurants, tennis, golf. **Credit cards** Not accepted. **Spoken** English. **Open** All year. **How to get there** (Map 18): 26km northwest of Auxerre. From south autoroute A6 exit 18 Villeneuve-sur-Yonne, then D89 Volgré, Senan. From Paris, A6 exit Joigny, then D89.

This is a charming house in a village, set back somewhat from a grass-covered walk planted with lime trees. It is very quiet. The interior is simple and well kept with some antique furniture. We recommend the large bedroom, which is reserved for a minimum of two nights. It is bright and pleasant with its waxed wood floor, its new striped wallpaper, its drapes and bedspread in tones of red and its splendid bathroom. Madame Defrance, who is very friendly, will ask you to choose where you would like to have breakfast: in your bedroom, the garden or the dining room.

161 - Les Lammes

89210 Venizy
(Yonne)
Tel. 03 86 43 44 42
(at meal times)
Mme Antoinette Puissant

Rooms 2 suites (2-4 pers.) and 1 family suite (5-8 pers.) with kitchen, sitting room, bath and WC. **Price** 420F/64,02€ (2 pers.), +120F/18,29€ (extra bed). Child's bed free. **Meals** Breakfast incl. No communal meal. **Facilities** Swimming pool, fishing. **Pets** Dogs allowed on request. **Nearby** Restaurants, tennis; Wine Route, Fontenay abbey. **Credit cards** Not accepted. **Spoken** English, German, Italian. **Closed** Oct 15 – Easter (possible weekly or weekend rental of apartment). **How to get there** (Map 18): 30km northeast of Auxerre via N77. Go through Saint-Florentin and take D30 towards Venizy; 300m after l'Auberge de Pommerats on the left.

Located in a vast farmhouse surrounded by a moat and in the house next door (where you can enjoy complete privacy), the bedrooms at Les Lammes are all suites with a corner salon and a kitchen area. Patchwork bedcovers and antique furniture make for a pleasant atmosphere, and many rooms have a view of the large swimming pool. Breakfast is served in a huge well-decorated room or outside under a canopy. You will receive an enthusiastic welcome.

162 - Domaine de Montpierreux

Route de Chablis
89290 Venoy
(Yonne)
Tel. 03 86 40 20 91
Fax 03 86 40 28 00
Françoise and François Choné

Rooms 4 and 1 suite with bath or shower and WC. **Price** 280-300F/42,68-45,73€ (2 pers.); suite 340F/51,83€ (2 pers.), 450F/68,60€ (3 pers.), 500F/76,22€ (4 pers.). **Meals** Breakfast incl. No communal meal. **Pets** Animals not allowed. **Nearby** Restaurants (3km, Chablis and Auxerre), hiking, tennis in village, hiking (GR), all sports (10km); Chablis and Auxerre Wine Route, Cistercian Abbey of Pontigny, village of Noyers-sur-Serein. **Credit cards** Not accepted. **Spoken** English. **Closed** Dec 15 – Jan 15. **How to get there** (Map 18): 10km east of Auxerre. A6 exit Auxerre-sud, then D965 towards Chablis, then signs: house in 3km on right (don't go to Venoy).

Lying in the midst of the country, this large farm produces wine and truffles. You will enjoy very pleasant bedrooms. The largest can be adjoined to a smaller one to make a suite for families. Located on the second étage (third floor), they are comfortable, personalized and each has a small bathroom which is kept immaculate. Breakfasts are served in a room reserved for guests or in the garden in good weather. The Chonés are very friendly and helpful.

163 - Domaine de Sainte-Anne
Allée de Sainte Anne
Soleines-le-Haut
89290 Venoy
(Yonne)
Tel. 03 86 94 10 16
Fax 03 86 94 10 12
Mme Genest
E-mail: info@domainesaintanne.com
Web: www.domainesaintanne.com

Rooms 3 with bath or shower, WC and tel. **Price** 330-410F/50,30-62,50€ (2 pers.), +80F/12,19€ (extra bed). **Meals** Breakfast incl. No communal meal. **Facilities** Sitting room (TV, library). **Pets** Dogs not allowed. **Nearby** Restaurants, historic sites, museums, visit to the wine cellars and wine tasting, Chablis (12km), vineyard, Auxerre's monuments, Vézelay, shows, concerts, walks on the banks of the Yonne, hiking, swimming pool, bikes, canoeing, fishing. **Credit cards** Not accepted. **Spoken** English. **Closed** Jan 15 – Feb 28. **How to get there** (Map 18): 8km east of Auxerre. Autoroute A6, exit Auxerre-sud, take towards Chablis, then 3rd road on left Soleines and 2nd on right.

On a slight rise facing the small valleys of the Auxerre region, the Domaine de Sainte Anne is an elegant, very comfortably appointed house. The delightful bedrooms are bright and cheerful, and their baths gleaming. The hearty breakfasts are served in two small dining rooms decorated in bright colors. In summer, tables are set out on the lawn, signaling the opening of Madame Genest's country tea room, which is the most popular in the region.

B R I T T A N Y

164 - La Tarais

22100 Calorguen
(Côtes-d'Armor)
Tel. and fax 02 96 83 50 59
Deborah and Bernard Kerkhof
E-mail: tarais@worldonline.fr
Web: //perso.worldonline.fr/tarais/index.htm

Rooms 4 with shower and WC. **Price** 225-300F/34,30-45,73€ (2 pers. for 1 night), 750F/114,33€ (2 pers. for 3 nights), +75F/11,43€ (extra bed). **Meals** Breakfast incl. (English breakfast possible +20F/3,04€). Meals at separate tables beg Apr – end Sept 125F/19,05€ (wine incl.). **Facilities** Sitting room. **Pets** Dogs not allowed. **Nearby** Restaurants (3km), swimming pool, tennis, hiking along the Rance, golf; seaside; Saint-Malo, Mont Saint-Michel. **Credit cards** Not accepted. **Spoken** English, German, Dutch. **Open** All year, by reservation. **How to get there** (Map 6): 7km south of Dinan via D12 towards Léhon. In Léhon, take road to Calorguen, then signs. **No smoking** in bedrooms.

In a little hamlet deep in the Breton countryside, this typical old farmhouse has been completely refurbished by an Anglo-Dutch couple. The bedrooms are simple country-style, but well-kept and brightened up by pretty flowered quilts. They all face the stunning garden, brimming with perennials. Here, as soon as weather permits, Deborah and Bernard set up the tables so that guests can have their breakfast outdoors. Otherwise, meals are served in the sitting-dining room, which is also used for afternoon tea. A friendly, inviting place, good value for the price.

165 - Le Char à Bancs

Plélo
22170 Chatelaudren
(Côtes-d'Armor)
Tel. 02 96 74 13 63
Fax 02 96 74 13 03
Family Lamour
E-mail: charabanc@wanadoo.fr

Rooms 5 (2-4 pers.) with bath or shower and WC. **Price** 300F/45,73€ (1 pers.), 380-500F/57,93-76,22€ (2 pers.), 480-600F/73,17-91,46€ (3 pers.), 600-680F/91,46-103,66€ (4 pers.). **Meals** Breakfast incl. No communal meal. Farmhouse-auberge 500m ("potée", "galettes", "crêpes") or restaurants. **Facilities** Lounge, paddle boats on the river, ponies. **Credit cards** Not accepted. **Open** Mid Jun – mid Sept (2 nights min.). In low season by reservation. **How to get there** (Maps 5 and 6): Between Saint-Brieuc and Guingamp. 4km north of the Paris-Brest highway, exit Plélo; signposted.

Here is a pleasant spot intelligently run by an active, warm-hearted family. Part of the family live at the farmhouse-inn where meals are served and where you can taste the traditional Breton stew ("potée"), simmered over an open fire and served with thin buckwheat crêpes ("galettes"). Other family members will welcome you at the quiet guest house, set deep in the country, apart from the hectic life the inn. The style is rustic but refined and all the rooms are comfortable (exposed beams, flowered quilts, vintage furniture) and have nice shower rooms. Breakfast is excellent and quite copious. Nearby, a museum shows how farm life was in the olden days. The welcome is cordial.

166 - Le Logis du Jerzual

25, 27 rue du Petit Fort
22100 Dinan
(Côtes-d'Armor)
Tel. 02 96 85 46 54
Fax 02 96 39 46 94
M. and Mme D. Ronsseray

Rooms 3 (1 with kitchen) with bath or shower, WC and 2 rooms with private shower but communal WC; TV on request. **Price** 300-420F/45,73-64,02€ (2 pers.); +100F/15,24€ (extra bed). **Meals** Breakfast incl. No communal meal. **Restaurants** Many restaurants at port 100m away. **Facilities** Sitting room, tel., fax. **Pets** Dogs allowed on request. **Credit card** Visa. **Spoken** English, German understood. **Open** All year. **How to get there** (Map 6): In Dinan, towards Le Port; 100m from port of Dinan. In front of old bridge, take Rue du Petit Fort (Le Jerzual): one-way street except for brief stopping. Leave luggage, park on port or Rue du Roquet beyond the washhouse.

From the old port, a splendid medieval street climbs upward to the center of the upper town (you may want to stop in the middle to catch your breath) and leads you to this charming home dating from the 15th and 18th centuries. Tucked away behind the facade is a little garden with a fine view of the old port. The guest house is just next to the home of Monsieur and Madame Ronsseray. The bedrooms are furnished with antique pieces and have the cozy feel of a private guest room. Our favorites are one flight up. There are two small breakfast rooms and in fine weather breakfast is served outside.

167 - Château de Bonabry

22120 Hillion
(Côtes-d'Armor)
Tel. 02 96 32 21 06
Fax 02 96 32 21 06
Vicomte and Vicomtesse
Louis du Fou de Kerdaniel

Rooms 1 with bath and WC. 2 suites (room and sitting room, 4-5 pers.) with bath or shower, WC (1 with whirlpool). Also one 16th-century house for rent (2 bedrooms, sitting room, kitchen and bath). **Price** Room 450F/68,60€ (2 pers.); suites 600-700F/91,46-106,71€ (2 pers.), +150F/22,86€ (extra pers.); house 7000F/1067,14€/week (4 pers.). **Meals** Breakfast incl. in room and suite. No communal meal. **Facilities** Sitting room, fishing on rocks, horse stalls paddocks (possible riding for experienced riders). **Pets** Dogs allowed in kennel only. **Nearby** Restaurants (5km), golf, seaside; Cap Fréhel, Mont Saint-Michel, Bréhat. **Credit cards** Not accepted. **Spoken** English. **Open** Easter – Sept 30. **How to get there** (Map 6): 12km northeast of Saint-Brieuc. On N12, exit Yffiniac/Hillion. In Hillion, towards La Granville. 300m from Hillion, entrance to property on left.

Bonabry spreads out over fields, woods, and cliffs, with the lanes of the château leading to an immense beach. The façade as well as the stables, the pigeon loft and the chapel have been left in their original state, while the interior of the château has just been very tastefully refurbished. The two suites, each with an immense private salon, are superb. The decor essentially includes antique furniture, family paintings and hunting trophies. You will enjoy authentic château life at Bonabry, and very friendly hospitality.

168 - Manoir de Troezel Vras

22610 Kerbors
(Côtes-d'Armor)
Tel. 02 96 22 89 68
Fax 02 96 22 90 56
Françoise and Jean-Marie Maynier

Rooms 5 with shower and WC. **Price** 300F/45,73€ (2 pers.), +100F/15,24€ (extra bed). **Meals** Breakfast incl. Evening meals at separate tables 95F/14,48€ (wine not incl.). **Facilities** Sitting room. **Nearby** Hiking (GR 34, 2km), seaside (3km); pink Granite Coast, Bréhat. **Credit cards** Not accepted. **Spoken** English. **Closed** Nov 1 – beg Apr. **How to get there** (Map 5): In Paimpol, take dir. Tréguier. 2km after Lézardieux, take on right dir. Pleumeur-Gautier. At village, towards Kerbors, the house is 2km farther on.

Not far from the Pink Granite Coast, this former farmhouse is surrounded by a magnificent garden with box hedge, perennial flowers and rare shrubs... Especially designed to accommodate guests, the interior will please all those who like an ascetic look. The bedrooms walls are in color-tinted whitewash, hung with little paintings by local artist Mathurin Méheut, antique wardrobes, floors of unpolished terra cotta. The effect is elegant, almost monastic, scrupulously clean. Breakfast (buffet style) and dinner are served in a large, rather formal room done in shades of yellow and blue. The welcome is pleasant and professional.

169 - Ferme de Malido

Saint-Alban
22400 Lamballe
(Côtes-d'Armor)
Tel. 02 96 32 94 74 / 06 07 14 65 38
Fax 02 96 32 92 67
M. and Mme Robert Legrand

Rooms 6 with shower, WC (1 with balcony). **Price** 200F/30,48€ (1 pers.), 200-260F/30,48-39,63€ (2 pers.), 300F/45,73€ (Euphonia, 2 pers.), +80F/12,19€ (extra pers.). Special rates for weekend and 10-17 pers. depending season. **Meals** Breakfast incl. No communal meal; barbecue in the garden. **Facilities** Sitting room, tel. **Pets** Dogs allowed on request (+20F/3,05€). **Nearby** Restaurants, swimming pool, tennis, fishing, riding, sailing, golf. **Credit cards** Not accepted. **Spoken** English. **Open** All year. **How to get there** (Map 6): 21km northeast of Saint-Brieuc. Take N12 to Lamballe, then D791 north from Lamballe towards Le Val André. At Saint-Alban, take the Saint-Brieuc road for 2km.

A plain simple farmhouse, some 4 km from the sea, where families are warmly welcomed. The house has been extensively renovated and is organized around a courtyard brimming over with flowers. The bedrooms are simple and well-kept. We especially recommend those on the ground floor and also "Euphonia," situated in a small outbuilding and very open on the garden. The dining room lacks warmth but the little sitting room could come in handy for children in bad weather.

170 - Manoir de Kerguéréon

Ploubezre
22300 Lannion
(Côtes-d'Armor)
Tel. 02 96 38 91 46
M. and Mme de Bellefon

Rooms 2 with bath and WC. **Price** 500F/76,22€ (2 pers.), +100F/15,24€ (extra pers.). **Meals** Breakfast incl. No communal meal. **Restaurants** 8km away, and "Les Côtes d'Armor" in Plestin-les-Grèves (10km). **Facilities** Sitting room. **Pets** Dogs allowed on request. **Nearby** Water sports, tennis, riding, golf; châteaux of Rosanbo, Kergrist and Tonquedec, chapels, Lannion, Tréguier, Morlaix, Pink Granite coast, concerts and folklore festivals (summer). **Credit cards** Not accepted.**Spoken** English. **Open** Easter – Nov 1. **How to get there** (Map 5): 10km south of Lannion via D11, then at Kerauzern D30 towards Ploumillau; 4th road on the left after the railway line.

Standing in the middle of the countryside beside a small stud farm, this is the archetypal Breton manor house, with a tower and Gothic arched doorways. The superb interior contains beautiful furniture and pottery and has kept its old character. The two large and beautiful bedrooms have been beautifully done, full of charm and comfort. You will enjoy excellent breakfasts (home made crêpes and jams) and a very warm welcome.

171 - Le Colombier

Coat Gourhant
Louannec
22700 Perros-Guirec
(Côtes-d'Armor)
Tel. 02 96 23 29 30
M. and Mme Fajolles

Rooms 4 with shower and WC. **Price** 250F/38,11€ (1 pers.), 280F/42,68€ (2 pers.). **Meals** Breakfast incl. No communal meal. **Facilities** Sitting room, library. **Pets** Dogs not allowed. **Nearby** Restaurants, seaside, golf, tennis, riding, sea fishing; Côte des Ajoncs. **Credit cards** Not accepted. **Spoken** English. **Open** Mar – Oct. In low season on request. (2 nights min.). **How to get there** (Map 5): Coming from Lannion, at the large traffic circle in Perros-Guirec, turn right towards Louannec for 20m, then 1st small road on right; signs. (Colombier in 2,5km.)

This old, well-renovated farmhouse is in the middle of the countryside, yet only a few minutes from the sea. You will be warmly greeted here. The bedrooms with their mansard ceilings are light, comfortable, and pretty, each with its own color scheme. In the small sitting room there is a mass of tourist information. Excellent breakfasts are served in a large room, elegant and rustic, where children are delighted to find a huge aquarium stocked with local fish species. Le Colombier is a good, economical place to stay.

172 - Demeure de Rosmapamon

Louannec
22700 Perros-Guirec
(Côtes-d'Armor)
Tel. 02 96 23 00 87
Mme Annick Sillard

Rooms 2 and 2 suites with bath and/or shower and WC. **Price** Rooms 330-370F/50,30-56,40€ (1 pers.), 380-420F/57,93-64,02€ (2 pers.), suites 370-420F/56,40-64,02€ (1 pers.), 420-470F/64,02-71,65€ (2 pers.), +100F/15,24€ (extra bed). **Meals** Breakfast incl. No communal meal. **Facilities** Sitting room, tel. **Pets** Dogs not allowed. **Nearby** Restaurants, seaside, water sports, seawater therapy, bird watching, golf; Pink Granite Coast. **Credit cards** Not accepted. **Spoken** English. **Open** Apr 1 – Sept 30. **How to get there** (Map 5): 2km east of Perros-Guirec on D6.

A few hundred meters from the sea and the port of Perros-Guirec, Rosmapamon stands on a hillside in a beautiful wooded park. The house, which once belonged to Ernest Renan, is simple and elegant. You will be very pleasantly greeted. The bedrooms are quiet and charming; those on the north enjoy a view of the sea beyond the large trees. Recently renovated, the suites are the nicest and most cheerful. In the "blue suite", as well as in the "Renan" room, you can make a fire in the fireplace. In the morning, a good breakfast with fresh orange juice and homemade pastries is served in the dining room or on the terrace, which faces south. There is a small, pretty sitting room decorated with antiques.

173 - Malik

Chemin de l'Étoupe
22980 Plélan-le-Petit
(Côtes-d'Armor)
Tel. 02 96 27 62 71 / 06 09 92 35 21
Martine and Hubert Viannay

Rooms 1 suite (2 pers.) with sitting room and 1 suite of 2 bedrooms (2-4 pers.) with shower and WC. **Price** 280F/42,68€ (1 pers.), 310F/47,25€ (2 pers.), 410F/62,50€ (3 pers.), 480F/73,17€ (4 pers.). **Meals** Breakfast incl. No communal meal. **Facilities** Sitting room. **Nearby** Restaurants, tennis, riding, golf, seaside (25km); Saint-Malo, Mont Saint-Michel. **Credit cards** Not accepted. **Spoken** English, Spanish. **Open** Apr 1 – Oct 31. **How to get there** (Map 6): 12km west of Dinan towards Saint-Brieuc via N176 (or E401), exit Plélan-le-Petit Centre. In front of Mairie, take D91 towards Saint-Maudez, then 2nd street on right.

This is one of our rare contemporary guest houses. Built entirely of wood, with large bay windows, it stands at the edge of the village, and opens generously on a pretty flower garden and a terrace. Delicious and lovingly prepared breakfasts are served here in summer. The bedrooms and white-tiled shower rooms are small but very cheery and decorated with a fine eye for detail: some antique furniture, kilims, patchworks, objects of great charm. They give onto a small sitting room. You will be independent, yet received with true hospitality.

174 - Manoir de Kergrec'h

22820 Plougrescant
(Côtes-d'Armor)
Tel. 02 96 92 59 13
Fax 02 96 92 51 27
Vicomte and Vicomtesse
de Roquefeuil

Rooms 5 and 2 suites with bath and WC. **Price** 550F/83,84€ (2 pers.); suites 750F/114,33€ (3 pers.), 850F/129,58€ (4 pers.). **Meals** Breakfast incl. No communal meal. **Facilities** Tel., coastal walks. **Pets** Dogs allowed on request. **Nearby** Restaurants (2km), beach, windsurfing, sea fishing, tennis, golf; island of Bréhat, Pink Granite Coast, road of golden gorse. **Credit cards** Not accepted. **Spoken** English. **Open** All year. **How to get there** (Map 5): Between Perros-Guirec and Paimpol; 7km north of Tréguier via D8 exit Guingamp, signposted.

With a park stretching along the Pink Granite Coast, the Manoir de Kergrec'h is charming and the hosts are very friendly. The bedrooms have recently been tastefully renovated; each has antique furniture and a character of its own. Breakfast, served around the dining room table or in the bedrooms, consists of crêpes, far breton (a custard pie with prunes), fruit and homemade jams. This is a very beautiful place.

175 - Château de Kermezen

22450 Pommerit-Jaudy
(Côtes-d'Armor)
Tel. and fax 02 96 91 35 75
Comte and Comtesse de Kermel

Rooms 4 and 1 suite (4 pers.) with bath and WC. **Price** Rooms 460-550F/70,12-83,84€ (2 pers.), +120F/18,29€ (extra pers.); suite 780F/118,91€ (4 pers.). **Meals** Breakfast incl. No communal meal. **Facilities** Sitting room, fishing and Kermezen path. **Pets** Animals allowed. **Nearby** Restaurants (2km), riding, equestrian center (2km), tennis, golf, seaside; island of Bréhat, Pink Granite Coast, road of golden gorse. **Credit card** Amex. **Spoken** English. **Open** All year. **How to get there** (Map 5): 10km south of Tréguier via D8 to La Roche-Derrien and Pommerit-Jaudy; signposted.

Kermezen stands in the beautiful, green, rolling Breton countryside. You will receive a marvelous welcome from the owners, whose family has lived here for 500 years. The bedrooms are extremely pleasant (the Aux Coqs and Pavillon rooms are knockouts); families will be delighted to find two rooms with a loft, which are perfect for children. Excellent breakfasts are served in the bedrooms, on the terrace, or in an imposing 17th-century dining room.

176 - Le Clos du Prince

10, rue Croix-Jarrots
22800 Quintin
(Côtes-d'Armor)
Tel. and fax 02 96 74 93 03
Mme Marie-Madeleine Guilmoto

Rooms 2 and 1 suite (3 pers.) with bath or shower and WC. **Price** 270F/41,16€ (1 pers.), 350-380F/53,35-57,93€ (2 pers.), +150F/22,86€ (extra bed). **Meals** Breakfast incl. Meals at communal or separate tables in low season 100F/15,24€ (wine not incl.) **Facilities** Lounge, tel. **Pets** Dogs allowed on request. **Nearby** Tennis (200m), riding, fishing, 18-hole golf course (25km), pond, hiking trail; châteaux, museums. **Credit cards** Not accepted. **Open** All year. **How to get there** (Map 6): 300m from town center of Quintin. At Mairie, take Rue des Douves, then Rue des Forges, Rue Saint-Yves and Rue Croix-Jarrots.

Located at the edge of the street and covered with Virginia creeper, this house is one of the many vestiges of the historic city of Quintin, which flourished until the 18th century. Madame Guilmoto has a passion for antiques and has furnished her guestrooms with taste and personality. The 1930s, Art Déco and Retro objects are coordinated with selected furniture and beautiful fabrics. The house is very comfortable throughout. Delicious breakfasts are served in a vast living room with fireplace and exposed stone, or in the garden. You will be enthusiastially welcomed.

177 - Le Presbytère

Les Hautes Mares
22630 Saint-André-des-Eaux
(Côtes-d'Armor)
Tel. and fax 02 96 27 48 18
M. and Mme Mousquey-Piel
E-mail: mous1849@wanadoo.fr
Web: perso.wanadoo.fr/mousquey.piel

Rooms 3 with bath or shower and WC. Rooms cleaned on request. **Price** 300F/45,73€ (2 pers.), +100F/15,24€ (extra bed). **Meals** Breakfast incl. No communal meal. **Facilities** Sitting room, tel. **Nearby** Restaurants (5km) or in Dinan (10km), fishing (500m), riding (3km), sailing, surfboarding, canoeing, kayaking (Bettineuc Lake, 500m), 18-hole golf course (30km); Dinan, Valley of the Rance, Saint-Malo, the Emerald Coast, Paimpont (40km). **Credit cards** Visa, Eurocard. **Spoken** English. **Closed** Nov 15 – Mar 1. **How to get there** (Map 6): 10km south of Dinan via Lehon, Saint-André-des-Eaux. Or via Rennes, Bécherel, Evran and Saint-André-des-Eaux.

When a family of artists decides to open their home to guests, it has got to be something special. And so it is. At Le Presbytère, the garden is like an Impressionist painting, and the colored woodwork in the dining room and salon highlight the pastel pictures and sculptures which are on permanent display. The bedrooms have been freshly refurbished and yet have retained their charm of the past. The view over the flower garden is marvelous. This is a lovely, tranquil place, and the owners are charming.

178 - Château du Val d'Arguenon

Notre-Dame-du-Guildo
22380 Saint-Cast
(Côtes-d'Armor)
Tel. 02 96 41 07 03
Fax 02 96 41 02 67
M. and Mme de La Blanchardière

Rooms 4 and 1 suite (2 pers. + 1 child) with bath or shower and WC. **Price** Rooms 450-650F/68,60-99,09€ (2 pers.), suite 850F/129,58€ (3 pers.). **Meals** Breakfast incl. No communal meal. **Facilities** Sitting room, tennis, fishing, horse stalls, beach. **Pets** Dogs not allowed. **Nearby** Restaurants (400m), golf, riding, sailing; Mont-Saint-Michel, Saint-Malo, Dinan, Cape Fréhel, Emerald Coast. **Credit cards** Not accepted. **Spoken** English. **Open** Apr – Sept (on request in winter). **How to get there** (Map 6): 16km west of Dinard via D786; just after Guildo bridge.

This château by the edge of the sea, built in the 16th century and modified in the 18th, has been in the same family for 200 years. In the rooms are objects, paintings and furniture belonging to previous generations. The bedrooms are all pleasant, comfortable and nicely decorated. They face the park, from which one can have a glimpse of the sea. All the rooms are different: our favorite is called "Bonne maman", the others are plainer but also charming. A nice breakfast is served in the dining room. Comfortable sitting room. Nice walks on the estate along the the sea. Pleasant smiling welcome.

179 - La Corbinais

22980 Saint-Michel-de-Plelan
(Côtes-d'Armor)
Tel. 02 96 27 64 81
Fax 02 96 27 68 45
M. and Mme Beaupère
E-mail: corbinais@corbinais.com
Web: www.corbinais.com

Rooms 3 with bath or shower and WC. **Price** 220F/33,53€ (2 pers.), +70F/10,67€ (extra pers.). **Meals** Breakfast 25F/3,81€. Evening meals at communal table, by reservation 80F/12,19€ (wine not incl.). **Facilities** Sitting room, horse stalls, 9-hole golf course and practice green (http://pro.wanadoo.fr/corbinais/golf/), golf lessons on request. **Nearby** Riding, golf. **Credit cards** All major. **Spoken** English. **Open** All year. **How to get there** (Map 6): 17km west of Dinan via N176 towards Plélan, then right onto D19 for 3km towards Plancoët through Plélan-le-Petit.

This small, granite Breton house and its pretty flower garden are set in a countryside criss-crossed by hedges and trees. There is a warm, country-style room with a tall fireplace, antique furniture, and a long wooden table where very good dinners are served. Upstairs there are three bedrooms, simple but charming. Their decoration is very rustic, with wood paneling and pretty fabrics in pale colors and with small bathrooms. You can practice your golf here (even without your own clubs) and you will enjoy a particularly kind welcome.

180 - La Ferme du Breil

22650 Trégon
(Côtes-d'Armor)
Tel. and fax 02 96 27 30 55
Comtesse de Blacas

Rooms 4 with (1 with mezzanine), bath and WC. **Price** 400-500F/60,97-76,22€ (2 pers.); +110F/16,76€ (extra pers.), +60F/9,14€ (child). If you stay 7 days, 1 day is free. **Meals** Breakfast incl. No communal meal. **Facilities** Sitting room. **Pets** Dogs allowed on request. **Nearby** Restaurants (2km), golf, riding, tennis, seaside, sailing school; Mont-Saint-Michel, Saint-Malo, Dinan, Pink Granite Coast, Cap Fréhel. **Credit cards** Not accepted. **Spoken** English. **Open** Jul and Aug (3 nights min.) **How to get there** (Map 6): 10km west of Dinard towards Saint-Brieuc through Ploubalay; after 2km turn left towards Plessix-Balisson.

This charming farmhouse, with its well-kept garden, is very close to both the sea and the road, but this does not disturb the peace of the bedrooms under the sloping roof. These lovely rooms are very cozy with their floral fabrics, engravings and antique furniture. All have pleasant, modern bathrooms. There is an elegant sitting room with deep, green leather chairs for the use of guests, and breakfast is served there at separate tables. This is a pleasant, comfortable place to stay.

181 - L'Ancien Presbytère

22420 Tregrom
(Côtes-d'Armor)
Tel. and Fax 02 96 47 94 15
Nicole de Morchoven

Rooms 3 with bath or shower and WC. **Price** 300F/45,73€ (2 pers.); possible weekly rental in west wing (2-6 pers.) 3500F/533,57€/week. **Meals** Breakfast incl. Evening meals on request. **Facilities** Sitting room. **Pets** Dogs allowed on request (+30F/4,57€/day). **Nearby** Restaurants (4-7km), fishing, riding, tennis, golf, walks, seaside (20km); pink granite coast, Paimpol, Tréguier, Lannion, Morlaix, Roscoff. **Credit cards** Not accepted. **Spoken** English. **Open** All year. **How to get there** (Map 5): 20km south of Lannion. On N12 between Saint-Brieuc and Morlaix turn off at Louargat; in Lourgat, take D33 to left of church, then go 7km to Tregrom.

This former presbytery that stands facing the front of the church is a house full of charm. The bedrooms vary in size but all still have an air of the past, with glowing antique furniture and elegant wallpaper, though some details have unfortunately aged. When the house is full you may be offered accommodation in the nearby "gîte rural." Although the house is pretty, we do not recommend the room. Breakfast is served in the vast kitchen, bright and gay in shades of blue and yellow.

182 - Manoir de Kervezec

Kervezec
29660 Carantec
(Finistère)
Tel. 02 98 67 00 26
Family Bohic

Rooms 5 with bath or shower and WC. **Price** 230-330F/35,06-50,30€ (1 pers.), 280-380F/42,68-57,93€ (2 pers.), +70F/10,67€ (extra bed). 50F/7,62€ reduction out of season and long weekends. **Meals** Breakfast incl. No communal meal. **Facilities** Sitting room, tel., game area, horses, llamas. **Nearby** Restaurants in Carantec (1.5km), sailing, 9-hole golf course, hiking trail along the coast (GR34); Callot Island, Armorique Park, tumulus, museums, churchyards. **Credit cards** Not accepted. **Open** May – Sept. **How to get there** (Map 5): 12km north of Morlaix via D58 towards Roscoff, then turn right towards Carantec. Sign on left at entrance to village.

Surrounded by truck farms, the handsome 19th-century Manoir de Kervezec enjoys an outstanding location and a splendid panoramic view from the terrace looking due south over the Breton coast and the Atlantic. There are small and large bedrooms, all of which are quiet, simple and bright, often done in tones of brown and beige. Recent renovations have added a more cheerful touch. Breakfasts are served on the terrace or in a room decorated with furniture typical of the Finistère region.

183 - Kerfornedic

29450 Commana
(Finistère)
Tel. 02 98 78 06 26
M. and Mme Le Signor

Rooms 2 with shower and WC. **Price** 280F/42,68€ (1 pers.), 320F/48,78€ (2 pers.); 2 nights min., and 4 nights min. in Jul and Aug. **Meals** Breakfast incl. No communal meal. **Pets** Dogs allowed on request. **Nearby** Restaurants (6km), crêperies (2km); riding, tennis, mountain biking, walks, lake, bathing, windsurfing, fishing (200m), Crêtes d'Arrée hiking path, local history museums. **Credit cards** Not accepted. **Open** All year. **How to get there** (Map 5): 41km southwest of Morlaix via N12 to Landivisiau, then D30 and D764 to Sizun, then D30 after Sizun to Saint-Cadou, then towards Commana; it's on the right after 2km.

This very old rambling house, surrounded by flowers, is set in the superb landscape of the Arrée Mountains. Once over the threshold, you will be captivated by the beauty of the simple but agreeable decoration. Everywhere, there are whitewashed walls, beams, dried flowers and well-chosen decorative objects. The bedrooms are just as lovely. The hosts are friendly and Kerfornedic is a charming place.

184 - Manoir de Kervent

29100 Douarnenez
(Finistère)
Tel. 02 98 92 04 90
Mme Lefloch

Rooms 3 (2-3 pers.) and 1 family suite (4 pers.) with shower and WC. **Price** Rooms 250-280F/38,11-42,68€ (2 pers.), family suite 440F/67,07€. **Meals** Breakfast incl. No communal meal. **Facilities** Sitting room. **Pets** Dogs allowed on request. **Nearby** Restaurants in Douarnenez, beach (3km), tennis, riding, golf; Pointe du Raz, Locronan, Port-Museum in Douarnenez, Quimper. **Credit cards** Not accepted. **Open** All year. **How to get there** (Map 5): In Douarnenez, take D765 dir. Audierne and, 400m after the last traffic lights, take the small road on the right in the Pouldavid quarter.

In this family home set in the heart of the countryside, the guest rooms were once the children's bedrooms. Cozy and comfortable, they still have their vintage furniture. Of the upstairs rooms, the first one on the left is too small. Madame Lefloch is quite a personality, friendly and full of humor. She knows the area very well and is always willing to advise you what's worth seeing in the surroundings. Breakfast is served to all the guests at the large table in the dining room.

185 - Ty Va Zadou

Bourg
29253 Île-de-Batz
(Finistère)
Tel. 02 98 61 76 91
Marie-Pierre and Jean Prigent

Rooms 3 with bath or shower, WC and 1 family suite (2-4 pers.) with bath and private WC (but outside the room). **Price** 230F/35,06€ (1 pers.), 300F/45,73€ (2 pers.), 390F/59,45€ (3 pers. in suite), 450F/68,60€ (4 pers. in suite). **Meals** Breakfast incl. No communal meal. **Facilities** Sitting room. **Pets** Animals not allowed. **Nearby** Horse farm (1km), bicycle rentals, sailing school, ocean cruising. **Credit cards** Not accepted. **Open** Mar 1 – Nov 15. **How to get there** (Map 5): In Roscoff, take the boat for Ile-de-Batz (15-min. crossing). The house is 10 mins. from boat landing on right of church.

This is the perfect place from which to visit Batz and discover the life of this small fishing and farming village. Madame Prigent is very friendly and she will surely make you fall in love with this island, where her family has lived for generations. The two small rooms on the ground floor still have their old regional furniture, while upstairs the bedrooms have just been refurbished. They are charming, cheerful and impeccable, and they enjoy an exceptional view over the small port, a string of islands and the continent. This is a place not to be missed, and be sure to reserve in advance.

186 - Château du Guilguiffin

29710 Landudec
(Finistère)
Tel. 02 98 91 52 11
Fax 02 98 91 52 52
M. Philippe Davy

Rooms 4, 2 suites (3-4 pers.) with bath, WC, TV and 1 spare room. **Price** 650-800F/99,09-121,95€ (2 pers.); suite 900-1100F/137,20-167,69€ or 1100-1300F/167,69-198,18€ (3/4 pers.); depending on season, spare room 200F/30,48€ (2 pers.) depending season. **Meals** Breakfast incl. No communal meal. **Facilties** Sitting room, pay tel. **Pets** Small dogs allowed. **Nearby** Restaurants, bike and boat rentals, golf; Pointe du Raz, Concarneau, Pont-Aven, Port-Museum in Dournanenez. **Credit cards** Not accepted. **Spoken** English, German. **Open** Mar 1 – Nov 15. **How to get there** (Map 5): 13km west of Quimper via D784 towards Audierne; property 3km before Landudec.

The Château du Guilguiffin is an architectural masterpiece with its concentric colonnaded enclosures, its splendid gardens and a façade in the purest 18th-century tradition. Philippe Davy has a passion for his château and receives his guests like old friends. The splendid bedrooms have been impeccably refurbished and the bathrooms are beautiful. The drawing rooms with their original 18th-century wood paneling are magnificent. There is a warm cozy room where breakfast is served. The château is a very distinguished place to stay.

187 - La Grange de Coatélan

29640 Plougonven
(Finistère)
Tel. 02 98 72 60 16
Charlick and Yolande de Ternay

Rooms 3 with bath and WC. **Price** 200-250F/30,48-38,11€ (1 pers.), 250-350F/38,11-53,35€ (2 pers.), +80-100F/12,19-15,24€ (extra bed). **Meals** Breakfast incl. "Crêperie" or barbecue in the evenings (not Wed) (about 120F/18,29€). **Facilities** Hiking. **Pets** Dogs not allowed. **Nearby** Riding, seaside; Arrée hills, Calvary of Plougonven. **Credit cards** Not accepted. **Spoken** English. **Open** Apr 1 – Nov 1. (2 days min.). **How to get there** (Map 5): 7km south of Morlaix via D109 towards Plourin-lès-Morlaix, then Plougonven; signposted in Coatélan.

Lying close to the Arrée Mountains, La Grange was once a weaver's farm. On the ground floor there is a bright, small auberge in pale wood with an open fireplace, and a bar area in the shape of a boat's hull. The cuisine is excellent and the atmosphere delightful. The two bedrooms are tastefully decorated and have unusual bathrooms. La Grange de Coatélan is a magical place.

B R I T T A N Y

188 - Le Manoir de Lanleya

Lanleya
29610 Plouigneau
(Finistère)
Tel. 02 98 79 94 15
M. Marrec
E-mail: manoir.lanleya@libertysurf.fr
Web: www.multimania.com/lanleya

Rooms 5 with shower, WC, and 1 with spare room, and 4 houses (2-7 pers.) with shower and WC. **Price** 290F/44,21€ (1 pers.), 340F/51,83€ (2 pers.), +100F/15,24€ (extra pers.); house 1350-2350F/205,80-358,25€ (2 pers.), 1650-2750F/251,54-419,23€ (4 pers.), 1950-3400F/297,27-518,32€ (7 pers.), depending on season. **Meals** Breakfast incl. No communal meal. **Facilities** Sitting room. **Pets** Dogs not allowed. **Nearby** Restaurants and crêperies, beaches and water sports; Morlaix, châteaux of Rosambo and Kerjean. **Credit cards** Not accepted. **Open** All year. **How to get there** (Map 5): 10km east of Morlaix via N12, towards Saint Brieuc. Take exit for Plouigneau and take towards Lanmeur. Signs. 3.5km from N12.

Part 15th-century manor house, part 18th-century mansion, Lanleya was saved from ruin and energetically restored. Here and there, however, an old stone fireplace, a handsome staircase, or a piece of antique Breton furniture remind you how old this place really is. The bedrooms are impeccably kept and many are ideal for families. The decoration is rather irregular — in our opinion, the most successful and coziest is the "Catherine du Plessis" room. The flower garden is lovely and the welcome is kind, if a little timid.

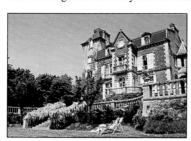

189 - Roch Ar Brini

29600 Ploujean / Morlaix
(Finistère)
Tel. and fax 02 98 72 01 44
Armelle and Étienne Delaisi
E-mail: rochbrini@aol.com
Web: www.brittanyguesthouse.com

Rooms 2 with bath or shower, WC and 1 suite (2/4 pers.) with bath and WC. **Price** Rooms 420F/64,02€ (2 pers.), suite 420F/64,02€ (2 pers.), 670F/102,14€ (4 pers.). **Meals** Breakfast incl. No communal meal. **Facilities** Sitting room, billards, riding. **Pets** Dogs not allowed. **Nearby** Restaurants in Morlaix (3km), hunting weekend on request, 9-hole golf course; Roscoff, Carantec, parish close, Monts d'Arrée. **Credit cards** Not accepted. **Spoken** English. **Open** All year. **How to get there** (Map 5): 3km northeast of Morlaix. In Morlaix take the right bank of the river towards La Dourduff for 3km, then on right signs.

This manor house was built at the end of the 19th century by the father of the poet Tristan Corbière. It stands in a vast park and proudly dominates a little valley cut by a saltwater river flowing to the port of Morlaix. Totally renovated by its young owners, the interior is stunning, the rooms bright and comfortable. The decoration is very much in tune with today's trends: sober, classical forms, noble materials, a fine choice of fabrics. With charming bedrooms, splendid bathrooms and an inviting atmosphere, this is a quality address.

B R I T T A N Y

190 - Pen Ker Dagorn

9, rue des Vieux-Fours
29920 Port de Kerdruc-en-Nevez
(Finistère)
Tel. 02 98 06 85 01
Fax 02 98 06 60 46
Family Brossier-Publier

Rooms 3 with bath or shower and WC (4th room possible in summer). **Price** 330F/50,30€ (2 pers.). **Meals** Breakfast incl. No communal meal. **Facilities** Sitting room. **Pets** Dogs not allowed. **Nearby** Restaurants in Kerduc, oyster farm, beaches, bicycle and boat rentals, tennis, riding, golf; Belon, Pont-Aven. **Credit cards** Not accepted. **Open** May 1 – Oct 30 (on request in winter). 2 nights min. **How to get there** (Map 5): 4km south of Pont-Aven via D783 towards Trégunc and Concarneau. 200m after gendarmerie, take north exit from Pont-Aven and on the left, rue des Fleurs in direction of Le Henan-Kerdruc on CD number 4 road. Or at the intersection of Croaz Hent Kergoz, take D77 dir. Névez. In Névez Kerdruc, take C number 8 road in direction of Kerdruc Port. At entrance to Kerdruc, take Chemin des Vieux-Fours on the small square.

A very attractive country house set amid lush greenery, Pen Ker Dagorn is 200 meters from the port of Kerdruc. It has been charmingly decorated. Each bedroom has a style of its own; all are large, comfortable and light, and some of the amusing bathrooms are hidden in deep closets. Excellent breakfasts are served and Monsieur and Madame Publier are pleasingly attentive.

191 - Les Hortensias

Kernec
29310 Querrien
(Finistère)
Tel. 02 98 71 35 22
M. and Mme Guillerm

Rooms 2 with bath or shower and WC can be rented together for 4 persons. **Price** 230F/35,06€ (1 room, 2 pers.). **Meals** Breakfast incl. Evening meals at communal table 80F/12,19€ (wine incl.). **Facilities** Sitting room, bikes. **Pets** Dogs not allowed. **Nearby** Riding, swimming pool, seaside, 18-hole golf course; Quimperlé, Carnoêt forest, "Les Roches du Diable", Saint-Fiacre. **Credit cards** Not accepted. **Spoken** English, German,Spanish. **Closed** Christmas – New Year. **How to get there** (Map 5) : 15km northwest of Quimperlé towards Le Faouët. In Querrien dir. Guiscriff to Kernec. Turn right after the Calvary. **No smoking** in bedrooms.

At the edge of a country hamlet, this simple little house with its flowered garden is most suitable for families, who can take the upstairs rooms both together for a nice family stay. One of them has its own shower and wash basin. Another bathroom down the hall offers more privacy. The rooms are simple and pleasant with their rustic wooden flooring. Downstairs you will enjoy the sitting room and the veranda that extends off it, where breakfasts and simple dinners are shared with the young owners, who reserve for guests a smiling and spontaneous welcome.

192 - La Maison d'Hippolyte

2, quai Surcouf
29300 Quimperlé
(Finistère)
Tel. 02 98 39 09 11
Mme Lescoat

Rooms 2 with bath or shower, WC and 2 with bath or shower, shared WC. Rooms cleaned on request. **Price** 240F/36,58€ (1 pers.), 270F/41,16€ (2 pers.), +100F/15,24€ (extra bed). **Meals** Breakfast incl. No communal meal. **Facilities** Lounge, salmon and trout fishing, canoes-kayaks rentals, participation in "Photography in November". **Nearby** Restaurants and "crêperies", riding, golf; Pont-Aven, Quimperlé, permanent exhibit of paintings. **Spoken** English. **Open** All year. **How to get there** (Map 5): 50m behind the Surcouf Office de Tourisme, near the river. A short walk from the railway station (TGV).

In the heart of the charming village of Quimperlé, this house stands on the banks of the Laïta. The house is small but friendly, simple and pleasant in style, and the reigning ambience is artistic and a bit bohemian. You will be surely be won over by the great kindness of Madame Lescoat. Herself a lover of painting and photography, she is happy to display on her walls the works of Breton artists. The same style is found in the comfortable and well-kept bedrooms. They each have a small but well-designed shower room. Excellent breakfasts are served outdoors as soon as the weather permits, in the shade of a fig tree on a terrace facing the river.

193 - Mescouez

29450 Le Tréhou
(Finistère)
Tel. and fax 02 98 68 86 79
Tel. 02 98 68 83 39
Élisabeth Soubigou

Rooms 5 with bath or shower and WC. **Price** 210F/32,01€ (1 pers.), 250F/38,11€ (2 pers.). **Meals** Breakfast incl. Communal meals (except Jul 15. – Aug 15.), by reservation 85F/12,95€ (1/4 bottle wine per person). **Facilities** Lounge, microwave, tel., tennis. **Pets** Animals not allowed. **Nearby** Restaurants (5km), hiking trails, mountain bikes, fishing, hiking, 18-hole golf course (12km); architectural, cultural and natural points of interest (churchyards, villages, sites and coastline). **Credit cards** Not accepted. **Spoken** English. **Open** All year. **How to get there** (Map 5): 4km north of Le Tréhou. In village, follow signs for 1km direction Sizun, turn left at sign "Gîte rural - Chambres d'hôtes - Mescouez", then go 2.5km.

Elisabeth Soubigou, whose parents, farmers by profession, completely restored and refurbished this house, now runs it with kindness and efficiency. The rooms are comfortable and impeccably kept, full of charm and decorated in cool colors. Some are classic while others are more youthful in style. They look out onto the garden or the courtyard of the farm. The breakfasts are excellent and the dinners are based on good local products. The prices are very reasonable.

194 - La Tremblais

35320 La Couyère
(Ille-et-Vilaine)
Tel. and fax 02 99 43 14 39
M. and Mme Raymond Gomis
Web: www.la-raimonder.com

Rooms 1 and 1 suite (4 pers.) with independent entrance, sitting room, shower and WC. 1 gîte (independent accommodation) also for rent. **Price** Room 300F/45,73€ (2 pers.); suite 350F/53,35€ (2 pers.), +70F/10,67€ (extra bed). **Meals** Breakfast incl. Communal or independent tables 100F/15,24€ and "soirée en amoureux" on request: 780F/118,91€ (2 pers. all incl.). **Facilities** Summer sitting room. **Pets** Dogs not allowed. **Nearby** Riding, lake fishing, megalithic monuments of La Roche aux Fées, Vitré Château. **Credit cards** Not accepted. **Spoken** English, Spanish. **Open** All year. **How to get there** (Map 15): 25km southeast of Rennes, take Autoroute to Vitré-Janzé. In Janzé, take D92 towards La Couyère-Châteaubriant. The house is in the village of La Tremblais. Or take the TGV to Rennes.

A pretty bedroom, nicely decorated in shades of green and yellow, and a duplex suite, rustic style, with a wood fire in the fireplace await you in this old farmhouse refurbished for today's tastes. Opposite the house is a barn, also well-restored and open on the surrounding greenery, in which breakfast and dinner are served. The overall effect is cheery and pleasant. Very hospitable and an excellent cook, Madame Goumis cares for her guests as well as she does the beautiful flowers in her garden.

195 - Manoir de la Duchée

La Duchée
Saint-Briac-sur-Mer
35800 Dinard
(Ille-et-Vilaine)
Tel. 02 99 88 00 02
Fax 02 99 88 92 57
Jean-François Stenou
Web: //pro.wanadoo.fr/manoir.duchee/

Rooms 3 (1 is a duplex) and 2 suites with bath, WC, hairdryer and TV. **Price** 350-500F/53,35-76,22€ (2 pers.), 550F/83,84€ (3-4 pers. duplex), 600F/91,46€ (suite with 2 baths). **Meals** Breakfast incl. No communal meal. **Facilities** Sitting rooms, exhibition gallery, pay phone, riding, mountain bikes, park, collection of antique horse-drawn carriages. **Pets** Dogs not allowed. **Nearby** Restaurants, thalassotherapy, golf; Mont-Saint-Michel, Saint-Malo, Dinan. **Credit cards** Not accepted. **Open** Mar 1 – Dec 31 and School vacations. **How to get there** (Map 6): In Saint-Malo, go towards Saint-Brieuc via D168, then D603 towards Saint-Briac; then first road to left on entering town; signs. Coming from Dinard, via D786 towards Camping Municipal. Signs.

This small manor house, whose origins go back to the 16th century, lies deep in the countryside. The very comfortable bedrooms for the most part have late 19th-century furniture painted with floral motifs. On the ground floor, a beautiful room with beams and exposed stonework serves as a slightly theatrical background for good breakfasts. The atmosphere is created by a cheerful log fire, a large chandelier, antique furniture and objects, and music. Breakfast is also served in the winter garden. Note that the staircase to some bedrooms is steep, to say the least.

196 - La Corne de Cerf

Le Cannee
35380 Paimpont
(Ille-et-Vilaine)
Tel. 02 99 07 84 19
M. and Mme Morvan

Rooms 3 with shower and WC. **Price** 300F/45,73€ (2 pers.), +70F/10,67€ (extra bed). **Meals** Breakfast incl. No communal meal. **Facilities** Sitting room. **Nearby** Restaurants (3km), lake (water sports), equestrian center, hiking, golf (20km); Brocéliande, various events scheduled in summer. **Closed** Jan. **How to get there** (Map 6): 2.5km south of Paimpont. At the big traffic circle to Beignon for 2km. At the first crossroads, it's the big house with broad windows. **No smoking** in bedrooms.

Set in the heart of the Forest of Brocéliande, the domain of King Arthur and his Knights of the Round Table, the beautiful stone "Stag's Horn" has been entirely renovated with modern amenities. Opening capaciously onto a carefully tended garden filled with flowers, it offers guests three colorful, comfortable bedrooms, each with a modern bath. Breakfasts are served in a beautiful room decorated with works by the owners (a painter and a decorator), or on a small terrace at the edge of the garden.

197 - La Treberdière

Place de l'Église
35380 Plélan-le-Grand
(Ille-et-Vilaine)
Tel. 02 99 06 83 05
Mme de Floris

Rooms 1 with bath or shower, WC and 1 suite (2-4 pers.) with bath and private WC but outside the room. **Price** 300F/45,73€ (2 pers.), 450F/68,60€ (4 pers.). **Meals** Breakfast incl. No communal meal. **Facilities** Sitting room. **Pets** Dogs not allowed. **Nearby** Restaurants in village, tennis and swimming pool in village, hiking and horse trekking, concerts and various events scheduled in summer, 18-hole golf course (25km); Brocéliande forest, Château de Trécesson. **Credit cards** Not accepted. **Spoken** English. **Open** All year, by reservation. **How to get there** (Map 6): in the village of Plélan.

This house, which stands on the village square near the apse of the church, looks like a 19th-century building although it is really much older. Madame de Floris is a friendly, amusing and spontaneous hostess. She has decorated the place with a nice collection of antique objects and furniture in all styles and from all horizons. The guest bedrooms are very comfortable and have brand new bathrooms. The other rooms are extremely inviting, especially the dining room with its large fireplace. Their old woodwork and parquet floors are charmingly uneven. In summer, breakfast is served in a delightful little garden brimming with flowers.

B R I T T A N Y

198 - Château du Bois Glaume

35320 Poligné
(Ille-et-Vilaine)
Tel. 02 99 43 83 05
Fax 02 99 43 79 40
M. and Mme Berthélémé

Rooms 2 and 2 suites (3 pers.) with bath or shower and WC (TV in suites). **Price** Rooms 450F/68,60€ (2 pers.), suite 650F/99,09€ (2 pers.), +150F/22,86€ (extra bed). **Meals** Breakfast 50F/7,62€. Lunch and evening meals at separate tables on request 150F/22,86€ (wine not incl.). **Facilities** Sitting rooms, fishing and park. **Pets** Dogs allowed on request +50F/7,62€/days. **Nearby** Tennis, equestrian center, golf; Duguesclin circuit, Vitré. **Spoken** English, Spanish. **Open** Jun 1 – Oct 1. **How to get there** (Map 14): 22km south of Rennes. Highway N137 to Nantes, exit Poligné. Follow signs from the village center.

The Berthélémés have recently restored this graceful, early 18th-century château, which is surrounded by a park with magnificent trees generously shading the banks of a lake: a lovely place to relax. The immense suites, with light streaming in through their many windows, have spacious bathrooms, as do the large, tastefully decorated bedrooms. Spacious and welcoming, the salons and the dining room are furnished with antiques.

199 - Château des Blosses

35460 Saint-Ouen-de-la-Rouërie
(Ille-et-Vilaine)
Tel. 02 99 98 36 16
Fax 02 99 98 39 32
M. and Mme Jacques Barbier

Rooms 5 with bath and WC. **Price** 650-850F/99,09-129,58€ (2 pers.). **Meals** Breakfast incl. Half board 520-630F/79,27-96,04€/pers. in double room (3 nights min.). Evening meals at separate tables (except Sun), by reservation 260F/39,63€ (wine incl.). **Facilities** Sitting room. **Pets** Dogs not allowed. **Nearby** Golf, swimming pool; Mont-Saint-Michel. **Credit cards** Amex, Visa. **Spoken** English. **Open** Mar 15 – Oct 25. **How to get there** (Map 7): 28km northwest of Fougères via D155 to Antrain, then D296 for 4km; signs. Coming from Pontorson/Mont-Saint-Michel, take N175 towards Rennes for 9km, then D97; signposted.

Built in the 19th century, this château set in a vast wooded park has belonged to the same family for seven generations. It still contains innumerable souvenirs of the ancestors (furniture, objects, paintings, hunting trophies...). The bedrooms are well-appointed, comfortable, pleasant and full of charm. Some evenings dinner is served (at separate tables) in the dining room and you can round off the evening lingering in the lounge over a cup of coffee in the company of Monsieur and Madame Barbier.

200 - Le Petit Moulin du Rouvre

35720 Saint-Pierre-de-Plesguen
(Ille-et-Vilaine)
Tel. 02 99 73 85 84
Fax 02 99 73 71 06
Mme Annie Michel-Québriac

Rooms 4 with bath, WC, TV, hairdryer, kettle, hot drings. **Price** 300F/45,73€ (1 pers.), 380F/57,93€ (2 pers.), +120F/18,29€ (extra pers.). **Meals** Breakfast incl. No communal meal. **Restaurants** Crêperie and auberge (3km) and others in Dinan (12km). **Facilities** Sitting room, lake fishing. **Pets** Dogs not allowed in bedrooms. **Nearby** Golf; Mont-Saint-Michel, the banks of the Rance, Dinan. **Credit cards** Not accepted. **Spoken** English. **Open** All year, by reservation. **How to get there** (Map 6): On N137 between Rennes and Saint-Malo. From Saint-Pierre-de-Plesguen center, towards Lanhélin via D10; follow signs for 2.5km. **No smoking** in bedrooms.

It's hard not to fall under the charm of this little mill standing all by itself at the edge of a pond. Even more so when you've seen the inside: endearing little rooms, sparkling clean and overflowing with antique furniture. The sitting room is often illuminated by the reflection of the sun on the water. The same careful attention has been paid to the bedrooms, which are cozy and charming and most of which face the pond. The one that faces the countryside has a broad picture window on the eastern side. An ideal place for total relaxation in the peace and quiet of nature. The restful quality is enhanced by the kind welcome.

201 - Les Mouettes

Grande-Rue
35430 Saint-Suliac
(Ille-et-Vilaine)
Tel. 02 99 58 30 41
Fax 02 99 58 39 41
Isabelle Rouvrais

Rooms 5 with bath or shower and WC. **Price** 220-260F/33,53-39,63€ (1 pers.), 250F/38,11€ (2 pers., Nov 15 – Easter)-290F/44,21€ (2 pers., high season).**Meals** Breakfast incl. No communal meal. **Facilities** Sitting room. **Pets** Dogs not allowed. **Nearby** Restaurants (150m), beach (200m) with water sports facilities, tennis, mountain bikes; Saint-Suliac, Saint-Malo, Dinan. **Spoken** English, Spanish. **Open** All year. **How to get there** (Map 6): 3km north of Châteauneuf (near Saint-Malo). On highway Rennes/Saint-Malo, exit Châteauneuf, go into village then follow signs for Saint-Suliac.

This house is situated directly on a street, perhaps not an ideal location, but this shortcoming is more than made up for by the liveliness of the little village of Saint-Sulic and its charming seaside promenade. Inside, the house is most pleasant, tastefully decorated with a personal touch (blond wood, pastel-colored fabrics): the bedrooms are small but comfortable. A further asset, the excellent breakfasts prepared by Isabelle with a true sense of hospitality. This house is a good bet in off-season (starting at Easter the prices become a bit steep and the summer crowds in the village spoil the peace and quiet.)

202 - Château de la Villouyère

35630 Vignoc
(Ille-et-Vilaine)
Tel. 02 99 69 80 69
M. and Mme Bruchet-Mery

Rooms 2 with bath or shower and WC. **Price** 500F/76,22€ (2 pers.), +180F/27,44€ (extra bed). **Meals** Breakfast incl. No communal meal. **Facilities** Sitting room, Ping-pong, badminton, bicycles, library, possibility baby-sitting. **Nearby** Restaurants (4km), tennis, riding, 18-hole golf course (10km); Rennes, Saint-Malo, Dinan, Dinard, Cancale, Combourg, Channel Islands. **Spoken** English. **Open** May – Oct and weekends all year on request. **How to get there** (Map 6): 15km north of Rennes by the highway N137 to Saint-Malo, exit Vignoc. At the traffic circle to La Mézière and 500m on right (sign posted).

Standing in a park planted with rare tree species, the small 18th-century Château de la Villouyère has been restored extremely skillfully by a young couple who love beautiful things. You will find two large bedrooms with antique furniture, one of which can be transformed into a suite with a small salon. History buffs can share their passion with Monsieur Bruchet-Mery, and everyone is sure to enjoy the family atmosphere at this delightful château.

203 - Ty Horses

Le Rouho - Route de Locmaria
56520 Guidel
(Morbihan)
Tel. 02 97 65 97 37
M. and Mme Hamon

Rooms 4 with shower and WC (TV on request). **Price** 230F/35,06€ (1 pers), 280-300F/42,68-45,73€ (2 pers.), +80F/12,19€ (extra pers.). **Meals** Breakfast incl. No communal meal. **Facilities** Possibility to receive guests with horses (stall and paddock). **Nearby** Restaurants (2km), seaside, Salmon fishing in river, Queven golf course (6km); Pont-Aven, Lorient, Carnac. **Credit cards** Not accepted. **Spoken** English. **Open** All year. **How to get there** (Map 5): 4km north of Guidel. Autoroute Nantes-Brest exit Guidel, go around church towards Centre Commercial, then Route de Locmaria for 4km: lane on left indicated.

M and Mrs Hamon, both born in Brittany, now live here the entire year, in this house they had built in the country not far from the sea. The house has a thatched roof and two wings, one of which is for the guests. It includes an entrance, the bedrooms and a veranda divided into a living area and a dining area (where you have your breakfast). Though the furniture is without great character, the decoration is fresh and pleasant. A tranquil bucolic spot, surrounded by meadows. You can watch the horses grazing and they will even come up to greet you.

204 - Les Cormorans

Rue du Chalutier
Les Deux Ange
56590 Île-de-Groix
(Morbihan)
Tel. 02 97 86 57 67
Mobile 06 81 19 49 85
Mme Hardy

Rooms 3 with private shower and WC. **Price** 300F/45,73€ (2 pers.), +50F/7,62€ (extra bed). **Meals** Breakfast 25F/3,81€. No communal meal. Cooking possibilities +100F/15,24€/day. **Facilities** Collection of books on boating. **Pets** Dogs allowed on request. **Nearby** Restaurants (200m), beach, fishing, sailing, seamanship lessons, riding, tennis, sea kayak; ecomuseum, "Maison de la réserve" (wildlife, flora…). **Spoken** English. **Open** All year. **How to get there** (Map 5): 45 min. by boat to Lorient. On the island 400m of the seaport.

Typical of Southern Brittany, this small white, blue-shuttered house is of recent construction. It offers you three bedrooms with a private entrance, whose tasteful decor and bright bathrooms are indications of the attention Madame Hardy pays to her guests. Breakfast in summer is served in the delightful garden or in the charming living room, where you can browse through the books in the library. "The Cormorants" is a great place to spend a vacation.

205 - Ty Mat

Penquesten
56650 Inzinzac-Lochrist
(Morbihan)
Tel. and fax 02 97 36 89 26
M. and Mme Spence

Rooms 4 with bath and WC. **Price** 300F/45,73€ (2 pers.), +70F/10,67€ (extra bed). **Meals** Breakfast incl. No communal meal. **Facilities** Sitting room, bikes. **Pets** Small dogs allowed on request. **Nearby** Restaurants (4km), canoeing, riding, tennis, golf; Hennebont, Port-Louis. **Spoken** English. **Open** All year, by reservation and deposit. **How to get there** (Map 5): 4km north of Hennebont via dir. Inzinzac-Lochrist. In Lochrist after the 2nd bridge, on right dir. Penquesten Bubry (D23). Go 4km (signs, house on left). **No smoking** in bedrooms.

This large family home enjoys a quiet site and a great location to discover Brittany. You will be received with kindness by the young owners who have come to live here with their family. The large, comfortable living room with its wood-paneled walls is at your disposal. The bedrooms are spacious and elegant, charming with with their antique furniture and well-chosen objects. Breakfast is simple but good and in fine weather it is served outdoors facing the broad lawn or at the very long table in the dining room which, although it has been brightly painted in yellow, is still a bit dark.

206 - La Carrière

8, rue de la Carrière
56120 Josselin
(Morbihan)
Tel. 02 97 22 22 62
Fax 02 97 22 34 68
M. and Mme Bignon
E-mail: albiguon@club-internet.fr

Rooms 6 with bath or shower, WC and 2 for children without bath or shower. **Price** 250-350F/38,11-53,35€ (1 pers.), 300-400F/45,73-60,97€ (2 pers.), 400-500F/60,97-76,22€ (3 pers.). **Meals** Breakfast incl. No communal meal. **Facilities** Sitting room. **Pets** Dogs allowed on request. **Nearby** Restaurants (500m), sailing on Lac aux Ducs, 9-hole golf course (12km), riding (12km); Josselin, Rochefort-en-Terre. **Credit cards** Visa, Eurocard, MasterCard. **Spoken** English, German. **Open** All year. **How to get there** (Map 6): RN24 between Rennes and Lorient.

La Carrière and its beautiful garden stand on a hill just outside the small town of Josselin, with its famous medieval château. It is a vast, very refined house. The beautiful reception rooms are bright and furnished with antiques, and they open onto a magnificent hall with 18th-century gilt paneling. The bedrooms are upstairs and are named after colors. All are pretty and classic, but our favorites are "Rouge" and "Blanche". All in all, a nice place to stop at.

207 - Kerdelan

Locqueltas
56870 Larmor-Baden
(Morbihan)
Tel. 02 97 57 05 85
Fax 02 97 57 25 02
Marie-Claude Hecker

Rooms 4 with bath or shower and WC (usually outside the room). **Price** 300-350F/45,73-53,35€ (2 pers.). **Meals** Breakfast incl. No communal meal. **Facilities** Sitting room, billiard, library. Small beach with pontoon (fishing). **Pets** Dogs allowed on request. **Nearby** Restaurants (2km), sea fishing, 18-hole golf course; Auray, port de St-Goustan. **Spoken** English, German, Spanish, some Italian. **Closed** Jul 15 – Aug 30. **How to get there** (Maps 5 and 14): 12km west of Vannes to Auray via D101, then Larmor-Baden (10km). On "Carrefour des quatre chemins" drive 1.6km; house on left.

Kerdelan is a large white villa built on the Gulf of Morbihan seashore, offering you three ground-floor bedrooms on a terrace facing the sea. Giving onto the garden, the fourth room is large and has a lovely bath. Its bed, like most of the furniture in the house, is beautifully original. At the foot of a flowery garden, a small beach is a good departure point for fishing. Kerdelan's exceptional location and Madame Hecker's genuine hospitality make it a perfect vacation spot.

208 - Le Cosquer-Trélécan

56330 Pluvigner
(Morbihan)
Tel. 02 97 24 72 69
Fax 02 97 24 90 45
Bernard and Françoise Menut

Rooms 1 suite (4 pers.) with bath, WC (+ washbasin in each bedroom). Small independent house (gîte) also for rent. **Price** 200F/30,48€ (1 pers.), 270F/41,16€ (2 pers.), 350F/53,35€ (3 pers.), 400F/60,97€ (4 pers.). **Meals** Breakfast incl. No communal meal. **Facilities** Sitting room. **Pets** Animals not allowed. **Nearby** Restaurants (7km), seaside, riding; Camors forest, Gulf of Morbihan, Saint-Goustan. **Credit cards** Not accepted. **Spoken** English. **Open** All year (May – Sept 2 days min.). **How to get there** (Map 5): 32km northwest of Vannes via N165 to Auray and D768 towards Pontivy. At Pluvigner take D102 towards Languidic, then signs for "Le Cosquer-Télécan".

This pretty and authentic thatched house stands in a quiet setting amid the greenery of the countryside. As a part of the house is reserved just for you, you will enjoy the space and feeling of independence. Downstairs, there is a very large sitting room with a fireplace, decorated with antique furniture chosen by Madame Menut, who used to be an antique dealer. Upstairs are two small, cozy rooms and a bathroom, perfect for a family. Breakfast is delicious, including home-made jam and honey from Mr. Menut's beehives. Children are made to feel welcome here and the reception could not be friendlier.

209 - Ty Maya

Kervassal
56670 Riantec
(Morbihan)
Tel. and Fax 02 97 33 58 66
M. and Mme Watine
E-mail: gonzague.watine@wanadoo.fr

Rooms 3 with shower and WC. **Price** 290F/44,21€ (2 pers.), +80F/12,19€ (extra bed). **Meals** Breakfast incl. No communal meal. **Facilities** Small sitting room. **Pets** Dogs not allowed. **Nearby** Restaurants (1.5km), seaside, riding, tennis, golf; Port-Louis, Carnac, Auray. **Credit cards** Not accepted. **Spoken** English, Spanish, Portuguese. **Open** All year by resevation and deposit. **How to get there** (Map 5): From Rennes N24 (from Vannes via N165), exit and dir. Port-Louis (D781). 3.2km after the exit (traffic circle of Kernours) dir. Port-Louis/Riantec; 1km, on left dir. Fontaine-Galeze to Kervassal. **No smoking.**

In a little country hamlet not far from the sea, this authentic thatched cottage dating from the 17th century offers two lovely bedrooms and a third one that is just as pretty but not quite so independent as to reach it you have to go through the owners' living room. The bath and shower rooms are impeccable and the bedrooms are brightened up by attractive fabrics (cushions, drapes, etc.), as is the charming little guests' sitting room, where breakfast is served. The food is delicious as well as pleasing to the eye. The small garden (unfortunately bordered by the metal roof of a nearby hangar) is nevertheless quiet, pleasant and overflowing with flowers.

B R I T T A N Y

210 - Château de Talhouët

56220 Rochefort-en-Terre
(Morbihan)
Tel. 02 97 43 34 72
Fax 02 97 43 35 04
M. Jean-Pol Soulaine

Rooms 7 with bath, WC, tel. and 1 with shower, WC and tel. **Price** 700-990F/106,71-150,92€ (2 pers.). **Meals** Breakfast incl. Half board 530-725F/80,79-110,53€ /pers. in double room. Evening meals at separate tables 230F/35,06€ (wine not incl.). **Facilities** Sitting room. **Nearby** Tennis, fishing, golf. **Credit cards** Amex, Visa, Eurocard, MasterCard. **Spoken** English. **Open** All year. **How to get there** (Map 14): 33km northwest of Redon via D775 towards Vannes, then D774; turn right towards Rochefort-en-Terre. Go through Rochefort and take D774 towards Malestroit for 4km, then left to Château de Talhouët.

Standing at the edge of a forest and overlooking a beautiful countryside, Talhouët is a château in true Breton style. The interior is absolutely splendid and has been been restored in excellent taste. There is a magnificent series of rooms on the ground floor, including a salon, billiards room, and dining room. Some of the bedrooms are vast and extraordinarily comfortable, and have well-equipped bathrooms. Our favorites are the upstairs ones, the others are more classic. Antique furniture, objects and paintings are found throughout. Jean-Pol Soulaine is an excellent host and he has managed to breathe new life into this lovely home where the atmosphere is one of calm and peacefulness. A perfect lovers' tryst.

211 - Château de Castellan
Auberge et chambres d'hôtes
56200 Saint-Martin-sur-Oust
(Morbihan)
Tel. 02 99 91 51 69
Fax 02 99 91 57 41
M. and Mme Cossé
E-mail: auberge@club-internet.fr
Web: www.castellan.fr.st.

Rooms 4 and 1 suite of 2 bedrooms (4 pers.), bath or shower and WC. **Price** 450-600F/68,60-91,46€ (2 pers.), +110F/16,76€ (extra bed). **Meals** Breakfast incl. Evening meals at separate tables 110-150F/16,76-22,86€ (wine not incl.). **Pets** Dogs not allowed. **Nearby** Tennis, seaside (45km); Rochefort-en-Terre, Josselin (medieval castle), La Gacilly (artisans' village), Saint-Marcel Museum. **Spoken** English. **Open** All year. **How to get there** (Map 14): 20km northwest of Redon via D764 towards Malestroit, then in Peillac, turn right towards Les Fougerêts; then, before the village, towards Saint-Martin. On leaving village, D149 for 1.5km, then road on right; signs.

This 18th-century château in the heart of the countryside has been in the same family for several generations. It used to be a working farm, today the commons have been made into an auberge. The bedrooms are in the château. Their size varies but all are nicely furnished and pleasantly decorated. The prettiest one, called "Médaillon," has beautiful woodwork. Excellent breakfasts and fine dinners are served at the auberge in a spacious room decorated in rustic style. The welcome is pleasant, dynamic and smiling.

212 - Lann Kermané

56470 Saint-Philibert
(Morbihan)
Tel. 02 97 55 03 75
Fax 02 97 30 02 79
M. and Mme Cuzon du Rest

Rooms 2 with bath or shower and WC. **Price** 450F/68,60€ (2 pers., 1 night), or 400-450F/60,97-68,60€ (2 pers., depending on season). **Meals** Breakfast incl. No communal meal. **Facilities** Sitting room. **Pets** Dogs not allowed. **Nearby** Restaurants (300m), beach, tennis, water sports, golf; cruises on Morbihan Gulf, Carnac, Belle-Île. **Credit cards** Not accepted. **Spoken** English. **Open** All year. **How to get there** (Map 5): 10km south of Auray. Coming from Vannes, D165 exit Carnac-Locmariaquer, then D28. At the Chat Noir intersection, take D781 for 500m; at the "Congre" intersection, take road on left for 300m and first on left: Rue des Paludier for 200m and the first on left: Rue des Peupliers. House at the end of impasse on right at number 13.

This house built with vintage materials is located in a small hamlet a hundred meters from an inlet off the gulf of Morbihan. It has a beautifully kept garden. Inside it is comfortably appointed in classic style with fine antique furniture and some carefully chosen objects. The bedrooms are quiet and pleasant, although rather small. The sitting room is furnished in classic fashion and enlivened in winter by a lovely wood fire in the grate. A classic setting with a courteous reception.

213 - La Maison du Latz

56470 La Trinité-sur-Mer
(Morbihan)
Tel. 02 97 55 80 91
Mobile 06 85 42 44 09
Fax 02 97 30 14 10
Nicole Le Rouzic
Web: www.charme-gastronomie.com

Rooms 3 with bath, WC, tel., and 1 suite with bedroom, sitting room, TV, bath, WC, tel., and 1 studio with independent entrance, basin, WC, kitchen and tel. **Price** 290-350F/44,91-53,36€ (2 pers.); suite 400F/60,98€ (2 pers.), 500F/76,22€ (3 pers.); studio 450F/68,60€ (2 pers.). **Meals** Breakfast incl. No communal meal. **Facilities** Sitting room (hi-fi, video, library); private parking, garden chairs at the water's edge. **Nearby** Restaurants; Morbihan Gulf; golf, tennis, riding, sailing. **Credit cards** Not accepted. **Spoken** English. **Open** All year. **How to get there** (Map 5): 10km south of Auray via D768 for 4.5km, then turn left towards La Trinité-sur-Mer via D186 for 4km; turn left towards Le Latz (before La Trinité); signs.

This unpretentious little house enjoys a fine location on a small sound. Excellent breakfasts are served on a sunny veranda overlooking the countryside. The bedrooms are simple, comfortable, pretty and very quiet. The one with the corner windows has the nicest view. The suite is also comfortable. The wood-paneled bedroom is the smallest. You will feel at home here and you can relax on deck chairs set up in the garden by the water's edge. A warm welcome and a convivial atmosphere.

C E N T R E

214 - Château de La Verrerie

Oizon
18700 Aubigny-sur-Nère
(Cher)
Tel. 02 48 81 51 60
Fax 02 48 58 21 25
Comte and Comtesse B. de Vogüé
E-mail: laverrerie@wanadoo.fr

Rooms 11 and 1 suite with bath and/or shower, WC and tel. **Price** 880-1100F/134,16-167,69€ (2 pers.), +250F/38,11€ (extra pers.); suite 1300F/198,18€ (2 pers.). **Meals** Breakfast 60F/9,14€. Evening meals at communal table, by reservation 280F/42,68€ (wine not incl.), or restaurant in the park (menus 100-195F/15,24-29,72€). **Facilities** Sitting room, tennis, riding, hunting and shooting, fishing, horse stalls, lake. **Pets** Dogs allowed on request. **Nearby** Golf; village of La Borne (pottery), route Jacques-Coeur (châteaux), vineyards (Sancerre, Menetou). **Credit cards** Visa, Eurocard, MasterCard. **Spoken** English, German, Spanish, Italian. **Open** Jan 15 – Dec 15. **How to get there** (Map 17): 35km south of Gien via D940 to Aubigny-sur-Nère; then D89 to La Verrerie.

Standing on the edge of the water and the forest, this ducal château was built just after the Hundred Years' War. The interior is absolute perfection: vast, sumptuous, comfortable, authentic. You can have dinner either with the owners or in the small 17th-century farmhouse restaurant in the park. The welcome is very friendly and exceptionally attentive.

215 - Domaine de Vilotte

Ardenais
18170 Le Châtelet-en-Berry
(Cher)
Tel. and fax 02 48 96 04 96
M. Jacques Champenier

Rooms 5 with bath and WC. **Price** 360-430F/54,88-65,55€ (2 pers.), +100F/15,24€ (extra pers.). **Meals** Breakfast incl. Meals at communal table 140F/21,34€. **Facilities** Sitting room, tel.; pond, fishing, woods and park on property. **Nearby** 18-hole golf course (30km), water sports center, tennis, riding, châteaux, Noirlac Abbey, Nonant House, Tronçais Forest. **Credit cards** Not accepted. **Spoken** English. **Open** All year, by reservation from Nov to Mar. **How to get there** (Map 17): 21km southwest of Saint-Amand-Montrond (exit A71 Autoroute Clermont-Ferrand), towards Orval, then La Châtre-Culan, then Fosse-Nouvelle. Go towards Le Châtelet. In village of Ardenais, turn left towards Culan on D38 and follow signs.

Nestling in the gentle, peaceful Berry countryside not far from the Loire Valley, the Domaine de Vilotte is an ancient Roman site. Monsieur and Madame Cheval, who are friends of the owners, offer beautiful, elegant guest rooms which are tastefully furnished and look out over a vast garden (except for "Marguerite," which can be combined with a small room for families). The decoration of the house itself is quite attractive and includes numerous collections of objects found in antique shops nearby: old phonographs and radios, antique tools and the like... The hospitality is very friendly and the location very quiet.

216 - Manoir d'Estiveaux

Estiveaux
18170 Le Châtelet-en-Berry
(Cher)
Tel. 02 48 56 22 64
Mme de Faverges

Rooms 4 and 1 suite of 2 bedrooms with bath or shower, WC and TV. **Price** 350-550F/53,35-83,84€ (1-2 pers.), +100F/15,24€ (extra pers.); suite 650F/99,09€ (1-2 pers.). **Meals** Breakfast incl. Evening meals at communal or separate tables, by reservation from 150F/22,86€ (wine incl.). **Facilities** Large no-smoking sitting room and small smoking sitting room, game and fitness room, tel., fishing. **Nearby** Swimming pool, 18-hole golf course, tennis; Romanesque churches, châteaux. **Credit cards** Not accepted. **Open** All year. **How to get there** (Map 17): 46km north of Montluçon via D943 to Culan, then D65 to Le Châtelet; then D951 for 1.5km, towards La Châtre.

This country mansion stands in a park with a lake close to the Route Jacques-Cœur and its many châteaux. The house is beautifully kept and has four quite large bedrooms which are classically and tastefully decorated. Madame de Faverges' hospitality is warm and unaffected. Ask her advice on touring the area; she participates in numerous cultural activities and knows the region well. Dinners are served in the large dining room or in the small private salon.

217 - Ferme du Château ✓

Levéville
28300 Bailleau-L'Évêque
(Eure-et-Loir)
Tel. and fax 02 37 22 97 02
Nathalie and Bruno Vasseur

Rooms 3 with bath or shower and WC. **Price** 200F/30,48€ (1 pers.), 290 and 320F/44,21 and 48,78€ (2 pers.), +90F/13,72€ (extra pers.). **Meals** Breakfast incl. Meals at communal or separate tables from 90F/13,72€ (wine incl.). **Facilities** Tel. **Pets** Dogs not allowed. **Nearby** 18-hole golf course (15km); Chartres cathedral, museums. **Credit cards** Not accepted. **Spoken** English. **Open** All year. **How to get there** (Map 8): 8km northwest of Chartres. Towards Dreux via RN154 at Pont de Poisvilliers, leave via D133 towards Fresnay, then D134[10] towards Bailleau-L'Évêque; follow signs for "Chambres d'Hôtes".

The quadrangular enclosure of this beautiful farm is adjacent to a magnificent château and from the fields all around, you can see the solitary spires of Chartres cathedral rising up to the sky. The hospitality here is very friendly and refined, and the comfortable bedrooms are tastefully decorated with cheerful colors, and have excellent bathrooms. Dinners and breakfasts are served in a living room reserved for guests but which could profit from a more alluring decor. The farmhouse is nevertheless lovely, well kept, and reasonably priced.

218 - Le Château de Jonvilliers

17, rue d'Épernon - Jonvilliers
28320 Ecrosnes
(Eure-et-Loir)
Tel. 02 37 31 41 26
Fax 02 37 31 56 74
Virginie and Richard Thompson
Web: www.chateaudejonvilliers.com

Rooms 4 with shower, WC, and 1 suite (double bed + single bed) with shower, WC, TV on request.
Rooms cleaned on request. **Price** 300F/45,73€ (2 pers.); suite 350F/53,35€ (2 pers.), +60F/9,14€
(extra bed). **Meals** Breakfast incl. Evening meals at communal tables (only Sun and Mon)
100F/15,24€ (wine incl.). **Facilities** Sitting room. **Nearby** Restaurants (5km), swimming pool, golf,
riding. **Spoken** English. **Closed** Beg Nov – Feb. **How to get there** (Map 9): Aut. A11, exit Ablis, then
N10 to Chartres. In Essart, on right towards Saint-Symphorien, follow Bleury. In Bleury, on right
towards Ecrosnes. In Ecrosnes, on right and on left to Jonvilliers. **No smoking** in bedrooms.

Built in the late 18th century, Jonvilliers nestles in the midst of a vast, densely
wooded park. Richard and Virginie Thompson, a friendly young couple, have
recently converted the château into a bed and breakfast, designing it to be
welcoming, simple, and compatible with their family life. The small guest
rooms are pretty, comfortable, and well kept ("Chartres" is our favorite).
You'll find a spacious salon with period furniture from different epochs and
an attractive dining room where, on Sunday and Monday, you can enjoy a
light dinner around the family dining table.

219 - Manoir de la Motte

28340 La Ferté-Vidame
(Eure-et-Loir)
Tel. 02 37 37 51 69 / 06 11 01 79 54
Fax 02 37 37 51 56
Mme Anne Jallot
E-mail: manoir.de.la.motte.lfv@wanadoo.fr

Rooms 1 and 1 suite (2-4 pers.) with bath and WC. **Price** 420-520F/64,02-79,27€ (2 pers.),
660F/100,61€ (3 pers., suite), 800F/121,95€ (4 pers., suite). Possible 1 child's room. Special rates
after 2 nights and in low season. **Meals** Breakfast incl. No communal meal. **Facilities** Lounge, tel.,
small sports room, 3-hole golf, jogging path. **Pets** Dogs allowed on request. **Nearby** Restaurants
(1km), equestrian center, golf; Le Perche, La Ferté-Vidame. **Spoken** English, some German. **Open**
All year. **How to get there** (Map 8): 1.5km north of La Ferté-Vidarne via D921 dir. Verneuil. In 1.5km,
turn left into tree-lined lane just before "Les Rableux".

In the heart of the country, this small manor house dating from 1850 is just a
few minutes away from the beautiful region of the Perche. Delightfully
decorated in shades of blue, green, or yellow, the bedrooms have a broad
view of the park. Quite spacious and comfortable, they are appointed with
embroidered sheets, a scattering of antique furniture, and charming objects.
A warm and cheerful hostess, Madame Jaillot is anxious to make your stay
pleasant, as you will see from her brunches served in a pretty, oak-panelled
dining room.

220 - Château de Boisrenault

36500 Buzançais
(Indre)
Tel. 02 54 84 03 01
Fax 02 54 84 10 57
M. and Mme Y. du Manoir
E-mail: yves.dumanoir@wanadoo.fr
Web: www.chateau-du-boisrenault.com

Rooms 7 with bath or shower, WC, and 2 rooms with shared shower and WC. **Price** 355-510F/54,11-77,74€ (1 pers.), 395-560F/60,21-85,37€ (2 pers.), 525-625F/80,03-95,28€ (3 pers.). Posibility to rent for 1 week an apart. with kitchen (4-7 pers.). **Meals** Breakfast incl. No communal meal. **Facilities** Sitting room, swimming pool. **Nearby** Golf, tennis; Brenne (lake), Loire châteaux. **Credit cards** Amex, Visa. **Spoken** English. **Closed** Jan. **How to get there** (Map 16): 25km northwest of Châteauroux via N143 towards Buzançais, then D926 towards Levroux; turn right 3km from the village.

Boisrenault is a neo-Gothic château standing in a park near the Thousand Lakes of La Brenne. Some of the bedrooms are immense, like the Les Faisans room, others more intimate, but all are beautiful and are decorated with antiques. The studied elegance of the decor includes details such as the motifs painted on the bathroom tiles, which harmonize with the fabrics in each bedroom. This magnificent, very welcoming château also has two handsome apartments for guests wishing to stay longer.

221 - La Maison des Moines

1, route de Neuillay
36500 Méobecq
(Indre)
Tel. 02 54 39 44 36 (before 9:00AM
or around 7:00PM)
Mme Cécile Benhamou

Rooms 2 with private bath or shower and communal WC on the ground floor. **Price** 300F/45,73€ (2 pers.), +100F/15,24€ (extra bed). **Meals** Breakfast incl. No communal meal. **Restaurant** "Le Boeuf Couronné" in Mézières-en-Brenne (18km). **Facilities** Sitting room. **Nearby** Golf (10km), swimming in "Bellebouche" Lake, swimming pools, tennis, hiking paths; La Brenne (lakes and forests), villages. **Credit cards** Not accepted. **Spoken** English. **Open** All year. **How to get there** (Map 16): 30km west of Châteauroux via D925 towards Châtellerault. After 18km, on left D27 towards Neuillay-Les-Bois, then continue on D27, towards Méobecq; house behind church.

Located behind a small church, the "Monks' House" is a pleasant departure point for exploring the splendid Parc des Mille Etangs – Thousand Lakes Park – of the Brenne region. The two guest rooms are bright, decorated with provincial furniture and pretty, colorful fabrics, and they are very well kept. In the large room, the bathroom has not been partitioned in order to respect the proportions of the room. The breakfasts are pleasant and cheerfully served in charming rooms or near a lovely garden.

222 - Château de Dangy

36260 Paudy-Reuilly
(Indre)
Tel. 02 54 49 42 24
Fax 02 54 49 42 99
Mme Lucie Place

Rooms 5 and 1 suite with bath or shower, WC (1 with tel.). **Price** 400F/60,97€ (1 pers.), 500-600F/76,22-91,46€ (2 pers.), +100F/15,24€ (extra bed) - possibility of one extra room - suite 1100F/167,69€ (5 pers.). **Meals** Breakfast incl. Evening meals at communal table 150F/22,86€. Dinner by candlelight 200F/30,48€ (wine not incl.). **Facilities** 4 lounges, tel. with meter, jacuzzi (with suppl.). **Pets** Animals allowed on request. **Nearby** Hot-air balloons, ULM, tennis, golf; Valençay Château, Nohant, Bourges. **Credit cards** Not accepted. **Spoken** English **Open** Easter – Nov 1 (except for special circumstances). **How to get there** (Map 17): 28km south of Vierzon. Autoroute A71, exit Vierzon-centre, then N20 to Issoudun/Châteauroux. Exit 8 Massay/Reuilly, then follow signs beginning in Massay center.

The Château de Dangy is set on a small hill in the center of a vast estate with century-old trees and carefully tended gardens. Very welcoming hosts, Monsieur and Madame Place have restored the château magnificently with period furnishings, very comfortable, beautiful bedrooms, and many communal rooms. Near a window in the salon, old games will delight children and take "grown-up children" back a few years. The dinners, with game in season, are sumptuous.

223 - Manoir de Villedoin

36330 Velles
(Indre)
Tel. 02 54 25 12 06
Fax 02 54 24 28 29
M. and Mme Limousin
Web: www.villedoin.com

Rooms 4 with bath or shower, WC and tel. **Price** 393-453F/60-69€ (1 pers.), 426-492F/65-75€ (2 pers.), +131F/20€ (extra pers.). **Meals** Breakfast incl. Evening meals at separate tables 164F/25€ (wine not incl.). **Facilities** Sitting room, tennis, river, fishing, boat, pedalo, ping-pong. **Pets** Dogs allowed on request (+50F/7,62€). **Nearby** 18-hole golf course, swimming pool, sailing, riding, gliding, ULM; George Sand's house in Nohan, Argenton, archeological sites, La Brenne Lakes. **Credit cards** Not accepted. **Open** All year. **How to get there** (Map 17): 19km south of Châteauroux via A20, exit 5 towards Velles (D14); then D40 between Velles and Mosnay.

The Manoir de Villedoin is set on an isolated wooded site, high above the winding Bouzanne River. The comfortably decorated rooms are very inviting, with many decorative objects, paintings, etc., and they are impeccably kept. The bedrooms are vast and very comfortable. In summer, breakfasts are served on a charming terrace overlooking the river and the communal meal is mouthwatering. The surrounding park is well tended and at night, several stone Venuses watch over the flowers and the abundant garden furniture.

224 - Château du Gerfaut

37190 Azay-le-Rideau
(Indre-et-Loire)
Tel. 02 47 45 40 16
Fax 02 47 45 20 15
Mme Salles
E-mail: le.gerfault@wanadoo.fr

Rooms 7 with bath or shower and WC. **Price** 450-635F/68,60-96,80€ (2 pers.). Possible weekly rental of apt. **Meals** Breakfast incl. No communal meal. **Facilities** Sitting room, tel., tennis, lake. **Pets** Dogs not allowed. **Nearby** Golf; châteaux, wine cellars. **Credit cards** All major. **Spoken** English, Spanish. **Open** Apr 1 – Nov 1. **How to get there** (Map 16): 18km northeast of Chinon via D751 towards Tours, then leaving Azay-le-Rideau take the Villandry road; signposted. In Tours, D751 dir. Chinon, Azay-le-Rideau. Turn right before the forest (23km).

This impressive turn-of-the-century château, surrounded by its vast estate, was used as a hunting lodge by the grandfather of Madame Salles, as witnessed by the trophies displayed in the entrance and on the monumental stairway leading to the bedrooms. Of varying size, these all contain furniture or objects belonging to the family and have the antiquated charm of an old family home. In three of them, the bathrooms are lacking in privacy as their separating walls do not reach the ceiling. Breakfast is served in the large sitting room, which has some remarkable Empire furniture. The welcome is courteous.

225 - Château du Vau

37510 Ballan-Miré
(Indre-et-Loire)
Tel. 02 47 67 84 04
Fax 02 47 67 55 77
Bruno and Nancy Clément

Rooms 4 with bath and WC. **Price** 480F/73,17€ (1 pers.), 510F/77,74€ (2 pers.), +100F/15,24€ (extra pers.) **Meals** Breakfast incl. No communal meal. **Facilities** Sitting room, tel. **Pets** Small dogs allowed. **Nearby** Restaurants (2km), golf, squash, health center, riding, swimming pool; Villandry, Saché, Azay-le-rideau, Langeais, Chinon. **Credit cards** All major. **Spoken** English, German. **Open** All year. **How to get there** (Map 16): 13km southwest of Tours. Aut. A10, exit 24 (south of Tours), then D751 at Ballan-Miré and on right at the 3rd traffic light before the level crossing.

This château built in the 16th century and modified in the 17th is situated very close to Tours and shares its large quiet grounds with a farm that produces foie gras. It has been the family of Bruno Clément for 100 years and now receives guests in three of its bedrooms. They are all large, bright, furnished and decorated in a sober but pleasant manner and are equipped with very nice bathrooms. Antique pieces or family heirlooms are scattered here and there. The dining room was not yet completed when we were there, but it is sure to be a pleasant setting for breakfast which, in good weather, is also served outdoors. A friendly welcome and relaxed atmosphere.

226 - Manoir de Montour

176, rue Véron
37420 Beaumont-en-Véron
(Indre-et-Loire)
Tel. and fax 02 47 58 43 76
Mme Valérie Arbon
E-mail: valerie.arbon@wanadoo.fr

Rooms 3 (1 for 4 pers. and 1 for 3 pers.) with bath and WC. **Price** 360F/54,88€ (2 pers.), 480F/73,17€ (4 pers.). **Meals** Breakfast incl. No communal meal. **Facilities** Sitting room, tel. **Pets** Small dogs allowed. **Nearby** Swimming pool, tennis, riding, fishing, golf; Azay-le-Rideau, Fontevraud, Giseux, Langeais, Villandry, Saumur, Rigny-Ussé. **Open** Easter – Nov 1. **How to get there** (Map 16): 5km northwest of Chinon via D749 towards Avoine and Bourgueil until Coulaine, then towards Savigny-en-Véron via D118.

The old building materials and traditional fireplaces give this lovely house a truly authentic character. The new owner has done extensive renovations, particularly in the bathrooms, for the greater comfort of the guests. A new sitting room has been created, larger and brighter than before. The beds have been adapted to suit today's norms but the bedroom with the charming old four-poster is still there and it still has its Louis XIII feel. This house has gained in comfort and is gradually beginning a new life in its calm and peaceful setting.

227 - La Garenne

37350 La Celle-Guénand
(Indre-et-Loire)
Tel. 02 47 94 93 02
M. and Mme Devaulx de Chambord

Rooms 3 with bath, shower and WC. **Price** 325F/49,54€ (1 pers.), 350F/53,35€ (2 pers.). **Meals** Breakfast incl. No communal meal. **Restaurant** "La Promenade" in Le Petit-Pressigny (3km). **Pets** Animals not allowed in rooms. **Nearby** Tennis (10km), riding (10km), 18-hole golf course (24km); Prehistoric Museum of Le Grand Préssigny, Angle-sur-Anglin, Parc de la Haute Touche. **Spoken** Some English. **Open** All year, by reservation. **How to get there** (Map 16): 24km southeast of Loches. Autoroute A10 towards Loches, then Ligueil D59, then D50 towards Preuilly for 12km. As you leave La Celle-Guénand, house on the left towards Preuilly.

La Garenne is a 19th-century family mansion, very typical in this region of the Loire. The mansion is superbly decorated with beautiful antique furniture, family portraits and hunting trophies. (The Loire has been a favorite hunting region for centuries.) The bedrooms are lovely, warm and cheerful, with beautifully coordinated carpets and fabrics. This is a beautiful mansion and the owners are very friendly.

C   E   N   T   R   E

228 - Ferme de Launay

37210 Chançay
(Indre-et-Loire)
Tel. and fax 02 47 52 28 21
M. Jean-Pierre Schweizer

Rooms 3 rooms with bath or shower and WC. **Price** 400-500F/60,97-76,22€ (2 pers.). Reduction after 3 nights and in low season. **Meals** Breakfast incl. Communal meals on request 150F/22,86€ (wine not incl.). **Facilities** Sitting room. **Pets** Dogs allowed on request. **Nearby** River fishing, tennis, swimming pool, canoeing (Loire), 18-hole golf course (15km); Wine Route, Loire châteaux. **Credit cards** Not accepted. **Spoken** English, German, Italian. **Closed** All year. 2 nights min. from May to Oct. **How to get there** (Map 16): 15km northeast of Tours via N152, north bank, towards Amboise. In Vouvray, take D46 towards Vernou, then Chançay. Signs before Chançay. **No smoking**.

This very old farmhouse is on the edge of the touristic road (deserted at night) which leads to the vineyards. In the fields, three thoroughbred horses have taken the place of the calves, cows and pigs. The inside of the house is comfortable, classic and cheerful. There are very pleasant small bedrooms (our favorites are on the premier étage); good breakfasts and outstanding dinners are served outside in good weather. This is a very good, refined place to stay, where you will be greeted with great hospitality.

229 - La Varenne

37120 Chaveignes
(Indre-et-Loire)
Tel. 02 47 58 26 31
Fax 02 47 58 27 47
Joëlle and Gérard Dru-Sauer
Web: www.la-varenne.com

Rooms 3 with bath and WC. **Price** 450, 500 and 600F/68,60, 76,22 and 91,46€ (2 pers.), +160F/24,39€ (extra pers.). **Meals** Breakfast incl. No communal meal. **Facilities** Sitting room, heated swimming pool, bicycles, ping-pong. **Pets** Dogs not allowed. **Nearby** Restaurants (4km), hiking; Richelieu, Loire Valley (châteaux de la Loire), Futuroscope. **Spoken** English, some German. **Open** All year. **How to get there** (Map 16): 4km southeast Richelieu via D757 to Tours for 2km, then on right D20, "route de Braslou" for 2km to Chizeray. Entrance 200m further.

Just several minutes from the city built for Cardinal de Richelieu, this 17th-century family mansion stands in a vast, unspoiled countryside. After walking through a leafy courtyard dappled with the clear water of a heated swimming pool (with wave-making apparatus), you will discover a lovely interior. The bedrooms are beautiful and comfortable (some are immense), and we felt right at home in them. The new bathrooms are just perfect, the breakfasts excellent, and the hospitality delightful.

230 - Domaine de Pallus

Cravant-les-Côteaux
37500 Chinon
(Indre-et-Loire)
Tel. 02 47 93 08 94
Fax 02 47 98 43 00
M. and Mme B. Chauveau

Rooms 2 rooms and 1 suite with bath and WC. **Price** 500-550F/76,22-83,84€ (2 pers.), +150F/22,86€ (extra pers. in suite). **Meals** Breakfast incl. No communal meal. **Restaurants** "L'Océanic" in Chinon and "Château de Marçay". **Facilities** Sitting room, tel., swimming pool. **Pets** Dogs not allowed. **Nearby** Fishing, golf, riding; châteaux of the Loire. **Credit cards** Not accepted. **Spoken** English, German. **Open** All year. **How to get there** (Map 16): 8km east of Chinon on D21 to Cravant-les-Côteaux; leaving the village, Pallus is on the right after 1.5km.

The little road that runs through vineyards to Chinon will take you to this beautiful house made up of several buildings and benefiting from double exposure. Inside, the furniture and objects of different eras have been carefully chosen with clearly affirmed taste. Each bedroom has its own personality and the bathrooms are comfortable. The charming suite with its sloping ceiling and its own living room has a whole floor to itself. The sitting room is also pleasant, with its woodwork and large fireplace. The atmosphere is one of harmony and refinement. The garden is lovely, the welcome agreeable and the breakfasts are excellent.

231 - La Butte de l'Épine

37340 Continvoir
(Indre-et-Loire)
Tel. 02 47 96 62 25
Fax 02 47 96 07 36
M. and Mme Michel Bodet

Rooms 3 (twin beds) with bath and WC (independent entrance). **Price** 300F/45,73€ (1 pers.), 330F/50,30€ and 300F/45,73€ from 3 nights (2 pers.), +100F/15,24€ (extra pers.), +80F/12,15€ (child's bed). **Meals** Breakfast incl. No communal meal. **Facilities** Sitting room, parking. **Pets** Animals not allowed. **Nearby** Restaurants, 18-hole golf course, riding, lake, tennis, walks; vineyards, châteaux, museums. **Credit cards** Not accepted. **Spoken** English. **Closed** Christmas. **How to get there** (Map 16): 13km north of Bourgeuil via D749 towards Château-la-Vallière, then right on D15 to Continvoir. In Continvoir take D64. **No smoking.**

La Butte de l'Epine is the realization of the owners' dream, which was to build a 17th-century-style house using materials of the period. In the center is a large and prettily decorated beamed room which serves as both sitting room and dining room. Two of the bedrooms are simple and charming, and are decorated with pretty floral wallpaper. A third bedroom has just been opened on the upper floor. Breakfast is served at a communal table inside or outside, depending on the weather. The Bodets are friendly hosts.

232 - Château de Girardet

37370 Épeigné-sur-Dême
(Centre)
Tel. 02 47 52 36 19
Fax 02 47 52 36 90
M. and Mme Chesnaux

Rooms 4 and 1 suite (4 pers.) with bath or shower and WC. **Price** 290-590F/44,21-89,94€ (2 pers.).
Meals Breakfast incl. No communal meal. **Facilities** Sitting rooms, ping-pong, bicycle rentals. **Pets**
Dogs not allowed in bedrooms (kennel). **Nearby** Restaurants (7km), riding, millpond, tennis; Tours,
Amboise, Le Loir, Lavardin, la Possonière (Dom. de Ronsard). **Credit cards** Not accepted. **Spoken**
English, German. **Open** All year, by reservation in winter. **How to get there** (Map 16): 30km north of
Tours via D29. In Chemillé-sur-Dême, go on D29 (don't take dir. Épeigné) for 2km.

This little château with its two turrets (from the 15th and 19th centuries) has
undergone several transformations since it was first built. Madame Chesnaux
has just redone all the interior decoration and will soon start to refurbish the
garden. The bedrooms are all different, furnished with an assortment of
vintage objects and real antiques, and each one evokes a different epoch. Our
favorites are the "1900" and the "Suite anglaise." The "Louis XVI" has a
circular view and the "Louis XIII" is most theatrical. Breakfast is served in a
large, country-style kitchen, a charming room with a nice fireplace, and a
pleasant welcome is reserved for all.

233 - Le Moulin de la Roche

37460 Genillé
(Indre-et-Loire)
Tel. 02 47 59 56 58
Fax 02 47 59 59 62
Josette and Clive Miéville
E-mail: clive.mieville@wanadoo.fr
Web: www.moulin-de-la-roche.com

Rooms 3 and 2 suites (3-4 pers.) with shower and WC. **Price** 340F/51,83€, +90F/13,72€ (extra
bed in suite). **Meals** Breakfast incl. No communal meal. **Facilities** Sitting rooms (satellite TV), river
fishing. **Pets** Dogs not allowed. **Nearby** Riding, U.L.M., swimming pool, hiking, mountain bike
rentals; Loches, Chenonceau, Amboise, "Labyrinthus", Futuroscope (1 hour). **Spoken** English,
Spanish. **Closed** Dec 20. – Jan 4. **How to get there** (Map 16): 21km south of Bléré. Take D31 to
Loches. In Saint-Quentin-sur-Indrois, on left to Genillé. After 6km on right, follow signs. **No smoking**
in bedrooms.

This is an authentic mill standing above an arm of water whose torrents are
more or less tumultuous depending on the season. Just renovated, the
bedrooms are comfortable, immaculately kept, and delightfully furnished in
a beautiful country spirit. You can enjoy the charming living room with its
antique furniture, and good, copious breakfasts. We found this a beautiful
place to stay, with informal and energetic hosts.

234 - Château de Pintray

37400 Lussault-sur-Loire
(Indre-et-Loire)
Tel. 02 47 23 22 84
Fax 02 47 57 64 27
M. and Mme Rault-Couturier
E-mail: marius.rault@wanadoo.fr

Rooms 3 and 1 family suite of 2 bedrooms with bath and WC. **Price** 500F/76,22€ (1 pers.), 550F/83,84€ (2 pers.), +140F/21,34€ (extra pers.). **Meals** Breakfast incl. No communal meal. **Facilities** Sitting room, billiards, tel., tasting of wines from property. **Pets** Dogs not allowed. **Nearby** Restaurants (2.5km), riding, hiking, tennis, swimming pool, 9-hole golf course (28km), châteaux and houses of Loire Valley writers, Touraine Aquarium (5 mins.). **Credit cards** Not accepted. **Spoken** English. **Open** All year. **How to get there** (Map 16): 7km southwest of Amboise via D751 towards Tours. At the church in Lussault, take D283 towards Saint-Martin-le-Beau: Château located 2km at end of lane of plane trees.

Once owners of a bookshop on the Ile de Ré and now winegrowers, Monsieur and Madame Rault have renovated this elegant small château with taste and an appreciation for modern amenities. They will make you feel extremely welcome here. Vast, bright, with pretty fabrics on the walls, the bedrooms are very smart, as are the bathrooms. There is a pleasant salon for guests and a beautiful garden which is extended by the vineyards of the estate.

235 - Les Hauts Noyers

Les Hauts Noyers
37530 Mosnes
(Indre-et-Loire)
Tel. 02 47 57 19 73
Fax 02 47 57 60 46
M. and Mme Saltron

Rooms 1 and 1 suite (4 pers.) with bath and WC. **Price** 310F/47,25€ (2 pers.), +100F/15,24€ (extra pers.). **Meals** Breakfast incl. No communal meal. **Restaurant** "La Chancelière" in Chaumont (5km). **Facilities** Sitting room, bicycles, jeux de boules. **Pets** Dogs not allowed. **Nearby** Riding, forest, canoeing, kayaks, 18-hole golf course (10km), châteaux of Loire, Wine Route, Chaumont Gardens. **Credit cards** Not accepted. **Open** All year. 2 nights min. **How to get there** (Map 16): 10km east of Amboise via D751 towards Blois and Chaumont. In Mosnes, follow signs. **No smoking** in bedrooms.

At the edge of vineyards and less than a kilometer from the Loire, this entirely renovated house offers two charming, very well-kept guest rooms with fabric-covered walls. The room on the ground floor is decorated predominantly in blue, while the Jaune Room, just beneath the roof, is like a vast family suite. Each room has a private garden where in summer the very copious breakfasts are served. A sitting room-dining room with fireplace is reserved for guests. The owners are especially hospitable and the prices truly reasonable. This house won a First Prize for its breakfast and another for its garden in 1998.

236 - Château des Ormeaux

37530 Nazelles
(Indre-et-Loire)
Tel. 02 47 23 26 51
Fax 02 47 23 19 31
M. Merle
E-mail: chateaudesormeaux@wanadoo.fr.
Web: www.chateaudesormeaux.com

Rooms 6 with bath, WC and tel. **Price** 550-650F/83,84-99,09€ (2 pers.). **Meals** Breakfast incl. Evening meals, by reservation 250F/38,11€ (wine incl.). **Facilities** Sitting room (satellite TV), swimming pool, vineyard, antiques, river fishing, mountain bikes. **Pets** Small dogs allowed on request. **Nearby** Tennis, golf; Loire châteaux, vineyard (Vouvray). **Credit cards** Not accepted. **Spoken** English, German, Spanish, Italian. **Open** All year. **How to get there** (Map 16): 4km north of Amboise. Autoroute A10, exit Amboise, dir. Autreche, then Saint-Ouen-les-Vignes, Pocé-sur-Cisse; in Nazelles (D1) dir. Noizay for 2km (sign posted).

Nestled in greenery atop a cliff, this house with its south-facing terrace has a sweeping view over the countryside. It has been converted into a guest house but has lost none of its former character. The rooms are all spacious and their decoration is colorful. The sitting room has a large fireplace, the bedrooms have their original painted woodwork, the dining room is vast and the bathrooms not only large but spotlessly clean. Throughout the house the old furniture and paintings are a testimony to Monsieur Merle's love for antiques. This lovely estate is a haven of calm and tranquility.

237 - Domaine de Beauséjour

37220 Panzoult
(Indre-et-Loire)
Tel. 02 47 58 64 64
Fax 02 47 95 27 13
Mme Marie-Claude Chauveau
E-mail: gdc37@club-internet.fr

Rooms 2 and 1 suite of 2 bedrooms with bath or shower and WC. **Price** 350-500F/53,36-76,22€ (2 pers., depending on rooms and season); suite 580-700 F / 88,42-106,71 € (3-4 pers.). **Meals** Breakfast incl. No communal meal. **Facilities** Sitting room, swimming pool. **Pets** Dogs allowed on request. **Nearby** Restaurants (6km), tennis, golf, riding, fishing; Loire châteaux. **Credit cards** Not accepted. **Spoken** English. **Open** All year. **How to get there** (Map 16): 12km east of Chinon via D21 to Panzoult; on the left before the village.

Beauséjour is a charming vineyard property. The bedrooms are comfortable and nicely furnished with antique pieces. They have beautiful views over vineyards and the plain below. The sitting room reserved for guests has a terrace with teak furniture, and even a laundry room and a large refrigerator. A swimming pool is also at your disposal. There is no table d'hôte meal, but many restaurants nearby. If you are interested in wine, a member of the family will invite you to a tasting, affording you a pleasant and sure means of becoming acquainted with the regional wines.

238 - Le Clos Saint-Clair

Départementale 18
37800 Pussigny
(Indre-et-Loire)
Tel. 02 47 65 01 27
Fax 02 47 65 04 21
Mme Anne-Marie Liné

Rooms 3 with shower and WC (2-4 pers.). **Price** 220F/33,53€ (1 pers.), 280-320F/42,68-48,78€ (2 pers.), 340-380F/51,83-57,93€ (3 pers., double bed and single bed), 420F/64,02€ (4 pers.), +100F/15,24€ (extra pers.), possibility baby bed free. 10% reduction after 5 nights. **Meals** Breakfast incl. No communal table. **Facilities** Sitting room, tennis, fishing, bicycle rentals. **Pets** Dogs not allowed. **Nearby** Restaurants in the village and in Vienne valley (4km), golf, swimming pool; Romanesque churches, châteaux, wine cellars, Futuroscope (50km). **Credit cards** Not accepted. **Open** All year. **How to get there** (Map 16): 50km south of Tours via A10, exit Sainte-Maure, then right on RN10 to Port-de-Piles, then right on D5 towards Pussigny for 2km, then left for 1km; in front of Mairie.

At the entrance to a pretty Touraine village you will find these two old houses in a flowery, well-tended garden. The charming bedrooms are rustic yet elegant, with some antique pieces of furniture, colorful fabrics and many charming details. Excellent breakfasts are served on a bright veranda which opens onto the garden in good weather. Madame Liné is delightfully hospitable.

239 - Château de Chargé

37120 Razines
(Indre-et-Loire)
Tel. 02 47 95 60 57
Fax 02 47 95 67 25
M. and Mme d'Asfeld

Rooms 3 with bath or shower and WC. **Price** 350-600F/53,35-91,46€ (1 pers., depending on rooms), 400-650F/60,97-99,09€ (2 pers., depending on rooms). **Meals** Breakfast incl. No communal table. **Restaurants** in Razines, Bouchard Island and Chinon. **Facilities** Sitting room, tel., swimming pool. **Pets** Dogs allowed on request. **Nearby** Fishing, 18-hole golf course; Futuroscope, châteaux. **Credit cards** Not accepted. **Spoken** English, German, Spanish, Russian. **Open** May 1 and Oct 31. By reservation in low season. Deposit. **How to get there** (Map 16): 7km southeast of Richelieu. Aut. A10, exit Sainte-Maure-de Touraine towards Richelieu. D749 dir. Châtellerault. After 7km of Razines; after the village on right.

Once a fortress that housed the governors of Richelieu and Chinon, this château exists thanks to the determination of Claude and Marie-Louise d'Asfeld. Perched on a hilltop amid fields and vineyards, with a chapel as well, it has been restored with rigor and precision. Each bedroom has its own character, ranging from the 14th to 18th centuries, with furniture to match. The bathrooms are small but impeccable.

240 - Les Religieuses

24, place des Religieuses
and 1, rue Jarry
37120 Richelieu
(Indre-et-Loire)
Tel. and Fax 02 47 58 10 42
Mme Le Platre-Arnould

Rooms 4 and 1 suite (3 pers.) with bath or shower and WC. **Price** Rooms 260F/39,63€ (1 pers.), 280 and 360F/42,68 and 54,88€ (2 pers.); suite 360F/54,88€ (2 pers.), 500F/76,22€ (3 pers.). **Meals** Breakfast incl. No communal meal. **Facilities** Sitting room. **Pets** Dogs not allowed. **Nearby** Restaurants (300m), swimming pool, tennis, golf; châteaux of the Loire, Chinon, Azay-le-Rideau. **Credit cards** Not accepted. **Closed** Dec 15 – Jan 15. **How to get there** (Map 16): 29km northwest of Châtellerault via A10 then D749; signposted in Richelieu.

Situated within the ramparts of Richelieu, this mansion is truly delightful. Madame Le Platre-Arnould is charming and will take pleasure in showing you around the house, which is full of antiques and curios. Everything is clean and shiny and smells of fresh polish, and the comfortable bedrooms are well kept. The house is reasonably quiet for a small town. In summer, breakfast is served in the sunlit garden.

241 - Les Tilleuls

La Sablonnière
37190 Saché
(Indre-et-Loire)
Tel. 02 47 26 81 45
Fax 02 47 26 84 00
Mme Piller

Rooms 3 and 1 suite with bath or shower and WC. **Price** Rooms 300F/45,73€ (1 pers.), 400F/60,97€ (2 pers.), 500F/76,22€ (3 pers.), +100F/15,24€ (extra pers.); suite 580F/88,42€ (3 pers.). **Meals** Breakfast incl. No communal meal. **Facilities** Sitting room. **Pets** Dogs allowed on request. **Nearby** Restaurants (6km), châteaux de Saché, Azay-le-Rideau and Loire Valley (châteaux de la Loire). **Spoken** English. **Closed** Nov 15 – Mar 15, by reservation. 2 night min. **How to get there** (Map 16): 6km east of Azay-le-Rideau via D84 to Artannes, 500m on left before the bridge of Saché.

Madame Piller cares for her garden and her house with tireless energy, enormous taste, and admirable attention to detail. Smartly waxed furniture and charming bric à brac fill the house, while comfortable beds and tiled baths await you in the bedrooms. Breakfasts are a treat and discussing gardening with the hostess is a true delight.

242 - Le Prieuré des Granges

15, rue des Fontaines
37510 Savonnières
(Indre-et-Loire)
Tel. 02 47 50 09 67
Fax 02 47 50 06 43
M. and Mme Salmon
E-mail: salmon.eric@wanadoo.fr
Web: chateauxcountry.com

Rooms 5 and 1 suite (2-4 per.) with bath or shower, WC and tel. **Price** Rooms from 420F/64,02€, +170F/25,91€ (extra bed); suite 750F/114,34€ (2 pers.), 900F/137,20€ (3 pers.), 1100F/167,69€ (4 pers.). **Meals** Breakfast incl. No communal meal. **Facilities** Sitting room (TV), swimming pool. **Pets** Dogs allowed on request. **Nearby** Restaurants (600m), tennis, fishing, riding, golf. **Spoken** English, Spanish, some German. **Open** Feb – end Nov. **How to get there** (Map 16): 11km from Tours. In Tours, go towards Tours Sud/Villandry to Savonnières. Autoroute A10, exit 24 Joué-les-Tours, follow signs Villandry to Savonnières. **No smoking** in bedrooms.

High in the hills of Savonnières (known for its lovely white wine), this charming house dating from the 17th, 18th and 19th centuries is very attractive, with its antique objects and furniture that go together so harmoniously. The bedrooms are outstanding for their comfort as well as their beautiful decoration. The family suite is very refined and the bathrooms are also very pleasant. There is an elegant 18th-century dining room decorated in shades of blue to match the Dresden china. The salon is warm and inviting. The Prieuré looks out onto a flowery private park. Monsieur and Madame Salmon are kind and gracious hosts.

243 - Le Prieuré Sainte-Anne

10, rue Chaude
37510 Savonnières
(Indre-et-Loire)
Tel. 02 47 50 03 26
Mme Caré

Rooms 1 suite (2-4 pers.) with shower and WC. **Price** 220F/33,53€ (1 pers.), 330F/50,30€ (2 pers.), +100F/15,24€ (extra pers.). **Meals** Breakfast incl. No communal meal. **Facilities** Sitting room. **Pets** Dogs allowed on request. **Nearby** Restaurants (200m), 18-hole golf course; châteaux. **Credit cards** Not accepted. **Open** Mar – Nov. **How to get there** (Map 16): 13km west of Tours via D7 towards Villandry; in the village, on the Druye road, take Rue du Paradis before the Mairie, then turn right.

This 15th-century house is somewhat set back from a quiet village street and is furnished in lovely rustic style with old polished furniture, antique plates on the wall, immense fireplaces, and comfortable wool mattresses in the bedrooms. It is a simple, well-kept place, which transports the visitor to another era. Friendly Madame Caré serves good breakfasts next to the fireplace or outside in the lovely flower garden which is protected from the wind by old stone walls.

244 - La Ferme des Berthiers

37800 Sepmes
(Indre-et-Loire)
Tel. and Fax 02 47 65 50 61
Mme Anne-Marie Vergnaud

Rooms 5 and 1 suite with bath or shower, WC, possible extra bed and 1 child's room. Room cleaned every 3 days. **Price** 200F/30,48€ (1 pers.), 250-290F/38,11-44,21€ (2 pers.), 300-340F/45,73-51,83€ (3 pers.); suite 360F/54,88€ (3 pers.). **Meals** Breakfast incl. Evening meals, by reservation the day before 110F/16,76€ (wine and coffee incl.). **Pets** Dogs allowed on request. **Nearby** Loire châteaux, wine cellars. **Credit cards** Not accepted. **Spoken** English, Dutch, German. **Open** All year. **How to get there** (Map 16): 40km south of Tours via A10 exit Sainte-Maure-de-Touraine, then D59 towards Ligueil; after Sepmes, signposted.

You will be warmly welcomed to this beautiful farmhouse with its large interior courtyard and shady garden. The comfortable bedrooms are prettily decorated and have superb bathrooms; our favorites are the Blue and the Yellow bedrooms. There is a magnificent terra-cotta floor. Anne-Marie Vergnaud prepares excellent evening meals and hearty breakfasts. Children are welcome here.

245 - Manoir de Foncher

37510 Villandry
(Indre-et-Loire)
Tel. 02 47 50 02 40
Fax 02 47 50 09 94
M. and Mme Salles

Rooms 1 suite (of 2 bedrooms) with bath and WC. **Price** 650F/99,09€ (1 bedroom, 1-2 pers.), 950F/144,82€ (2 bedrooms, 3-4 pers.). **Meals** Breakfast incl. No communal meal. **Facilities** Sitting room. **Nearby** Restaurants, riding, golf; Loire châteaux. **Credit cards** Not accepted. **Spoken** English. **Open** Apr – Sept. **How to get there** (Map 16): 15km west of Tours via D7 towards Villandry. At Savonnières, cross the bridge and turn left along the right bank of the Cher for 3km.

At the tip of a spit of land between the Loire and the Cher, this manor house surely looks the same as it did in the 15th-century, with its mullioned windows, exterior gallery and an exceptional spiral staircase. Breakfast is served on an immense convent table in a room with a huge fireplace, where you will be greeted with very friendly hospitality. The very comfortable bedrooms and the suite are beautiful and authentic. The bathrooms are charming. This is a magical place to stay while visiting the châteaux of the Loire.

246 - Domaine des Bidaudières

Rue du Peu Morier
37210 Vouvray
(Indre-et-Loire)
Tel. 02 47 52 66 85
Fax 02 47 52 62 17
M. and Mme Suzanne
Web: www.bandb-loire.valley.com

Rooms 6 with bath or shower, WC, tel. and TV. **Price** 600F/91,46€ (1 pers.), 650F/99,09€ (2 pers.), +100F/15,24€ (extra bed). **Meals** Breakfast incl. No communal meal. **Restaurant** in Vouvray, Vernou-sur-Brenne and Tours. **Facilities** Sitting room, greenhouse, heated swimming pool, lake. **Nearby** Golf, tennis, riding; Loire châteaux, Tours. **Credit cards** Not accepted. **Spoken** English, German. **Open** All year. **How to get there** (Map 16): 14km east of Tours. Autoroute A10 exit 20 Vouvray, then N152 dir. Amboise. In Vouvray dir. Vernou-sur-Brenne via D46. After the TGV bridge, 2nd road on left.

This wine growing property from the 18th century has been completely restored since 1996. The property includes a superb heated swimming pool, a recently-created pond and a pretty garden. An elevator goes up to the bedrooms, which are decorated in a tasteful contemporary style with several period touches. All face the countryside except for the "Clos Chapon," but it too is full of charm. They all have air-conditioning and very nice bathrooms. Breakfast is served in a stone-walled room carved into the tufa or else on the terrace. The welcome is smiling and dynamic.

247 - La Farge

41600 Chaumont-sur-Tharonne
(Loir-et-Cher)
Tel. 02 54 88 52 06
Fax 02 54 88 51 36
M. and Mme de Grangeneuve
E-mail: sylvie.lansier@wanadoo.fr
Web: www.web.de.loire.com/C/41h1034.htm

Rooms 1, 1 suite (2-4 pers.) and 1 studio (3-4 pers. with living room, fireplace, TV, kitchen), bath and WC. Special rates for more than 3 days. **Price** Room 350F/53,35€ (2 pers.); suite 500F/76,22€; studio 450-550F/68,60-83,84€. **Meals** Breakfast incl. No communal meal, cooking possible in evening. **Facilities** Living room with fireplace and TV, swimming pool, equestrian center, footpaths. **Pets** Dogs allowed on request. **Nearby** Restaurants (5km); Loire châteaux. **Credit cards** Not accepted. **Spoken** English. **Open** All year. **How to get there** (Map 16): 5km east of Chaumont-sur-Tharonne, take C2 towards Vouzon. La Farge 4km on right. (35km south of Orléans via N20). Follow signs for Centre Equestre.

Set in the midst of a forest, this is a beautiful group of 17th-century buildings. The comfortable bedrooms are pleasantly furnished and the bathrooms are wonderful. The apartment is outstanding with its beautiful small, attractive salon, fireplace and kitchen. Breakfasts are served in a beautiful, spacious room. Copper pots, hunting trophies and handsome old furniture create a warm atmosphere in this welcoming place.

248 - Le Clos Bigot

Route le Buchet
41700 Cheverny
(Loir-et-Cher)
Tel. 02 54 44 21 28
M. and Mme Bravo-Meret

Rooms 1 suite (4 pers.) with bath, WC and 1 apartment (500 ft-) in the outbuildings with 1 bedroom, sitting room, bath and WC. **Price** suite 340-380F/51,83-57,93€ (2 pers.); apart. 500F/76,22€ (2 pers.), 700F/106,71€ (4 pers.). **Meals** Breakfast incl. No communal meal. **Restaurants** Cheverny (2km). **Facilities** Sitting room, swimming pool. **Pets** Dogs allowed on request. **Nearby** 18-hole golf course (3km), tennis, riding; Sound and Light at Loire châteaux. **Credit cards** Not allowed. **Spoken** English, Spanish. **Open** All year, but by reservation from Nov 1 to Mar 31. **How to get there** (Map 16): 2km from Cheverny via the road, follow signs.

This prim little longère, a long, low house typical of Sologne, has been very well-renovated, with an interior which is ravishing. The suite, which is upstairs under the slope of the roof, is very nicely appointed. The apartment is in a separate little house and has its own sheltered terrace. Breakfasts are served outside or in a charming room with handsome furniture and old paintings. The owners are hospitable and will give you good advice on touring the region.

249 - Ferme des Saules

41700 Cheverny
(Loir-et-Cher)
Tel. 02 54 79 26 95
Fax 02 54 79 97 54
M. and Mme Merlin
E-mail: merlin.cheverny@infonie.fr
Web: www.chez.com/fermedessaules

Rooms 4 with bath or shower and WC. **Price** 210F/32,01€ (1 pers.), 285-350F/43,44-53,35€ (2 pers., depending on room). **Meals** Breakfast incl. Evening meals at communal table 110-135F/16,76-20,58€ (wine incl.). **Facilities** Heated swimming pool. **Pets** Dogs allowed on request. **Nearby** Riding, tennis, hot-air ballon, mountain bikes, golf; châteaux, festivals, antiques. **Credit cards** Not allowed. **Spoken** English, German, Spanish, Dutch. **Closed** Dec 15 – Jan 15, by reservation and deposit. **How to get there** (Map 16): 2km south of Cheverny. Autoroute A10, exit Blois towards Vierzon. Crossing Cour-Cheverny towards Cheverny, then D102 towards Contres. At 1500m, on right after the gate of the château.

Situated near the château of Cheverny, this former farm of "The Willows" has been restored by Didier and Anita, to receive their guests in a setting of forest and field. The two upstairs bedrooms are nicely decorated with checkered fabrics, the bathrooms have roof windows. We prefer the ones in the former bakehouse, which are larger: one has a small terrace, the other its own little courtyard. There is a warm welcome for all and Didier, a professional cook, proposes menus according to the season. In summer the nearby camping site (500 meters away) may be a little noisy.

250 - La Rabouillère

Chemin de Marçon
41700 Contres
(Loir-et-Cher)
Tel. 02 54 79 05 14
Fax 02 54 79 59 39
Mme Thimonnier
E-mail: rabouillere@wanadoo.fr
Web: //rabouillere.ifrance.com/

Rooms 4, 1 suite and 1 small house with bath, WC (TV on request). **Price** Rooms 300F/45,73€ (1 pers.), 360F/54,88€ (2 pers.); suite 550F/83,84€ (2 pers.), 650F/99,09€ (3 pers.); small house 650F/99,09€ (2 pers.), 800F/121,95€ (3-4 pers.). **Meals** Breakfast incl. No communal meal but kitchen available. **Restaurants** In Court-Cheverny and Contres. **Facilities** Sitting room, tel. **Pets** Dogs not allowed. **Nearby** Tennis, riding, fishing, golf; Loire châteaux. **Credit cards** All major except Amex. **Spoken** English. **Open** All year. **How to get there** (Map 16): 19km south of Blois via D765. At Cheverny take D102 towards Contres for 6km; signposted "Chambres d'hôtes".

This traditional Sologne farmhouse is surrounded by 12 1/2 acres of woods and meadows, with a beautiful garden near the house. The bedrooms are all pleasant and decorated with taste and elegance. The small house is a haven of happiness with its dining room, fireplace and two bedrooms. Monsieur and Madame Thimonnier love their home and open it to guests with evident pleasure. When the weather is cold, an open fire burns in the living room, which opens wide onto the garden.

251 - Le Béguinage

41700 Cour-Cheverny
(Loir-et-Cher)
Tel. 02 54 79 29 92
Fax 02 54 79 94 59
Brice and Patricia Deloison
E-mail: le.beguinage@wanadoo.fr
Web: www.multimania.com/beguinage/

Rooms 6 with bath or shower and WC. **Price** 270-320F/41,16-48,78€ (1 pers.), 290-360F/44,21-54,88€ (2 pers.), +80F/12,19€ (extra bed); children under 4 free. **Meals** Breakfast incl. Evening meals at communal table, by reservation 100F/15,24€ (wine incl.), 85F/12,95€ (children). **Facilities** Tel. with meter, river, pond. **Pets** Dogs allowed on request. **Nearby** Tennis, riding, fishing, golf; Loire châteaux. **Credit cards** Not accepted. **Spoken** English. **Open** All year, by reservation and deposit. **How to get there** (Map 16): Autoroute A10 exit Blois towards Châteauroux/Vierzon via D765. Exit Cour-Cheverny centre.

At Cour-Cheverny, on the Château Road, this "Béguinage," a former convent, has begun a new life in its quiet tree-shaded park with a pool and a river. Patricia and Brice have installed independent rooms in the different buildings, with large beds, brightly colored fabrics and lovely bathrooms with bath or shower. Our preference goes to the "Bouton d'Or" where, if you like, you can have a wood fire (40 F / 6.09 Euros extra). The "Rouge" and "Jaune" rooms are separated from their bathrooms by swinging "saloon" doors. Breakfast served on the terrace or in the dining room with its pale green beams.

252 - La Borde

41160 Danzé
(Loir-et-Cher)
Tel. 02 54 80 68 42
Fax 02 54 80 63 68
M. and Mme Kamette

Rooms 3 and 2 suites of 2 bedrooms with shower and WC. **Price** 180-260F/27,44-39,63€ (1 pers.), 240-320F/36,58-48,78€ (2 pers.); suites 410-450F/62,50-68,60€ (3 pers.), 470-510F/71,65-77,74€ (4 pers.). Special rates after 2 nights. **Meals** Breakfast incl. No communal meal. **Restaurants** In Danzé (2km) and in La Ville-aux-Clercs (3km). **Facilities** Sitting room, tel., fishing, covered swimming pool. **Pets** Dogs not allowed. **Credit cards** Not accepted. **Nearby** Riding, tennis, golf; Loir châteaux, Loir valley. **Spoken** English, Spanish. **Open** All year. **How to get there** (Map 16): 15km north of Vendôme via D36 to Danzé, then D24 towards La Ville-aux-Clercs.

La Borde is a beautiful 1930s mansion in a large park. All the bedrooms overlook the park; they are comfortable, handsomely decorated and some are huge. The Bleue room is our favorite, but all are pleasant. Good, hearty breakfasts are served in a large, bright room which is both the television/living room and the breakfast room. You can enjoy a lovely covered, heated swimming pool, along with charming hospitality, and reasonable prices.

253 - Château de la Vaudourière

41360 Lunay
(Loir-et-Cher)
Tel. and fax 02 54 72 19 46
M. Clays and M. Venon

Rooms 2 with bath and WC. **Price** 450-580F/68,60-88,42€ (2 pers.). **Meals** Breakfast incl. Communal meals on request. **Facilities** Sitting room (TV), tel., swimming pool, park and forest (4 hectares). **Nearby** Restaurants (10km), tennis, millpond, fishing, 9-hole golf course; Loir Valley, Loire Valley, châteaux (Blois, Amboise, Chaumont, Tours). **Credit card** Visa. **Spoken** English. **Open** All year. **How to get there** (Map 16): 17km west of Vendôme towards Montoire D5, then Lunay on right D82. 3km of village: at the church follow signs.

The father of French poet Alfred de Musset was born in this lovely house lost in the country at the edge of a forest. The two bedrooms are just above the sitting room and can be reached by a remarkable spiral staircase carved in walnut. Luxuriously appointed with antique furniture (from the 16th to 19th centuries), decorated with shimmering fabrics, paintings and art objects, they express an art of gracious living, refined and very comfortable. Superb bathrooms with salon area. Very good breakfasts are served out of doors to the sound of songbirds. A friendly welcome.

254 - Le Clos

9, rue Dutems
41500 Mer
(Loir-et-Cher)
Tel. 02 54 81 17 36
Fax 02 54 81 70 19
Mme Mormiche
Web: www.france.bonjour.com/mormiche/

Rooms 4 and 1 suite of 2 bedrooms (4 pers.) with bath or shower and WC. **Price** 290-350F/44,21-53,35€ (2 pers.); suite 580F/88,42€ (4 pers.) depending on season. **Meals** Breakfast incl. No communal meal. **Facilities** Sitting room, billiards and bike rentals. **Pets** Dogs not allowed. **Nearby** Swimming pool, tennis, fishing, 18-hole golf course (15km); châteaux of Chambord, Blois, Talcy and Beaugency. **Credit cards** Eurocard, MasterCard, Visa. **Spoken** English. **Open** All year. **How to get there** (Map 16): Between Blois and Beaugency on N152, Autoroute A10 exit Mer-Chambord; then follows signs for Centre ville. The Rue Dutems is a semi-pedestrian street between the Place de Halle and the church.

You reach this 16th-century house via a pedestrian street. It is very quiet because of a vast shady garden in the back. Newly renovated, the interior is bright, tastefully and simply decorated in tones of écru. The very pleasant bedrooms have some antique furniture (from Directoire to 1900s style), elegant fabrics and impeccable bathrooms. The breakfasts are sumptuous and the young owners are extremely friendly.

255 - Manoir de Clénord

Route de Clénord
41250 Mont-près-Chambord
(Loir-et-Cher)
Tel. 02 54 70 41 62
Fax 02 54 70 33 99
Mme Renauld
E-mail: sg@clenord.com
Web: www.clenord.com

Rooms 4 with bath, WC and 2 suites (2-4 pers.). **Price** 390-690F/59,45-105,18€ (2 pers.), suites 950-1200F/144,82-182,94€. **Meals** Breakfast incl. Evening meals, by reservation. **Facilities** Sitting room, swimming pool, tennis, bicycles. **Nearby** 18-hole golf course; forest, Loire châteaux, wine cellars. **Credit card** Visa. **Spoken** English. **Closed** Dec 15 – Feb 15. **How to get there** (Map 16): From Paris, A10 exit Blois, towards Vierzon via D765. In village of Clénord, turn left on Mont-Près-Chambord; entrance 200m.

You drive down a small path to this 18th-century manor house. Here, Madame Renauld will greet you very warmly and show you the bedrooms, which are pretty and tastefully, elegantly decorated with antique furniture and lovely fabrics. All look out onto the formal gardens. Breakfast is served in a rustic dining room or on the terrace, weather permitting. You will find a very pleasant and restful atmosphere.

256 - Château de Colliers

41500 Muides-sur-Loire
(Loir-et-Cher)
Tel. 02 54 87 50 75
Fax 02 54 87 03 64
M. and Mme de Gélis

Rooms 4 and 1 suite (4 pers.) with bath and WC. **Price** 600-750F/91,46-114,33€ (2 pers.); suite 1000F/152,44€ (4 pers.). Plus local taxes depending on season. **Meals** Breakfast incl. No communal meal. **Facilities** Sitting room, tel., swimming pool in Jul and Aug, hot-air balloon and helicopter rides departing from the property. **Nearby** Restaurants (1km), kayak, 18-hole golf course, equestrian center, water sports, Loire châteaux. **Credit cards** Not accepted. **Spoken** English, Spanish. **Open** All year, by reservation in winter. **How to get there** (Map 16): Autoroute A10, exit Mer, follow towards Chambord to Muides-sur-Loire, then D951 towards Blois. Colliers on right, on bank of Loire, 300m after last house.

This fanciful 18th-century house enjoys an outstanding location on the banks of the Loire. The interior is truly elegant: the salons are superbly furnished, the dining room is covered with original frescos and the pretty bedrooms have cheerful fireplaces. Almost all have a splendid view over the Loire. (One has an amusing private terrace on the roof.) The owners are pleasant and discreet.

257 - En Val de Loire

46, rue de Meuves
41150 Onzain
(Loir-et-Cher)
Tel. 02 54 20 78 82
Mobile 06 07 69 74 78
Fax 02 54 20 78 82
Mme Langlais

Rooms 5 with bath or shower and WC. **Price** 350F/53,35€ (2 pers.). **Meals** Breakfast incl. No communal meal. **Facilities** Sitting room. **Pets** Dogs not allowed. **Nearby** Swimming pool, tennis, riding, golf; Loire châteaux. **Credit cards** Not accepted. **Spoken** English. **Open** Easter – Nov 1. **How to get there** (Map 16): 15km southwest of Blois via N152 towards Amboise, then right on D58 at Chouzy towards Monteaux as far as Onzain.

A long garden leads up to this pretty house surrounded by flowers. It is small and welcoming and has been decorated by Monsieur and Madame Langlais themselves, who have created a model of good taste and rustic comfort. The bedrooms are furnished with antiques and some have upholstered walls with matching lampshades. There is an inviting sitting room-dining room with deep armchairs in front of the fire. Breakfast includes 21 different types of preserves. This is a very beautiful place.

258 - Prieuré de la Chaise

8, rue du Prieuré
41400 Saint-Georges-sur-Cher
(Loir-et-Cher)
Tel. 02 54 32 59 77
Fax 02 54 32 69 49
M. and Mme Duret
E-mail: prieuredelachaise@yahoo.fr
Web: www.prieuredelachaise.com

Rooms 2 and 1 suite (6 pers.) with bath or shower and WC. **Price** 390F/59,45€ (2 pers.); suite 880F/134,15€ (6 pers.). **Meals** No communal meal. **Facilities** Sitting room, tel. ping-pong, billard, wine tasting. **Pets** Dogs not allowed. **Nearby** Restaurants (5km), tennis, riding, bicycle rentals, golf; Cheverny, Loire châteaux, vineyards. **Credit cards** Not accepted. **Spoken** English. **Open** All year, by reservation and deposit. **How to get there** (Map 16): 30km south of Tours. Autoroute A10, exit Amboise towards Montrichard, then towards Chissay-en-Touraine. After the bridge in Saint-Georges-sur-Cher, dir. La Chaise, then follow signs. **No smoking** in bedrooms.

This former priory, first built in the 12th century and reconstructed in the 16th, still has the original chapel on its grounds where the village feast-day is celebrated. The meadows and vineyards all around provide quiet and a broad vista. The house combines comfort and old-fashioned charm, with its wooden beams and old stone fireplaces. The brightly-colored bedrooms have antique furniture and comfortable bathrooms. The suite consists of three bedrooms, a bathroom and two toilets. The importance of wine in this region is shown by the old wine press and by a small museum where tools are displayed. And you can also sample the local vintages.

259 - Le Moulin de Choiseaux

8, rue des Choiseaux Diziers
41500 Suèvres
(Loir-et-Cher)
Tel. 02 54 87 85 01
Fax 02 54 87 86 44
Marie-Françoise and André Seguin
E-mail: choiseaux@wanadoo.fr
Web: //le-village.ifrance.com/choiseaux

Rooms 4 and 1 suite with bath or shower and WC. **Price** Rooms 300-370F/45,73-56,40€ (2 pers.); suite 450F/68,60€ (2 pers.), +100F/15,24€ (extra bed). **Meals** Breakfast incl. No communal meal. **Restaurants** "Les Calanques" (5km). **Facilities** Lounge (TV), swimming pool, bikes. **Pets** Animals not allowed. **Nearby** Restaurants (7km), karting, water sports on Loire, 2 golf courses; Châteaux of Chambord and Cheverny; Sologne Forest. **Spoken** English. **Open** All year. **How to get there** (Map 16): 15km northeast of Blois. Autoroute A10, exit "Mer", 3km after "Mer", turn on right. Signs via Diziers.

You will receive a most cordial welcome in this 18th-century mill with its little stream and water wheel, and a swimming pool for sunny days. On the ground floor, the dining room is warm and cozy with its old beams and rustic furniture. Upstairs are the bedrooms, some quite beautiful – we have a particular preference for the one called "Les Vieux Livres." The sitting room is now in the part that was the miller's home, where the bedroom "Le Pressoir" and the suite with its own little salon are also located. All the rooms are very quiet and the bathrooms are impeccable.

260 - Château de La Voûte

41800 Troo
(Loir-et-Cher)
Tel. 02 54 72 52 52
M. and Mme Provenzano
E-mail: chatlavout@aol.com

Rooms 5 with bath or shower and WC. **Price** 450-600F/68,60-91,46€ (2 pers.). **Meals** Breakfast incl. No communal meal. **Nearby** Restaurants (200m), 9-hole golf course in Ouques; Vendôme, Loir Valley, Loire Valley. **Credit cards** Not accepted. **Spoken** English. **Open** All year. **How to get there** (Map 16): 48km north of Tours, take D29 to Chartre sur-Loire, then on right via D305 and D917 to Troo.

The Château de la Voute stands with its back to the hillside and faces out onto two terraced gardens. Inside, the bedrooms each have a distinctive style and are furnished with attractive antiques. All of them have a view over the most charming of countrysides. Breakfast is served in the bedrooms or if weather permits on the flower-covered terrace. The whole place is friendly and comfortable, and just beside a lovely village that you can explore.

261 - Château de la Giraudière

41220 Villeny
(Loir-et-Cher)
Tel. 02 54 83 72 38
Mme Anne Giordano-Orsini

Rooms 2 with bath, WC, 3 with private bath, shared WC; 1 apart. (4 pers.), with 2 bedrooms, bath, WC, sitting room, kitchen. **Price** Rooms 380F/57,93€ (2 pers.); apart. (except in Jul and Aug): 2000F/304,89€, 3 nights min.; +400F/60,97€ (extra night). **Meals** Breakfast incl. No communal meal. Light meals possible. **Facilities** Sitting room (piano), tennis. **Pets** Dogs not allowed. **Nearby** Restaurants, fishing, riding, golf. **Credit cards** Not accepted. **Spoken** English. **Open** Easter – Nov 1. **How to get there** (Map 17): 25km south of Beaugency in D925 (exit aut. A10 in Meung/Loire), then 10km before la Ferté-Saint-Cyr, on right before the crossroads with the D18. 800m on right.

This attractive Louis XIII château has beautifully kept grounds and lies in mid-forest off a small lane. The interior is lovely, with light streaming in through the large living room windows, illuminating the elegant furniture. The bedrooms are very refined and have a lovely view over the gardens. The château is an excellent place to stay while visiting the Sologne. You will be made very welcome.

C   E   N   T   R   E

262 - Château de la Ferté

45240 La Ferté-Saint-Aubin
(Loiret)
Tel. 02 38 76 52 72
Fax 02 38 64 67 43
Catherine and Jacques Guyot
E-mail: catherine.guyot@worldonline.fr

Rooms 1 and 1 suite (2-3 pers.) with bath and WC. **Price** Rooms 1000F/152,44€ (2 pers.); suite 1100F/167,69€ (2 pers.), 1500F/228,67€ (3 pers.). **Meals** Breakfast incl. No communal meal. **Facilities** Sitting room, park (animal park, small farm), historic stables. **Pets** Dogs allowed on request. **Nearby** Health center, 27-hole golf course (1km); Chambord Château (30km), La Sologne, lakes. **Spoken** English. **Open** Easter – Nov 11. **How to get there** (Map 17): 18km south of Orléans. Follow N20, turn left at entrance to La Ferté-Saint-Aubin (still on N20).

This late 17th-century château, which is open to visits, is irresistibly charming and one of the most elegant in this part of France. The welcome is warm and friendly. The interior, which is being renovated, is already splendid (some rooms can be visited). Overlooking the moat, the bedrooms and suites have retained all their original character. Some are immense, but all are comfortable. There are beautiful, old-fashioned bathrooms. Excellent breakfasts are served in the bedrooms or in a salon reserved for guests.

263 - Sainte-Barbe

Route de Lorris - Nevoy
45500 Gien
(Loiret)
Tel. 02 38 67 59 53
Fax 02 38 67 28 96
Mme Annie Le Lay
E-mail: annielelay@aol.com

Rooms 2 with bath, WC, and 1 with shower, WC. 1 small house (5 pers.) with washroom, 2 WCs. **Price** 220-270F/33,53-41,16€ (1 pers.), 350F/53,35€ (2 pers.), 420F/64,02€ (3 pers.), +70F/10,67€ (extra pers.), small house en week-end 800F/121,95€ (2 pers.), 1200F/182,93€ (4-5 pers.). **Meals** Breakfast incl. Evening meals (separate tables) 150F/22,86€ (wine not incl.). **Pets** Dogs allowed in kennels. **Facilities** Sitting room, tennis, fishing, swimming pool. **Nearby** Riding, ball-trap, golf. **Credit cards** Not accepted. **Spoken** English. **Open** All year on request. **How to get there** (Map 17): 5km northwest of Gien via D44, Lorris road.

Despite its deceptively simple appearance, this old house, surrounded by fields and woods, offers guests gorgeous bedrooms furnished and decorated with taste and attention to detail. You will be made very welcome and can enjoy a sitting room for guests' use. The furniture, much of it Haute Epoque, a Chesterfield sofa, and numerous objects connected with hunting and riding lend special charm to Sainte-Barbe. Note also the "little house," which is ideal for a stay in a country setting. This is a lovely place.

264 - Ferme des Foucault

45240 Ménestreau-en-Villette
(Loiret)
Tel. and fax 02 38 76 94 41
Mobile 06 83 39 70 94
Mme Rosemary Beau

Rooms 3 with bath and shower, WC and TV. **Price** 360-420F/54,88-64,02€ (2 pers.), +100F/15,24€ (extra bed). **Meals** Breakfast incl. No communal meal. **Pets** Dogs allowed on request. **Nearby** Restaurants in the village and nearby, lake fishing, bikes, mountain bikes, riding, golf; Saint-Benoît Monastery, châteaux (Sully-sur-Loire, Chambord, Cheverny, Orléans). **Credit cards** Not accepted. **Spoken** English, German. **Open** All year, by reservation. **How to get there** (Map 17): 6km south of Marcilly-en-Villette via D64 towards Senneley for 6km. On right, follow signs Les Foucault; turn right at the end of the path, at the mailbox. **No smoking.**

In a truly calm setting in the heart of the Sologne forests, this old brick farmhouse offers impeccably-kept bedrooms (the years the owner spent in America have left her with both good humor and a no-nonsense attitude.) The downstairs bedroom has a lovely bath, an exit to the surrounding lawn and also an adjoining room with a convertible couch where one can laze or where a child can sleep. Upstairs under the sloping roof, the two other bedrooms (one with a terrace) are large and light. Copious breakfasts are served in a large sunlit room.

265 - La Mouche

45130 Meung-sur-Loire
(Loiret)
Tel. 02 38 44 34 36
Fax 02 38 46 52 49
M. and Mme Perrody
E-mail: perrody@3dnet.fr

Rooms 3 with bath, shower and WC. **Price** 350F/53,35€ (1 pers.), 390F/59,45€ (2 pers.). **Meals** Breakfast incl. No communal meal. **Restaurants** In Meung-sur-Loire and Saint-Ay. **Facilities** Sitting room. **Nearby** Fishing in the Loire (with permit), tennis, swimming pool, mountain bikes, fishing, kayaking, hiking, 18-hole golf course (20 km); châteaux (Chambord, Blois, Cheverny...), Orléans, Vendôme. **Credit cards** Not accepted. **Spoken** English. **Open** All year, by reservation from Nov to Mar. **How to get there** (Map 17): Autoroute A10 exit Meung-sur-Loire, then N152. 200m after the exit, towards Orléans, 1st road on right.

This 18th-century mansion on the banks of the Loire has a four-hectare park, a pond with water lilies, an orchard and a small French-style garden. Two bedrooms face the river. They are decorated with antique furniture and have large and very pleasant bathrooms. The third one, in Empire style, faces west toward the sunset. Breakfast is delicious, with homemade fresh fruit juice, and is served on the terrace in summer. The only weak point is the decoration of the common room, which ought to have a more delicate treatment.

266 - Château du Plessis

45530 Vitry-aux-Loges
(Loiret)
Tel. 02 38 59 47 24
Fax 02 38 59 47 48
M. and Mme de Beauregard

Rooms 3 with bath or shower and WC. **Price** 550F/83,84€ (2 pers.) and 1 child's room (no WC): 350F/53,35€ (2 pers.). **Meals** Breakfast incl. Evening meals, by reservation 200F/30,48€ (all incl.). **Facilities** Swimming pool and pond fishing. **Pets** Dogs not allowed. **Nearby** Riding, 18-hole golf course (7km); Orléans forest, Château de Sully, Château de Chamerolles. **Spoken** English, German. **Closed** Christmas and Aug. **How to get there** (Map 17): Autoroute A10, exit Orléans-nord, to Montargis. In Chateauneuf-sur-Loire, take on left Vitry-aux-Loges. In the village on left take: rue Pasteur and follow signs "Le Plessis".

Dating from the 17th century, the Château du Plessis is a ravishing edifice surrounded by a moat and set in a vast wooded estate. Bathed with light, the rooms are adorned with beautiful family furniture, much of which is 18th century and well represents the joyful nature of the decorative arts of that period. The guest rooms are elegant (we especially like the Jaune room), with traditional furnishings and full baths – some are just next to the room, but all are private. Monsieur and Madame de Beauregard are unaffected, refined, friendly hosts.

267 - Rue du Moulin

5, rue du Moulin
10190 Bucey-en-Othe
(Aube)
Tel. 03 25 70 34 09
M. and Mme Poisson-Dallongeville

Rooms 1 suite (2-3 pers.) with shower and WC. **Price** 330F/50,30€ (2 pers.), +100F/15,24€ (extra bed). **Meals** Breakfast incl. Evening meals at communal table, by reservation 180F/27,44€ (all incl.). **Facilities** Lounge, tel. **Pets** Small dogs allowed on request. **Nearby** Tennis (500m), mountain bikes; Cider Route, Troyes (history of the Middle Ages and Renaissance). **Spoken** Some English. **Closed** End Oct – end Feb. **How to get there** (Map 10): From Paris, autoroute A5, exit 19 Vulaines, or coming from east or north, autoroute A5, exit 20 Torvilliers. Dir. Estissac, then Bucey-en-Othe. 1st road on right going up hill.

Monsieur and Madame Poisson-Dallongeville, who lived abroad for years, today enjoy introducing guests to the points of interest in their adopted region and taking turns cooking the evening meal. The suite has its own entrance and adjoins the owners' lounge, where you are always welcome. You can also enjoy the beautiful garden which surrounds this quiet village house.

268 - La Maison de Marie

11, rue de la Motte
52220 Droyes
(Haute-Marne)
Tel. 03 25 04 62 30
(at meal times preferably)
Sylvie Gravier

Rooms 1 suite of 2 bedrooms (2-5 pers.) with sitting room, bath and WC. **Price** 270F/41,16€ (2 pers.), +100F/15,24€ (extra pers.), +50F/7,62€ (children 4-10 year); -15% for stay more 3 days +1F/0,15€/night. **Meals** Breakfast incl. No communal meal. **Facilities** Sitting room. **Nearby** Restaurants (400m), riding, mountain bikes, water sports at Lake Der Chantecoq, tennis; Montier-en-Der Stud Farm, migration of grey cranes. **Credit cards** Not accepted. **Spoken** English, Spanish. **Open** All year. **How to get there** (Map 11): 30km southeast of Vitry-le-François via D396, then D13 at Frignicourt, towards Lac de Der. In Giffaumont, towards Montier-en-Der, then D174 to Droyes. Follow signs.

This beautiful house is an excellent example of a local half-timbered architectural style. You will find an immense, very spacious suite, which has been recently installed and is ideal for a family or group of friends. With many windows, light parquet floors, a corner library and comfortable beds with elegant eiderdowns, it is an invitation to stay on. Excellent breakfasts are served in a pleasant room or outside near the bread oven. Youthful Sylvie Gravier will welcome you with friendly hospitality to this lovely place.

CHAMPAGNE-ARDENNE

269 - Domaine de Boulancourt

Longeville-sur-la-Laisne
Boulancourt
52220 Montier-en-Der
(Haute-Marne)
Tel. 03 25 04 60 18
Christine and Philippe Viel-Cazal

Rooms 5 with bath or shower and WC. **Price** 220 and 280F/33,53 and 42,68€ (2 pers., depending on bedroom), +75F/11,43€ (extra bed). **Meals** Breakfast 25F/3,81€. Evening meals (7:30PM) at communal or separate tables, by reservation 130F/19,81€ (aperitif and wine incl.); 80F/12,19€ (children). **Facilities** Sitting room, tel., fishing. **Pets** Dogs not allowed. **Nearby** Hiking, mountain bikes, tennis (2km); migration of grey cranes (Mar and Nov), churches, Lake. **Spoken** English, some German. **Open** All year. **How to get there** (Map 11): Autoroute A26, exit Arcis-sur-Aube, dir. Brienne-le-Château, then dir. Nancy, Saint-Dizier, Montier-en-Der via D400. In Louze, on left D182 dir. Longeville-sur-Laines. Cross D174 Longeville; 1km before the exit, first crossroads on the left.

Once called the Ferme du Désert, this guest house is set in quiet surroundings, with a very pleasant garden and a lake and river below. It is beautifully decorated with cheerful, bright colors. The refurbished bedrooms are charming and comfortable. Excellent evening meals often include local game. The fish comes from the nearby lake and boars are raised on the property. You will receive a very warm welcome.

270 - A Tarrazza

192, Marina di Fiori
20137 Porto-Vecchio
(Corse)
Tel. 04 95 70 33 57
M. and Mme Mesana

Rooms 1 suite (2-4 pers.) with shower, WC and TV. Rooms cleaned twice a week. **Price** 400F/60,98€ (2 pers., Jun and Sept), 500F/76,22€ (2 pers., Jul and Aug), 300F/45,73€ (2 pers., Oct 1 – May 30), +150F/22,87€ (extra bed). **Meals** Breakfast incl. No communal meal. **Restaurants** Nearby and clubhouse in residence in summer. **Facilities** Swimming pool, tennis. **Nearby** Beach (50m), diving, yacht harbor, 2 golf courses (5 and 25km); archeological sites, Aiguilles de Bavella, Bonifacio. **Spoken** English, Spanish, Italian. **Open** All year. **How to get there** (Map 36): 2km north of Porto-Vecchio. Telephone for directions.

Tucked away amidst oak and olive trees, La Terrazza is part of a residence and enjoys the use of four tennis courts, a huge swimming pool, and the beach. The bedroom (or family suite) is elegant, sober, and comfortable, opening onto a large terrace where a delicious breakfast is served in the shade of a bougainvillea. With its flowers, southern fragrances, and wonderfully warm hospitality, this is a delightful place from which to explore Corsica.

271 - Château Cagninacci

20200 San-Martino-di-Lota
(Corse)
Tel. 04 95 31 69 30
Fax 04 95 31 91 15
Family Cagninacci

Rooms 4 (1 with terrace) with bath and WC. Rooms cleaned every 2/3 days. **Price** 400-440F/60,97-67,07€ (2 pers., depending on season), +100F/15,24€ (extra bed). **Meals** Breakfast incl. No communal meal. **Facilities** Lounge, tel. **Pets** Animals not allowed. **Nearby** Restaurants (1km), tennis and beach (8km); Ethnography Museum, Bastia. **Spoken** English, Italian. **Closed** Oct 1 – May 15. **How to get there** (Map 36): 8km northwest of Bastia, take road for Cap Corse, then in Pietra Néra, take D131 to San Martino di Lota. House 500m before village.

A former 17th-century convent, rebuilt in the 19th century in the spirit of the patrician villas of northern Italy, this is one of the most beautiful châteaux in Corsica. Progressively renovated, the interior still has much of its original character, with huge, bright rooms and a monumental staircase. The pleasant bedrooms are simply furnished with antiques and are illuminated by a lovely columned window; the modern baths are immaculate. Delicious breakfasts are served on a terrace overlooking the luxuriant countryside, with the sea and the Island of Elba in the distance.

F R A N C H E - C O M T É

272 - Chez les Colin

Maison d'Hôtes de La Fresse
25650 Montbenoît
(Doubs)
Tel. 03 81 46 51 63
Christiane and Jacques Colin

Rooms 6 with shower and WC. **Price** 2150F/327,76€/week in summer, 3100F/472,59€/week in winter (per pers. in full board). **Meals** Breakfast incl. Communal meals at lunch and dinner. **Facilities** Sitting room, tel., watercolor and Yoga lessons in summer; week with cross-country skiing in winter; fitness packages. **Pets** Dogs not allowed. **Nearby** Cross-country skiing. **Credit cards** Not accepted. **Spoken** English, German. **Closed** Apr 15 – Jul 1; Sept 15 – Dec 20, by reservation. Special rates by telephone. 6 nights min. **How to get there** (Map 20): 10km east of Pontarlier via D47.

This former customs station on the peaks of the Jura Mountains offers inviting guest rooms furnished with pale-wood Franche-Comté furniture, thick eiderdowns and decorative objects. Each room has a washroom which is cleverly integrated into the decoration; the other bathroom facilities, all well-kept, are in the corridor. Guests come here for cross-country ski holidays organized by Jacques Colin, as well as for his wife's outstanding cuisine. This is a warm and friendly place to stay.

273 - Château d'Andelot

Rue de l'Église
39320 Andelot-les-Saint-Amour
Tel. 03 84 85 41 49
Fax 03 84 85 46 74
Mme and M. Susan
and Harry Belin

Rooms 5, 1 suite. **Price** Rooms 950F/144,82€ (2 pers.); suite 1295F/197,42€ (2 pers.). **Meals** Breakfast incl. Evening meals (regional cooking) at separate tables 220F/33,53€ (wine not incl.). **Facilities** Sitting room. **Pets** Animals not allowed. **Nearby** River fishing, riding, hiking or bicycling, 9-and 18-hole golf course; Jura Wine Route, Lakes of Vouglans. **Spoken** English. **Credit cards** All major. **Open** All year. (3 rooms in the keep closed Nov – Easter). **How to get there** (Map 19): 30km south of Lons-le-Saunier via A40, exit Bourg-Vriat, then N83 to Saint-Amour, then D3 to Andelot-les-Saint-Amour.

This 12th-century fortress-château towers over the foothills of the Jura, offering total peace and quiet. Our favorite bedrooms are those in the outbuildings, especially Number 4, which is decorated in shades of blue and overlooks the valley. Those in the keep still have a certain medieval austerity despite the lovely antiques with which they are furnished. You can enjoy regional specialties in the barrel-vaulted dining room or on the small terrace; and relax in front of the fireplace in the large salon. History buffs shouldn't miss the library with its books on the history of the Franche Comté.

274 - Abbaye
de Baume-les-Messieurs

39210 Baume-les-Messieurs
(Jura)
Tel. 03 84 44 64 47
M. Ghislain Broulard

Rooms 3 with bath or shower, WC and TV. **Price** 390F (1 or 2 pers.)/59,45€, +105F/16€ (extra pers.). **Meals** Breakfast incl. **Restaurant** "Ghotique Café" lunch and dinner except Mon: about 100F/15,24€ (wine not incl.). **Facilities** Sitting room, tel. Visit of the Abbey Jul 15 – Sept 15 from 10:00AM to 6:00PM; the rest of the year by reservation. **Pets** Dogs allowed (+30F/4,57€/day). **Nearby** Golf (20km), tennis, riding, lakes, swimming pool, sightseeing tours, hiking, mountain biking; Baume-les-Messieurs, Château Cholons. **Credit cards** All major. **Open** All year. **How to get there** (Map 19): 15km northeast of Lons-le-Saulnier via N183 dir. Poligny, then on right towards Voiteur, then Nevy-sur-Seille and Baume-les-Messieurs.

For a holiday steeped in history, this magnificent and beautifully preserved medieval abbey offers three guest rooms that are quite spacious yet a little spartan. The hospitality is kind and the restaurant meals are good even though the menu is limited. In summer meals are served out of doors and you can enjoy a lovely view of the valley. Many excursions available in the area to explore the Jura and its vineyards.

275 - Rue du Puits

3, rue du Puits
39100 Gevry
(Jura)
Tel. 03 84 71 05 93
Fax 03 84 71 08 08
M. and Mme Pilloud

Rooms 5 with bath or shower and WC. **Price** 310F/47,25€ (1 pers.), 460F/70,12€ (2 pers.), 610F/92,98€ (3 pers.). **Meals** Breakfast and dinner incl. (communal table). **Facilities** Sitting room. **Nearby** Tennis, riding, golf; Jura and Burgundy vineyards, forest of Chaux. **Credit cards** Not accepted. **Spoken** English, German. **Open** All year. Arrival from 16.00 (except by special arrangement at time of reservation). Half board only. **How to get there** (Map 19): 8km south of Dole via N73 towards Chalon-Beaune, then left on N5 towards Genève. Or Autoroute A39 exit Dole-sud; in 1.5km towards Geneva. First village on right.

Formerly a village farm, this large house still has its original beams and pillars. The sitting room is pleasant and bright, and the beautiful bedrooms have been redone, comfortably furnished, and decorated with prettily colored fabrics. With the first nice weather, the excellent, copious evening meal is served in the garden. The Picards are cheerful, humorous, and welcoming, and the breakfasts are superb.

F R A N C H E - C O M T É

276 - Château de Salans

39700 Salans
(Jura)
Tel. 03 84 71 16 55
Fax 03 84 79 41 54
M. and Mme Oppelt

Rooms 3 and 1 suite (3 pers.) with bath and WC. **Price** Rooms 450F/68,60€ (1 pers.), 550F/83,84€ (2 pers.); suite 650F/99,09€ (2 pers.), 750F/114,33€ (3 pers.). **Meals** Breakfast incl. No communal meal. **Restaurants** "La Marine" in Ranchot, "Le Tisonnier" in Velesmes-Essarts. **Facilities** Sitting rooms. **Pets** Dogs allowed on request. **Nearby** Fishing (Doubs), 9-and 18-hole golf course; Salines d'Arc-et-Senans, Dole and Besançon. **Spoken** English, German. **Open** All year. **How to get there** (Map 19): 18km west of Besançon. Autoroute A36, exit Gendrey, follow Dampierre, Saint-Vit. In Saint-Vit, to Salans.

Situated on the Doubs River, this château with its neo-classical facade is truly a delight. On its wooded grounds grow wildflowers, peonies, and irises along the banks of a little stream. The rooms have been tastefully refurbished, without ostentation and with a good eye for the past. Two rooms and the suite face the grounds, the third looks out on a church and the countryside. Full of refinements like embroidered sheets, bouquets of roses, two charming sitting rooms (one in Directoire style) and a large dining room, not to mention the discretion of the owners. An excellent address.

277 - Les Égrignes

Le Château
Route d'Hugier
70150 Cult
(Haute-Saône)
Tel. and fax 03 84 31 92 06
Mobile 06 84 20 64 91
Fabienne Lego-Deiber

Rooms 1 and 2 suites (with lounge) with bath or shower, WC. **Price** Room 310F/47,25€ (2 pers.), suites (2-4 pers.) 310-350F/47,25-53,35€ (2 pers.), +100F/15,24€ (extra pers.). **Meals** Breakfast incl. Evening meals at communal table 110F/16,76€ (wine incl.). **Facilities** Sitting room. **Pets** Dogs allowed on request. **Nearby** Besançon, Dole. **Spoken** English, German. **Open** All year. 2 days min. in Jul and Aug. **How to get there** (Map 19): 20km southwest of Besançon. Autoroute A36 exit 3 Besançon-Ouest, then D67 dir. Gray. 20km of Gray dir. Besançon. In Cult, follow signs.

At the edge of the village, in a lovely little park filled with flowers, this small château rebuilt under Louis XVIII is a rare example of Restoration style. Inside, many of the original features are still preserved: a fine columned stairway, trompe-l'oeil decoration, stuccos, lintels and fireplaces. The bedrooms have been renovated and decorated with great care and are most comfortable. Excellent breakfasts and dinners are served in the yellow dining room, beside a beautiful faïence stove. The owners, who care about the quality of the products they serve, have their own vegetable garden. A fine address with truly warm hospitality.

278 - La Maison Royale

70140 Pesmes
(Haute-Saône)
Tel. and fax 03 84 31 23 23
M. and Mme Hoyet

Rooms 7 with bath and WC. **Price** 450F/68,60€ (2 pers., 1 night), 400F/60,97€ (2 pers., from 2 nights). **Meals** Breakfast incl. No communal meal. **Facilites** Sitting room, mountain bikes and bicycles. **Pets** Dogs not allowed. **Nearby** Restaurants, fishing, riding, beach, golf (50km); abbey of Acey, small châteaux, Arc-et-Senans. **Spoken** English, German, Italian, Spanish, Japanese. **Closed** Oct 15 – Mar 31, by reservation. **How to get there** (Map 19): Autoroute A6 Dijon, A39 Dijon-Dole, exit Dole, to Gray, Pesmes (15km). **No smoking.**

Located in the center of the lovely village of Pesmes, the "Royal House" is a restored fortress dating from the 14th and 15th centuries, today offering guest rooms. All the bedrooms are different, those on the top floor overlook the countryside or the roofs of the old village. The Oiseaux room is inviting and cozy; Amarante, with its red dais, pays hommage to nearby Burgundy, once a powerful duchy. Breakfasts are served in a small room overlooking the spacious salon. The library is a restful place to read and to play chess or billiards.

279 - Le Clos Thibaud de Champagne

Le Petit Cessoy
77520 Cessoy-en-Montois
(Seine-et-Marne)
Tel. 01 60 67 32 10
Fax 01 64 01 36 50
M. and Mme Dineur

Rooms 2 with shower, WC and 1 suite (5 pers.) with 2 bedrooms, bath and shower, WC; TV and Tel. on request. **Price** 450F/68,60€ (2 pers.), +150F/22,86€ (extra bed). **Meals** Breakfast incl. Lunch and evening meals at communal table or not about 200F/30,48€ (wine incl.). Half board and full board (3 days min.). **Facilities** Sitting room, riding, bicycles, hot-air balloon on request. **Pets** Dogs allowed on request. **Nearby** Tennis, swimming pool, golf; Fontainebleau, Vaux-le-Vicomte. **Spoken** English, German, Spanish. **Open** All year. **How to get there** (Map 10): 12km southeast of Nangis. Autoroute A5, exit Châtillon-la-Borde, dir. Nangis, then Rampillon, Meigneux, Le petit Cessoy.

A 19th-century farm in the heart of wheatfields — a true haven of calm. Upstairs, all the bedrooms are comfortable: "Lavande" and "Vanille" have fine showers; "Canelle" is the largest and can be rented along with another room for the children. Its bathroom has a large tub, a shower and two wash basins. There is a garden and a billiard room and breakfast can be taken by the fireplace in the living room. Added to this, inventive cuisine featuring dishes based on market availability.

280 - Le Manoir de Beaumarchais

77610 Les Chapelles-Bourbon
(Seine-et-Marne)
Tel. 01 64 07 11 08
Fax 01 64 07 14 48
M. and Mme Charpentier
E-mail: Hubert.Charpentier@wanadoo.fr
Web: www.le-manoir-de-beaumarchais.com

Rooms 1 suite (2 pers.) with bath and WC (poss. TV). **Price** 700F/106,71€ (1 pers.), 750F/114,33€ (2 pers.). **Meals** Breakfast incl. No communal meal. **Facilities** Sitting room, pond (boat), bicycles. **Pets** Small dogs allowed on request. **Nearby** Restaurant (8km), tennis, swimming pool, golf; Vaux-le-Vicomte, Fontainebleau, Disneyland. **Spoken** English, German, Spanish. **Open** All year. **How to get there** (Map 9) : 43km east of Paris. Paris, Porte de Bercy dir. Metz-Nancy, exit 13, dir. Provins via 231. In Villeneuve-le-Comte, dir. Tournan (D96). 250m after Neufmoutiers, on left, follow signs.

This large manor house in late 17th-century Anglo-Norman style was in fact built in 1927 by the grandfather of the present owner, but the talent of the architect and the materials used make it look quite authentic. The light streams in through the large arcaded windows, giving the salon a warm inviting look. The suite for guests consists of a large bedroom and a delightful little round boudoir. It is comfortable and pleasant, furnished and decorated with pieces belonging to the family. The vast grounds surrounding the house assure perfect tranquility. The welcome is courteous.

ÎLE - DE - FRANCE

281 - La Ferme de Vosves

155, rue de Boissise
Vosves
77190 Dammarie-les-Lys
(Seine-et-Marne)
Tel. 01 64 39 22 28
Fax 01 64 79 17 26
Mme Lemarchand

Rooms 3 with bath or shower and WC. **Price** 250F/38,11€ (1 pers.), 280F/42,68€ (2 pers.), 380F/57,93€ (3 pers.), 480F/73,17€ (4 pers.). **Meals** Breakfast incl. No communal meal. **Restaurant** "L'Île aux Truites" in Vulaine. **Pets** Dogs allowed on request. **Facilities** Big garden. **Nearby** Châteaux of Vaux-le-Vicomte and Courances; towpath along the Seine and canal locks, Forest of Fontainebleau, Barbizon. **Credit cards** Not accepted. **Spoken** English, Italian. **Open** All year. **How to get there** (Map 9): 15km northwest of Fontainebleau (A6 Exit 12). N7 towards Fontainebleau. After Ponthierry, left on N472 for 3km, then right to Vosves.

Madame Lemarchand will receive you with great hospitality at this farmhouse located on the edge of the small village of Vosves. She is an artist and has decorated her house with excellent taste. You can choose between the bedroom, decorated in an elegant country style, or the atelier, very nice for families, with its high beams and large roof window. There is also a charming small, independent house with its big wood stove. The breakfasts are excellent and the prices truly reasonable.

282 - Bellevue

77610 Neufmoutiers-en-Brie
(Seine-et-Marne)
Tel. 01 64 07 11 05
Fax 01 64 07 19 27
Isabelle and Patrick Galpin
E-mail: ipgalpin@club-internet.fr
Web: www.club-internet.fr/perso/ipgalpin

Rooms 5 with shower, WC and TV. **Price** 230F/35,06€ (1 pers.), 270-290F/41,16-44,21€ (2 pers.), +90F/13,72€ (extra bed). 2 independent lodges 390F/59,45€ (2 pers.), +90F/13,72€ (extra pers.) **Meals** Breakfast incl. Communal evening meals by reservation 95F/14,48€ (wine not incl.), 60F/9,14€ (child). **Facilities** Sitting room, tel., bicycle rentals, pond, Ping-pong, game area for children. **Pets** Dogs allowed on request. **Nearby** Eurodisney (10km), concerts in churches. **Credit cards** Not accepted. **Spoken** English. **Open** All year. **How to get there** (Map 9): 40km east of Paris. Autoroute A4 towards Metz, exit 13 to Villeneuve-Lecomte; then towards Neufmoutiers-en-Brie. At church, follow signs.

Don't be alarmed by the houses you see as you drive up: Bellevue stands at the edge of the village and looks out on a vast expanse of fields. The five well-appointed bedrooms with mezzanines and the beautiful lodge are all comfortable and nicely decorated in shades of blue and white. Here and there you'll see a lovely object, a fine piece of furniture. A large room with a huge table and a smaller living room area are at your disposal. The welcome is a pleasant one. A good place to know, quite close to Paris, for individual travelers or families.

ÎLE - DE - FRANCE

283 - Le Manoir des Freyculs

Le Manoir des uns et des hôtes
77930 Perthes-en-Gâtinais
(Seine-et-Marne)
Tel. 01 60 66 03 31
Fax 01 60 66 07 21
Mme Michèle del Rio

Rooms 5 with bath, WC, tel. and TV. **Price** 650-750F/99,09-114,33€ (2 pers.). **Meals** Breakfast incl. Communal meals noon and evening by reservation 250F/38,11€ (wine incl.). **Facilities** Swimming pool, river fishing, riding on request (with suppl.), sauna, Ping-pong, gift shop. **Pets** Dogs allowed on request (+60F/9,14€/day). **Nearby** Golf; Fontainebleau Forest, Barbizon, antique market first Sun of every month. **Credit cards** Not accepted. **Spoken** English, Spanish. **Open** All year. **How to get there** (Map 9): 18km south of Evry. 45km from Paris via A6 towards Fontainebleau. 1st exit (Cély), turn left, cross Autoroute bridge, then first left and follow signs for "Freyculs" (about 2km).

This is a former canons' house situated deep in the countryside though not far from Paris. Five beautiful bedrooms here have just been tastefully redone and all have vast, ultra-modern bathrooms. There is a great amount of space around the house, but it is a shame that with the west wind you can sometimes hear the noise from the autoroute 600 meters away. Madame del Rio will welcome you enthusiastically and you can enjoy beautiful walks in the Fontainebleau Forest and its environs. You can go biking, have a swim in the swimming pool, or just relax by a nice open fire.

284 - Mont au Vent

2, route de Maule
Herbeville
78580 Maule
(Yvelines)
Tel. 01 30 90 65 22
Fax 01 34 75 12 54
Mme Turmel

Rooms 5 (2 with tel., TV) and 1 suite with bath and WC. **Price** 380-450F/57,93-68,60€ (2 pers.), +100F/15,24€ (extra pers.); suite 800F/121,95€ (4 pers.). **Meals** Breakfast incl. Evening meals on request 120F/18,29€ (wine not incl.). **Facilities** Sitting room; tennis, swimming pool, Jacuzzi. **Nearby** Versailles, Saint-Germain-en-Laye, Giverny (Monet's house), Thoiry, Saint-Nom-la-Bretèche Golf Club, forest and lake (500m.). **Credit cards** Not accepted. **Open** All year. **How to get there** (Map 9): 33km of Paris and 7km east of Orgeval, Autoroute exit Poissy, then towards Orgeval. In Orgeval (N13), turn left towards Maule. After village Les Alluets-le-Roi, first left towards Herbeville; first house on right after entering village.

Offering vast, sunny, traditionally furnished guest rooms, a swimming pool, tennis courts, a jacuzzi and other recreational possibilities, the "Windy Mountain" is a good place to stay for a country weekend near Paris. When you reserve a bedroom, ask only for one of the rooms on the ground floor, their carpets coordinated with beautiful fabrics in autumnal colors and each with a pleasant bath. In summer, breakfasts are served on the terrace with a magnficient view over the countryside.

285 - Domaine de la Bonde
30, route de Caudebronde
11390 Cuxac-Cabardès
(Aude)
Tel. 04 68 26 57 16
Fax 04 68 26 59 94
Mmes and M. Yager-Grandin
E-mail: welcome@labonde-cuxac.com
Web: //labonde-cuxac.com

Rooms 5 with shower and WC. **Price** 310F/47,25€ (1 pers.), 350-380F/53,36-57,93€ (2 pers.), +80F/12,19€ (extra bed). **Meals** Breakfast incl. Communal evening meals 150F/22,86€ (wine incl.). **Facilities** Sitting room, swimming pool. **Pets** Dogs allowed on request. **Nearby** Tennis, riding, mountain bikes, fishing, golf; Cathar Châteaux, Carcassonne, Canal du Midi, Corbières, Montagne Noire, Village du Livre. **Credit cards** Not accepted. **Spoken** English, German, Spanish, Italian. **Closed** Nov – mid Mar. **How to get there** (Map 31): 23km from Carcassone via D118 dir. Mazamet. Follow Cuxac-Cabardès, chambres d'hôtes.

This former textile mill, once part of a royal factory, has begun its new life as a guest house with charm and dignity. Breakfast is served beside the swimming pool or upstairs in the large salon, while dinner is in the spacious ground floor dining room, with beams of celadon green. The stately and often elaborate dinners contain such dishes as wild mushrooms with cream or magret de canard. All the bedrooms face south on the garden. The largest of them is decorated all in tones of white. The bathrooms are of Jura stone with showers level with the floor.

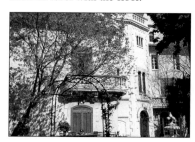

286 - Lou Castelet
Place de la République
11200 Fabrezan
(Aude)
Tel. 04 68 43 56 98
Fax 04 68 43 56 98
M. and Mme Wouters-Machiels
E-mail: lou.castelet@bigfoot.com
Web: //lou.castelet.free.fr

Rooms 4 and 1 suite with bath or shower and WC. **Price** 290-320F/44,21-48,78€ (1-2 pers.), +50F/7,62€ (extra bed); suite 435-480F/66,31-73,17€ (4 pers.). **Meals** Breakfast 35F/5,33€. Communal evening meals 120F/18,29€ (wine incl.). **Facilities** Sitting room, tel., swimming pool. **Nearby** Tennis, mountain bikes, canoeing, fishing, golf; Cathar Châteaux, Carcassonne, Lagrasse, Fontfroide Abbey, Minerve. **Credit cards** All major. **Spoken** English, German, Spanish, Dutch. **Open** All year. 3 days min. **How to get there** (Map 31): 30km west of Narbonne. A61 - E80 exit Lézignan. On left Fabrezan for 6km. At the village follow signs.

This "little castle" in a quiet little town in Cathar country was built in the mid-19th century and restored by a Belgian couple. The bedrooms, on the upper floors, are decorated with cheerful fabrics and have a marked character. Each has a particular feature: a balcony, a large bathroom (modern or traditional), a bed in an alcove. The suite is done in Provençal colors. Meals are served in the dining room, pure 19th century, or outdoors under a large umbrella. They may feature local specialties, vegetarian dishes or other on request. The terraced garden is still quite new, and one can do some star-gazing from the tower.

LANGUEDOC - ROUSSILLON

287 - La Ferme de la Sauzette

Route de Villefloure-Cazilhac
11570 Palaja
(Aude)
Tel. 04 68 79 81 32
Fax 04 68 79 65 99
Diana Warren and Chris Gibson

Rooms 5 with bath or shower and WC. **Price** 300-350F/45,73-53,35€ (1 pers.), 345-395F/52,59-60,21€ (2 pers.), +100F/15,24€ (extra pers.). **Meals** Breakfast incl. Communal evening meals on request 150F/22,86€ (all incl.). Half board from 645F/98,32€/day (2 pers.). **Facilities** Sitting room, tel., mountain bikes (extra charge). **Pets** Dogs not allowed. **Nearby** 18-hole golf course, tennis, lake, kayaking, swimming pool; Carcassonne, Cathar Châteaux, Fontfroide Abbey, medieval villages, caves. **Credit cards** Not accepted. **Spoken** English, German. **Closed** Feb and Nov 2 days min. between Jun and Sept. **How to get there** (Map 31): 5km from Carcassonne, at the foot of the city, go towards Palaja, Cazilhac for about 2km. In center of Cazilhac, follow signs. About 2km after village.

Only five kilometers from the very touristic city of Carcassonne, this old farmhouse is part of another world, set on a tranquil rise, cooled by a gentle breeze, and surrounded by vineyards and countryside. You will find five mansard bedrooms which are simple and comfortable. From their many travels, Diana Warren and Chris Gibson have absorbed an openness and sense of hospitality which confer warmth and conviviality to this beautiful place.

288 - L'Abbaye de Capversy

11600 Villardonnel
(Aude)
Tel. and fax 04 68 26 61 40
M. and Mme Meilhac

Rooms 3 with bath or shower and WC. **Price** 225F/34,30€ (1 pers.), 250F/38,11€ (2 pers.), 330F/50,30€ (3 pers.), 400F/60,97€ (4 pers.), 450F/68,60€ (5 pers.). **Meals** Breakfast incl. Communal evening meals 120F/18,29€ (wine incl.). **Facilities** Sitting room, tel., swimming pool, lake. **Pets** Dogs not allowed. **Nearby** Tennis, riding, golf; Carcassonne, Cathar Châteaux. **Credit cards** Not accepted. **Spoken** German. **Open** All year. **How to get there** (Map 31): 17km north of Carcassonne via D118 dir. Mazamet. In Les Auberges, on left sign "Abbaye de Capversy".

Of the former abbey tucked away in the Montagne Noire countryside, all that is left are several 16th century doors. Breakfast is served in a large room with a fire in season, and there is a cozy sitting room to watch television or do some reading. Behind the house, the former barn is open to the surroundings and serves dinner in summer with guinea hen fricassee and homegrown vegetables. The bedrooms are simple, white with a green trim of grape leaves. Two have a mezzanine where children can sleep.

LANGUEDOC-ROUSSILLON

289 - Le Cèdre

97, place Émile Jamais
30670 Aigues-Vives
(Gard)
Tel. 04 66 35 93 93
Fax 04 66 35 56 37
Abigail Barthélemy

Rooms 5 with bath or shower, WC and tel. **Price** 400-600F/60,97-91,46€ (2 pers.). **Meals** Breakfast incl. No communal meal. **Facilities** Sitting room. **Pets** Dogs allowed on request. **Nearby** Restaurants in the village and 3km, tennis, riding, beaches, mountain bikes, golf; Aigues-Mortes, Nîmes, La Camargue, Les Cévennes. **Credit cards** Not accepted. **Spoken** English, Italian. **Open** All year. **How to get there** (Map 32): 19km from Nîmes. Autoroute A9 exit 26 Gaillargues. At the entrance on right Aigues-Vives, sign in the village.

Between an elegant and thoughtful hostess, bedrooms decorated in perfect taste and a simply beautiful swimming pool, this place fairly oozes with charm. This typical southern stone house with its century-old cedar beside it stands right in the village and contains a wealth of treasures. Breakfast is served under wisteria vines. Bedroom floors have coconut matting and bedsteads of antique carpets. Everything is appealing down to the last details. Our favorites are the one with the Moorish-inspired bathroom-salon and the yellow suite upstairs.

290 - Le Rocher Pointu
Plan-de-Dève
30390 Aramon
(Gard)
Tel. 04 66 57 41 87
Fax 04 66 57 01 77
Annie and André Malek
E-mail: amk@imaginet.fr
Web: www.imaginet.fr/~amk

Rooms 4 with bath or shower and WC. 2 apart. and 2 studios with bath or shower and WC. **Price** 360-445F/54,88-67,83€ (2 pers.); studio 475F/72,41€ (2 pers.); apart. 510-600F/77,74-91,46€ (2 pers.); +65F/9,90€ (extra pers.).**Meals** Breakfast not incl. No communal meal. (Possibility summer kitchen). **Facilities** Sitting room, swimming pool. **Pets** Dogs not allowed. **Spoken** English. **Open** All year. **How to get there** (Map 33): 12km west of Avignon dir. Nimes by road along the Rhône. Before Aranon, at the SANOFI sign, go right dir. Saze for 2.3km, then follow signs.

In the heart of the countryside not far from Avignon, the "Pointed Rock" enjoys an outstandingly beautiful view of the environs. Everything evokes Provence here: the house, the pink oleanders, the crickets, the olive trees, the jovial atmosphere....The buildings are arranged around a central courtyard where you can cool off in summer. Inside, there is a large living room with several salon areas. The bedrooms are simply decorated, while the apartments are pleasantly decorated with wood, stone, and lovely fabrics. Served outside on several tables, breakfast is a mini-brunch. For meals, a small summer kitchen is at your disposal.

LANGUEDOC-ROUSSILLON

291 - Domaine de la Sérénité

Place de la Mairie
30430 Barjac
(Gard)
Tel. and fax 04 66 24 54 63
Mme Catherine L'Helgoualch

Rooms 1 with bath, WC; 1 suite (2 pers.) with lounge, bedroom, library, bath, shower and WC; 1 family suite (4 pers.) with 2 bedrooms, bath and WC. **Price** Room 340F/51,83€ (2 pers.); suite 500F/76,22€ (2 pers.), 690F/105,18€ (3 pers.); family suite 815F/124,24€ (4 pers.). **Meals** Breakfast incl. No communal meal. **Facilities** Lounge. **Nearby** Restaurants in Barjac, tennis (free for guests), riding, speleology, canoeing, rivers, swimming pool, natural 6-hole golf (7km). **Open** All year, by reservation. **How to get there** (Map 32): 40km from Bollène. Autoroute A7, exit Bollène, then dir. Pont-Saint-Esprit, then Barjac. In the village.

With the Place de l'Eglise behind, this luxurious 18th-century house overlooks a sumptuous panorama and the mountains of the Cévennes. Madame L'Helgoualch, an antique dealer, has tastefully preserved the character of the house, while fitting it with modern amenities. The bedrooms and suites are all charming and beautiful, with antique furniture and objects, old-fashioned or shimmering fabrics, and gorgeous bathrooms. The magnificent view is omnipresent, with the lush garden partly ringed by small, old stone walls and vaulted blockhouses.

292 - Mas de la Ville

Rue Basse
30430 Barjac
(Gard)
Tel. and fax 04 66 24 59 63
Mme Claudy Ciaramella

Rooms 4 with bath or shower and WC. **Price** 310-340F/47,25-51,83€ (1-2 pers.), 470F/71,65€ (3 pers.) - Special rates for 7 nights 2100F/320,14€ (1 pers.), 2300F/350,63€ (2 pers.), 3200F/487,83€ (3 pers.) and 1 family room (2 pers., 2 children) 550F/83,84€/1 night, 3800F/579,30€/7 nights. **Meals** Breakfast incl. No communal meal. Cold lunch served on request 60F/9,15€ (wine incl.). **Restaurants** in Barjac. **Facilities** Sitting room, swimming pool. **Pets** Dogs allowed on request. **Nearby** Golf course; Avignon. **Credit cards** Not accepted. **Spoken** English, German. **Open** All year, by reservation. **How to get there** (Map 32): 40km from Bollène, A7 exit Bollène, then towards Pont-Saint-Esprit, then Barjac.

This 18th-century village house looks austere from the street but on closer inspection, we discovered a large flower garden and a pretty swimming pool. The façade on the garden is charming with its small stairways, numerous balconies, and nooks and crannies everywhere. The bedrooms are all pleasant but our favorite has a small balcony and direct access to the garden. The two others overlook the Rue Basse, which is not noisy, and the room on the top floor has the advantage of a larger bathroom. The owner's welcome is very friendly.

293 - Mas Escombelle

La Villette
30430 Barjac
(Gard)
Tel. and fax 04 66 24 54 77
Isabelle and Antoine Agapitos

Rooms 3 with shower and WC. **Price** 250F/38,11€ (1 pers.), 300F/45,73€ (2 pers.), +50F/7,62€ (child's bed), +100F/15,24€ (extra bed). **Meals** Breakfast incl. Evening meals at communal table in summer 100F/15,24€ (wine incl.). **Restaurant** in Barjac. **Facilities** Lounge, swimming pool. **Nearby** Riding, canoeing on Cèze and Ardèche Gorges, 6-hole natural golf course; French Song Festival in Barjac in Jul; antiques (brocante) in Barjac (Easter and Aug). **Spoken** English. **Open** All year. **How to get there** (Map 32): 40km from Bollène. Autoroute A7, exit Bollène, then dir. Pont-Saint-Esprit, then Barjac. In Barjac, go towards Gendarmerie (Vallon, Pont d'Arc road); house is 300m beyond.

You will be captivated by the friendliness and good humor of the Agapitos family. Their mas, a traditional Provençal farmhouse, is very charming: from its shady courtyard with stone arcades, several steps lead to the flower garden and swimming pool. The comfortable bedrooms are tastefully decorated, each with its own theme: Campagne, Bateau and Contemporaine (which, with its stone vault, is very cool in summer.) We advise you not to take the bedroom next to the kitchen which is rented in high season. The dinners are very pleasant and the prices truly reasonable.

294 - Domaine des Clos

Route de Bellegarde
30300 Beaucaire
(Gard)
Tel. 04 66 01 14 61 / 06 11 81 62 78
Fax 04 66 01 00 47
M. and Mme Ausset

Rooms 5 with shower and WC. 3 apartments with bath, WC, Kitchen and lounge. **Price** 300-350F/45,73-53,35€ (2 pers., depending on season). Apart. 2000-4500F/304,89-686,02€/week (6 pers.). **Meals** Breakfast incl. in room. No communal meal. **Facilities** Swimming pool. **Pets** Dogs not allowed. **Nearby** Restaurant (1km), riding, boating, golf; Nîmes, Arles, Avignon, Les Baux de Provence, La Camargue, Pont du Gard. **Spoken** English, German. **Open** All year. **How to get there** (Map 33): In Beaucaire, take D38 dir. Bellegarde. 6km on left, follow signs.

This large traditional mas surrounded by orchards and vineyards has just been completely renovated. Upstairs, the bedrooms are all whitewashed in lovely pastel colors, with traditional brass or wrought iron beds, some nice vintage furniture, some charming antique pottery. The effect is sober and elegant, though still a bit stiff. Outside there are two fireplaces (with grill) with awnings, very useful in summer. The swimming pool is large enough to accommodate all the guests of this spacious farmhouse. Sandrine and David Ausset are most hospitable.

LANGUEDOC-ROUSSILLON

295 - La Maison des Rêves

Le Village
30260 Bragassargues
(Gard)
Tel. and fax 04 66 77 13 45
M. and Mme Chapman
E-mail: chapreve@aol.com

Rooms 2 with bath or shower. **Price** 280F/42,68€ (1 or 2 pers.). **Meals** Breakfast incl. Evening meals on request 100F/15,24€ (wine incl.). **Facilities** Lounge. **Pets** Dogs not allowed. **Nearby** Restaurants (4-7km), fishing (2km), riding, 18-hole golf (23km). **Spoken** English. **Open** All year. **How to get there** (Map 32): 23km northeast of Nîmes. D999 dir. Quissac. **No smoking.**

The "House of Dreams" is a dream come true for an English painter and his costume-maker wife, who fell in love with the colors of the region and the countryside. In the heart of the village next to a small square, the house can be recognized by its balcony and veranda giving onto a flower-covered terrace. On the ground floor, a bedroom in natural shades opens onto a private courtyard. The guest room upstairs is prettily decorated. Each has a private entrance. This is an inviting, quiet house on the road to Provence, where you will be greeted with friendly informality by an English couple (who still speak English better than they do French!)

296 - Le Mas du Seigneur

Altayrac
30530 Chamborigaud
(Gard)
Tel. and fax 04 66 61 41 52
M. and Mme Bertrand
E-mail: altayrac@club-internet.fr
Web: www.i-france.com/seigneur

Rooms 4 and 1 suite with shower and WC. **Price** 330-380F/50,30-57,93€ (2 pers., depending on season); suite 530F/80,79€ (4 pers.). Children under 5 (free). **Meals** Breakfast incl. Evening meals 95-110F/14,48-16,76€ (all incl.). Half board, 7 nights 250F/38,11€ (pers., double room). **Facilities** Sitting room, swimming pool, river fishing. **Pets** Dogs allowed on request. **Spoken** English, Spanish, Italian. **Closed** Nov 1 – Easter, except by reservation. 2 nights min. **How to get there** (Map 32): 4km north of Chamborigaud. Follow signs from the village.

If you love nature and peaceful surroundings, please persevere. Because once you're in Chamborigaud, you still have to drive up a small, winding road before you reach this beautiful 16th-century Cévennes mas. You won't regret the effort when you see the lovely, elegantly simple bedrooms (one ideal for a family), whitewashed and brightened with colorful Provençal fabrics. Each has a modern shower room. All around, you can take a deep breath of country air, relax, and enjoy the magnificent view far out over the Cévenne Mountains. In the evening, dinner is served beneath the celestial vault.... No wonder it's called "The House of the Lord".

297 - Le Mas Parasol
Rue Damon
30190 Garrigues
(Gard)
Tel. 04 66 81 90 47
Fax 04 66 81 93 30
Geoffroy Vieljeux
E-mail: gvieljeux@masparasol.fr
Web: www.masparasol.fr

Rooms 6 and 1 suite (in caravan) with bath or shower and WC. **Price** 500-900F/76,22-137,20€ (2 pers.). **Meals** Breakfast incl. Evening meals 2/week 140F/21,34€ (wine not incl.). **Restaurants** "Les Fontaines" in Uzès, "La Table de l'Horloge" in Saint-Quentin (10km). **Facilities** Sitting rooms, tel., swimming pool, parking, theme holidays. **Pets** Animals not allowed. **Credit Cards** Visa, Eurocard, MasterCard. **Spoken** English. **Open** Mar 15 – Nov 15. **How to get there** (Map 32): 8km west of Uzès via road to Anduze (D982). Just before the sign of Garrigues, go right on Avenue du Pigeonnier. Signs.

On the far side of the village facing the countryside, this old mas is an elegant expanse of terraces, stairways, and loggias. Decorated with extremely good taste, the very comfortable bedrooms are all simply lovely, with rough, painted walls, and carefully selected fabrics, furnishings, paintings, and engravings. Travelers who like their independence will enjoy the suite installed in an old wooden caravan that has kept its original woodwork. Breakfast/brunch is served on a large terrace in the garden or in a very pleasant room whose glassed-in arcades open onto the trees and the swimming pool. The owner is a young, very friendly host.

298 - Mas des Garrigues

La Leque
30580 Lussan
(Gard)
Tel. 04 66 72 91 18
Fax 04 66 72 97 91
Mme Sylvia Dollfus

Rooms 4 with shower and WC. **Price** 305F/46,49€ (1 pers.), 340F/51,83€ (2 pers.), 420F/64,02€ (3 pers.) depending on season. **Meals** Breakfast incl. Communal meals, by reservation. **Facilities** Sitting room, swimming pool, tennis (50F/7,62€/hr.), riding (90F/13,72€/hr.), French billards. **Pets** Dogs allowed on request. **Nearby** Swimming and fishing in rivers, canoeing, kayaking, golf; La Cocalière Caves, the Cévennes, Pont du Gard. **Credit cards** Not accepted. **Spoken** English, German. **Open** Mar – end Dec. 7 nights min. **How to get there** (Map 32): 30km west of Bagnols-sur-Cèze towards Alès for 25km; turn right towards Barjac for 7km to La Leque. At the entrance to village.

Lying at the foot of a hundred-year-old hamlet, this beautiful family house has retained all its original character. The pretty bedrooms are decorated with polished antique furniture and cheerful cotton fabrics. We loved the large salon with fireplace and billiard table, the beautiful dining room and the terrace where breakfast is served. For dinner, just cross the road to reach the little auberge kept by the owner's children. A pleasant welcome, an ideal place to spend a holiday.

LANGUEDOC-ROUSSILLON

299 - Château de Ribaute

30720 Ribaute-les-Tavernes
(Gard)
Tel. 04 66 83 01 66
Fax 04 66 83 86 93
M. and Mme Chamski-Mandajors
E-mail: chateau.de-ribaute@wanadoo.fr

Rooms 5 and 1 suite with bath and WC. **Price** Rooms 350-500F/53,35-76,22€ (2 pers.); suite 600F/91,46€ (3 pers.); +80F/12,19€ (extra bed). **Meals** Breakfast 40F/6,09€. Evening meals at communal table or not, Sat, and twice weekly in summer 200F/30,48€ (wine incl.) or 130F/19,81€ (wine not incl.). **Facilities** Restaurants (1km), sitting room, tel., swimming pool. **Pets** Dogs allowed (50F/7,62€/day). **Nearby** Tennis (free), riding, golf, cross-country and alpine skiing (35km). **Credit cards** All major except Amex and Diners. **Spoken** English. **Closed** Jan and Feb. **How to get there** (Map 32): 10km south of Alès via N110 dir. Montpellier. In Tavernes, on right D106 to Ribaute.

This château is a large family home integrated in the village, with a stunning 18th-century monumental staircase that leads to the reception rooms and the bedrooms. The bedrooms are large and comfortable, with antique furniture, but can be a bit austere in winter. As soon as there are enough guests, nice dinners are served in the large dining room or in the courtyard. Julie is in charge of the cooking while her parents take care of the guests. There is a spontaneous and family-style atmosphere. The garden is pleasant and a small swimming pool is wonderful for a dip after a day's sightseeing.

300 - Mas de l'Amandier

30720 Ribaute-les-Tavernes
(Gard)
Tel. 04 66 83 87 06
Fax 04 66 83 87 69
Sophie Lasbleiz and
Dominique Bernard

Rooms 3 and 1 family room with bath and WC. **Price** 390F/59,45€ (2 pers.); family room 640-760F/97,56-115,86€ (4-6 pers.). Children under 5 (free). **Meals** Breakfast incl. Evening meals, by reservation 130F/19,81€ (wine incl.). **Facilities** Sitting room, pond. **Nearby** Tennis, river swimming, 6-hole golf course; Nîmes, Saint-Jean-du-Gard, Uzès. **Spoken** English, Spanish, some Italian. **Open** All year. **How to get there** (Map 32): 10km east of Anduze. Dir. Nîmes for 7km, then on left dir. Alès. Follow signs from Ribaute-les-Tavernes.

Located in a pastoral hamlet, the beautiful old "Almond Tree Mas" has just been redone by its jovial young owners, who have installed four whitewashed bedrooms for guests. Old red floor-tiles, softly colored bedspreads, and large bathrooms contribute to an ambiance of relaxation and comfort. Breakfast with homemade preserves is served in the shade of a large chestnut tree or in a delightful small dining room. And everywhere you look, you'll have a magnificent view of the Cévennes.

301 - Le Moulin de Cors

30200 La Roque-sur-Cèze
(Gard)
Tel. and fax 04 66 82 76 40
or 06 08 51 73 13
M. and Mme Hedouin

Rooms 4 houses (5-8 pers.) with sitting room, kitchen, 1-2 bath, TV, hi-fi, tel., laundry, dishwasher, towels. Poss. housework 50F/7,62€/hr. **Price** House in low season 2000-4000F/304,89-609,76€ (heating not incl.), middle season 3500-6500F/533,57-990,91€, high season 5500-8500F/838,46-1295,81€ (heating and electricity incl.). 4 bedrooms week-ends in low season 800F/121,95€. **Facilities** Swimming pool, river fishing, mountain bikes, canoeing/kayaks. **Nearby** tennis (membership card provided). **Pets** Small dogs allowed. **Open** All year with deposit: 20%. 7 days min. (poss. week-ends in low season on request, 2 days min.). **How to get there** (Map 33): 10km southeast of Pt-St-Esprit. A7 exit Bollène, then Pont-Saint-Esprit, then Bagnols and "route de Barjac". Road after 7km on left.

In a remote site of southern Ardèche, this ancient mill, amid a profusion of flowers, stands above the waters of the River Cèze. Made up of several units, each with its own entrance and terrace. Beautifully renovated with excellent taste (terra cotta floors, walls in warm colors, harmonious furnishings), it has calm and comfort and a large swimming pool. A dream location for a holiday in Ardèche.

302 - Mas de Casty

Boisson
Allègre
30500 Saint-Ambroix
(Gard)
Tel. 04 66 24 82 33
M. and Mme Mesnage

Rooms 6 with shower, WC, and 1 apart. with 1 bedroom, sitting room, kitchenette, shower, WC, and 1 apart. with 1 bedroom, sitting room, kitchen, shower, WC, terrace and garden. **Price** 240-650F/36,58-99,09€; apart. 2900F/442,10€/week (2 pers. + 1 child); apart. 4100F/625,04€/week (2 pers. + 1 baby). Possibily to rent for 1 week 1 house (6 pers.). **Meals** Breakfast 35F/5,33€. No communal meal. **Restaurant** In Allègre. **Facilities** Sitting room, swimming pool. **Nearby** Golf, canoeing, Kayaking, Pont du Gard. **Credit cards** Not accepted. **Spoken** English. **Open** All year. 3 nights min. **How to get there** (Map 32): 48km northwest of Pont du Gard via D981 towards Uzès, then D979 through Lussan and D37. In Pont-d'Auzon, right on D16 towards Barjac for 2km.

Michèle and Alain Mesnage have restored by themselves this small paradise in the midst of the country. Located in two houses, the comfortable bedrooms are pretty and have some antique furniture. Breakfast is served on one of the terraces or in the summer dining room surrounded by a rock garden. The landscaped grounds cover five hectares and you can enjoy a garden full of flowers, a lovely swimming pool, and a very friendly welcome.

303 - Indeo

Hameau de Vacquières
30580 Saint-Just-et-Vacquières
(Gard)
Tel. 04 66 83 70 75
Fax 04 66 83 74 15
Mme Nicole Henderson

Rooms 5 rooms with shower and WC. **Price** 500F/76,22€ (2 pers.). **Meals** Breakfast 40F/6,09€. Communal meals, by reservation 200F/30,48€ (wine incl.). **Facilities** Sitting room, swimming pool, mountain bikes. **Nearby** Rock climbing, hiking, 9-hole golf course (15km), Uzès, Avignon, Orange, the Cévennes. **Credit cards** Visa, Mastercard. **Spoken** English, Italian. **Open** All year, by reservation. **How to get there** (Map 32): 15km northwest of Uzès via Alès. After Euzet, turn right onto D7 towards Saint-Just-et-Vacquières; in 4km, turn right towards Vacquières, go past Auberge Saint-Just and take first road on right. House with yellow shutters. **No smoking.**

Monsieur and Madame Henderson travelled the world before deciding to settle in this out of the way hamlet. On either side of a small lane, their two houses are decorated with utmost care and with many (sometimes fragile) souvenirs of their travels. The atmosphere is friendly, the bedrooms brightly colored and everything is meticulously clean. The blue room and the green one are a bit small, but especially pleasant in summer. Breakfast is outstanding, and served in summer on a terrace covered with flowers. A nice place for all who seek quiet and who like pretty things.

304 - Mas de la Fauguière

30610 Saint-Nazaire-des-Gardies
(Gard)
Tel. 04 66 77 38 67
Fax 04 66 77 11 64
Mme Edna Price

Rooms 2 with bath, shower, WC, and 2 with private shower, communal WC. **Price** 300-375F/45,73-57,16€ (1 pers.), 350-450F/53,35-68,60€ (2 pers.), +100F/15,24€ (extra pers.). **Meals** Breakfast incl. No communal meal. **Facilities** Sitting room, tel., swimming pool, riding. **Pets** Dogs not allowed. **Nearby** Restaurants (8.5km and 11km), tennis, fishing, mountain bikes, 18-hole golf course (40km); prehistoric caves, silk industry, medieval villages. **Credit cards** Not accepted. **Spoken** English, German, Dutch. **Open** All year. **How to get there** (Map 32): 15km southwest of Alès toward Montpellier, Saint-Christol-lez-Alès, then Lezan. Go around Lezan on left via circular road, then towards Quissac. In Canaules, take towards Saint-Nazaire-des-Gardies. Signs at Mairie. **No smoking.**

This old silkworm farm overlooks the vineyards and garrigue of the Gard plain, the countryside extending over both the Cévennes and the Lozère regions. The country character of this mas stops there, for the comfortable bedrooms and the beautiful garden are traditionally English in charm. Madame Price is a helpful and gracious hostess and her house offers you quiet, relaxation and sunshine in the heart of nature.

LANGUEDOC-ROUSSILLON

305 - Hôtel de l'Orange

7, rue des Baumes
30250 Sommières
(Gard)
Tel. 04 66 77 79 94
Fax 04 66 80 44 87
M. Philippe de Frémont

Rooms 6 with bath or shower, WC, TV and tel. **Price** 300-340F/45,73-51,83€ (1 pers., depending on season), 340-400F/51,83-60,97€ (2 pers., depending on season). Special rates for 1 week in autumn and winter. **Meals** Breakfast 40F/6,09€. Evening meals, by reservation. **Restaurants** "Olivette" and "L'Evasion" in Sommières. **Facilities** Sitting room (piano), swimming pool. **Pets** Dogs allowed (+30F/4,57€/day). **Nearby** 18-hole golf course (30km), tennis; Château de Sommières, villages nearby, Nîmes (30km). **Credit cards** Not accepted. **Spoken** English, German. **Open** All year. **How to get there** (Map 32): In village of Sommières on leaving Nîmes via D40.

This wonderful 17th-century mansion stands on a rocky slope in the center of town, dominating the little medieval houses all around. The centerpiece of the house is an outstanding monumental staircase, around which are spacious rooms carefully decorated in refined taste. The bedrooms are most comfortable, sober and elegant. There is a rooftop swimming pool surrounded by a pleasant terrace. Breakfast is excellent. This is a very fine address, halfway between a guest house and a small hotel.

306 - Cruviers

Route de Saint-Ambroix
Cruviers-Larnac
30700 Uzès
(Gard)
Tel. 04 66 22 10 89
Fax 04 66 22 06 76
Thérèse Delbos

Rooms 4 with shower and WC. **Price** 320F/48,78€ (2 pers.), 380F/57,93€ (3 pers.), 440F/67,07€ (4 pers.). **Meals** Breakfast incl. Half board +110F/16,76€ per pers. Evening meals, by reservation. **Facilities** Sitting rooms, swimming pool. **Pets** Dogs allowed on request. **Nearby** 9-hole golf course, tennis, riding (4km); Uzès, Pont du Gard, Gardon gorges, Nîmes, Anduze, Avignon. **Credit cards** Visa, MasterCard, Eurocard. **Open** All year. **How to get there** (Map 33): 5km north of Uzès towards Lussan (autoroute: Remoulins-Pont du Gard exit).

In this nicely-renovated little inn, four bedrooms have been installed for guests, all with southern exposure. Provided with mezzanines (convenient for families), they are simple but comfortable, but some have a drawback of inadequate soundproofing. At dinner, you will be served in a charming small dining room brightened by ravishing Provençal fabrics. Meals are prepared with products from the farm (ducks, chickens, vegetables, fruits...) and homemade preserves are served at breakfast. The young owner is most hospitable.

307 - Demeure Monte-Arena
Place de la Plaine, 6
Montaren and Saint-Médiers
30700 Uzès
(Gard)
Tel. 04 66 03 25 24
Fax 04 66 03 12 49
F. Plojoux-Demierre
E-mail: fplojoux.demierre@wanadoo.fr

Rooms 1 with shower and WC. 1 duplex suite (4/6 pers.) with bath and WC. **Price** Room 400F/60,97€ (2 pers.); suite 500F/76,22€ (2 pers.); +150F/22,86€ (extra bed). **Meals** Breakfast incl. Meals at communal table or not, lunch and dinner on request 90-160F/13,72-24,39€ (wine incl.). **Facilities** Tel., festival (theater, movie, music) in Aug, drawing classes all year, gatherings at the estate. **Pets** Dogs allowed on request. **Nearby** Tennis, boating, riding, golf; Uzès, Natural park of the Cévennes, Avignon, Camargue. **Credit cards** Visa, MasterCard, Eurocard. **Spoken** English, German, Italian. **Open** All year. **How to get there** (Map 33): 4km northwest of Uzès dir. Alès to Montaren. On right at the traffic light, after the church square, first street on left. House situated on château terrace.

Built in a portion of the château that is right in the heart of the village, this large house offers one bedroom and one duplex suite. It stands on a sunny terrace but is quite cool in summer. Just across the way is a delightful little garden full of greenery, next to a large vaulted room where meals are served. You will find a sympathetic welcome and an ambience filled with love for art and music.

308 - Le Grand Logis

Place de la Madone
30210 Vers-Pont-du-Gard
(Gard)
Tel. 04 66 22 92 12
Fax 04 66 22 94 78
Mme Florence Hopital and
M. Thierry Léger

Rooms 3 with bath or shower and WC. Rooms cleaned on request. Linens changed every 3 days. **Price** 350 and 400F/53,35 and 60,97€ (1 pers.), 400 and 450F/60,97 and 68,60€ (2 pers.), +130F/19,81€ (extra bed). **Meals** Breakfast incl. No communal meal. **Facilities** Sitting room. **Pets** Small dogs allowed. **Nearby** Restaurants (2-6km), swimming in La Gardon, tennis in village; Pont du Gard, Uzès, Avignon, Nîmes. **Credit cards** Not accepted. **Spoken** English. **Closed** Nov 15 – Mar 1, except by reservation. **How to get there** (Map 33): Autoroute 9, Remoulins exit, then towards Uzès/Pont du Gard Rive Gauche, D981, then 1st road on right after La Bégude-de-Vers.

Tastefully renovated by a former antiques dealer, this very pretty house has a beautiful façade with a superb balcony and wrought-iron railing. The shutters are closed during the day to keep the inside cool. A stairway (with worn-out steps) leads to the bedrooms which are furnished in a very simple, traditional style. The embroidered bed linens, the beautifully patinated walls and the small decorative friezes are lovely. There is a delightful garden and a terrace on the last floor, where you can sunbathe. Note that Le Grand Logis is indicated with a copper sign reading Chambres d'Hôtes (guest rooms).

309 - Château Massal

Bez et Esparon
30120 Le Vigan
(Gard)
Tel. and Fax 04 67 81 07 60
Mme du Luc

Rooms 3 with bath or shower and WC. **Price** 300-400F/45,73-60,97€ (1 pers.), 350-450F/53,35-68,60€ (2 pers.), +50F/7,62€ (extra bed). **Meals** Breakfast incl. Evening meals at communal table 100F/15,24€ (wine incl.). **Facilities** Sitting room, tel. **Nearby** Tennis, horse trekking, hiking, river, fishing, mountain bikes, riding; Guiherm Abbey, Tarn gorges, Millau, Le Vigan, the Causses. **Credit cards** Not accepted. **Spoken** English, Spanish. **Open** All year. **How to get there** (Map 32): 60km southeast of Millau via D999 dir. Ganges.

This "château" situated at the foot of Mont Aigual, just beyond Le Vigan, is really is stately family home of the 19th century. Its atmosphere is still familial and it is quiet despite its roadside location. Antique furniture adorns the living room, which opens on a garden. Here, next to a fountain, breakfast is served (including homemade fruitcake). The bedrooms upstairs, which you reach through a tower, are large, with a rather stately "Old French" air. One has a piano, another a lovely mosaic on the floor but only a half-size bathtub. The table d'hôte meals include such specialties as sautéed veal and civet of rabbit.

310 - Domaine de la Redonde

Montels
34310 Capestang
(Hérault)
Tel. 04 67 93 31 82
M. and Mme Hugues
de Rodez Bénavent

Rooms 1 suite with bath and WC (pers.) 2 nights min. 1 studio (4 pers.) with bath and WC 1week min. Room cleaned on request. **Price** Suite 600F/91,46€/night, studio 3500F/533,57€/week. Rental for 1 or 2 weeks (according to season). **Meals** Breakfast incl. in suite. No communal meal. **Facilities** Sitting room, swimming pool. **Pets** Small dogs allowed on request. **Nearby** Restaurants, tennis, riding, golf, barge trips on the Midi Canal, seaside; Narbonne, Carcassonne, Fontfroide Abbey, Minerve. **Credit cards** Not accepted. **Spoken** English, Spanish. **Open** All year. **How to get there** (Maps 31 and 32): 21km southwest of Béziers. Take D11 towards Capestang. South of Capestang on D16.

You will be warmly welcomed to this small château surrounded by vineyards, where you will find a pleasant suite reserved for guests. There is also a studio, which we do not recommend, as it looks a bit faded and worn. The interior has been tastefully decorated and handsomely furnished and the rooms are of spacious proportions. You can enjoy a garden full of flowers, a lovely swimming pool, and a very friendly welcome. A shady path leads to the swimming pool where you can enjoy the classic elegance of the château. You will be comfortable at this charming place, whose young owners are very hospitable, and allow you much privacy.

311 - Aux 3 Cèdres

166, avenue des Deux-Ponts
34190 Cazilhac-Ganges
(Hérault)
Tel. 04 67 73 50 77
Mme Isnard

Rooms 1 and 1 suite of 2 bedrooms (3 pers) with bath or shower and WC. **Price** 250-280F/38,11-42,68€ (1 pers.), 300-320F/45,73-48,78€ (2 pers.), +100F/15,24€ (extra bed). **Meals** Breakfast incl. No communal meal. **Restaurants** "Jocelyn-Melodie" (800m) and "Ferme Auberge Blancardy" (8km). **Facilities** Sitting room, access to swimming, fishing on property. **Nearby** Tennis, riding, hiking, mountain bikes, canoeing, kayaks in village, 18-hole golf course (18km), seaside (50km); Demoiselles Caves (7km), Eco Silk Museum, Cevennes Museum. **Credit cards** Not accepted. **Open** All year by resevation only. **How to get there** (Map 32): 45km northeast of Montpellier. From Montpellier, D986 to Ganges, 45km. In Ganges, D25, towards Cazhillac for 500m.

Aux 3 Cèdres is a former silk factory that Madame Isnard has converted into a warm and very comfortable home. It is decorated with many flowers and pretty colors, which relieve the austere look of the house from the street. Hikers and sports enthusiasts will particularly appreciate the hearty breakfasts which have been thoughtfully prepared for the numerous guests engaging in the many outdoor activities nearby. Note: Slippers are even provided for guests who return with muddy shoes!

312 - Domaine du Pous

Notre-Dame-de-Londres
34380 Hérault
(Hérault)
Tel. 04 67 55 01 36
Mme Élisabeth Noualhac

Rooms 6 with bath or shower and WC. **Price** 250F/38,11€ (1 pers.), 280-300F/42,68-45,73€ (2 pers.), +50F/7,62€ (extra bed). **Meals** Breakfast incl. No communal meal, but you can order a dinner from a nearby restaurant and have it delivered. **Facilities** Sitting room. **Pets** Dogs not allowed. **Nearby** Sailing, canoeing/kayaks, tennis, 9-hole golf course; Romanesque church, Saint-Guilhem, Demoiselles caves. **Open** All year. **How to get there** (Map 32): 30km north of Montpellier. Dir. Ganges via N986. 6km after Saint-Martin-de-Londres, on right D1E dir. Ferrière-les-Verreries. 2km, signs "Chambres d'hôtes".

The Domaine du Pous is an ancestral home whose courtyard opens out into a terrace facing an immense scrubland and a huge sky. You will find six luminous bedrooms with a scattering of antique furniture, two of which can be joined to make very pleasant suites for families or groups of friends. Most often, guests spend their time outdoors, enjoying life in the virgin wilderness. Or you might prefer the unique square sitting room, whose barrel vault is supported at the four corner by caryatids representing the four seasons. Madame Noualhac couldn't be nicer, and her prices are very reasonable for this superb place to stay.

313 - La Bergerie de l'Étang

34310 Montels
(Hérault)
Tel. 04 67 93 46 94
Fax 04 67 93 42 56
M., Mme and Marion Delaude
E-mail: delaude@infonie.fr
Web: bergerie.web-france.net.

Rooms 4 and 2 suites (with kitch.) with air-conditioning, bath or shower and WC. **Price** 400-500F/60,97-76,22€ (2 pers.), 700-800F/106,71-121,95€ (4-5 pers. in suite). **Meals** Breakfast incl. No communal meal. **Facilities** Sitting room, tel., swimming pool to be completed in 2000, yoga, hunting, fishing, mountain bikes. **Pets** Dogs not allowed. **Nearby** Restaurants (3km); golf; Cathar country, Canal du Midi, Montagne Noire, beaches, Wine Route. **Spoken** English, Spanish, Italian. **Open** All year, by reservation. **How to get there** (Maps 31 and 32): 10km north of Narbonne. From Narbonne D413 dir. Cuxac, Capestang, (from Béziers D11 dir. Capestang, then D413 Cuxac Narbonne) then Montels. On right in the village.

In a flat landscape of reed-fringed ponds, at the end of a little path, this old sheepfold combines charm, quiet and modernity. The house has just been tastefully restored, in soft harmonious colors and with attention to details. A large sitting room has soft deep couches to relax in a cool corner and there is a spacious terrace for breakfast in the sun. The bedrooms are all different, decorated with vintage pieces recalling visits to Africa and the glory of the south in blue and yellow. The bathrooms are modern and impeccable.

314 - Château de Quarante

25, avenue du Château
34310 Quarante
(Hérault)
Tel. 04 67 89 40 41
Fax 04 67 89 40 41
M. and Mme Neukirch
E-mail: chateau.quarante@wanadoo.fr

Rooms 4 and 1 suite with bath, shower and WC. **Price** 425F/64,79€ (1 pers.), 550-650F/83,84-99,09€ (2 pers.), +150F/22,86€ (extra bed); suite 750F/114,33€ (2 pers.), +150F/22,86€ (extra bed). **Meals** Evening meals at communal table or not 170F/25,92€ (wine not incl.). **Facilities** Sitting room, tel., pond, pétanque, bicycles. **Pets** Dogs not allowed. **Nearby** Fishing, riding, mountain bikes; Carcassonne, Canal du Midi, Cathar castles, Thau lake, beaches. **Spoken** English, German. **Closed** Jan 1 – Apr 1. **How to get there** (Map 31): 22km west of Béziers. From A9, exit Béziers-Ouest, D11 dir. Mazamet, via D11, crossing Montady and Capestang. 5km after Capestang, turn on D184 dir. Quarante (4km). At the entrance of the village.

This little 19th-century château stands at the edge of the village and is surrounded by a romantic park. Each room has been lovingly furnished, their styles varying with favorite objects installed here and there: some lovely antique furniture, modern paintings, family photos... all blend to create a cheery atmosphere. Table d'hôte with some very fine meals, but be sure to ask what costs extra. A very nice address.

315 - La Cerisaie

1, avenue de Bédarieux
34220 Riols
(Hérault)
Tel. 04 67 97 03 87
Fax 04 67 97 03 88
Mme Degenaar and M. Weggelaar
E-mail: cerisaie@wanadoo.fr

Rooms 5 and 1 studio (2 pers.) with bath or shower and WC. 2 small independent houses (2-4 pers.). **Price** 340-420F/51,83-64,02€ (2 pers.), +95F/14,48€ (extra bed); houses 490-550F/74,70-83,84€ (2-4 pers.). **Meals** Breakfast incl. Evening meals separate tables (except Wed) 130F/19,81€ (wine incl.). **Facilities** Lounge, tel. with meter, fax, swimming pool. Pets Animals allowed (+40F/6,09€). **Nearby** River fishing, tennis in village, riding, canoeing. **Spoken** English, German, Dutch. **Open** All year. **How to get there** (Map 31): 4km southeast of Saint-Pons de Thomières, dir. Béziers via N221; go 1km, turn left on D908. After the church on left.

A young Dutch couple will welcome you to this large family home which is named after the cherry trees planted in the garden. The simple, bright rooms are furnished with several antiques, and the bathrooms and showers are equipped with modern amenities. In summer, breakfast and dinner are served outside in a flower garden with large shade trees. An atmosphere of the past and youthful owners give a special touch to this village house.

316 - Les Mimosas

Avenue des Orangers
34460 Roquebrun
(Hérault)
Tel. and fax 04 67 89 61 36
M. and Mme La Touche
E-mail: la-touche.les-mimosas@wanadoo.fr
Web: perso.wanadoo.fr/les-mimosas/

Rooms 4 (2 for 1 suite) with shower and WC. 1 apart.weekly rental. Rooms cleaned every day. **Price** 365-445F/55,64-67,83€ (2 pers.). **Meals** Breakfast incl. Evening meals at communal table or not 155-175F/23,62-26,67€ (wine not incl.). **Facilities** Sitting room. **Nearby** Fishing, river swimming, canoeing/kayaks, archery, climbing, hiking, 9-hole golf course; Minerve, Oppidum d'Ensérune, caveaux (Saint-Chinian). **Spoken** English. **Open** All year. By reservation Nov – Feb. **How to get there** (Maps 31 and 32): 30km northeast of Béziers via D14 dir. Maraussan, then Cazouls-lès-Béziers, Cessenon, then Roquebrun. After the bridge, turn on left. Opposite the school. **No smoking.**

This charming village house, whose owners are connoisseurs of French wine and gastronomy, offers four large bright bedrooms tiled with local red tomettes. Some rooms are on the street but the village, traversed by the Orb River, is quiet. Meals are served on a delightful terrace in the shade of an arbor. It's a beautiful place to stay in the the magnificent Haut Languedoc Regional Park.

LANGUEDOC-ROUSSILLON

317 - Le Mas de Bombequiols

34190 Saint-André-de-Buèges
(Hérault)
Tel. and fax 04 67 73 72 67
Anne-Marie Bouëc and
Roland Dann

Rooms 4, 2 suites and 2 studios (kitchenette, lounge), with bath, shower and WC. **Price** Rooms 450F/68,60€, suites 600F/91,46€, studios 700F/106,71€ (price for 2 pers.); +150F/22,86€ (extra bed). **Meals** Breakfast incl. Evening meals at communal table or not 150F/22,86€ (all incl.). **Facilities** Lounge, tel., swimming pool, lake, possibility to rent an apartment with kitchenette (for week). **Pets** Animals not allowed. **Nearby** 18-hole golf course, skiing. **Open** All year, by reservation. **How to get there** (Map 32): 45km north of Montpellier via D986 towards Ganges to Saint-Bauzille-de-Putois, then turn left dir. Brissac via A108. In Brissac, on left dir. Saint-jean-de-Buèges for 5km, on left Bombequiols.

Set on a magnificent 125-acre estate with the remains of an abandoned golf course, this medieval stone house, partly restored over the centuries, welcomes you beneath the barrel vaults of a former shepherd's house which is today the dining room. Arranged around the interior courtyard, the bedrooms and apartments are huge, simply furnished and comfortable (some have a working fireplace), and all have a private entrance. You will enjoy a restful, quiet stay here, facing the incomparable beauty of the Seranne Massif.

318 - Le Mas de Gourgoubès

34190 Saint-André-de-Buèges
(Hérault)
Tel. 04 67 73 31 31
Mobile 06 03 50 72 84
Fax 04 67 73 30 65
M. and Mme Fauny-Camerlo
Web: www.intel-media.fr/gourgoubes

Rooms 6 (poss. suites) with bath or shower, WC (TV in some rooms). **Price** 500F/76,22€ (1 or 2 pers.), suites 700F/106,71€ (3 pers.), 900F/137,20€ (4 pers.), 1200F/182,93€ (4-6 pers.) and 1 apart. (weekly rental); +100F/15,24€ (extra bed). **Meals** Breakfast 50F/7,62€. Communal meals, by reservation 180F/27,44€ (all incl.). **Facilities** Sitting room, tel., swimming pool, theater. **Pets** Dogs allowed on request. **Nearby** Golf; prehistoric caves, Romanesque churches. **Credit cards** Not accepted. **Spoken** English, Spanish, Italian. **Open** All year, 3 days min. in summer. **How to get there** (Map 32): 45km north of Montpellier. In Montpellier, towards Ganges via D986 to Saint-Bauzille-de-Putois, then turn left toward Brissac via D108. In Brissac, turn left towards Saint-Jean-de-Buèges for 5km; turn right towards Gourgoubès.

This is a big, very old country house whose spacious bedrooms Madame Camerlo has made elegant and comfortable. Ingenious double-doors can be opened to convert the rooms into apartments which are perfect for families or groups of friends. Surrounded by beautiful, luxuriant countryside on the edge of the Cévennes, Le Mas de Gourgoubès is ideal for those who enjoy restful, genuine places and simple, friendly hospitality.

LANGUEDOC-ROUSSILLON

319 - Domaine de Saint-Clément

34980 Saint-Clément-de-Rivière
(Hérault)
Tel. 04 67 66 70 89
Fax 04 67 84 07 96
M. and Mme Bernabé

Rooms 3 and 1 suite with bath or shower and WC. **Price** 450-550F/68,60-83,84€ (1-2 pers.), 800F/121,95€ (4 pers. in suite). **Meals** Breakfast incl. No communal meal. **Facilities** Sitting room, tel., swimming pool. **Pets** Dogs allowed on request. **Nearby** Restaurant (2km), hiking, mountain bikes, riding, tennis, golf; Montpellier, Aigues-Mortes, Saint-Guilhem-le-Désert, prehistoric museum, Romanesque churches, the Cévennes. **Spoken** English, German, Spanish. **Open** All year. **How to get there** (Map 32): 7km north of Montpellier. Autoroute A9 exit Vendargues, then dir. Millau, Ganges, then on right D112 facing the greenhouses.

Just a few minutes from Montpellier, this 18th-century mansion and its swimming pool stand hidden from view by a pine forest. One of the downstairs bedrooms is always cool, as is the large salon-library with its decorative woodwork. The other bedrooms are upstairs, built around an old tiled patio. They are all large, with family furniture and modern paintings, a passion of the owners. The bathrooms are adorned with mosaics. Breakfast is served in a dining room giving onto the garden.

320 - Leyris

48240 Saint-Frézal-de-Ventalon
(Lozère)
Tel. and fax 04 66 45 43 60
M. and Mme Bonnecarrère
E-mail: leyrisba@club-internet.fr
Web: //perso.club-internet.fr/leyrisba

Rooms 1 with shower, WC and 2 bedrooms with shared shower and WC. **Price** 300F/45,73€ (1 pers.), 350F/53,35€ (2 pers.). **Meals** Breakfast incl. Evening meals at communal table, by reservation 100F/15,24€ (vine incl.); picnic basket on request. **Facilities** Sitting room. **Pets** Dogs allowed on request. **Nearby** Swimming, riding; Mont Lozère, springs of the Tarn. **Spoken** English, Spanish. **Open** May – end Oct, reservation by mail. **How to get there** 32): On N106 between Alès/Florac towards Saint-Frézal-de-Ventalon for 9.4km. At Plan de la Fougasse, on right, dir. Collet-de-Dèze for 1km, then on right dir. Leyris (2.7km). Last house (cul de sac).

This old mas stands alone amid calm and beauty in the heart of the Cévennes. You have to follow a long winding road to reach it, but the trip is well worth the effort. The house has been elegantly renovated and offers the comfort and refinement of light-walled bedrooms opening on a splendid landscape of woods and sky. Substantial breakfasts and dinners often made with home-grown garden vegetables are served on the terrace or in the pretty old-fashioned kitchen. The welcome is kind and thoughtful. Good for those fond of hiking or of pure relaxation.

LANGUEDOC-ROUSSILLON

321 - Mas Senyarich

66700 Argelès-sur-Mer
(Pyrénées-Orientales)
Tel. and fax 04 68 95 93 63
Mme Roméro

Rooms 5 with bath or shower and WC. **Price** 310F/47,25€ (2 pers.). **Meals** Breakfast incl. Evening meals, by reservation 110F/16,76€ (all incl.). **Facilities** Sitting room, swimming pool. **Nearby** Beach, sailing, water skiing, fishing, mountain bikes, 18-hole golf course (7km); Collioure, Catalogne, Romanesque architecture, vineyard (Banyuls, Rivesaltes), Tautavel (prehistoric sites). **Spoken** English, Spanish. **Open** All year. **How to get there** (Map 31): 3km northwest of Argelès. Red light, dir. Sorède, take under the bridge, then follow signs for 3km.

It's hard to believe that this large house, surrounded by aromatic Mediterranean vegetation with the smell of vacation in the air, is only a stone's throw from the crowded beaches on the coast. But you'll know it's true when you look out of the beautiful dining room: the sea is right there. The bedrooms are decorated simply but they are comfortable and some have a private entrance. In the evening, Madame Roméro will be delighted to serve you the specialties and wines of her lovely region.

322 - Mas Saint Jacques

66300 Caixas
(Pyrénées-Orientales)
Tel. and fax 04 68 38 87 83
Mobile 06 12 29 69 05
Ian Mayes
E-mail: MasStJacq@aol.com

Rooms 2 and 1 suite (4 pers.) with bath or shower and WC. 1 small house (2-3 pers.) with kitchen, sitting room/dining room, terrace, garden. **Price** 300F/45,73€ (2 pers.), suite 550F/83,84€. Small house 3000F/457,34€ (2 pers.)/week. **Meals** Breakfast incl. in bedrooms. Evening meals, by reservation 100F/15,24€ (all incl.); wine list includes vintage wines of the region; special menu with winetasting (wines of Roussillion) 150F/22,86€. **Facilities** Sitting room, tel., swimming pool. **Pets** Dogs allowed on request. **Nearby** Golf; Collioure, Museum of Modern Art in Céret. **Spoken** English, German. **Open** All year. **How to get there** (Map 31): 30km west of Perpignan. Aut. A9 exit Perpignan-sud toward Thuir. In Thuir, towards Elne for 2km then towards Céret for 5km. At Fourques, on right toward Caïxas via D2 for 44km. In Caïxas towards Mairie-église and signs.

Perched on a hillside is one of the rare houses in Caïxas: the Mas Saint-Jacques. It offers a suite and five simple, light bedrooms where wood is used extensively in the decor (two bedrooms are located in the garden annex.) There is a large, convivial, inviting sitting room for those in search of cool relaxation, and the swimming pool looks out over the countryside with the snow-capped Canigou Mountains in the distance. The hosts are friendly and attentive at this lovely place to stay in a beautiful region.

LANGUEDOC-ROUSSILLON

323 - Le Mas Félix

66300 Camelas
(Pyrénées-Orientales)
Tel. 04 68 53 46 71
Fax 04 68 53 40 54
Lucie Boulitrop
E-mail: lucie.boulitrop@wanadoo.fr

Rooms 4 and 1 suite with bath or shower, WC and TV. **Price** 290F/44,21€ (1 pers.), 330F/50,30€ (2 pers.), +80F/12,19€ (extra bed); 590F/89,94€ (4 pers. in suite). **Meals** Breakfast incl. Evening meals at communal table 130F/19,81€ (wine incl.). **Facilities** Sitting room, tel., ping-pong, pétanque. **Pets** Dogs not allowed. **Nearby** Hiking, mountain bikes, swimming pool, golf; Cathar castles, Perpignan, Castelnou (2km). **Spoken** English, German, Spanish. **Open** Apr 1 – Sept 15. **How to get there** (Map 31): 10km from Thuir dir. Ille/Têt. 5km after the last traffic circle, just before the Camelas bridge, road on left Mas Félix.

On a hilltop between vineyards and garrigue, this old mas enjoys a splendid view as well as superb calm. The bedrooms, named after Impressionist painters, all have direct access. They look a bit austere but are always cool in summer. The dinners prepared by the owner have the mingled savors of the Mediterranean, from Greece, Catalonia and North Africa, and are served on the terrace in fine weather. A reading corner for culture buffs and a shady music corner to laze away an afternoon.

324 - La Volute

1, place d'Armes
66210 Mont-Louis
(Pyrénées-Orientales)
Tel. and fax 04 68 04 27 21
Mme Schaff

Rooms 3 with shower and WC. **Price** 250F/38,11€ (1 pers.), 310F/47,25€ (2 pers.), +85F/12,95€ (extra bed). **Meals** Breakfast incl. No communal meal. **Facilities** 2 sitting rooms. **Pets** Dogs not allowed. **Nearby** Restaurants in Mont-Louis, swimming pool, pond and tennis in Mont-Louis; lake, rivers, sailing; Font-Romeu, Villefranche de Conflent, Andorre. **Spoken** English, Spanish. **Closed** Jun 1 – 15 and Nov 11 – 30. **How to get there** (Map 31): 74km southwest of Perpignan. In Mont-Louis, house on top of the entrance vault of the Mont-Louis citadel.

La Volute is situated in the former quarters of the governors of the old fortified town of Mont-Louis. It is on the ramparts, just over the postern entrance. The interior has been extensively renovated but still preserves some old elements. The entire effect is simple but inviting: pleasant bedrooms, all white, comfortable and well-kept (we prefer the one facing the garden). Excellent breakfasts are served with music in a small sitting room or outside facing the peaks of the Pyrenees. A very hospitable welcome.

LANGUEDOC-ROUSSILLON

325 - Las Astrillas

12, Carrer d'Avall
66500 Taurinya
(Pyrénées-Orientales)
Tel. and fax 04 68 96 17 01
M. Loupien

Rooms 5 and 1 suite with shower and WC. **Price** Rooms 260F/39,63€ (2 pers.), +70F/10,67€ (extra bed); suite 450F/68,60€ (4 pers.). **Meals** Lunch and evening meals at communal table, by reservation 100F/15,24€ (all incl.). **Facilities** Sitting room. **Nearby** Swimming pool, tennis, canoeing/kayaks, mountain bikes, golf practice, horse trekking, cross-country; Font-Romeu, Romanesque art, Festival Pablo Casals (Jul and Aug). **Spoken** English, Spanish. **Open** All year. **How to get there** (Map 31): 5km south of Prades dir. Taurinya. At the entrance of the village on left.

In the land of Romanesque art, music, and hiking, an old farmhouse has recently been converted into this pretty, welcoming guest house. It offers five bedrooms, simple and comfortable, with immaculate bathrooms. Meals are served in a beautiful dining room, lent atmosphere by antique furniture and objects. The prices are reasonable and Monsieur Loupien is a courteous host.

326 - La Casa del Arte

Mas Petit
66300 Thuir
(Pyrénées-Orientales)
Tel. and fax 04 68 53 44 78
Mme Fourment
E-mail: casadelarte@wanadoo.fr

Rooms 5 and 1 suite with bath, WC, minibar, tel. and TV. **Price** Rooms 420F/64,02€ (2 pers.); suite 650F/99,09€ (2 pers.). **Meals** Breakfast incl. **Facilities** Sitting room, swimming pool. **Pets** Dogs allowed on request. **Nearby** Tennis, sea and 18-hole golf course (30km); Font-Romeu (60km), Tautavel (prehistoric site), Prades Festival (summer). **Open** All year, by reservation. **How to get there** (Map 31): 15km southwest of Perpignan. Aut. La Catalane, exit Perpignan sud. Dir. Thuir, then dir. Ille-sur-Têt for 2km; signs on left.

Standing between the sea and the mountains in the land of apricot and nectarine orchards, the Casa del Arte is a small cottage of pink stone surrounded by luxuriant vegetation watered by the streams that trickle through the property. Pictures and works of art are hung to great effect in the house, creating an atmosphere of fantasy and tranquillity. The bedrooms and baths are spacious and have modern conveniences. The large living room and the swimming pool enhance the attractive, unusual charm of the house.

327 - Moncabirol

09500 La Bastide-de-Bousignac
(Ariège)
Tel. 05 61 68 88 42
Mme Hillari

Rooms 3 houses (1 with wheelchair access; 2 with 2 bedrooms) for 4-5 pers. with kitchen or kitchenette, sitting room or lounge, bath or shower and WC. Rooms cleaned on request with suppl. **Price** 300F/45,73€ (1 pers.), 350F/53,35€ (2 pers.), +50F/7,62€ (extra pers.). **Meals** Breakfast incl. No communal meal. **Facilities** Swimming pool. **Pets** Small dogs allowed. **Nearby** Restaurants (5km), Cathar castles, lakes. **Credit cards** Not accepted. **Spoken** Spanish. **Open** All year. Rental by night or week in summer and week the rest of the year. **How to get there** (Map 31): 6km from Mirepoix dir. Pamiers. In Besset, dir. Senesse de Senabugue-Mazerolles dir. Saint-Julien-de-Gras-Capou, signs Moncabirol.

In the charming hamlet of Montcabirol, not far from Mirepoix, you will find three little independent houses. The owner, Maryse, is dynamic and imaginative and endowed with an infectious good humor. With patience and talent, she has succeeded splendidly in transforming the houses with charm and comfort. Each house contains furniture, objects and fabrics of various styles, all blending in to make you feel right at home. For breakfast, Maryse provides all the necessary ingredients in advance, so that you can prepare your breakfast at any time that suits you.

328 - Le Poulsieu

Cautirac
09000 Serres-sur-Arget
(Ariège)
Tel. 05 61 02 77 72
Jenny and Bob Brogneaux

Rooms 4 with shower and WC. **Price** 180-200F/27,44-30,48€ (1 pers., top price Jul/Aug), 230-250F/35,06-38,11€ (2 pers., top price Jul/Aug), +50F/7,62€ (extra pers.). **Meals** Breakfast incl. Evening meals at communal table 70F/10,67€ (all incl.). At lunchtime there is a kitchenette for guests' use. **Facilities** Sitting room, riding, swimming pool, trips in 4-wheel drive. **Credit cards** Not accepted. **Spoken** English, German, Dutch, Spanish. **Open** Apr 1 – Nov 1. **How to get there** (Map 30): 12km west of Foix; in Foix head for Saint-Girons, then D17 towards Col de Marrons. After 10km at La Mouline; left opposite the bar; signposted (4km).

Having traveled the world, Jenny and Bob Brogneaux now welcome other travelers to their home in this old, isolated mountain village, which stands all by itself amid 70 hectares of woods and fields. The whitewashed bedrooms are simple, fresh and rustic in style. Evening meals are informal and in summer, dinner is served outside on a terrace overlooking the valley. There is plenty of horse riding in this remote but charming region and can you even have lessons in the art of harnessing horses.

329 - Ferme-Auberge de Quiers

Compeyre
12520 Aguessac
(Aveyron)
Tel. 05 65 59 85 10
M. and Mme Lombard Pratmarty

Rooms 6 with bath or shower and WC (1 for 4-5 pers. with mezzanine). Rooms cleaned once a week. **Price** 210F/32,01€ (2 pers.), mezzanine bedroom 310F/47,25€ (4 pers.), +30F/4,57€ (extra pers.). **Meals** Breakfast 30F/4,57€. Half-board except when Ferme-Auberge is closed 215F/32,77€/day and per pers. in double room (2 days min.). Evening meals in the Ferme-Auberge (except Mon all year and Sun in low season), only by reservation (separate tables) 90-105F/13,72-16€ (wine not incl.). **Open** Apr 1 – Nov 15, by reservation. **How to get there** (Maps 31 and 32): At Millau take N9 towards Severac. At Aguessac, N9, 500m on right to Compeyre; signs.

Not far from the medieval village of Compeyre, the Ferme-Auberge de Quiers overlooks an enchanting landscape of rolling hills. The bedrooms, in a converted barn, open directly onto the outside; they are pleasant and charming with white walls, natural wood furniture and a few touches of pink or blue. Dinner, served in the rustic dining room, is healthful and copious, based almost entirely on homegrown products. A friendly and inviting place for a holiday.

330 - Château de Camboulan

12260 Ambeyrac
(Aveyron)
Tel. and fax 05 65 81 54 61
M. and Mme Prayssac

Rooms 2 and 1 suite (4-5 pers. with bath, shower and 2 WC) with bath or shower, WC and TV. **Price** 300 and 350F/45,73 and 53,35€ (1 pers.), 350, 400 and 600F/53,35, 60,98 and 91,46€ (2 pers.), suite 700F/106,71€ (3 pers.); +80F/12,19€ (extra pers.). **Meals** Breakfast incl. No communal meal. **Facilities** Sitting room, tel., swimming pool, ping-pong, pétanque, 2 mountain bikes. **Nearby** Restaurants (7km), canoeing/kayaking; Lot, Saint-Cirq-Lapopie. **Pets** Dogs not allowed. **Closed** Nov 1 – Apr 30, by reservation. **Spoken** English, German, Dutch. **How to get there** (Map 31): 18km southwest of Figeac via D662 (Lot Valley) via Faycelles, Frontenac to cross roads Saint-Pierre Toirac. Cross railroad tracks, bridge over the Lot River, then D86 via Ambeyrac.

The elegant 13th- to 16th-century facade of this château towers over the valley of the Lot and you can enjoy this lovely view from the terrace swimming pool and its surrounding green lawn. The interior is decorated with period furniture, usually Louis XIII, but the renovation has removed some of the old charm. The rooms are all comfortable, with special mention for "Aliénor," the most expensive but really superb. Lovely breakfasts are served in a vast sitting room with a fireplace and the welcome is warm and jovial.

331 - Le Bouyssou

12800 Crespin
(Aveyron)
Tel. 05 65 72 20 73
Marie-Paule and Philippe Wolff

Rooms 4 houses to rent from Sat to Sat. Down payment required. Accommodates 2-3 pers., up to 6 pers. depending on house. Room cleaning responsibility of guest. **Price** 1900-3400F/289,65-518,32€/week (off-season, welcome meal included; activities not included); 3800-5800F/579,30-884,20€/week (in summer with activities). **Facilities** Dish- and clothes-washer, radio, CD player, Tel., sheets and towels (extra charge). **Pets** Small dogs allowed on request. **Facilities** Swimming pool, bicycles, mountain bikes, ateliers (pottery, photo and sculpture), hiking paths. **Nearby** River fishing, tennis, riding. **Closed** Nov 1 – Easter. **How to get there** (Map 31): 10km southeast of Naucelle dir. Rodez and Crespin, then dir. Lespinassol during 4km, then follow signs on left.

For a culturally stimulating vacation in beautiful natural surroundings, you won't find another place like Le Bouyssou, which offers four small houses each equipped with a kitchen and designed with a rare sense of well-being and comfort. The owners do everything to ensure that you enjoy interesting experiences and encounters. Apart from the swimming pool and the various crafts and artistic activities offered, you can even pick your own vegetables from the garden and make your own bread. It's a veritable art of living that is cultivated here.

332 - Vilherols

Vilherols
12600 Lacroix-Barrez
(Aveyron)
Tel. 05 65 66 08 24
Fax 05 65 66 19 98
Jean Laurens

Rooms 3 (1 with laundry, terrace and TV) and 1 family suite, (2-5 pers.) with shower and WC. **Price** 280F/42,68€ (2 pers.), 400F/60,97€ (2 pers., bedroom with terrace), +100F/15,24€ (extra bed). **Meals** breakfast incl. No communal meal. **Facilities** Lounge (TV), children's pool, bikes. **Pets** Not accepted. **Nearby** Restaurants (4km), riding, fishing, tennis, fitness center; Conques. **Open** Jul 1 – Aug 30. **How to get there** (Map 24): 5km south of Mur-de-Barrez via D904 dir. Entraygues-Rodez. 1km before Lacroix-Barrez, turn left dir. Vilherols. Signs.

Located in magnificent country, Vilherols is a dream village that has been inhabited for centuries by the charming Laurens family and their ancestors. Covered with traditional lauze stone like its neighbors, the main house contains a ravishing family suite, the breakfast room with beautiful regional furniture, and an immense fireplace. The other bedrooms are in a specially arranged annex. Pretty, comfortable, cheerful, they have huge bay windows which open onto the trees or a large terrace.

333 - La Manufacture

2, rue des Docteurs Basset
31190 Auterive
(Haute-Garonne)
Tel. and Fax 05 61 50 08 50
Mme Balansa

Rooms 4 with bath or shower and WC. **Price** 290F/44,21€ (1 pers.), 380F/57,93€ (2 pers.), 490F/74,70€ (3 pers.); +90F/13,72€ (extra bed). **Meals** Breakfast incl. No communal meal. **Facilities** Sitting room, swimming pool, fishing (Ariège), bicycles, mountain bikes, ping-pong. **Pets** Dogs allowed on request. **Nearby** Tennis, riding, hiking, mountain bikes, canoeing/kayaking, 18-hole golf course (30km); Toulouse, Canal du Midi, medieval villages, Cathar castles, grottoes of Ariège. **Open** All year. **How to get there** (Map 30): 32km south of Toulouse. RN20 dir. Foix-Andorre. In Auterive, 2nd traffic light on left dir. Centre-ville. After the bridge, in the street opposite the Post Office.

This beautiful building, which was a textile factory in the 18th century, is situated in a peaceful quarter of Auterive, near the banks of the Ariège River. The rooms are arranged around a superb central staircase and the decor (18th and 19th century) is charming and authentic. The bedrooms are of considerable proportions and the furniture, though antique, is quite comfortable. The bathrooms are modern and pleasant and the welcome is cordial.

334 - Serres d'en Bas

Route de Nailloux
31550 Cintegabelle
(Haute-Garonne)
Tel. and fax 05 61 08 41 11
M. and Mme Deschamps

Rooms 5 with bath or shower and WC. **Price** 220F/33,53€ (1 pers.), 250-275F/38,11-41,92€ (2 pers.), +80F/12,19€ (extra bed); suite 480F/73,17€ (4 pers.). **Meals** Breakfast incl. Evening meals at communal table 90F/13,72€ (all incl.). Half board from 5 days. Gourmet weekend (1 night, 2 meals and breakfast) 750F/114,33€ (2 pers., wine incl.). **Facilities** Sitting room, tel., laundry room, swimming pool, volleyball, croquet, badminton, tennis. **Pets** Dogs not allowed. **Nearby** Water sports (Lake); Cintegabelle, Montgeard. **Credit cards** Not accepted. **Spoken** Spanish. **Open** Easter – Nov 1. **How to get there** (Map 30): 40km south of Toulouse. Exit RN20 in Toulouse, go past Auterive for 7km, go left towards Cintegabelle, then towards Nailloux for 3.5km.

Perched on a hillock in gently rolling countryside, this inviting rustic house, named "The Greenhouses Down Below," opens out onto a luxuriant carpet of grass and shrubs. The bedrooms and the suite are comfortably equipped with modern bathroom facilities. With the first sunny weather, guests enjoy relaxing outdoors and admiring the splendid view over the hillsides. The owners are very welcoming and helpful. A nice place for a family visit.

335 - Château de Larra

Larra
31330 Grenade-sur-Garonne
(Haute-Garonne)
Tel. 05 61 82 62 51
Baronne de Carrière

Rooms 3 with suite with bath or shower and WC. **Price** 350-400F/53,35-60,97€ (2 pers.); suite 500F/76,22€ (3-4 pers.). **Meals** Breakfast incl. Evening meals at communal table 130F/19,81€ (wine incl.). **Facilities** Sitting room. **Pets** Dogs allowed on request. **Nearby** Riding, golf; Belleperche Abbey, Caumont, Pibrac, Montauban, Toulouse. **Credit cards** Not accepted. **Open** Easter – Nov 1. **How to get there** (Map 30): 30km northwest of Toulouse. On A62 exit 10, then N20 towards Grisolles, Ondes, Grenade. At Grenade, signposted. It's on D87.

The 18th-century ambience of the Château de Larra remains intact, with Louis XV furniture and painted fabrics in the salon, plasterwork in the dining room, and an impressive staircase with unusual wrought-iron bannisters. The bedrooms and the suites are large, pleasant, and old fashioned, but charming. The aging bathrooms, however, could do with a good renovation to add some modern amenities. You will enjoy excellent breakfasts and dinners, and Madame de Carrière is a vivacious hostess.

336 - Stoupignan

31380 Montpitol
(Haute-Garonne)
Tel. and fax 05 61 84 22 02
Mme Claudette Fieux

Rooms 4 with bath or shower and WC. **Price** 300F/45,73€ (1 pers.), 500F/76,22€ (2 pers.), +100F/15,24€ (extra bed). **Meals** Breakfast incl. No communal meal. **Restaurants** "Le Club" and "L'Auberge de la pointe". **Facilities** Sitting room, tennis, lake on property. **Pets** Dogs allowed on request. **Nearby** Riding (18km), swimming pool (4.5km), Palmola golf (7km); Verfeil (village), Lavaur (Cathedral). **Credit cards** Not accepted. **Spoken** English, Spanish. **Open** All year. **How to get there** (Map 31): 20km north of Toulouse via N88, towards Albi; or via A68, exit 3, to Montastruc. 500m after the traffic light, D30 towards Lavaur-Montpitol, then turn right to Stoupignan.

Madame Fieux will receive you with extremely warm hospitality at this beautiful Louis XIII house. The four bedrooms are spacious, decorated with antiques and very elegant, as are the bathrooms. Beautiful linens and silverware add a further refined touch to the communal dining table where, on request, a delicious regional meal is served. There is a lovely private park with trees and a beautiful view over the valleys nearby. Stoupignan is truly a charming place to stay.

337 - Domaine de Ménaut

Auzas
31360 Saint-Martory
(Haute-Garonne)
Tel. 05 61 90 21 51
(at meal times)
Mme Jander

Rooms 1 and 1 suite (2 bedrooms, 4 pers.) with bath and WC. **Price** 350F/53,35€ (2 pers.), 600F/91,46€ (3-4 pers.). **Meals** Breakfast incl. Evening meals on request 70F/10,67€. **Facilities** Sitting room, garage, lakes, fishing, swimming. **Pets** Animals not allowed. **Nearby** Tennis, skiing, golf, photo safaris; museums, tours of Cathar country. **Credit cards** Not accepted. **Spoken** English, German. **Open** All year. **How to get there** (Map 30): About 20km east of Saint-Gaudens, Toulouse N117. In Boussens towards Mancioux, then D33; 5km before D52 (Saint-Martory/Aurignac) go right and follow the fence.

Situated on a vast wooded property containing three small lakes, the Domaine de Ménaut seems far from all civilization. This 225-acre estate lies in the midst of a lovely, unspoiled forest. The immaculate interior is tastefully decorated, with elegant antique-style furniture in the dining room and sitting room. The comfortable bedrooms have beautiful bathrooms and there is a sunny terrace for summer breakfasts and dinners. Nature lovers and all those who seek peace and quiet will find the Domaine to their taste.

338 - Château du Bousquet

31570 Saint-Pierre-de-Lages
(Haute-Garonne)
Tel. 05 61 83 78 02
Fax 05 62 18 98 29
M. and Mme de Lachadenède

Rooms 1 suite (2 pers.) with 1 room (2 pers), shower, WC, tel. and TV. Rooms cleaned on request. **Price** 350F/53,35€ (2 pers.), 600F/91,46€ (4 pers.). **Meals** Breakfast incl. No communal meal. **Facilities** Lake fishing, pétanque, ping-pong. **Pets** Animals not allowed. **Nearby** Restaurants (4.5km in Fonvegrives), golf, tennis, riding; Toulouse, La Montagne Noire, medieval villages (Revel). **Closed** Christmas. **How to get there** (Map 31): 15km southeast of Toulouse. Dir. Castres, Mazamet (or exit 17 by the Rocade), for 8km, then on right, dir. Saint-Pierre-de-Lages. At the exit of Saint-Pierre-de-Lages on left, dir Vallesvilles for 800m.

Just nine miles from Toulouse yet in the heart of the country, this solid, pink-brick château is surrounded by well-proportioned buildings and an immense park with large trees. It offers guests a delightful suite with a small salon and television, to which the adjacent bedroom can be joined. The ensemble is bright and cheerful, and it has a panoramic view of the bucolic countryside. The pleasant breakfast room and the quiet spots in the garden put a charming finishing touch on this friendly place to stay.

339 - Le Petit Roquette

31570 Sainte-Foy-d'Aigrefeuille
(Haute-Garonne)
Tel. and fax 05 61 83 60 88
M. and Mme Chanfreau-Phidias

Rooms 1 with bath or shower, WC and 1 suite (2-4 pers.) with bath and WC. **Price** 270F/41,16€ (1 pers.), 300F/45,73€ (2 pers.); suite 350F/53,35€ (2 pers.), +120F/18,29€ (extra bed). **Meals** Evening meals 100F/15,24€ (wine incl.). **Facilities** Sitting room, tel., swimming pool. **Nearby** Restaurants (3km), fishing, tennis, golf; Albi, Cordes, Carcassonne, Montagne Noire, Cathar castles. **Spoken** English, German, Spanish. **Open** All year. **How to get there** (Map 30): 14km northeast of the center of Toulouse dir. Castres. In Quint-Fonsegrive, at the town hall, on right D18 dir. Quint/Revel. From sign exit of Quint, 2nd on right. 3km to Roquette.

This long low farmhouse has been renovated and transformed into an opulent home. We particularly recommend the family suite, with a rustic style bedroom, which is both lovely and comfortable, and a private sitting room that can sleep one person. Fine breakfasts and dinners are served next door, in a large sitting room with lots of antique furniture and in good weather, under an awning facing the garden. Nice view over the Lauraguais valleys. The owners, a youthful retired couple, are friendly and helpful.

340 - Au Soulan de Laurange

Juilles
32200 Gimont
(Gers)
Tel. and fax 05 62 67 76 62
M. Crochet and M. Petit

Rooms 3 with bath or shower and WC. **Price** 310F/47,25€ (1 pers.), 350F/53,35€ (2 pers.), 450F/68,60€ (3 pers.). **Meals** Breakfast incl. Evening meals at communal table or not, by reservation 120F/18,29€ (wine incl.). **Facilities** Sitting room, tel., swimming pool. **Nearby** Mountain bikes, tennis, riding, golf; Planselve and Cistercian abbeys, Auch, Lectoure. **Spoken** English, Spanish, Italian. **Open** All year. **How to get there** (Map 30): 25km from Auch dir. Toulouse via N124 for 22km. In Gimont dir. Saramon (D12) for 3km and signs on right.

Soulan means sunny, a good description of this beautiful 18th-century house that stands atop a hillside in Gers and, with its pink coating, resembles a Tuscan villa. The bedrooms are on the ground floor. Two of them face a valley planted with wheat and corn. All have been redone with vintage objects and furniture found in local antique shops. The bathrooms are modern and pleasant. There is a table d'hôte meal with local specialties (magret de canard with honey, fresh vegetable pie...) and an inviting swimming pool when the weather is fine.

341 - Castelnau de Fieumarcon

32700 Lagarde-Fimarcon
(Gers)
Tel. 05 62 68 99 30
Fax 05 62 68 86 91
M. Jean Calviac
E-mail: Castelnau@lagarde.org

Rooms 15 rooms located in 10 houses. **Price** 500F/76,22€ (1 pers.), 600F/91,24€ (2 pers.). **Meals** Breakfast 50F/7,62€. Communal meals 150-250F/22,86-38,11€ (wine not incl.). **Facilities** Tel. **Pets** Dogs not allowed. **Nearby** Restaurants (10km), tennis, riding, swimming pool, walking, mountain bikes, golf; Gers, Lectoure, Condom, Auch, concerts. **Spoken** English, German, Portuguese. **Credit cards** All major. **Closed** Feb. **How to get there** (Map 30): 8km west of Lectoure dir. Condom D7. 4km on right, Lagarde-Fimarcon.

This little fortified village overlooking the beautiful Gascon countryside is a privileged spot, preserved and protected by its owner. It is unusual in that its rooms are located in ten different houses. They have been carefully restored and are furnished and decorated in a manner that is simple but elegant and well-adapted to the local style: terra cotta, wooden floors, paintings, vintage furniture... The bedrooms, usually large and bright, face either the hamlet, the valley or the little garden. The bathrooms are modern. There are kitchen facilities for those who want to cater for themselves. A stopover here feels like living in another time.

342 - Le Moulin de Mazères

32450 Lartigue
(Gers)
Tel. 05 62 65 98 68
Fax 05 62 65 83 50
Régine and Raymond Bertheau

Rooms 4 with shower and WC. Rooms cleaned on request. **Price** 280F/42,68€. **Meals** Breakfast 30F/4,57€. Evening meals at communal table 125F/19,05€ (all incl.). **Facilities** Sitting room, swimming pool, fishing, riding, horse stalls and track. **Nearby** Tennis, squash, riding, in Auch 18-hole golf course (20km), Auch Cathedral, Castelnau, Barbarens, fortified churches. **Credit cards** Not accepted. **Spoken** English. **Open** All year. **How to get there** (Map 30): 17km southeast of Auch, towards Toulouse, in Aubiet take D40, go past Castelnau dir. Héréchou and go 3.5km on D40.

Located on the edge of a small road, this very pretty old mill, which has been tastefully restored, is surrounded by cool, lush vegetation. From the four spacious bedrooms you will hear the soft, reposing sound of the water tumbling through the mill; from the large bay window of one room, you can see the water flowing below. Riders with their horses are welcome at the Moulin de Mazères. The swimming pool and the rich breakfasts prepared by Madame Bertheau complete the feeling of relaxation and pleasure to be enjoyed here.

343 - Le Vieux Pradoulin

32700 Lectoure
(Gers)
Tel. 05 62 68 71 24
Mme Martine Vetter

Rooms 1 suite of 1 room and sitting room and 2 rooms sharing 1 bath, and WC. **Price** 200F/30,48€ (1 pers.), 250F/38,11€ (2 pers.). **Meals** Breakfast incl. No communal meal. **Restaurant** "Le Bastard" (1km). **Facilities** Sitting room, tel. **Nearby** Swimming pool, tennis, fishing, riding, golf; Cistercian Abbey, cloisters, châteaux. **Credit cards** Not accepted. **Open** All year. **How to get there** (Map 30): North of Auch via N21 towards Agen. Just before Lectoure, crossroads; take the road to Condom, turn left after 500m.

A very quiet house despite the road, Le Vieux Pradoulin is built on a Gallo-Roman site and on display are ancient oil lamps, terra cotta fragments and other treasures; the overall effect has a hint of kitsch. The lovingly arranged bedrooms overlook the garden and have comfortable antique beds. The bathroom is shared, but this is a small drawback at this charming, informal place where you will be welcomed like friends. The owner, a seasoned traveler, has been to the ends of the earth and can beguile guests with a multitude of tales.

344 - La Tannerie

32170 Miélan
(Gers)
Tel. and fax 05 62 67 62 62
M. and Mme Bryson

Rooms 3 (1 with TV) with bath and WC. **Price** 275-320F/41,92-48,78€ (2 pers.). **Meals** Breakfast incl. No communal meal. **Facilities** Sitting room, TV, refrigerator. **Nearby** Restaurants (2-6km), tennis in village, riding (1km), in Tillac 9-hole golf course (10km), water sports (14km), swimming in Miélan (1km), fishing; Cirque de Gavarny, villas and churches. **Credit cards** Not accepted. **Spoken** English, Spanish. **Closed** Dec, Jan, Feb and 2 weeks in Jun. **How to get there** (Map 30): 40km southwest of Auch, N21 towards Tarbes; in Miélan, before the church, turn right on small street.

We were totally charmed by this beautiful house, its handsome balustraded terrace, the garden, the paintings hung in the staircase, and above all, by its delightful owner, Madame Bryson. The three bedrooms are bright and spacious, though the one with pine furniture is simpler than the others. In the elegant room that serves for reading and watching television, there is an electric kettle for making coffee or tea. With the first sunny days, breakfasts and dinners are served outside at tables with parasols. La Tannerie is delightful for its hospitality, tranquility and the charming view of the hillsides nearby.

345 - La Garlande

Place de la Mairie
32380 Saint-Clar
(Gers)
Tel. 05 62 66 47 31
Fax 05 62 66 47 70
Nicole and Jean-François Cournot
E-mail: nicole.cournot@wanadoo.fr

Rooms 3 with shower and WC; possibility suites. 2 child's rooms (1 with basin, shower and 1 with a private washroom but on the lower floor). **Price** 280-320F/42,68-48,78€ (2 pers.). **Meals** Breakfast incl. Evening meals, by reservation 90F/13,72€ (wine incl.). **Facilities** Sitting room. **Pets** Dogs not allowed. **Nearby** Tennis, Saint-Clar lake (swimming, pedalo…), riding, swimming pool, 9-hole golf course; Saint-Clar, Condom, Lectoure, Fourcès. **Spoken** English. **Closed** 1 week in Aug. **How to get there** (Map 30): 35km northeast of Auch via N21, then D953 at Fleurance. In the center of Saint-Clar.

Standing in the heart of a tranquil old village with its beautiful covered market, this large 17th-century house is majestically oriented around an imposing stone staircase. Still graced with traditional character, the bedrooms are comfortably decorated, their baths modern. The kitchen, where breakfast is served, is delightful. You can relax in the large living room or in the garden, and you will be greeted with friendly hospitality.

346 - La Lumiane

Grande Rue
32310 Saint-Puy
(Gers)
Tel. 05 62 28 95 95
Fax 05 62 28 59 67
M. and Mme Scarantino
E-mail: la.lumiane@wanadoo.fr

Rooms 5 with bath or shower, WC and tel. **Price** 380F/57,93€ (2 pers.). **Meals** Breakfast incl. Evening meals at communal table 140F/21,34€ (wine incl.). **Facilities** Sitting room, swimming pool. **Nearby** Tennis (free, 100m), 18-hole golf course (18km); Condom, Lavardens, Lectoure, Larressingle, Flaran Abbey, Vic-Fezensac. **Spoken** English, Italian. **Credit cards** All major. **Open** All year. **How to get there** (Map 30): 11km southeast of Condom to Fleurance.

This fine 17th-century mansion is situated in the heart of the village next to a lovely garden and a very beautiful church. The bedrooms have been newly created and are cheery, comfortable and refined. The pleasant sitting room is decorated in a spirit that is classic yet up to date. A large swimming pool surrounded by flowers offers a lovely panorama over the Gers valley. Breakfasts are excellent and the welcome most attentive.

347 - En Bigorre

32380 Tournecoupe
(Gers)
Tel. 05 62 66 42 47
Jacqueline and Jean Marqué

Rooms 5 with shower and WC. Rooms cleaned on request. **Price** 280F/42,68€ (2 pers.). **Meals** Breakfast incl. Half board 220F/33,54€ per pers. (in double room). Evening meals at communal table 80F/12,19€ (all incl.) **Facilities** Sitting room, tel., swimming pool, putting green, fishing. **Nearby** Tennis, golf; Saint-Clar, Cologne, Avezan, Solomiac. **Credit cards** Not accepted. **Open** All year. **How to get there** (Map 30): 40km south of Agen via N21 towards Lectoure, then left on D27. Before Lectoure follow signs for Saint-Clar and Tournecoupe.

This is a renovated village house surrounded by a spacious garden. The bedrooms are pleasantly decorated. Breakfast and dinner are served in a pretty dining room or under a canopy (equipped with a barbecue) beside the swimming pool. You will enjoy good regional cuisine at very reasonable prices. The hosts are charming.

348 - Le Rive Droite

1, chemin de Saint-Jacques
32730 Villecomtal-sur-Arros
(Gers)
Tel. 05 62 64 83 08
Fax 05 62 64 84 02
Philippe and Myriam Piton
E-mail: rivedroite2@wanadoo.fr

Rooms 1 suite with 1 large bedroom, 1 small bedroom and 1 sitting room, bath and WC. **Price** 400F/60,97€ (2 pers.), 640F/97,56€ (3 pers.), 690F/105,18€ (4 pers.). **Meals** Breakfast incl. No communal meal. Restaurant is part of the house (service 12:00PM-1:30PM, 8:00PM-9:00PM), menus + carte (spec. foie gras). **Facilities** Parking, visits of canning plant. **Pets** Dogs not allowed. **Nearby** Golf, riding, water sports and Jazz festival in Marciac (15km); Saint-Sever Abbey, Pyrénées Natural park and skiing (40km), Lourdes (40km). **Credit cards** Amex, Diner's. **Closed** period of "Toussaint" holiday (end Oct) - By reservation. **How to get there** (Maps 29 and 30): 25km north of Tarbes. In the village, near the church on N21.

The reputation of "La Rive Droite" as a quality restaurant had long been established when the owners, taking advantage of its setting in a beautiful 19th-century house, decided to install a suite for guests. The main bedroom, large and comfortable, owes its charm to its windows opening on three sides to a garden shaded by tall trees. Although the road is nearby, the double-glazed windows filter out all noise. The second bedroom is smaller but just as comfortable. The large sitting room is an inviting spot to chat or relax. The welcome is smiling and considerate.

349 - Château de Cousserans

46140 Belaye
(Lot)
Tel. 05 65 36 25 77
Fax 05 65 36 29 48
M. and Mme Georges Mougin
E-mail: château.cousserans@wanadoo.fr

Rooms 5 with bath and WC. **Price** 750F/114,33€ (2 pers.), 950F/144,82€ (3 pers.). **Meals** Continental breakfast incl. No communal meal; possible cold meal on request. **Facilities** Music room (organ and 2 pianos), swimming pool, fishing. **Nearby** Restaurants (4km); Prehistoric sites, medieval villages, music festivals, Wine Route. **Credit cards** Not accepted. **Spoken** English, Spanish. **Open** Easter – Nov 1. **How to get there** (Map 30): 30km from Cahors via D911. At Castelfranc, towards Belaye, then towards Montcuq via D45 on left for 3km.

This amazingly well-preserved castle of the 15th century stands amid a cluster of trees, just off a side road. Its medieval appearance contrasts sharply with the interior, which has been remodeled with an eye to maximum comfort. An elevator takes you to the bedrooms on the upper story. These are fully carpeted, soberly decorated in pale colors and furnished with some nice antique pieces. The delightful music room is more authentic in appearance, as is the bedroom on the ground floor. Breakfast is served in a bright dining room or outside on the terrace of the castle.

350 - Château La Gineste

46700 Duravel
(Lot)
Tel. 05 65 30 37 00
Fax 05 65 30 37 01
M. and Mme Lamothe

Rooms 3 with bath, WC, tel, TV and 2 suites (4 pers.) with bath, WC, tel. and TV. **Price** 671F/102,29€ (1 pers.), 726F/110,67€ (2 pers.); +165F/25,15€ (extra bed). Suite 870F/132,63€ (1 pers.), 946F/144,21€ (2 pers.); +165F/25,15€ (extra bed). **Meals** Breakfast incl. Lunch and evening meals at communal table or not 165F/25,15€ (wine not incl.). **Facilities** Sitting room, tel., swimming pool. **Nearby** Tennis, riding, golf; Bonaguil, fortified bastides. **Credit cards** All major. **Spoken** English, Spanish, Portuguese. **Open** All year. **How to get there** (Map 30): 35km from Cahors or Villeneuve via D911.

This large winery is situated within a loop of the Lot River. It is an old family mansion built in the 13th and 18th centuries and remarkably renovated by Monsieur and Madame Lamothe. Here you will find luxury without ostentation. It lies in the beauty of the materials, the quality of the antique furniture, the sober comfort of the bathrooms done in a timeless modern style. Each bedroom is impeccable, a perfect synthesis of refined elegance. Breakfast and dinners are of the same quality, as is the gracious hospitality.

M I D I - P Y R É N É E S

351 - Domaine de Labarthe

46090 Espère
(Lot)
Tel. 05 65 30 92 34
Fax 05 65 20 06 87
M. and Mme Claude Bardin

Rooms 2 and 1 suite (with kitchenette, TV), with bath and WC. **Price** 350F/53,35€ (1 pers.), 400-600F/60,97-91,46€ (2 pers.). **Meals** Breakfast incl. No communal meal. **Facilities** Sitting room, tel., swimming pool, barbecue, garden. **Pets** Dogs allowed on request. **Nearby** Restaurants (5km), tennis (500m), 9-hole golf course (40km), caving, hiking, riding; very historic region (Cahors, Lot, Dordogne, Périgord). **Credit cards** Not accepted. **Spoken** English. **Open** All year, by reservation. **How to get there** (Map 30): 10km west of Cahors via D911, towards Villeneuve-sur-Lot; on the Place d'Espère turn left at tel. booth.

You will be courteously greeted at this beautiful, vast mansion of white stone. The classic bedrooms are restful and have a lovely view of the park. The breakfasts are generous and refined, and they are served in a room reserved for guests. The pigeon loft has a suite, including a kitchen, and a small private garden. In good weather, you can relax around the beautiful swimming pool which is surrounded by trees and shrubs.

352 - Moulin de Fresquet

46500 Gramat
(Lot)
Tel. 05 65 38 70 60 / 06 08 85 09 21
Fax 05 65 38 70 60
M. and Mme Ramelot

Rooms 5 with shower and WC (TV on request). **Price** 290-410F/44,21-62,50€ (2 pers.), +80F/12,19€ (extra pers.). **Meals** Breakfast incl. Evening meals at communal table 115F/17,53€ (wine incl.). **Facilities** Sitting room, fishing, boating, footpath. **Pets** Dogs not allowed. **Nearby** Riding, swimming pool, tennis, mountain biking, canoeing/kayaks; Rocamadour, Padirac, Loubressac. **Credit cards** Not accepted. **Spoken** Some English. **Open** Mar 15 – Nov 1. **How to get there** (Map 24): 800m southeast of Gramat; in Gramat, take N140 towards Figeac, then turn left in 500m; path 300m long. **No smoking** in bedrooms.

This old mill is in a peaceful setting close to Gramat, with greenery all around. It has been beautifully restored throughout. The bedrooms are beautifully decorated and two overlook the water. There is a charming sitting room-library and Claude and Gérard will greet you warmly. The evening meal is remarkably good and so is the aperitif-foie gras, which is served on request.

353 - L'Ermitage

46230 Lalbenque
(Lot)
Tel. 05 65 31 75 91
Mme and M. Daniel Pasquier

Rooms 3 independent studios with shower, WC, kitchenette and tel. Room cleaning guests' responsibility. **Price** 200F/30,48€ (2 pers.). **Meals** No communal meal. **Restaurant** "Chez Bertier" in the village. **Nearby** Tennis, riding; Saint-Cirq-Lapopie, Gallic ruins. **Credit cards** Not accepted. **Spoken** German. **Open** All year. **How to get there** (Map 30): 16km south of Cahors via D6; turn left at sign at the entrance to Lalbenque.

In a forest of truffle oaks, L'Ermitage consists of three small houses where you can live like a veritable hermit. Completely circular, they are spotlessly clean, cool in summer and warm in winter. They have a kitchenette where you can prepare your meals, a shower room and a comfortable (though somewhat narrow) bed. This an unusual place to stay and the price is very reasonable.

354 - Le Mas Azemar

Rue du Mas de Vinssou
46090 Mercuès
(Lot)
Tel. 05 65 30 96 85
Fax 05 65 30 53 82
Sabine and Claude Patrolin
Web: www.masazemar.com

Rooms 6 with bath or shower (for 1 room) and WC. **Price** 390-450F/59,45-68,60€ (2 pers.), +90F/13,72€ (extra bed). **Meals** Breakfast incl. Evening meals at communal table 150F/22,86€ (wine and coffe incl.). **Facilities** Sitting room, library, tel., heated swimming pool. **Pets** Dogs allowed (+25F/3,81€ per day). **Nearby** Canoeing/kayaks and boats on the Lot, tennis; Saint-Cirq-Lapopie (30km), vineyard of Cahors, Lot Valley and Célé Valley, Dordogne, Périgord. **Open** All year, by reservation. **How to get there** (Map 30): 8km west of Cahors dir. Villeneuve-sur-Lot via D911. In Mercuès; sign posted.

We were struck by the beautifully harmonious proportions of the rooms in the spacious 17th-century Mas Azemar. The large rooms still have their traditional charm and character, the windows in most bathrooms highlighting the impression of space. A beautiful room with exposed stone walls serves as the breakfast room. The dining room and the salons with warm, cheerful paneling add to the pleasure of relaxing over the evening meal. Outside, a delightful garden gives onto the fields skirting the house.

355 - Le Cayrou

Le Bourg
46310 Saint-Chamarand
(Lot)
Tel. 05 65 24 50 23
M. and Mme Beauhaire

Rooms 2 with bath or shower and WC. **Price** 290-340F/44,21-51,83€ (2 pers.). **Meals** Breakfast incl. Evening meals at communal table, by reservation 90F/13,72€ (wine incl.). **Facilities** Small sitting room, swimming pool. **Pets** Dogs not allowed. **Nearby** Tennis, mountain bikes; Cahors, Sarlat, Rocamadour, caves of Cougnac and Lascaux, Padirac chasm, châteaux. **Spoken** English. **Closed** Nov 1 – Apr 1, in winter by reservation. **How to get there** (Map 23): 35km north of Cahors via N20 (Limoges/Toulouse), then D704 dir. Périgueux via Saint-Chamarand. In the village, in front of the church.

This pleasant house situated in a well-preserved little village boasts a lovely enclosed garden with a terrace and a swimming pool. The bedrooms are independent with doors that open directly on the outside. They have all been carefully and comfortably appointed with some antique objects and furniture and pretty fabrics that are fresh and cheery. The largest of the bedrooms opens on the garden and its bathroom is extremely bright. You will have dinner with the owners at the large table in the inviting family kitchen with its ocher walls and green beams, or else outside under the arbor in summer.

356 - Château d'Uzech

46310 Uzech-les-Oules
(Lot)
Tel. and fax 05 65 22 75 80
M. and Mme Brun

Rooms 4 studios (1-3 pers.) with bath or shower, WC, kitchenette and TV. **Price** 500F/76,22€ (2 pers.), +100F/15,24€ (extra bed). **Meals** Breakfast incl. Evening meals on request 120F/18,29€ (all incl.). **Facilities** Lounge, swimming pool, ping-pong, boules. **Pets** Animals not allowed. **Nearby** 9-hole golf course (10mn), riding, tennis, canoeing/kayaks; Padirac Chasms, Rocamadour, Bonaguil, Cahors Spring Festival, Saint-Céré Festival. **Spoken** English, Spanish, Portuguese. **Open** All year, only by reservation. **How to get there** (Map 23): 23km north of Cahors, dir. Villeneuve-sur-Lot via D911. Outside of Mercuès, dir. Gourdon via D12. After Saint-Denis-Catus, go 4km. In village on left, dir. école (school), château.

This lovely house situated just outside a little village in Quercy boasts a pleasant swimming pool and a superb view of the countryside. The accommodation facilities have been well designed: they are independent and built mainly of wood and stone. Often the bedrooms are installed in a loft. You will have a kitchenette but it would be a pity to miss out on the excellent cooking of Madame Brun. This is a refined and hospitable address.

357 - Manoir de la Barrière
46300 Le Vigan
(Lot)
Tel. 05 65 41 40 73
Fax 05 65 41 40 20
M. and Mme Auffret
E-mail: manoirauffret@aol.com
Web: www.france-bonjour.com/manoir-le-barriere/

Rooms 5 (3 in outbuildings) with bath and WC. **Price** 350-450F/53,35-68,60€ (2 pers.), +100F/15,24€ (extra pers.). **Meals** Breakfast incl. Evening meals at communal table or not 170F/25,91€ (wine incl.). **Facilities** Sitting room, swimming pool, fishing. **Pets** Dogs not allowed. **Nearby** Tennis, riding, hiking and bicycles (G.R.64), golf; prehistoric sites, Les Eyzies, Sarlat, Rocamadour. **Spoken** English, German. **Open** Easter – Nov 1, by reservation. **How to get there** (Map 23): 21km south of Souillac via N20 dir. Cahors. After Peyrac, on right dir. Le Vigan for 5km. At the pond, small road.

The origins of this beautiful Périgord house go back to the 13th century. While conserving its traditional old charm, the new owners have renovated the Manoir de la Barrière with all the modern conveniences. The five tastefully decorated, spacious bedrooms have large, beautiful baths. The big flowery garden traversed by a small winding river, Monsieur Auffret's delectable cuisine (he is a former chef), and the couple's delightful hospitality put lovely finishing touches on this restful place to stay.

358 - Château du Tail
Route de Goux
65700 Castelnau-Rivière-Basse
(Hautes-Pyrénées)
Tel. 05 62 31 93 75
Fax 05 62 31 93 72
M. and Mme Ongyert
E-mail: chateau.du.tail@wanadoo.fr
Web: www.sudfr.com/chateaudutail

Rooms 3 and 1 suite with bath or shower and WC. **Price** 350F/53,35€ (2 pers.), +100F/15,24€ (extra bed). **Meals** Breakfast incl. Evening meals at communal table, by reservation 130F/19,81€ (all incl.). **Facilities** Sitting room, library, swimming pool, fitness center. **Pets** Dogs allowed on request. **Nearby** Tennis, fishing, riding, bicycles, golf; vineyard (Madiran), Marciac (jazz). **Spoken** English, German, Italian. **Open** All year. **How to get there** (Map 29): 25km southeast of Aire-sur-l'Adour via dir. Tarbes. In Castelnau, dir. village center, then dir. Goux and on left 300 m after the end of the village. **No smoking** in bedrooms.

A former wine château, this large house is surrounded by flowers and greenery. The three rooms and one suite are in one of the outbuildings. They are carefully decorated, with some fine pieces of furniture adding a note of real refinement. Each guest will find a favorite corner here, whether the library or a quiet spot in the shade of the tall trees. Meals are served in the main house, at a magnificent table in the dining room. A good holiday address.

359 - Les Rocailles

65100 Omex / Lourdes
(Hautes-Pyrénées)
Tel. 05 62 94 46 19
Fax 05 62 94 33 35
M. and Mme Fanlou

Rooms 3 (2 with air-conditioning) with bath or shower, WC, tel. and TV. **Price** 250F/38,11€ (1 pers.), 330F/50,30€ (2 pers.), +70F/10,67€ (extra bed). **Meals** Breakfast incl. Evening meals at communal table 100F/15,24€ (wine incl.). **Facilities** Swimming pool. **Nearby** Mountain bikes, rafting, paragliding, tennis, 18-hole golf course; Lourdes, Gavarnie, Cauteret, Pic du Midi. **Spoken** English. **Closed** Mid Nov – end Jan. **How to get there** (Map 29): 4km west of Lourdes dir. Saint-Pée-Bhétarram, then take Omex Bridge, then follow signs.

Perched in the mountains above Lourdes, this beautifully-renovated former presbytery enjoys a superb view of the snow-capped peaks of the Pyrenees. All the bedrooms have blond wood parquet floors and a four-poster bed in local country style (with flowered print or checkered fabric), some have a bed in an alcove for a child. Antique furniture and a host of little details give them further charm and one of them has its own terrace. The bathrooms are not very large, but impeccably kept. The meals are largely based on regional specialties and carefully served by the owners. This house is a rare find.

360 - Domaine de Jean-Pierre

20, route de Villeneuve
65300 Pinas
(Hautes-Pyrénées)
Tel. and fax 05 62 98 15 08
Mme Marie Colombier
E-mail: marie.colombier@wanadoo.fr

Rooms 3 with bath and WC. **Price** 250F/38,11€ (1 pers.), 280F/42,68€ (2 pers.), +70F/10,67€ (extra pers.). **Meals** Breakfast incl. No communal meal. **Restaurants** "Chez Maurette" and "Le Relais du Castera" (5 and 7km) and "Le Pré Vert" at the golf. **Facilities** Sitting room, library, piano, horse stalls. **Nearby** Lannemezan 18-hole golf course (3km); Lourdes, Saint-Bertrand-de-Comminges, the Pyrénnées. **Credit cards** Not accepted. **Spoken** English, Spanish. **Open** All year. **How to get there** (Map 30): 30km east of Tarbes. Aut A64, exit 16 Lannemezan, dir. Toulouse via N117. 5km from Lannemezan. At the Pinas' Church take D158 dir. Villeneuve: The house is on the right (800m).

In a peaceful setting on the edge of the village, this beautiful house is covered with Virginia creeper and surrounded by a very well-kept garden. The quiet bedrooms look out over the garden; each has antique furniture and a color scheme of its own. The modern bathrooms are huge. The decor is tasteful throughout. Madame Colombier is very welcoming and prepares excellent breakfasts, which are served on the terrace in good weather.

361 - Le Grand Cèdre

6, rue du Barry
65270 Saint-Pé-de-Bigorre
(Hautes-Pyrénées)
Tel. 05 62 41 82 04
Fax 05 62 41 85 89
M. Christian Peters
E-mail: grand.cedre@sudfr.com
Web: www.sudfr.com/grand.cedre

Rooms 4 with bath or shower, WC, TV on request. **Price** 300F/45,73€ (1 pers.), 350F/53,35€ (2 pers.), +80F/12,19€ (extra bed). **Meals** Breakfast incl. **Facilities** Sitting room, pond, swimming pool (children). **Pets** Dogs allowed on request. **Nearby** Swimming pool, tennis, canoeing/kayaks, mountain bikes, fishing in the Gave, golf, cross-country and alpine skiing (40km); Lourdes, Pau, Gavarnie, Sacred Music Festival (Easter). **Spoken** English, German, Spanish. **Open** All year. **How to get there** (Map 29): 25km southeast of Pau, dir. Lourdes via Bétharram. In Saint-Pé, "Place des Arcades", road on the right of the "Mairie" (town hall).

Its style highly typical of the Bigorre region, this huge 17th-century house is like a place from another country with its four beautiful bedrooms all in different styles, which you reach via a gallery with an exotic colonial touch. Shaded by a magnificent century-old cedar, the garden has a grassy expanse on one side, as well as a vegetable garden laid out in formal French style, à la Versailles. Meals made with local produce are festively served by Monsieur Peters, who is a most attentive host. The "Big Cedar" has all the charm of yesteryear.

362 - Château de Sombrun

65700 Sombrun
(Hautes-Pyrénées)
Tel. 05 62 96 49 43
Fax 05 62 96 01 89
M. and Mme Brunet
E-mail: chateaudesombrun@sudfr.com

Rooms 3 with bath and WC. **Price** 320F/48,78€ (2 pers.), +50F/7,62€ (extra bed); suite 450F/68,60€ (4 pers.). **Meals** Evening meals at communal table 120F/18,29€ (aperitif and wine incl.). **Facilities** Sitting room, swimming pool, pond, ping-pong, billiard, mountain bikes. **Pets** Dogs not allowed. **Nearby** Tennis (100 m), riding, ponies, 9-hole golf course (30km), skiing (70km); Madiran Wine Route, Romanesque church and chapel, Marciac Festival (15km). **Spoken** English. **Closed** Dec 1 – Jan 31. **How to get there** (Maps 29 and 30): 50km south of Aire-sur-l'Adour via D935 dir. Tarbes to Maubourguet. At the entrance of the village, on right dir. Lembeye, then first road on right after the train stop.

Shaded by the century-old trees in its beautiful park, the Château de Sombrun offers extremely spacious guest rooms with parquet floors and old fireplaces of character and charm. The bathrooms have modern amenities in a lovely atmosphere of the past. A handsome salon and dining room add smart touches to this beautiful château set in a highly interesting region.

363 - Les Écuries du Château

Allée du Château
65140 Tostat
(Hautes-Pyrénées)
Tel. and fax 05 62 31 23 27
Catherine Rivière d'Arc

Rooms 4 (1 for disabled persons) with bath or shower and WC **Price** 290F/44,21€ (2 pers.), +50F/7,62€ (extra bed). **Meals** Breakfast incl. Evening meals at communal table or not, by reservation 80F/12,19€ (wine incl.). **Facilities** Sitting room, river fishing. **Pets** Dogs allowed on request. **Nearby** Tennis, swimming pool, 18-hole golf course (12km), skiing (60km), hiking in mountains; cirque de Gavarnie, Saint-Jacques-de-Compostelle road. **Spoken** Spanish. **Open** All year. **How to get there** (Maps 29 and 30): 10km south of Rabastens-de-Bigorre. Drive for 10km dir. Tarbes, then on right (2km).

Appointed with tasteful simplicity, the former stables of this lovely 18th-century château contain four guestrooms, light and spacious, sober and comfortable, with a view of the countryside. The welcome is smiling and pleasant. A fine address for a restful stay.

364 - Château de la Serre

81580 Cambounet-sur-le-Sor
(Tarn)
Tel. 05 63 71 75 73
Fax 05 63 71 76 06
Chantal and Guy
de Limairac-Berthoumieux
Web: www.la-serre.com

Rooms 2 and 1 suite with bath and WC. Rooms cleaned on request. **Price** 550F/83,84€ (2 pers.), 700F/106,71€ (3 pers.); 10% reduction beginning with 2nd night. **Meals** Breakfast incl. Communal meals possible on request 150-180F/22,86-27,44€. **Facilities** Sitting room, billiard, tel., swimming pool. **Nearby** Restaurants (6km), tennis, riding, golf; Castres, Goya Museum, Albi. **Credit cards** Not accepted. **Spoken** English, Spanish, Italian. **Closed** Nov – Apr. **How to get there** (Map 31): 11km east of Castres towards Toulouse via N126. Go 9km, then turn right towards Vielmur and Sémalens. In Cambounet-sur-le-Sor, after the church, first turning on left; follow signs.

This old family château stands on a hillside looking out over the gentle countryside of the Tarn River. It was restored at the turn of the century by Madame Limairac-Berthoumieux's grandparents and she herself has tastefully decorated and arranged the magnificent suite and the bedrooms, including three new ones, smaller but each with personalized decoration. No detail has been overlooked, from the period furnishings to the ultra-modern baths, all designed for your comfort and pleasure. The owners' warm, thoughtful hospitality further adds to the pleasure of a stay here.

365 - Aurifat

81170 Cordes-sur-Ciel
(Tarn)
Tel. 05 63 56 07 03
M. and Mme Wanklyn

Rooms 3 and 1 suite (4 pers.) with bath or shower and WC. **Price** 300F/45,73€ (2 pers.), suite 550F/83,84€ (4 pers.) -10% for stay over 7 nights. **Meals** Breakfast incl. No communal meal. **Facilities** Kitchen at guests' disposal, lounge, library, swimming pool, boules. **Pets** Animals not allowed. **Nearby** Tennis, river fishing; Circuit des Bastides, Albi. **Spoken** English, Spanish. **Closed** End Sept – May 1 (3 nights min.). **How to get there** (Map 31): In Cordes, from the lower town, take dir. Cité on right of the Maison de la Presse for 500m; then left dir. Le Bouysset and Aurifat. After hair-pin turn, go 200m. Sign.

A five-minute walk from the center of medieval Cordes, this large house was built over the years around the old watchtower of the village. The bedrooms and the suite look out over the valley, each enjoying an independent entrance and a small private terrace. There is no evening meal, but the barbecue pit is at guests' disposal: just one indication of the Thornleys' simple, warm hospitality. This is a beautiful, quiet spot in one of the best preserved historic villages of France.

366 - Manoir La Maysou

81800 Coufouleux
(Tarn)
Tel. 05 63 33 85 92
Fax 05 63 40 64 24
M. and Mme Silver
E-mail: tonysilver@compuserve.com
Web: www.manoir-maysou.8m.com

Rooms 4 with bath or shower, WC and 1 suite with bath, shower, WC and TV. **Price** 330F/50,30€ (2 pers.); suite 475F/72,41€ (2 pers.). **Meals** Breakfast incl. Evening meals on request. Half board 270-352,50F/41,16-53,73€ per pers. per night, depending on season and room. **Facilities** Sitting room (TV), swimming pool, ping-pong, mountain bikes. **Nearby** Tennis, riding, golf, U.L.M.; Floral Park, vineyard, bastides. **Spoken** English, German, Spanish, Dutch. **Open** All year. **How to get there** (Map 31): 3.5km northeast of Saint-Sulpice. A68, Toulouse Albi, exit n. 6. In Saint-Sulpice, dir. Coufouleux D13 for 3km; house on left. **No smoking** in bedrooms.

Monsieur and Madame Silver spent their vacations in the Tarn département for years, finally deciding to live here for good. They found an immense 18th-century house which makes a perfect bed and breakfast. The bedrooms have been renovated with great attention paid to comfortable amenities while highlighting the traditional character of the old house. The immaculate bathrooms, the shady park, the charming salon, and the festive atmosphere around the dining table, where excellent local specialties are served with a smile, are good reasons to unpack your bags at the Manoir La Maysou, and stay a while.

367 - Lucile Pinon

8, place Saint-Michel
81600 Gaillac
(Tarn)
Tel. 05 63 57 61 48
Fax 05 63 41 06 56
Mme Pinon

Rooms 5 with bath, WC, tel., and 1 suite with lounge, bath, shower and WC. **Price** 240F/36,58€ (1 pers.), 260F/39,63€ (2 pers.), suite 360F/54,88€ (2 pers.). **Meals** Breakfast incl. No communal meal. **Restaurants** "Les Sarments" (200m) and "Le Relais de la Portanelle" (300m). **Facilities** Sitting room, TV. **Nearby** Swimming pool, tennis, golf courses; Compagnonage (Skilled Workers) Museum; the château and Le Nôtre Garden, Natural History Museum, Saint-Michel Abbey Church, Cordes (27km), Albi (20km), Toulouse (49km). **Credit cards** Not accepted. **Spoken** English. **Open** All year. **How to get there** (Map 31): In Gaillac, in front of the Saint-Michel Abbey Church.

With its monumental staircase, its high ceilinged, wood paneled rooms and parquet floors, this handsome 17th-century mansion is full of character, yet the bedrooms have modern bathrooms and all the comfort one could want. The decoration is elegant wherever you look, with a predilection for Napoleon III style. Breakfast is served on a covered terrace facing the abbey church of Saint Michel and overlooking the Tarn River. A charming place that is inviting as well as authentic.

368 - Château de Garrevaques

81700 Garrevaques
(Tarn)
Tel. 05 63 75 04 54
Fax 05 63 70 26 44
Mme Barande and Mme Combes
E-mail: m.c.combes@wanadoo.fr
Web: www.qarrevaques.com

Rooms 7 (2-3 pers.) and 1 suite with bath and WC. **Price** 650F/99,09€ (2 pers.); suites from 1100F/167,69€ (4-6 pers.). **Meals** Breakfast incl. Half board 450F/68,60€/pers. in double room (2 days min.). Evening meal at communal table, by reservation 150F/22,86€ (wine incl.). **Facilities** Sitting rooms, tcl., swimming pool, tennis, billiards. **Credit cards** Amex, Visa, Diner's. **Pets** Small dogs allowed on request. **Nearby** Golf, antiques; sightseeing, flying club (about a mile away), chauffeur-driven tours available. **Spoken** English, Spanish. **Open** All year, only by reservation. **How to get there** (Map 31): 50km southeast of Toulouse via D1. At Revel turn onto D79F (opposite the police station) for 5km.

Burned down during the Revolution and restored at the beginning of the 19th century, Garrevaques has been inhabited by fifteen generations of the same family. It stands in a large park with a swimming pool and a tennis court. The beautiful living rooms are filled with Empire and Napoleon III furniture. We recommend the premier étage bedrooms and suites, which are large, well furnished and comfortable. The traditional cuisine is good and the owners are very welcoming.

M I D I - P Y R É N É E S

369 - Meilhouret

81140 Larroque
(Tarn)
Tel. and fax 05 63 33 11 18
Minouche and Christian Jouard

Rooms 2 with bath or shower and WC. Rooms cleaned and linens changed every 3 days. **Price** 260F/39,63€ (1 pers.), 290F/44,21€ (2 pers.), +80F/12,19€ (extra bed). **Meals** Breakfast incl. No communal meal. In summer poss. to rent a kitchenette. **Facilities** Sitting room, swimming pool. **Nearby** Restaurants in the village, fishing in lake and water sports in Monclar, tennis, riding, Circuit des Bastides, concerts in summer. **Spoken** English. **Credit cards** Not accepted. **Open** Apr 1 – Oct 1. (2 nights min. in Jul and Aug). **How to get there** (Map 31): 25km northwest of Gaillac via D964, towards Caussade. 4km before Larroque, left on D1 towards Monclar (15km) for 3km, then turn right at "Chambres d'Hôtes" sign, and go 2km in the woods, 2nd house, tar road.

Lost at the end of narrow road through the woods, this fine regional house will offer you a warm welcome. The bedrooms are most comfortable, carefully and tastefully furnished and decorated, just as if they were the guest room of a private house. Fine breakfasts are served by the fire in cool weather, or outdoors under the oak trees facing a breathtaking view. A place full of charm that's worth knowing.

370 - Chez M. et Mme Audouy

Rue de l'Église
81440 Lautrec
(Tarn)
Tel. 05 63 75 95 11
M. and Mme Audouy

Rooms 2 and 1 suite (with TV) with bath and WC. **Price** 270F/41,16€ (2 pers.); suite 400F/60,97€ (3 pers.). **Meals** Breakfast incl. No communal meal. **Restaurants** In the village and farm-auberge (3km). **Facilities** Tel., locked garage, sitting room. **Pets** Dogs allowed on request. **Nearby** Several golf courses, tennis and water sports, riding (3km), hiking from the village; Albi (30km), Castres (12km), Le Sidobre (10km). **Spoken** English, Spanish. **Closed** Nov 1 – Easter, except by reservation. **How to get there** (Map 31): 30km south of Albi towards Castres; 3km after Réalmont on right, towards Lautrec. Blue door next to pharmacy.

In this large family house located in the heart of the beautiful village of Lautrec you will find three very comfortable bedrooms and a suite, as well as a breakfast room decorated with authentic panoramic wallpaper dating from 1810. An extraordinary terraced garden overlooks the small valleys of the Tarn countryside. The hosts are friendly and informal at this very beautiful place to stay.

371 - Château de Montcuquet

81440 Lautrec
(Tarn)
Tel. 05 63 75 90 07
M. and Mme Vene

Rooms 2 with bath and WC, and 1 spare room without bath or shower. **Price** 300F/45,73€ (1-2 pers.), +100F/15,24€ (extra pers.). **Meals** Breakfast incl. Evening meals at communal table (except Sun) 100F/15,24€ (wine incl.). **Facilities** sitting room (TV), reading room; fishing in river and lake on property. **Nearby** water sports in Lautrec, 19-hole golf course (15km); Sidobre, châteaux, Cordes. **Credit cards** Not accepted. **Open** All year. **How to get there** (Map 31): 15km from Castres. Go towards Lautrec. Château is 4km from Lautrec on the road to Roquecourbe.

A gigantic green oak and boxwood garden frames the entrance to this handsome U-shaped château with its 14th-century tower. The interior has preserved all its ancestral character. The family suite contains two vast bedrooms (one of them in the tower) and has a magnificent view. The other bedroom has its own charm, with its attractive small bathroom and a beautiful view over the shady terrace, where breakfasts are served in summer. The owners' good nature and simplicity help make the Château de Montcuquet a lovely place to stay.

372 - La Bousquétarié

81700 Lempaut
(Tarn)
Tel. and fax 05 63 75 51 09
Monique and Charles
Sallier-Larenaudie

Rooms 2 and 2 suites (3-4 pers.) with bath or shower and WC. **Price** 360F/54,88€ (2 pers.); suites 400F/60,97€ (2 pers.), 500F/76,22€ (3 pers.), +100F/15,24€ (extra bed). Special rates for long stays. **Meals** Breakfast incl. Communal meals on request 120-130F/18,29-19,81€ (all incl.). **Facilities** Sitting rooms, swimming pool, tennis, lake fishing, mountain bikes (with suppl.). **Pets** Dogs not allowed in bedrooms. **Nearby** Castres Festival. **Credit cards** Not accepted. **Spoken** Some English. **Open** All year. **How to get there** (Map 31): 18km southwest of Castres. Towards Toulouse to Soual, then towards Revel. In Lescout, turn right towards Lempaut via D46. House 2km further, on right, follow signs.

If you enjoy the comforting atmosphere of large family houses, with all those little touches that only time confers, you won't want to leave La Bousquétarié, a vast manor house built in the early 19th century in the heart of a farming estate. The quiet, the space, the Empire style wallpaper, the big house generously opened to guests and the family dining room are all evocative of old-fashioned vacations. The owners are energetic and friendly.

373 - Montpeyroux

81700 Lempaut
(Tarn)
Tel. 05 63 75 51 17
M. and Mme Adolphe Sallier

Rooms 1 with bath, WC, and 4 with shower, WC, (2 with shared shower, WC). Rooms cleaned twice a week and on request. **Price** 250-300F/38,11-45,73€ (1-2 pers.). **Meals** Breakfast incl. Evening meals at communal table 100-120F/15,24-18,29€ (all incl.). **Facilities** Sitting room, swimming pool, tennis. **Pets** Dogs not allowed. **Nearby** Riding, golf; Saint-Féréol lake, Albi, Toulouse, Carcassonne. **Credit cards** Not accepted. **Open** Apr 1 – Oct 1. **How to get there** (Map 31): 12km northeast of Revel via D622 towards Castres for 9km, then left on D12. At Lempaut left, on D46 towards Blan, then turn left before cemetery.

Montpeyroux is a very quiet, old residence in a luxuriant setting. Beautiful antique furniture – 18th- and early 19th-century – enhances the decor of the sitting room as well as the comfortable bedrooms, one with a bathroom, the others with showers. Two of them also have a shared toilet. Dinners are excellent and, in good weather, breakfasts are served outside under an awning. In front of the house, a tall tree also provides welcome shade. The owners are informal and very friendly.

374 - Villa Les Pins

81700 Lempaut
(Tarn)
Tel. 05 63 75 51 01
Mme Delbreil

Rooms 5 with bath, shower, WC and 2 small rooms sharing shower and WC. Rooms cleaned twice weekly. **Price** 180F/27,44€ (1 pers.), 350-450F/53,35-68,60€ (2 pers.), 500F/76,22€ (3 pers.). **Meals** Breakfast incl. Evening meals at communal table on request (meals for special diets on request) 130F/19,81€ (aperitif and wine incl.). **Facilities** Sitting room, river fishing, ping-pong. **Pets** Dogs not allowed. **Nearby** 18-hole golf course (30km), tennis, riding, lake (12km); Cathar castles, Montagne Noire, Castres. **Credit cards** Not accepted. **Spoken** English. **Open** May 15 – Oct 15. **How to get there** (Map 31): 12km northeast of Revel via D622 towards Castres for 9km, then left on D12. At Lempaut, left on D46 towards Blan, then take 2nd turn left.

This lovely Italian-style villa was built at the beginning of the last century and has been completely renovated with excellent taste and attention to detail. The bedrooms are charming and bright, with flowered wallpaper, and beautiful family furniture; the largest has a pleasant semi-circular balcony. The park has a view of the Montagne Noire. The hosts are friendly and welcoming.

375 - Château d'En Pinel

81700 Puylaurens
(Tarn)
Tel. and fax 05 63 75 08 62
M. and Mme Viguié

Rooms 1 and 1 suite with bath and WC. **Price** 400F/60,97€ (1 pers.), 500F/76,22€ (2 pers.), +150F/22,86€ (extra bed). **Meals** Breakfast incl. Communal table d'hôte meal on the night of arrival 95F/14,48€ (wine incl.). **Facilities** Sitting room, tel., swimming pool. **Nearby** Restaurants (3km), tennis, riding, mountain bikes, hiking, sailing, swimming, golf; Montagne Noire, Sidobre, Lauraguais, Cathar castles, Carcassonne, Toulouse. **Credit cards** Not accepted. **Spoken** English, Spanish. **Open** Apr – end Oct. **How to get there** (Map 31): N126 from Toulouse to Puylaurens, then dir. Revel. 2km, right dir. Saint-Sernin, then right dir. Pechaudier, En Pinel is 800m further.

This lovely family home in the Lauragais countryside is filled with beauty, history and peacefulness. The entrance hall has a Florentine mosaic floor and opens onto a terrace from which you have a breathtaking view. The white bedrooms upstairs are soberly decorated in warm colors with refined touches like the lovely leaf arrangements done by the mistress of the house. The bathrooms are traditional in appearance but are actually modern and very pleasant. A youthful and courteous reception for a delightful stay.

376 - La Bonde

Loupiac
81800 Rabastens
(Tarn)
Tel. and fax 05 63 33 82 83
M. and Mme Maurice Crété

Rooms 2 with bath or shower, WC and TV. **Price** 270F/41,16€ (1 pers.), 290F/44,21€ (2 pers.). **Meals** Breakfast incl. Communal meals 95F/14,48€ (all incl.). **Facilities** Tel. **Pets** Dogs not allowed. **Nearby** Swimming pool in park (6km), lake (12km), tennis (4km), riding (9km), golf (15km); Toulouse (45km), Albi (35km), village festivals (Jul, Aug), Gaillac Wine Festival, Lavaur Church, Saint-Géry Château. **Credit cards** Not accepted. **Spoken** English, Spanish. **Closed** Dec 15 – Jan 15. (3 days min. in Jul and Aug). **How to get there** (Map 31): 7km east of Rabastens towards Loupiac. At the cemetery, follow signs.

"A guest who arrives is a friend when he leaves." — that is Madame Crété's motto and we take her at her word, having sampled her kind hospitality and outstanding cooking. Add to this the feel of a genuine family home with antique furniture, books, souvenirs, very comfortable bedrooms always nicely decorated, and you will certainly want to return (as we did) "as friends."

377 - Le Barry

Faubourg Saint-Roch
82270 Montpezat-du-Quercy
(Tarn-et-Garonne)
Tel. 05 63 02 05 50
Fax 05 63 02 03 07
M. Bankes and M. Jaross

Rooms 5 with bath or shower and WC. **Price** 325F/49,54€ (2 pers. except Jul and Aug), 350F/53,35€ (2 pers, Jul and Aug). **Meals** Breakfast incl. Evening meals at communal table on request 125F/19,05€ (all incl.). **Facilities** Lounge, swimming pool. **Pets** Animals allowed on request. **Nearby** Riding, golf; Moissac (Romanesque art), Saint-Cirq-Lapopie. **Spoken** English, German, Italian. **Open** All year, only by reservation in winter. **How to get there** (Map 30): 25km south of Cahors via N20 in dir. Montauban; go about 2.5km, turn right dir. Montpezat-du-Quercy. In the village, go past the Café de l'Union on right, go about 50m; signs on left.

This handsome village house perched on the old ramparts overlooks a vast and varied landscape. The bedrooms all enjoy this lovely view and each of them has its own distinctive charm. The style is warm and rustic, yet with comfort and refinement. The sitting room-library is built around a central fireplace and decorated with an impressive collection of modern paintings and drawings. The elegant dining room provides a convivial setting for delicious dinners. The hospitality is imaginative and courteous.

378 - Château d'En Haut

59144 Jenlain
(Nord)
Tel. 03 27 49 71 80
Fax 03 27 35 90 17
M. and Mme Demarcq

Rooms 6 with bath or shower and WC. **Price** 290-400F/44,21-60,97€ (2 pers.), 400F/60,97€ (3 pers.), 450F/68,60€ (4 pers.). **Meals** Breakfast incl. No communal meal. **Facilities** Sitting room. **Pets** Dogs not allowed. **Nearby** Restaurants, golf; Mormal forest. **Credit cards** Not accepted. **Spoken** English. **Open** All year. **How to get there** (Map 3): 8km southeast of Valenciennes (Aut A2 exit 22a) via N49 towards Maubeuge. **No smoking.**

This delightful flower-filled château is nestled in a large park, a short distance from the autoroute, and reached through the "Grand'Rue" of the village. Inside, it is extremely comfortable, with handsome carpets, rugs, and antique furniture, all enhanced by lovely color schemes. There are very pleasant bedrooms, and breakfast is served in one of three dining rooms. You will enjoy a friendly welcome and very good value for the money.

379 - La Gacogne

La Gacogne
62310 Azincourt
(Pas-de-Calais)
Tel. and fax 03 21 04 45 61
Marie-José and Patrick Fenet

Rooms 4 with washbasin, shower and WC. **Price** 250F/38,11€ (2 pers.). **Meals** Breakfast incl. No communal meal. **Restaurants** In Hesdin, Fruges and Azincourt. **Facilities** Sitting room. **Pets** Dogs not allowed. **Nearby** Seaside, tennis, riding, fishing; Azincourt Museum. **Credit cards** Not accepted. **Spoken** English. **Open** All year. **How to get there** (Map 2): 41km northeast of Abbeville via D928 towards Fruges. In Ruisseauville, towards Azincourt, Blangy, Tramecourt. At the crossroads La Gacogne, towards Tramecourt.

This welcoming house is on the historical site of Agincourt, on the spot where the English camp once stood. The bedrooms are in a small separate building, which has a sitting room, kitchen and fireplace. They are all charming and unusual. Breakfast is served at a communal table in an attractively decorated room, and the atmosphere here is convivial.

NORTH - PAS-DE-CALAIS

380 - Le Clos Grincourt

18, rue du Château
62161 Duisans
(Pas-de-Calais)
Tel. and fax 03 21 48 68 33
Annie Senlis

Rooms 1 and 1 suite (4 pers.) with bath or shower and WC. **Price** 180F/27,44€ (1 pers.), 260F/39,64€ (2 pers.), +50F/7,62€ (extra bed), children under 5 (free); suite 430F/65,55€ (4 pers.). **Meals** Breakfast incl. No communal meal. **Restaurants** Many in Arras. **Facilities** Sitting room, hiking (G.R. 121) on property. **Nearby** Tennis in village, 18-hole golf course (4km), riding; old Arras, Route du Camp du Drap d'Or, Flower Route, Air-sur-la-Lys, Saint-Omer Marsh. **Credit cards** Not accepted. **Spoken** English. **Open** All year. **How to get there** (Map 2): 7km west of Arras via N39, then D56 towards Duisans, then follow signs. **No Smoking** in bedrooms.

Le Clos Grincourt is a beautiful family house surrounded by a private park filled with flowers. The hospitality, the interior decoration and the family photos make you feel immediately at home. We especially recommend the Chambre d'Amis, the Friends' Room, which is delightfully retro, large and very comfortable. One room is reserved for guests, where breakfast is served and you can gather tourist information, and watch a videotape on the region.

381 - La Grand'Maison

62179 Escalles
(Pas-de-Calais)
Tel. 03 21 85 27 75
Fax 03 21 85 27 75
Jacqueline and Marc Boutroy

Rooms 4 and 1 studio (2 pers.) with bath or shower and WC. Rooms cleaned on request. **Price** 240-300F/36,58-45,73€ (2 pers.), +80F/12,19€ (extra pers.). **Meals** Breakfast incl. No communal meal. **Facilities** Sitting room, mountain biking on large hiking trail (G.R. 120), donkey tours available. **Pets** Dogs not allowed. **Nearby** Restaurants (1km), tennis, riding, seaside (1.4km), golf; coastline paths, Cap Blanc-Nez, Cap Gris-Nez. **Credit cards** Not accepted. **Spoken** English. **Open** All year. **How to get there** (Map 1): 15km southwest of Calais via D940 (by sea); access to Escalles via highway (A16), exit Blanc-Nez (11 or 10), Peuplingues, then D243. Village of La Haute Escalles. Turn 1st house on left, then on the place n. 3.

A stone's throw from the splendid coastline of Cape Blanc-Nez, you will find La Grand'Maison, a vast farm laid out in a rectangle, with beautiful flower beds and a melodic pigeon house in the center. You will be greeted with warm hospitality. The bedrooms are large, beautiful, very comfortable and are furnished with handsome, tall wardrobes, Voltaire-style chairs, engravings and pretty carpets. (The two studios on the ground floor are less attractive.) Good breakfasts are served in a warm, pretty room.

382 - Le Manoir du Meldick

2528, avenue du Général de Gaulle
Le Fort Vert
62730 Marck
(Pas-de-Calais)
Tel. and fax 03 21 85 74 34
M. and Mme Houzet

Rooms 5 with bath or shower and WC. **Price** 250F/38,11€ (1 pers.), 300F/45,73€ (2 pers.), +50F/7,62€ (extra bed). **Meals** Breakfast incl. No communal meal. **Facilities** Sitting room. **Pets** Dogs not allowed. **Nearby** Restaurants (4km), riding, recreation area, mountain bikes, land sailing, parachuting, golf (30km); the Flandres, the coast, the Coupole in Saint-Omer. **Open** All year. **How to get there** (Maps 1 and 2): 7km east of Calais. Aut. A16, exit 19, Marck-Ouest dir. Fort-Vert, then D119 on right.

Situated in the lowlands, not far from the nature reserve of Oye, this typical house is well worth a stop. There are no major tourist attractions in the vicinity, but the kind welcome of the owners is a definite asset. Upstairs, the bedrooms (Jacinthes and Pâquerettes) have mansard roofs and are full of family souvenirs. Those on the ground floor are large and warm with vast bathrooms (except for Coquelicots, a little smaller). The breakfasts are indeed of mammoth quantities with homemade fruitcake and freshly squeezed orange juice. On cool days, there's a wood fire in the sitting room.

383 - La Chaumière

19, rue du Bihen
62180 Verton
(Pas-de-Calais)
Tel. 03 21 84 27 10
M. and Mme Terrien
Web: //perso.worldonline.fr/lachaumiere

Rooms 4 with shower, WC and TV. **Price** 290F/44,21€ (2 pers.). **Meals** Breakfast incl. No communal meal. **Pets** Dogs not allowed. **Nearby** Restaurants, beach (3km), different sports in Berck; 6 golf courses (less than 15km); Parquenterre Park, Valloire Abbey, Authie Valley, Montreuil-sur-Mer, Le Touquet. **Credit cards** Not accepted. **Open** All year. **How to get there** (Map 1): 3km southeast of Berck. In Abbeville, take N1 towards Boulogne to Wailly-Beaucamp, then D142 towards Verton. Or autoroute A16 (Paris/Calais), exit Beck n. 25. **No smoking** in bedrooms.

The beaches are only three kilometers from this thatched-roof cottage built twenty years ago. Isolated from the village by a garden of flowers and trees, it offers guests very well-kept small bedrooms, cheery, comfortable and each of them different, all with elegant shower rooms. Breakfasts are served in a bright dining room with 1930s furniture. The owners are friendly and gregarious.

384 - Château d'Asnières-en-Bessin

14710 Asnières-en-Bessin
(Calvados)
Tel. 02 31 22 41 16
M. and Mme Heldt

Rooms 2 with bath and WC. **Price** 450F/68,60€ (2 pers.). **Meals** Breakfast incl. No communal meal. **Restaurants** Beside the sea. **Pets** Dogs not allowed. **Nearby** Tennis, riding, seaside; Normandy landing beaches, Bayeux, Château de Bessin, Balleroy forest. **Credit cards** Not accepted. **Spoken** English. **Open** All year. **How to get there** (Map 7): 20km northwest of Bayeux via N13 towards Isigny-sur-Mer; right on D98 towards Asnières.

The beautiful Château d'Asnières is charmingly reflected in the ornamental pond in front. Handsomely decorated, it is a home that is obviously happily lived in. The pleasant bedrooms are very large, and are furnished with traditional antiques. The excellent breakfasts are served around a large table in the beautiful dining room with 18th-century wood paneling. This lovely place is especially outstanding for its owners' marvelous hospitality.

385 - Château de Vaulaville

Tour-en-Bessin
14400 Bayeux
(Calvados)
Tel. 02 31 92 52 62
Fax 02 31 51 83 55
Mme Corblet de Fallerans

Rooms 2 with bath, WC, and 1 suite (3 pers. and 2 children), bath, WC. **Price** 350F/53,35€ (1 pers.), 500F/76,22€ (2 pers.); suite 700F/106,71€ (3 pers.). **Meals** Breakfast incl. Evening meals at separate tables, by reservation 150 and 200F/22,86 and 30,48€ (all incl.). **Facilities** Sitting room. **Pets** Dogs allowed on request. **Nearby** Golf, seaside; Bayeux, Memorial museum, Normandy landing beaches. **Credit cards** Not accepted. **Spoken** English. **Open** Easter – Nov 1. **How to get there** (Map 7): 7km west of Bayeux via N13 towards Tour-en-Bessin; signposted.

This small, perfectly proportioned 18th-century château is surrounded by a graceful moat. The bedrooms are totally authentic in style, with antique furniture, carpets, and engravings. The long bathrooms are adequately equipped and have a sweeping view over the countryside. Breakfasts and excellent dinners are served in a magnificent circular room, a veritable masterpiece furnished with signed antiques.

386 - Chez Mme Hamelin

Le Bourg
14430 Beuvron-en-Auge
(Calvados)
Tel. 02 31 39 00 62
Mme Hamelin

Rooms 2 (2 pers.) with bath or shower and WC (Possibility of one extra room with bunk beds). **Price** 280F/42,68€ (2 pers., 1 night) and 260F/39,63€ (2 pers., from 2 nights), +80F/12,19€ (extra bed). **Meals** Breakfast incl. No communal meal. **Restaurants** "La Forge", "La Boule d'Or", "Le Pavé d'Auge" in Beuvron-en-Auge and the Crêperie. **Pets** Small dogs allowed. **Nearby** 18-hole golf course; pretty villages. **Credit cards** Not accepted. **Spoken** English. **Open** Easter – Nov 1. **How to get there** (Map 7): 27km east of Caen via N175, then D49; in front of La Boule d'Or at the entrance to village. **No smoking** in bedrooms.

This pretty house is located in a splendid Norman village with flower-filled balconies and half-timbered houses. The house is built around a small pretty flower garden with a path to the pastures beyond. Two bedrooms are reserved for guests, one at garden level and the other upstairs. Their decoration is elegant and warm, as is that of the pretty dining room where breakfasts are served. Madame Hamelin is friendly and open, and the prices are very reasonable.

387 - Château des Riffets

14680 Bretteville-sur-Laize
(Calvados)
Tel. 02 31 23 53 21
Fax 02 31 23 75 14
Anne-Marie and Alain Cantel

Rooms 2 with bath, WC and 2 suites (2-4 pers.) 1 with whirlpool, WC and 1 with multi-jet shower, WC. **Price** 550F/83,84€ (2 pers.), +160F/24,39€ (extra pers.); 50F/7,62€ children under 10. **Meals** Breakfast incl. Evening meals at communal table or not 240F/36,58€ (all incl.); 1/? price (children under 13). **Facilities** Sitting room, swimming pool, horse stalls. **Pets** Dogs not allowed. **Nearby** 18-hole golf course (5km); Beauvron-en-Auge, Beaumont, Deauville, Cabourg, Caen. **Credit cards** Not accepted. **Spoken** English, German. **Open** All year. **How to get there** (Map 7): 10km south of Caen via N158 towards Falaise. At La Jalousie, D23 and D235 before the village; signposted.

Surrounded by a beautiful, hilly park, the Château des Riffets dominates the church and the château of Quilly. The edifice has undergone many changes over the years and no longer has its original allure. But the bedrooms, like the baths, are large, comfortable, and decorated in classic and traditional styles with a scattering of antiques. In the blue and yellow salon/dining room, you will be treated to Madame Cantel's marvelous, copious breakfasts and hearty dinners. They are served by her husband, who enjoys chatting and joking with guests.

388 - Manoir des Tourpes
3, chemin de l'Église
14670 Bures-sur-Dives
(Calvados)
Tel. 02 31 23 63 47
Fax 02 31 23 86 10
Mme Landon and M. Cassady
E-mail: mcassady@mail.cpod.fr
Web: www.cpod.com/monoweb/mantourpes

Rooms 3 with bath or shower and WC. **Price** 300-400F/45,73-60,97€ (2 pers.), +50F/7,62€ (extra pers.). **Meals** Breakfast incl. No communal meal. Picnic possible in garden. **Facilities** Sitting room. **Pets** Dogs not allowed. **Nearby** 18-hole golf course, tennis, swimming pool, riding, sailing; Caen, the Auge region, marshlands. **Credit cards** Not accepted. **Spoken** English. **Open** Mar 15 – Nov 15. **How to get there** (Map 7): 15km east of Caen via A13, exit 30, then N175; in Troarn, D95 towards Bures-sur-Dives; beside the church.

Next to a church, this elegant 18th-century manor house overlooks a countryside of pastures traversed by a small river. The Franco-American owners are warm and friendly, and their ravishing bedrooms are tastefully and comfortably furnished, with coordinated wallpaper and curtains which complement the antique furniture. There is a beautiful sitting room-dining room for fireside breakfasts, and a lovely garden on the edge of the Dives.

389 - Domaine de la Picquoterie
14230 La Cambe
(Calvados)
Tel. 02 31 92 09 82 / 06 62 09 09 82
Fax 02 31 51 80 91
M. and Mme Laloy
E-mail: picquoterie@wanadoo.fr
Web: www.picquoterie.com

Rooms 2 (double or four-poster bed), 1 suite and 1 room for 1 pers. with bath, shower, WC. Rental of small house. **Price** Rooms 550F/83,84€, suite 1000F/152,44€ (2 pers.), 1300F/198,18€ (3 pers.). Small house 2500F/381,12€/week; 400F/60,97€/night (2 pers.), 800F/121,95€/night (4 pers.). **Meals** Breakfast 50F/7,62€. No communal meal. **Pets** Dogs not allowed. **Nearby** Restaurants, golf, sea. **Credit cards** Visa, Eurocard, Mastercard. **Spoken** English, German, Italian. **Open** All year, by reservation. **How to get there** (Map 7): 20km west of Bayeux via RN13. Exit Saint-Pierre-du-Mont, D204; follow signs "La Picquoterie" (from Cherbourg RN13, exit La Cambe D113, then signs). Guests should plan to arrive before 6 p.m. **No smoking.**

The artist Jean-Gabriel Laloy has made his house a very special place. You will find a garden full of perennials and rare plants and rooms which are designed like veritable paintings. The bedrooms are both contemporary and traditional. The Domaine is warm, restful and very comfortable. The breakfasts are excellent and the young host is very friendly.

390 - Ferme Savigny

14230 La Cambe
(Calvados)
Tel. 02 31 22 70 06
M. and Mme Maurice Le Devin

Rooms 3 with bath and WC. **Price** 200F/30,48€ (1 pers.), 250F/38,11€ (2 pers.). **Meals** Breakfast incl. No communal meal. **Restaurants** "La Marée" and "La Belle Marinière" (3km). **Pets** Dogs not allowed. **Nearby** Tennis, riding, 27-hole golf course, seaside; Pointe du Hoc (3km), Normandy landing beaches, Bayeux (Tapestry, museum, cathedral), marshland park of Cotentin. **Credit cards** Not accepted. **Open** All year. **How to get there** (Map 7): 25km west of Bayeux via N13 to La Cambe; then at the roadside cross take D113 to the right, towards Grandcamp-Maisy; signposted.

In the Bessin region of Normandy, this farmhouse is covered with graceful Virginia creeper, which is just a prelude to the charming interior. A stone staircase leads to beautiful, country-style bedrooms which are very well kept and have recently installed bathrooms. Breakfasts are served in a rustic room brightened by red-and-white checked tablecloths. The Ferme Savigny is simple and very charming.

391 - Manoir de Cantepie

Le Cadran
14340 Cambremer
(Calvados)
Tel. 02 31 62 87 27
M. and Mme Gherrak

Rooms 3 with bath and private WC (but 1 outside the room). **Price** 300F/45,73€ (2 pers.). **Meals** Breakfast incl. No communal meal. **Pets** Animals not allowed. **Nearby** Restaurants (1.5km), tennis (1km), Saint-Julien golf course in Pont-Lévêque; Auge country, Lisieux. **Spoken** English, German, Swedish. **Open** All year. **How to get there** (Map 8): 14km west of Lisieux via N13 dir. Caen. In La Boissière, take D50 dir. Cambremer for 5km. 30m before "Le Cadran" (house with a clock), sign on left.

Built in 1610, this magnificent manor house was furnished in the 19th century by a certain Monsieur Swann, a friend of Marcel Proust. It is outstanding in both architecture and decoration: wood paneling, sculptured wooden staircase, painted ceiling, lovely furniture and objects (and even the prices are attractive). The bedrooms are pleasant, large and bright, with one overlooking a small valley. All have a bathroom but one is downstairs. Breakfasts are served in the beautiful dining room with a view of the park. Madame Gherrak will welcome you with elegance, kindness, and simplicity.

392 - Les Marronniers

14340 Cambremer
(Calvados)
Tel. 02 31 63 08 28
Fax 02 31 63 92 54
Mme Darondel

Rooms 3 with bath or shower and WC. **Price** 250-320F/38,11-48,78€ (2 pers.), +75F/11,43€ (extra bed). **Meals** Breakfast incl. No communal meal - Use of kitchen. **Pets** Animals not allowed. **Facilities** Walks on the estate. **Nearby** Restaurants (2km), tennis, swimming pool, riding, 18-hole golf course; Auge country, Deauville. **Spoken** English. **Open** All year (2 days min.). **How to get there** (Map 8): 15.5km west of Lisieux via N13 to La Boissière, then D50 dir. Cambremer. In Cambremer, church square, dir. Dozulé for 3.8km; opposite the stop sign, take the road on left for 1.8km.

Its architecture, unusual in the region, Les Marronniers (Chestnut Trees) affords an almost ethereal view. The bedrooms are located in a simpler outbuilding covered by Virginia creeper and are attractively appointed: white walls, fresh, cheerful cotton fabrics, immaculate baths. Our favorites are Diane with its view over the garden, and Vénus, a very bright room. In the morning, Madame Darondel will greet you cheerfully over a delicious breakfast in the dining room, the summer salon or on the flowery terrace.

393 - Le Courtillage

14320 Clinchamps-sur-Orne
(Calvados)
Tel. 02 31 23 87 63
Mme Hervieu

Rooms 3 and 1 suite (3-4 pers.) with bath and WC. **Price** 300F/45,73€ (1 pers.), 400F/60,97€ (2 pers.), +50F/7,62€ (baby's bed); suite 400F/60,97€ (2 pers.), 500F/76,22€ (3 pers.), +100F/15,24€ (extra bed). **Meals** Breakfast incl. No communal meal. **Pets** Dogs not allowed. **Facilities** Sitting rooms. **Nearby** Restaurants (2km), golf; Typical landscapes of "La Suisse normande,", Normandy landing beaches, festival (classical music). **Spoken** English, German. **Open** All year, reservation by mail. **How to get there** (Map 7): 12km south of Caen dir. Flers to Laize-la-Ville, then right dir. Evrecy for 2km. In Clinchamps, on left. At church 1st on left. **No smoking** in bedrooms.

This large 19th-century family home, which stands outside the village, has a lovely flower garden and an eventful history. Recently converted into an inviting guest house, its bedrooms are all carefully decorated in such different styles as "Beaumarchais," "Suédoise," "Provençal" or the delightful "Chambre de l'Ecrivain,"with its red draperies and are as comfortable as they are refined. Two of them can be turned into a suite. A brunch composed of various homemade products is served until 11.30 a.m. and will give you the fortitude you need for a day of heavy touring.

394 - Le Haras de Crépon

Le Clos Mondeveille
14480 Crépon
(Calvados)
Tel. 02 31 21 37 37
Fax 02 31 21 12 12
Mme Pascale Landeau

Rooms 4 (2 of them can be turned into a suite) with bath or shower and WC. **Price** 390-550F/59,45-83,84€ (2 pers.), +135F/20,58€ (extra bed). **Meals** Breakfast incl. Evening meals at communal table or not, by reservation 150F/22,86€ (wine not incl.). **Pets** Dogs allowed (+35F/5,33€/day). **Facilities** Sitting room (piano), kitchen area, bicycles, horse-riders welcomed, visits of horse farms. **Nearby** Tennis, beach, sailing club, golf; Normandy landing beaches, Bayeux, Caen. **Spoken** English, Spanish. **Open** All year, by reservation and deposit. **How to get there** (Map 7): 20km northwest of Caen. On the road Caen/Cherbourg, exit D158B. At the stop, dir. Creully, then Saint-Gabriel-Brécy, then Arromanches. In Villiers-le-Sec, turn right and immediatly left (2km).

A haras is a horse farm and this stately manor house, dating from the 16th century and carefully restored, is , as its name indicates, a place where horses are raised. Three large comfortable bedrooms are named after horses raised on the property, some of them winners of major races. The fourth bedroom is smaller but it is very light, with two windows and a fine view. The bathrooms are very nicely designed. Dinner is served in a spacious dining room and in good weather breakfast is outdoors beside a pretty garden.

395 - Manoir de Crépon

Route de Caen-Arromanches
14480 Crépon
Tel. 02 31 22 21 27
Fax 02 31 22 88 80
Mme Anne-Marie Poisson

Rooms 2 and 1 suite (3 pers. with spare bedroom) with bath or shower, WC, TV (on request). **Price** 330F/50,30€ (1 pers.), 400F/60,97€ (2 pers.), +100F/15,24€ extra bedroom (suite) and 1 suite with 2 bedrooms, bath and WC 600F/91,46€ (4 pers.). **Meals** Breakfast incl. No communal meal. Ferme de la Rançonnière (500m). **Facilities** Lounge, tel. **Nearby** Sailing, tennis, riding, beach sailing, hiking, golf; landing beaches, Bayeux. **Credit cards** All major except Amex. **Spoken** English. **Open** All year, by reservation in Jan and Feb. **How to get there** (Map 7): 10km east of Bayeux. From Paris, take dir. Cherbourg, exit 7 dir. Creuilly-Arromanches.

A few minutes from the sea and the historic site of Arromanches, this is a very elegant small manor house from the late 17th century. A welcoming hostess, Madame Poisson has arranged the pleasant guest rooms with great taste. Their decoration is fresh, with just the right amount of classicism and antique furniture to combine charm with the comfort and taste of today. There is a delightful small blue suite for families, and a huge lounge. Breakfasts are served in a warm, rustic kitchen where an open fire burns in the winter.

396 - Manoir de L'Hermerel

14230 Géfosse-Fontenay
(Calvados)
Tel. and fax 02 31 22 64 12
Agnès and François Lemarié

Rooms 4 with shower and WC. **Price** 250F/38,11€ (1 pers.), 300F/45,73€ (2 pers.), +100F/15,24€ (extra pers.). **Meals** Breakfast incl. No communal meal. **Facilities** Sitting room. **Pets** Dogs not allowed. **Nearby** Tennis, golf, sailing, fishing; Bayeux, châteaux, manors, Normandy landing beaches. **Credit cards** Not accepted. **Spoken** English. **Open** Apr 1 – Nov 11, or by reservation. **How to get there** (Map 7): 7km north of Isigny-sur-Mer via RN13. In Osmanville, D514 towards Grandcamp-Maisy then left on D199A; 2nd road on the right.

This 17th-century farmhouse, with its beautiful architecture and façade, could pass for a château. The pleasant bedrooms have high ceilings and combine comfortable amenities with rustic charm. The rooms are all different but each one has its own particular charm. Breakfast is served in a large, attractive room. A large relaxation room and a summer sitting room have been installed in a chapel, classified as a landmark building. Madame Lemarié is very welcoming and will advise you on tourist activities.

397 - Château de Dramard

14510 Houlgate
(Calvados)
Tel. 02 31 24 63 41
Fax 02 31 91 05 00
Luce and Alexis Straub

Rooms 2 small and 2 large suites (2-4 pers.) with bath or shower and WC. **Price** Small suites 700F/106,71€ (2 pers.); large suites 800F/121,95€ (1 bedroom, 2 pers.), 1200F/182,93€ (2 bedrooms, 4 pers.). **Meals** Breakfast incl. Communal meals (6 pers. min.) 200-300F/30,48-45,73€ (all incl.). **Facilities** Sitting room. **Pets** Small dogs only allowed on request. **Nearby** Beach (3km), 18-hole golf courses; Route des Haras (Stud Farms), Route des Marais (marshlands). **Credit card** Visa. **Spoken** English, German. **Open** All year. **How to get there** (Map 7 and 8): Autoroute A13 exit Dozulé toll station. Take towards Cabourg and Dives. In Dives, D45 towards Lisieux. At top of hill, in 3km on left, small road to Dramard. Château in 1km: white gate

The sea surges by the small road and then disappears, making way for a forest which opens onto a clearing and the Château de Dramard. Energetic and very hospitable, Luce and Alexis have created a cheerful, warm interior. The suites have a salon, their decoration combining antique and period furniture with some modern pieces. The four-poster beds, the upholstered walls and the attractive carpets all form a comfortable and elegant ensemble. Breakfasts and dinners are served in a magnificently beautiful dining room.

398 - Château de Vouilly

Vouilly
14230 Isigny-sur-Mer
(Calvados)
Tel. 02 31 22 08 59
Fax 02 31 22 90 58
Marie-José and James Hamel

Rooms 5 with bath and WC. **Price** 280-340F/42,68-51,83€ (1 pers.), 320-380F/48,78-57,93€ (2 pers.), +80F/12,19€ (extra pers.). **Meals** Breakfast incl. No communal meal. **Restaurants** Auberge "La Piquenotiére" and seaside restaurants. **Facilities** Sitting room. **Pets** Dogs allowed on request. **Nearby** Tennis, lake fishing, golf; regional marshland park of Contentin and Bessin, Bayeux (Tapestry, cathedral). **Credit cards** All major. **Spoken** English. **Open** Mar – Nov. **How to get there** (Map 7): 8km southeast of Isigny-sur-Mer via D5 towards Vouilly; signposted.

Close to the village yet very quiet, Vouilly is a charming small château surrounded by a moat. The bedrooms are large, comfortable, and some are furnished with antiques. All have a very beautiful view over the garden and the countryside. Three rooms, L'Orangerie, Delavier and the Giverny, also have handsome, smartly polished parquet floors. Breakfasts are served in a lovely dining room, which was the American press room during the Normandy landings. The owners are very pleasant and you'll get good value for your money.

399 - Le Magnolia

7, rue du Docteur Boutrois
14230 Isigny-sur-Mer
(Calvados)
Tel. 02 31 21 12 33 / 02 31 21 18 75
M. and Mme Jacques Le Devin

Rooms 1 duplex bedroom with kitchen, bath, shower, WC and TV. **Price** 200F/30,48€ (1 pers.), 240F/36,58€ (2 pers.), +40F/6,09€ (extra bed). **Meals** Breakfast incl. No communal meal. **Restaurants** "La Petite Normande" (300m), or "La Trinquette" in Grandcamp-Maisy (5km). **Pets** Small dogs only allowed. **Nearby** Tennis (500m), lake fishing (500m), port (500m), sea excursions, hiking path along coast (5km); D-Day landing beaches, Marais (marshlands) Regional Park, museums. **Credit cards** Not accepted. **Open** All year. **How to get there** (Map 7): 30km west of Bayeux. Take N13 towards Cherbourg, then Isigny Centre, then towards Grandcamp and Rue du Docteur Bontrois.

When you see the Magnolia's charming garden, you will quickly forget the unattractive road in front of the house. And your bedroom looks out onto this flowery setting. It is a small duplex (kitchen downstairs, bedroom above) which is comfortable, elegant and very well kept. Breakfasts are served outside with the first sunny weather. The owners extend familial, youthful and pleasant hospitality.

400 - Manoir du Carel

14400 Maisons par Bayeux
(Calvados)
Tel. 02 31 22 37 00
Fax 02 31 21 57 00
M. and Mme Aumond

Rooms 3 with bath and shower, WC, tel., TV, and 1 independent house with bedroom, living room (sofa bed), kitchen, bath and shower, WC, tel. and TV. Rooms cleaned on request. **Price** 400F/60,97€ (1 pers.), 600F/91,46€ (2 pers.); house 850F/129,58€/day or flat rate for long stay. **Meals** Breakfast 45F/6,86€. No communal meal. **Facilities** Sitting room, tel., tennis, riding. **Pets** Dogs not allowed. **Nearby** Restaurants, 27-hole golf course (2km); seaside (3km). **Credit cards** All major. **Spoken** English, some German. **Open** All year. **How to get there** (Map 7): 5km from Bayeux. D6 towards Port-en-Bessin: itinerary sent by fax on request.

Three kilometers from the sea and very near the D-Day landing beaches, you will find this 16th-century manor house whose beautifully austere stone and wood are enhanced by extremely comfortable modern amenities. You can choose between the tastefully decorated bedrooms (antique furniture, lovely fabrics, charming details) or the small house which can be rented for a single night or a longer stay. The bathrooms are also splendid. The excellent, copious breakfasts are served in a superb Haute Epoque dining room. There is an inviting small salon and the owner is very hospitable.

401 - Le Cotil

14140 Le Mesnil-Simon
(Calvados)
Tel. and fax 02 31 31 47 86
Mme Mecki Dauré

Rooms 2 independent, 1 with shower, WC, and 1 with bath, WC; 1 with kitchen. 1 small house with kitchen, bedroom, sitting room (fireplace, satellite TV), bedroom/study. **Price** 300F/45,73€ (2 pers.). Small house 400F/60,98€ (2 pers.). **Meals** Breakfast incl. No communal meal. **Pets** Animals allowed on request. **Nearby** Restaurants (3km), golf; Auge country, Lisieux, Livarot. **Spoken** English, German. **Open** Easter – Nov 11 (2 nights min.). **How to get there** (Map 8): 10km southeast of Lisieux via D511 dir. Saint-Pierre-sur-Dives. After La Corne driving during 3km on D511 then in the turn on right, take the small road on left, follow signs "Peintures sur bois".

This lovely half-timbered house has a superb view over the valley. The tastefully decorated bedrooms and the hand-painted furniture are the work of Madame Dauré herself. The rooms are spacious, bright and comfortable. The one in the main building is on the mezzanine and overlooks its own private sitting room. The other one is in the mansard roof of an outbuilding. The little guest house is charming, perfect for a longer holiday. Good breakfasts, nice prices and a warm welcome.

402 - La Varinière

La Vallée
14310 Monts-en-Bessin
(Calvados)
Tel. 02 31 77 44 73
Fax 02 31 77 11 72
Pippa and David Edney

Rooms 4 rooms and 1 suite with bath or shower and WC. **Price** 200F/30,48€ (1 pers.), 330F/50,30€ (2 pers.), 390F/59,45€ (3 pers.), 465F/70,88€ (4 pers.). **Meals** Breakfast incl. No communal meal. Picnic possible. **Facilities** Sitting room. **Pets** Dogs not allowed. **Nearby** Restaurants (4km), tennis, riding, covered swimming pool, lake and sea fishing, sea (30km), golf; Normandy landing beaches, Bayeux, Caen. **Credit cards** Not accepted. **Spoken** English. **Open** All year (except Dec 23 – 27). **How to get there** (Map 7): From Caen, autoroute A84 dir. Rennes/Mont-saint-Michel, exit 45, on right D92 towards Monts-en-Bessin, straight at the crossroads, right before the château, signs, 2nd house on left. **No smoking** in bedrooms.

Surrounded by typically Norman hedgerows, La Varinière is a traditional house which has recently been redecorated by a friendly young British couple. Prettily coordinated wallpapers and cotton fabrics create a color scheme in each room: yellow for the dining room, and blue or rose for the bedrooms. Throughout, the house is bright, extremely well kept and elegantly furnished. The quiet, comfortable bedrooms are conducive to sleeping deliciously late. This is a beautiful place to stay at reasonable prices.

403 - La Ferme des Poiriers Roses

14130 Saint-Philibert-des-Champs
(Calvados)
Tel. 02 31 64 72 14
Fax 02 31 64 19 55
M. and Mme Lecorneur

Rooms 6 (2 of which for 4 pers.) and 1 suite with sitting room, all with bath and WC. **Price** 350-500F/53,36-76,22€ (2 pers.). **Meals** Gourmet breakfast 52F/7,93€. No communal meal. **Restaurant** "Le Dauphin" in Breuil-en-Augc. **Facilities** Sitting room, bicycles. **Pets** Dogs not allowed. **Nearby** 27-hole golf course, tennis, riding, man-made lake; tour of manors. **Credit cards** Not accepted. **Spoken** English. **Open** All year. **How to get there** (Map 8): A13 exit Pont-l'Evêque, then D579 towards Lisieux. In Ouilly, left on D98 through Norolles, then D284; 700m before the village.

In the heart of the country and surrounded by a lovely garden full of flowers, the "Farmhouse With the Pink Pear Trees" and its half-timbered buildings are truly a world apart. It's more like a stage set than a house as it's sometimes difficult to move among the excessive accumulation of furniture, bric à brac, skirted tables, carpets, objects, engravings, photos, and bouquets of dried flowers hung from the ceiling beams. The guest rooms and bathrooms are extremely well appointed and tasteful, and decorated in the same spirit as the house. We loved them, and the breakfasts are a gourmet feast.

404 - Le Prieuré Boutefol

14130 Surville
(Calvados)
Tel. 02 31 64 39 70
M. and Mme Colin

Rooms 3 with bath and WC. **Price** 300F/45,73€ (1 pers.), 350F/53,35€ (2 pers.), +50F/7,62€ (extra bed). **Meals** Breakfast incl. No communal meal. **Facilities** Sitting room. **Pets** Animals not allowed. **Nearby** Restaurants (1km), 4 18- and 27 golf courses (about 10km); Honfleur (15km), Deauville and Trouville (12km), Normandy landing beaches (40km). **Credit cards** Not accepted. **Spoken** English. **Open** All year. **How to get there** (Map 8): 1km southeast of Pont-l'Évêque. Road Rouen/Paris, past "Intermarché", under highway bridge. Entrance 300m on left after the bridge. **No smoking** in house.

This former priory near Pont-l'Evêque was entirely remodeled by its owner at around the turn of the century. Today, guests have their breakfast in the salon, where the dark woodwork and checkered couch combine to give it a very English look. In winter the aperitif is served here in front of a wood fire. Upstairs, a large bedroom full of charm has a vast 1930s style bathroom. The other two bedrooms, smaller and simpler, are in the former stables. The only flaw — when the wind is from the south you can hear the hum of the autoroute.

405 - Château de Colombières

Colombières
14710 Trévières
(Calvados)
Tel. 02 31 22 51 65
Fax 02 31 92 24 92
Comtesse E. de Maupeou

Rooms 1 with bath and 2 suites (2-4 pers.) with bath and WC. **Price** 800-1000F/121,95-152,44€ (1-2 pers.), +200F/30,48€ (extra pers.). **Meals** Breakfast 40F/6,09€. No communal meal. **Facilities** Sitting room, tennis, fishing, horse stalls. **Pets** Dogs not allowed. **Nearby** Restaurants, 27-hole golf course; Bayeux Tapestry, marshland park. **Credit cards** Not accepted. **Spoken** English. **Open** Jun – Sept. **How to get there** (Map 7): 20km west of Bayeux via N13 towards Mosles, signposted 'Monument historique'.

Built in the 14th and 15th centuries and subsequently restructured, notably in the 18th century, the Château de Colombières is a beautiful example of architectural harmony. The suites are large, quiet, and pleasant, each with its own style. In the oldest part of the château, you reach the largest suite via a rare, wooden spiral staircase. The other suite, on the ground floor, is more classic. Our favorite is the bedroom, located upstairs and appointed with family furniture and objects. The bathroom amenities could be improved. Breakfasts are served in the large, bright dining room. Countess de Maupeou is a courteous, refined hostess.

406 - Ferme de l'Abbaye

Ecrammeville
14710 Trévières
(Calvados)
Tel. 02 31 22 52 32
Fax 02 31 22 47 25
M. and Mme Louis Fauvel

Rooms 2 suites (3-4 pers.) with bath or shower and WC. **Price** 200F/30,48€ (1 pers.), 240F/36,58€ (2 pers.), 300F/45,73€ (3 pers.), 400F/60,97€ (4 pers.). **Meals** Breakfast incl. Evening meals at communal table 90F/13,72€ (cider incl.). **Pets** Dogs not allowed. **Nearby** Swimming pool, tennis, 27-hole golf course, seaside; Normandy landing beaches, Bayeux. **Credit cards** Not accepted. **Open** All year. **How to get there** (Map 7): 19km west of Bayeux via N13, exit Formigny Trévières, then D30 towards Trévières, then on right D80 and D29, then on right towards Saint-Lô. Before the calvary, on right continue D29 for 1km, then D124 on right towards Ecrammeville. Turn on right after the church: house on left.

This large farm, set in a pretty village, is surrounded by lovely grounds. The rooms are ideal for families. Those in the farmhouse are prettily decorated with antique furniture; the other occupies a small house of its own and is more soberly decorated. We recommend it particularly for the summer. Monsieur and Madame Fauvel are very friendly hosts.

407 - Pomme Reinette

56, avenue de la
Brigade Piron
14640 Villers-sur-Mer
(Calvados)
Tel. and fax 02 31 81 17 88
M. and Mme Verbelen

Rooms 2 with bath, WC and TV. **Price** 330 and 360F/50,30 and 54,88€ (2 pers.), +70F/10,67€ (child's bed). **Meals** Breakfast incl. Evening meals at communal table, by reservation 130F/19,81€ (all incl.). **Facilities** Sitting room, heated swimming pool (May – Oct). **Spoken** Some English, Dutch. **Open** All year, only by reservation. **How to get there** (Maps 7 and 8): go out of the town dir. "Gare" and Lisieux. On the avenue, pass the "gendarmerie" and go up the road to No. 56. **No smoking** in bedrooms.

We selected this small house for its location on the coast, its extensive view in the direction of Deauville, and the warm hospitality of Monsieur and Madame Verbelen. Of recent construction, the house is built with quality materials and is surrounded by a large expanse of land. The dining room/sitting room is inviting, with a fireplace, old and contemporary furniture, sofas, and a farm table where breakfast is served. Cheerful and comfortable, the bedrooms are appointed with English-style pine furniture. The most attractive room, located upstairs, has a king-size bed.

408 - Les Aubépines

Aux Chauffourniers
27290 Appeville-Annebault
(Eure)
Tel. and fax 02 32 56 14 25
M. and Mme Closson-Maze

Rooms 2 with bath and WC. **Price** 240F/36,58€ (1 pers.), 270F/41,16 € (2 pers.), +100F/15,24€ (extra pers.). **Meals** Breakfast incl. Evening meals, by reservation 100F/15,24€ (all incl.). **Pets** Dogs allowed only on request. **Facilities** Sitting room, ping-pong, mountain bikes, croquet and games. **Nearby** Swimming pool, tennis; Pont-Audemer, Abbeys, Brotonne Regional park, Honfleur, Normandie bridge. **Spoken** English, Spanish. **Closed** Sept 30 – Mar. In low season by reservation. **How to get there** (Maps 1 and 8): 13km southeast of Pont-Audemer. Aut. A13, exit 26, dir. Pont-Audemer for about 1km. At the Médine crossroads D89 dir. Evreux. Straight on after the sign "Les Marettes", on left dir. Rondemare, then Les Chauffourniers and straight on. **No smoking.**

This is a typical Norman house with its half-timbered walls with red brick insets. It stands well off the road, surrounded by a vast garden facing a pretty valley. There are two pleasant bedrooms with private bath and toilets. Meals are served in a large dining room or a splendid kitchen. The Aubépines (Hawthorn Blossoms) makes a good base for exploring the region.

409 - Château de Boscherville

27520 Bourgtheroulde
(Eure)
Tel. and fax 02 35 87 62 12
M. and Mme Henry du Plouy

Rooms 5 with bath or shower and WC (Tel. and fax on request). **Price** 270F/41,16€ (2 pers.), +60F/9,14€ (extra bed). **Meals** Breakfast incl. No communal meal. **Facilities** Sitting room, fitness track. **Nearby** Restaurants (3km), swimming pool, tennis, riding, 18-hole golf course (10km); Château du Champs de bataille, Regional Park of Brotonne, le Bec-Hellouin (abbey), Rouen, Seine valley. **Spoken** English. **Open** All year, by reservation: (24 hours before for 1 night or 8-15 days before for longer stay.). **How to get there** (Maps 1 and 8): From Paris autoroute A13, exit Maison Brûlée. At the 1st traffic circle dir. Brionne, on left at the 3rd traffic circle then follow signs.

Built in the 18th century, the Château de Boscherville is a family estate where you will be warmly greeted by Monsieur and Madame du Plouy. The three comfortable bedrooms upstairs are well appointed, family objects and linen sheets conferring them with the charm of the past. The bedrooms on the upper floor are a bit smaller and have mansard roofs. The bathrooms have modern amenities, although one has a hip bath. Jean de la Fontaine stayed on the property several times in his day. It is still a very nice place to stop.

410 - Le Vieux Pressoir

Le Clos Potier
27210 Conteville
(Eure)
Tel. and fax 02 32 57 60 79
Mme Anfray

Rooms 5 with bath or shower and WC. **Price** 280F/42,68€ (2 pers.). **Meals** Breakfast incl. Evening meals at communal table, by reservation 120F/18,29€ (cider incl.). **Facilities** Sitting room, visit to the 18th-century cider press, bicycle rentals. **Pets** Small dogs allowed on request. **Nearby** Swimming pool, tennis, golf, seaside (12km); Honfleur, abbeys. **Credit cards** Not accepted. **Spoken** Some English. **Open** All year. **How to get there** (Map 8): 12km east of Honfleur via D180 towards Pont-Audemer, then left on D312 at Fiquefleur to Conteville; signposted.

This is an adorable small Norman farmhouse with working farm buildings and a duck pond. In the sitting room, the dining room and bedrooms, there is a charming retro decor of dried flowers, pretty lace and thick quilts on the beds.The bathrooms are well kept (the new baths in the small house are especially pleasant.) Madame Anfray is a kind hostess and there is an excellent evening meal.

411 - Les Ombelles

4, rue du Gué
27720 Dangu
(Eure)
Tel. 02 32 55 04 95
Fax 02 32 55 59 87
Mme de Saint-Père
E-mail: vextour@aol.com
Web: //vextour.ifrance.com

Rooms 2 with bath or shower and WC. **Price** 300-330F/45,73-50,30€ (2 pers.). **Meals** Breakfast incl. Half board (2 days min.) 250F/38,11€ per pers. in double room (wine incl.). Evening meals at communal table (except Sat) 130F/19,81€ (wine incl.). "Grandmother's dinner" without alcohol 90F/13,72€. **Facilities** Sitting room, painting courses or lessons in family cooking available on request. **Pets** Dogs not allowed. **Nearby** Giverny (Monet house and garden), Gisors, Rouen. **Credit cards** Not accepted. **Spoken** English. **Open** Mar 1 – Dec 15 (year round by reservation). **How to get there** (Map 9): 8km west of Gisors on D181.

Located in the village, this simple house has a sheltered terrace and a garden on a pretty river. The decoration is elegant. The bedroom on the street is small but charming with its bed in an alcove; double windows keep out noise from the street. The other room looks out onto the garden and both are prettily furnished with antiques; only the baths are somewhat old-fashioned. Les Ombelles is a hospitable place to stay.

412 - La Réserve

27620 Giverny
(Eure)
Tel. and fax 02 32 21 99 09
M. and Mme Didier Brunet

Rooms 5 with bath or shower (1 for disabled pers.) and WC. **Price** 480-680F/73,17-103,66€ (2 pers., depending on size). Special rates for family. **Meals** Breakfast incl. No communal meal. **Facilities** Sitting room, billiard, library, bicycles. **Nearby** Restaurants (2km), tennis, 18-hole golf course; Giverny Museum, Seine valley and Risle valley. **Spoken** English. **Open** All year, by reservation with credit card number. **How to get there** (Map 8): 4km north of Vernon (autoroute A13). At the entrance of Giverny, on left Rue Claude Monet. After the church go 400m, turn on left, Rue Blanche Hochedé Monet. Go 1.2km in the wood, then on left at the white arrow and immediatly on right for 800m. **No smoking.**

In the hills above Giverny, this large inviting house surrounded by prairies offers five large bright guest rooms. Each one has its own character, but all have been appointed with good taste and attention to detail. Carefully prepared breakfasts are served in a beautiful dining room and there is a warm pleasant sitting room for relaxing moments. Considerate hospitality.

413 - Le Four à Pain

8, rue des Gruchets
27140 Saint-Denis-Le-Ferment
(Eure)
Tel. 02 32 55 14 45
Madeleine Rousseau

Rooms 2 with shower and WC. **Price** 210F/32,01€ (1 pers.), 250-280F/38,11-42,68€ (2 pers.), 320F/48,78€ (3 pers.). **Meals** Breakfast incl. No communal meal. **Restaurant** "L'Auberge de l'Atelier" (500m). **Facilities** Sitting room. **Pets** Dogs not allowed. **Nearby** Riding, tennis, forest, fishing, 2 18-hole golf courses (15km), hiking; Lyons-la-Forêt, Gisors castle, Gerberoy, Giverny, Château-Gaillard. **Credit cards** Not accepted. **Spoken** English. **Open** All year. **How to get there** (Maps 1 and 9): 6km northwest of Gisors via D14bis towards Bézu and Rouen; then D17 towards Saint-Denis-le-Fervent. In the village, turn left at 2nd "Chambres d'Hôtes" sign, then Rue des Gruchets.

This charming Norman house offers guests two lovely bedrooms. One, decorated in autumnal shades, is located beneath the high, beamed-ceilings of the roof. The other is installed in the old bread oven (four à pain) in the garden. With its terra cotta floors, its charming floral fabrics and a kitchenette, it is ideal particularly for long stays. Several pieces of antique furniture and a large fireplace lend charm to the living/dining room. Good breakfasts are served with courtesy and charm.

414 - La Fèvrerie

Sainte-Geneviève
50760 Barfleur
(Manche)
Tel. 02 33 54 33 53
Fax 02 33 22 12 50
Marie-France Caillet

Rooms 2 (double bed or twin beds) with bath or shower and WC. **Price** 300-350F/45,73-53,35€ (2 pers.), +100F/15,24€ (extra bed). **Meals** Breakfast incl. No communal meal. **Facilities** Sitting room, bicycles, horse stalls (+60F/9,14€/day). **Pets** Dogs allowed on request. **Nearby** Restaurants and crêperies (3km), tennis in village, golf, sea (2km); Barfleur, Tatihou Island, Pointe de la Hague, Hôtel de Beaumont in Valognes. **Credit cards** Not accepted. **Open** All year, in winter by reservation. **How to get there** (Map 7): 3km west of Barfleur via D25 towards Quettehou, then 2nd road on right; signs. **No smoking** in bedrooms.

La Fèvrerie, a beautiful farm/manor house dating from the 16th and 17th centuries, is set in the heart of the countryside not far from the splendid Pointe de Barfleur. The interior is both warm and refined. The delightfully charming bedrooms are comfortable, prettily furnished with antiques and brightened with beautiful fabrics. Breakfasts and dinners are served in front of a large fireplace in the pleasant living room. This is a remarkable place to stay where you will be greeted with warm hospitality.

415 - Manoir de Caillemont

Saint-Georges-de-la-Rivière
50270 Barneville-Carteret
(Manche)
Tel. 02 33 53 81 16
Fax 02 33 53 25 66
Éliane Coupechoux

Rooms 1 studio (2 pers.) with kitchenette, shower, WC, and 2 suites (2-4 pers.) with bath or shower, WC and tel. **Price** Studio 340F/51,83€; suites 560F/85,37€ (2 pers.), +100F/15,24€ (extra pers. in bedroom), extra room 250F/38,11€ (2 pers.) **Meals** Breakfast incl. No communal meal. **Restaurant** "La Marine" in Carteret (5km). **Facilities** Swimming pool, billiard, ping-pong. **Pets** Dogs allowed on request. **Nearby** Tennis, riding, golf, sea; Cap de la Hague, Mont-Saint-Michel, Channel Islands. **Credit cards** Not accepted. **Spoken** English. **Open** May – Oct, by reservation in low season. **How to get there** (Map 6): 35km south of Cherbourg via D903. At Barneville-Carteret head for Coutances. Phone for directions.

This old Norman manor has a studio and two suites consisting of a bedroom and a sitting room which are very comfortable, quiet and well kept. The studio is decorated in country style. The bedrooms are more classic, the one upstairs quite attractive with Louis XV wood paneling. Excellent, hearty breakfasts are served. There is a heated swimming pool hidden by a terrace. Madame Coupechoux is a very friendly hostess.

416 - Les Rousselières

Château de Brucheville
50480 Brucheville
(Manche)
Tel. 02 33 71 52 55
Mme Touraille

Rooms 1 small house (3-4 pers.) with equipped kitchen, sitting room (bed, 1 pers.) room (double bed), shower (basin, shower, bidet), separate WC, tel. (02 33 42 05 00). **Price** 1400-2200F/213,42-335,38€/week depending on season (electricity incl.) or 370F/56,40€ per day (week-end only). Possibility sheet rentals and housework. **Pets** Animals not allowed. **Nearby** Utah Beach (7km), riding, tennis, golf. **Open** Easter – Nov 1, by reservation, Contract; deposit and guarantee: 1000F/152,44€. **How to get there** (Map 7): 8km southeast of Sainte-Mère-l'église. Phone for directions.

If you enjoy your independence, you can rent a small house in an outbuilding here, which shares the courtyard with this beautiful 16th-century manor house; there is a large meadow in the back. Comprising three ground-floor rooms and a well-equipped shower room, it is furnished and decorated with taste and personality: antique furniture, decorative objects, engravings, a piano. The salon and the bedroom are spacious, with beamed ceilings and terra cotta floor tiles.

417 - Château de Coigny

50250 Coigny
(Manche)
Tel. and fax 02 33 42 10 79
Mobile 06 07 27 02 17
Mme Ionckheere

Rooms 2 (1 with an extra bed) with bath and WC. **Price** 450F/68,60€ (1 pers.), 500F/76,22€ (2 pers.), 600F/91,46€ (3 pers.). **Meals** Breakfast incl. No communal meal. **Facilities** Sitting room. **Pets** Dogs not allowed. **Nearby** Restaurants, riding, golf; museums, Mont-Saint-Michel, Carentan bridge, marshlands, sea. **Credit cards** Not accepted. **Open** Easter – Nov 1, in low season by reservation. **How to get there** (Map 7): 11k west of Carentan via D903 towards Barneville, then D223; after the sign for Coigny take the first entrance on the left.

Built by the ancestor of one of Louis XV's marshals, Coigny is a beautiful 16th-century château. Inside, the antique furniture has been replaced by reproductions, but the decor is lovely. The bedrooms are comfortable, quiet and have a pretty view onto the courtyard or the moat. Good breakfasts are served in an immense salon with a stunning Italian Renaissance stone fireplace, an Historic Monument, decorated with sculptures and marble studs. Madame Ionckheere is a very open, friendly hostess.

418 - Belleville

Route de Saint-Marc
50530 Dragey-l'Église
(Manche)
Tel. 02 33 48 93 96
Fax 02 33 48 59 75
Florence and Olivier Brasme
E-mail: belleville@waika9.fr

Rooms 2 with bath and WC. **Price** 300F/45,73€ (1 pers.), 340F/51,83€ (2 pers.), +80F/12,19€ (extra pers.). **Meals** Breakfast incl. No communal meal. **Restaurants** "Le Marquis de Tombelaine" (4km) and "Les Jardins de l'Abbaye" in Saint-Pierre Langers (7km). **Pets** Dogs not allowed. **Nearby** 18-hole golf course (15km), tennis, sea, crossing Mont-Saint-Michel Bay on foot or horseback, with guide. **Credit cards** Not accepted. **Spoken** English. **Open** All year. **How to get there** (Map 6): 12km northwest of Avranches. On 4-lane highway in Avranches, take exit Gare SNCF, then D911 towards Vains-Jullouville (coast road). On leaving Genêts, continue towards Dragey. Sign for Dragey-l'Eglise in 2km. **No smoking** in bedrooms.

From the beach beyond which rises the silhouette of Mont-Saint-Michel, it will take you only a few minutes to reach this 17th-century house. Located at the edge of the village, it faces the lush green paddocks where Olivier Brasne trains his foals. The bedrooms are simple, elegant, cheerful and very comfortable with very pleasant bathrooms. Refined breakfasts include excellent kinds of bread and fresh orange juice. The young owners are hospitable and informal.

419 - Le Homme

Le Bourg
Bourg de Poilley
50220 Ducey
(Manche)
Tel. 02 33 48 44 41
Jeanine and Victor Vaugrente

Rooms 1 (2-4 pers.) with bath, WC, and 1 with private bathroom, WC but outside the room. **Price** 260F/39,63€ (2 pers.), +90F/13,72€ (extra pers.). **Meals** Breakfast 20F/3,04€. No communal meal. **Facilities** Sitting room. **Pets** Dogs not allowed. **Nearby** Restaurants, golf, tennis, canoeing/kayaks, seaside; Mont-Saint-Michel, Château de Fougères. **Credit cards** Not accepted. **Spoken** English. **Open** All year (2 nights min.). **How to get there** (Map 7): 10km southeast of Avranches. Autoroute A84 exit Poilley via RN176 towards Ducey.; Go 2km, then on right. In the village.

Near Mont Saint Michel, this village house offers guests a large, luminous bedroom appointed with family furniture and objects. Located upstairs next to the owners' bedroom, it has a washbasin which can be concealed by a folding screen, and a large private bathroom on the other side of the landing. If you want more privacy, ask for the second family room beneath the eaves on the second étage, which is simpler but lovely and has its own bathroom. Breakfast is served in the large bright kitchen overlooking the pretty garden.

420 - Grainville

50310 Fresville
(Manche)
Tel. 02 33 41 10 49
Fax 02 33 21 59 23
M. and Mme Brecy
E-mail: b.brecy@wanadoo.fr
Web: //perso.wanadoo.fr/grainville/

Rooms 3 with bath or shower and WC. **Price** 280-300F/42,68-45,73€ (2 pers.), +70F/10,67€ (extra bed). **Meals** Breakfast incl. No communal meal. **Facilities** Lounge, meter tel. **Nearby** Restaurants, sea, beaches, sailing school, riding, tennis, 9-hole golf course (7km); Normandy landing beaches, Sainte-Mère-l'Eglise Museum, Tatihou Island, Hôtel de Beaumont in Valognes, marshlands. **Spoken** English, Spanish, German. **Open** All year. **How to get there** (Map 7): 5km northwest of Sainte-Mère-l'Eglise. On 4-lane highway, exit Fresville to Grainville. Signs.

We loved the character and charm of this 18th-century country house on the edge of the Cotentin Park. A stone staircase with inlaid wood leads to the bedrooms upstairs, where a family atmosphere is felt immediately: most of the decor and the furniture have not changed for generations. Their original charm is intact, but they are also comfortably equipped and cheerful. Breakfasts are served in a large room with beamed ceilings, exposed stone walls, and old Norman furniture.

421 - Château de la Roque

50180 Hébécrevon
(Manche)
Tel. 02 33 57 33 20
Fax 02 33 57 51 20
Family Delisle
E-mail: mireille.delisle@wanadoo.fr
Web: www.chateau-de-la-roque.fr

Rooms 15 (2 with handicap access) with bath or shower, WC, tel. and TV. **Price** 280F/42,68€ (1 pers.), 400F/60,97€ (2 pers., double bed) and 420F/64,02€ (2 pers., twin bed), 480F/73,17€ (3 pers.). **Meals** Breakfast incl. Half board 600F/91,46€ (2 pers. in double room). Evening meals at communal table 100F/15,24€ (wine incl.). **Facilities** Sitting room, tennis, bicycles. **Pets** Dogs on a lead allowed on request. **Nearby** Riding, fishing, golf; Bayeux, Mont-Saint-Michel. **Credit card** Visa. **Spoken** English, German, Spanish. **Open** All year. **How to get there** (Map 7): 6km northwest of Saint-Lô via D972 towards Coutances. At Saint-Gilles take D77 towards Pont-Hébert for 3km.

This elegant 18th-century château is built around a lovely central garden. The bedrooms are very prettily decorated, comfortable, and are equipped with telephone and TV. The sitting room and dining room may be used by guests on request. The Château de la Roque is so professional it could be a hotel, but the hospitality and the evening meals lend it special personality.

422 - Le Manoir

Barfleur
50760 Montfarville
(Manche)
Tel. 02 33 23 14 21
M. and Mme Gabroy

Rooms 2 (incl. 1 with extra bedroom for 1 pers.) with shower and WC. **Price** 250F/38,11€ (1 pers.), 300F/45,73€ (2 pers.), +100F/15,24€ (extra room, 1 pers.). **Meals** Breakfast incl. No communal meal. **Restaurants** In 800m and "Le Bouquet de Cosqueville" in 5km. **Facilities** Sitting room. **Pets** Dogs not allowed. **Nearby** Sea and beach (300m), riding (5km), sailing school (800m); Tatihou Island, Barfleur, visits to manor houses and gardens. **Credit cards** Not accepted. **Open** All year. **How to get there** (Map 7): 1km south of Barfleur via D1 towards Saint-Vaast. On leaving Barfleur, 2nd on right then 1st on left; follow signs. **No smoking** in bedrooms.

Originally a feudal estate, this manor house has witnessed the vicissitudes of many wars. Today it is a welcoming house overlooking a few poetic cauliflower fields and the blue waters of the English Channel beyond. The interior is pleasant, comfortable and well kept, as are the bedrooms, which are bright and quite large. The beautiful garden is filled with flowers. Breakfast is served in a living room with a view over the sea.

423 - Le Château

50340 Le Rozel
(Manche)
Tel. 02 33 52 95 08
Mme Grandchamp

Rooms 1 with shower and private WC; poss. suite. **Price** 480F/73,17€; suite 200F/30,48€ (1 pers.). House rental (contract on request), (4-5 pers.) 2100-2800F/320,14-426,85€/week, depending on season + electricity. **Meals** Breakfast incl. (in room) No communal meal. **Facilities** Sitting room, poss. kitchen. **Pets** Animals allowed on request. **Nearby** Restaurants, sea (1.5km), bicycle rentals, tennis, equestrian center, golf. **Spoken** English, German. **Open** All year. (except winter on request). **How to get there** (Map 6): 15km north of Carteret via D904 dir. Les Pieux. 3km before Les Pieux (signs) take on left dir. Le Rozel. At the exit of Rozel on right.

You can enjoy bed and breakfast in the main building of this imposing fortified farmhouse dating from the 18th century. Beautiful and built on a human scale, it is decorated with tastefully chosen old furniture and objects. The shower room, located in a turret, is somewhat cramped but the excellent breakfast compensates for this drawback. You can also rent a pleasant, charmingly decorated house in a wing of the building; or another small, attractive house, but its spiral staircase is somewhat dangerous.

424 - Château de la Brisette

50700 Saint-Germain-de-Tournebut
(Manche)
Tel. 02 33 41 11 78
Fax 02 33 41 22 32
Inès and Gentien de la Hautière
Web: www.Normandy-Tourist ORG

Rooms 3 with bath, WC, tel. and TV. **Price** 450-500F/68,60-76,22€ (2 pers.), +100F/15,24€ (extra bed); Children under 5 (free). **Meals** Breakfast incl. No communal meal. **Facilities** Sitting room, pond fishing. **Pets** Dogs not allowed. **Nearby** Restaurants (8km), tennis and riding (6km), 18-hole golf course (6km); sea (10km), animal park (4km); Hôtel de Beaumont in Valognes, Old Barfleur, Nez de Jobourg, Sainte-Marie-l'Eglise. **Credit cards** All major except Amex. **Spoken** English. **Open** All year, only by reservation in winter. **How to get there** (Map 7): 8km east of Valognes via D902, road to Quettehou for 6km, then signs at intersection.

The Château de la Brisette, which is splendidly isolated, is a beautiful example of classic 18th-century architecture. The rooms are nobly proportioned, particularly the large salon with its beautiful gilt-wood paneling and its tall French doors. Looking out on the lovely lake and the countryside, the pleasant bedrooms are furnished with antiques, which vary from austere Haute Epoque to elegant Empire styles. If you're fond of antique cars, you'll appreciate those of Monsieur de la Hautière.

425 - La Hogue marine

152, rue de la Hogue
50380 Saint-Pair-sur-Mer
(Manche)
Tel. 02 33 50 58 42
Fax 02 33 50 64 92
Madame Nicole Elie
E-mail: elie.nicole@wanadoo.fr

Rooms 2 with bath or shower, WC and tel. **Price** 240F/36,58€ (1 pers.), 320F/48,78€ (2 pers.), 470F/71,65€ (3 pers.), 550F/83,84€ (4 pers.), +80F/12,19€ (extra bed) and 1 extra bedroom (no bath) 150F/22,86€ (1 pers.), 230F/35,06€ (2 pers.). **Meals** Breakfast incl. No communal meal. **Facilities** Lounge. **Nearby** Restaurants. **Spoken** English. **Closed** Oct 1 – Easter. By reservation, preferably in writing (3 night min. in Jul and Aug). **How to get there** (Map 6): 5km south of Granville via the coast road, in dir. Saint-Pair. In Saint-Pair, pass the church, take Rue Saint-Michel, then right onto Rue Mallais, again right. **No smoking** in bedrooms.

A stone's throw from the beach, this turn-of-the-century house is in the heart of the Saint-Pair residential quarter. Two guest rooms are tastefully arranged. The Granvillaise room has a very cozy, classic decor in tones of old pink and white. Upstairs, the Cancalaise bedroom is more youthful in style and is decorated in shades of blue and yellow. Both are very well kept and enjoy modern conveniences. Hospitable Madame Elie serves delicious breakfasts on a veranda reserved for guests. Prices are moderate and babies are welcome (the house is equipped.)

426 - Manoir de Bellauney

50700 Tamerville
(Manche)
Tel. 02 33 40 10 62
M. and Mme Allix-Desfauteaux

Rooms 3 with bath or shower and WC. **Price** 250-330F/38,11-50,30€ (2 pers.), +60F/9,14€ (extra bed). **Meals** Breakfast incl. No communal meal. **Facilities** Sitting room, mountain bikes. **Pets** Dogs not allowed. **Nearby** Restaurants (4km), sea, beach, water sports, tennis, 18-hole golf course (12km); Le Cotentin, Barfleur, Sainte-Mère-l'Eglise. **Spoken** English. **Closed** Nov 15 – Mar 15. **How to get there** (Map 7): 3.5km east of Valognes via D902 dir. Quettehou. House on left after the crossroads of Tamerville.

Twelve kilometers from the sea, this former monastery was built in the late fifteenth and early sixteenth centuries, becoming a farmhouse in the nineteenth century. In the same family since 1880, it has recently been made into a bed and breakfast. The bedrooms reflect the owners' wish to recreate a decor inspired by each epoch of the house: Norman, medieval and Louis XV style. Ask for one of the rooms upstairs, which are large and luminous. The bathrooms are modern and well equipped, and the Manoir overall is economical and pleasant, with kind and discreet owners.

427 - Le Prieuré Saint-Michel

61120 Crouttes
(Orne)
Tel. 02 33 39 15 15
Fax 02 33 36 15 16
M. and Mme Pierre Chahine

Rooms 3 with shower and WC. (Rent house/week 4-8 pers.). **Price** 400-600F/60,97-91,46€ (2 pers.), +50F/7,62€ (extra pers.). **Meals** Breakfast 50F/7,62€. No communal meal. **Facilities** Sitting room, art center, concerts and theatre. **Pets** Dogs not allowed. **Nearby** Golf; Ducs de Normandie Road, Route of Parks and Gardens of Lower Normandy, Honfleur, Deauville, Bagnoles-de-l'Orne. **Credit card** Visa. **Spoken** English, German, Spanish. **Closed** Nov 1 – Mar 31. **How to get there** (Map 8): 34km south of Lisieux via D579. In Vimoutiers take D916 towards Argentan; signposted "Monuments Historiques".

Once part of Jumièges Abbey, this priory looks out over lovely Norman countryside. Guests enjoy their privacy in this quiet environment. The half-timbered buildings contain very beautiful, comfortable and tastefully decorated bedrooms, and are set in a magnificently landscaped park. In the summer the monumental old cider press is used as a sitting room-dining room. Be sure to see the chapel and the 12th-century barn.

428 - La Grande Noë

61290 Moulicent
(Orne)
Tel. 02 33 73 63 30
Fax 02 33 83 62 92
Pascale and Jacques de Longcamp
E-mail: grandenoe@wanadoo.fr

Rooms 3 with bath and WC. **Price** 500-600F/76,22-91,46€ (2 pers.); +100F/15,24€ (extra bed), +80F/12,19€ (extra child's bed). **Meals** Breakfast incl. Evening meals at communal table (4 pers. min.) 250F/38,11€ (all incl.); 80F/12,19€ (children). **Facilities** Sitting room, horse stalls, horse carriage. **Pets** Dogs allowed in kennel. **Nearby** Tennis, swimming pool, 18-hole golf course; Trappe Abbey, manor houses, Old Mortagne. **Credit cards** Not accepted. **Spoken** English, Spanish. **Closed** Nov 30 – Apr 1, by reservation in winter. **How to get there** (Map 8): 24km southwest of Verneuil-sur-Avre via N12 towards Alençon. At the Sainte-Anne intersection, towards Longny via D918, then left for 4km towards Moulicent; house 800m on right.

The Grande Noé, a family mansion built in the 15th and 18th centuries, is set in the heart of the countryside. The bedrooms are gorgeous, with lovely old furniture and elegant fabrics; the bathrooms have modern amenities. There is a splendid stairwell with beautiful trompe-l'œil marble and early 19th-century stucco, and a vast, handsomely decorated salon with a fireplace. The dining room, with 18th-century natural-oak paneling, is lovely, and the hospitality is very charming.

429 - Les Gains

61310 Survie
(Orne)
Tel. 02 33 36 05 56
Fax 02 33 35 03 65
M. and Mme C. C. Wordsworth
E-mail: christopher.wordsworth@
libertysurf.fr

Rooms 3 with bath or shower and WC. **Price** 230F/35,06€ (1 pers.), 330F/50,30€ (2 pers., 1 night), 300F/45,73€ (2 pers., from2 nights), +80F/12,19€ (extra bed). **Meals** Breakfast incl. Communal meals 130F/19,81€ (wine and cider incl.). **Facilities** Sitting room. **Pets** Dogs not allowed. **Nearby** Trout fishing in village, riding; Haras du Pin (Stud Farm) (10km), Mont-Ormel Museum, Châteaux of O, Médavy and Carrouges; "Norman Switzerland". **Credit cards** Not accepted. **Spoken** English. **Closed** Dec, Nov and Feb. **How to get there** (Map 8): 10km south of Vimoutiers. In Lisieux, take D579 towards Vimoutiers, then D16 and D26 towards Exmes. In village of Survie, 20m on right behind church (sign). **No smoking** in bedrooms.

The Wordsworths left England and chose this beautiful, rolling part of Normandy on which to start a farm. The countryside today is dotted with sizeable flocks of sheep and apple trees. You will find a pleasant family atmosphere here, with charming bedrooms. Good breakfasts with homemade bread are served in summer in the pergola beside a tiny stream and a lovely garden.

430 - Le Château

Place de l'Église
76750 Bosc-Roger-sur-Buchy
(Seine-Maritime)
Tel. 02 35 34 29 70
M. and Mme Preterre Rieux

Rooms 4 with bath or shower and WC. **Price** 250F/38,11€ (1 pers.), 360F/54,88€ (2 pers.), 430F/65,55€ (3 pers.), 480F/73,17€ (4 pers.). **Meals** Breakfast incl. No communal meal. **Restaurants** In Buchy (1km). **Facilities** Sitting rooms, horse stalls, bicycles, theme weekends (gardens, hiking, golf). **Pets** Animals not allowed. **Nearby** Tennis, swimming pool, 18-hole golf course, Mortemer Abbey, park of Forges-les-Eaux. **Credit cards** Not accepted. **Spoken** English. **Closed** Dec – Feb. **How to get there** (Maps 1 and 8): 27km northeast of Rouen via A28 or N28 towards Neufchâtel, right on D919 towards Buchy, then right towards Bosc-Roger. Access possible by quiet side roads; phone for instructions.

Opposite the church in a tiny village, this small château charms immediately with its restful atmosphere. The reception rooms are prettily decorated, comfortable and fresh. The bedrooms are very pleasant and colorful, with cane or pale wood furniture, and they overlook the park (our favorites are the rotunda rooms). The bathrooms are large and also overlook the park. The owners are lively and welcoming, and you will enjoy excellent breakfasts.

431 - La Villa Florida

24, chemin du Golf
76200 Dieppe-Pourville
(Seine-Maritime)
Tel. 02 35 84 40 37
Fax 02 35 84 32 51
M. Noel

Rooms 3 with bath or shower (incl. 1 with shower and bath) and WC. **Price** 320-350F/48,78-53,35€ (2 pers.). **Meals** Breakfast incl. No communal meal. **Facilities** Sitting room, Yoga and relaxation sessions on the property. **Nearby** Restaurants (300m), 18-hole golf course (adjoining the property), sea (1.5km), water sports, heated seawater swimming pool, tennis; organ concerts, churches, château of Guy de Maupassant. **Credit cards** Not accepted. **Spoken** English. **Open** All year. **How to get there** (Maps 1): 2km west of Dieppe. Et the entrance of Dieppe, go down and turn on left towards Pourville via D75. Go 2km, then left just before the golf.

When seen from the rear this contemporary house may look somewhat austere, but as soon as you cross the threshold you will be surprised by the bright cheerfulness of its multicolored decor. It has a broad view of the lovely Gulf of Dieppe and offers three comfortable bedrooms equipped with well designed bathrooms. Each bedroom has a little corner of terrace. For those who like the beach, the sea is just nearby. Pleasant smiling hospitality.

432 - Château du Mesnil Geoffroy

76740 Ermenouville
(Seine-Maritime)
Tel. 02 35 57 12 77
Fax 02 35 57 10 24
Prince and Princesse H. Kayali
E-mail: chateaumesnil.geoffroy@wanadoo.fr

Rooms 4 and 2 suites (incl. 1 for 3 pers.) with bath and WC. **Price** 380-500F/57,93-76,22€ (2 pers.); suites 550-650F/83,84-99,09€ (2 pers.), 600F/91,46€ (3 pers.). **Meals** Breakfast (brunch) 50F/7,62€. Communal meals (except Sun and Mon) 250F/38,11€/pers. (dinner by candlelight, all incl.). **Facilities** Bicycles and exotic bird-garden. **Pets** Dogs not allowed. **Nearby** Golf, tennis, beach. **Credit cards** Visa, MasterCard, Eurocard. **Spoken** English, Spanish. **Open** All year. **How to get there** (Map 1): 7km south of Veules-les-Roses. A13, exit 25 Pont-de-Brotonne, Yvetot. In Yvetot, take D37 towards Saint-Valéry-en-Caux, go 2km beyond Sainte-Colombe, then turn right towards Fontaine-le-Dun (D70). Château 2km on left (signs).

We fell in love with the elegance and harmony of this small château, the exact symmetry of the windows with light flickering through them, the superb 18th-century woodwork in the succession of salons. The very pleasant bedrooms with walls covered with fabric or wood paneling (some rooms are small.) There is antique or period furniture. Dinners by candle light and excellent brunches (with homemade jams and cakes) are served in a lovely dining room and the owners are very friendly.

433 - Villa Les Charmettes

Allée des Pervenches
76790 Étretat
(Seine-Maritime)
Tel. 02 35 27 05 54
Fax 02 35 28 45 08
M. and Mme Renard

Rooms 3 with bath and WC. **Price** 320F/48,78€ (1 pers.), 350F/53,35€ (2 pers.), +80F/12,19€ (extra bed), +120F/18,29€ (small extra room). **Meals** Breakfast incl. No communal meal. **Nearby** Restaurants (500 m), riding, tennis, sailing, hiking, golf; Étretat, Maurice Le Blanc Museum, Terres-Neuvas Museum in Fécamp. **Spoken** English, German. **Open** All year. **How to get there** (Map 8): In Étretat. From the Town Hall, Parc des Roches (park), Rue Jules Gerbeau (2nd street on right, no camping-cars), then 2nd on right, Allée des Pervenches, to the very end.

This handsome family home was built on the heights of Etretat in the mid-19th century and enjoys tranquility and joy of living of a world of good taste and personality. The bedrooms on the upper floors are all very sunny and furnished in a "seaside" style. They face the town and the sea and their bathrooms are small but pleasant. One has an extra small room suitable for children. When the weather is fine breakfast is served on the terrace, where one can then relax stretched out on deck chairs. The young owners are courteous and discreet.

434 - Le Clos Valentin

Manoir du Val
76510 Freulleville
(Seine-Maritime)
Tel. 02 35 04 27 78
Mme Barthélémy

Rooms 1 with bath and WC. **Price** 350F/53,35€ (2 pers.) **Meals** Breakfast incl. No communal meal. **Facilities** Sitting rooms. **Pets** Animals not allowed. **Nearby** Restaurants (5 or 15km), golf; Cider Route, Pays de Bray museum. **Spoken** English, German, some Spanish. **Open** All year, by reservation. 2 days min. **How to get there** (Map 1): 15km southeast of Dieppe dir. Arques-la-Bataille, then dir. Torcy. In Saint-Germain-d'Étable, dir. Freulleville via D107 and D98. At "Manoir du Val", first house on left. **No smoking.**

In the heart of the countryside, this small, entirely renovated farmhouse has a sweeping view out over the beautiful, pastoral valley below. The house is bright and delightful, with cheerful painted beams, white walls, English pine furniture, fabrics, cushions, paintings and innumerable small decorative objects. It's a quiet house, with a family of cats snoozing peacefully in their baskets. The delightful bedrooms and private baths are small but tastefully decorated. Madame Barthélémy is a friendly hostess and her breakfasts copious and healthful.

435 - Le Val de la Mer

76400 Senneville-sur-Fécamp
(Seine-Maritime)
Tel. 02 35 28 41 93
Mme Lethuillier

Rooms 3 with bath or shower and WC. **Price** 250F/38,11€ (1 pers.), 320F/48,78€ (2 pers.), 390F/59,45€ (3 pers.). **Meals** Breakfast incl. No communal meal. **Restaurants** "La Marée" in Fécamp, "Le Maritime" (3km), "Le Relais des Dalles" (7km). **Pets** Dogs not allowed. **Nearby** 18-hole golf course (in Etretat, 18km). **Credit cards** Not accepted. **Closed** Aug. **How to get there** (Map 8): At Fécamp take D925 towards Dieppe; in the village close to the church.

Built by Monsieur Lethuillier in the local style, this house is situated in a very quiet village. It takes its name from the little road bordering its garden. The upstairs rooms are small but cozy and attractive. The one on the ground floor (our favorite) is quite large and bright with lots of windows opening on a flower-filled garden. The bathroom is private but situated across the hall. Breakfast is good and served at the large table in the living-dining room with its profusion of knick-knacks. A simple, friendly and smiling welcome.

436 - La Folie

44130 Bouvron
(Loire-Atlantique)
Tel. 02 40 56 33 03
Mme Rouget and M. Martin

Rooms 3 (1 with tel., Wheelchair access) with bath or shower and WC. **Price** 265F/40,39€ (2 pers.), +65F/9,90€ (extra bed). **Meals** Breakfast incl. No communal meal. **Facilities** Sitting room on mezzanine, riding (experienced riders only), bicycles. **Pets** Dogs allowed on request. **Nearby** Restaurants (5km), tennis, swimming pool, 18-hole golf course (5km); Canal de Nantes in Brest, Gavre forest, La Brière (canals, birds). **Spoken** English. **Closed** 2 weeks/year. **How to get there** (Map 14): 35km northwest of Nantes. Aut. exit Châteaubriant, then N171 dir. Blain for 5km and follow signs on left.

Madame Rouget, a costume designer, and Monsieur Martin, a teacher of martial arts, have entirely renovated this small 19th-century farmhouse with the idea of exercising their respective jobs and receiving guests here. Three bedrooms (one of which is equipped for handicapped people) are decorated with cheerful colors and a scattering of antique furniture. You will find a quiet, comfortable setting at La Folie, and youthful, friendly hospitality.

437 - Le Tricot
8, rue du Tricot
44350 Guérande
(Loire-Atlantique)
Tel. 02 40 24 90 72
Fax 02 40 24 72 53
M. and Mme de Champsavin
E-mail: letricot@chateauxcountry.com
Web: www.chateauxcountry.com/chateaux/letricot

Rooms 2 with bath or shower, WC, and 1 without bath (poss. suite). **Price** 420-480F/64,02-73,17€ (2 pers.); suite 850F/129,58€ (4 pers.), +120F/18,29€ (extra bed); One night free for each week reserved. **Meals** Breakfast incl. No communal meal. **Facilities** Sitting room. **Pets** Dogs not allowed. **Nearby** Seaside (5km), riding, golf; Old Guérande. **Spoken** English, German. **Closed** Nov 1 – Apr 1, poss. in winter by reservation. **How to get there** (Map 14): inside the medieval walls of Guérande, go to Chapelle de Notre-Dame la Blanche, then Rue du Tricot.

Behind the old ramparts of Guérande stand a number of beautiful old mansions, mainly from the 17th century. This one has a garden just next to the old sentry path. Beyond the wall lie the outer quarters, then the swamp land. The place is gradually being renovated with tasteful elegance and all amenities. The bedrooms, classic in style, have antique furniture. The public rooms have remained as they were, with old objects, equestrian etchings and hunting accessories... Breakfasts are refined and copious. A noble house, a little on the expensive side, particularly off-season, when its nearness to the sea is of lesser importance.

PAYS DE LA LOIRE

438 - La Ferme des Forges

44650 Legé
(Loire-Atlantique)
Tel. 02 40 04 92 99
Fax 02 40 26 31 90
Francette and René Peaudeau

Rooms 2 with shower and WC. **Price** 280F/42,68€ (2 pers.), +40F/6,09€ (extra bed). **Meals** Breakfast incl. No communal meal. **Facilities** Lounge, tel. **Pets** Dogs allowed on request. **Nearby** Swimming pool, lake fishing; Château du Bois Chevalier (17th cent.), Vendée Memorial, Saint-Philibert Abbey. **Spoken** English. **Closed** Last 3 weeks of Jan. **How to get there** (Map 14): 40km south of Nantes via D937 dir. La Roche-sur-Yon (Bordeaux). In La Rocheservière, dir. Les Lucs. In about 5km, turn right dir. Legé. Signs.

Carefully modernized, this family farmhouse enjoys a beautiful and very quiet country setting. Two guest bedrooms have been installed in the former haylofts; they are bright, cheery and spacious. The beds are comfortable (with mattresses and linens of high quality), and the bathrooms are well designed and impeccably kept. A very nice address for a "back to nature" holiday. And the welcome is simple, youthful and considerate.

439 - La Mozardière

Richebonne
44650 Legé
(Loire-Atlantique)
Tel. 02 40 04 98 51
Fax 02 40 26 31 61
M. and Mme Desbrosses
E-mail: lamozardiere@wanadoo.fr

Rooms 2 with bath and WC (possibility of one extra room). **Price** 275F/41,92€ (1 pers.), 295F/44,97€ (2 pers.), +95F/14,48€ (extra bed). Child under 3 (free). **Meals** Breakfast incl. Meals at communal table or not 120F/18,29€ (wine incl.). **Facilities** Sitting room, kitchen facilities in summer, ping-pong, bicycles. **Pets** Dogs allowed on request. **Nearby** Sports area (800m). **Credit cards** Not accepted. **Spoken** English, Spanish. **Open** All year. **How to get there** (Map 14): 1km from Legé. In the center of town, before church, take towards Touvois. 20m before leaving town, at barred Legé sign, turn left onto the small road indicating Richebonne. In 300m. **No smoking.**

This is a lengthwise old Vendée house of freestone set in a quiet, carefully tended park. Christine and Gérard accept a limited the number of reservations in order to devote maximum time to their guests, who feel very much at home here. You can choose between the blue room, decorated in retro style, and the green room with rattan furniture, which gives directly onto the garden. The good communal meal is occasionally served in beautiful enameled ceramic ware, which was made by Christine. This is a lovely, simple place to stay and the prices are very reasonable.

440 - Château Plessis-Brézot

44690 Monnières
(Loire-Atlantique)
Tel. 02 40 54 63 24
Fax 02 40 54 66 07
Mme Calonne

Rooms 5 with bath or shower and WC. **Price** 470-670F/71,65-102,14€ (1-2 pers.). **Meals** Breakfast incl. No communal meal. **Facilities** Sitting room, swimming pool, Visits to winecellars. **Pets** Dogs allowed (50F/7,62€/day) - Horses boarded (80-100F/12,19-15,24€/day). **Nearby** Restaurants (5km), mountain bikes, fishing, golf; Clisson, Puy-du-Fou, Nantes, Route du Muscadet, Atlantic seacoast. **Credit cards** Not accepted. **Spoken** English. **Open** Apr 1 – Oct 30, by reservation and deposit. In winter only by reservation. **How to get there** (Map 15): Autoroute A11, exit Nantes, then dir. Bordeaux via N149. Exit Le Pallet/La Haye/Fouassière, then N149. Before Le Pallet, on right, D7 dir. Monnières.

This 17th-century wine château stands amid acres of vineyards that produce muscadet wine. The owners have worked hard at finding old materials with which to restore the house, thus giving it a new lease on life. The grand salon is very bright with Regency woodwork in green and yellow. The entrance to the bedrooms also has carved wood and a stone floor. All the bedrooms are furnished with antiques, one of those on the second floor looks out over the roofs and the vineyards. The little chapel in the courtyard is quite pretty and the winecellars can be visited.

441 - La Cour de la Grange

2, rue des Templiers
44330 Le Pallet
(Loire-Atlantique)
Tel. 02 40 80 46 79
Mobile 06 82 38 17 45
Mireille and Alain Clémot

Rooms 1 with bath and WC; 1 suite (2-4 pers.) with shower and WC. ("Lovebird special" - Nuptial Suite). Rooms cleaned on request. **Price** 330-420F/50,30-64,02€ (2 pers.); suite 390F/59,45€ (2 pers.), +120F/18,29€ (extra pers.). **Meals** Breakfast incl. No communal meal. **Facilities** Sitting room, river fishing (boat). **Nearby** Restaurants (50m), golf, beach (45 mn). **Spoken** English. **Open** Apr 1 – Nov 1. **How to get there** (Map 15): 20km southeast of Nantes, via N249 dir. Cholet/Poitiers.Take dir. Le Pallet and cross the village. Turn 2nd road on left after the church. **No smoking** in bedrooms

With a square courtyard enclosed by old walls, this family mansion whose origins go back to the 11th century is certainly not lacking in character. The charm begins with a ravishing garden which slopes down to a small river. Inside, you will find beautiful elements of the ancient building which remain despite extensive restoration. The bedrooms, which can be transformed into family suites, are comfortable and tastefully appointed, the room on the premier étage upstairs being the most charming. Breakfasts are excellent and the young owners are pleasantly hospitable.

442 - Le Jardin de Retz

Avenue du Général de Gaulle
44210 Pornic
(Loire-Atlantique)
Tel. 02 40 82 02 29 / 02 40 82 22 69
M. and Mme Blondeau-
Raederstoerffer

Rooms 3 with bath, shower and WC. **Price** 275-295F/41,92-44,97€ (2 pers.). **Meals** Breakfast incl. No communal meal. **Facilities** Orangerie-sitting room, theme holidays, 4 pers. minimum (gardening lessons, antiquing tours...). **Pets** Dogs not allowed. **Nearby** Restaurants in Pornic, beach (150m), scenic coastal path, water sports, 18-hole golf course (400m); Pornic, sea, fishing, Noirmoutier. **Open** All year. **How to get there** (Map 14): in Pornic, pass under the arches of the castle. After 100m turn on right, follow signs "Pépinière". **No smoking** in bedrooms.

The owners, who are keen tree-growers and antique-hunters, have made their lovely home the very model of a guest house. The rooms, decorated in light natural colors, have a romantic charm. They have the warmth and comfort of a real guest room, although the sanitary facilities are a bit small. Breakfasts are well-prepared, served in a beautiful living room or outside amid shrubs and flowers (sometimes rare species). Hospitality is as serene as the site itself.

443 - La Cariote

11, route de la Carioterie
44117 Saint-André-des-Eaux
(Loire-Atlantique)
Tel. 02 40 01 20 84
M. Caldray

Rooms 1 with bath and private WC but outside the room. **Price** 290F/44,21€ (2 pers.), +80F/12,19€ (extra bed) and 1 spare bedroom 220F/35,53€. **Meals** Breakfast incl. No communal meal. **Restaurants** On seaside. **Facilities** Lounge. **Nearby** Beach (8km), salt-water therapy, 18-hole golf course; salt marshes, ornithology. **Pets** Dogs allowed on request if well behaved. **Closed** Aug 31 – Easter. **How to get there** (Map 14): 8km northeast of La Baule via N171 between La Baule and Saint-Nazaire, then Saint-André-des-Eaux. In village, take "Toutes Directions". In 1.2km, turn right towards Kermeans, then straight on. In 800m on left, signs "Chambres d'Hôtes, artiste peintre, La Cariote". **No smoking**.

In the Brière Regional Park, this house is as welcoming as the hosts who will greet you. Comfortable and very cheerfully arranged, La Cariote is decorated with a number of paintings by Madame Caldray, who formerly ran an interior decoration boutique with her husband. The small but very cozy bedroom upstairs opens into the painting atelier, where a small lounge is reserved for you. The bathroom is pleasant and, with the first rays of sunshine, breakfast is served outside.

444 - La Plauderie

1, rue du Verdelet
44680 Sainte-Pazanne
(Loire-Atlantique)
Tel. 02 40 02 45 08
Mme Mignen

Rooms 3 with bath or shower and WC. Rooms cleaned every 2 days. **Price** 270-400F/41,16-60,97€ (2 pers.). **Meals** Breakfast 35F/5,33€. No communal meal. **Restaurant** "Le Col Vert" in Fresnay-en-Retz. **Facilities** Sitting room. **Pets** Dogs allowed on request. **Nearby** Tennis, seaside, golf; Breton marshes, Noirmoutier Island. **Credit cards** Not accepted. **Spoken** English. **Open** May 1 – Oct 30. **How to get there** (Map 14): 28km southwest of Nantes via D751 towards Pornic/Noirmoutier. In Port Saint-Père left on D758 towards Bourgneuf-en-Retz/Noirmoutier.

Right beside a church, this beautiful house is hidden in a delightfully romantic garden. Madame Mignen's hospitality is reason enough to recommend La Plauderie, but you will also find very prettily decorated, comfortable accommodations. The bedrooms are elegant, and you can make yourself a cup of coffee or tea there. This is a charming place with many interesting things to do nearby.

445 - Palais Briau

Rue de la Madeleine
44370 Varades
(Loire-Atlantique)
Tel. 02 40 83 45 00
Fax 02 40 83 49 30
M. and Mme Devouge
E-mail: palaisbrio@aol.com
Web: //welcome.to/palais-briau

Rooms 3 and 1 suite with bath or shower and WC. **Price** 550-850F/83,84-129,58€ (1-2 pers.). **Meals** Breakfast incl. No communal meal. **Facilities** Sitting room. **Pets** Dogs not allowed. **Nearby** Restaurants (banks of the Loire, 1 km), swimming pool, tennis, canoeing, fishing, 18-hole golf course; Loire châteaux, Angers, Château du Pin Garden. **Credit cards** Not accepted. **Spoken** English. **Closed** Dec, Jan and Feb, by reservation and deposit. **How to get there** (Map 15): 40km west of Angers and 44km of Nantes. Autoroute A11 exit Beaupréau via N23 dir. Nantes. In Varades, 1st traffic circle, on left Palais Briau.

This palace in Palladian style was built in 1854 by Edouard Mol for François Briau, who made his fortune in railroads under Napoleon III. The building with its vast park is perched on a hillside facing the Loire valley and the abbey church of Montglonne at St-Florent-le-Vieil. It has kept much of its original furniture. The bedrooms upstairs have been entirely redone in Napoleon III style with lovely bathrooms. The view from the back bedroom is adequate. Breakfast is served in the small salon. All in all the house is rather amazing and the welcome is a pleasant one.

P A Y S   D E   L A   L O I R E

446 - Château des Briottières

49330 Champigné
(Maine-et-Loire)
Tel. 02 41 42 00 02
Fax 02 41 42 01 55
Hedwige and François de Valbray
E-mail: briottieres@wanadoo.fr
Web: www.briottieres.com

Rooms 9 with bath, WC and tel. **Price** 650, 900 and 1500F/99,09, 137,20 and 228,67€ (2 pers.). **Meals** Breakfast 60F/9,14 €. Half board 810F/123,48€ per pers. in double room. Evening meals at separate tables, by reservation 300F/45,73€ (all incl.). **Facilities** Sitting room, French billiards, heated swimming pool (Jun 1– Oct 15), horse stalls, fishing, bicycles. **Nearby** Tennis, riding, 18-hole golf courses (5 and 15km); Anjou. **Credit cards** Visa, Eurocard, MasterCard. **Spoken** English. **Open** All year, by reservation from Jan 1 to Mar 1. **How to get there** (Map 15): 25km north of Angers towards Laval. At Montreuil-Juigné, right on D768 through Feneu, then Champigné.

The enterprising owners of the Château des Briottières have successfully conserved its noble allure of centuries passed, making it a highly sought-after place to stay in the region. Inside, the immense hallway leading to the reception rooms and the antique furniture say much about the beauty of the bedrooms. Small or large, they are lovely and welcoming. You will enjoy good, family-style cuisine (whose price is justified by the elegance of the château) and marvelous hospitality.

447 - Beauregard

22, rue Beauregard - Cunault
49350 Chênehutte-les-Tuffeaux
(Maine-et-Loire)
Tel. 02 41 67 92 93
Fax 02 41 67 95 35
M. and Mme Tonnelier

Rooms 1 suite (4 pers.) 2 bedrooms with bath, WC and TV. **Price** 380F/57,93€ (2 pers.), 500F/76,22€ (3 pers.), 620F/94,51€ (4 pers.). **Meals** Breakfast incl. No communal meal. **Facilities** Fishing in the Loire. **Pets** Small dogs allowed on request. **Nearby** Restaurants (5km), equestrian center, golf, hiking; churches of Trèves-Cunault, Le Thoureil, Montreuil-Bellay, Saumur. **Credit Cards** Not accepted. **Spoken** English. **Open** Apr 1 – Nov 1. **How to get there** (Map 15): 10km west of Saumur on D751 towards Gennes; before the village of Cunault, on left on the Loire.

This handsome manor house, built in the 15th century, enlarged in the 16th and again in the 19th, has a superb view over the Loire. Monsieur Tonnelier inherited it from his father, an artist and antique dealer, who must have been a man of taste to judge by the many objects and furniture of various epochs which are still there to be seen. The bedrooms are in the oldest part of the house. They are refined and comfortable and their bathrooms are charming. Breakfast is served in the dining room, appointed in a rather classic manner. Monsieur and Madame Tonnelier are excellent hosts as well as impassioned classical music lovers.

448 - La Cour Pavée

374, route de Montsoreau
49400 Dampierre-sur-Loire
(Maine-et-Loire)
Tel. 02 41 67 65 88
Fax 02 41 51 11 61
M. Jehanno

Rooms 2 and 1 suite with bath or shower and WC. Rooms cleaned on request. **Price** Room 390F/59,45€ (2 pers.); suite 650F/99,09€ (4 pers.). Special rates for more than 3 days. **Meals** Breakfast incl. Evening meals (except Sun), by reservation 150-180F/22,86-27,44€ (wine incl.). **Pets** Dogs not allowed. **Facilities** Sitting room **Nearby** 18-hole golf course (14km); Saumur, Wine Route, Fontevraud, Ussé. **Open** All year. **How to get there** (Map 15): 4km east of Saumur dir. Fontevraud, Chinon. Just at the entrance of Dampierre.

The "Paved Courtyard" owes its name to the flagstones from the nearby Abbey of Fontevraud which have been laid in the courtyard. The house is narrowly separated from the Loire by a road, which is dominated by the terrace planted with century-old trees. Guests are offered spacious, comfortable bedrooms decorated with shimmering fabrics and painted furniture; the bathrooms are immense. Jean-Jacques Jehanno is a warm and hospitable host, and prepares excellent breakfasts beautifully served with fine china and silverware. A spacious, lovely home.

449 - Malvoisine

49460 Ecuillé
(Maine-et-Loire)
Tel. and fax 02 41 93 34 44
Mobile 06 88 90 15 76
M. and Mme de La Bastille
E-mail: bastille-pr@wanadoo.fr
Web: www.malvoisine-bastille.com

Rooms 3 with bath and WC. **Price** 280-350F/42,68-53,35€ (2 pers.), +90F/13,72€ (extra bed). **Meals** Breakfast incl. Evening meals at communal table or not 130F/19,81€ (wine incl.). **Facilities** Walk and bicycles, painting studio available. **Nearby** Fishing, 18- hole golf course, boat rentals; route du Roi René (châteaux), music and singing lessons available. **Spoken** English **Open** All year, by reservation in winter. **How to get there** (Map 15): 18km north of Angers via N162 dir. Laval, then D768 in Montreuil-Juigné, dir. Champigné; 5km after Feneu, pass the small crossroads and drive 1km on D768, then on right "La Roche Malvoisine" and first road on left.

The welcoming young de La Bastille family has recently renovated this charming small Anjou farmhouse with a sure sense of good taste. Apart from the guest room in a corner of the ground floor, all the bedrooms are lovely, with beautifully coordinated colors, tasteful furniture, and high-quality decorative materials; they enjoy a sweeping view over a magnificent countryside. The breakfasts are good, the dinners mouthwatering (game is occasionally served in winter). A must.

450 - Le Clos du Rocher

Chemin des Bigottières
Dép. 191
49460 Feneu
(Maine-et-Loire)
Tel. and fax 02 41 32 05 37
M. and Mme Pauvert

Rooms 2 with bath or shower (1 with private WC but outside the room). **Price** 300-370F/45,73–56,40€ (2 pers.). **Meals** Breakfast incl. **Facilities** Swimming pool, kayak, piano. **Nearby** Riding, 18-hole golf course (10km), boating center, river fishing; Château du Plessis-Bourré, Château du Plessis-Macé, Angers. **Spoken** Some English. **Open** All year. **How to get there** (Map 15): 13km northwest of Angers via D770 dir. Sablé. In Feneu, take the road of Grez-Neuville for 2.5km then follow signs on road n° 191.

Built about thirty years ago, Le Clos du Rocher is surrounded by a park full of flowers and trees. You will be greeted with marvelous hospitality and ushered into an elegant and inviting interior with traditional old French furniture. Decorated in shades of yellow, the ravishing guest rooms are quiet, comfortable, and truly irresistible, especially the Azalée room. The delicious breakfast is served outdoors or in a lovely dining room.

451 - Le Domaine de Mestré

49590 Fontevraud-l'Abbaye
(Maine-et-Loire)
Tel. 02 41 51 72 32 / 02 41 51 75 87
Fax 02 41 51 71 90
M. and Mme Dominique Dauge
E-mail: domaine-de-mestre@wanadoo.fr
Web: www.dauge-fontevraud.com

Rooms 11 and 1 suite with bath and WC. **Price** 325F/49,54€ (2 pers.), +50F/7,62€ (extra pers.); suite 590F/89,94€ (4 pers.). **Meals** Breakfast 40F/6,10€. Half board 330F/53,35€ per pers. in double room (1 week min.). Lunch and evening meals at separate tables (except Sun and Thurs), by reservation 145F/22,11€ (wine not incl.). **Facilities** Sitting room. **Pets** Small dogs allowed. **Nearby** Golf; Loire châteaux. **Credit cards** Not accepted. **Spoken** English, German. **Closed** Dec 20 – Feb 1. Open only weekends in Feb and Mar. With reservation confirmation by mail or fax. **How to get there** (Maps 15 and 16): 12km southeast of Saumur via D947 towards Chinon, then head for Fontevrault-l'Abbaye; between Montsoreau and Fontevrault.

This beautiful house was once the farm of the monks of Fontevrault Abbey. The comfortable bedrooms have been very prettily decorated, while their traditional elegance has been conserved. Excellent, generous dinners are served in a lovely dining room at elegant separate tables. (Meal prices are based on the farm produce used, including meats, vegetables, and dairy products, which are prepared as in the past). Perfumed soaps are also made on the premises using an ancient process, and they are for sale.

452 - La Croix d'Etain

2, rue de l'Écluse
49220 Grez-Neuville
(Maine-et-Loire)
Tel. 02 41 95 68 49
Fax 02 41 18 02 72
M. and Mme Bahuaud

Rooms 4 with bath and WC. **Price** 380-480F/57,93-73,17€ (2 pers.), +100F/15,24€ (extra bed). **Meals** Breakfast incl. Evening meals served occasionally, by reservation 170F/25,91€ (wine not incl.). **Facilities** Sitting room (TV). **Nearby** Restaurants, golf, fishing, tennis, riding, houseboat rental; châteaux, vineyards. **Credit cards** All major. **Open** All year. **How to get there** (Map 15): 3km southeast of Lion-d'Angers. RN162 from Angers towards Laval. In Grez-Neuville, between church and Mayenne River (access Rue de l'Ecluse).

This distinctive house in old Grez-Neuville has been entirely restored and has pleasant modern amenities. The bedrooms are quite modern, spacious and light because of their corner location; they are very tastefully furnished. In good weather you can enjoy the large park behind the house or stroll along the banks of the Mayenne, which is only a few steps away.

453 - Château du Plessis

49220 La Jaille-Yvon
(Maine-et-Loire)
Tel. 02 41 95 12 75
Fax 02 41 95 14 41
Paul and Simone Benoist
E mail: plessis.anjou@wanadoo.fr
Web: perso.wanadoo.fr/plessis

Rooms 8 (2 with balcony) with bath and WC. **Price** 780-820F/118,91-125€ (2 pers.). **Meals** Breakfast incl. Half board 660F/100,61€ per pers. in double room. Evening meals (except Sun) at communal table, by reservation 280F/42,68€ (all incl.). **Facilities** Sitting room, tel., horse stalls, hot-air ballooning. **Pets** Dogs allowed on request. **Credit cards** Visa, Amex, Diners. **Spoken** English, Spanish. **Open** Apr 1 – Oct 31. **How to get there** (Map 15): 11km north of Lion-d'Angers via N162. Go 11km then take D189 and follow signs.

Madame Benoist loves flowers, and fresh bouquets adorn the Château du Plessis throughout the seasons. Your hosts are naturally hospitable and Monsieur Benoist is expert at advising guests on touring the region. The bedrooms are very well decorated, and the bathrooms irreproachable. You will enjoy delicious evening meals, which are served in a lovely dining room with 1930s frescos.

454 - Manoir Saint-Gilles

La Cirottière
49160 Longué-Jumelles
(Maine-et-Loire)
Tel. 02 41 38 77 45
Fax 02 41 52 67 82
M. and Mme Claude Naux
E-mail: cmcnaux@aol.com

Rooms 3 and 1 suite with bath or shower and WC. Rooms cleaned every 3 days. **Price** 350F/53,36€ (room 1 pers.), 380-400F/57,93-60,98€ (2 pers.), suite 680F/103,67€ (3 pers.). **Meals** Breakfast incl. No communal meal. **Facilities** Sitting room. **Pets** Dogs not allowed. **Nearby** Restaurants (1.5km), golf, fishing in the Loire. **Credit cards** Not accepted. **Open** Apr 1 – Nov 1. By request in low season (2 nights min. end May – Sept). **How to get there** (Map 15): 15km from Saumur via RN147. In Longué, at the traffic circle (Super U), on right towards Blou, Saint-Philibert, Vernantes, go straight on to the stop. At the first intersection turn on right, road on left (sign voie sans issue), turn left again, then right 400m farther on. Entrance to La Cirottière 100m ahead. **No smoking** in bedrooms.

Anne du Bellay was the first known owner of this beautiful 15th-century manor house. It is surrounded by flower beds, a rose garden and small formal gardens that enhance the refinement of its façade. The bedrooms are cheerful and very comfortable; several modern pieces mingle with antique furniture and much of the floor is in superb terra-cotta. All combine to form a very tasteful whole, which is further enhanced by the owners' great hospitality.

455 - La Poirière

49320 Maunit-Chemellier
(Maine-et-Loire)
Tel. 02 41 45 59 50
Fax 02 41 45 01 44
Mme Edon
E-mail: daniel.edon@wanadoo.fr

Rooms 3 with bath or shower and WC. **Price** 260F/39,63€ (2 pers.), +90F/13,72€ (extra bed). **Meals** Breakfast incl. Evening meals at communal table or not 110F/16,77€ (wine incl.). **Facilities** Sitting room **Pets** Dogs not allowed. **Nearby** Tennis, pond, fishing, 18-hole golf course (9km). **Open** All year. **How to get there** (Map 15): 25km south of Angers via dir. Niort, Poitiers. In Brissac-Quincé, take D761. In Alleuds, on left D90 dir. Chemellier. **No smoking** in bedrooms.

Set in a farming hamlet and fronted by a carefully tended garden, La Poirière is a small lengthwise house – a longère typical of the Angers region. Its delightful guest rooms are comfortable, well kept, and the bathroom facilities are impeccable (our favorite rooms are upstairs). On the ground floor, guests can enjoy a charming living room and a small dining room, where Madame Edon serves delicious family cooking in the evening. The "Pear Tree" is a simple, good bed and breakfast for very reasonable prices.

456 - Château du Montreuil

49140 Montreuil-sur-Loir
(Maine-et-Loire)
Tel. 02 41 76 21 03
M. and Mme Bailliou

Rooms 4 with bath or shower and WC. **Price** 330F/50,30€ (1 pers.), 380F/57,93€ (2 pers.), +100F/15,24€ (extra bed). **Meals** Breakfast incl. Evening meals at communal table 135F/20,58€ (wine incl.). **Facilities** Sitting room, tel. **Nearby** Boating on the Loir, swimming pool, tennis, riding, mountain bikes, golf; Champigné, Sablé, Angers, châteaux (Plessis, Bourré, Mt Geoffroy, Brissac, Serrant), national stud farms, Wine Route, Saumur, Fontevraud Abbey. **Spoken** English. **Closed** Nov 15 – Mar 15, by reservation and deposit. **How to get there** (Map 15): 22km north of Angers. Autoroute A11, exit Seiches-sur-Loir, then dir. Seiches, then D74 dir. Tiercé and Montreuil. At the village exit.

In the heart of Anjou, this curious château was built in 1840 in "troubadour" style by the architect Hodé. Its broad terrace overlooks the Loir and the large wooded park. There is a neo-gothic reading room, heated in winter by a large fireplace. The mistress of the house prepares her homemade specialties (onion tart, farm-raised chicken or poultry dishes Anjou style) and serves them in the little dining room. The bedrooms are upstairs, they have antique furniture and a view of the river. Our favorite is "L'Evêque," done in shades of blue.

457 - Le Jau

Route de Nantes
49610 Murs-Érigné
(Maine-et-Loire)
Tel. 02 41 57 70 13
Mobile 06 83 26 38 80
Mme Terriere
Web: le.jau@anjou-et-loire.com

Rooms 3 with bath or shower and WC (poss. TV.). 2 houses rentals in summer. **Price** 300-350F/45,73-53,35€ (2 pers.), +100F/15,24€ (extra bed). **Meals** Breakfast incl. Evening meals at communal tables or not, by reservation 130F/19,81€ (wine incl.). **Facilities** Sitting room (TV), tel. **Pets** Dogs not allowed. **Nearby** River fishing, golf. **Open** All year, by reservation Nov 1 – Easter. **How to get there** (Map 15): 12km south of Angers via N160 dir. Cholet, then Les Ponts-de-Cé, Érigné and dir. Murs, Route de Châlonnes (corniche Angevine). 100m on left after the red light. **No smoking** in bedrooms.

You will be given a warm welcome in this large house from the early 19th century. It is situated not far from Angers, in a village with a stream running through, where you can go fishing, and its grounds face the church, separating it from the built up part of town. The pink bedroom with its fruitwood furniture is a true joy. Another bedroom, more sober in style, still contains the library of the elder daughter, and the third is the simplest of all. Breakfast is served in the huge blue and yellow kitchen and dinner in a pleasant sitting-dining room very open to the outside.

PAYS DE LA LOIRE

458 - Château du Goupillon

49680 Neuillé
(Maine-et-Loire)
Tel. and fax 02 41 52 51 89
Monique Calot

Rooms 2 and 1 suite (5 pers.) with bath or shower and WC. **Price** 350-450F/53,35-68,60€ (2 pers.), +90F/13,72€ (extra pers.); suite 750F/114,33€ (5 pers.). **Meals** Breakfast incl. No communal meal. **Restaurants** Many in Saumur. **Facilities** Sitting room. **Pets** Dogs allowed on request. **Nearby** Swimming pool, tennis, golf; Loire Valley (châteaux de la Loire), Anjou Natural Park. **Credit cards** Not accepted. **Open** All year. **How to get there** (Map 15): 9km north of Saumur towards Longué. At the La Ronde traffic circle take D767 towards Vernantes for 2km, then left on D129 towards Neuillé. 1km before Neuillé take the Fontaine-Suzon road, then follow signs.

In the heart of the Anjou natural park, this 19th-century château is built in Napoleon III style and its stately windows illuminate a very inviting interior. You will find lovely old paneling with stripped down wood, linen-covered walls and some fine antiques. The Louis XVI room is charming with its 18th-century furniture and its pretty bathroom. The other bedroom is also nice, but simpler in style. The suite is spacious, with its appealing little boudoir and pleasant bathroom. Breakfast is served in the dining room. You will not fail to be won over by the kindness of Madame Calot and her love for her house.

459 - La Bouquetterie

118, rue du Roi-René
49250 Saint-Mathurin-sur-Loire
(Maine-et-Loire)
Tel. 02 41 57 02 00
Fax 02 41 57 31 90
Claudine Pinier

Rooms 6 (2 in the 18th-century outbuildings) with shower and WC. **Price** 215-275F/32,77-41,92€ (1 pers.), 300-350F/45,73-53,35€ (2 pers.). Special rates for more than 3 days. **Meals** Breakfast incl. Evening meals at communal table, by reservation 125F/19,05€ (wine incl.). Kitchenette reserved for guests. **Facilities** Sitting room, tel. (France Télécom card), organisation of 6 weekends "découvertes insolites" per year in low season. **Pets** Dogs not allowed. **Nearby** Fishing in Loire, swimming pool; Loire Valley (châteaux de la Loire). **Credit cards** Not accepted. **Spoken** English, Italian. **Open** All year. **How to get there** (Map 15): 20km southeast of Angers via D952 (touristic route along Loire), towards Saumur; 1km before Saint-Mathurin-sur-Loire.

This large 19th-century house stands near the banks of the Loire with an expanse of garden and orchard behind it. The owner, Claudine Pinier, is always ready to share her passion for the history of the region. She and her children will greet you in a relaxed and friendly atmosphere. Only a road separates the house from the Loire (though it has a certain amount of traffic). The rooms are simple but quite large, with 19th-century furniture. The quietest ones are at the rear. The others have double-glazed windows. Two bedrooms have been installed in what used to be the stables, both modern with kitchen facilities.

PAYS DE LA LOIRE

460 - Château de Beaulieu

Route de Montsoreau
49400 Saumur
(Maine-et-Loire)
Tel. 02 41 67 69 51
Fax 02 41 67 63 64
Andréa and Jean-Christian Michaut

Rooms 6 and 1 suite (4 pers.) with bath and WC. **Price** Room 370-450F/56,40-68,60€ (2 pers.), suite 500F/76,22€ (2 pers.), +120F/18,29€ (extra bed). **Meals** Breakfast incl. **Facilities** Sitting room, meter tel., heated swimming pool, billiards. **Nearby** Water sports and swimming in Loire, 9-hole golf course; Fontevraud, Wine Route. **Credit card** Visa. **Spoken** English, German. **Closed** Dec and Jan. **How to get there** (Map 15): 2km east of Saumur via D947 towards Chinon. Go along the Loire to the "Gratien et Meyer" wine cellars; sign.

Protected from the road by a wall and several century-old trees, this château is located some fifty meters from the banks of the Loire. Youthful and welcoming, André and Jean-Christian have comfortably arranged the sitting room, the billiard room and the dining room with a combination of antique and modern furnishings. The bedrooms are classic and well furnished: our favorite by far is the Rose room and the suite. Dinners, which are a very convivial moment, are served outdoors in good weather.

461 - La Croix de la Voulte

Route de Boumois
Saint-Lambert-des-Levées
49400 Saumur
(Maine-et-Loire)
Tel. 02 41 38 46 66
M. and Mme Jean-Pierre Minder

Rooms 4 with bath or shower and WC. **Price** 350-450F/53,35-68,60€ (2 pers.). **Meals** Breakfast 35F/5,33€. No communal meal. **Restaurants** "Le Relais", "Les Forges de Saint-Pierre" in Saumur (5km) and "La Toque Blanche" in Rosiers-sur-Loire (9km). **Facilities** Sitting room, swimming pool. **Pets** Dogs allowed on request. **Nearby** Golf, Saumur, Fontevraud, Langeais, Boumois, Montreuil-Bellay. **Credit cards** Not accepted. **Spoken** English, German. **Open** Apr 15 – Oct 15. **How to get there** (Map 15): 4km northwest of Saumur via D229 towards Château de Boumois.

This is a lovely group of houses made of native limestone; all are very old and have been beautifully restored. The bedrooms are tastefully decorated, with antique furniture lending each a special style. Breakfasts are truly delicious and are charmingly served on a flower-filled terrace, or in a small dining room. The bedrooms are spacious, and in good weather you can enjoy the park, which has plenty of garden furniture.

462 - Domaine du Marconnay

Route de Saumur
Parnay
49400 Saumur
(Maine-et-Loire)
Tel. 02 41 67 60 46
Fax 02 41 50 23 04
M. and Mme Goumain

Rooms 3 and 1 suite (4 pers.) with bath or shower and WC. **Price** 260-300F/39,63-45,73€ (2 pers.), +65F/9,90€ (extra pers.). **Meals** Breakfast 32F/4,87€. No communal meal. **Facilities** Sitting room with TV, swimming pool, visit to wine cellar and tasting, troglodyte caves. **Pets** Dogs allowed on request. **Nearby** Restaurants, 18-hole golf course; banks of Loire, Saumur, Montsoreau, Fontevraud, Ussé, Loire châteaux. **Credit cards** Not accepted. **Spoken** English, German. **Open** Apr 1 – Nov 11. **How to get there** (Map 15): 6km east of Saumur via D947 towards Chinon, then 6km and signs.

In a charming village on the banks of the Loire, you will be warmly welcomed in this late 19th-century house, which is part of a wine estate. Here you will find the three characteristics of the region: saumur-champigny wines, houses of white tufa and troglodyte dwellings. The house has been simply adapted for guests; bedrooms and bathrooms are both done in sober good taste. The "château" stands just opposite, built in the 15th century and remodeled in the 18th, and behind it, carved out of the rock, an amazing labyrinth of caves. An impressive set of buildings on lovely grounds.

463 - Château de Mirvault

Azé
53200 Château-Gontier
(Mayenne)
Tel. and fax 02 43 07 10 82
Brigitte and François d'Ambrières

Rooms 2 with bath, WC, and 2 spare rooms. **Price** 300F/45,73€ (1 pers.), 400F/60,97€ (2 pers.), +100F/15,24€ (extra pers.). **Meals** Breakfast incl. No communal meal. **Restaurant** Nearby, on other bank of river (1km). **Facilities** Sitting room (piano), pond and river (water sports), fishing, bicycles, horse stalls. **Pets** Dogs not allowed. **Nearby** Golf, tennis, swimming pool, cruise boats on the Mayenne; Château-Gontier. **Credit cards** Not accepted. **Spoken** English. **Open** Apr 1 – Nov 1 (by request in low season). **How to get there** (Map 15): 1km from Château-Gontier by the bypass, avenue "René Cassin", exit traffic circle "route de Laval" (N162), then signs

On the outskirts of Château-Gontier, but perfectly protected by its spacious grounds, this large estate, which has been in the same family since 1573, is located near the Mayenne. The welcome in this old family home is courteous and gracious. The large reception rooms are superbly furnished and provide space in which to be alone. The bedrooms are beautiful as well as comfortable (those on the second floor are ideal for families). And if you like, in the evening, you can take a boat and dine in a little restaurant across the river.

PAYS DE LA LOIRE

464 - Château du Bas du Gast

6, rue de la Halle-aux-Toiles
53000 Laval
(Mayenne)
Tel. 02 43 49 22 79
Fax 02 43 56 44 71
M. and Mme Williot

Rooms 3 with bath, WC, and 1 suite (4 pers.) with bath, shower and WC. **Price** Rooms 550-650F/83,84-99,09€ (2 pers.); suite 1150F/175,31€ (2 pers.), +150F/22,86€ (extra child's bed), +250F/38,11€ (extra bed). **Meals** Breakfast 50F/7,62€, 80F/12,19€ (English). No communal meal. **Restaurants** 5 good in Laval. **Facilities** Sitting room. **Pets** Dogs allowed on request. **Nearby** Golf, swimming pools, cruising, fishing, riding. **Credit cards** Not accepted. **Spoken** English. **Closed** Dec and Jan. **How to get there** (Map 7): In Laval near the town hall and the Perrine Garden.

This 18th-century mansion in purest Classical style (and classified as a historic monument) stands in the heart of Laval and has a garden of clipped boxwood extended by a romantic park. Monsieur and Madame Williot, both fascinated by history and architecture, will be happy to tell you the story of their home and advise you on your local touring. The reception rooms, and some of the bedrooms as well, have lovely old woodwork. The bedrooms are as handsome as they are comfortable, many are quite spacious and decorated with family furniture, objects and etchings, and adorned with beautiful fabrics.

465 - Le Vieux Presbytère

53640 Montreuil-Poulay
(Mayenne)
Tel. 02 43 00 86 32
Fax 02 43 00 81 42
M. and Mme Legras-Wood
E-mail: 101512.245@compuserve.com.

Rooms 2 with bath, shower and WC. **Price** 320F/48,78€ (2 pers.). **Meals** Breakfast incl. No communal meal but kitchen available. **Facilities** Sitting rooms. **Nearby** Restaurants, lake with sports facilities (4km), riding (4km), 18-hole golf course (15km); Old Laval, Lassay and Jublain Châteaux (Roman vestiges). **Spoken** English, German, Spanish. **Credit cards** Not accepted. **Closed** In winter. **How to get there** (Map 7): 11km north of Mayenne. RN12 between Javron and Mayenne, take D34 towards Lassay-Bagnols-de-l'Orne. Follow signs from Montreuil Church.

Former foreign correspondents, Patricia and Denis finally put their suitcases down in this elegant house. You will be very hospitably received here, where you will find a pleasantly rustic and inviting interior. With attractive wallpaper, engravings and magazines, the guestrooms have the air of friends' rooms; the bathrooms have comfortable amenities. You can also enjoy a vast, carefully tended flower garden which is traversed by a small brook. There is a pleasant summer sitting room installed in an outbuilding.

466 - Logis de Villeprouvé

53170 Ruillé-Froid-Fonds
(Mayenne)
Tel. and fax 02 43 07 71 62
M. Christophe Davenel

Rooms 4 with bath or shower and WC. **Price** 170F/25,91€ (1 pers.), 250F/38,11€ (2 pers.), 310F/47,25€ (3 pers.). **Meals** Breakfast incl. Half board 200F/30,48€ per pers. in double room. Evening meals at communal table 80F/12,19€ (wine not incl.). **Facilities** Sitting room, fishing. **Pets** Small dogs allowed on request. **Nearby** Solesmes Abbey, La Trappe. **Credit cards** Not accepted. **Spoken** English. **Open** All year. **How to get there** (Map 15): 25km south of Laval via N162 to Villiers-Charlemagne, then D109; signposted in the village.

We love this 17th-century farmhouse, which is as pretty as its natural surroundings. A very beautiful wooden staircase leads to the comfortable bedrooms, which have been carefully decorated in a warm, rustic style with elegant fabrics, thick carpets and lace curtains. They are all very pleasant and have impeccable small bathrooms. Only home-grown farm produce is used in the excellent evening meals, which are cheerfully served by Madame Davenel, and the grog flambé au calvados is spectacular (and delicious).

467 - Le Logis et les Attelages du Ray

53290 Saint-Denis-d'Anjou
(Mayenne)
Tel. 02 43 70 64 10
Fax 02 43 70 65 53
Martine and Jacques Lefebvre

Rooms 3 with shower and WC. **Price** 350-395F/53,35-60,21€ (2 pers.), 540F/82,32€ (3 pers.), +150F/22,86€ (child's bed). −10% from 3 to 4 nights and −15% from 5 to 7 nights. **Meals** Breakfast incl. Evening meals on Sat, by reservation (6 pers. min.) 160F/24,39€ (all incl.). **Facilities** Sitting room, theme rides in horsedrawn carriage with lunch in country; carriage school. **Pets** Dogs not allowed. **Nearby** Restaurant (800m), golf, fishing. **Credit card** Visa. **Spoken** English. **Open** All year. **How to get there** (Map 15): 9km southwest of Sablé-sur-Sarthe via D27 towards Angers; in Saint-Denis-d'Anjou. Follow signs for "Chambres d'Hôtes - Attelages du Ray".

You will find a friendly and attentive welcome in this very well-restored old house. The bedrooms, decorated in blue and tastefully furnished, are very charming. Two of them – including the one with the four-poster bed – have a superb floor of antique terracotta tiles. The excellent breakfasts are served in a ravishing dining room with beautiful 18th-century furniture. In summer Monsieur Lefebvre, an enthusiastic horseman, will invite you for a carriage ride. Unfortunately, there is not yet a sitting room for guests.

PAYS DE LA LOIRE

468 - La Maison du Roi René

4, Grande-Rue
53290 Saint-Denis-d'Anjou
(Mayenne)
Tel. 02 43 70 52 30
Fax 02 43 70 58 75
M.-C. and P. de Vaubernier
E-mail: roi.rene@wanadoo.fr

Rooms 4 (incl. 1 with small sitting room) with bath or shower, TV and tel. Special rates for long stays. **Price** 350-450F/53,35-68,60€. **Meals** Breakfast 50F/7,62€. **Restaurant** On property, menus: 80-250F/12,19-38,11€, also à la carte. **Nearby** Tennis in village, swimming pool (5km), 27-hole golf course (5km), carriage rides (weekends); Malicorne pottery factory, Solesmes Abbey, Lion d'Angers stud farm, river boating. **Credit cards** All major. **Spoken** English, Italian, German. **Open** All year. **How to get there** (Map 15): 10km south of Sablé towards Angers. In the village in front of antiques shop. Or TGV train to Sablé: 1 hour 15. mins. from Paris.

Located in a medieval village, this 15th-century house has three delightful bedrooms that are beautiful, comfortable, and still have much of their old charm. There is an excellent restaurant where a fire is permanently ablaze in the monumental fireplace. In the summer, drinks and meals are served in the flower-filled garden. You will be warmly received at "King René's House."

469 - Château de Saint-Paterne

72610 Alençon - Saint-Paterne
(Sarthe)
Tel. 02 33 27 54 71
Fax 02 33 29 16 71
Mme and M. de Valbray
E-mail: paterne@club-internet.fr
Web: www.chateaux-saintpaterne.com

Rooms 3 and 3 suites (3 pers.) with bath or shower, WC and tel. **Price** Rooms 450-650F/68,60-99,09€ (2 pers.), suites 850F/129,58€; 1 "pigeon loft" 450F/68,60€/night, 1800F/274,40€/week. **Meals** Breakfast 50F/7,62€ (7:30AM to 12:00PM). Evening meals (8:00PM) at separate tables, by reservation 220F/33,53€ (aperitif and coffe incl.). **Facilities** Sitting room, tennis, horse stalls, parking. **Pets** Dogs allowed on request. **Nearby** Golf, riding; Haras du Pin (stud farm), Mont-Saint-Michel, Chartres, Le Perche. **Credit cards** Amex, Visa, Eurocard, MasterCard. **Spoken** English, Spanish. **Closed** Jan 15 – Mar 15, by reservation in low season. **How to get there** (Map 8): 2km southwest of Alençon on D311 towards Mamers-Chartres; in Saint-Paterne center.

The village of Saint-Paterne is on the edge of Alençon, but this château is secluded behind a beautiful walled park. With youthful enthusiasm, the owner has completely restored it. Classic or déco in style, the bedrooms are all beautiful. The small dovecote is lovely, too, and those with an independent spirit will love it. Antique furniture and elegant fabrics also decorate the salon and the dining room.

470 - Manoir des Claies

72430 Asnières-sur-Vègre
(Sarthe)
Tel. 02 43 92 40 50
Fax 02 43 92 65 72
M. Anneron

Rooms 2 and 1 suite (3-4 pers.) with bath, WC and TV on request. **Price** 390F/59,45€ (1 pers.), 440F/67,07€ (2 pers.), +160F/24,39€ (extra pers. in suite). **Meals** Breakfast incl. Evening meals at communal table, by reservation 150F/22,86€ (all incl.). **Facilities** Lounge, tel., river fishing, boat, bicycles, mountain bikes, access to the private swimming pool. **Pets** Animals allowed on request. **Nearby** 27-hole golf, tennis, riding, swimming pools; Solesmes Abbey, Asnières medieval village, summer theatre, music festivals. **Open** All year, by reservation. **How to get there** (Map 15): 45km southwest of Le Mans. Autoroute A81, exit Joué-en-Charnie.

This manor house, located in a very attractive region, is a good example of the architecture of its time. Under the very high ceilings, the tastefully decorated rooms have small windows (in keeping with the traditional style) and are quite comfortable. The sitting room and dining room have kept their old-fashioned charm. They are furnished with taste and have a warmth that matches that of Monsieur Anneron, who clearly loves old buildings. The suite is rustic and full of charm and installed in an old farm building that opens directly on the garden.

471 - Garencière

72610 Champfleur
(Sarthe)
Tel. 02 33 31 75 84
Denis and Christine Langlais

Rooms 5 (3 on ground floor, including 1 in small house in photo, and 2 upstairs; 2 with roof windows) with bath or shower and WC. **Price** 200F/30,48€ (1 pers.), 260F/39,63€ (2 pers., double bed), 280F/42,68€ (2 pers., twin beds). **Meals** Breakfast incl. Half board 235F/35,82€ per pers. in double room. Meals at communal table 110F/16,77€ (all incl.). **Facilities** Small sitting room, covered and heated swimming pool. **Pets** Dogs allowed on request. **Credit cards** Not accepted. **Spoken** English. **Open** All year. **How to get there** (Map 8): 5km southeast of Alençon via N138 towards Le Mans, then left on D55 towards Champfleur. In Champfleur, continue on D55 to Bourg-le-Roi.

You will be warmly welcomed to this hillside farmhouse. The bedrooms are tastefully decorated with prettily colored fabrics and old-fashioned furniture. The small house is ideal for families; the ground floor is rustic and we especially loved the lovely upstairs bedroom. Breakfast and dinner are served in a bright dining room. The excellent cuisine is made with products from the farm.

472 - La Maridaumière

Route de Tulièvre
72510 Mansigné
(Sarthe)
Tel. and fax 02 43 46 58 52
Mme Hamandjian-Blanchard

Rooms 4 with bath or shower and WC. **Price** 280-380F/42,68-57,93€ (2 pers.), +60F/9,14€ (extra bed) and 1 room (no WC) 150F/22,86€. **Meals** Breakfast incl. Brunch on Sun, by reservation 80F/12,19€. No communal meal. **Facilities** Sitting room; theme weekends organized (jam-making, floral decoration) 50F/7,62€/day. **Pets** Dogs not allowed. **Nearby** Restaurant (6km). **Spoken** English. **Open** All year, by reservation Oct – Mar. **How to get there** (Map 16): Aut. A11, exit Le Mans-Est then, dir. Château-du-Loir; in Arnage D307 Le Lude and D77 dir. Requeil. In Requeil, Mansigné road, signs on left (3km). **No smoking** in bedrooms.

Set deep in the countryside, La Maridaumière has recently been converted into a bed and breakfast. The guest rooms, comfortable and kept immaculately, are attractively decorated in a half-English, half-country style. Prepared with the same refinement, breakfast is a civilized treat and the Sunday brunch (on reservation) can easily take the place of lunch.

473 - Château de Monhoudou

72260 Monhoudou
(Sarthe)
Tel. 02 43 97 40 05
Fax 02 43 33 11 58
Marie-Christine and Michel
de Monhoudou

Rooms 6 with bath or shower, WC and 1 child's room with washbasin. **Price** 450-650F/68,60-99,09€ (2 pers.), 200F/30,48€ (child's room). **Meals** Breakfast incl. Meals at communal or separate tables "Dîner aux chandelles" 195F/29,72€ (all incl.) - "Dîner prestige" in the library 320F/48,78€ (Champagne). **Facilities** Sitting room, piano, tel., lake fishing, bicycles. **Nearby** 18-hole golf course, tennis; Le Mans, Orne châteaux, Perche forests. **Credit cards** All major. **Spoken** English. **Open** All year. **How to get there** (Map 8): From Paris, autouroute A11, exit La Ferté-Bernard, towards Mamers, then left on D27 towards Marolles and right towards Monhoudou.

To get to this elegant small château, you must turn off the road, follow a lane and go through fields and a wood. The interior has been very tastefully redone in bright colors and still has its beautiful antique furniture and family paintings throughout. The bedrooms are equally comfortable and very beautiful. All look out over the immense English-style park which is inhabited by sheep, swans, horses and peacocks. The beautiful reception rooms are open to guests.

474 - Château de la Renaudière

72240 Neuvy-en-Champagne
(Sarthe)
Tel. 02 43 20 71 09
Fax 02 43 20 75 56
M. and Mme de Mascureau

Rooms 2 (double) with bath, WC; 1 (twin beds) with shower, WC and 1 small room for children. **Price** Double 600F/91,46€; twin 500F/76,22€, +100F/15,24€ (extra bed); small room 200F/30,48€. **Meals** Breakfast incl. Evening meals at communal table 250F/38,11€ (all incl.). **Facilities** Lounges, lake fishing, forest. **Pets** Animals not allowed. **Nearby** Solesmes, Music Festival in Jul. **Spoken** English. **Closed** Oct 15 – May 15. **How to get there** (Map 7): 20km west of Le Mans. Autoroute A81, exit Le Mans-Ouest, take road dir. Laval to Coulans-sur-Gée, then dir. Conlie for 6km. After the village of Saint-Julien-le-Pauvre, 300m on right.

This lovely château stands amid its large grounds and overlooks a bucolic countryside dotted with small ponds. You will get the warmest of welcomes. The dining room is magnificent with its wood paneling and handsome fireplace. The salons and small boudoirs have been tastefully appointed by the different generations of the family. A lovely spiral staircase leads to the spacious and elegant bedrooms, which have kept all their old style. Only the one on the top floor, although comfortable, lacks the charm of the others.

475 - Le Fresne

Route de Beaucé
72300 Solesmes
(Sarthe)
Tel. and fax 02 43 95 92 55
Marie-Armelle and Pascal Lelièvre

Rooms 3 (1 with mezzanine) with bath or shower and WC. Big house rental. **Price** 250-260F/38,11-39,63€ (2 pers.), +70F/10,67€ (extra pers.). Special rates for more than 4 nights. **Meals** Breakfast incl. Meals at communal table, by reservation 120F/18,29€ (wine incl.). **Facilities** Fishing in pond. **Pets** Dogs allowed on request (+30F/4,57€). **Nearby** Golf, riding, boating on Sarthe River, Asnières-sur-Vègre, Solesme Abbey, Malicorne pottery factory. **Credit cards** Not accepted. **Spoken** English, German. **Open** All year. **How to get there** (Map 15): 7km east of Sablé towards Solesmes; follow signs beginning at pharmacy. House in 3km. (TGV train station in 7km).

This modest farmhouse outside the village and its famous abbey, is a pleasant and inexpensive address and the young owners will give you a friendly welcome. The ground floor bedrooms were installed by the hosts in former outbuildings.They offer independence, calm and comfortable amenities (with very pretty bathrooms). Simply and soberly decorated, they are enlivened by brightly colored fabrics. It is a place where one can feel at home, and the dinners are shared moments of warmth and friendliness.

476 - Le Domaine du Grand Gruet

Route de Challes
72440 Volnay
(Sarthe)
Tel. and fax 02 43 35 68 65
Mobile 06 87 42 50 58
Mme Eveno-Sournia

Rooms 2 studios with kitchenette, shower, WC, and 2 apart. with lounge, shower and WC. Rooms cleaned on request. **Price** 450F/68,60€ (2 pers.), 500 and 650F/76,22 and 99,09€ (2 pers.), +70F/10,67€ (extra pers.). Reduction after 2 nights. **Meals** No communal meals. **Facilities** Sitting rooms. **Pets** Small dogs allowed on request (+50F/7,62€). **Nearby** Restaurants (6km), equestrian center; Loire valley. **Credit cards** Not accepted. **Spoken** German. **Open** Feb 15 – Dec 31 (in winter on request). **How to get there** (Map 16): Chartres Autoroute A11, exit Ferté-Bernard towards Le Mans. At Connerré, towards Grand-Lucé for 15km. Exit at Volnay and take D90 towards Challes. In 600m after Volnay on left, dirt road.

Anne Sournia is a painter who restored this beautiful house with an expert eye. The garden is ravishing and the apartments, located on the ground floor, are very attractively appointed: totally indepedent, they are perfect for relaxing in the heart of quiet countryside. The studios are simpler. Overall, the Domaine du Grand Gruet is cheerful, modern, and comfortable, with art exhibited in the living room and dining room.

477 - Le Logis de Beaumarchais

85470 Brétignolles-sur-Mer
(Vendée)
Tel. and fax 02 51 22 43 32
Mme Robet

Rooms 3 with bath or shower and WC. **Price** 450F/68,60€ (1 pers.), 520-620F/73,27-94,51€ (2 pers.), +100F/15,24€ (extra bed). **Meals** No communal meals. **Facilities** Sitting room, tel. **Pets** Dogs not allowed. **Nearby** Restaurants (4km), golf; Apremont, "Le Marais insolite", Islands (Saint-Gilles-Croix-de-Vie, 10km). **Credit cards** Not accepted. **Spoken** English. **Closed** Nov – Apr, except by reservation - Confirmation with 30% deposit. **How to get there** (Map 14): 42km southwest of La Roche-sur/Yon. Dir. Saint-Gilles-Croix-de-Vie via Aizenay-Coëx. At the exit, on left La Chaize Giraud. Cross the village, right on D12 for 1.5km; right on the Avenue, at the lower end on left Logis de Beaumarchais.

Five kilometers from the sea, in a stretch of countryside still unspoiled by the concrete accretions of other seasides, this guest house occupies an outbuilding of one of the loveliest châteaux in the region. Refurbished from top to bottom, it offers pleasant bedrooms with antique furniture and soberly beautiful decoration, brightened by an elegant choice of fabrics. The breakfasts are equally fine, served outdoors or in a vast ground floor dining room facing south directly on the garden. You can enjoy calm, hospitality and refinement.

478 - Manoir de Ponsay

Saint-Mars-des-Prés
85110 Chantonnay
(Vendée)
Tel. 02 51 46 96 71
Fax 02 51 46 80 07
M. and Mme de Ponsay
E-mail: manoir.de.ponsay@wanadoo.fr

Rooms 8 with bath or shower and WC. **Price** 300-570F/45,73-86,89€ (2 pers.); suite 600F/91,46€ (2, 3 or 4 pers.). **Meals** Breakfast (brunch) 45F/6,86€. Evening meals at communal table or not 180F/27,44€ (wine incl.). **Facilities** Sitting room, tel., horse stalls and exercise areas. **Nearby** Swimming pool, tennis, seaside, golf; Yeu Island, Poitou marshes, Puy-du-Fou. **Pets** Dogs not allowed. **Credit card** Amex. **Spoken** English, German. **Open** Apr 1 – Nov 30 (on request in winter). **How to get there** (Map 15): 35km east of La Roche-sur-Yon via D948 and D949bis to Chantonnay and Saint-Mars-des-Prés; signposted. Autoroute A83 exit Bournezeau (14km).

Overlooking a beautiful landscape of rolling hills, this manor house has been in the same family since the 17th century. The interior has preserved much of its authenticity, in particular the lovely dining room and the bedrooms in the main building, nicely decorated and with antique furniture. The "rose" room is wonderful and the "suite" is perfect for families. The other bedrooms, located in the wing, are more ordinary but also less costly. The entire house is beautifully kept. A hospitable place in the heart of Vendée.

479 - Logis de Chalusseau

111, rue de Chalusseau
85200 Doix
(Vendée)
Tel. and fax 02 51 51 81 12
M. and Mme Gérard Baudry

Rooms 2 with bath or shower and WC. Rooms cleaned every 3 days. **Price** 200F/30,48€ (1 pers.), 250F/38,11€ (2 pers.), +60F/9,14€ (extra pers.). **Meals** Breakfast incl. No communal meal but independent kitchen for guests. **Facilities** Sitting room. **Pets** Dogs not allowed. **Nearby** Swimming pool, tennis, seaside (40km), riding, golf; Poitou marshes, Mervent Forest, Romanesque art, Maillezais Abbey, Nieul-sur-L'Autize Cloisters, La Rochelle (40km). **Credit cards** Not accepted. **Open** Apr 1 – Nov 15 (2 nights min.). **How to get there** (Map 15): 9km south of Fontenay-le-Comte via D938ter towards La Rochelle, then left on D20 for 4km towards Fontaines-Doix.

The vast reception rooms in this very beautiful 17th-century Vendée house still have their original exposed beams and stone fireplaces. The bedrooms are very spacious, bright and are prettily decorated with charming regional furniture. The hearty breakfasts can be served in the pleasant garden. Beautifully situated, this is a wonderful place and you will be warmly welcomed.

480 - Château de la Flocellière

85700 La Flocellière
(Vendée)
Tel. 02 51 57 22 03
Fax 02 51 57 75 21
Erika Vignial

Rooms 5 and 3 suites with bath, WC and tel. **Price** Rooms from 550F/83,84€ (2 pers.); suite from 750F/114,33€. **Meals** Breakfast 50F/7,62€. Evening meals at communal table or not, by reservation 250F/38,11€ (all incl.). **Facilities** Lounges, billiards, ping-pong, croquet, swimming pool. **Pets** Dogs allowed on request. **Nearby** Tennis, golf; Le-Puy-du-Fou (7km). **Spoken** English, German, Italian. **Open** All year. **How to get there** (Map 15): 25km southeast of Cholet via D752 in dir. Pouzauges. In Saint-Michel-Mont-Mercure, turn left at the traffic light dir. La Flocellière. In the village, Place de la Mairie. Sign.

This magnificent château is itself a lesson in history, and the Vignial family runs the Flocellière with a feeling for beautiful things and warm hospitality. The bedrooms are often quite elegant, with modern bathrooms, and some of them can be converted into suites. All enjoy a beautiful view. The reception rooms are wonderful, warm and generously open to the guests and the welcome is particularly kind. A quality address.

481 - Le Logis d'Elpénor

5, rue de la Rivière
85770 Le Gué-de-Velluire
(Vendée)
Tel. 02 51 52 59 10
Fax 02 51 52 57 21
Christiane and Michel Ribert

Rooms 5 with bath or shower, WC and TV on request. **Price** 220F/33,53€ (1 pers.), 280F/42,68€ (2 pers.), +70F/10,67€ (extra pers.). **Meals** Breakfast incl. Evening meals at communal table 100F/15,24€ (wine incl.). **Facilities** Sitting room, tel. **Nearby** Hiking, tennis, river fishing, bicycles, 18-hole golf course, boat rental; Poitou marshes, Maison du Petit Poitou, Mervent Forest, Nieul-sur-Autize, Vouvrant. **Credit cards** Not accepted. **Closed** Nov 15 – Jan 31. **How to get there** (Map 15): 30km northeast of La Rochelle. From Niort N148 towards Fontenay-le-Compte, then D938ter, towards La Rochelle, then N137 towards Nantes, then in Marans D938ter towards Fontenay-le-Compte.

Le Logis, which is located at the bottom of a village street, is simple and charming. There are terra cotta floors (particularly lovely in the hall), doors of natural wood, wide-board parquet floors, and the bedrooms are bright, cheerful and generally quite large. There is a pleasant walled garden, behind which a path runs along the waters of the Vendée. The delicious family cooking features regional specialties.

P A Y S D E L A L O I R E

482 - Le Cabanon des Pêcheurs

49, rue Saint Hilaire
85350 L'île d'Yeu
(Vendée)
Tel. 02 51 58 42 30
Lysiane and Claude Groisard

Rooms 2 (in a small independent house) with bath or shower and WC. **Price** 320F/48,78€ (2 pers.), 280F/42,68€ (low season). **Meals** Breakfast incl. No communal meal. **Facilities** Sitting room. **Nearby** Restaurants (1.5km), beach (800m), mountain bikes, all sports. **Spoken** English. **Open** All year. **How to get there** (Map 14): 1.5km south of Port-Joinville. In Port-Joinville, take the Citadelle road; house opposite the Saint-Arnaud chapel.

Lysiane and Claude Groisard, hospitable hosts that they are, have decorated a small guest house (shown in the photo) at the far end of their garden; it contains two small bedrooms with white walls and very simple furnishings. Good breakfasts are served in an attractive room in the main house or on a terrace surrounded by flowers just in front. From "The Fishermen's Cabin", you can bike to the sea and the beaches, just a stone's throw away. And if you don't want to go out for dinner, you can have platters of shellfish delivered and enjoy them on the small private terraces outside the rooms.

483 - Le Petit Marais des Broches

7, chemin des Tabernaudes
85350 L'île d'Yeu
(Vendée)
Tel. and fax 02 51 58 42 43
Chantal and Jean-Marcel Hobma

Rooms 5 (2 with loft) with shower, WC. **Price** 360-450F/54,88-68,60€ (2 pers., depending on length of stay and season), +110F/16,76€ (extra pers.). **Meals** Breakfast incl. Meals at communal table 150F/22,86€ (all incl.). **Pets** Animals not allowed. **Nearby** Beach (300m), bicycles, mountain bikes, water sports, riding, tennis; summer concerts. **Open** All year. **How to get there** (Map 14): northeast of island. 300m from Anse des Broches. Boat from Fromentine (information 02 51 49 59 69) or from Noirmoutier Island in summer (information 02 51 39 00 00) and Saint-Gilles-Croix-de-Vie (information 02 51 54 15 15).

The Petit Marais des Broches is a contemporary house typical of the Island of Yeu, set just 300 meters from the sea and the breathtaking Côte Sauvage, Wild Coast. The attractive bedrooms are simply decorated – like a vacation house on the seaside (we found only the Coquillage room less appealing). Madame Hobma prepares excellent dinners with the catch-of-the-day and serves them on the terrace facing the ravishing garden in good weather. In Port-Joinville, you can rent bicycles and tour this beautiful island.

484 - Chez Mme Bonnet

69, rue de l'Abbaye
85420 Maillezais
(Vendée)
Tel. 02 51 87 23 00
Fax 02 51 00 72 44
Liliane Bonnet

Rooms 5 with bath or shower and WC. **Price** 340-370F/51,83-56,40€ (2 pers.), 410F/62,50€ (3 pers.). **Meals** Breakfast incl. No communal meal. **Restaurants** "Auberge de la Rivière Velluire" farmhouse-auberge in Saint-Michel-de-Cloucq. **Facilities** Sitting room (library), tennis, fishing, boating trips, private enclosed parking, bicycles; theme visits or weekends in low season. **Pets** Dogs not allowed. **Nearby** Riding, Forests, Maillezais and Nieul Abbeys, La Rochelle, Ré Island. **Credit cards** Not accepted. **Spoken** English, Spanish. **Open** All year (2 nights min.). **How to get there** (Map 15): 28km northwest of Niort via N148 towards Fontenay-le-Comte, then left on D15 to Maillezais.

Perhaps the main attraction of this typical Vendean home is its lovely garden bordering the canal, with a boat on which you can explore the surrounding marshes. One small bedroom done in rustic style looks out on this garden. The others are upstairs in the main house. They are decorated and appointed with great simplicity, but all are quiet and comfortable. The kind welcome, the quality of the breakfasts and the old-fashioned charm of the decor complete the appeal of this house situated in a marshland village.

485 - Le Logis de la Cornelière

85200 Mervent
(Vendée)
Tel. 02 51 00 29 25
Lyse and Jean-Raymond
de Larocque Latour
E-mail: corneliere.mervent@libertysurf.fr

Rooms 3 and 1 suite (4-5 pers.) with bath and WC. **Price** 400-500F/60,97-76,22€ (2 pers.); suite 600F/91,46€ (2 pers.); +100F/15,24€ (extra pers.). **Meals** Breakfast 45F/6,86€ (brunch). Meals at communal table, by reservation from 150F/22,86€. Summer kitchen at guests' disposal. **Facilities** Sitting room, games room, heated swimming pool, exercise room (body building), mushroom gathering in forest (12,355 acres), mountain bikes, ping-pong. **Credit cards** Not accepted. **Spoken** English. **Open** All year. **How to get there** (Map 15): In Fontenay-le-Comte go towards Bressuire, then road to Mervent; go through Mervent and continue to "Les Ouillières"; then towards "La Châtaigneraie" for 3km; follow signs "Monument historique".

The Cornelière, a stunning spectacle with its old roofs and golden stones, lies in a lovely valley on the edge of a beautiful forest. The interior has retained all of its old charm, with antique furniture, family objects and beautiful sculpted fireplaces. The bedrooms are vast, very comfortable and really attractive; the "Rose" room is superb and the suite is perfect for families. The outstanding breakfasts are served in exquisite family dishes. The welcome is warm and convivial. A very nice place to know.

486 - Le Château

85450 Moreilles
(Vendée)
Tel. 02 51 56 17 56
Fax 02 51 56 30 30
Mme Danièle Renard

Rooms 3 and 3 suites (3-4 pers.) with bath or shower, WC and tel. **Price** Room 350F/53,35€ (1 pers.), 400-500F/60,97-76,22€ (2 pers.); suite 550F/83,84€ (2 pers.), +100F/15,24€ (extra pers.); children under 12 (1/2 price). **Meals** Breakfast 50F/7,62€. Half board 405-500F/61,74-76,22€ per pers. in double room. Evening meals at separate tables 185F/28,20€ (wine not incl.). **Facilities** Swimming pool. **Pets** Dogs allowed on request. **Nearby** Fishing, golf; La Rochelle, Poitou marshes. **Credit cards** Not accepted. **Spoken** English. **Open** All year (on request Oct – Mar). **How to get there** (Map 15): 35km north of La Rochelle via the Nantes road N137; at the entrance to the village on the right.

This "Château" is in fact a large, handsome family home where you will be given a generous welcome, yet have all your independence. Only the veranda built on at the rear somewhat spoils the appearance. Breakfast and dinner are served at separate tables in the dining room. The sitting room is pleasant and the bar very cozy. The upstairs bedrooms are very nice, with period furniture and some old family pieces. The bedroom in the annex holds the bed of "La Belle Otero." Unfortunately, the noise from the road disturbs the calm of the garden and swimming pool.

487 - Logis du Ranquinet

85200 L'Orbrie
(Vendée)
Tel. 02 51 69 29 27
M. and Mme Reigner

Rooms 1 suite (3 pers.) with 2 rooms with bath or shower and WC. Rooms cleaned on request. **Price** Room 250F/38,11€ (2 pers.); suite 200F/30,48€ (1 pers.), 250F/38,11€ (2 pers.), 400F/60,97€ (3 pers.). **Meals** Breakfast incl. No communal meal. **Restaurant** "Le Chouan Gourmet" in Fontenay-le-Comte (3km) or crêperie. **Facilities** Lounge, tel. **Nearby** Riding, tennis, river and lake fishing; Puy-du-Fou (40km), forest, Atlantic (30km). **Open** All year. **How to get there** (Map 15): 3km northwest of Fontenay-le-Comte. From Niort, take dir. Mervent, L'Orbrie. House on right at first stop sign.

The atmosphere is warm and inviting in this beautiful Vendée stone house. You will find a small guest room with beautiful antique furniture; it can be converted into a suite with the neighboring bedroom and modern bathroom, all tastefully arranged. Your breakfast is served in a pretty, bright dining room or, in summer, in the garden full of flowers. The spacious sitting room has just been refurbished for pleasant evenings with a large fireplace. A quiet house where the hospitality is most thoughtful.

PAYS DE LA LOIRE

488 - Château du Breuil

85170 Saint-Denis-la-Chevasse
(Vendée)
Tel. and fax 02 51 41 40 14
Monique and Pierre Maestre

Rooms 3 (incl. 1 suite with tel.) with bath and WC. **Price** 300-450F/45,73-68,60€ (1-2 pers.), +100F/15,24€ (extra bed); suite 650F/99,09€ (3-4 pers.) **Meals** Breakfast 45F/6,86 €. Evening meals 180-250F/27,44-38,11€ (wine incl.). **Facilities** Sitting room, heated swimming pool. **Pets** Dogs allowed on request. **Nearby** Tennis, golf. **Credit card** Visa. **Spoken** English, Spanish. **Closed** Nov 1 – Easter (in winter on request) - Confirmation: deposit or credit card number. **How to get there** (Map 15): 45km south of Nantes via A83, E03, D763 dir. La Roche-sur-Yon. Exit Saint-Denis-la-Chevasse. In front of the church, dir. Belleville/Vie, then left 500m.

This 19th-century château stands on grounds containing century-old trees of South American origin. Once it lived its independent life amid the bocage country of Vendée. Today it has been restored and takes in guests. The bedrooms are done in blue, yellow or pink, with large bathrooms, all furnished with antiques. The pink one has another little adjoining room with a bow window. Before dinner (monkfish à l'armoricaine, scallops à l'estouffade and products of the vegetable garden), guests are invited to have an aperitif in the grand salon.

489 - Château de la Millière

85150 Saint-Mathurin
(Vendée)
Tel. and fax 02 51 22 73 29
Tel. 02 51 36 13 08
Danielle and Claude Huneault

Rooms 5, (incl. 1 suite) with bath and WC. **Price** 500F/76,22€ (2 pers.), +100F/15,24€ (extra bed); suite 750F/114,33€ (4 pers.). 10% reduction in May, Jun and Sept. **Meals** Breakfast 40F/6,09€. No communal meal. (Barbecue possible in garden). **Facilities** Sitting room, swimming pool, lake, French billiards, horse stalls, ping-pong, fishing. **Pets** Small dogs allowed on request. **Nearby** Restaurants, 18-hole golf course (3km); salt marshes, Saint-Gilles, La Rochelle, Noirmoutier. **Credit cards** Not accepted. **Spoken** English. **Open** May – Sept. **How to get there** (Map 14): 8km north of Les Sables-d'Olonne via N160 towards La Roche-sur-Yon, Les Sables-d'Olonne; 1km on left before Saint-Mathurin and just before marker km81.

You will enjoy a splendid view from the beautiful 19th-century Château de la Millière which overlooks a private park with large trees and a lake. The interior has been newly restored, combining various styles of furniture with a profusion of carpets. The very comfortable bedrooms are vast, the bathrooms are luxurious and the château is quiet.

P A Y S   D E   L A   L O I R E

490 - Le Fief Mignoux

85120 Saint-Maurice-des-Noués
(Vendée)
Tel. 02 51 00 81 42
M. and Mme Schnepf

Rooms 2 sharing bathroom with shower and WC. Rooms cleaned every three days. **Price** 250F/38,11€ (1 pers.), 300F/45,73€. **Meals** Breakfast incl. No communal meal. **Pets** Dogs not allowed. **Nearby** Restaurants, tennis, riding, lake; Mervent Forest, Vouvant, Poitou marshes, Maillezais Abbey. **Credit cards** Not accepted. **Open** May 1 – Nov 1. **How to get there** (Map 15): 25km northeast of Fontenay-le-Comte via D938ter towards La Châtaigneraie. In L'Alouette take D30 towards Vouvant. After Saint-Maurice-des-Noués right on D67 towards Puy-de-Serre.

Le Fief Mignoux is a charming 17th-century Vendée house which is filled with light and surrounded by two gardens full of flowers. The main bedroom is immense, bright, and very pleasantly furnished in country style; there is a private shower room opposite. For families or groups, it is possible to annex a second bedroom, which is large and beautiful. The owners are very welcoming.

491- Château de la Cacaudière

85410 Thouarsais-Bouildroux
(Vendée)
Tel. 02 51 51 59 27
Fax 02 51 51 30 61
Mme Montalt

Rooms 5 (2 with twin beds) and 2 suites (3-4 pers.) with bath or shower, WC, tel. in 3 rooms and TV on request. **Price** 400F/60,98€ (1 pers.), 450-620F/68,60-94,51€ (2 pers.), 680F/103,66€ (3 pers.), 780F/118,91€ (4 pers.). **Meals** Breakfast incl. No communal meal. **Facilities** Sitting rooms, billiard, piano, tel., heated swimming pool. **Pets** Small dogs only allowed on request. **Nearby** Lake fishing, 18-hole golf course (45km). **Spoken** English, German, Spanish. **Closed** Sept 30 – Jun 1, by reservation in low season. **How to get there** (Map 15): 20km north of Fontenay-le-Comte via D23 towards Bressuire; 4km after Saint-Cyr-des-Gâts, take GC39 on right towards Thouarsais-Bouildroux. Château in first small village in front of the barn.

La Cacaudière is a small, charming 19th-century château set in a lovely park filled with trees. It is furnished with antiques, and the salon, billard room and dining room are at your disposal. The bedrooms have been entirely renovated; they are extremely comfortable and subtly decorated with English wallpapers, elegant fabrics and very tasteful furniture. You will find a romantic atmosphere here, and very friendly hosts.

P I C A R D I E

492 - La Ferme de Léchelle

Hameau de Léchelle
02200 Berzy-le-Sec
(Aisne)
Tel. 03 23 74 83 29
Fax 03 23 74 82 47
Nicole and Jacques Maurice

Rooms 2 with bath or shower, WC; 2 rooms share 1 shower, WC. **Price** 180-230F/27,44-35,06€ (1 pers.), 200-250F/30,48-38,11€ (2 pers.). **Meals** Breakfast incl. Evening meals at communal table, by reservation 100F/15,24€ (wine not incl.). **Facilities** Sitting room, pool, bicycles. **Nearby** 18-hole golf course, tennis; forest, Romanesque churches, archaeological tours, Château de Longpont. **Credit cards** Not accepted. **Spoken** English, Spanish. **Open** All year, by reservation Nov – Apr. **How to get there** (Maps 2 and 10): 10km south of Soissons via N2 towards Paris. At Chaudun intersection, turn left on D172 towards Vierzy for 4km, then go left on D177 towards Lechelle.

Built on a 12th-century foundation, this opulent farm is outstanding in many ways, including its magnificent garden, its harmonious, elegant interior decoration and the owners' warm hospitality. The guest rooms are homey, comfortable and look out over a beautiful wooded countryside. The excellent, very generous breakfasts are served in a bright room with a beautiful, large fireplace and antique fruitwood furniture. Superb dinners are prepared with poultry and vegetables from the farm.

493 - Le Clos

Le Clos
02860 Chérêt
(Aisne)
Tel. 03 23 24 80 64
M. and Mme Simonnot

Rooms 1 with a 1 small in suppl. with bath, WC; 2 rooms with shower and WC on the ground floor; 2 rooms share 1 shower, WC on the first floor. **Price** 200-280F/30,48-42,68€ (2 pers.). **Meals** Breakfast incl. Evening meals at communal table 95F/14,48€ (wine incl.). **Facilities** Sitting room. **Pets** Dogs not allowed. **Nearby** Tennis, swimming pool, riding, golf; medieval town of Laon, Saint-Gobain forest, Reims Cathedral (40km). **Credit cards** Not accepted. **Open** Apr 15 – Oct 15. **How to get there** (Maps 3 and 10): 8km south of Laon via D967 towards Fismes, then D903; signposted.

This fine 17th-century building is now the family home of Monsieur Simonnot, a very nice retired farmer who presides over the table d'hôte meals with warmth and good humor. The house has retained its antique furniture. Each bedroom bears the name of a flower. "Iris" is very pleasant with a nice bathroom and little "Bleuet" is pretty even though its facilities are shared. The others are much simpler. An authentic and hospitable house with a relaxed family atmosphere.

494 - La Ferme
sur la Montagne

02290 Ressons-le-Long
(Aisne)
Tel. 03 23 74 23 71
Fax 03 23 74 24 82
M. and Mme Ferté

Rooms 5 with bath or shower and WC. **Price** 200F/30,48€ (1 pers.), 300F/45,73€ (2 pers.), +100F/15,24€ (extra pers.). **Meals** Breakfast incl. No communal meals. **Facilities** Sitting room, tel., tennis. **Pets** Dogs allowed on request. **Nearby** Restaurants (700m), riding, mountain bikes, swimming pool, golf; Pierrefonds château, Longpont Abbey, Soissons, Compiègne. **Spoken** English, German. **Credit cards** Not accepted. **Open** All year. **How to get there** (Map 10): 15km west of Soissons. N2 Paris/Soissons exit Villers-Cotterêts, then dir. Vic-sur-Aisne and Ressons on right.

This large farmhouse, most of which dates back to the 14th century, overlooks the valley of the Aisne River. The owners, somewhat bohemian in personality, offer large bedrooms with parquet floors, nice views and small bathrooms equipped with showers. The one called the Bureau is on the ground floor on a garden. The Chambre du Moine (Monk's Room) is sober with old woodwork and La Tourelle has a mansard roof and flowered fabrics. The remaining two (Bûcher and Lavoir) are smaller, having been remodeled from a former work area. Our only reservation is about the breakfast room, which should be redone in a warmer manner.

495 - Domaine des Jeanne

Rue Dubarle
02290 Vic-sur-Aisne
(Aisne)
Tel. and fax 03 23 55 57 33
M. and Mme Martner

Rooms 5 and 1 studio with shower, WC and TV. **Price** 320-380F/48,78-57,93€ according to season. **Meals** Breakfast incl. Evening meals at separate tables 100F/15,24€ (wine not incl.). **Facilities** Sitting room, telephone, swimming pool, tennis, secondhand shop, artist's studio available in the Medieval tower. **Pets** Dogs allowed on request. **Nearby** Golf; châteaux of Pierrefond, Compiègne, hunting museum in Senlis. **Credit card** Visa. **Spoken** English. **Open** All year. **How to get there** (Maps 2 and 10): 16km west of Soissons on N31 towards Compiègne.

This handsome house located in the village stands on pleasant grounds with a river at one end. The view is not attractive on all sides, but it is often shielded by the tall trees. The bedrooms are comfortable and harmoniously decorated and face the greenery. They each have a private shower room. The sitting room and dining room are classically appointed but very inviting. The cooking is family style (as is the welcome) and meals are served at separate tables. Some people might be disturbed, between October and December, by the odor from a sugar refinery 3 kilometers away.

496 - Domaine des Patrus

La Haute Epine
02540 L'Épine-aux-Bois
(Aisne)
Tel. 03 23 69 85 85
Fax 03 23 69 98 49
Mary-Ann and Marc Royol
E-mail: contact@domainedespatrus.com
Web: www.domainedespatrus.com

Rooms 5 with bath and WC. **Price** 350-480F/53,35-73,17€ (2 pers.), +130F/19,81€ (extra bed). **Meals** Breakfast incl. Evening meals at communal table 140-160F/21,34-24,39€ (wine incl.). **Facilities** Sitting room, horse stalls, fishing in the lakes, bicycles. **Nearby** Golf; Château-Thierry. **Credit card** Visa. **Spoken** English, German. **Open** All year. **How to get there** (Map 10): 10km west of Montmirail via D933 towards La-Ferté-sur-Jouarre. At La Haute-Epine, D863 towards L'Epine-aux-Bois; signposted.

This splendid farmhouse is very pleasantly decorated and surrounded by green countryside. The bedrooms are comfortable and very elegant with white walls and antique furniture. The Blue bedroom is magnificent. In the charming dining room decorated with antique pitchers, you can enjoy traditional French country dishes like potée champenoise – a heavy cabbage and vegetable soup with champagne, and blanquette de veau – a creamy veal stew. Homemade preserves are served at breakfast.

497 - Ferme du Château

02130 Villers-Agron
(Aisne)
Tel. 03 23 71 60 67
Fax 03 23 69 36 54
Christine and Xavier Ferry
E-mail: xavferry@club-internet.fr

Rooms 4 with bath or shower and WC. **Price** 360-430F/54,88-65,53€ (2 pers.). **Meals** Breakfast incl. Evening meals at communal table, by reservation (except weekend) 180F/27,44€ (wine incl.). **Facilities** Sitting room, tennis, 18-hole golf course. **Nearby** Swimming pool, riding (10km), canoeing/kayaks, Eurodisney (45mn via A4), Champagne wine route, forest walks, châteaux and abbeys. **Credit cards** Not accepted. **Spoken** English, German. **Open** All year. **How to get there** (Map 10): 25km west of Reims and 30km northeast of Château-Thierry. Exit autoroute A4 n. 21, in Dormans, then D980, then D801 towards Golf de Champagne; signposted.

This old (13th-18th century) château has a peaceful and verdant park that extends to a golf course traversed by a small river. The interior is very tastefully decorated, elegant and comfortable. The beautiful bedrooms have cheerful fabrics on the walls and are furnished with antiques. Game in season and other local products are served at the excellent dinners, hosted by the friendly young owners.

P I C A R D I E

498 - Chez Mme Gittermann

26, rue Nationale
60110 Amblainville
(Oise)
Tel. 03 44 52 03 22
Fax 03 44 22 41 49
Mme Gittermann

Rooms 4 with shared 1 bath and 2 showers and WC. **Price** 220F/33,53€ (2 pers.). **Meals** Breakfast incl. No communal meal. **Restaurants** In Le Coudray, Nesles-la-Vallée and Méru. **Facilities** Sitting room, pottery workshop. **Pets** Dogs allowed on request. **Nearby** Regional Park in Vexin, hiking or bicycles, river and lake fishing, riding, tennis, 18-hole golf course; Château de Chantilly (horse museum), Beauvais (museum, cathedral), Gerberoy, Giverny, Auvers-sur-Oise, Royaumont Abbey. **Spoken** English, German. **Open** All year. **How to get there** (Map 9): Autoroute A86, Cergy-Pontoise, exit Marine, "Centre hospitalier régional" to the first red light dir. Beauvais, D927 Amblainville.

With her cats, dogs, turtle doves and parrots, Madame Gittermann's house is something of an annex to Noah's Ark. In the heart of the village, surrounded by trees and shrubs, it has an inviting yellow living room with green plants, making a cheerful venue for breakfast. The small bedrooms with twin beds are decorated in blue, green, pink, or yellow for the room with a double bed. They share a large bathroom with a tub or two small shower rooms.

499 - La Bultée

60300 Fontaine-Chaalis
(Oise)
Tel. 03 44 54 20 63
Fax 03 44 54 08 28
Annie Ancel

Rooms 5 with shower, WC and TV. **Price** 300F/45,73€ (2 pers.), +80F/12,19€ (extra pers.). **Meals** Breakfast incl. No communal meal. **Facilities** Sitting room, parking. **Pets** Dogs not allowed. **Nearby** Restaurants (3km), swimming pool, riding, golf; Chantilly, Compiègne, Pierrefond, Jean-Jacques Rousseau Park. **Credit cards** Not accepted. **Spoken** Some English. **Open** All year. **How to get there** (Map 9): 8km southeast of Senlis (A1) via D330a towards Nanteuil-le-Haudouin; house after Borest and before Fontaine-Chaalis. (Roissy Airport, 20km).

The inner courtyard of this farmhouse has great character. You will be independent here, sharing with the owners a large living room with a fireplace, where breakfast is served when the weather is not good enough to eat outside. Entirely renovated, the bedrooms are beautiful, comfortable, simple and impeccably well-kept, as are the bathrooms. They all overlook a pretty flower garden.

500 - Château de Fosseuse

104, rue du Vert Galant
60540 Fosseuse
(Oise)
Tel. and fax 03 44 08 47 66
M. and Mme Marro
E-mail: chateau.fosseuse@wanadoo.fr

Rooms 1 suite with shower, WC, and 1 with bath and WC. **Price** 300F/45,73€ (1 pers.), 420F/64,03€ (2 pers.), +90F/13,72€ (extra bed); 380F/57,93€ (2 pers.); 1 child's room 90F/13,72€/bed. **Meals** Breakfast incl. Evening meals at communal table 120F/18,29€ (wine incl.). **Facilities** Sitting room, fishing. **Pets** Dogs allowed on request. **Nearby** Swimming pool, tennis, pony-club, riding, golf; Auvers-sur-Oise, Royaumont abbey, Chantilly. **Spoken** English. **Open** Apr 1 – Nov 1. (or on request). **How to get there** (Map 9): 15km northeast of Isle Adam. Paris-Beauvais N1, exit Bornel, then Fosseuse for 2km.

This splendid brick château of the 16th century boasts large grounds, a pond, and a delightful monastic garden. Two rooms, rented to the same family, are in the main building and share a bathroom. The nicest room, in the square tower, has two immense windows. You have to go through the toilet to reach the little shower at the top of the tower, but this in no way spoils the charm of the place. Fine cooking and warm welcome.

501 - La Maison du sculpteur Hugard

32, route de Clermont
60660 Rousseloy
(Oise)
Tel. 03 44 56 25 94 / 03 44 56 42 90
Hugard

Rooms 1 with bath, WC, and 1 spare bedroom with private bath, shared WC. (tel. in 1 room). **Price** 300 and 390F/45,73 and 59,45 € (2 pers.). **Meals** Breakfast 20 or 35F/3,04 or 5,33€. No communal meal. **Restaurants** Auberge du Tillet and restaurants (2km). **Facilities** Sitting room. **Pets** Dogs allowed on request. **Nearby** Hiking in forest starting from house, several golf courses; Senlis, Saint-Leu Church (music), Creil Theater. **Credit cards** Not accepted. **Open** All year. **How to get there** (Map 9): 70km north of Paris via A1 towards Lille, Senlis exit, then towards Beauvais. At the "Kuom" traffic circle, towards Mouy. Go about 3km, then towards Rousseloy. In the village, in front of bus stop.

This pretty village house conceals a lovely garden. The main bedroom is set up in the artist's studio in the barn. You will sleep on one of the large mezzanines surrounded by drawings and sculptures in a rather bohemian atmosphere. The other bedroom, with a mansard roof, has only roof windows and the amenities are quite simple. The bathrooms are in the rooms themselves. This is a nice place to come if you want to rest or take long walks in the surrounding countryside. The welcome is cordial.

P I C A R D I E

502 - Abbaye de Valloires

Valloires - Service Accueil
80120 Argoules-par-Rue
(Somme)
Tel. 03 22 29 62 33
Fax 03 22 29 62 24
Association de Valloires

Rooms 6 (4 with bedroom annex) with bath, WC and tel. **Price** 370F/56,41€ (1 pers.), 460F/70,13€ (2 pers.), 540F/82,32€ (3 pers.), +80F/12,19€ (extra pers.) **Meals** Breakfast incl. No communal meal. **Facilities** Sitting room, tour of the Abbey and the garden. **Pets** Dogs not allowed. **Nearby** Restaurants, 18-hole golf course (6km). **Credit cards** Not accepted. **Spoken** English. **Open** All year. **How to get there** (Map 1): 31km north of Abbeville via N1 to Nampont-Saint-Martin, then D192 towards Argoules.

This huge Abbey built in the 12th century and rebuilt in the 18th is today managed by an association. A broad gallery leads to six lovely bedrooms, once reserved for the abbot and his guests. Large, comfortable and beautifully decorated, many of them still have their wood paneling and recessed beds. A wonderful view of the outstanding gardens. Breakfast is served in the former refectory. The Abbey has retained its vocation as a place of hospitality. During the day, there are occasional visits by groups of tourists.

503 - Château des Alleux

Les Alleux
80870 Behen
(Somme)
Tel. and fax 03 22 31 64 88
M. and Mme René-François
de Fontanges

Rooms 4 with bath or shower and WC. **Price** 250F/38,11€ (1 pers.), 300F/45,73€ (2 pers.) and 1 child's bedroom +80F/12,19€/extra pers. 10% reduction after 2 nights and 20% after 3 nights. **Meals** Breakfast incl. Evening meals at communal table, by reservation 130F/19,81€ (drinks incl.). **Facilities** Sitting room, living room with fireplace and independent kitchen for guests; pony riding, bicycles. **Pets** Dogs not allowed. **Nearby** Golf, tennis, seaside (20km); Somme bay, Marquenterre Park. **Credit cards** Not accepted. **Spoken** English, Spanish. **Open** All year. **How to get there** (Map 1): 10km south of Abbeville via D928 towards Rouen, turn right at the hamlet Les Croisettes; or get off Autoroute A28 via Monts Caubert exit, and turn right to Les Croisettes and follow signs "Les Alleux Chambres d'hôtes" and not Behen.

Lying secluded in a lovely 30-acre park, the small Château des Alleux offers three attractive, well-decorated guest rooms which are located in small outbuildings, and a fourth room in the main house. The table d'hôte dinners are excellent and we loved the delightful family atmosphere. It all comes for a reasonable price.

504 - Château de Yonville

80490 Citernes
(Somme)
Tel. and fax 03 22 28 61 16
M. and Mme des Forts

Rooms 3 and 1 suite of 2 bedrooms (1 in annex, 50m) with bath and WC. **Price** 300F/45,73€ (1 pers.), 330F/50,30€ (2 pers.), +100F/15,24€ (extra pers.); child under 2 (free). Special rates on request. **Meals** Breakfast incl. No communal meal. **Facilities** Sitting room in summer, tennis. **Pets** Dogs not allowed. **Nearby** Restaurants (5km), 18-hole golf course (20km), riding, seaside; lakes of the Somme, Marquenterre Park, châteaux, archeological site. **Credit cards** Not accepted. **Spoken** Some English. **Open** All year. **How to get there** (Map 1): 15km south of Abbeville. Autoroute A16, exit Beauvais, then D901 towards Abbeville to Airaines, then D936 towards Le Tréport. In Oisemont, D53 to Citernes. At entrance to village, towards Yonville, then signs (300m). **No smoking** in bedrooms.

You will surely be as charmed as we were by Monsieur and Madame des Forts' hospitality, as well as by the pleasant atmosphere of their château. This is a real family home in which the furniture, objects and paintings often have an interesting history. The bedrooms have just been renovated, but their authentic style and elegance have been preserved. They are very comfortable, as are the bathrooms, and they offer excellent value for the price.

505 - Château de Foucaucourt

80140 Oisemont
(Somme)
Tel. 03 22 25 12 58
Mme de Rocquigny

Rooms 2 (1 small) with bath or shower, WC, and 2 rooms with shared bath and WC. **Price** 300, 350 and 400F/45,73, 53,35 and 60,97€ (2 pers.). **Meals** Breakfast incl. Lunch and evening meals at communal table 60 or 110F/9,14 or 16,76€ (wine not incl.). **Facilities** Sitting room, tel., riding, horse stalls. **Pets** Dogs allowed on request. **Nearby** 18-hole golf course (28km), tennis (5km), boating center (12km); Somme Bay, Tréport, Mers-les-Bains, Rambure Château. **Credit cards** Not accepted. **Spoken** English. **Open** All year. **How to get there** (Map 1): 25km south of Abbeville via N28 to Saint-Maxent, then D29 to Oisemont and D25 towards Senarpont.

This charming 18th-century château is set in attractive grounds outside the village. The reception rooms still evoke the past, and the sitting room has a happy mixture of furniture from different periods. The suite is pleasant and the two bedrooms on the park have private baths. The two other rooms share a bathroom which has just been redone. You will find a friendly, family atmosphere. Alas, the quality of the meals varies.

506 - Château d'Omiécourt
Route de Chaulnes
80320 Omiécourt
(Somme)
Tel. 03 22 83 01 75
Fax 03 22 83 21 83
M. and Mme Dominique de Thezy
E-mail: thezy@terre-net.fr
Web: www.isasite/chateau-omiecourt/

Rooms 3 and 1 suite with bath and WC. **Price** Rooms 280F/42,68€ (1 pers.), 330F/50,30€ (2 pers.); suite 500F/76,22€ (4 pers.); +70F/10,67€ (extra pers.). Children under 7 (free). **Meals** Breakfast incl. Evening meals at communal table, by reservation 80 or 130F/12,19 or 19,81€ (Wine incl.). **Facilities** Sitting room, ping-pong, football table and pétanque. **Pets** Dogs not allowed. **Nearby** Pony Club (2.5km); Museum of World War I ("Historial de la Grande Guerre") and Roye ("cité gastronomique") 13km. **Credit cards** Not accepted. **Spoken** English. **Open** All year - Confirmation: deposit 30%. **How to get there** (Maps 2 and 9): 40km east of Amiens dir. Saint-Quentin, then Roye. Go round Roye, dir. Peronne and go 13km. In the village, 1st on left after the church, then follow signs. **No smoking** in bedrooms.

The Château d'Omiécourt is an ancient family home surrounded by a large park filled with trees. The three bedrooms are bright and spacious, with cheery and colorful fabrics, modern bathrooms, and have kept all their old style. The atmosphere is young and familial and children are welcome. The reception is courteous for all.

507 - Le Bois de Bonance

80132 Port-le-Grand
(Somme)
Tel. 03 22 24 11 97
Fax 03 22 31 63 77
M. and Mme Jacques Maillard
E-mail: maillard.chambrehote@binance.com

Rooms 3 with bath, WC, and 1 suite of 2 bedrooms (4 pers.) with bath, WC, kitchen, sitting room. **Price** 300F/45,73€ (1 pers.), 400F/60,97€ (2 pers.), +100F/15,24€ (extra pers.); suite 700F/106,71€ (4 pers.). **Meals** Breakfast incl. No communal meal. **Restaurants** In Saint-Valéry-sur-Somme and Le Crotoy. **Facilities** Swimming pool, park. **Pets** Small dogs allowed. **Credit cards** Not accepted. **Spoken** English, German. **Closed** Nov 15 – end Feb. **How to get there** (Map 1): 8km northwest of Albertville via D40 towards Saint-Valéry-sur-Somme; sign at the entrance to the village. Autoroute A28, exit Baie de Somme and from north (Calais) A16, exit Abbeville-nord, then towards Saint-Valéry-sur-Somme, on Bay of the Somme.

Standing alone in the countryside, this welcoming family house is surrounded by lovely grounds open to visitors. The interior is very elegant. Each beautiful, comfortable bedroom is furnished with antiques, mostly Louis XVI pieces. The nicest are those in the main house. The small cottages have a direct entrance on a pretty garden but their furnishing is much more sober. Breakfast is served in an attractively decorated dining room furnished with graceful "lyre" chairs. An excellent address.

508 - La Grande Métairie

Oyer
16700 Bioussac-Ruffec
(Charente)
Tel. 05 45 31 15 67
Fax 05 45 29 07 28
M. and Mme Moy

Rooms 1 room and 1 suite (4 pers.) with shower and WC. Rooms cleaned on request. **Price** 180F/27,44€ (1 pers.), 230F/35,06€ (2 pers.), +60F/9,14€ (extra pers. in suite). −10% off for 1 week. **Meals** Breakfast incl. No communal meal. **Facilities** Sitting room, swimming pool. **Pets** Dogs not allowed. **Nearby** Restaurants (3km), hiking, tennis, riding, fishing, canoeing; Nanteuil-en-Vallée, Verteuil, discovery of rural heritage, markets. **Credit cards** Not accepted. **Spoken** English. **Open** End Mar − beg Nov. **How to get there** (Map 23): 6km east of Ruffec via D740 towards Confolens. After Condac, sign towards Bioussac via D197 then left, 1st farm: Oyer.

Nestling deep in the country, this lovely little farmhouse gives you the choice of a bedroom or of a family suite. The suite is charming with its old flagstone floor, stone niches, and its two Louis-Philippe beds. A small kitchen is at your disposal, allowing you to prepare your meals with organic produce grown in the garden. Upstairs, the pretty little bedroom is decorated in nice cool colors. The breakfasts are good and the atmosphere is relaxed.

509 - Logis de Boussac

Boussac
16370 Cherves-Richemont
(Charente)
Tel. 05 45 83 22 22
Fax 05 45 83 21 21
M. and Mme Méhaud

Rooms 3 (incl. 1 large in annex for family with shower and bath) with bath or shower and WC. **Price** 350F/53,35€ (1-2 pers.), +100F/15,24€ (extra bed). **Meals** Breakfast 50F/7,62€. Evening meals at communal table, by reservation 180F/27,44€ (wine incl.). **Facilities** Lounge, tel., swimming pool, river fishing. **Nearby** Riding at "Les Ecuries de Boussac", Club next to the property, golf; Romanesque churches, vineyards. **Spoken** English. **Open** All year. **How to get there** (Map 22): 5km north of Cognac. Exit Cognac via D731 dir. Saint-Jean-d'Angély. In 5km, in the small village of L'Epine, turn left dir. Richemont. Property on left soon after the bridge over river.

This handsome and imposing residence was built in the 17th century by a wealthy merchant in wines and spirits and its authenticity was carefully respected by the present owners when they carried out their modernization. The salon with antique furniture and the large dining room have retained their original style. Two large, simply decorated bedrooms (one with a very beautiful bathroom) have all the modern amenities. The family bedroom installed in the former paper mill has a more countrified air, with its windows facing the garden and the river below. The hospitality is courteous.

POITOU - CHARENTES

510 - La Ronde

Saint-Amand-de-Nouère
16170 Rouillac
(Charente)
Tel. and fax 05 45 96 82 10
Mobile 06 82 29 13 67
M. and Mme de Prévost
E-mail: Johelle@infonie.fr

Rooms 1 with bath, WC, and 1 suite (2-3 pers.) with shower and WC. Rooms cleaned on request. **Price** 350-380F/53,35-57,93€ (2 pers., depending on season); suite 450-480F/68,60-73,17€ (3 pers.). **Meals** Breakfast incl. Evening meals, by reservation. **Facilities** Sitting room (TV, fireplace), swimming pool. **Pets** Dogs not allowed. **Nearby** Restaurants, riding, tennis, hiking ("via Agrippa"), 18-hole golf course. **Spoken** English. **Open** All year. **How to get there** (Map 22): 18km west of Angoulême via D939 towards La Rochelle. Pass Saint-Genis d'Hiersac; 3km on left, signs "La Ronde". From Cognac, towards Jarnac, Rouillac, then D939 towards Angoulême.

Behind a handsome stone portal, you will discover this converted 18th-century farmhouse with its buildings arranged around a huge courtyard in characteristic Charentes style. On the ground floor, the sitting room/library and the dining room are handsomely appointed with pale wood furniture (walnut and cherry), and old objects. The spacious, elegant bedrooms are decorated with imagination and flair. The former orchard has been transformed into a garden, with a swimming pool at the back surrounded by trees. Breakfast is served outside in summer. La Ronde is a beautiful place to stay between Cognac and Angoulême.

511 - Logis de Romainville

16440 Roullet-Saint-Estèphe
(Charente)
Tel. and fax 05 45 66 32 56
Francine Quillet

Rooms 3 with bath, WC, and 1 family suite (2 rooms) with shared bath and WC. Rooms cleaned every day, except making beds (guests' responsibility). **Price** 250F/38,11€ (1 pers.), 300F/45,73€ (2 pers.), +70F/10,67€ (extra bed). **Meals** Breakfast incl. Evening meals at communal table (except Thurs and Sun), by reservation 120F/18,29€ (wine incl.). **Facilities** Sitting room, swimming pool, bicycles. **Nearby** Golf, tennis, riding, fishing; Cognac, Angoulême. **Credit cards** Not accepted. **Spoken** English, Italian. **Open** Apr 15 – Oct 15. **How to get there** (Map 22): 12km south of Angoulême via bypass towards Bordeaux and N10, exit Roullet, go through village via D42 towards Mouthiers; house in 2km, signs.

We love the Logis de Romainville and its comfortable, pretty rooms, soft carpets, white or patchwork bedcovers, and its soft pastel wallpapers. The rooms are immaculate and have lovely bathrooms. Breakfasts and delicious dinners are served in a handsome, spacious room with antique furnishings. In summer, meals are served outdoors so that you can enjoy the splendid panoramic view. A friendly and relaxed welcome.

512 - Le Maurençon

10, rue de Maurençon
Les Moulins
17400 Antezant
(Charente-Maritime)
Tel. and fax 05 46 59 94 52
Mobile 06 11 11 03 35
Marie-Claude and Pierre Fallelour

Rooms 1 (twin beds) with shower, WC and 1 suite with 2 rooms: 1 bed (160cm) and 2 beds (120cm) with bath and WC. Rooms cleaned twice a week on longer stays. **Price** 240-270F/36,58-41,16€ (2 pers.), +70-90F/10,67-13,72€ (extra pers.). **Meals** Breakfast incl. Evening meals at communal table, by reservation (not Sun and holidays), 95F/14,48€. **Facilities** Sitting room, fishing, billiards. **Pets** Dogs not allowed. **Nearby** Golf, swimming pool, riding, tennis; Saintes, Saint-Jean-d'Angély, Cognac, Poitou marshes, châteaux, Romanesque churches. **Credit cards** Not accepted. **Open** All year. **How to get there** (Map 22): 6km northeast of Saint-Jean-d'Angély via D127 towards Dampierre; house at the entrance to the village.

The River Boutonne once powered the mill but is now simply a romantic border to the garden. The bedrooms, which are furnished with handsome old furniture, are light and pleasant. The sitting room has a billiards table. Excellent breakfasts are served outside in good weather. Madame Fallelour is a very welcoming hostess.

513 - La maison de Caroline

17, rue de la Clairière
17580 Le Bois - Plage en Ré
Île-de-Ré
(Charente-Maritime)
Tel. 05 46 09 34 81
Mme Caroline Chenue

Rooms 4 with shower and WC. **Price** 280-310F/42,68-47,25€ (2 pers.). **Meals** Breakfast incl. No communal meal. **Nearby** Restaurant (300m), beach (water sports), bicycles, riding, tennis, golf practice; museum of the salt marshes, bird preserve, museum of the sea (Cognac), Chapeliers Abbey. **Spoken** German. **Closed** Jan. By reservation and deposit. **How to get there** (Map 14): 2km of Saint-Martin-de-Ré. At the exit of the bridge, 10km by the southern itinerary dir. Saint-Martin. At Bois-Plage, 5th road on left, pass the Moulin La Bouvette, At the no entry sign on right, then signs.

The building reserved for guests stands at the foot of a garden just at the edge of Saint-Martin. It is of recent construction but is built in the style of the traditional low houses of Ile de Ré. It offers four bedrooms with showers, all small and unpretentious. The surrounding countryside assures you of quiet. There is no sitting room but in summer breakfast is served under a flowered awning. A nice place for a stopover on the island in good weather.

POITOU-CHARENTES

514 - Logis de Louzignac

2, rue des Verdiers
17800 Brives-sur-Charente
(Charente-Maritime)
Tel. 05 46 96 45 72
Fax 05 46 96 16 09
Mme van Nispen tot Sevenaer

Rooms 2 with bath or shower and WC. **Price** 300-400F/45,73-60,97€ (2 pers., depending on season). **Meals** Breakfast (Dutch) +50F/7,62€ (extra pers.). No communal meal. **Facilities** Sitting room, swimming pool. **Nearby** Restaurant (4km), riding, tennis, boating on the river, fishing, 18-hole golf courses, seaside (45km); Romanesque churches, Saintes concerts and festival (Jul), Cognac. **Spoken** English, German, Dutch. **Closed** Oct 1 – Apr 30. 2 days min. **How to get there** (Map 22): 17km east of Saintes. Autoroute A10 exit Saintes, dir. Cognac, then on right dir. Cognac/Chaniers via Charente Valley (D24); at Treuil on right dir. Brives (D135), then signs.

The Logis of Louzignac was once the main house of a former wine estate of Saintonge. It is of good proportions and the salon is surprisingly bright. Everywhere there are antique pieces, paintings, family carpets. The two bedrooms and their shower rooms are carefully appointed and very comfortable. In summer, breakfast is served in a pleasant walled garden. This is a fine house with considerate and energetic hosts.

515 - Château de Crazannes

17350 Crazannes
(Charente-Maritime)
Tel. 06 80 65 40 96
Fax 05 46 91 34 46
M. and Mme de Rochefort

Rooms 6 and 2 suites (2-4 pers.) with bath or shower and WC. **Price** Rooms 500-900F/76,22-137,20€ (2 pers.); suite 800-1200F/121,95-182,93€ (2 pers.). Poss. weekly rental of the keep (donjon) or a house. **Meals** Breakfast 50F/7,62€. No communal meal. **Facilities** Sitting rooms. **Pets** Dogs not allowed. **Nearby** Restaurants (3km), equestrian center, tennis, river fishing, boat rentals on the Charente, beaches (35km), 18-hole golf course; Romanesque art of Saintonge, châteaux, Crazannes. **Spoken** English. **Credit card** Visa. **Open** Mar – Nov, except by reservation. **How to get there** (Map 22): 12km north of Saintes via N137 towards Rochefort, then D119 towards Plassay; follow signs "Château de Crazannes".

In the heart of Romanesque Saintonge and not far from the Atlantic beaches, the Château de Crazannes radiates the charm and serenity of a beautiful Renaissance edifice with its lovely views out over the park, a Romanesque chapel, an imposing keep, and terraces surrounded by a moat. The interior is one of comfort and authentic period style: large salons, a panelled library, huge bedrooms and suites, each with a private bath. The hospitality is friendly and thoughtful.

POITOU - CHARENTES

516 - Le Clos Bel Ebat

17, rue de la Grainetière
17630 La Flotte-en-Ré
(Charente-Maritime)
Tel. 05 46 09 61 49
M. and Mme Jambut

Rooms 3 (incl. 2 as a suite with kitchenette, small sitting room, clothes-washer, tumble dryer, dishwasher) with bath and WC. **Price** 300F/45,73€ (1 pers.), 400F/60,97€ (2 pers.) - Poss. of reserving the whole place (4-5 people) 800-900F/121,95-137,20€ /night, 4500-6000F/686,02-914,69€/week. **Meals** Breakfast incl. No communal meal. **Restaurants** In La Flotte. **Facilities** Sitting room, parking. **Pets** Small dogs only allowed. **Nearby** Beach, golf. **Credit cards** Not accepted. **Spoken** English, German. **Open** Easter – Nov 1 and school vacations. 2 nights min. and by the week in Jul, Aug and long weekends. **How to get there** (Map 22): In La Flotte -en-Ré. At the Port of La Flotte, towards Saint-Martin. At the village exit, street on left, signs for Grainetière, then turn right, then left.

The rooms are quite small but charming and nicely installed in the former storerooms. They are cheerful, comfortable and carefully decorated with antique beds, engravings, and the like. They face the flowered terrace and the walled garden with many trees, from which you can unfortunately hear the noise of the road. There is an equipped kitchen so you can be independent. Madame Jambut is a most welcoming hostess and every evening she will provide the ingredients (croissants, homemade jam...) for your breakfast.

517 - Le Logis de l'Épine

17250 Plassay
(Charente-Maritime)
Tel. 05 46 93 91 66
Mme Charrier

Rooms 1 with shower and WC; 1 with private shower and WC but outside the room; 2 with washbasin, shared shower and WC. **Price** 350F/53,35€ (2 pers., 1 night), 280-320F/42,68-48,78€ (2 pers., from 2 nights). **Meals** Breakfast incl. No communal meal. **Facilities** Sitting room. **Pets** Dogs allowed on request. **Nearby** Restaurants (5km), swimming pool, tennis, riding, seaside, golf; Romanesque Saintonge. **Credit cards** Not accepted. **Spoken** English. **Closed** Nov 15 – Mar 15. **How to get there** (Map 22): 10km northwest of Saintes via N137, then D119; house on the way out of the village.

In its large shaded park, this 18th-century house, which once served as headquarters of a large wine estate (producing pineau and cognac) seems to be protected from the modern world. Madame Charrier is very hospitable. The rooms are well appointed, sober in taste with some old traditional furniture. Breakfast is served outdoors under the oak trees or in the magnificent room covered with 19th-century frescos of fruits and foliage. A simple place at quite reasonable prices.

518 - 33, rue Thiers

33, rue Thiers
17000 La Rochelle
(Charente-Maritime)
Tel. 05 46 41 62 23
Fax 05 46 41 10 76
Mme Maybelle Iribe
E-mail: 106510.2775@compuserve.com

Rooms 6 with bath or shower and WC. **Price** 440F/69,09€ (1 pers.), 480-610F/73,17-92,99€ (2 pers.). **Meals** Breakfast 40F/6,09€. Evening meals at separate tables 180F/27,44€ (wine not incl.). **Facilities** Sitting room, tel., cooking lessons. **Pets** Dogs allowed on request. **Nearby** Sailing, golf; Ré Island, Poitou marshes. **Credit cards** Not accepted. **Spoken** English. **Open** All year. **How to get there** (Map 22): in La Rochelle follow the Centre Ville signs and go around the main square; in front of the cathedral at the traffic lights, take first left, rue Gargoulleau, which becomes rue Thiers further on.

This beautiful house in the very pretty town of La Rochelle has a pleasant inner garden where breakfast is served in summer. The bedrooms, on two floors, are quiet, very comfortable, and remarkably decorated with pictures and family objects. Some of them have their bathrooms across the hall. There is a pleasant sitting-room/library for guests. Don't miss the evening meal, because Madame Iribe is an outstanding gourmet cook. This is a house full of personality.

519 - Château des Salles

17240 Saint-Fort-sur-Gironde
(Charente-Maritime)
Tel. 05 46 49 95 10
Fax 05 46 49 02 81
Sylvie Couillaud

Rooms 5 with bath or shower, WC and tel. **Price** 430-600F/65,55-91,46€ (2-3 pers.). **Meals** Breakfast 50F/7,62€. Half board 400-450F/60,97-68,60€/pers. in double room (3 days min.), 560F/85,37€ (1 pers., single room). Evening meals at separate tables, by reservation 160F/24,39€ (wine not incl.). **Facilities** Sitting room, fax. **Pets** Dogs not allowed. **Nearby** Cognac, La Rochelle. **Credit card** Visa. **Spoken** English, German. **Open** Mar – Oct. Reservation by mail or fax. **How to get there** (Map 22): 14km from the A27 Mirambeau-Royan exit; at the crossroads of D125 towards Saint-Fort-sur-Gironde and D730 towards Royan. **No smoking** in dining room.

Built in the 15th century and renovated in the 19th, this château has five pleasant guest bedrooms with views over the park.Two bedrooms appointed with antique furniture have just been entirely redone, their walls covered with lovely fabrics. One is beneath the eaves but the ceiling is almost nine feet high. Watercolors painted by the owners add further aesthetic appeal. Breakfast can be served in your room or in the dining room (smoking is not allowed).

520 - Rennebourg

Saint-Denis-du-Pin
17400 Saint-Jean-d'Angély
(Charente-Maritime)
Tel. 05 46 32 16 07
Michèle and Florence Frappier

Rooms 5 (poss. 1 suite) with bath, WC, and 1 suite of 2 bedrooms (3-4 pers.) with 1 bath and WC. **Price** 320-350F/48,78-53,35€ (2 pers.). **Meals** Breakfast 35F/5,33€. Evening meals 110F/16,76€ (all incl.). **Facilities** Sitting rooms, swimming pool. **Pets** Dogs not allowed. **Nearby** Tennis, golf, seaside; La Rochelle, Cognac, Poitou marshes, Romanesque Saintonge. **Credit cards** Not accepted. **Spoken** English, German understood. **Open** All year. **How to get there** (Map 22): 7km north of Saint-Jean-d'Angély (A10 exit 34), via N150; signposted.

In the heart of the Saintonge countryside, this traditional house has several rooms with 18th-century paneling, fine old provincial furniture and, throughout, antique curios and paintings. All the bedrooms are different, as they are in a real family home. In one of the barns there is a splendid swimming pool, sheltered from the wind and surrounded by a summer salon. The other barn displays an impressive collection of antique toys and costumes. Excellent dinners are served in a beautiful dining room, and the kind hospitality of Michèle and Florence Frappier makes this place even more appealing.

521 - Domaine de la Baronnie

21, rue Baron de Chantal
17410 Saint-Martin-de-Ré
(Charente-Maritime)
Tel. 05 46 09 21 29
Fax 05 46 09 95 29
Florence and Pierre Pallardy

Rooms 3 and 2 suites (2 connecting rooms for 3 pers.) with shower or bath and WC. **Price** 500-750F/76,22-114,33€ (2 pers.), +100F/15,24€ (extra bed). **Meals** Breakfast 50F/7,62€. No communal meal. **Restaurants** "L'Écailler"in La Flotte and "La Baleine" in Saint-Martin. **Facilities** Sitting rooms, Fitness training (M. Pallardy is an osteopath and dietician). **Pets** Dogs not allowed. **Nearby** All sports, beaches (500m); salt marshes (bicycles), Clergeotte museum. **Spoken** English. **Closed** Nov 15 – Mar 30. 2 nights min. **How to get there** (Maps 14 and 22): in Saint-Martin, in the street leading away from the port, facing the small island. **No smoking**.

We would never have guessed that behind the massive door of the Domaine de la Baronnie, we were about to enter one of the most noble residences on the Island of Ré. In fact, this 18th-century mansion, facing onto a courtyard and onto a garden, is intimately linked with the history of the island. The bedrooms are beautiful but simply appointed so as to call attention to their style. The elegant salons, which are progressively being renovated, are at your disposal. The breakfasts are not only good: they are good for you!

POITOU-CHARENTES

522 - Le Clos

La Menounière
20, rue de la Légère
17310 Saint-Pierre-d'Oléron
(Charente-Maritime)
Tel. 05 46 47 14 34
Fax 05 46 36 03 15
Micheline Denieau
Web: //perso.wanadoo.fr/denieau-gites

Rooms 5 (3 with mezzanine for children and 1 with handicap access) with shower and WC. **Price** 260F/39,63€ (2 pers.), 320F/48,78€ (3 pers.), 370F/56,40€ (4 pers.), +50F/7,62€ (extra pers.). **Meals** Breakfast incl. No communal meal. **Facilities** Room with kitchen, TV and sitting room. **Pets** Dogs allowed on request. **Nearby** Restaurants, golf, fishing, bicycle rental, riding, tennis, hiking and biking tours, seaside (500m); bird sanctuary. **Credit cards** Not accepted. **Spoken** English, Spanish. **Open** All year. **How to get there** (Map 22): 4km west of Saint-Pierre d'Oléron via D734; at Saint-Pierre turn left at the traffic lights after the Shell station, then follow signs for La Menounière.

On entering the village, you will find this small house, which is bordered by vineyards and has a pretty flower garden. The guest bedrooms are simple, attractive, and well kept. Three have a loft, making them ideal for families, and a small ground-level terrace. Two small kitchens make it possible for guests to prepare a small meal occasionally, which they can have in the large sitting-dining room, heated by a wood fire in winter. "The Enclosure" is a good, reasonably priced bed and breakfast.

523 - Château de la Tillade

17260 Saint-Simon-de-Pellouaille
(Charente-Maritime)
Tel. 05 46 90 00 20
Fax 05 46 90 02 23
Vicomte and Vicomtesse
Michel de Salvert
E-mail: la.tillade@t3a.com

Rooms 3 with bath or shower and WC. **Price** 420-500F/64,02-76,22€ (2 pers.). **Meals** Breakfast incl. Meals at communal table 180F/27,44€ (wine incl.). **Facilities** Sitting room, drawing and painting lessons, poss. horseback riding accompanied by the owner (80F/12,19€/hour), bikes lent. **Pets** Dogs not allowed. **Nearby** Swimming pool (4km), 18-hole golf course (20km); Romanesque Saintonge, Saintes, Talmont. **Credit cards** Not accepted. **Spoken** English. **Open** All year. **How to get there** (Map 22): 4km north of Gémozac on road to Saintes on left. Autoroute A10, exit n. 36.

The Château de la Tillade is a vast wine-growing estate located in very quiet surroundings. The interior is elegant and decorated as it was in the past; there are modern amenities. Upstairs, the bedrooms have just been renovated and decorated with 18th- and 19th-century furniture, soft pastel colors, and shimmering fabrics; all are exemplary of Madame de Salvert's artistic tastes (she gives courses in watercoloring). The bathrooms are impeccable. The communal meals are mouthwatering.

524 - Château de Cherveux

79410 Cherveux
(Deux-Sèvres)
Tel. and fax 05 49 75 06 55
M. and Mme Redien
E-mail: fredien@minitel.net
Web: château-de-cherveux.com

Rooms 2 and 1 suite (2-6 pers.) with bath or shower, private WC incl. 1 outside the room. **Price** 220-270F/33,53-41,16€ (1 pers.), 270-320F/41,16-48,78€ (2 pers.); suite 300F/45,73€ (2 pers.), 500F/76,22€ (4-6 pers.). **Meals** Breakfast incl. Meals at communal table or not 90F/13,72€ (wine incl.). **Facilities** Sitting room, fishing in moat and tour of Château, horse stalls. **Pets** Dogs allowed on request. **Nearby** Golf; Poitou marshes, Futuroscope. **Credit cards** Not accepted. **Open** All year. **How to get there** (Map 15): 13km north of Niort towards Parthenay-Saumur via RD743, then leave town via RD8 via St-Gelais; or autoroute A10, exit 32, towards St-Maixent/Niort. At the croosroads: St-Maixent. 1st on left D7 Cherveux.

Originally a fortress belonging to the Lusignan feudal lords in the 13th century, Cherveux was rebuilt in the 15th century by the Scots. Today it is a vast farm with superb, dramatic architecture. We recommend only the two bedrooms located in the salle des gardes (guard room), especially the large room. They are pleasant and have acceptable bathroom facilities. For dinner and breakfast, you can choose between several rooms: ask for the very rustic kitchen, which is much less austere than the other rooms. Lovers of old architecture and a rustic lifestyle will appreciate this house.

525 - Château de Saint-Loup

79600 Saint-Loup-Lamairé
(Deux-Sèvres)
Tel. 05 49 64 81 73
Fax 05 49 64 82 06
M. de Bartillat
E-mail: saint-loup@wfi.fr
Web: www.chateaudesaint-loup.com

Rooms 12 (4 and 1 suite (2-4 pers.) in the donjon, 7 in the château (many with 4-poster beds) with bath or shower and WC. **Price** Rooms 550-1150F/83,84-175,31€ (2 pers.). **Meals** Breakfast 60F/9,14€. Evening meals, by reservation from 250F/38,11€ (wine not incl.). **Facilities** Sitting room, canal, river fishing and gardens 17- and 18-century - Poss. boat, horse carriage by reservation. **Pets** Dogs allowed on request. **Spoken** English, German. **Credit cards** Not accepted. **Open** All year, by reservation and 50% deposit. **How to get there** (Map 15): 19km northeast of Parthenay via D938 dir. Thouars/Saumur for 15km, then right D46 dir. Airvault/Saint-Loup. In Saint-Loup, at the end of the main street.

This magnificent château in the Thouet valley has been classified as a historic landmark. In addition to a flower garden and a vegetable garden, it has an orchard and an orangerie, rehabilitated according to the original plans At the end of the canal stands a charming little house. In the keep (donjon), dating from the 15th century, the rooms are decorated after a medieval manner. Despite an austere appearance they are all comfortable, with well-appointed bathrooms. The top floor suite is more simply arranged. The other bedrooms are in the 17th-century château.

526 - La Gatinalière

86100 Antran
(Vienne)
Tel. 05 49 21 15 02
Fax 05 49 85 39 65
M. Bernard Claret de la Touche
E-mail: bdelatouche@minitelnet
Web: www.chateaux-france.com

Rooms 1 suite in annex and 1 suite in the château (lounge) with bath and WC and 2 houses. **Price** 650-800F/99,09-121,95€ (2-3 pers.); houses 2000 and 4000F/304,89 and 609,79€/week. **Meals** Breakfast incl. Candlelit dinner 200F/30,48€ (all incl.). **Facilities** Sitting room, tel, fax, bicycles, mountain bikes. **Pets** Dogs allowed on request. **Nearby** Hot-air ballooning, 18-hole golf courses; Futuroscope, Loire châteaux. **Spoken** English, Spanish. **Open** Easter – Nov 1, by reservation in winter. **How to get there** (Map 16): 5km north of Châtellerault, exit autoroute then dir. Richelieu; go 5km. In La Gerbaudière, turn left onto D75; in 500m on right.

Surrounded by a large park and flower garden at the end of a cool avenue of lindens, this small 18th-century château offers guests the choice of two suites: one is simple and independent, with the air of a country house; the other, in the château, features an amazing bathroom/lounge of tremendous charm. A large salon and a beautiful, inviting dining room add to the beauty of La Gatinalière.

527 - La Talbardière

86210 Archigny
(Vienne)
Tel. 05 49 85 32 51/05 49 85 32 52
Fax 05 49 85 69 72
M. and Mme Lonhienne
E-mail: jacques.lonhienne@interpc.fr
Web: www.interpc.fr/mapage/lonhienne/
indexhtm

Rooms 3 (2-3 pers.) with bath or shower, WC, and 1 studio (5 pers.) with bath, WC, kitchen, tel. and TV. **Price** 300F/45,73€ (2 pers., 1 night), 270F/41,16€ (2 pers., 2-3 nights), 260F/39,63€ (2 pers., 4-6 nights), 240F/36,58€ (2 pers., from 7 nights). **Meals** Breakfast incl. No communal meal. **Pets** Dogs not allowed. **Nearby** Restaurants (15km), fishing, riding, tennis, golf. **Credit cards** Not accepted. **Spoken** English, German, Italian, Russian. **Open** All year. **How to get there** (Map 16): 18km southeast of Châtellerault via D9 towards Monthoiron, then D3 towards Pleumartin; signs after 1km.

This house deep in the countryside goes back to the 17th century and was once a guard house. It has large windows and a handsome oak staircase that leads up to the bedrooms. The first of these is immense, simply but comfortably furnished, with a floor of terra cotta flagstones. Its bathroom might be more cheerful. The second is smaller, with parquet flooring, and well appointed (its bath as well). Another large bedroom is comfortably installed in the rustic setting of what used to be the stables. Breakfast, with homemade bread and jams, is served in the bedrooms or outdoors. The welcome is smiling and pleasant.

528 - La Veaudepierre

8, rue du Berry
86300 Chauvigny
(Vienne)
Tel. 05 49 46 30 81 / 05 49 41 41 76
Fax 05 49 47 64 12
M. and Mme J. de Giafferri

Rooms 4 and 1 suite (3 pers.) with bath or shower, WC (incl. 1 room with bath outside room). **Price** 180-250F/27,44-38,11€ (1 pers.), 230-300F/35,06-45,73€ (2 pers.), 360F/54,88€ (3 pers.). **Meals** Breakfast incl. **Facilities** Sitting room; cultural stays in Poitou organized. **Pets** Dogs not allowed. **Nearby** 18-hole golf course, tennis and swimming pool (village), Romanesque abbeys and churches, Saint-Savin, Fort Chauvigny, Futuroscope (25km). **Credit cards** Not accepted. **Spoken** English. **Closed** Nov 1 – Easter, except for school holidays and by reservation. **How to get there** (Map 16): In the village.

La Veaudepierre is a Directoire house which is located in a medieval village surmounted by an imposing fortress. The owners are warm and helpful. The house is richly furnished with antiques while retaining provincial charm. The pleasant bedrooms open onto a lovely garden which is surrounded by the old walls of the village. This is a very delightful place and a good base for discovering the hidden treasures of the Poitou region.

529 - Le Logis du château du Bois Dousset

86800 Lavoux
(Vienne)
Tel. and fax 05 49 44 20 26
Vicomte and Vicomtesse
Hilaire de Villoutreys

Rooms 3 (2 with room for children) with bath and WC (incl. 1 with bath outside room). **Price** 300-350F/45,73-53,35€ (2 pers.). **Meals** Breakfast incl. Evening meals, by reservation 60F/9,14€ (all incl.). **Facilities** Sitting room, château and logis both classified as historic landmarks, French (formal style) garden. **Pets** Dogs allowed on request. **Nearby** Restaurants (5km), golf, riding, sailing, canoeing, kayaks; Romanesque art of Poitou, Brenne lakes, châteaux, Futuroscope. **Credit cards** Not accepted. **Spoken** English, Spanish. **Open** All year. **How to get there** (Map 16): 12km east of Poitiers. Autoroute A10 exit Poitiers-Nord, towards Limoges, then in 5km towards Bignoux. Logis on D139 between Bignoux and Lavoux.

The Logis is an outbuilding of a superb château, a landmarked monument admirably located in the heart of an immense private park. In a small, newly restored wing, there are two comfortable guestrooms with tasteful decoration and beautiful bathrooms. The large (450 sq. ft.) third room upstairs is magnificently furnished and lighted by tall windows, but its bath facilities are old-fashioned. Breakfasts are pleasant and are served in a sunny room looking out on the beautiful formal garden.

530 - Château de Vaumoret

Rue du Breuil-Mingot
86000 Poitiers
(Vienne)
Tel. 05 49 61 32 11
Fax 05 49 01 04 54
M., Mme and Melle Vaucamp

Rooms 3 with bath and WC. **Price** 300-370F/45,73-56,40€ (1 pers.), 350-430F/53,35-65,55€ (2 pers.), 470-520F/71,65-79,27€ (3 pers.), 590F/89,94€ (4 pers.). **Meals** Breakfast incl. No communal meal. (Guests may use kitchen.). **Facilities** Sitting room, bicycles. **Pets** Dogs allowed on request. **Nearby** Restaurants (2km), golf, riding; Futuroscope. **Credit cards** Not accepted. **Spoken** English, Spanish. **Open** All year. **How to get there** (Map 16): 8km east of Poitiers. Autoroute A10 exit Poitiers-Nord, towards Limoges via bypass, exit 5km towards Montamisé, La Roche-Posay on D3; then on right, towards Sèvres-Anxaumont (D18); entrance to château in 2.5km on right.

The small, 17th-century Château de Vaumoret, located on the outskirts of Poitiers but nevertheless still in the country, has been classified as a historic landmark. One wing is reserved for the guest rooms, which are lovely and have superb bathrooms. Each very comfortable room has its own style, which is created by a tasteful choice of furniture, paintings and fabrics. Breakfast is served in a salon decorated with old engravings, many depicting hunting scenes. This is a welcoming and elegantly luxurious place to stay.

531 - Le Bois Goulu

86200 Pouant
(Vienne)
Tel. 05 49 22 52 05
Mme Marie-Christine Picard

Rooms 2 with bath or shower and WC (possible child's rooms). **Price** 260F/39,63€ (2 pers.), +60F/9,14€ (children with suppl.). **Meals** Breakfast incl. No communal meal. **Restaurants** In Pouant and Richelieu. **Facilities** Sitting room, bicycle rentals. **Pets** Dogs allowed on request. **Nearby** Swimming pool, fishing, golf, hunting; Loire châteaux, Chinon, Villandry, Richelieu, Futuroscope (50km). **Credit cards** Not accepted. **Open** All year. **How to get there** (Map 16): 15km east of Loudun towards Richelieu via D61; on leaving village, avenue of linden trees.

The impressive avenue of linden trees leading to the Bois Goulu is quite in keeping with the size of the buildings set around the courtyard of this handsome farm complex. The bedrooms are simply appointed with their parquet floors, large wardrobes and comfortable beds. One of them has an adjoining children's room. The other is more romantic in character. The salon is comfortably furnished and bright, with double exposure. Breakfast (with nice homemade jam) is served at the big table in the dining room. You are welcomed with kindness and simplicity.

532 - Château de Prémarie

86340 Roches-Prémarie
(Vienne)
Tel. 05 49 42 50 01
Fax 05 49 42 07 63
M. and Mme Jean-Pierre de Boysson

Rooms 4 with bath or shower and WC. **Price** 400-500F/60,97-76,22€ (2 pers.). **Meals** Breakfast incl. No communal meal. **Restaurant** In Saint-Benoit (8km) and in Smarves (4km). **Facilities** Sitting room, swimming pool, tennis. **Pets** Dogs not allowed. **Nearby** Equestrian center (12km), 18-hole golf course (10km); Romanesque art, Futuroscope (23 km). **Credit cards** Not accepted. **Spoken** English. **Open** Easter – Nov 1. **How to get there** (Map 16): 14km south of Poitiers via D741 towards Smarves-Confolens.

Once an English fortress, this small château is inviting and comfortable. The rooms are very charming and cheerful, as are the bathrooms. Everything is admirably well-kept, the atmosphere seems authentic and the welcome feels warm and genuine. The breakfasts are excellent and the heated swimming pool is open from springtime onwards.

533 - Château de Cibioux

86250 Surin
(Vienne)
Tel. 05 49 87 04 89
Fax 05 49 87 46 30
M. Jean-Claude Corbin

Rooms 1 suite (2-3 pers.) with bath, WC, TV and tel. **Price** 450F/68,60€ (1 pers.), 550F/83,84€ (2 pers.), +100F/15,24€ (extra bed). **Meals** Breakfast incl. Communal meals 100F/15,24€ (wine incl.). Half board from 3 days. **Facilities** Sitting room. **Nearby** Tennis (400m), riding (5km); abbeys of Charroux, Laréau and Nantueil-en-Vallée, Romanesque sites and châteaux, Futuroscope. **Credit cards** Not accepted. **Spoken** English. **Open** All year. **How to get there** (Map 23): 10km south of Civray. N10 exit Ruffec or Couhé. From Couhé take D7 to Civray, then D35 towards Genouillé for 4km. At entrance to village on right.

A fortified castle in the 15th century, Cibioux later became a seigneurial manor house and endured many trials and tribulations before it was finally saved by Jean-Claude Corbin. Each epoch has left its imprint here, the most charming of which is the small 15th-century wing. It is here that you will find the suite. Very comfortable and decorated in authentic style, it gives onto a superb loggia where breakfasts and dinners can be served unless you prefer the charming, rustic dining room which has great character.

534 - La Boulinière

Journet
86290 La Trimouille
(Vienne)
Tel. 05 49 91 55 88
Fax 05 49 91 72 82
M. and Mme Earls

Rooms 4 with bath or shower and WC. **Price** 420F/64,02€ (2 pers.). **Meals** Breakfast incl. Communal evening meals 95F/14,48€ (wine incl.). **Facilities** Sitting room, swimming pool, lake fishing, GR 48. **Pets** Small dogs allowed. **Nearby** Mountain bikes, riding, canoes, kayaks; Fresco valley, Saint-Savin. **Credit cards** Not accepted. **Open** All year. **How to get there** (Map 16): 10km south of Montmorillon via D727 dir. La Trimouille; sign (4km).

The entire Earls family came over from England to raise sheep (700 head) and take in guests. Their 19th-century farmhouse, situated deep in the countryside, is nicely decorated in English taste: bright colors, a collection of engravings, wallpaper with flowery borders... The bedrooms are large and pleasant and benefit from attentive care. The bathrooms are all perfectly adequate. Nice breakfasts are served in an attractive green room.

535 - Château de Régnier

86290 La Trimouille
(Vienne)
Tel. and fax 05 49 91 60 06
M. and Mme de Liniers

Rooms 4 with bath or shower and WC. Rooms cleaned on request. **Price** 250-400F/38,11-60,97€ (2 pers.), +50F/7,62€ (extra bed), children under 10 (free). **Meals** Breakfast incl. Evening meals at communal tables 100-150F/15,24-22,86€ (wine incl.). **Facilities** Sitting room, lake and river (fishing and swimming), hunting (by reservation). **Pets** Dogs allowed on request. **Nearby** Fresco valley, church of Saint-Savin, site of Argentomagus, Angle-sur-l'Anglin. **Spoken** English, Spanish. **Open** All year. **How to get there** (Map 16): 30km south of Le Blanc via D975 to La Trimouille then D675 towards Limoges, Le Dorat; house on left after 5km.

The Château de Régnier, which existed in the 13th century, was extensively rebuilt in the 19th century. From its elevated position, it commands a magnificent view over a countryside of rivers, fields, and woods. Inside, there is the simple, somewhat bohemian atmosphere of an old mansion of the past. We recommend the ravishing Rouge room, which overlooks the impressive panorama; and the delightful Rose room, despite the somewhat spartan bathroom facilities. Breakfast is served in the delightfully old-fashioned kitchen, there is antique furniture throughout, and the owners couldn't be nicer.

POITOU-CHARENTES

536 - Château de Ternay
Ternay
86120 Les Trois-Moutiers
(Vienne)
Tel. 05 49 22 97 54
Fax 05 49 22 34 66
Caroline and Loïc de Ternay
E-mail: chateauternay@wanadoo.fr
Web: //perso.wanadoo.fr/chateau.ternay/
accueil.html

Rooms 3 with 4-poster beds (incl. 1 with twin beds) and 1 suite (4 pers.) with bath and WC. **Price** Rooms 420-480F/64,02-73,17€ (2 pers.); suite 700F/106,71€. **Meals** Breakfast 40F/6,09€. Evening meals, by reservation 250F/38,11€ (all incl.). **Facilities** Sitting rooms, swimming pool, horse stalls. **Pets** Dogs not allowed. **Nearby** Golf; abbey of Fontevrauld, Loire châteaux. **Spoken** English. **Open** All year. **How to get there** (Map 15): 30km south of Saumur via N147. In Montreuil-Bellay, towards Les Trois-Moutiers, then towards Ternay.

A 15th-century castle built around an even older keep, the Château de Ternay did not escape some 19th-century remodeling. But it still has its Gothic chapel and impressive appearance with a handsome courtyard and some authentic decoration. The bedrooms are large and quiet, with antique furniture and fabric-covered walls. Modernity is present in the form of nice functional bathrooms. Table d'hôte dinner in a friendly atmosphere.

537 - Les Hauts de Chabonne

Chabonne
86210 Vouneuil-sur-Vienne
(Vienne)
Tel. 05 49 85 28 25
Florence and Antoine Penot

Rooms 5 with bath or shower, WC (incl. 1 private but outside room). **Price** 270-290F/41,16-44,21€ (2 pers.), +80F/12,19€ (extra pers.). **Meals** Breakfast incl. Communal meals, by reservation 95F/14,48€. **Facilities** Sitting room. **Pets** Dogs allowed in 3 rooms only. **Nearby** Water sports (6km), tennis (2km), riding (4km), 18-hole golf course (6km); bird sanctuary and forest (500m), Futuroscope (15km). **Credit cards** Not accepted. **Spoken** English. **Open** All year. **How to get there** (Map 16): 12km south of Châtellerault via RN10, then D749 at Châtellerault, then at Vouneuil-sur-Vienne, follow signs.

Situated at the edge of a bird sanctuary, this old, extensively renovated farmhouse offers six pretty bedrooms. With a tiled floor, two spacious, ground-floor rooms are perfect in good weather. The others (except for the small blue room) are also charming. Breakfasts are served in the main house, where you will find an elegant salon and dining room, both furnished with antiques and beautiful, cheerful fabrics. The young owners are delightful hosts.

538 - Le Pigeonnier

Rue du Château
04280 Céreste
(Alpes-de-Haute-Provence)
Tel. 04 92 79 07 54
Fax 04 92 79 07 75
Mme Exbrayat

Rooms 4 (incl. one extra large with double bed and 2 single beds) with bath or shower and WC; and 1 with private shower and private WC. **Price** 260-315F/39,63-48,02€ (2 pers.), +75F/11,43€ (extra bed). **Meals** Breakfast incl. No communal meal. **Restaurants** "L'Aiguebelle" (500m away) and "L'Auberge de Carluc" (regional specialties). **Facilities** Sitting room, garden, private lighted parking lot, bicycles. **Pets** Dogs allowed on request. **Nearby** Swimming pool and tennis in village, riding, hiking, biking path, 18-hole golf course (20km); Lubéron Regional Park, Gordes, Bonnieux, Roussillon, Lacoste. **Credit cards** Not accepted. **Spoken** English. **Open** Easter – Nov 1. **How to get there** (Map 33): 20km from Manosque via N100 towards Apt.

"The Pigeon Loft" is a very old village house with a small enclosed garden next to it, and especially lovely interior decoration. Each bedroom has its own color scheme for the bedcovers, lampshades, paintings and objects, all of which are prettily set off by the white walls. The bathrooms are immaculate. Good breakfasts are served in a beautiful living room with a wonderful sweeping view of the village and the countryside.

539 - Foulara

04230 Cruis
(Alpes-de-Haute-Provence)
Tel. 04 92 77 07 96
M. and Mme Hartz

Rooms 5 with bath or shower and WC. **Price** 220F/33,53€ (1 pers.), 260F/39,63€ (2 pers.); 320F/48,78€ (1 room, 3 pers.). **Meals** Breakfast incl. Evening meals at communal table 80F/12,19€ (wine incl.). **Facilities** Sitting room, pétanque, garden swing set for children. **Pets** Dogs not allowed. **Nearby** Tennis, swimming pool, riding, mountain bikes; Cruis church, Montagne de Lure. **Credit cards** Not accepted. **Spoken** English. **Closed** Dec – Mar, or by reservation. Confirmation with 25% deposit. Arrival before 7:00PM. **How to get there** (Map 34): 20km north of Forcalquier. Autoroute A51, exit Peyruis dir. Avignon via D4A. Go through N96 dir. Saint-Étienne-les-Orgues via D101 then D951. In Cruis, take D16 dir. Montlaux then follow signs (2km). Access by the road on right.

Situated in the center of a 30-hectare estate, this old farmhouse built in a U-shape has just been completely renovated but has lost none of its charm. It offers five simple and comfortable bedrooms enhanced by some nice antique furniture. There is lots of space around the house, shaded or otherwise sheltered. The table d'hôte meals are convivial and served outdoors when the weather is fine. Added to the smiling hospitality, it makes this a lovely place for a holiday.

540 - Château d'Esparron

04800 Esparron-de-Verdon
(Alpes-de-Haute-Provence)
Tel. 04 92 77 12 05
Fax 04 92 77 13 10
Charlotte-Anne and Bernard
de Castellane
E-mail: bernard.de.castellane@wanadoo.fr

Rooms 4 and 1 suite of 2 bedrooms with bath and WC. **Price** Room 700-1300F/106,71-198,18€ (2 pers.); suite 800F/121,95€ (2 pers.); + 100F/15,24€ for 1 night, +150F/22,86€ (extra bed). **Meals** Breakfast incl. No communal meal. **Facilities** Sitting room, tel. **Pets** Dogs allowed on request. **Nearby** Restaurants (200m), swimming and boats (Esparron Lake). **Credit cards** Visa, Eurocard, MasterCard. **Spoken** English. **Closed** Nov – Easter. **How to get there** (Map 34): Autoroute A51 exit Manosque. Go to Gréoux-les-Bains, then Esparron. In the village. **No smoking** in bedrooms.

This château that looks down over the village and the lake of Esparron has been in the same family since the 12th century. The young owners have renovated it with good taste and sensitivity. The large comfortable bedrooms are simply furnished with nice antiques, decorated with fine fabrics and equipped with impeccable bathrooms. The stately sitting room is built around a fireplace and the charming dining room, where you will be served a delicious and copious breakfast, has been installed in what used to be the kitchen. A superb address and most inviting.

541 - Les Méans

La Fresquière
04340 Meolans Revel
Tel. and fax 04 92 81 03 91
M. and Mme Millet
E-mail: lesmeans@chez.com
Web: www.chez.com/lesmeans/

Rooms 4 and 1 suite with bath, shower and WC. **Price** Rooms 280F/42,68€ (1 pers.), 320F/48,78€ (2 pers.); suite 640F/97,56€ (4 pers); +100F/15,24€ (extra bed). **Meals** Breakfast incl. Evening meals at communal table or not 98F/14,94€ (wine not incl.). **Facilities** Sitting room, Tel. **Pets** Dogs allowed, +20F/3,04€/day. **Nearby** Hiking (GR), rafting, mountain bikes, canyon, climbing, Serre-Ponçon Lake, La Cayolle pass, Mercantour Park. **Credit cards** Visa, Eurocard, MasterCard. **Spoken** English, Spanish, Italian. **Closed** Oct 15 – May 15. **How to get there** (Map 34): 10km of Barcelonnette. On D900 Gap-Barcelonnette. After crossing La Fresquière, 500m on left: indicated on large wooden sign.

Just above Barcelonnette, Les Méans has dominated the valley since the 16th century. The building is vast and opulent and has preserved a number of its original features, such as the wooden staircase or the large vaulted common room. This has been made into a bright and cheery sitting room with a kitchen area near the large fireplace, where spit-roasted meats are prepared for dinner. The bedrooms have a more spartan air: choose the ones with a double bed, better proportioned than the others. They are simply furnished but the bathrooms are comfortable. The welcome you get is natural, sporty and pleasant.

542 - L'Escapade

Le Bourg
04200 Noyers-sur-Jabron
(Alpes-de-Haute-Provence)
Tel. 04 92 62 00 04
M. Guirand and M. Fontaine
E-mail: escapades.en.jabron@wanadoo.fr

Rooms 1 suite (4 pers.) with shower and WC. **Price** 350F/53,35€ (2 pers.), 500F/76,22€ (4 pers.). **Meals** Breakfast incl. No communal meal. **Facilities** Sitting room, tel. **Nearby** Restaurants (100m), hiking; route of Romanesque chapels, Sisteron. **Credit cards** Not accepted. **Spoken** English, Italian. **Closed** Nov 1 – Easter. **How to get there** (Map 34): 10km southwest of Sisteron. Between Sisteron and Château-Arnoux, take N85, then D946. House at the entrance of the village. **No smoking.**

Standing at the entrance to the village, this "Escapade" is an amusing family home from the turn of the century. The visitor pushing open the gate will walk up an alley of boxwood, climb a staircase and find himself in a house that is retro and meticulously cared for at the same time. There is a certain "Proustian" air about it all, recalling the home of "Tante Léonie." The two-room suite for guests is most elegant, and makes up for the fatigue of getting here. The welcome is hospitable and the breakfasts, served on the terrace in summer, are both refined and delicious.

543 - Le Jas de la Caroline

Chenebotte
04200 Noyers-sur-Jabron
(Alpes-de-Haute-Provence)
Tel. and fax 04 92 62 03 48
Monique and Henri Morel

Rooms 2 with bath, WC, and 1 with bath, WC, sitting room, kitchenette and tel. with card. **Price** 250F/38,11€ (1 pers.), 300F/45,73€ (2 pers.); -10% from 2 nights; suite 300F/45,73€ (1 pers.), 400F/60,97€ (2 pers.), +100F/15,24€ (extra pers.). **Meals** Breakfast incl. Evening meals, by reservation 100F/15,24€ (wine incl.). **Facilities** Sitting room, mountain-bike rides. **Pets** Dogs allowed on request (+20F/3,04€/day). **Nearby** Tours in the footsteps of writers Giono, Magnan and P. Arène, secondhand shop, festivals. **Credit cards** Not accepted. **Spoken** English, Italian. **Open** All year. **How to get there** (Map 34): 12km southwest of Sisteron, dir. Aix and Digne for 3km; then turn right towards Noyers-sur-Jabron. On leaving village, 1st road on right, then follow signs. **No smoking**.

Standing on the flank of a hill in a magnificent, unspoiled site, this converted 16th-century shepherd's cottage with traditional stone walls offers you three cool, comfortable guest rooms. You can enjoy resting and relaxing in the quiet surroundings, and lovely moments on the terrace where breakfast and dinners (we're told they are delicious) are usually served. Monique and Henri Morel's cheerful hospitality will add a big plus to your stay.

545 - Les Granges de Saint-Pierre

04150 Simiane-la-Rotonde
(Alpes-de-Haute-Provence)
Tel. 04 92 75 93 81
Fax 04 92 75 93 81
M. and Mme Tamburini

Rooms 3 with shower and WC. **Price** 330F/50,30€ (2 pers.), 290F/44,21€ (2 pers., +5 nights). **Meals** Breakfast incl. No communal meal. Equipped kitchen at guests' disposal. **Facilities** Tel. with card, swimming pool. **Nearby** Restaurants (50m), mountain bikes, riding; Luberon Valley, Simiane village and rotunda, "Provençal Colorado". **Spoken** English, Italian. **Open** All year, only by reservation Nov 15 – Mar 30. **How to get there** (Map 33): 22km northeast of Apt via D22 dir. Banon. In Simiane, house on right, at the entrance of village. **No smoking** in bedrooms.

Simiane is halfway between the mountains of Luberon and Ventoux. This house is situated in the former barns of an 18th-century bastide, whose garden you pass as you walk to the swimming pool, set on a rugged terrain, half wild, half cultivated. The interior is surprisingly warm and modern. The decoration, both in the vast sitting room and the comfortable bedrooms, is sober and elegant: shades of ecru, natural wood, pretty cotton fabrics... Breakfast is served on a terrace-solarium, which is very inviting and makes up for the small size of the garden. The welcome is friendly and the prices very reasonable.

546 - La Maurissime

Chemin des Oliviers
04180 Villeneuve
(Alpes-de-Haute-Provence)
Tel. and fax 04 92 78 47 61
Nicole Mouchot

Rooms 3 and 1 suite (2-4 pers.) with bath or shower and WC. **Price** Room 250-300F/38,11-45,76€ (2 pers.), +50F/7,62€ (extra bed); suite 250-500F/38,11-76,22€ (2-4 pers.). **Meals** Breakfast incl. Evening meals at communal table 90F/13,72€ (aperitif incl., wine not incl.). **Facilities** Sitting room. **Pets** Dogs allowed. **Nearby** Sainte-Croix and Esparron Lakes, golf; Sisteron. **Spoken** English. **Open** All year, by reservation in winter. **How to get there** (Map 34): 10km northeast of Manosque. A51 exit La Brillanne, take on left, then at the traffic circle N96 towards Manosque, then Villeneuve and follow signs "Chambres d'hôtes". **No smoking** in bedrooms.

La Maurissime is new and still lacks the warmth of age but its marvelous view, charming decor, and Madame Mouchot's lovely hospitality compensate for that small drawback. Sober, comfortable, and cheerful, the guest rooms and private baths are immaculately kept, and some enjoy a private terrace. The pleasant living rooms are prettily decorated and look out over a huge terrace where breakfast is served in the morning sun. As for the dinners, they are simply outstanding. The place is a must.

547 - La Girandole

Brunissard
05350 Arvieux-en-Queyras
(Hautes-Alpes)
Tel. 04 92 46 84 12
Fax 04 92 46 86 59
Isabelle and Noël Morel

Rooms 5 and 1 suite (4 pers.) with bath and WC. **Price** Rooms 250F/38,11€ (1 pers.), 350F/53,35€ (2 pers.), +150F/22,86€ (extra bed); suite 500F/76,22€ (4 pers.). **Meals** Breakfast incl. No communal meal. Poss. half board. Equipped kitchen at guests' disposal. **Facilities** Sitting room (fireplace, piano, music), lounge, sauna, gym apparatus and games room (children), whirlpool swimming pool in summer. **Nearby** Restaurants (100m), mountain bikes, rafting, paragliding, skiing; snowshoeing, dogsleds; Val d'Azur. **Spoken** English. **Open** All year. By reservation, confirmation with contract and 25% deposit. 2 days min. **How to get there** (Map 27): 60km from Briançon towards Gap to Mont-Dauphin then Guillestre. Follow Col de Izoard to Brunissard (in summer from Briançon via Col de Izoard).

Located in a little village well off the beaten path, this spacious old house, typical of Queyras, has been tastefully refurbished with talent and imagination. Antique furniture and objects, colorful fabrics and wood everywhere make for a feeling of warmth and brightness in the bedrooms and the living room as well. There is also a small café, where an afternoon snack is served. Ideal for a mountain holiday in summer or winter. A welcome that is kind and considerate.

548 - Le Parlement

Quartier de Charance
05000 Gap
(Hautes-Alpes)
Tel. and fax 04 92 53 94 20
M. and Mme Drouillard

Rooms 5, 1 suite (2-4 pers.) with bath and/or shower, WC, TV (on request) and 1 studio (5 pers.) with bath, shower, WC, kitchen (laundry and dishwasher), small garden, TV (black and white), linens changed and room cleaned on departure. **Price** Room 360-400F/54,88-60,97€ (2 pers.), suite 500F/76,22€ (2 pers.); +100F/15,24€ (extra pers.), +50F/7,62€ (children under 12); studio 2500-3500F/381,12-533,57€/week, depending season. **Meals** Breakfast incl. No communal meal. Summer kitchen at guests' disposal on request. **Facilities** Sitting room, tel., swimming pool, sauna. **Pets** Animals not allowed. **Spoken** English. **Open** All year. **How to get there** (Maps 27 and 34): 5km northwest of Gap in dir. Orange/Valence, then at the 3 Cascades intersection, dir. Charance; signs. **No smoking** except evenings in the sitting room.

In this pretty, rather unusual house dating from the 18th century, the bedrooms are very pleasant and tasteful, as are the baths. Guests in the suite enjoy a balcony with a beautiful view. There is also an independent studio, comfortable and well kept. Bruno Drouillard, who is a mountain guide, will help you select what sports you'd like to try and, if you wish, he can organize outings for you.

549 - La Bastide du Bosquet

14, chemin des Sables
06160 Antibes
(Alpes-Maritimes)
Tel. and fax 04 93 67 32 29
Tel. 04 93 34 06 04
Sylvie and Christian Aussel

Rooms 3 with bath or shower, WC. Rooms cleaned every 3 days. **Price** 390-480F/59,45-73,17€ (2 pers.) depending on season; +100-120F/15,24-18,29€ (extra bed). **Meals** Breakfast incl. No communal meal. **Pets** Dogs not allowed. **Nearby** 18-hole golf course, beach (5 min. walk); Picasso Museum, Jazz Festival in Juan-les-Pins (Jul). **Credit cards** Not accepted. **Spoken** English. **Closed** Feb, by reservation. 3 days min. **How to get there** (Map 35): From Cannes via Jean-les-Pins towards Palais des Congrès (at bottom of Chemin des Sables); Autoroute exit Antibes, towards "Centre Ville", then Cap d'Antibes. On the seafront, take towards Juan-les-Pins (not Antibes). In front of the synagogue.

This 18th-century Provençal house is located some distance from the busy streets of Antibes even though it is in the heart of the city and a short walk to the beaches. It is a family house which is as beautiful inside as out. The bedrooms are sunny and quiet, with pretty Provençal fabrics and tastefully furnished. The bathrooms are very pleasant and are decorated with large, colorful pottery motifs. Breakfasts are served in a pretty dining room or on the terrace.

550 - Villa Panko

17, chemin du Parc Saramartel
06160 Cap d'Antibes - Juan-les-Pins
(Alpes-Maritimes)
Tel. 04 93 67 92 49
Fax 04 93 61 29 32
M. and Mme Bourgade

Rooms 2 with bath and WC. **Price** 500-730F/76,22-111,28€ (2 pers., depending on room, season and service), +100F/15,24€ (extra bed). **Meals** Breakfast incl. No communal meal. **Facilities** Sitting room, piano, tel. with card. **Pets** Dogs allowed on request. **Nearby** Restaurants (10 min. walk), music festivals (jazz, opera, classical). **Credit cards** Not accepted. **Spoken** English, Italian. **Closed** Christmas and Jan 1, by reservation. 3 nights min. and 5 in high season. **How to get there** (Map 35): From center of Antibes, take towards Cap d'Antibes direct (twice), then turn right onto Chemin du Crouton, then 1st on left (dead-end). At end of dead-end, on left. **No smoking** incl. in the garden.

Located at the end of a quiet dead-end street ten minutes by foot from the beach, this house and its garden are small but it is a haven of tranquillity in the heart of Cap d'Antibes. The shaded terrace reserved for guests is a delightful place for a rest and Madame Bourgade is a wonderful hostess, attentive to your every need. The breakfasts are delicious and the prices quite reasonable off-season. A nice place for a longer holiday.

551 - Le Clos de Saint-Paul

71, chemin de La Rouguière
06480 La Colle-sur-Loup
(Alpes-Maritimes)
Tel. and fax 04 93 32 56 81
Mme Ronin-Pillet
E-mail: leclossaintpaul@hotmail.com

Rooms 3 with bath or shower and WC. **Price** 320-400F/48,78-60,97€ (2 pers.), +60F/9,14€ (extra bed). **Meals** Breakfast incl. No communal meal. **Facilities** Swimming pool, ping-pong. **Pets** Dogs allowed on request. **Nearby** Restaurants (600m), sailing, golf, skiing; Saint-Paul-de-Vence (Fondation Maeght), Nice, Antibes. **Spoken** English, German. **Open** All year. **How to get there** (Map 34): 12km west of Nice. In Nice, towards Saint-Paul-de-Vence. After the church of Colle-sur-Loup, at the red light on right to the small village. Follow signs "Groupe scolaire P. Teisseire". Pass arrow pointing left and take 1st road on right, Chemin de la Rouquière.

Located at the foot of beautiful St. Paul de Vence, this house is part of a residence built 15 years ago. Since then, the vegetation has had time to grow, so that the whole place is now swathed in greenery. Charming rooms decorated with Provençal fabrics are comfortable and well-kept. The excellent breakfast can be taken on the veranda (facing the large swimming pool) or in the garden. Pleasant welcome.

552 - La Bastide de la Citadelle

13, montée de la Citadelle
06610 La Gaude
(Alpes Maritimes)
Tel. and fax 04 93 24 71 01
M. and Mme Martin

Rooms 2 with bath or shower and WC. **Price** 250-300F/38,11-45,73€ (2 pers.), +100F/15,24€ (extra pers.). **Meals** Breakfast incl. Evening meals at communal table, on request in the morning 90F/13,72€ (wine incl.). **Facilities** Sitting room. **Pets** Dogs not allowed. **Nearby** Seaside, trout fishing, golf; Saint-Paul-de-Vence. **Spoken** English. **Open** All year, by reservation with deposit. **How to get there** (Map 35): 8km from Vence. Autoroute A8, exit n. 47 towards Cagnes-sur-Mer. In Cagnes, towards La Gaude for 7km. After the dome, on left Place du Marronnier, then Rue du Marronnier behind the grocer's shop; at the top of the rise of the Citadelle.

Perched on a hill in the little village of La Gaude, near Vence, this appealing old house is a wonderful spot for a holiday. The duplex bedroom with its large balcony is just right for families. Those who like their independence will choose the one on the garden. Here comfort invites to farniente. Meals are served on a pleasant terrace. The breakfasts are copious and dinners are prepared following the inspiration of the market. The welcome is courteous and considerate, the vegetation is lush and the view is delightful.

553 - Le Coteau de Malbosc

210, avenue Saint-Exupéry
06130 Grasse
(Alpes-Maritimes)
Tel. and fax 04 93 36 41 31
M. and Mme Malbrel

Rooms 2 with shower and WC. Rooms cleaned on request. **Price** 400-450F/60,97-68,60€ depending on season. **Meals** Breakfast incl. No communal meal. **Restaurants** "La Jarrerie" (5 km), "La Dragonnière" (2 km). **Facilities** Sitting room with TV, tel., swimming pool, boules court, ping-pong. **Pets** Animals not allowed. **Nearby** Hikes organized by Monsieur Malbrel, tennis, 18-hole golf (3km), Marineland (Biot beach); Maeght Foundation in Saint-Paul-de-Vence, Picasso Museum in Antibes, Matisse Museum in Nice. **Closed** Nov 1 – Mar 1, by reservation. 2 nights min. **How to get there** (Map 34): In the village of Grasse-Est (East Grasse). Map sent on request. Via Autoroute A8, exit Grasse, highway. **No smoking.**

You will enjoy a very pretty view over the plain of Grasse and La Napoule Bay from this contemporary house perched on the Malbosc hillside. There are two independent bedrooms (one is located in a small house near the swimming pool) which overlook the flower garden and swimming pool, as well as a living room with fireplace and television. Breakfast is served on the covered terrace.

554 - La Villa Renée

464, avenue Joffre
06140 Vence
(Alpes-Maritimes)
Tel. 04 93 58 87 01 / 06 12 68 07 83
Fax 04 92 02 87 10
M. and Mme Labica
E-mail: villa-renee@wanadoo.fr

Rooms 2 with bath and WC. **Price** 360-460F/54,88-70,12€ (2 pers., depending on season); +50F/7,62€ (extra bed). **Meals** Breakfast incl. No communal meal. **Facilities** Sitting room, swimming pool. **Nearby** Restaurants (200m), hiking (Gorges du Loup), bicycles, Baous ascent, beach, paragliding, tennis, 18-hole golf course (12km), skiing; Matisse Chapel, château de Villeneuve, château des Fleurs, Maeght Foundation, Saint-Paul-de-Vence. **Spoken** English. **Open** All year. (2 or 3 days min.). **How to get there** (Map 34): 400m northeast of Vence. At the entrance of the town, take towards Saint-Jeannet, then after the bridge, on left, come back towards Vence.

Dating from the late 19th century, the Villa Renée occupies a quarter of Vence which is somewhat apart, facing the side of the town built on the other side of a tiny valley. It is ideal for those who enjoy independence and who wish to explore the countryside behind Nice. The elegant bedrooms are adjacent to a small room reserved for guests and furnished with a leather sofa, a television, and a breakfast table. You can also enjoy the swimming pool surrounded by a terraced garden. The Labicas are pleasant, discreet hosts.

555 - La Pauline

Chemin de la Fontaine des Tuiles
Les Pinchinats
13100 Aix-en-Provence
(Bouches-du-Rhône)
Tel. 04 42 17 02 60
Fax 04 42 17 02 61
M. and Mme Macquet

Rooms 4 with bath, WC, terrace, tel and TV. 1 suite with 2 bedrooms, sitting room, terrace, bath, WC, tel. and TV. **Price** 750-850F/114,33-129,58€ (2 pers.); suite 1600F/243,91€ (2-4 pers.); 1 caravan 400F/60,97€. **Meals** Breakfast 60F/91,14€. No communal meal. **Facilities** Swimming pool. **Pets** Dogs not allowed. **Nearby** Restaurants in Aix (2km), riding, tennis. **Credit cards** Visa, Amex. **Spoken** English. **Closed** Dec 15 – Feb 15, deposit of 30% (retained in case of cancellation). **How to get there** (Map 33): Autoroute A51 exit Aix, Les Platanes (N12) then signs, house 1 km further.

This 18th-century villa stands at the entrance to Aix, in surroundings that are still unspoiled. The outbuildings reserved for guests have been renovated with style and elegance. The bedrooms are all on the ground floor. Most of them have walls in warm colors, Provençal furniture with the patina of age, lovely coordinated fabrics and luxurious bathrooms. Breakfast consists of a copious buffet which can be eaten in the dining room or taken back to your room to have on your private terrace. The garden, laid out on several levels, is beautifully cared for and overlooks the countryside.

556 - Le Petit Romieu

Villeneuve
13200 Arles
(Bouches-du-Rhône)
Tel. 04 90 97 00 27
Fax 04 90 97 00 52
M. Blanchet

Rooms 5 with bath or shower and WC. **Price** 400F/60,97€ (1 pers.), 450F/68,60€ (2 pers.); +50F/7,62€ (extra bed). **Meals** Breakfast incl. Evening meals at communal table 100F/15,24€ (wine incl.). **Facilities** Sitting room with TV, tel., tennis. **Nearby** Riding, bicycles, beaches, 9- and 18-hole golf courses; Nîmes and Arles bullfights, Camargue races, Avignon and Orange festivals. **Closed** Sept 1 – Mar 1, 2 days min. **How to get there** (Map 33): 10km south of Arles via D570 dir. Les Saintes-Maries-de-la-Mer, then D36 dir. Salin-de-Giraud; then D36b dir. Gageron-Villeneuve; signs on the road to Fielouse.

This 1125-acre property is located very near Vaccarès Lagoon in the region of marshlands and prairies where bulls and small horses are traditionally raised. The mas is tastefully and elegantly decorated with beautiful materials, local colors – predominantly yellow-ochre – and Provençal furniture and fabrics. The pretty, pleasant, comfortable bedrooms are upstairs on either side of a handsomely furnished corridor. Jacqueline, the caretaker, prepares typical regional specialties for the evening meal.

557 - Les Quatre-Vents

Favery - Route de Lascours
13400 Aubagne
(Bouches-du-Rhône)
Tel. 04 42 03 76 35
Fax 04 42 18 98 58
M. and Mme Arlès
E-mail: lesquatrevents@free.fr

Rooms 2 and 1 suite with bath and WC. **Price** 400F/60,97€ (1 pers.) to 700F/106,71€ (4 pers.). -10% for more than 3 nights. **Meals** Breakfast incl. Evening meals on request. **Facilities** Swimming pool, tennis. **Pets** Dogs not allowed. **Nearby** Restaurants (3km), 18-hole golf (10km); Aix-en-Provence, Sainte-Baume Gorge, Cassis' calanques (deep coves); Marseille museums. **Credit cards** All major. **Spoken** English. **Open** All year. **How to get there** (Map 33): 20km east of Marseille. Autoroute A50 dir. Nice, exit Aubagne-Nord, then RN96 dir. Pont-de-l'Etoile. At intersection, Napollon Parc des Activités, take D43f and D44e (sign), dir. Lascours and follow signs.

This recent, Provençal-style house is located on a vast property at the edge of Marcel Pagnol's famous hills, with a sweeping view over the Garlaban Peak. Two independent bedrooms with beamed ceilings, terra cotta floors and pretty Provençal furniture, as well as a lovely lounge in the same spirit, are at guests' disposal. This quiet spot nestled amid lush flowers and foliage is perfect for relaxing or walking in the beautiful countryside.

558 - Le Balcon des Alpilles

Quartier du grand Verger
D 24 A
13930 Aureille
(Bouches-du-Rhône)
Tel. and fax 04 90 59 94 24
M. and Mme Gatti

Rooms 5 with bath and WC. **Price** 500-700F/76,22-106,71€ (2 pers.). **Meals** Breakfast incl. Evening meals, only by reservation 200-300F/30,49-45,73€ (all incl.). **Facilities** 2 sitting rooms (fireplace, TV), swimming pool, tennis (clay court), putting green. **Pets** Dogs not allowed. **Nearby** Restaurants (village), 9- and 18 golf courses, 18-hole Ballesteros golf course (23km); Les Alpilles, Aix-en-Provence, Avignon, Arles, La Camargue. **Open** All year, only by reservation. **How to get there** (Map 33): 15km northwest of Salon-en-Provence. Autoroute A54, exit Les Baux. Follow dir. Eyguières then Aureille. Map sent on reservation. **No smoking** in bedrooms.

Nearby Luberon may be trendy, but Aureille has remained a genuine Provençal village. Every year at the start of summer, it still celebrates the departure of its flocks to their mountain pastures. The Balcon des Alpilles stands at the edge of the village, on spacious grounds planted with poplars and olive trees and a lawn worthy of a luxury golf course. The house has been enlarged and now offers several Provençal style bedrooms, all large and very comfortable. If you are fortunate enough to taste the cooking, you will see that the hosts are a couple of real professionals.

P R O V E N C E - R I V I E R A

559 - Le Mas de la Tour

13, rue de la Tour
13990 Fontvieille
(Bouches-du-Rhône)
Tel. 04 90 54 76 43
Fax 04 90 54 76 50
Mme Monique Burnet
E-mail: m-burnet@club-internet.fr.

Rooms 4 and 1 studio (3 pers.) with bath or shower, WC, tel. and TV. **Price** 450-600F/68,60-91,46€. **Meals** Breakfast incl. Evening meals at communal table twice weekly, by reservation 150F/22,86€ (wine incl.). **Facilities** Sitting rooms, swimming pool. **Pets** Dogs allowed on request. **Nearby** Restaurants (5-10 min. walk), golf. **Spoken** English, Italian. **Credit cards** not accepted. **Open** All year, by reservation. **How to get there** (Map 33): 8km east of Arles via D17 towards Saint-Rémy-de-Provence to Fontvielle (if coming from other direction, phone for instructions).

A walled garden and luxuriant vegetation make this beautiful mas, built in the 17th and 18th centuries, a very peaceful place to stay. It is comfortably appointed with huge bedrooms in a style both classic and contemporary (one has a tiny salon decorated by Jean Cocteau). Its old walls keep the house cool in summer, and there is a lovely area for relaxation around the swimming pool. Last but not least, Madame Burnet's genuine and kind hospitality add further appeal to the lovely Mas de la Tour.

560 - Mas Ricard

107, avenue Frédéric Mistral
13990 Fontvieille
(Bouches-du-Rhône)
Tel. 04 90 54 72 67
Fax 04 90 54 64 43
M. and Mme Ricard-Damidot

Rooms 2 with bath and WC. **Price** 450F/68,60€ (1 pers.), 500F/76,22€ (2 pers.), 550F/83,84€ (3 pers.). **Meals** Breakfast incl. No communal meal. **Restaurants** "La Reyalido", "Le Chandelier", "Le Chat gourmand" and "Le Planet" in Fontvielle. **Pets** Not accepted. **Nearby** 9-hole golf course (7km); the Camargue, Montmajor Abbey, Les Baux. **Spoken** English. **Closed** Nov 1 – Apr 1, 2 nights min. **How to get there** (Map 33): 30km south of Avignon via N570 dir. Arles for 24km; turn left onto D33 dir. Fontvielle. In the village.

Located in the center of the village on a street which is rather busy but quiet at night, the beautiful, luxurious Mas Ricard has a lovely garden and is very elegantly decorated. Guest rooms are in an independent building adjacent to Monsieur and Madame Ricard's house, and you will be made to feel as if you are visiting friends. In the salon and in the bedrooms upstairs, you will find handsome period furniture, beautiful objects, paintings and silverware.

PROVENCE - RIVIERA

561 - La Chardonneraie

60, rue Notre-Dame
13910 Maillane
(Bouches-du-Rhône)
Tel. and fax 04 90 95 80 12
Claudine and Roland Achard

Rooms 3 (1 with mezzanine for 3 pers.) and 1 duplex (with sitting room for 3 pers.) with shower and WC. **Price** 320F/48,78€ (1 pers.), 350F/53,35€ (2 pers.), +100F/15,24€ (extra bed), duplex 450F/68,60€ (2 pers.). **Meals** Breakfast incl. No communal meal. **Facilities** Sitting room (TV), swimming pool. **Pets** Not accepted. **Nearby** Restaurants (village), golf; Frédéric Mistral Museum in Maillane, Avignon festival, Saint-Rémy-de-Provence, Les Baux-de-Provence. **Spoken** English. **Open** All year, 2 nights min. in Jul and Aug. **How to get there** (Map 33): 15km south of Avignon. Autoroute A7, exit Avignon-Sud; then D28 dir. Chateaurenard; D5 dir. Maillane. At the village take the street in front of the Maison de la presse, then follow signs.

Claudine and Roland Achard have settled down in this large farmhouse in the poet Frédéric Mistral's native village. In the central part of the house, they have installed very comfortable guest rooms pleasantly decorated with antique furniture and Provençal fabrics. The beautiful bathrooms are adjacent. You can enjoy la bella farniente in the garden or beside the swimming pool, as well as sightseeing in the beautiful region. A simple place with relaxed hospitality.

562 - Mas Sainte-Anne

3, rue d'Auriol
13790 Peynier
(Bouches-du-Rhône)
Tel. 04 42 53 05 32
Fax 04 42 53 04 28
Mme Lambert

Rooms 4 with bath or shower and WC. **Price** 360-400F/54,88-60,97€ (2 pers., depending whether bath or shower); +120F/18,29€ (extra pers.). **Meals** Breakfast incl. Evening meals, by reservation. **Facilities** Sitting room, swimming pool. **Pets** Animals not allowed. **Nearby** Restaurants, 18-hole golf course (4km). **Spoken** English. **Closed** 3 weeks in Aug, (2 nights min.) **How to get there** (Map 33): 18km east of Aix-en-Provence. Autoroute A8 towards Nice, exit Le Canet, then D6 towards Trets. 4km before Trets, D57 on right towards Peynier. Rue d'Auriol is beside the post office before the village center. **No smoking.**

Madame Lambert will greet you with warm and informal hospitality in this beautiful, quiet Provençal mas which once belonged to the painter Vincent Roux and whose decoration she has conserved. The artist's former bedroom, appointed with family furniture and red bedcovers, features an unusual bathroom in green and brown Sainte Zacharie ceramic tiles. Guests in another bedroom will enjoy a view over Mont Sainte Victoire, often painted by Cézanne. Hearty American-style breakfasts are served in the dining room or on the terrace.

P R O V E N C E - R I V I E R A

563 - Mas de la Rabassière

Route de Cornillon
13250 Saint-Chamas
(Bouches-du-Rhône)
Tel. and fax 04 90 50 70 40
Michael Frost
E-mail: michaelfrost@rabassiere.com
Web: www.rabassiere.com

Rooms 2 (with air-conditioning in summer) with bath, shower and WC. **Price** 400F/60,97€ (1 pers.), 700F/106,71€ (2 pers.). **Meals** Breakfast incl. Meals at communal table 130F/19,81€ (lunch) and 180F/27,44€ (dinner) (wine incl.). **Facilities** Sitting room (piano), library, TV, fireplaces, swimming pool, garden, tennis, croquet, theme holidays organized (cooking, Provençal decoration, music...). **Pets** Dogs not allowed. **Nearby** Golf; Aix, Avignon, Arles, the Luberon. **Spoken** English, German. **Open** All year, by reservation. **How to get there** (Map 33): Between Saint-Chamas and Cornillon. Ask Monsieur Frost to send you a map. Pick-up free of charge at airport or Miramas railway station.

With its view over the plain and Lake Berre, its lovely garden of climbing roses, olive trees, a croquet lawn; its elegant decoration and modern amenities in good Anglo-Saxon fashion, the Mas de la Rabassière has everything it takes for a delightful stay. But there's still more going for it in the personality of Michael Frost, his enthusiasm, his helpfulness, and his sense of humor. Thevi is a marvelous cook and Michael makes sure that you'll have a memorable stay, friendly and fun.

564 - Le Mas des Bartavelles

Chemin des Savoyards
13100 Saint-Marc-Jaumegarde
(Bouches-du-Rhône)
Tel. 04 42 24 92 98
Fax 04 42 24 92 99
Mme Mattei

Rooms 1 apart. (2-4 pers.) with, sitting room, fireplace, 2 bedrooms, shower and WC. 1 studio with bedroom, kitchen, shower and WC. **Price** Apart. 650F/99,09€ (2 pers.), 750F/114,33€ (3 pers.), 800F/121,95€ (4 pers.). Children under 2 free. Studio 550F/83,84€ (2 pers)/day (1-3 nights). **Meals** Breakfast incl. No communal meal. **Facilities** Swimming pool. **Pets** Small dogs allowed on request (+30F/4,57€/day). **Nearby** Aix country, Lyric Music festival (Jul). **Credit cards** Not accepted. **Spoken** English. **Open** All year, by reservation. **How to get there** (Map 33): 6km north of Aix-en-Provence. On Boulevard Extérieur take towards Vauvenargues via D10 for 6km. At the Les Savoyards bus stop, left onto Chemin des Savoyards for 800m; green door on right.

Nestled amid pine woods, this is a beautifully appointed though rustic little house. Nicely decorated in the spirit of Southern France, the bedrooms are perfect for a longer stay (one has a sitting room with fireplace, the other a kitchenette). Madame Mattei is a cheerful and generous hostess, thinking of every little detail that can make your stay enjoyable. Breakfast is served in a friendly sitting room or on the terrace overlooking the pines and vineyards. A most appealing place.

565 - Mas de Cornud
Route de Mas Blanc
13210 Saint-Rémy-de-Provence
(Bouches-du-Rhône)
Tel. 04 90 92 39 32
Fax 04 90 92 55 99
Nitockrees and David Carpita
E-mail: mascornud@compuserve.com
Web: www.mascornud.com

Rooms 5 and 1 suite with bath and WC. **Price** 720-990F/109,76-150,92€ (2 pers.); suite 1200F/182,93€ (2 pers.), 1400F/213,42€ (3 pers.), 1600F/243,91€ (4 pers.). **Meals** Breakfast incl. Communal meals, by reservation from 250F/38,11€ (aperitif and wine incl.). **Facilities** Sitting room, tel., checks accepted in all currencies; cooking courses, swimming pool, visit of winecellars with wine tasting. **Pets** Dogs allowed on request (+50F/7,62€/day). **Nearby** Hiking and biking paths, horse trekking, golf; Avignon, Arles, Camargue. **Credit cards** Not accepted. **Spoken** English. **Closed** Jan and Feb (2 nights min.). **How to get there** (Map 33): 3km west of Saint-Rémy-de-Provence via D99 towards Tarascon for about 3km; turn left onto D27 towards Les Baux, then 1st on left; 200m on left.

Guests at this 18th-century mas love the way it has been renovated by Nito and David. The Mas de Cornud is also special in that it is devoted to Mediterranean, and more particularly Provençal, cuisine. Nito Carpita and several brilliant chefs from the region give cooking courses here from time to time. Dishes prepared with fruits and vegetables from the garden make up the meal which crowns the day's lesson. This is a friendly, hospitable place.

566 - Mas Shamrock

Chemin de Velleron et
du Prud'homme
13210 Saint-Rémy-de-Provence
(Bouches-du-Rhône)
Tel. 04 90 92 55 79
Fax 04 90 92 55 80
Mme Christiane Walsh

Rooms 5 with bath and WC. **Price** 450F/68,60€ (1 pers.), 500F/76,22€ (2 pers.), +100F/15,24€ (extra bed). **Meals** Breakfast incl. No communal meal. **Restaurants** In Saint-Rémy-de-Provence (2km). **Facilities** Sitting room, swimming pool, riding (tour on horseback +100F/15,24€/hour). **Nearby** Tennis, golf, bicycle rentals; Gallo-Roman remains, sites painted by Van Gogh. **Spoken** English, German. **Open** Easter – Feb. **How to get there** (Map 33): 2km north of Saint-Rémy-de-Provence via dir. Avignon. Leave Saint-Rémy-de-Provence, after the bus stop "Mas Bruno", turn on left just before the bus stop "Lagoy", 5th house on right. **No smoking**.

A great amount of care and attention to detail has gone into renovating this 18th-century farmhouse, which is arranged to offer you a cool haven of comfort and informal hospitality for your stay in Saint-Rémy. The bedrooms on the south overlook a park shaded with century-old plane trees and all are very large and bright, with pretty fabrics in cool colors and immaculate bathrooms. You can enjoy swimming in the huge pool or riding in the Alpilles with Monsieur Walsh; he provides the horses.

567 - Rue du Château
24, rue du Château
13150 Tarascon
(Bouches-du-Rhône)
Tel. 04 90 91 09 99
Fax 04 90 91 10 33
Yann and Martine Laraison
E-mail: ylaraison@wanadoo.fr
Web: www.chambres-hotes.com

Rooms 5 with bath or shower and WC. Rooms cleaned twice weekly. **Price** 350-450F/53,35-68,60€ (2 pers.). **Meals** Breakfast incl. No communal meal. **Facilities** Sitting room. **Nearby** Restaurants in Tarascon, water sports (1.5km), riding, ULM, 2 golf courses (15km); château, Charles Demery Museum, Tartarin House, Sainte-Marthe Crypt, Les Baux. **Spoken** English, Spanish. **Open** All year, by reservation in winter. **How to get there** (Map 33): in Tarascon. At the château, take the small pedestrian street just in front (residents' cars are allowed). Public parking 50m away. **No smoking**.

This beautiful group of houses is located in the medieval village of Tarascon, a stone's throw from the royal château. Christiane and Henry, both artists, have restored the Rue du Château with inspiration and talent. The materials used are the finest, the colors soft and tasteful, and the modern conveniences perfect: it's difficult to recommend one bedroom over another. Antique and contemporary styles harmonize beautifully and charmingly.

568 - Le Mistral
8, rue Frédéric Mistral
13122 Ventabren
(Bouches-du-Rhône)
Tel. 04 42 28 87 27
Fax 04 42 28 87 37
Mme Mc Donald
E-mail: lynnmcd@aix.pacwan.net
Web: www.lemistral.com

Rooms 4 with bath, WC, tel. and TV (CNN satellite). **Price** 600-840F/91,46-128,05€ (2 pers.). **Meals** Breakfast incl. Communal meals on request 100F/15,24€ (wine incl.). Or kitchen at guests' disposal. **Facilities** Sitting room and terrace with barbecue on roof. **Pets** Dogs allowed on request. **Nearby** Restaurants (10m.), access to club (swimming pools, tennis, squash, golf, riding) for about 100F/15,24€ (6km); wine festivals, antique fairs, Aix-en-Provence. **Credit cards** Not accepted. **Spoken** English, Spanish. **Open** All year. 3 nights min. **How to get there** (Map 33): 13km west of Aix-en-Provence. Autoroute exit Aix-en-Provence Ouest, towards Berre via D10. Park in Ventabren, Place de la Mairie.

Standing at the top of the picturesque village of Ventabren, Le Mistral has very charming guest rooms with colorful decor (we like the yellow room less). Hearty, elegant breakfasts are served either in the spacious living room, which is entirely at your disposal, or on the terrace, where you will enjoy a breathtaking view of the region. You are welcome to prepare a light meal at the house, or you can go to the restaurant just next door. Madame McDonald is a dynamic, generous hostess.

569 - Mas de Castellan

13670 Verquières
(Bouches-du-Rhône)
Tel. 04 90 95 08 22
Fax 04 90 95 44 23
M. Pinet

Rooms 4 with bath or shower and WC. **Price** 450F/68,60€ (2 pers.). **Meals** Breakfast incl. No communal meal. **Facilities** Sitting room, tel., swimming pool. **Pets** Dogs not allowed. **Nearby** Bicycles, 18-hole golf course (10km), riding. **Closed** Jan (2 nights min. in summer). **How to get there** (Map 33): 8km northwest of Saint-Rémy. Detailed instructions by phone.

Designed and inhabited by a decorator who mixes styles skillfully (trompe l'oeil decoration and an intimate atmosphere), this mas is truly one of our most beautiful Provençal houses. You'll surely enjoy as much as we did the antique and Baroque furniture, the profusion of decorative objects, the lush winter garden with its curtain of jasmine overlooking the park, and the discreet swimming pool set amidst trees and shrubs. The bedrooms are beautiful and comfortable and most have ravishing bathrooms with antique terra cotta floors.

570 - Les Cancades

Chemin de la Fontaine-de-Cinq-Sous
Les Cancades
83330 Le Beausset
(Var)
Tel. 04 94 98 76 93
Fax 04 94 90 24 63
Mme Zerbib

Rooms 2 with bath and WC; 2 with bath (1 private but outside the room), shared WC and terrace, and 1 little room. Room cleaning responsibility of guest or on request. **Price** 300-400F/45,73-60,97€ (2 pers.). **Meals** Breakfast incl. No communal meal. Use of summer kitchen. **Restaurants** In Le Beausset. **Facilities** Sitting room, swimming pool. **Pets** Dogs not allowed. **Credit cards** Not accepted. **Open** All year. **How to get there** (Map 34): 20km northwest of Toulon via N8 towards Aubagne; opposite "Casino" supermarket, Fontaine-de-Cinq-Sous road for 1.3km then dirt road on the left; 50 meters after the 90° turn.

After passing through a small housing development, you will discover this large Provençal-style villa standing in a landscape of pine and olive trees. Recently built and tastefully decorated, it has two beautiful guest bedrooms, one with a private terrace opening onto the garden and swimming pool; the other, somewhat smaller, has been prettily redecorated with lovely Provençal fabrics. There is a magnificent garden lush with trees and shrubs. You can also rent the studio by the week.

571 - La Bastide Rose

358, chemin du Patelin
83230 Bormes-les-Mimosas
(Var)
Tel. 04 94 71 35 77
Fax 04 94 71 35 88
Isabelle and Didier Lardaud

Rooms 3 and 1 suite (2-3 pers.) with bath or shower and WC. **Price** Rooms 500-700F/76,22-106,71€ (2 pers., depending on season); suite 600-900F/91,46-137,20€ (depending on season). **Meals** Breakfast incl. No communal meal. **Facilities** Sitting room, tel. and fax; swimming pool. **Nearby** Restaurants, beaches, tennis, riding, 18-hole golf course; Les Îles d'Or, Chartreuse de la Verne, Wine Route. **Credit cards** Not accepted. **Spoken** English, Italian, Spanish. **Closed** Sept 30 – Apr 1, only by reservation. **How to get there** (Map 34): 20km east of Hyères towards Le Lavandou. At entrance to Bormes, turn right to Cabasson-Brégançon. Follow sign after 800m.

Not far from the coast, the "Pink Farmhouse" is a converted old winemaker's bastide in the deep countryside, offering you five guest bedrooms, one of which is located in a modern building nestling among trees and greenery. Comfortably appointed, prettily decorated with sponge-painted walls, elegant fabrics, a scattering of old furniture..., they boast especially beautiful bathrooms. Although an occasional detail may be a bit haphazard, this is still a pleasant and inviting place for a holiday in summer.

572 - La Grande Maison

Domaine des Campaux
6987, Route du Dom
83230 Bormes-les-Mimosas
(Var)
Tel. 04 94 49 55 40
Fax 04 94 49 55 23
Laurence Lapiney

Rooms 3 with bath or shower, WC, and 2 suites, with 2 rooms, bath. **Price** Rooms 500F/76,22€ (2 pers.); suite 600 and 800F/91,46 and 121,95€ (4 pers.). **Meals** Breakfast 45F/6,86€. Evening meals at communal table 160F/24,39€ (wine not incl.). **Facilities** Sitting room, swimming pool, lakes. **Nearby** Riding, golf; Chartreuse de Laverne, Provence villages, gulf of Saint-Tropez. **Spoken** English. **Closed** Jan. **How to get there** (Map 34): 15km from Cogolin. In Cogolin, N98 towards Bormes-les-Mimosas. Signposted (15km).

This imposing 18th-century Provençal house stands high above a magnificent landscape of woods, fields, and vines which produce the estate's wine. With sure taste and a myriad of good ideas, Laurence has transformed La Grande Maison into an irresistible bed and breakfast. Spacious, cheerful, and sunny, the comfortable bedrooms are handsomely decorated with pale wood antique furniture. Overlooking the panorama, the beautiful shady terrace is your venue for breakfast. The excellent dinners, the youthful, friendly, informal hospitality all contribute to making "The Big House" a must.

573 - La Bastide Collombe

83119 Brue Auriac
(Var)
Tel 04 94 80 91 60
M. and Mme Domont

Rooms 3 with shower and WC. **Price** 280-310F/42,68-47,29€ (2 pers.), +50F/7,62€ (extra bed).
Meals Breakfast 30F/4,57€. Evening meals at separate tables, by reservation 110F/16,76€ (wine
incl.). Poss. of picnic baskets. **Facilities** Ping-pong. **Nearby** Tennis, riding, swimming pool, 18-hole
golf course; Saint-Maximin, gorges of the Verdon, Sainte-Baume Lake. **Open** Easter – end Oct or by
reservation. **How to get there** (Map 34): 10km northeast of Saint-Maximin. Autoroute A8 exit Saint-
Maximin, dir. Barjos for 10km then, on left follow signs. 1km before the village of Brue-Auriac.

Large and imposing with its stone walls dating back to the 12th century, this
house offers three bedrooms specially arranged for guests. Each one has a
small corner of terrace and their bright color schemes give them a cheery
look. Copious breakfasts and dinners with Mediterranean flavors are
prepared by the mistress of the house and served outdoors or in a friendly
sitting room. An energetic welcome helps make this a favorite country
address for those who value their independence.

574 - L'Aumonerie

620, avenue de Font-Brun
83320 Carqueiranne
(Var)
Tel. 04 94 58 53 56
M. and Mme Menard

Rooms 1 with shower, WC; and 2 bedrooms with bath or private shower, communal WC; and 1 small
house with 1 bedroom (double bed), kitchen, clothes-washer. **Price** Rooms 320-380F/48,78-57,93€
(2 pers., depending on season); 420-480F/64,02-73,17€ (2 pers., depending on season), +100F/
15,24€ (extra bed); house 550F/83,84€, +100F/15,24€ (extra bed). **Meals** Breakfast incl. in rooms.
No communal meal. **Restaurants** In Carqueiranne. **Facilities** Private beach at the end of garden. **Pets**
Dogs not allowed. **Nearby** Tennis, golf, thalassotherapy. **Credit cards** Not accepted. **Spoken** English.
Open All year. **How to get there** (Map 34): 15km east of Toulon via Autoroute towards Nice Le Pradet,
exit 2 Le Pradet-Carqueirane. After Carqueiranne sign, go past 3 traffic circles, then 2nd road on right.

At "The Chaplain's House", the sea is literally just beyond the garden and its
small private beach. The bedrooms are comfortable and well furnished.
Upstairs, the more spacious ones have private bath or shower rooms but share
a toilet. The room downstairs is somewhat small. Those who like to be more
independent should choose the pleasant little house. You can enjoy breakfast
in your room or in the garden. The owners are especially jovial and friendly.
You should reserve well in advance.

575 - Bastide de Peyroles

83570 Entrecasteaux
(Var)
Tel. and fax 04 94 04 40 06
Mobile 06 03 23 26 36
M. d'Argencé

Rooms 2 with bath, WC; and 1 small house (3 pers.) with lounge, kitchen, 1 room (2 pers.) with shower, WC and terrace. **Price** Room 550F/83,84€ (1 pers.), 600F/91,46€ (2 pers.); house 4000F/609,79€/week. **Meals** Breakfast incl. No communal meal. **Facilities** Swimming pool. **Nearby** Restaurants (4km), tennis, trout fishing in lake and river, riding club, 18-hole golf course (18km); Le Thoronet Abbey, Verdon Gorges, Saint-Tropez (50km). **Spoken** English, Italian. **Open** All year, only by reservation. **How to get there** (Map 34): Autoroute A6, exit Le Luc, then N7 dir. Vidauban for 500m; then Le Thoronet, D84 and D562 dir. Carcès, then D31. Before the village on left D50 towards Cotignac for 3km and right to Piste de Riforan for 800m.

Nestling on a hillside in the beautiful Var département, this 18th-century bastide has been restored in its original style. The long terrace shaded by plane trees and the swimming pool are an irresistible invitation to sit back and relax. The bedrooms in the bastide and in the small independent house all enjoy a typical Provençal view of vineyards and olive trees. Monsieur Argencé is an artist and a very helpful host. A pleasant reception in a house of refinement.

576 - Aubanel

83560 Ginasservis
(Var)
Tel. 04 94 80 11 07
Fax 04 94 80 11 04
Fatia and Michel Lazes

Rooms 3 (1-4 pers.) with bath and WC. Rooms cleaned every 3 days. **Price** 300F/45,73€ (2 pers.), +80F/12,19€ (extra bed). **Meals** Breakfast incl. Meals at communal table or not 100F/15,24€ (wine incl.). **Facilities** Sitting room, tel., mountain bikes, archery; organization of half-days devoted to gastronomy, oenology or botanical walks. **Nearby** Fishing, golf, gliding; Verdon Gorges, Esparron Lake. **Credit cards** Not accepted. **Spoken** English. **Open** All year. **How to get there** (Map 34): 3km south of Ginasservis. Autoroute exit Saint-Maximin, then towards Sisteron and Rians. Before entrance to village, on right, follow signs for "Aubanel - Chambres d'Hôtes".

Any children visiting here will be delighted by the geese, peacocks and purebred Arab horses raised on this vast Provençal farm. Large plane trees provide generous shade over this house and its outbuildings in which there are three beautiful, simply and tastefully decorated bedrooms. Two have a small private terrace. For dinner, Fatia and Michel prepare copious meals based on seasonal products that guests may enjoy at a common table or separately. Fine breakfasts and a discreet and smiling welcome.

577 - Le Mazet des Mûres

Route du Cros d'Entassi
Quartier Les Mûres
83310 Grimaud
(Var)
Tel. 04 94 56 44 45
Mme B. Godon-Decourt

Rooms 5 studios (1-4 pers.) with shower, WC, kitchenette and TV. **Price** 380F/57,93€ (2 pers.), 450F/68,60€ (3 pers.). **Meals** Breakfast incl. Evening meals on request. **Restaurants** In Grimaud, Port-Grimaud, Gassin, Saint-Tropez. **Nearby** Beaches, sailing, golf, riding, tennis. **Spoken** English, German. **Closed** Oct 15 – Dec 20 and Jan 10 – Feb 20. **How to get there** (Map 34): N98 between Sainte-Maxime and Saint-Tropez; at the traffic circle, follow "Les Mûres" signs.

This house, close to Saint-Tropez, has a garden and several terraces where breakfast is served. Four studio-bedrooms are located in one of the outbuildings just in front of the house and give onto the garden. The fifth room is in the house. They are tastefully, simply and prettily decorated and have a kitchenette decorated with Salernes tiles (the one on the north side is more austere). Two of the bedrooms are adjoining, so are practical for a family or group of friends. With its informal atmosphere, this is a nice place for a stay in summer, but the surroundings may soon be spoiled by a housing development.

578 - Leï Méssugues

Domaine du Cros d'Entassi, N°86
83310 Grimaud
(Var)
Tel. and fax 04 94 56 03 16
M. and Mme Casazza

Rooms 2 rooms and 2 studios (with kitchenette) with shower and WC. **Price** Rooms 350F/53,35€ (2 pers.), studios 350-380F/53,35-57,93€ (2 pers., depending on season), +50F/7,62€ (extra child's bed), +100F/15,24€ (extra bed). **Meals** Breakfast 35F/5,33€. No communal meal. **Facilities** Swimming pool, private parking. **Pets** Dogs allowed on request. **Nearby** Restaurants (1km), all sports, beaches, 18-hole golf course (1.5km); old villages, Saint-Tropez, Grimaud, Ramatuelle. **Open** Easter – Oct 10. **How to get there** (Map 34): N98 on the seaside traffic circle, 6km west of Sainte-Maxime. Itinerary given at time of reservation.

Surrounded by vegetation and a pretty garden, Leï Méssugues is part of a group of houses located several minutes from the beaches. You will have the choice of two small guest rooms, comfortable and charming, or two studios, each with a kitchenette; our favorite is the studio on the ground floor. The house is meticulously kept and we were especially pleased with Monsieur and Madame Casazza's hospitality and their laudable efforts to satisfy their guests.

579 - Château de Roux

Le Cannet-des-Maures
83340 Le Luc-en-Provence
(Var)
Tel. 04 94 60 73 10
Fax 04 94 60 89 79
Family Giraud-Dyens

Rooms 1 with bath, WC, and 1 suite (4-6 pers.) with shower and WC. **Price** 300F/45,73€ (2 pers.), 600F/91,46€ (4 pers., in suite), +60F/9,14€ (extra bed). **Meals** Breakfast incl. Evening meals at communal table 150F/22,86€ (wine incl.). **Facilities** Sitting room, tel., lake fishing. **Nearby** Tennis, swimming pool (800m); vineyard, Maures Mountains, Thoronet Abbey, old villages. **Spoken** English, German, Spanish, Italian. **Open** All year. **How to get there** (Map 34): Autoroute A8 exit Le Cannet-des-Maures, then Saint-Tropez road. Follow signs on left (2.5km).

Facing the dramatic Massif des Maures, this imposing 18th-century bastide lies in a vast wine-growing estate in the heart of the Côtes de Provence region. Decorated with family furniture and objects from many epochs and many countries, the interior is delightfully authentic. There is an atmosphere of the past in the attractive guest rooms, each with a private bath or shower room (it is modern in the Jaune room and more old-fashioned in the suite). Prepared with excellent local produce and lots of aromatic spices à la provençale, the dinners are delectable. The Giraud-Dyenses are a hospitable family and their prices are most reasonable.

580 - L'Amandari

Vallat d'Emponse
83120 Plan-de-la-Tour
(Var)
Tel. 04 94 43 79 20
Fax 04 94 43 10 52
Mme de Wasseige and M. Remy

Rooms 6 with bath or shower and WC (1 with TV). **Price** 350-500F/58,35-76,22€ (2 pers.). –30% for long stays (6 nights min.) in low season. **Meals** Breakfast 45F/6,86€. Lunch and evening meals at communal table or not 100-140F/15,24-21,34€ (wine incl.). **Facilities** Sitting room (TV), tel., fax, swimming pool, pétanque. **Pets** Dogs allowed (+20-40F/3,04-6,09€/day). **Nearby** Tennis, riding, seaside, mountain bikes, golf; Gassin, Saint-Tropez, Ramatuelle, Grimaud, La Garde-Freinet. **Spoken** English, Dutch. **Open** All year, 2 days min. **How to get there** (Map 34): 6km from Sainte-Maxime. Autoroute A8, exit Sainte-Maxime, dir. Plan-de-la-Tour then signs. At the traffic circle Plan-de-la-Tour follow Amandari.

With its lush vegetation and a stream running by, this charming house has a surprising air of Asia about it. A bridge bordered by bamboo plants leads up to the front door and the interior decoration is in tones of blue and white. On either side of the patio you find the bedrooms, which are small but pleasant, bright and comfortable. Thanks to the warm welcome of Martine and Jacques, guests quickly get to know each other around an excellent table d'hôte. The atmosphere is refined, amusing and cosmopolitan, and the conversations tend to be lively.

P R O V E N C E - R I V I E R A

581 - Le Mas du Rouge

83120 Plan-de-la-Tour
(Var)
Tel. 04 94 43 75 88
Mme Roques

Rooms 2 with shower and WC. 1 studio with shower and WC. **Price** 300F/45,73€, 270F/41,16€ (from 4 nights); studio 420F/64,02€, +50F/7,62€ (extra bed), 380F/57,93€ (from 4 nights). **Meals** Breakfast incl. No communal meal. **Pets** Animals not allowed. **Facilities** Swimming pool. **Nearby** Tennis, 18-hole golf course (12km). **Spoken** English, German, Italian. **Closed** Sept 30 – end May, 2 nights min. **How to get there** (Map 34): 3.5km northeast of Plan-de-la-Tour via D44 towards Le Muy.

Not far from Saint Tropez, Le Mas du Rouge enjoys a quiet setting in a beautiful countryside of vineyards and oaks. You have a choice of two bedrooms, simply but tastefully decorated, and a studio giving onto a small, private garden near the swimming pool; it has a fireplace, exposed beams, a terra-cotta floor, and armchairs with white cotton slipcovers. Breakfast is served on the terrace. Le Mas du Rouge is an informal bed and breakfast, with reasonable prices for the region.

582 - Saint-Ferréol

Domaine de Saint-Ferréol
83670 Pontevès
(Var)
Tel. 04 94 77 10 42
Fax 04 94 77 19 04
M. and Mme de Jerphanion

Rooms 2 and 1 suite (4 pers.) with bath or shower and WC. Rooms cleaned on request. **Price** 300-350F/45,73-53,35€ (2 pers.), 480F/73,17€ (4 pers.). **Meals** Breakfast incl. No communal meal. Kitchen reserved for guests. **Facilities** Sitting room, swimming pool. **Pets** Animals not allowed. **Nearby** Restaurants, tennis (3km), hiking; Verdon Gorges, Thoronet Abbey, Upper Var. **Credit cards** Not accepted. **Spoken** English, German. **Open** Mar – Nov. **How to get there** (Map 34): 21km northeast of Saint-Maximin via D560 towards Barjols. In Barjols, towards Draguignan. 2.5km from Barjols, take dirt road on left just after the sign "Bienvenue à Pontevès".

Standing on a gentle slope in the heart of the countryside, this lovely 18th-century farmhouse is part of a vast wine estate. The bedrooms are situated in one of the four wings around a square courtyard sheltered from the wind. Simply and tastefully appointed, they are often large, well-proportioned and have nice bathrooms. Breakfast is served in a large rustic room on the ground floor. A warm and smiling hospitality.

583 - Mas des Graviers

Route de Rians - Chemin Cézanne
83910 Pourrières
(Var)
Tel. 04 94 78 40 38
Fax 04 94 78 44 88
Mme Andréa Mc Garvie Munn
E-mail: masdesgraviers@wanadoo.fr
Web: www.foolscap.com/mas/

Rooms 2 with bath or shower and WC; 2 suites (1 Family suite; 1 for 5 pers., 3 rooms). **Price** Rooms 400F/60,97€ (1 pers.), 500F/76,22€ (2 pers.); suites 700 and 1000F/106,71 and 152,44€. **Meals** Breakfast incl. Evening meals at communal table or not, on request 150F/22,86€ (wine not incl.). **Facilities** Sitting room, swimming pool, tennis. **Pets** Dogs allowed on request. **Nearby** Sainte-Baume, museums of Aix-en-Provence. **Spoken** English, German. **Open** All year. 2 nights min. **How to get there** (Map 33): 30km southeast of Aix-en-Provence. Autoroute A8, exit Le Canet, then N7 towards Saint-Maximin. Take on left towards Pourrières, then towards Rians and follow signs.

Surrounded by vines, fields of lavender and groves of trees, this inviting mas enjoys a dream location facing the Montagne Sainte Victoire of Cézanne fame. Decorated in a warm Provençal style, its magnificent rooms are hung with contemporary art. The bedrooms are attractive and comfortable. The baths are private but not always next to the room, which accentuates the feeling that this is not a guest house but truly a house for friends. Breakfast is served beneath the old mulberry trees on the terrace, in front of the swimming pool.

584 - Vasken

Les Cavalières
83520 Roquebrune-sur-Argens
(Var)
Tel. 04 94 45 76 16
M. and Mme Kuerdjian

Rooms 5 with bath or shower and WC. 1 studio (2 pers. + 1 child), with shower, WC, kitchen and 1 bedroom/living room (TV on request). Rooms cleaned on request. **Price** 350F/53,35€ (1 pers.), 400F/60,97€ (2 pers.), studio 500F/76,22€. **Meals** Breakfast 40F/6,09€. No communal meal. **Facilities** Sitting room, swimming pool. **Pets** Dogs not allowed. **Nearby** Restaurants (2km), water skiing, riding and tennis (2 km), hiking, mountain biking, golf (2km); Roquebrune (traditional glassworks), Nice, Fréjus. **Credit cards** Not accepted. **Open** All year, by reservation in low season. **How to get there** (Map 34): 12km west of Fréjus via N7 between Le Muy and Le Puget-sur-Argens, then D7 towards Roquebrune. In the village, 1st right. At the cemetery, Blvd. du 18 Juin for 1.5km and then follow Vasken signs.

Monsieur Kuerdjian, a retired pastry chef, makes fresh croissants for your breakfast at Vasken, a house which he built himself. Made of the warm red stones of the region, his pretty, L-shaped house is set amidst the aromatic shrubs and trees of Provence. Decorated in simple, rustic style, the ground-floor bedrooms open onto the garden and each has a private terrace. Madame Kuerdjian will welcome you with enthusiastic and friendly hospitality.

585 - Mas de Fontbelle

Hameau des Molières
83136 La Roquebrussanne
(Var)
Tel. and fax 04 94 86 84 16
Bernadette and Roger Buyle

Rooms 2 with bath or shower and WC. 1 suite (2-4 pers.) of 2 bedrooms with lounge, bath and WC. **Price** 410-430F/62,50-65,55€ (2 pers.); suite 470F/71,65€ (2 pers.), +100F/15,24€ (extra pers.). **Meals** Breakfast incl. Evening meals at communal table or not 180F/27,44€ (wine incl.). **Facilities** Sitting room, tel., swimming pool, cooking lessons, hiking (GR). **Pets** Dogs not allowed. **Nearby** Tennis (free, 2km), beach, U.L.M., golf. **Spoken** English, Spanish, Dutch. **Closed** Nov 11 – Mar 20. **How to get there** (Map 34): 30km north of Toulon. Autoroute A8, exit Saint-Maximim, then N7 to Tourves, then D205 (becoming D5) to La Roquebrussanne, then follow Chemin des Molières and signs. **NO smoking** in bedrooms.

After running a well-known restaurant in Belgium, Monsieur and Madame Buyle settled here in this old mas, which they have very tastefully renovated. The bedrooms are attractive, decorated, as is the whole house, with great refinement (early 19th-century furniture, lovely objects, paintings...). Genuine comfort, breakfasts and dinners of high quality, a true sense of hospitality and a beautifully tended garden are the other assets of this charming house.

586 - La Vieille Bastide

Plan de Chibron
83870 Signes
(Var)
Tel. 04 94 90 81 45
Mme Françoise Penvern

Rooms 2 with private bath or shower and WC. **Price** 310F/47,25€ (2 pers.). **Meals** Breakfast incl. Evening meals at communal table, by reservation 95F/14,48€ (wine not incl.). **Facilities** Sitting room, tel., ornamental pool, stall and field for 1 horse. **Pets** Dogs not allowed. **Nearby** Hiking path for Sainte-Baume Mountain, Les Glacières, swimming pool, tennis, 18-hole golf course (25km), seaside (35km). **Credit cards** Not accepted. **Open** All year. 2 nights min. **How to get there** (Map 34): 1.5km west of Signes. In Signes, take towards Marseille for 1.5km; in the curve take the path parallel to the one with a red and white barrier.

After a long and somewhat bumpy drive on a dirt road you will discover, standing on a hillside, a beautifully renovated 18th-century bastide. Its two bedrooms are comfortable and attractive, perfect for families. The kitchen, a room full of character on the ground floor, says a lot about the quality of the cooking. Dinner is served in a superb sitting room decorated with antique furniture, painting, objects of beauty. The shaded terrace, where you can have breakfast, is another plus, as is the friendly welcome.

587 - La Prévôté

354, chemin d'Exploitation
84210 Althen-les-Paluds
(Vaucluse)
Tel. 04 90 62 11 16
Fax 04 90 62 12 61
Mme Pasquier

Rooms 5 with bath and WC (TV on request). **Price** 400F/60,97€ (1 pers.), 500-550F/76,22-83,84€ (2 pers.), +150F/22,86€ (extra bed). **Meals** Breakfast incl. No communal meal. **Facilities** Sitting room, tel., swimming pool, ping-pong, pétanque, baby-foot, bicycles. **Pets** Dogs allowed only on request (+40F/6,09€/day). **Nearby** Restaurants (500m), tennis, fishing (Sorgue), riding, golf; Avignon, Isle-sur-la-Sorgue, Luberon, Carpentras, Mont Ventoux. **Spoken** English, some German. **Open** All year. **How to get there** (Map 33): 10km north of Avignon. Autoroute A7 exit Avignon-Nord, dir. Carpentras via expressway, exit Althen-les-Paluds Est, then signs. **No smoking** in bedrooms.

This lovely mas surrounded by an orchard offers five comfortable, recently refurbished bedrooms. They are discreetly decorated and all have nice bathrooms. Outside, in a flower filled garden, a tall chestnut tree provides generous shade. A leafy arbor also offers a delightful shaded area. Just a stone's throw from Avignon, this is a good address to know.

588 - Le Massonnet

Résidence de vacances
Route Saint-Saturnin
84400 Apt
(Vaucluse)
Tel. and fax 04 90 04 66 15
Myriam Choisez and her staff

Rooms 1 with shower, WC, terrace, and 2 with shared bath, WC, and 4 apart. (4 pers.) with sitting room, kitchen, bath, WC, TV, (1 dishwasher in 2 apart.). Rooms cleaned once a week. **Price** 225-400F/34,30-60,97€ (2 pers., depending on season and room), apart. 2000-4500F/304,89-686,02€/week, depending on season and apart. **Meals** Breakfast 30F/4,57€ in room. No communal meal. **Facilities** Sitting room, swimming pool. **Pets** Dogs allowed on request. **Nearby** Restaurants, 18-hole golf course. **Spoken** English. **Open** All year. 7 days min in Jul and Aug. **How to get there** (Map 33): 3km northwest of Apt. In Apt, towards Saint-Saturnin.

An avenue of plane trees leads up to this beautiful property, a converted mill surrounded by a green and leafy park. Restored with simplicity and taste, it offers comfortable, spacious, well-furnished apartments, each with an equipped kitchen. At guests' disposal are the terraces and the private garden with a flowery arbor. Myriam Choisez and Danielle Denison will greet you warmly and advise you on things to see and do in this lovely region. Each spring, they organize a one-week musical seminar called "Key to Music".

P R O V E N C E - R I V I E R A

589 - Le Moulin de Mauragne
Route de Marseille
84400 Apt
(Vaucluse)
Tel. 04 90 74 31 37
Fax 04 90 74 30 14
Manuèle and Frédéric Miot
E-mail: info@moulin-de-mauragne.com.
Web: www.moulin-de-mauragne.com

Rooms 4 with bath and WC. **Price** 640-740F/94,56-112,81€ (1 pers.), 680-780F/103,66-118,91€ (2 pers.), +110F/16,76€ (extra bed), +40F/6,55€ (cradle). **Meals** Breakfast incl. Evening meals on Sat, by reservation 140F/21,34€ (wine not incl.). **Facilities** Sitting room, library, tel., swimming pool, river. **Pets** Dogs not allowed. **Spoken** English, Spanish. **Credit cards** Visa, MasterCard. **Closed** Feb 1 – Mar 10 and Nov 1 – Dec 10. Reservation 7 days before with 50% of total stay in advance + fax. **How to get there** (Map 33): 3km southeast of Apt. At the O.F.T. of Apt, D943 dir. Lourmarin. At the traffic circle, dir. Lourmarin for 800m. On left at electricity transformer, small road for 600m.

We were very taken with this old mill (whose origins go back to the 10th century), standing all alone in an ocean of greenery near many of finest sites of Luberon. Surrounded by trees and flowers, traversed by a river (the garden furniture is set up near a little waterfall) the house boasts a meticulous interior, decorated with a lovely blend of 18th-century and Far Eastern furniture, modern paintings and shimmering fabrics. The bedrooms are done in the same spirit and the bathrooms are also attractive. A pleasant and youthful welcome. Reserve well in advance.

590 - Richarnau

84390 Aurel
(Vaucluse)
Tel. and fax 04 90 64 03 62
Visnja and Christian Michelle
E-mail: c.richarnau@accesinter.com

Rooms 3 and 2 suites (3-4 pers.) with bath or shower and WC. **Price** Rooms 390F/59,45€ (2 pers.); suites 390-450F/59,45-68,60€ (2 pers.), 600F/91,46€ (4 pers.). **Meals** Breakfast incl. Communal meals, by reservation 135F/20,58€. **Facilities** Sitting room, tel. **Pets** Dogs not allowed. **Nearby** Swimming pool (6km), tennis (6km), mountain bikes, river swimming (8km); old villages, concerts in Simiane, Avignon Festival, Lavender Festival Aug 15 in Sault. **Credit cards** Not accepted. **Spoken** English, German, Italian. **Closed** Jan 5 – Feb 28. 2 nights min. **How to get there** (Map 33): 40km east of Carpentras via Sault; after going through Sault take towards Aurel and Montbrun for 4km, then turn left and follow signs for Richarnau.

In this land of honey and cherries, with sky and lavender fields as far as the eye can see, this big L-shaped building is shaded by a sumptuous century-old linden tree. Three bedrooms and two suites, different in size and exposure, are tastefully arranged for guests' comfort. Christian and Visjna Michelle's warm hospitality and good, varied cuisine give you the impression that you have come to stay with friends.

P R O V E N C E - R I V I E R A

591 - La Ferme Jamet
Domaine de Rhodes
Île de la Barthelasse
84000 Avignon
(Vaucluse)
Tel. 04 90 86 88 35
Fax 04 90 86 17 72
Étienne Jamet and his staff
E-mail: fermja@club-internet.fe
Web: avignon-et-provence.com/ferme-jamet/

Rooms 6 (2-4 pers.), 3 cottages (2-3 pers.) and 3 suites (4-6 pers;) with bath or shower and WC. **Price** 520-1100F/79,27-167,69€ (2 pers.). **Meals** Breakfast incl. No communal meal. **Pets** Animals not allowed. **Facilities** Sitting room (TV, piano), tel., swimming pool, tennis. **Nearby** Restaurants, rowing, golf. **Spoken** English, German. **Credit cards** Visa, Eurocard, MasterCard. **Open** Easter - Nov 1. 2 nights min (poss. 1 night if availability). Poss. long stays in low season. **How to get there** (Map 33): 7km from Avignon. Autoroute A7, exit Avignon-Nord, dir. Avignon-Centre, Pont Edouard Daladier. On the bridge to the right, Barthelasse Island. Signs.

The very old Jamet farmhouse lies on a lush island not far from the famous Papal city. The bedrooms, suites and an apartment are all in the main building. Those who like to feel independent can choose the cottages. Each bedroom has its charm. The ground floor one is dark, but cool in summer. We enjoyed our stay in this quiet place with considerable appeal. The prices are somewhat high, as Avignon is so close.

592 - Mas de la Lause
Chemin de Geysset
Route de Suzette
84330 Le Barroux
(Vaucluse)
Tel. 04 90 62 33 33
Fax 04 90 62 36 36
Corine and Christophe Lonjon
E-mail: info@provence-gites.com
Web: www.provence-gites.com

Rooms 4 and 1 suite (4 pers. with kitchenette) with shower and WC. **Price** Rooms 250F/38,11€ (1 pers.), 300-315F/45,73-48,02€ (2 pers.); suite 380F/57,93€ (2 pers.), 470F/71,65€ (3 pers.), 550F/83,84€ (4 pers.). −5% 3-5 nights; −10% from 6 nights. **Meals** Breakfast incl. Evening meals at communal table, by reservation (except Wed and Sun) 95F/13,72€ (aperitif incl., wine not incl.), 45F/6,86€ (children under 6). **Facilities** Boules. **Nearby** Lake swimming, riding; Vaison-la-Romaine. **Spoken** English, German. **Closed** Nov – end Mar. **How to get there** (Map 33): 15km north of Carpentras via D938 dir. Malaucène. Signs in Le Barroux.

The young, friendly owners, Corinne and Christophe, recently finished totally restoring this 19th-century mas surrounded by orchards and vineyards. The bedrooms, done in a sober Provençal style, are pleasant and well kept. A beautiful little structure has just been installed on the terrace, facing the Château du Barroux, where you can have tasty breakfasts and dinners (with homegrown fruits and vegetables). It is a nice addition to the small dining room, which could do with a warmer decoration. This is a quality address with reasonable prices.

593 - Aux Tournillayres

84410 Bédoin
(Vaucluse)
Tel. 04 90 12 80 94
Marie-Claire Renaudon

Rooms 4 studios (2 pers.) and 1 suite (4 pers.) with shower, WC, kitchenette, fireplace. Rooms cleaned once a week. **Price** 470F/71,65€ (2 pers.), +100F/15,24€ (extra bed); suite 600F/91,46€; children under 5 free. **Meals** Breakfast incl. No communal meal. **Facilities** Sitting room. **Pets** Animals not allowed. **Nearby** Swimming pool, riding; Avignon and Vaison-la-Romaine Festivals. **Spoken** Some English. **Closed** Nov 15 – Apr 1. 3 nights min. **How to get there** (Map 33): Autoroute A7, exit Bollène, dir. Sainte-Cécile-les-Vignes, Beaume-de-Venise, Vacqueyras, Caromb and Bédoin; road to Mont Ventoux via D974. After Bédoin, go 500m. At the "Des Lavandes" Garage, first road on left for 2km. Signs.

Facing a countryside of vineyards and scrubland, these four small houses were recently built at the foot of Mont Ventoux. The bedrooms are lovely with their four-poster beds and canopies in Provençal fabrics, old engravings, dried flowers, beamed ceilings... In addition, they each have a small kitchen, a fireplace and heating. In the morning, a breakfast tray with homemade preserves is set out in the private garden shaded by green oaks. This welcoming, beautiful spot is ideal for long stays.

594 - Bonne Terre

Lacoste
84480 Bonnieux
(Vaucluse)
Tel. and fax 04 90 75 85 53
M. Roland Lamy
E-mail: bonneterre@fr.st
Web: www.bonneterre.fr.st

Rooms 6 with bath or shower, WC, TV and terrace. **Price** 390 and 480F/59,46 and 73,17€ (1 pers., depending on season), 480 and 570F/73,17 and 86,89€ (2 pers., depending on season), +120F/18,29€ (extra pers.). **Meals** Breakfast incl. No communal meal. **Restaurants** In Lacoste and nearby (7-8km). **Facilities** Tel., swimming pool. **Pets** Dogs allowed (+40F/6,09€). **Nearby** Golf, tennis, riding, music and theater festivals, Luberon villages. **Spoken** English, German. **Closed** Dec **How to get there** (Map 33): East of Cavaillon via N100 towards Apt, then D106 towards Lacoste.

At the entrance to the beautiful village of Lacoste, you can enjoy a quiet stay with total privacy in this elegant, recently built house. Simple and cheerful, the guest rooms are comfortable and open directly onto the outside. Our favorites have a private terrace surrounded by trees and shrubs: a delightful spot for breakfast. The ravishing tiered garden has a swimming pool and a sweeping view over Mont Ventoux.

P R O V E N C E - R I V I E R A

595 - La Bouquière

Quartier Saint-Pierre
84480 Bonnieux
(Vaucluse)
Tel. 04 90 75 87 17
Fax 04 90 75 83 56
Françoise and Angel Escobar

Rooms 4 (ground floor on the garden) with bath or shower and WC. **Price** 385-450F/58,69-68,60€ (2 pers.), +85F/12,95€ (extra pers.). **Meals** Breakfast incl. No communal meal. Small kitchen at guests' disposal. **Facilities** Sitting room. **Pets** Dogs allowed on request. **Nearby** Restaurants, hiking in Lubéron National Park. **Credit cards** Not accepted. **Spoken** English, Spanish. **Open** All year. 2 nights min., 7 nights min. in Jul and Aug. **How to get there** (Map 33): 3km from Bonnieux via D3 towards Apt; then signs.

Surrounded by verdant countryside, La Bouquière enjoys a magnificent view of Mont Ventoux and has four comfortable guest bedrooms, very prettily decorated in Provençal style. Each bedroom has an independent entrance and opens onto a terrace where breakfast can be served. You can enjoy the use of the living room, the fireplace, and even a small, colorfully decorated kitchen.You will be pleasantly welcomed by Françoise and Angel Escobar and their young son.

596 - Les Trois Sources
Saint-Victor
84480 Bonnieux
(Vaucluse)
Tel. 04 90 75 95 58
Fax 04 90 75 89 95
Caroline Guinard and Paul Jeannet
Web: www.luberon-news.com/les-trois-sources.html

Rooms 1 with shower, WC, and 3 with shower, bath, WC, and 1 suite with 2 bathes and 2 WC. **Price** 350 and 500F/53,35 and 76,22€ (1-2 pers.); suite 850F/129,58€ (4 pers.); +100F/15,24€ (extra bed). **Meals** Breakfast incl. No communal meal. **Facilities** Sitting room, swimming pool. **Pets** Dogs allowed on request (ı 50F/7,62€/day). **Nearby** Restaurants (2km), Luberon villages, antique dealer, music and theater festivals. **Credit cards** All major. **Spoken** English. **Open** All year. **How to get there** (Map 33): 2km northwest of Bonnieux via D194 dir. Gordes, Goult. At edge of village 2 km further on the right after Château Luc, follow signs for Les Trois Sources.

This is a very old farmhouse and the facades facing the inner courtyard still have some Renaissance features. The bedrooms, most of them vast, sober and elegant, have been completely renovated and display a great deal of character: walls in natural colors, terra cotta floors, beamed ceilings... As soon as the weather permits, breakfast is served outdoors in the shade of a mulberry tree and sheltered from the wind. Your hosts are young and pleasant. The fine swimming pool is set amid the grape vines, from which you have a sweeping view of the villages of Lacoste and Bonnieux.

597 - La Bastide Sainte-Agnès

84200 Carpentras
(Vaucluse)
Tel. 04 90 60 03 01
Fax 04 90 60 02 53
Gerlinde and Jacques Apothéloz
E-mail: gerlinde@infonie.fr
Web: www.avignon-et-provence.com/sainte-agnes

Rooms 4 with bath or shower, WC, and 1 suite (4-5 pers.) with living, kitchen, 2 bedrooms, bath, WC, garden, parking, tel. and TV. **Price** 360-420F/54,88-64,03€ (1 pers.), 430-490F/65,55-74,70€ (2 pers.); suite 750F/114,33€ (2 pers.), 950F/144,82€ (4 pers.). **Meals** Breakfast incl. No communal meal. Poss. picnic and barbecue. **Facilities** Tel. and fax with meter, swimming pool. **Pets** Not accepted. **Nearby** Restaurants. **Spoken** English, German. **Open** Apr 1 – Oct 31. **How to get there** (Map 33): 3km northeast of Carpentras dir. Mont Ventoux-Sud via D974 and dir. Caromb via D13; turn left into Chemin de la Fourtrouse; entrance to house is 300m on right.

This extensively restored, very welcoming 19th-century farmhouse is located at the edge of Carpentras, isolated from the city by a beautiful garden planted with exotic and Provençal trees, which create a very pleasant small haven. The comfortable Provençal rooms have sponge-painted walls (avoid the "suite," which is too expensive, except for longer stays). The huge living room is discreetly contemporary in style, with wrought-iron or lacquered furnitiure, colored leather, gilt objects, and a fireplace. The breakfasts are excellent.

598 - Le Clos des Saumanes

519, chemin de la Garrigue
84470 Châteauneuf-de-Gadagne
(Vaucluse)
Tel. 04 90 22 30 86
Fax 04 90 22 30 68
Mme Lambert
E-mail: closaumane@aol.com

Rooms 5 with bath and WC. **Price** 400-650F/60,97-99,09€ (2-4 pers.). **Meals** Breakfast incl. No communal meal. **Facilities** Sitting room, pond. **Pets** Small dogs allowed on request. **Nearby** Restaurants (2km), tennis, jogging path, hiking, 18-hole golf courses; Avignon, Luberon, monts du Vaucluse, vineyards. **Spoken** English, Spanish, Italian, some German. **Closed** Nov – Mar, or by reservation. Confirmation: deposit of one night's stay in advance. **How to get there** (Map 33): 9km east of Avignon. Autoroute A7 exit Avignon-Nord dir. Carpentras. 1st exit dir. Vedène, straight on. Go through Saint-Saturnin. In Jonquerettes, on right Centre Ville D97. Go up to the village. 350m from sign "fin de village", on left (signs). **No smoking** in bedrooms.

Well protected from noise and heat by a shaded path and lush vegetation, this traditional bastide has five pleasant bedrooms equipped with modern bathrooms. In the sitting room the furniture, fabrics, objects and paintings combine to create a lovely atmosphere. The courtyard and the delightful walled garden are ideal spots for rest and relaxation, and the welcome is courteous.

599 - La Respelido

Au village
84110 Crestet
(Vaucluse)
Tel. and fax 04 90 36 03 10
M. and Mme Veit

Rooms 2 with bath or shower and WC. **Price** 250-300F/38,11-45,73€ (2 pers.), +100F/15,24€ (extra bed) **Meals** Breakfast incl. No communal meal. **Facilities** Sitting room, truffle-hunting weekends organized on request. **Pets** Small dogs allowed. **Nearby** Restaurants, riding, tennis; Vaison festival, Orange, Avignon. **Spoken** English, German. **Closed** 1 month in winter - Reservation with deposit. **How to get there** (Map 33): 5km from Vaison-la-Romaine via Malaucène-Carpentras road. In the village of Crestet. **No smoking** in bedrooms.

La Respelido, a former olive oil mill, is an ideal spot from which to visit the beautiful medieval village (closed to auto traffic) of Crestet and to explore the entire region between Drôme and Vaucluse. The large bedroom, our favorite, is a tasteful blend of furniture from different horizons and has a wonderful view over the old roofs of the village and the countryside beyond. The rest of the house is as appealing: salon-library, Provençal dining room, vaulted kitchen. Mouth-watering breakfasts are served in a small garden ringed with flowers and foliage. The hospital is friendly and generous.

600 - La Ribaude

84110 Crestet
(Vaucluse)
Tel. 04 90 36 36 11
Fax 04 90 28 81 29
Mme Lühmann

Rooms 1 suite (2 pers. and 2 children) and 4 suites (2 pers.) with bath or shower and kitchenette. **Price** 1000F/152,44€ (2 pers.). **Meals** Breakfast (brunch) 80F/12,19€. No communal meal. **Facilities** Sitting room, tel., swimming pool, children's pool. **Nearby** Restaurants (10km), bikes, riding in Malaucène or Entrechaux (5km), 18-hole golf course (40km); Mont Ventoux (16km). **Spoken** English, German. **Closed** Oct 15 – May 1. 3 nights min. **How to get there** (Map 33): 5km southwest of Vaison-la-Romaine. Go past Vaison-la-Romaine, then dir. Malaucène and Le Crestet. Sign.

This is a somewhat unusual bed-and-breakfast which will please lovers of (in the words of Beaudelaire) "luxe, calme, and volupté". The house is beautiful with its elegant, tasteful decoration, and it offers all the services of a fine hotel. Outside, the lovely terraces, patio, gardens and swimming pool enjoy a magnificent view of Mont Ventoux. The spacious suites are also superb and the whole house is run with love and care.

601 - Clos Saint-Vincent

84410 Crillon-le-Brave
(Vaucluse)
Tel. 04 90 65 93 36
Fax 04 90 12 81 46
Mme Vazquez

Rooms 5 with shower, WC, and 1 small house (4 pers.) with 2 bedrooms, bath, WC, sitting room, kitchen, terrace and TV. **Price** Rooms 460-510F/70,12-77,74€ (2 pers.); small house 800F/121,95€ (2 pers.), 1000F/152,44€ (4 pers.), +130F/19,81€ (extra bed). **Meals** Breakfast incl. Evening meals occasionally 150F/22,86€ (wine incl.). **Facilities** Sitting room, tel., swimming pool, fitness room, pétanque. **Pets** Animals not allowed. **Nearby** Restaurants, (500m). **Credit cards** Not accepted. **Spoken** English, Spanish. **Closed** Nov 15 – Feb 15. **How to get there** (Map 33): 12km from Carpentras, road to Bedoin, then towards Crillon-le-Brave. Clos Saint-Vincent indicated.

The Clos Saint-Vincent is so nicely situated, one almost feels like keeping it a secret. Madame Vasquez loves her house and will share her enthusiasm with you. The decoration is tasteful, original and pleasant with its antique furniture and fabrics from the region. It manages to express, without overstatement, the Provençal style and the joie de vivre that goes with it. Don't miss the breakfasts, which include homemade pastries and rice pudding. If dinner is suggested, don't miss that either!

602 - La Badelle

84220 Gordes
(Vaucluse)
Tel. 04 90 72 33 19
Fax 04 90 72 48 74
Mme Cortasse
E-mail: badelle@club-internet.fr
Web: guideweb.com/provence/bb/badelle

Rooms 5 and 1 suite (2-4 pers.) with bath or shower, WC and TV. **Price** 390F/59,45€ (1 pers.), 415F/63,26€ (2 pers.); suite 495F/75,46€ (3 pers.), +80F/12,19€ (extra pers.). **Meals** Breakfast incl. No communal meal. Equipped kitchenette at guests' disposal. **Facilities** Sitting room, pay phone, swimming pool. **Nearby** Restaurants, (in Gordes and Goult), tennis, riding, 18-hole golf course; villages of Lubéron and borie stone houses; Abbey of Sénanque. **Spoken** English, some German. **Open** All year. **How to get there** (Map 33): 17km northeast of Cavaillon. In Coustellet, N100 in dir. Apt, exit Notre-Dame-de-Lumières; signs after the Cave Coopérative.

On a gentle hillside with a very beautiful view, the outbuildings of this farm have been entirely renovated to form four ravishing bedrooms arranged around a gleaming swimming pool. Immaculate, prettily decorated with a dominant color matching the headboard and the fabrics, each room has a piece of antique furniture and a lovely bath. Breakfasts are served outside on the covered terrace.

603 - La Borie

Route de Murs
84220 Gordes
(Vaucluse)
Tel. and fax 04 90 72 13 14
Christine Le Marinel
Web: www.borie-provence.com

Rooms 2 with bath or shower, WC and TV. **Price** 475F/72,41€ (1 pers.), 500F/76,22€ (2 pers.). local tax: 6.60F/about 1€/pers. **Meals** Breakfast incl. No communal meal. **Facilities** Sitting room, tel., swimming pool. **Pets** Dogs allowed on request. **Nearby** Restaurant (500m), tennis (by agreement with Hotel La Gacholle, 500 meters away), 18-hole golf course. **Spoken** English. **Credit cards** Visa, Eurocard, MasterCard. **Open** All year. **How to get there** (Map 33): 800m from Gordes (Autoroute Avignon Sud, dir. Apt) on the Murs road.

Near the famous village of Luberon, this house consists of a 500 year-old stone borie (in which the kitchen is installed), and next to it the farmhouse, one part renovated, another modern. In front of the house is a terrace planted with typical trees of Southern France and overlooking a small valley with, set right in the middle, a lovely swimming pool. The interior is also exceptional, with an atmosphere of warmth and intimacy, a harmonious mixture of styles, bright colors, antique sculptures and beautiful views over the countryside. The bedrooms are small but very pleasant and the welcome is natural and enthusiastic. A must.

604 - Au Ralenti du Lierre

Les Beaumettes
84220 Gordes
(Vaucluse)
Tel. 04 90 72 39 22
Fax 04 90 72 43 12
T. Dulieu and S. Lhuillier
Web: //rdlierre.free.fr

Rooms 5 with bath or shower and WC. **Price** 380 and 460F/57,93 and 70,13€ (2 pers., view village), 550F/83,85€ (2 pers., view garden), +150F/22,87€ (extra pers.). **Meals** Breakfast incl. Evening meals 150F/22€ (all incl.). **Restaurant** "La Remise". **Facilities** Sitting room, swimming pool. **Pets** Dogs not allowed. **Nearby** 18-hole golf course, hiking, fishing, tennis, riding, canoeing, climbing; Gordes, Lacoste, Bonnieux, Sénanque abbey. **Credit cards** Not accepted. **Open** All year, by reservation in low season. **How to get there** (Map 33): 15km east of L'Isle-sur-la-Sorgue. Avignon-Sud Autoroute, exit towards Apt; in the village of Les Beaumettes.

This pleasant little village house dating back to the 18th century is refined yet strongly Provençal in style. In the bedrooms, colors, fabrics, period furniture and some antique pieces blend in nicely to give an effect that is cheerful, comfortable and elegant at the the same time. A "suite" of two vaulted rooms, one of them very dark and secluded, is most unusual. On the slope of the hillside, a lovely garden reaches to the rock at the top. The breakfasts are delicious and the hospitality very kind.

605 - Le Jas de Monsieur

84240 Grambois
(Vaucluse)
Tel. 04 90 77 92 08
M. and Mme Mazel

Rooms 2 and 1 suite (2-4 pers.) with bath or shower and WC. **Price** 300-350F/45,73-53,35€ (2 pers., depending on season), +80F/12,19€ (extra bed in suite). **Meals** Breakfast incl. No communal meal. **Facilities** Sitting room, swimming pool, marked discovery trails. **Nearby** Restaurants (3km), tennis, millpond, golf; Château d'Ansouis, old villages (Cucuron, Grambois), Aix Festival and La-Roque-d'Anteron Festival. **Spoken** English. **Open** All year. **How to get there** (Map 33): 15km west of Manosque. Autoroute Aix-Sisteron, exit Pertuis, then towards La Tour-d'Aigues and Grambois, then follow signs.

Great lovers of nature and of the Vaucluse, the owners of this authentic 18th-century farmhouse will greet you with warm hospitality. The guest rooms are simply but comfortably and handsomely decorated, and you will sleep between beautiful embroidered sheets. There is a great amount of tourist information at your disposal in the attractive reception rooms. Facing due south, a huge terrace overlooks the gardens and the swimming pool below, affording a magnificent view over the stunning countryside. "Monsieur's Sheepfold" is an economical and endearing place to stay.

606 - Mas du Clos de l'Escarrat

Route de Carpentras
84150 Jonquières
(Vaucluse)
Tel. and fax 04 90 70 39 19
Mobile 06 10 29 17 82
M. and Mme Charles Barail
Web: www.visit.to/provence

Rooms 2 studios (2 pers.) with shower, WC, kitchenette, TV, and 1 apart. Studios cleaned once weekly. **Price** 270F/41,16€ (1 pers.), 300F/45,73€ (2 pers.); 2000F/304,89€/week. Apartment 2800F/426,85€ (2 pers.) 3300F/503,08€ (3-4 pers.); price/week. **Meals** Breakfast 40F/6,09€. No communal meal. **Restaurants** In Orange (8km). **Facilities** Swimming pool. **Pets** Animals not accepted. **Spoken** English, Spanish. **Open** All year, by reservation in winter. **How to get there** (Map 33): 8km southeast of Orange. On D950 towards Carpentras; turn left onto lane bordered by a wall.

Surrounded by the fertile plain of the Comtat Venaissin, this old mas has just been handsomely renovated by Monsieur and Madame Barail, who have traveled widely and enjoy decorating their home with souvenirs of their trips. You will find two independent guest rooms, cheerful, comfortable and elegant; small shower rooms. You may have breakfast served in your room, beneath the large trees in the garden, or in a very pleasant dining room, unless you prefer to use the kitchenette in your studio and enjoy the view over Mont Ventoux and the Dentelles de Montmirail from your terrace.

P R O V E N C E - R I V I E R A

607 - La Ferme des 3 Figuiers

84800 Lagnes
(Vaucluse)
Tel. 04 90 20 23 54
Fax 04 90 20 25 47
M. and Mme Gouin

Rooms 4 (incl. 1 small outside the house) and 2 suites (incl. 1 for 2-6 pers.) with bath or shower and WC. **Price** Rooms 450 and 550F/68,60 and 83,84€ (2 pers.), +100F/15,24€ (extra bed); suites 600 and 700F/91,46 and 106,71€ (2 pers.), 800F/121,9 € (4 pers.). **Meals** Breakfast incl. Evening meals 160F/24,39€ (wine incl.). **Facilities** Sitting room, tel., swimming pool, cooking lessons. **Pets** Dogs not allowed. **Nearby** Riding, golf; Luberon. **Spoken** English. **Closed** Nov – Feb but open between Christmas and New Year's. **How to get there** (Map 33): 30km south of Avignon via D22 dir. Apt. Signs in 2km after Petit Palais.

Set slightly back from a road that is quite busy in high season, this big farmhouse offers guests modern conveniences that are almost on a par with those of a hotel. Monsieur and Madame Gouin invite you for an aperitif before dinner, which is served in the large, rustic dining room or on the covered terrace. The meals are excellent and lovingly prepared. The bedrooms are spacious and comfortable, and there is a studio with a kitchenette which can accommodate a family or group of friends. The warm colors, the cheerful fabrics and old furniture are typical of Provence, a region where hospitality and friendliness, too, are a tradition.

608 - Mas du Grand Jonquier

Route départementale 22
84800 Lagnes
(Vaucluse)
Tel. 04 90 20 90 13
Fax and anwsering machine
04 90 20 91 18
Monique and François Greck

Rooms 6 with shower, WC, TV and tel. **Price** 480F/73,17€ (1-2 pers.), +100F/15,24€ (extra pers.). **Meals** Breakfast incl. Evening meals at separate tables, by reservation 130F/19,81€ (wine not incl.). **Facilities** Sitting room, swimming pool, pétanque court. **Credit cards** All major. **Pets** Dogs not allowed. **Nearby** Golf; Luberon, Gordes and Avignon Festivals, antiques dealers in L'Ile-sur-la-Sorgue. **Credit cards** Not accepted. **Spoken** English, Italian, German, Spanish. **Open** All year, Jan and Feb only by reservation. **How to get there** (Map 33): 10km east of Cavaillon. On D22 between Avignon-Sud and Apt. Coming from Avignon: 1.5km after the sign indicating the village of Petit Palais.

This lovely old mas, something between an inn and a guest house, stands behind a thick wall of foliage that keeps out much of the noise from the nearby road. In high season, however, there is so much traffic that the place is still a bit noisy and we would not recommend it at this period. The house has been completely renovated and the bedrooms are comfortable and impeccably kept. The welcome, a bit timid at first, is simple and pleasant. Breakfast and dinner are tasty and elegant, served in a rustic dining room or in the shade of a tall chestnut tree.

P R O V E N C E - R I V I E R A

609 - La Pastorale

Les Gardiolles
84800 Lagnes
(Vaucluse)
Tel. 04 90 20 25 18
Fax 04 90 20 21 86
M. and Mme Negrel

Rooms 4 with bath or shower and WC. **Price** 330F/50,30€ (2 pers.), +80F/12,19€ (extra pers.). **Meals** Breakfast incl. No communal meal. Summer kitchen at guests' disposal **Facilities** Living room, tel. **Nearby** Restaurants (2km), swimming pool, tennis, river fishing, mountain bikes, 18-hole golf course (2km); Luberon villages and park; Avignon and music festivals. **Credit cards** Not accepted. **Spoken** English, German. **Open** All year. **How to get there** (Map 33): Autoroute A7 exit L'Isle-sur-la-Sorgue. In L'Isle-sur-la-Sorgue towards Apt for about 3km, then towards Fontaine-de-Vaucluse via D24. Do not enter Lagnes but continue for 1km on D24. Sign on left.

Skirted by a small road, La Pastorale is an 18th-century farmhouse which was tastefully restored by Monsieur and Madame Negrel, a friendly couple offering guests four comfortable bedrooms with antique furniture. The large garden offers you both sun and shade for relaxation. The atmosphere is pleasant and familial.

610 - Saint-Buc

Route de l'Isle
84800 Lagnes
(Vaucluse)
Tel. 04 90 20 36 29
Mme Delorme

Rooms 3 with bath and WC. **Price** 400-450F/60,98-68,60€ (1-2 pers.). **Meals** Breakfast incl. No communal meal. **Facilities** Sitting room, swimming pool. **Pets** Animals not allowed. **Nearby** Restaurants, 18-hole golf course, equestrian center; Luberon, Gordes, Avignon Festival, Fontaine-de-Vaucluse. **Credit cards** Not accepted. **Open** May 1 – Sept 5, only by reservation. **How to get there** (Map 33): 23km east of Avignon via N100 towards Apt. At Petit-Palais head for Fontaine-de-Vaucluse. At Lagnes take D99 towards Isle-sur-la-Sorgue.

Saint Buc is a recently built house located several minutes out of L'Isle-sur-la-Sorgue, famed for its antique markets. Attractively and simply decorated, the ground-level guest rooms here open onto the garden. Each has a large, functional bathroom whose tub is set into the floor. The large living room is beautified with antique objects. Madame Delorme is a very helpful hostess and her breakfasts truly delicious. They are often served on a covered terrace overlooking the trees and garden.

611 - La Carraire

84360 Lauris
(Vaucluse)
Tel. 04 90 08 36 89
Fax 04 90 08 40 83
Michel Cuxac
E-mail: www.dnweb.com/carraire

Rooms 5 with bath and WC. **Price** 350F/53,35€ (2 pers., except Jul/Aug), 450F/68,60€ (2 pers., Jul/Aug). **Meals** Breakfast 35F/5,33€. No communal meal. **Facilities** Sitting room, swimming pool, pond. **Pets** Dogs allowed on request. **Nearby** Restaurants, riding, bicycle rentals, hiking in le Luberon, golf; National Park of Luberon, festivals (Aix, La Roque-d'Antheron, Avignon). **Spoken** English. **Closed** Nov – Feb, except by reservation. 2 nights min. **How to get there** (Map 33): 2km south of Lourmarin. A7 exit Senas, then Malemort road, after the bridge, go towards Pertuis. In Lauris, take Lourmarin road; at the cemetery traffic circle, 800m signs on left.

An 18th-century family house that has been completely renovated. It faces a large stone-bordered irrigation basin. Sophie, always cheerful, will lead you to your rooms, all attractively done in old-fashioned pastel colors (our preference goes to the larger ones, with one bed). The old walls and southern-style decoration exude charm. You will be captivated by the swimming pool surrounded by vines and cherry trees. Delicious breakfasts and good value off-season.

612 - La Maison des Sources

Chemin des Fraisses
84360 Lauris
(Vaucluse)
Tel. and fax 04 90 08 22 19
Mobile 06 08 33 06 40
Mme Collart Stichelbaut

Rooms 4 with bath or shower, WC (1 with 4 beds, bath, shower). **Price** 370-390F/56,40-59,45€ (1 pers.), 430-450F/65,55-68,60€ (2 pers.), 530-550F/80,79-83,84€ (3 pers.), 650F/99,09€ (4 pers.). **Meals** Breakfast incl. Evening meals at communal table, by reservation 140F/21,34€ (all incl.). **Facilities** Sitting room, tel., ping-pong **Pets** Animals allowed on request **Nearby** Restaurants, golf, swimming pool. **Open** All year. **How to get there** (Map 33): 27km southeast of Cavaillon. Autoroute A7, exit Cavaillon, D973 dir. Pertuis/Cadenet via Lauris (signs on D973). At the bottom of the Lauris village.

The "House of the Springs" is surrounded by greenery and backs onto a rock where troglodyte dwellings can be seen. Bathed in light, the very spacious bedrooms are handsomely decorated and extremely comfortable. The bedroom called Les Nonnes is quite original: its four beds with canopies and white curtains are lined up rather like nuns in a row, thus the name. It's delightful to relax on the terrace in the shade of the acacias. Very nice breakfasts, pleasant dinners, and a warm and friendly welcome.

613 - Château Talaud
84870 Loriol-du-Comtat
(Vaucluse)
Tel. 04 90 65 71 00
Fax 04 90 65 77 93
Conny and Hein Deiters
E-mail: chateautalaud@infonie.fr
Web: www.chateautalaud.com

Rooms 5 and 1 suite with bath, WC, tel., TV satellite and 1 apart. (2-4 pers.) with lounge, kitchenette, bath, WC. 1 small mas (5 pers.) with lounge, kitchen, dinning room, 3 rooms, 2 showers, 2 WC. **Price** Room 750-950F/114,33-144,82€ (2 pers.); suite 1000F/152,44€ (2 pers.), +150F/22,86€ (extra bed). Apart. 5500F/838,46€/week. Mas 6500F/990,91€/week. **Meals** Breakfast incl. in room. Evening meals, by reservation 250F/38,11€ (wine incl.). **Facilities** Sitting room, swimming pool. **Pets** Dogs not allowed. **Cerdit cards** Visa, Eurocard, MasterCard (2 nights). **Spoken** English, German, Dutch. **Closed** Feb. 2 nights min. May 1 – Oct 30. **How to get there** (Map 33): Aut. exit 22 or 23 towards Carpentras, Monteux road (D107). **No smoking** in bedrooms.

A long driveway, a cluster of giant plane trees, and then, the elegant facade of this 18th-century château appears, surrounded by gardens and fountains. Splendidly renovated, the interior decoration is of outstanding quality. Fine antiques, comfortable beds, painting, carpets... The cooking too is a dream come true, with gourmet dinners prepared by Conny and excellent wines chosen by Hein. A wonderful atmosphere of refinement.

614 - Domaine de la Lombarde
BP 32 - Puyvert
84160 Lourmarin
(Vaucluse)
Tel. 04 90 08 40 60
Fax 04 90 08 40 64
M. and Mme Lèbre
E-mail: la.lombarde@wanadoo.fr

Rooms 4 with shower, WC, TV, and 2 studios (2-3 pers.) with bedroom, shower, WC and TV. **Price** 380-410F/57,93-62,50€ (1-2 pers.), +120F/18,29€ (extra bed); studio 2700F/411,61€/week (linen incl.) **Facilities** Sitting room, tel. and fax, swimming pool, ping-pong, volleyball, bicycles, pétanque. **Pets** Dogs not allowed. **Nearby** Riding, polo, golf; Luberon, Cassis, Verdon Gorges. **Spoken** English, Spanish. **Closed** Nov 1 – Mar 1. **How to get there** (Map 33): 30km from Aix-en-Provence. 2km of Lauris dir. Cadenet (don't take the new deviation at the bottom of Lauris, but go up into the village) and 5km from Cadenet dir. Lauris.

This renovated farmhouse stands facing a beautiful little valley planted with grape vines and cherry trees. The bedrooms face the rear, toward a long path bordered by thuja trees. Each has its own entrance with a covered terrace. They are small, simply decorated, comfortable, but rather dark with their low ceilings and small square windows. Breakfast is served in a lovely patio amid lush foliage and there is a nice swimming pool. A good place to go in fine weather.

615 - Villa Saint-Louis

35, rue Henri-de-Savornin
84160 Lourmarin
(Vaucluse)
Tel. 04 90 68 39 18
Fax 04 90 68 10 07
Bernadette Lassallette
E-mail: villasaintlouis@wanadoo.fr

Rooms 5 with bath or shower, WC, tel. and TV. Rooms cleaned on request. **Price** 350-450F/53,35-68,60€ (2 pers.). **Meals** Breakfast incl. No communal meal. **Restaurants** Many in village. **Facilities** Sitting room, mountain-bikes. **Nearby** 18-hole golf course (25km), tennis, swimming pool, riding, kayaking; Luberon Natural Park, Luberon villages, summer festivals. **Credit cards** Not accepted. **Spoken** English. **Open** All year. **How to get there** (Map 33): 50km east of Avignon via N7 and D973 towards Cavaillon, then Cadenet and left on D943 towards Lourmarin.

At the entrance to picturesque Lourmarin, the beautiful 17th-century Villa Saint-Louis is set in a charming walled garden. You are certain to share our enthusiasm for lovely interior decoration in which a profusion of furniture, wall fabrics, paintings, and objects tastefully combine different periods. (There is an endearingly carefree touch in this artistic, bohemian atmosphere.) Breakfasts are served outdoors or in an interesting dining room illuminated from above. The Villa is a place you'll want to return to, if only for Bernadette Lassallette's memorable hospitality.

616 - La Grange de Jusalem

Route de Malemort
84380 Mazan
(Vaucluse)
Tel. 04 90 69 83 48
Fax 04 90 69 63 53
Mme du Lac

Rooms 4 with bath or shower, WC (incl. 2 private baths but outside the room). **Price** 350-400F/53,35-60,97€ (2 pers.), +100F/15,24€ (extra bed). **Meals** Breakfast incl. Evening meals at separate tables 130F/19,82€ (wine incl.) **Facilities** Swimming pool. **Pets** Small dogs allowed. **Nearby** Riding, golf, skiing; Orange and Avignon festivals, Villeneuve-lès-Avignon, Vaison-la-Romaine, Gordes. **Spoken** English. **Open** All year. **How to get there** (Map 33): 30km northeast of Avignon via highway towards Monteux and Carpentras (airport Marignane, 80km).

This old farmhouse built around a shaded courtyard is located in the middle of a small winegrowing plain. One of the wings is occupied by a charming little restaurant which has already built up a reputation in the area. Its decoration is cream colored, with a fireplace , pretty tablecloths, vintage tableware... which clearly announce that the owners like to go antiquing in the region but the result is never overdone. The bedrooms vary in size and are decorated in the same spirit, to make one feel quite at home. Good breakfasts are served under a rose bower when the weather is fine. There is a nice swimming pool with a view of Venasque. A very friendly welcome.

617 - La Magnanerie

Le Roucas
84560 Ménerbes
(Vaucluse)
Tel. 04 90 72 42 88
Fax 04 90 72 39 42
Mme and M. Rohart
E-mail: magnanerie@aol.com
Web: www.magnanerie.com

Rooms 6 with bath and WC. **Price** 365-455F/55,64-69,36€ (1 pers., depending on season), 400-490F/60,97-74,70€ (2 pers., depending on season), +70F/10,67€ (extra pers.). **Meals** Breakfast incl. Evening meals at separate tables, by reservation 100F/15,24€ (wine not incl.). **Facilities** Sitting room (TV, video recorder), swimming pool, pétanque, ping-pong, parlor games. **Nearby** Mountain bike rentals, riding, golf; Bonnieux, Gordes, Roussillon. **Spoken** English, German. **Closed** Nov 11 – Mar 1, by reservation and deposit. 2 nights min. in Jul and Aug. **How to get there** (Map 33): 18km southeast of Cavaillon. Autoroute A7 exit Cavaillon, dir. Apt. Pass Robion dir. Ménerbes via D3. Leaves Ménerbes, on right dir. Bonnieux and go about 3km. **No smoking** in bedrooms.

This large 18th-century mansion is tucked away in a little valley and enjoys a beautiful view of the Luberon countryside. Renovated with a great deal of skill, it offers six bedrooms, all soberly but pleasantly furnished with antique pieces and with very fine bathrooms. Tasty breakfasts are served outside, in sun or shade, in a good setting for pure relaxation. The table d'hôte dinner is based on traditional Provençal dishes. Monsieur and Madame Rohart are friendly and considerate hosts.

618 - La Badiane

685, chemin de la Grangette
84170 Monteux
(Vaucluse)
Tel. 04 90 66 85 51
Mme Bigonnet

Rooms 2 with bath or shower and WC (poss. 1 extra room without bath). **Price** 250F/38,11€ (1 pers.), 350F/53,35€ (2 pers.). **Meals** Breakfast incl. Evening meals at communal table on request 100F/15,24€ (all incl.), 60F/9,14€ (children from 4). **Facilities** 2 sitting rooms, French billiards, piano, drums, books, swimming pool, fishing in Sorgues. **Nearby** Tennis, bicycle rentals, touring on horseback or in horse-drawn caravan, golf. **Spoken** English, Spanish. **Closed** Oct – Pentecost. 2 days min. **How to get there** (Map 33): Autoroute A7 exit Avignon-Nord, dir. Carpentras. Go to the Monteux traffic circle, head back in direction you came from until you pass Vahiné, 1st road on right (Chemin de Beauchamp) then on left, Chemin de la Grangette for 1km.

After cutting across the fields on a little dirt road you finally reach the Sorgue River and find on the riverbank a lovely house surrounded by trees and flowers. Two bedrooms are available here, both comfortable and relaxing, with an atmosphere of yesteryear. On the ground floor, an inviting living room with a fireplace and nice furniture, a billiard room and a piano. Outside an awning for meals and a garden with lots of hidden corners. A fine house with a warm welcome.

619 - Les Hauts de Véroncle

84220 Murs
(Vaucluse)
Tel. 04 90 72 60 91
Fax 04 90 72 62 07
Prisca and Didier Del Corso
E-mail: hauts-de-veroncle@wanadoo.fr

Rooms 5 with bath or shower, WC, and 1 apart. with living area/kitchen. **Price** 280-290F/42,68-44,21€ (2 pers.), +100F/15,24€ (extra bed). **Meals** Breakfast incl. Evening meals at separate tables 120F/18,29€ (aperitif, wine and coffee incl.). **Facilities** Sitting room. **Nearby** Tennis, swimming pool (1.5km), mountain bikes; Véroncle mills road (16th to 19th century). **Spoken** English, Italian. **Closed** Nov 5 – Mar 20. **How to get there** (Map 33): 6km east of Gordes. In Gordes-Centre, take Murs road for 6km and follow signs "Chambres d'hôtes".

Lost at the end of a long path through beautiful countryside, this house will enchant all those who seek nature, calm and solitude. There are many walks in the environs and its elevation guarantees a breath of fresh air even in midsummer. Prisca and Didier are young, friendly and hospitable. Their love of good food is evident from the quality of the dinners, served under the trellis thick with wisteria. The bedrooms are simple but perfectly adequate.

620 - Bastide Le Mourre

84580 Oppède
(Vaucluse)
Tel. 04 90 76 99 31
Fax 04 90 76 83 60
Mme Canac

House 4 (3-6 pers.), with: 1-3 rooms, 1-2 bath, 1-3 WC, kitchen, sitting room, terrace, tel., TV, laundry, dishwasher, towels, sheets. **Price** 1800F/274,40€/weekend; 5200-8500F/792,73-1295,81€ and 4200-6000F/640,28-914,69€/week depending on house and season. Contract with 20% deposit. House work 80F/12,19€/houre. **Facilities** Swimming pool. **Nearby** Golf, all sports; old villages in the Luberon. **Open** All year. 3 days min. in low season and 1 week Apr 1 – Oct 15. **How to get there** (Map 33): 10km east of Cavaillon.

Perched on a small hill, this estate that resembles a little hamlet enjoys a splendid panorama over the plain and the old village against its rocky background. Grouped around the main building, each house is independent. Madame. Canac has fitted them out as if each unit were for herself, and the result is an unqualified success, for the decoration (Provençal but not excessive), the beauty of the materials and the quality of the amenities. An elegant swimming pool overlooking the vineyards completes the idyllic scene.

PROVENCE - RIVIERA

621 - Le Domaine du Petit Crui

84580 Oppède
(Vaucluse)
Tel. 04 90 76 80 89
Fax 04 90 76 92 86
M. and Mme Goudin

Rooms 4 with bath or shower, WC, TV, minibar; and 2 apart. (weekly rental, or 2 week in Jul and Aug). Rooms not cleaned on Sun. **Price** 450-550F/68,60-83,84€; apart. 2800-8400F/426,85-1280,57€ (2-9 pers.; depending on season and number of bedrooms). **Meals** Breakfast incl. in bedrooms. No communal meal. **Facilities** Sitting room, outdoor kitchen, clothes-washer, swimming pool, ping-pong, table football, boules. **Pets** Dogs allowed on request. **Nearby** Restaurants (3km), 18-hole golf course (9km); old villages, second-hand dealing in l'Isle-sur-la-Sorgue. **Spoken** English, Spanish, Italian. **Closed** Nov 15 – Mar 1. No checkout on Sun. 2 days min. in low season and 5 nights min. from May to Sept. **How to get there** (Map 33): 10km east of Cavaillon via D2 towards Robion, then D3 to Ménerbes; 2.5km signs.

This handsome family mansion with its opulent outbuildings sits amid 18 hectares of cherry orchard. We were impressed by the kindness of Monsieur and Madame. Goudin and by the extraordinary brunch, served in the elegant dining room or on the terrace. The rooms are large, pleasant and impeccably clean (our favorite was the "Jaune"). Fine swimming pool facing the vast expanse of fruit trees. Generous and authentic, an excellent family address.

622 - Saint-Barthélémy

Chemin de la Roque
84210 Pernes-les-Fontaines
(Vaucluse)
Tel. and fax 04 90 66 47 79
Mme Mangeard
E-mail: mangeard.jacqueline@wanadoo.fr

Rooms 5 with bath or shower and WC. **Price** 240F/36,58€ (1 pers.), 300F/45,73€ (2 pers.), +100F/15,24€ (extra bed). **Meals** Breakfast incl. No communal meal. **Restaurant** "Au fil du temps" in Pernes. **Facilities** Sitting room, tel. with meter, swimming pool, river fishing (with permit), bikes, swimming in waterfall on property. **Pets** Animals not allowed. **Nearby** 18-hole golf course. **Spoken** English. **Open** All year. **How to get there** (Map 33): 5km south of Carpentras. Autoroute A7, exit Avignon-Nord, then Vedène via D6, Saint-Saturnin-les-Avignon, then Pernes-les-Fontaines (D28). Take the road to Mazan (D1). Signs on right in 2km.

Almost three centuries old, this house is undergoing renovation, revealing beautiful old vestiges such as the stair railing and the "missal hole" in a bedroom. The bathrooms are well kept, as are the pleasant bedrooms. The breakfast-buffet table is set out under an old weeping willow. There are many facilities for long stays, and a lovely garden (where you can hear some road noise) on the edge of a small river with a beautiful waterfall.

623 - La Cipionne

84160 Puyvert
(Vaucluse)
Tel. 04 90 08 40 58
M. Quentin Genicot

Rooms 3 with shower but without private WC (2 WC for 3 rooms), and 1 apartment (weekly rental) with 2 rooms and kitchen, shower and WC. **Price** 310F/47,25€ (1 pers.), 340F/51,83€ (2 pers.); studio 2400F/365,87€ (1 pers.), 2600F/396,36€ (2 pers.). **Meals** Breakfast incl. No communal meal. **Facilities** Sitting room, tel. on request, swimming pool. **Pets** Dogs not allowed. **Nearby** Restaurants (3km), mountain bikes, golf; Saint-Rémy-de-Provence, Luberon, antiquities. **Spoken** English. **Closed** Oct 15 – Mar 31, by reservation in low season. 2 days min. **How to get there** (Map 33): 30km north of Aix-en-Provence and 28km east of Cavaillon: itinerary sent at time of reservation.

This old stone farmhouse with an inner courtyard, oriented due south and facing an open vista, enjoys a wonderful location in the heart of the countryside. Here the atmosphere is relaxed and friendly. The rooms are simply decorated. There is a piano, which guests are invited to use, and a swimming pool set in a garden, restful and refreshing for a sunset dip. And in fine weather, another magical moment is having your breakfast outdoors while you savor the view.

624 - Domaine de Canfier

84440 Robion
(Vaucluse)
Tel. 04 90 76 51 54
Fax 04 90 76 67 99
Catherine and Michel Charvet
E-mail: canfier@aol.com

Rooms 2 with shower, WC, and 1 with separate WC and bath. **Price** 420F/64,02€ (2 pers.). **Meals** Breakfast incl. Communal meals, by reservation (3 or 4/week) 125F/19,05€ (all incl.). **Facilities** Sitting rooms, tel., swimming pool. **Pets** Dogs not allowed. **Nearby** Tennis (1km), canoeing, kayaks, mountain hikes, 9- and 18-hole gulf course (10km), riding; Luberon, Avignon Festival, Gordes, antiques in L'Isle-sur-la-Sorgue. **Credit cards** Not accepted. **Spoken** English, Spanish. **Open** All year. **How to get there** (Map 33): 5km east of Cavaillon. Autoroute A7 exit Cavaillon, then towards Apt and Digne. In Robion at the 2nd traffic light, turn left toward L'Isle-sur-la-Sorgue; go 1km (straight) and take small road on right. Do not go over the Coulon Bridge.

Located at the foot of the Luberon Mountains, this old farm mansion has been elegantly decorated by Catherine and Michel Charvet. Everything has been provided for your relaxation and pleasure: the tastefully but simply furnished bedrooms, the various nooks and crannies in the garden, the swimming pool and the sitting rooms are all available for your enjoyment, not to mention the family cooking and fruit from the orchard.

625 - Mamaison

Quartier Les Devens
84220 Roussillon
(Vaucluse)
Tel. 04 90 05 74 17
Fax 04 90 05 74 63
Marine and Christophe Guillemot

Rooms 4 and 2 suites (2-4 pers.) with bath or shower, WC and tel. **Price** Rooms 450-650F/68,60-99,09€ (2 pers.); suites 850F/129,58€ (2 pers.), +80F/12,19€ (extra bed). **Meals** Breakfast incl. No communal meal. Poss. snacks avalaible outside at night on request. **Facilities** Sitting room, swimming pool. **Pets** Dogs allowed on request. **Nearby** Restaurants, golf, tennis, riding. **Credit cards** Visa, Eurocard, MasterCard. **Spoken** English, Italian. **Closed** Nov 1 – Mar 15. **How to get there** (Map 33): 12km west of Apt. On N100 between Apt and Le Coustellet, take D149 towards Roussillon. Go 800m, sign on left.

Flowers, a stone vault, a beautiful swimming pool and the Vaucluse Plateau all around: the surroundings of this old mas are rivaled only by its very beautiful interior and cheerful, lively furnishings. The bedrooms are comfortable (the Oiseaux room is somewhat small), the furniture well chosen, and the predominant color is echoed in charming frescos; the bathrooms are equally attractive. Good breakfasts and light meals are served in a friendly, informal atmosphere.

626 - Mas d'Azalaïs

Clavaillan
84220 Roussillon
(Vaucluse)
Tel. and fax 04 90 05 70 00
Mme Lacombe

Rooms 1 with bath, shower, WC, and 1 suite for disabled persons, bath and shower, WC, tel. and TV. **Price** 570F/86,89€ (2 pers.); suite 680F/103,66€ (2 pers.), +130F/19,81€ (extra pers.). **Meals** Breakfast incl. Evening meals at communal table or not (3/week) 145F/22,10€ (wine not incl.). **Facilities** Swimming pool. **Pets** Animals not allowed. **Nearby** Restaurants, riding, 18-hole golf course; Luberon. **Spoken** English, Spanish. **Open** All year. **How to get there** (Map 33): 5km east of Gordes. Itinerary given at time of reservation.

A long walk through a pine forest leads to this typical Provençal house with a marvelous view. Built about ten years ago, it has incorporated many traditional elements (old stones, doors and beams and a beautifully sculpted fireplace in the suite). The rooms are comfortable and attractive, with abundant decoration. Quality furniture, paintings and knickknacks make them seem like real guest rooms at the home of a friend. And the welcome you get will also make you feel like a friend.

627 - La Forge
Notre-Dame-des-Anges
84400 Rustrel
(Vaucluse)
Tel. 04 90 04 92 22
Fax 04 90 04 95 22
D. Ceccaldi and C. Berger
E-mail: info@laforge.com.fr
Web: www.laforge.com.fr

Rooms 2 with bath and WC. 2 suites with shower and WC. **Price** 480F/73,17€ (2 pers.); suite 740F/112,81€ (4 pers.). **Meals** Breakfast 30F/4,57€. Communal meals 160F/24,36€ (all incl.). **Facilities** Sitting room, tel., swimming pool, hiking, riding and mountain-bike paths. **Pets** Dogs not allowed. **Nearby** 18-hole golf course (35km), tennis, water sports, riding; Luberon Park, Provençal Colorado, Apt open market (Tues, Sat), L'Isle-sur-la-Sorgue. **Credit cards** Not accepted. **Spoken** English. **Closed** Nov 17 – Dec 30 and Jan 6 – Feb 28. **How to get there** (Map 33): 8km from Apt. In Apt, towards Rustrel and Saint-Christol via D22 for 7.5km; on right towards Le Colorado, then follow signs "La Forge - Chambres d'Hôtes".

La Forge lies in the heart of "Provençal Colorado" at the edge of a protected forest teeming with flora and fauna. This old 19th-century foundry with its spectacular pyramid-shaped chimneys has been transformed into a residence. The strange place turns out to be comfortable, quiet and welcoming due to the design of the bedrooms, the garden, the swimming pool, as well as Dominique Ceccaldi and Claude Berger's hospitality.

628 - Chambre de séjour avec vue…

84400 Saignon-en-Luberon
(Vaucluse)
Tel. and fax 04 90 04 85 01
Kamila Regent and Pierre Jaccaud
E-mail: chambreavecvue@vox-pop.net

Rooms 3 and 1 studio with bath or shower and WC. **Price** Rooms 300F/45,73€ (2 pers.), +80F/12,19€ (extra bed); studio 350F/53,35€/day (or weekly rental). **Meals** Breakfast 40F/6,09€. Evening meals at communal table 140F/21,34€ (wine incl.). **Facilities** Sitting room, bicycles, pétanque, gallery of contemporary art. **Pets** Dogs allowed on request. **Nearby** Hiking, mountain bikes, 18-hole golf course (35km). **Spoken** English, Russian, Polish. **Open** All year. **How to get there** (Map 33): 4km southeast of Apt. **No smoking.**

A good address for lovers of contemporary art (and for gourmets, too), this 18th-century village house is a proof of its owners' passion for art and hospitality. A number of artists work, create and exhibit here. The bedrooms are simple but comfortable, contemporary yet warmly inviting, with bathrooms situated across the hall. In the summer Kamila and Pierre set up the large table under the cherry trees, creating an atmosphere of family picnics of days gone by, with culinary creations that are positively unforgettable!

629 - La Calade

84110 Saint-Romain-en-Viennois
(Vaucluse)
Tel. 04 90 46 51 79
Fax 04 90 46 51 82
M. Haggai and M. Terrisse

Rooms 4 with bath or shower and WC. **Price** 350F/53,35€ (1 pers.), 400F/60,97€ (2 pers.). **Meals** Breakfast incl. No communal meal. **Facilities** Sitting room, tel. **Pets** Dogs not allowed. **Nearby** Restaurants (3km), walking, biking, motorcycling, 18-hole golf course (40km); Vaison-la-Romaine, Nyons, Les Baronnies, Mont Ventoux **Spoken** English, Spanish, Italian. **Closed** Nov – Easter. **How to get there** (Map 33): 3km northwest of Vaison-la-Romaine dir. Nyons.

This charming old village house has undergone a successful renovation. Its sober but elegant decoration sets off the 19th-century fruitwood furniture, family pieces, glazed pottery, amusing etchings... Here the Provençal style is present, but not caricatured: the bedrooms are comfortable, with white walls, colorful Asian fabrics, marine lithographs, an overall effect that is calm, simple and attractive. In the evening you can have a drink on the roof terrace as you admire the last rays over the vineyards before the church is illuminated. And in the morning, an excellent breakfast is served in the flowered patio.

630 - Maison Garance

Hameau des Bassacs
84490 Saint-Saturnin-lès-Apt
(Vaucluse)
Tel. 04 90 05 74 61
Fax 04 90 05 75 68
M. Pascal Bennett

Rooms 6 with bath, shower, WC and tel. **Price** 600-750F/91,46-114,33€ (2 pers.). **Meals** Breakfast 50F/7,62€. Meals at communal table or not; lunch 120F/18,29€, dinner 150F/22,86€ (wine not incl.). **Facilities** Sitting room, tel., swimming pool. **Pets** Dogs not allowed. **Nearby** Bicycles and mountain bikes, 18-hole golf course, riding, tennis. **Credit card** Visa. **Spoken** English, Spanish. **Closed** Nov 15 – Jan 5, only by reservation. **How to get there** (Map 33): 12km east of Gordes via D2 towards Saint-Saturnin-lès-Apt. Go past La Tuillière; in 1.5km, turn left at the sign Les Bassacs and 2nd house on right.

In this charming hamlet, the Maison Garance opens onto a patio with a fig tree, lemon trees, and large jugs of flowers. A well-furnished veranda room gives onto the flower garden. From the swimming pool, the view over the Luberon is truly magnificent. In the five guest rooms, roughcast walls in bright Provençal shades of yellow, pink, and blue; furniture found in nearby antique shops and decorative objects combine to create a charming atmosphere. The bathrooms are exceptionally lovely, the cuisine is delightful, and the owner is a very pleasant host.

631 - Mas de Lumière

Campagne Les Talons
84490 Saint-Saturnin-lès-Apt
(Vaucluse)
Tel. 04 90 05 63 44
M. and Mme Bernard Maître

Rooms 3 (2 with independant entrance) with bath or shower and WC. **Price** 550-650F/83,84-99,09€ (2 pers.), +120F/18,29€ (extra pers.). **Meals** Breakfast incl. No communal meal. **Restaurants** "L'Estellan" and "La Bartavelle". **Facilities** Swimming pool. **Pets** Animals not allowed. **Nearby** 18-hole golf course (20 mn.), riding and tennis (10 mn), Luberon villages. **Credit cards** Not accepted. **Spoken** English, Spanish. **Open** All year, 2 nights min. in low season. **How to get there** (Map 33): 10km west of Apt via N100 towards Gordes, and D4 towards Roussillon-Murs, at the crossroads with D2 go 500m on D4, then turn right at the Les Talons sign.

Standing on a slight rise above a tiny hamlet, Mas de Lumière is lovely, both outside and within its cool walls. The bedrooms are luxurious and beautiful, with decor in soft colors. Several outside terraces offer guests privacy and comfort; (the terrace facing east is ideal for breakfast). There is a beautiful swimming pool overlooking the Luberon Plain. The owners are friendly and refined.

632 - Saint-Jean

84110 Séguret
(Vaucluse)
Tel. 04 90 46 91 76
Fax 04 90 46 83 88
Mme Augier

Rooms 1 and 2 suites (3-4 pers.) with shower, WC, tel. and minibar. **Price** 400-500F/60,98-76,22€ (1 pers.), 490-570F/74,70-86,89€ (2 pers.), 630-680F/96,04-103,66€ (3 pers.), +110F/16,76€ (extra pers.). **Meals** Breakfast incl. No communal meal. **Restaurants** "Le Mesclun" in Séguret and "Le Brin d'Olivier" in Vaison. **Facilities** Sitting room, swimming pool. **Nearby** Tennis; Wine Route, Séguret, Vaison-la-Romaine, Orange, Le Ventoux. **Spoken** English, Spanish. **Open** All year. **How to get there** (Map 33): 2km northeast of Séguret. At the bottom of Séguret, take on right the Route des Vins (D88). Signs 1.5km dir. Vaison (D88).

Backed up against a wall covered with greenery and lush foliage, Saint Jean offers large guest rooms whose decor is classic and cheerful. All are comfortable and have unusual layouts (one even has a greenhouse/lounge). You have to go around the fountain and walk up the steps to find the other garden and its beautiful swimming pool overlooking a panorama of vineyards and orchards. Madame Augier's cheerful disposition is communicative and her breakfasts are worth a detour.

633 - La Treille

84190 Suzette
(Vaucluse)
Tel. 04 90 65 03 77 / 04 90 62 92 05
M. and Mme Challier

Rooms 2, and 1 studio (2 pers.) and 1 suite (2-4 pers.) with bath or shower and WC. **Price** Room 330F/50,30€ (2 pers.), +70F/10,67€ (extra bed); studio 400F/60,97€ (2 pers.); suite 450F/68,60€ (2 pers.), 500F/76,22€ (4 pers.). **Meals** Breakfast 35F/5,33€. **Facilities** Sitting room. **Pets** Dogs allowed on request. **Nearby** Hiking; Avignon (Festival), Orange, Vaison-la-Romaine, Montmirail lace. **Spoken** English. **Open** All year. 2 days min. **How to get there** (Map 33): 38km northeast of Avignon via D942 towards Carpentras, then on left towards Beaumes-de-Venise. In Beaumes-de-Venise, D90, on right towards Suzette.

Well restored with old materials, this converted farmhouse enjoys a magnificent view over Mont Ventoux. Simple but comfortable, the bedrooms are handsomely decorated. Our favorite is the charming mazet, a small, independent two-story house adjacent to the farmhouse. It is decorated in country style, with white walls, beamed ceilings, and antique wardrobes. Reduced rates are available for long stays. The Challiers are delightful hosts.

634 - L'Évêché

Rue de l'Évêché
84110 Vaison-la-Romaine
(Vaucluse)
Tel. 04 90 36 13 46
Fax 04 90 36 32 43
M. and Mme Verdier
E-mail: eveche@aol.com

Rooms 4 with bath or shower, WC and tel. **Price** 350-400F/53,35-60,97€ (1 pers.), 400-440F/60,97-67,07€ (2 pers.). **Meals** Breakfast incl. No communal meal. **Restaurants** In Vaison. **Facilities** Sitting room, mountain bikes. **Pets** Dogs allowed on request. **Nearby** Swimming pool, tennis, riding, golf (miniature and practice) in the village, walks; Vaison-la-Romaine. **Credit cards** Not accepted. **Open** All year. **How to get there** (Map 33): 29km northeast of Orange via D975; in Vaison-la-Romaine follow Ville Médiévale signs.

Built in the 17th century in the medieval part of Vaison-la-Romaine, this former Bishop's Palace is immensely charming. A very comfortable residence with rooms of varying proportions, it opens onto several flower-covered terraces (one of which is delightful for breakfast.) The decoration is warm and inviting throughout, with antique furniture, books, paintings, lovely objects. But what is truly outstanding about L'Evêché is Aude and Jean-Loup Verdier's cheerful, informal hospitality.

635 - Mastignac

Route de Taulignan
84600 Valréas
(Vaucluse)
Tel. 04 90 35 01 82
Mme de Précigout

Rooms 5 with bath or private shower (1 with private WC); 2 with shared WC. **Price** 350-450F/53,35-68,60€ (2 pers.). **Meals** Breakfast incl. No communal meal. **Restaurants** "Au délice de Provence" in Valréas and "L'Eau à la bouche" in Grignan. **Facilities** Sitting room, swimming pool. **Pets** Small dogs allowed. **Nearby** Tennis, riding, 18-hole golf course (30km); Roman ruins, Romanesque churches and abbeys, Provence villages, Mont Ventoux. **Spoken** English. **Open** May 20 – Oct 1. **How to get there** (Map 33): 2km north of Valréas. Follow signs "Mastignac" from Valréas.

An old Provençal farmhouse with delightful gardens surrounded by vineyards, Mastignac is laid out in a rectangle around a huge patio. The antique furniture, the paintings and objects accumulated over the years endow it with the charm of a family home. Of average size (except for one bedroom at the end of the left wing), the guest rooms are elegant and pleasant. Breakfasts are served at a communal table on the patio or in a charming dining room. Madame de Précigout is a marvelous hostess.

636 - Villa Velleron

Rue Roquette
84740 Velleron
(Vaucluse)
Tel. 04 90 20 12 31
Fax 04 90 20 10 34
Simone Sanders and Wim Visser
E-mail: villa.velleron@wanadoo.fr

Rooms 6 with bath and WC. 1 small apart. weekly rental. **Price** 500-650F/76,29-99,09€ (2 pers.). **Meals** Breakfast incl. Meals at separate tables 160F/24,39€ (wine not incl.). **Facilities** Sitting room, tel., swimming pool. **Pets** Dogs not allowed. **Nearby** Tennis, riding, mountain bikes, 18-hole golf course (5km); Mont Ventoux, Luberon villages, L'Isle-sur-la-Sorgue (antiques, 3km), Avignon, Wine Route. **Credit cards** Not accepted. **Spoken** English, German, Dutch. **Closed** Nov 1 – Easter weekend. **How to get there** (Map 33): 25km east of Avignon. Autoroute A7, exit Avignon-Nord toward Carpentras. In Monteux, follow directions to Velleron, go 10km (D31). In Velleron, behind post office.

Set in the center of the village, this tastefully converted old oil mill is surrounded by a swimming pool, terraces and a small shady garden. Depending on the season, Wim Visser's meals are served outdoors or in a pretty dining room. The bathrooms are modern and the welcome is friendly.

637 - La Maison aux Volets Bleus

84210 Venasque
(Vaucluse)
Tel. 04 90 66 03 04
Fax 04 90 66 16 14
Mme Martine Maret
E-mail: voletbleu@aol.com

Rooms 5 with bath and WC (1 with shower, bath). **Price** 420-500F/64,02-76,22€ (2 pers.), +120F/18,29€ (extra pers.); suite 780F/118,91€ (4 pers.) **Meals** Breakfast incl. Evening meals (Mon, Wed and Sat) at separate tables 135F/20,58€ (wine not incl.). **Facilities** Sitting room, tel. **Nearby** Tennis, bicycles, footpaths; Sénanque Abbey, Fontaine-de-Vaucluse, Avignon, Luberon, L'Isle-sur-la-Sorgue. **Credit cards** Not accepted. **Spoken** English. **Open** Mar 1 – Nov 1. **How to get there** (Map 33): South of Carpentras via D4; signposted. In the village at the fountain: sign.

Perched on a rocky outcrop, Venasque dominates the plain below, as does "The House With Blue Shutters". A small, flowery courtyard, a huge living room delightfully decorated with dried flowers and antique furniture, a terrace with a breathtaking view where breakfast is served: such are the charming sights that await you here. Comfortable and quite large, the guest rooms are tastefully appointed and enjoy a spectacular view. Add delicious cuisine to all those delights and you will understand why you should reserve a long time in advance.

638 - Ferme Templière de la Baude

La Baude
84110 Villedieu (Vaucluse)
Tel. 04 90 28 95 18
Fax 04 90 28 91 05
Chantal and Gérard Monin
E-mail: labaude@pacwan.fr
Web: guideweb.com/provence/
chambres.hotes/baude

Rooms 2 suites (4-5 pers.) with bath, shower, WC, tel. and TV. **Price** Rooms 590F/89,94€ (2 pers.), suites 890F/135,67€ (4 pers.); +100F/15,24€ (extra bed).–20% Nov – end Mar (2 nights min.). **Meals** Breakfast incl. Evening meal at communal table 150F/22,86€ (wine and coffee incl.). **Facilities** Swimming pool, tennis. **Nearby** 9-hole golf (20km), downhill and cross-country skiing (Mont Ventoux 30km); Vaison-la-Romaine, Orange, Avignon. **Spoken** English, Italian. **Closed** Telephone for dates. **How to get there** (Map 33): 6km northwest of Vaison-la-Romaine, dir. Cave Coopérative, then Villedieu. The house is 500m from the village square.

After an extensive restoration, this old house (12th century in origin) has all at once come back to life. The bedrooms are pleasant and well kept, simply appointed in a modern Provençal style. We particularly recommend those that face the beautiful inner courtyard – they are brighter than the others. With the warm atmosphere created by Chantal and Gérard, the guests quickly get to know each other around the table (over fine dinners), at pétanque games, tennis tournaments, around the superb swimming pool and in summer at the villages fêtes.

R H Ô N E - A L P S

639 - Manoir de Marmont

01960 Saint-André-sur-Vieux-Jonc
(Ain)
Tel. 04 74 52 79 74
Geneviève and Henri
Guido-Alhéritière

Rooms 2 with bath or shower, WC, and 1 spare room with washbasin. **Price** 400F/60,97€ (1 pers.), 500F/76,22€ (2 pers.), 750F/114,36€ (4 pers.). Children under 8 free. 10% reduction beg. 3rd night. **Meals** Breakfast incl. No communal meal. **Restaurants** At golf course (400m), and "La Rolande" (3km). **Facilities** Sitting room. **Pets** Dogs allowed on request. **Nearby** 6- and 18-hole golf courses; Lakes of the Dombs Route, Châtillon-sur-Chalaronne, Pérouges, Bird sanctuary in Villars-les-Dombes. **Credit cards** Not accepted. **Spoken** English, Italian. **Open** All year. **How to get there** (Map 26): 14km southwest of Bourg-en-Bresse via N83 towards Lyon to Servas. At traffic light on right towards Condeissiat (D64) for 5km, then take the road with plane trees on left (500 m.).

This fine old house, built in the mid-19th century, still has its original wallpaper and the furniture appears never to have left its place. Monsieur and Madame. Guido are excellent hosts: he the straight-faced type, she lively, talkative, amusing, and eager to please the guests. There is everything to make you feel at home, even a number of books in the spacious bedrooms. Well-prepared breakfasts are served in the sitting room or in a charming winter garden.

640 - Les Petites Varennes

01190 Sainte-Bénigne
(Ain)
Tel. 03 85 30 31 98
Christine-Ariane Tréal

Rooms 2 and 1 suite (3 pers.) with bath or shower, WC, tel; and 1 spare room. **Price** 390 and 480F/59,45 and 73,17€ (2 pers.), +130F/19,81€ (extra pers.); suite 610F/92,99€ (3 pers.). **Meals** Breakfast incl. No communal meal. **Restaurant** 300m, gastronomic restaurants in 2km. **Facilities** Sitting room, heated and covered swimming pool (Apr – Oct). **Pets** Dogs not allowed. **Nearby** Tennis, golf; Mâcon vineyards, river port in Pont-de-Vaux. **Credit cards** Not accepted. **Spoken** English. **Open** All year, by reservation. 2 days min. **How to get there** (Map 19): 21km north of Mâcon. Autoroute A6; exit Tournus or Mâcon-Nord, then N6. In Fleurville take D933A toward Pont-de-Vaux for 2.5km via D2 toward Saint-Trivier. Signs in Sainte-Bénigne. **No smoking** in bedrooms.

We love this small, late 18th-century house with its charming colonial appearance on the south side. The comfortable bedrooms upstairs are extremely elegantly decorated (only the Pagode room is less appealing because it has a small shower). There is a delightful living room, also well decorated with paintings and antique furniture, where breakfasts are served when it's too cold to enjoy the terrace.

641 - Le Jeu du Mail

07400 Alba-la-Romaine
(Ardèche)
Tel. and fax 04 75 52 41 59
M. and Mme Maurice Arlaud
E-mail: lejeudumail@free.fr

Rooms 4 with bath or shower, WC, and 1 suite (4-6 pers.) of 2 bedrooms (with mezzanine) with 2 showers, 2 WCs, fridge. Rooms cleaned every 2 days. **Price** 290-350F/44,21-53,35€ (2 pers.); suite 650F/99,09€ (4 pers.). **Meals** Breakfast incl. No communal meal. **Facilities** Sitting room, swimming pool. **Pets** Dogs allowed on request (+30F/4,57€). **Nearby** Restaurants, tennis, riding, golf; medieval villages, Romanesque churches. **Credit cards** Not accepted. **Spoken** English, Italian. **Open** All year. **How to get there** (Maps 26 and 33): 18km west of Montélimar via N102. At Buis-d'Aps, D107 towards Viviers; it's 200m from the Château.

We like "The Mall Game" for its very homey atmosphere, the Arlauds' sincerity, and their perfect knowledge of the Ardèche. The many antique wardrobes, the simple but pleasant guest rooms (a few bathrooms are somewhat cramped), the very much lived-in dining and living room contribute to the half-rustic, half-artistic charm of the house. A small disappointment, however: the neglected look of the outside, which we hope will soon be improved.

642 - Le Couradou

07150 La Bastide-de-Virac
(Ardèche)
Tel. 04 75 38 64 75
Fax 04 75 38 68 26
Annie and Xavier Destrade
E-mail: lecouradou@wanadoo.fr

Rooms 6 with bath and WC. **Price** 475-750F/72,41-114,33€ (2 pers.); 3rd pers. +125F/19,05€, 725F/110,52€ (4 pers.). **Meals** Breakfast incl. Evening meals at communal table 180 or 270F/27,44 or 41,16€ (aperitif, wine and coffee incl.). **Facilities** Sitting room, swimming pool, theme weekends (list on request). **Pets** Dogs allowed on request. **Nearby** Hiking; gorges of the Ardèche, caves. **Spoken** English, Spanish. **Closed** Dec 1 – Jan 31, by reservation 48 hours in advance from Nov 15 to Mar 15. **How to get there** (Map 33): 8km northeast of Barjac via D979 towards Vallon Pont-d'Arc, then on right to Labastide-de-Virac; 500m before the village.

Overlooking a small back road, this highly renovated house enjoys a wonderful view over hills, fields and vineyards. The garden is filled with flowers but the swimming pool opposite the front door is sadly lacking in space. However, the interior makes up for it, with vaulted rooms on the ground floor, a cheerful and personalized decor, well-chosen furniture (each room has a theme), excellent amenities. A great success due largely to the youthful atmosphere, friendly and full of humor.

643 - Mounens

07270 Lamastre ·
(Ardèche)
Tel. 04 75 06 47 59
Max Dejour and
Mayèse de Moncuit-Dejour
E-mail: max.dejour@wanadoo.fr

Rooms 4 with bath or shower and WC. Rooms cleaned on request. **Price** 360-380F/54,88-57,93€ (2 pers.), +100F/15,24€ (extra bed). **Meals** Breakfast incl. Meals at communal table 120F/18,29€ (wine incl.). **Facilities** Sitting room, swimming pool. **Pets** Dogs not allowed. **Nearby** 18-hole golf (35km), tennis, fishing, riding, hiking; Le Mastrou touristic train, villages (Desaigues, Chalencon), châteaux. **Credit cards** Not accepted. **Spoken** English, Spanish. **Open** Easter – Nov 11. **How to get there** (Map 26): 6km south of Lamastre via D578 towards Le Cheylard. After Lapras, straight ahead for 800m; on left, take small uphill road; signs Mounens.

Mounens consists of two old houses on a hillside, connected by a lovely flower garden. One house has just been renovated for guests and is beautifully tasteful and comfortable with lovely printed cottons, elegant antique furniture, thick carpets and watercolors. Breakfast and dinner are served on the terrace when the weather is fine. This part of the Ardèche is particularly beautiful with its gentle hillsides covered with chestnut trees, terraced farms and verdant orchards.

644 - Chez Marcelle et Jean-Nicolas Goetz

07000 Pourchères
(Ardèche)
Tel. 04 75 66 81 99
M. and Mme Goetz

Rooms 3 with shower and WC. Rooms cleaned every 4 days. **Price** 460-530F/70,12-80,79€ (2 pers., with half board), +170F/25,91€ (extra pers.). Special rates for children under 5. **Meals** Evening meals at communal or separate tables. Vegetarian meals possible. **Pets** Well-behaved dogs allowed. **Credit cards** Not accepted. **Spoken** English, German. **Closed** 15 days in winter and 15 days mid-season. **How to get there** (Map 26): at Privas head for Les Ollières, at Petit Tournon 2nd left towards Pourchères; signs. **No smoking.**

This old house is built on a lava flow that is today covered with flowers. The dark stone contrasts with the verdant countryside. The bedrooms are modest but pleasant, and cool in summer (but avoid La Papesse room). Good dinners based on excellent regional products are served in a very charming room or outdoors in good weather. The view is superb from all vistas and the atmosphere will please those who love traditional Ardèche.

645 - La Désirade

07340 Saint-Désirat
(Ardèche)
Tel. 04 75 34 21 88
M. and Mme Meunier
E-mail: la-desirade@wanadoo.fr

Rooms 6 with bath or shower and WC. Rooms cleaned on request. **Price** 250F/38,11€ (2 pers.), +100F/15,24€ (extra bed). **Meals** Breakfast incl. Evening meals at communal table or not 95F/14,48€ (wine not incl.). **Facilities** Sitting room, tel.-metter. **Pets** Dogs allowed on request. **Nearby** Paragliding, mountain bikes, tennis, hiking, hot-air balloon, lakes, riding, 18-hole golf course; Alambic Museum and Wine House in village, Canson museum. **Spoken** English. **Open** All year. **How to get there** (Map 26): 70km south of Lyon. Autoroute A7 exit Chanas, then Annonay. In Serrières, towards Montpellier, Marseille via RN86 then follow signs.

Located at the entrance to the village of Saint-Désirat, this beautiful 19th-century house is surrounded by the Saint-Joseph vineyards which thrive on the surrounding hillsides. Inside, the walls are covered with fabric or painted in a variety of bright colors (somewhat violent in the Bleue room). The youthful, cheerful style is in perfect harmony with the Meuniers' charming hospitality. The bedrooms are simple and well kept, and the delicious table d'hôte dinners are served in a lovely small dining room.

646 - Le Moulinage Chabriol

Chabriol Bas
07190 Saint-Pierreville
(Ardèche)
Tel. 04 75 66 62 08
Fax 04 75 66 65 99
Lize and Ed de Lang
E-mail: chabriol@infonie.fr
Web: www.chabriol.com

Rooms 6 with shower and WC. **Price** 295-350F/44,97-53,35€ (2 pers.). **Meals** Breakfast incl. No communal meal. Kitchen on request. **Facilities** Sitting room (with fireplace), river fishing and swimming. **Pets** Animals not allowed. **Nearby** Restaurants (4-10km), hiking, bicycling, tennis. **Spoken** English, German, Dutch. **Open** All year, by reservation. **How to get there** (Map 26): 35km west of La Voulte. Autoroute A7, exit Loriol, then La Voulte and D120 towards Le Cheylar. In Saint-Sauveur-de-Montagu, D102 towards Alban. 4km before Alban. **No smoking** in bedrooms.

This old spinning mill is set on the edge of a small, clear river where you can swim, and where terraced fields and chestnut groves rise on either side. The very hospitable owners have decorated the Moulinage in a modern, deliberately spare style. An exhibit of photos entitled "The Silk Industry" is permanently on exhibit here. There are grey-tiled floors, white or exposed-stone walls, twin beds covered with colorful eiderdowns, and very pleasant, immaculately kept baths. Far from the traditional Ardèche style, Chabriol is the soul of simplicity and makes its past come alive.

647 - Domaine de Combelle

Asperjoc
07600 Vals-les-Bains
(Ardèche)
Tel. 04 75 37 62 77
Isabelle Meynadier

Rooms 5 with bath or shower and WC. **Price** 320-420F/48,78-64,09€ (1 pers.), 360-460F/54,88-70,12€ (2 pers.), +80F/12,19€ (extra pers.). Special rates for long stays. **Meals** Breakfast incl. Communal meal, by reservation. **Facilities** Sitting room, tel., swimming pool, small fitness room, game room, ping-pong, pony. **Pets** Dogs allowed on request (+35F/5,33€). **Nearby** Golf, skiing, riding, fishing, tennis, canoeing, mountain bikes; game, photography and documentary festivals; Gorges de l'Ardèche. **Credit cards** Not accepted. **Open** All year. (Nov 15 – Feb 28, by reservation). **How to get there** (Maps 25 and 26): 1.5km from center of Vals-les-Bains, towards Antraigues via D578, on left, take the private bridge.

You cross a small bridge over the swift currents of the Volane in order to reach the Domaine de Combelle, an early 19th-century house hidden in a grove of trees, its gardens and terraces climbing up the slope. The interior decoration and antique patinas have been scrupulously conserved. The bedrooms are elegant and have antique furniture (except for the "Familiale," which is more ordinary). There is a natural and relaxed hospitality.

648 - Ferme de Prémauré

Route de Lamastre
07240 Vernoux-en-Vivarais
(Ardèche)
Tel. and fax 04 75 58 16 61
Jeannine and Jean-Claude Gonzalez

Rooms 6 and 1 suite with bath or shower and WC. Rooms cleaned every 2 days. **Price** Rooms 320F/48,78€ (2 pers.), +105F/16€ (extra pers.); suite 420F/64,02€ (2 pers.), 465F/70,88€ (3 pers.), 590F/89,94€ (4 pers.). **Meals** Breakfast incl. Evening meals at communal table or not 100F/15,24€ (wine not incl.). **Facilities** Sitting room, swimming pool, stabling, theme weekends (spring and autumn). **Pets** Dogs allowed on request. **Nearby** Golf, swimming pool, tennis, millpond. **Credit cards** Not accepted. **Spoken** English, German, Spanish. **Open** Mar 1 – Nov 15. Or the weekend on request. **How to get there** (Map 26): Autoroute exit Valence-Nord or Sud then towards Saint-Peray-Le Puy. In Vernoux, go 8km on the Lamastre road, (D2); lane with signs on right

Clinging to the hillside, this old farmhouse has an exceptional view over the Ardèche mountains. The bedrooms are small and sometimes a bit dark but the space all around offers treasures for your leisure enjoyment (swimming pool, cozy nooks for reading, play areas for children). Meals are served in a sitting-dining room or on the flower-decked terrace in warm weather. For simple holidays in a natural setting.

649 - L'Eygalière

Quartier Coussaud
26300 Alixan
(Drôme)
Tel. 04 75 47 11 13
Fax 04 75 47 13 35
Jacques and Renée Crammer
E-mail: jcrammer@easynet.fr

Rooms 3 with bath or shower and WC. **Price** 350F/53,35€ (2 pers.). **Meals** Breakfast incl. **Facilities** Sitting room (TV), swimming pool. **Nearby** Tennis, golf, riding; Mozart Festival (Saou), Bach Festival (Saint-Donat), jazz (Crest and Vienne), the Vercors, the Ardèche. **Spoken** English. **Closed** Nov 3 – Mar 1, except for long stay. **How to get there** (Map 26): 8km south of Romans. Autoroute A7, exit Tain-l'Hermitage, towards Romans, then Chanos-Curson, towards Châteauneuf-sur-Isère to Alixan. In Alixan via D101, take towards Besayes for 500m, then on left for 100m; follow signs.

You will find this house on leaving the village of Alixan, just before the open flat country of the Drôme rises into the foothills of the Vercors. We took instant delight in the small garden filled with flowers and two nearby spots for relaxation: around the swimming pool and the covered terrace. Inside, L'Eyglière is lovely and charming, with antique furniture in the comfortable, tastefully decorated bedrooms. Monsieur Crammer presides over the cuisine, while his wife is the flower expert, and both are sure to welcome you in style.

650 - Les Terrasses

Chemin de la Tour
26230 Chamaret
(Drôme)
Tel. and fax 04 75 46 93 57
M. Vansteenberghe

Rooms 2 with bath or shower, WC, and 1 suite (2-4 pers.) with bath and WC. **Price** Rooms 320F/48,78€ (2 pers.), +60F/9,14€ (extra bed); suite 390F/59,45€ (2 pers.), +120F/18,29€ (extra bed). **Meals** Breakfast incl. No communal meal. **Facilities** Sitting room. **Pets** Dogs allowed on request. **Nearby** Restaurant in Grignan (3km), tennis, swimming, riding, hiking, 9-hole golf course (6km); Château Grignan, Vaison-la-Romaine, Mont Ventoux, Wine Route, villages. **Open** All year. **How to get there** (Map 33): 30km southeast of Montélimar. Autoroute A7 exit Montélimar-Sud, Grignan road. Just before Grignan, on right D71 to Chamaret.

You will find Les Terrasses at the top of this village, just at the foot of a 12th-century tower. From the rooms, the gardens, and the terraces, you can enjoy a magnificent view out over the old rooftops of Chamaret and the countryside as they are bathed by the sun from morning to evening. There is a spacious, modern living room and the attractive, comfortable bedrooms are furnished in a delightful Mediterranean style. The owner is most hospitable.

651 - Domaine du Grand Lierne

26120 Châteaudouble
(Drôme)
Tel. 04 75 59 80 71
Fax 04 75 59 49 41
M. and Mme Charignon-Champel

Rooms 2 (1-3 pers.) and 2 suites (1 with terrace, sitting room, TV, and 1 suite upstairs) with bath or shower and WC. **Price** Rooms 280F/42,68€, 310-410F/47,25-62,50€; suites 350-450F/53,35-68,60€ (2-3 pers.), 310-530F/47,25-80,79€ (4 pers.). **Meals** Breakfast incl. No communal meal. **Pets** Dogs not allowed. **Nearby** Restaurants (2.5km), golf; Bach festival (summer). **Credit cards** Not accepted. **Spoken** English. **Open** All year. **How to get there** (Map 26): 15km east of Valence via D68 towards Chabeuil; at the traffic circle at the entrance to Chabeuil go towards Romans; at the 2nd traffic circle 1.5km later, go right towards Peyrus; 1st house on the left after "Les Faucons". **No smoking.**

This beautiful house, typical of the Drôme département, has been carefully renovated and decorated with great taste. Family furniture, paintings, old objects and the like confer a classic, refined atmosphere throughout. The children's bedrooms, now turned into guest rooms, are done in the same spirit and one feels right at home in them, although the "rose room" is a bit small. In the summer, raspberries make a delicious addition to the breakfasts, which are attentively prepared by Madame Carignon. They are served in the beautiful dining room, or outdoors in a very sunny spot, which is sheltered from the wind.

652 - Maison forte de Clérivaux

26750 Châtillon-Saint-Jean
(Drôme)
Tel. 04 75 45 32 53
Fax 04 75 71 45 43
M. and Mme Josquin
E-mail: pierre.josquin@kyxar.fr

Rooms 4 with bath or shower and WC. **Price** 260F/39,63€ (1 pers.), 320F/48,78€ (2 pers.), +100F/15,24€ (extra bed), +80F/12,19€ (extra child's bed). **Meals** Breakfast incl. No communal meal. **Pets** Animals not allowed. **Nearby** Restaurants in the village and in Romans, tennis, riding, swimming pool, hiking, golf and skiing; Saint-Antoine abbaye, House of "Le Facteur Cheval", Museum of Shoes, Bach Festival in Saint-Donat. **Spoken** English, German. **Closed** Jan 9 – Feb 9. **How to get there** (Map 26): 9km northeast of Romans (26). In Châtillon-Saint-Jean, take dir. Parnans. After 1km, take on left dir. Saint-Michel then follow signs.

In the hollow of a lovely valley in the Drôme département, this is one of our most beautiful discoveries. Next to the superb 13th-century fortified house stands the 16th-17th-century farmhouse for guests. Renovated with the finest materials used in traditional building, Clérivaux is discreetly elegant, highlighted by a scattering of antique furniture. The bedrooms are comfortably equipped and the baths, with tiles or green Alpine marble, are outstanding. Good breakfasts are served on a terrace full of flowers.

653 - Le Balcon de Rosine

Route de Propiac
26170 Mérindol-les-Oliviers
(Drôme)
Tel. and fax 04 75 28 71 18
M. and Mme Bouchet-Poussier

Rooms 1 with bath, WC, TV (use of adjacent kitchen), and 1 with shower, WC, sitting room, terrace, kitchen, TV and tel. 1 small house with 2 bedrooms and terrace. Rooms cleaned on request. **Price** Rooms 240F/36,58€ (1 pers.), 300F/45,73€ (2 pers.) and 350F/53,35€ (2 pers.), 390F/59,45€ (3 pers.). House 2700-3000F/411,61-457,34€/week, 4 pers., depending on season. **Meals** Breakfast incl. in bedrooms. No communal meal. **Pets** Dogs allowed on request. **Nearby** Restaurant (1km), skiing, tennis, riding; festivals in summer, Vaison-la-Romaine, Wine Route. **Credit cards** Not accepted. **Spoken** English, Italian. **Closed** In Aug. **How to get there** (Map 33): 10km northeast of Vaison-La-Romaine via D938 towards Nyons, then D46 towards Puymeras, then left on D205. In Mérindol D147 towards Propiac for 1km.

Le Balcon de Rosine has an exceptional position overlooking the plain of Ouvèze, with a view of Mont Ventoux. The old farmhouse has a lovely garden and two tastefully decorated bedrooms, which have independent entrances. One of them is located in a small house next door. Breakfast is served on the terrace or in the sitting room. The welcome is friendly and relaxed.

654 - Les Grand'Vignes

26170 Mérindol-les-Oliviers
(Drôme)
Tel. and fax 04 75 28 70 22
Chantal and François Schlumberger
E-mail: lesgrandvignes@libertysurf.fr

Rooms 1 with shower, WC, fridge, and 1 studio with bath, WC, TV and fridge. Adjacent room with washbasin. Rooms cleaned on request. **Price** Rooms 260F/39,63€ (1 pers.), 300F/45,73€ (2 pers.); studio 350F/53,35€ (2 pers.); +80F/12,19€ (extra bed); adjacent room 160F/24,39€ (2 pers.). Poss. of renting an entire wing of the house (by the week). **Meals** Breakfast incl. No communal meal. Summer kitchen at guests' disposal. **Facilities** Swimming pool. **Pets** Well-behaved dogs allowed. **Nearby** Restaurant (100m). **Credit cards** Not accepted. **Spoken** English, Spanish. **Open** All year. 2 nights min. **How to get there** (Map 33): In Vaison, D938 towards Nyons then D46 towards Puyméras and D205. In Mérindol, D147; 1st house on the right on the Mollans road.

Amid rolling hills of vineyards and olive groves, this pretty house is comfortable and extremely inviting. The bedrooms are simply and pleasantly decorated, with pale wood furniture and enlivened by brightly colored fabrics that set off the pure white of the walls. Just a few steps away, across a garden full of trees and flowers, is a swimming pool. In fine weather the breakfast table is set up outside in the shade of a cherry tree and looking out over a superb landscape that one never grows tired of admiring.

655 - La Lumière

26170 Mérindol-les-Oliviers
(Drôme)
Tel. 04 75 28 78 12
Fax 04 75 28 90 11
Beth and Peter Miller
E-mail: miller@clubinternet.fr

Rooms 1 studio (2-3 pers.) with bath and WC. Rooms cleaned every 3 days. **Price** 350F/53,35€, +100F/15,24€ (extra bed). **Meals** Evening meals, by reservation 135F/20,58€ (wine incl.). **Facilities** Sitting room, swimming pool. **Nearby** Tennis (in the village); Wine Route, Mont Ventoux, Vaison-la-Romaine, old villages, Toulourenc valley. **Spoken** English. **Closed** Oct 15 – Apr 15, only by reservation. **How to get there** (Map 33): In Vaison D938 towards Nyons, then D46 towards Puyméras and D205. In Mérindol, at the restaurant "La Gloriette", take the small road on right.

A little road winding through vineyards and a pine wood leads to this modern villa nestled in a verdant landscape. A British couple, retired in France, will give you the warmest of welcomes and will take you to the one room they have to let. It is a duplex studio, cheerful and quite comfortable. From the terrace, a path amid the pine trees leads to a discreet and elegant swimming pool. The excellent cooking is a must.

656 - Les Tuillières

26160 Pont-de-Barret
(Drôme)
Tel. and fax 04 75 90 43 91
M. and Mme Jenny
E-mail: h.jen@infonie.fr

Rooms 5 with bath or shower and WC. **Price** 425F/64,79€ (1 pers.), 460F/70,12€ (2 pers.), +125F/19,05€ (extra bed). **Meals** Breakfast incl. Evening meal at communal table or not (except Mon and Thurs) 160F/24,39€ (wine incl.). **Facilities** Sitting room, tel., heated swimming pool, walk. **Pets** Animals not allowed. **Nearby** Tennis, riding, canoes, kayaks, golf. **Spoken** English, German, Italian. **Closed** Oct 5 – Apr 1. **How to get there** (Maps 26 and 33): 24km east of Montélimar. Autoroute A7, exit Montélimar-Nord, then dir. Dieulefit. In Sauzet, D6 dir. Cleon-d'Andran, then D9 to Charols, then D128 on left for 2km. Sign.

Dating partly from the 17th century, this beautiful house is set fairly high up a hillside in Provençal Drôme. Enclosed on three sides, the elegant courtyard/garden overlooks a small, green ravine. The bedrooms are very attractive, comfortable, decorated simply, and they are well kept. The baths are lovely. Monsieur and Madame Jenny are globe trotters who bring an elegant, cosmopolitan ambiance to their dinner table. The beautiful swimming pool is surrounded by nature.

657 - Mas de Pantaï

26230 Réauville
(Drôme)
Tel. 04 75 98 51 10
Fax 04 75 98 58 59
Sergio Chiorino
Web: perso.wanadoo.fr/masdepantai

Rooms 3 (1 for disabled persons) and 1 suite (2-4 pers.) with bath or shower and WC. Rooms cleaned on request. **Price** 480F/73,17€ (2 pers.), 780F/118,91€ (4 pers.). **Meals** Breakfast incl. Communal meals on request 180F/27,44€ (all incl.). **Facilities** Sitting room (music, satellite TV, web), swimming pool. **Pets** Dogs allowed on request. **Nearby** Golf; Grignan, Avignon and Orange Festivals. **Credit cards** Not accepted. **Spoken** Italian. **Open** All year. **How to get there** (Map 33): 20km southeast of Montélimar towards Avignon for about 10km, then turn left towards Grignan for 12km; left again towards Réauville for 2km; signs on right.

Like a veritable siren out of the Odyssey, Sergio Chiorino will thoroughly charm you with his verve and passion for the land where he lives. You will also be charmed by this pale old tiled-roof house snugly enclosed in a shady garden (we do not however recommend the independent lodgings). Surrounding it on all sides is a forest of great oaks, fields of lavender and a splendid view over the Provençal Drôme countryside with, in the distance, Mont Ventoux and the "lacy" peaks of the Dentelles de Montmirail.

658 - Le Buisson

Hameau Le Buisson
26230 Roussas
(Drôme)
Tel. 04 75 98 61 90
Patricia and René Berruyer

Rooms 2 with bath and WC. **Price** 390F/59,45€ (2 pers.), +100F/15,24€ (extra bed); and in summer 1 suite (2 bedrooms, 1 bath, WC) 320F/48,78€ (2 pers.), 550F/83,84€ (4 pers.). **Meals** Breakfast incl. No communal meal. **Facilities** Sitting room, swimming pool, tennis, mountain bikes. **Pets** Dogs not allowed. **Nearby** Restaurants, 18-hole golf course (15km); Wine Route, Château de Grignan. **Spoken** English. **Open** Easter – end Oct. **How to get there** (Map 33): 15km south of Montélimar. Autoroute A7 exit Montélimar-Sud, then Grignan road. In Roussas, take towards Aiguebelle (D203); house 2km after Roussas.

This entirely renovated old house stands just off a small road in the midst of a typical hilly landscape of southern France. You will surely appreciate, as we did, the warm welcome of René and Patricia Berruyer, who are simple, open and always ready to help. Each of the two rooms has its own front door. The one we prefer is "Poteries" – large, sober, elegant and gay, but the other, "Bleue," is also nice. Fine landscape of gardens and terraces, with a swimming pool just down the hill.

+44 7802 090100

Mobile + *

*

8705

2 later

8705 214000

659 - Les Aubes

26450 Roynac
(Drôme)
Tel. 04 75 90 43 92
Fax 04 75 90 44 92
Mme Sparks

Rooms 5 (1 for disabled pers.) with bath or shower and WC. **Price** 380F/57,93€ (2 pers.), +130F/19,81€ (extra bed). **Meals** Breakfast incl. Evening meals at communal table (5 days a week) 140F/21,34€ (wine incl.). **Facilities** Sitting room (fireplace), metered telephone, swimming pool with jaccuzi, boules. **Nearby** Golf (15km). **Spoken** English. **Open** All year. **How to get there** (Map 26): 20km northeast of Montélimar via D6 to Cléon-d'Andran, then D113, towards Roynac. 2km of Cléon-d'Andran, take on left "Les Aubes" road.

An old farmhouse set in the plain of the Drôme département, Les Aubes has just been converted into a bed and breakfast, adding modern amenities to the bedrooms and the baths. Decorated in elegant pastel shades, the rooms are cheerful and harmoniously furnished. The attractive dining room has been redecorated with stylish rattan and wrought-iron furniture. The cuisine – breakfast and dinner alike – is excellent.

660 - Mas de Champelon

Hameau de Saint-Turquois
26790 Suze-la-Rousse
(Drôme)
Tel. 04 75 98 81 95
Christiane and Michaël Zebbar

Rooms 4 with basin, WC (1 has private terrace). **Price** 250F/38,11€ (2 pers.). **Meals** Breakfast incl. Half board 220F/33,53€/pers. in double room. Evening meals at communal table. **Pets** Dogs not allowed. **Nearby** Gorges of the Ardèche, châteaux of Suze-la-Rousse and Grignan, Vaison-La-Romaine. **Credit cards** Not accepted. **Open** Apr 4 – Sept 30. **How to get there** (Map 33): From Bollène head towards Nyons; at Suze-la-Rousse towards Saint-Paul-Trois-Châteaux and Grignan via D117; the house is at the beginning of Saint-Turquois.

This small traditional farmhouse, very peaceful and completely renovated, is set back from the road and hidden between rows of vines and a small forest. The simple, comfortable bedrooms are hung with Provençal fabrics and overlook a flowering garden; each has a modern shower. Breakfast is generally served outside in the shade and includes a large choice of homemade preserves; the evening meals, based on local recipes, are very good. There is a friendly, family-style atmosphere.

661 - La Souche

Quartier Péquimbert
26460 Truinas
(Drôme)
Tel. 04 75 53 31 03
Fax 04 75 53 37 75
Mme Archer
E-mail: rapanello@wanadoo.fr

Rooms 1 with private showers, WC, and 1 with private shower, shared WC, and 1 suite with shower and WC. **Price** Rooms 300F/45,73€ (2 pers.), 360F/54,88€ (3 pers.) and 200F/30,48€ (1 pers.), 280F/42,68€ (2 pers.); suite 500F/76,22€ (4 pers.) to 600F/91,46€ (5 pers.). **Meals** Breakfast incl. Meals on request at communal or separate tables 120F/18,29€. **Facilities** Sitting room, tel. **Pets** Dogs allowed on request. **Nearby** Swimming pool, tennis, riding, mountain biking, rock climbing in Saou; Grignan, Saou Forest, Poët-Laval, jazz festival in Crest. **Credit cards** Not accepted. **Spoken** English, Italian. **Open** All year, only by reservation. **How to get there** (Maps 26 and 33): 9km northwest of Dieulefit towards Bourdeaux for about 7km, then sign on left for "La Souche", D233 towards Lovier.

At the end of a small road that crosses the valleys, a big, solid, inviting house awaits you at La Souche, with its unsurpassed view of the magnificently beautiful countryside. The bedrooms are arranged simply but tastefully, meals are prepared with products from the farm, and the bread is baked in the old bread oven. Giulia Archer's friendly hospitality will help you enjoy a relaxing stay in these beautiful surroundings.

662 - Les Volets Bleus

26460 Truinas
(Drôme)
Tel. 04 75 53 38 48
Fax 04 75 53 49 02
Pilar and Carlo Fortunato
E-mail: lesvolets@aol.com
Web: www.guideweb.com/provence/
chambres-hotes/volets-bleus

Rooms 5 with shower and WC. **Price** 260F/39,63€ (1 pers.), 300F/45,73€ (2 pers.), +70F/10,67€ (extra bed). **Meals** Breakfast incl. Evening meals at communal table or not 125F/19,05€ (wine incl.). **Facilities** Lounge, tel. possible, children's games. **Pets** Dogs allowed in some conditions (+30F/4,57€/day). **Nearby** Swimming pool, tennis, riding, mountain climbing; festivals, Provençal markets, châteaux. **Spoken** English, Spanish, Italian. **Open** All year. **How to get there** (Maps 26 and 33): 9km northwest of Dieulefit in dir. Bourdeaux for about 9km; turn left D192 dir. Truinas. House 900m farther. Signs.

Nestling in the hills surrounded by vegetation that already has the fragrance of Provence, this multi-colored house could be misleading from its façade. However, Madame Fortunato has put great talent into decorating her comfortable guest rooms with charming details and beautiful color schemes, all creating a cheerful, quiet, and very lovely atmosphere. Delicious dinners and breakfasts are served outdoors or in the pretty dining room.

663 - La Bruyère

La Bruyère
38490 Les Abrets
(Isère)
Tel. 04 76 32 01 66
Fax 04 76 32 06 66
M. and Mme Chavalle-Revenu

Rooms 4 and 2 suites (4 pers.) with bath and WC (TV on request). **Price** 350F/53,35€ (1 pers.), 450F/68,60€ (2 pers.); suite 500-550F/76,22-83,84€ (2 pers.); +100F/15,24€ (extra bed). **Meals** Breakfast incl. Communal meals, by reservation 200F/30,48€ (aperitif and wine incl.). **Facilities** Sitting room, tel., swimming pool. **Pets** Dogs not allowed. **Nearby** Tennis, ponies, 18-hole golf course (40km); lakes (Paladru, Aiguebelette, Le Bourget); La Chartreuse. **Credit cards** Not accepted. **Spoken** English. **Closed** 15 days in Nov. **How to get there** (Map 26): 2km from Abrets towards Autoroute A43; from the center of town, follow signs for "Chambres d'Hôtes".

Located between Savoie and Dauphiné, La Bruyère is an old barn which has unfortunately been too energetically restored. The interior has thus gained in modern comforts what it may have lost in charm, but the modern decoration of the bedrooms and the luxurious and sparkling clean bathrooms are really very nice. Breakfast includes an assortment of bread and pastries and dozens of homemade preserves. That alone makes the stay worthwhile, not to mention the good dinners and the friendly, natural welcome.

664 - La Ferme des Collines

Hameau Notre-Dame
38260 Gillonay
(Isère)
Tel. and fax 04 74 20 27 93
Marie and Jean-Marc Meyer

Rooms 3 and 2 suites (4 pers.) with shower and WC. **Price** 300F/45,73€ (2 pers.), 400F/60,97€ (4 pers., suite), +100F/15,24€ (extra bed). **Meals** Breakfast incl. Meals at communal table 100F/15,24€ (wine incl.). **Facilities** Sitting room; painting and sculpture lessons with professional artists, lake fishing. **Pets** Small dogs allowed on request. **Nearby** Gourmet restaurant (4km), swimming pool, mountain biking, Paladru and Charavines Lakes, tennis; Berlioz Museum, Saint-Antoine Abbey, Facteur Cheval House. **Credit cards** Not accepted. **Spoken** English. **Open** All year. **How to get there** (Map 26): 4km east of La-Côte-Saint-André. In La-Côte-Saint-André, go towards Grenoble, then follow signs in Gillonay.

This hospitable house on the top of a hill overlooks an immense plain that stretches to the banks of the Isère and the edge of the Vercors. The bedrooms are tastefully renovated, with pastel-tinted beams, white or sponge-painted walls and attractive fabrics, either flowered, or in a natural ecru tone. All in all, they are bright and cheery, as is the elegant sitting room well furnished with assorted pieces searched out in antique shops. A nice place for a quiet stay – just take care at night, the old wood floors make your every step audible.

665 - Château de Pâquier

38650 Saint-Martin-de-la-Cluze
(Isère)
Tel. and fax 04 76 72 77 33
M. and Mme Rossi

Rooms 5 with bath and WC. **Price** 250F/38,11€ (1 pers.), 310F/47,25€ (2 pers.), +80F/12,19€ (extra bed). **Meals** Breakfast incl. Evening meals at communal table 90F/13,72€ (wine incl.), 40F/6,09€ (child's menu). **Facilities** Sitting room, parking, ping-pong, mountain bikes, pony (children). **Pets** Small dogs allowed. **Nearby** Swimming pool; music festival in summer. **Credit cards** Not accepted. **Spoken** English, German. **Closed** Nov 1 – Mar, or by reservation. Confirmation with 1 night deposit. **How to get there** (Map 26): 25km south of Grenoble. N75 dir. Sisteron for 20km - level crossing - on left, dir. Saint-Martin-de-la-Cluze then follow signs. **No smoking** in bedrooms.

Rebuilt in the 16th century on the site of an old fortress, this little château combines the charm of yesteryear with modern comfort. The spacious bedrooms all have lovely bathrooms; one is installed in the former chapel, another has a fireplace, a third is very bright and enjoys a wonderful view. There are two new bedrooms (which we did not visit), one of which is a duplex for four persons. Although quite close to Grenoble, the house is in a quiet setting surrounded by nature. Madame Rossi prepares the meals with produce from the garden and serves outdoors when the weather is fine.

666 - Domaine de Champfleury

42155 Lentigny
(Loire)
Tel. and fax 04 77 63 31 43
Mme Gaume

Rooms 1 and 1 suite with 2 rooms. **Price** 350F/53,35€ (2 pers.), 500F/76,22€ (3-4 pers., suite). Possibility special rates. **Meals** Breakfast incl. No communal meal. Picnic table and refrigerator. **Facilities** Sitting room, tennis. **Pets** Dogs allowed on request. **Nearby** Restaurants (2km), millpond, golf; museum (showing local life in the 19th C.) in Ambierle, Abbeys of Bénisson-Dieu and of Charlieu, vineyard. **Spoken** German. **Open** Mar 15 – Nov 15, by reservation in winter. **How to get there** (Map 25): 8km southwest of Roanne. D53 towards Clermont-Ferrand for 8km. In Lentigny, beside the post office. **No smoking** in bedrooms.

There is vacation in the air at this beautiful square house dating from the last century. The two bright bedrooms, one of which can be transformed into a family suite, have immaculate bathrooms. You can relax in a quiet corner beneath the large trees in the park, or you might prefer to play tennis or one of the games at your disposal in the game room. Madame Gaume serves homemade preserves with breakfast and she will surely communicate her passion for the Roanne region, which is full of interesting things to do. The quiet, charming Domaine de Champfleury makes an ideal location for spending several days or more.

667 - Platelin

42370 Renaison
(Loire)
Tel. 04 77 64 29 12
Fax 04 77 62 14 79
Christine and Michel De Bats
E-mail: platelin@aol.com

Rooms 2 (1 for 4 pers. with sitting room and satellite TV) with bath or shower and WC. **Price** 240F/36,58€ (1 pers.), 290F/44,21€ (2 pers.), +50F/7,62€ (extra bed). **Meals** Breakfast incl. Evening meals at communal table or not 95F/14,48€ (regional wine incl.). **Facilities** Sitting room, tel., swimming pool. **Nearby** River (800m), tennis, riding, 9-hole golf course (12km); medieval village of Saint-Haon-le-Chatel, priory of Ambierle and museum, winegrowers of the Roanne coasts region. **Credit cards** Not accepted. **Spoken** English. **Closed** Jan and Feb. **How to get there** (Map 25): 12km of Roanne take dir. Roanne-Renaison airport or dir. Vichy (mountain road). Further details by phone.

This old farmhouse, totally renovated, stands in the middle of the country. In the part reserved for guests, there is a dining room with a mezzanine, where a pleasant sitting room-library has been installed. Here stand two prized possessions – a grand piano and a telescope. All the decoration is bright and youthful, with some nice antique pieces here and there. Comfortable bedrooms are done in pastel colors, set off by pretty checkered fabrics. The shower rooms are impeccable, the vast garden has a swimming pool, and the breakfasts and dinners are excellent. An attractive and inviting place.

668 - Le Plat

42330 Saint-Galmier
(Loire)
Tel. 04 77 54 08 27
Fax 04 77 54 18 94
Mme Catteau and Mme Vernay
"Chez Jacotte and Élia"
E-mail: cafecouettejacotte@minitel.net

Rooms 4 with bath or shower and WC. **Price** 280F/42,68€ (1 pers.), 330-350F/50,30-53,35€ (2 pers.), +100F/15,24€ (extra bed). Special rate from 3 days. **Meals** Breakfast incl. Communal meals for lunch or dinner, on request 120F/18,29€ (wine incl.). **Facilities** 2 sitting rooms, French billiards, tennis (clay court), pétanque. **Nearby** Swimming pool, riding, golf; Lyonnais and Forez mountains. **Credit cards** Not accepted. **Spoken** English, Spanish understood. **Open** All year. **How to get there** (Map 25): Autoroute A72, exit Montrond-Les Bains. In Saint-Galmier, D12 dir. Chazelles-sur-Lyon. At the Citroën garage, on right dir. La Bérinche, then straight on for 3.5km (house with blue shutters and cobbled court).

Le Plat is made up of two buildings joined together by a large central hall, in the traditional style of the region. The original house, which has all the charm of places that have been lived in for generations, is now for guests. It has a kitchen-dining room, a living room and three bedrooms. The former stables, done in ultra modern style, have become the main house. This faces on a pretty walled garden and contains another guest bedroom. The bathrooms have been nicely arranged. Everything has a spacious feel, which helps create a holiday spirit. And the the welcome is pleasant and informal.

669 - L'Échauguette

Ruelle Guy de la Mure
42155 Saint-Jean-Saint-Maurice
(Loire)
Tel. 04 77 63 15 89
M. and Mme Alex

Rooms 3 with bath and WC. Rooms cleaned on request or once/week. **Price** 240F/36,58€ (1 pers.), 290F/44,21€ (2 pers.), +50F/7,62€ (extra bed). **Meals** Breakfast incl. Evening meals at communal table or not, on request 115F/17,53€ (all incl.). **Facilities** Sitting room, library. **Nearby** Tennis, golf, cross-country skiing, small port on the lake; Ambierle abbey, Romanesque church. **Spoken** English, German, Italian. **Open** All year. **How to get there** (Map 25): 15km south of Roanne. Autoroute A72, exit Saint-Germain-Laval towards Roanne via D8 for 15km. In Saint-Maurice, beside the donjon follow signs.

In this lovely medieval village, at the foot of the surrounding hills, stand three small houses overlooking a lake. The pleasant sitting room faces this wonderful panorama, as does the superb kitchen, with its large bay window. You can enjoy the view from the terrace as well (where breakfast is served in summer), and from some of the bedrooms. These have been added recently and are very cheerful, elegantly decorated in modern taste; each one has a living area. This is a fine address and the welcome is smiling and thoughtful.

670 - Domaine du Château de Marchangy

42190 Saint-Pierre-la-Noaille
(Loire)
Tel. 04 77 69 96 76
Fax 04 77 60 70 37
Mme Marie-Colette Rufener

Rooms 2 and 1 suite (4 pers.) with bath, WC, tel. and TV. **Price** 430-530F/65,53-80,79€ (1 pers.), 480-580F/73,17-88,42€ (2 pers.); +80F/12,19€ (children under 10), +130F/19,81€ (extra pers.). **Meals** Breakfast incl. Communal meals 70-150F/10,67-22,86€. **Facilities** Sitting room, swimming pool, bicycle rentals. **Pets** Dogs allowed on request. **Nearby** Tennis, riding, 18-hole golf course hiking; Romanesque churches, Charlieu (medieval village). **Credit cards** Not accepted. **Spoken** English. **Open** All year. **How to get there** (Map 25): 4.5km northwest of Charlieu. Go toward Fleury-la-Montagne for 2km, then straight ahead toward Saint-Pierre-la-Noaille; follow signs.

This little château overlooks a hilly landscape of wood and pastureland where, in springtime, you can watch the newborn calves skip and frolic. It has been tastefully renovated with a good eye for detail and offers three guest bedrooms. These are luminous, refined and very comfortable. You will also enjoy the tasty dinners and breakfasts served in a cozy room with a wood fire in the fireplace. The welcome is particularly warm.

671 - Château de Bois-Franc

69640 Jarnioux
(Rhône)
Tel. 04 74 68 20 91
Fax 04 74 65 10 03
M. and Mme Doat

Rooms 2 suites (1-6 pers.) with bath or shower and WC. **Price** 400-900F/60,97-137,20€ (depending on suite and number of pers.). **Meals** Breakfast incl. No communal meal. **Facilities** Sitting room. **Pets** Dogs allowed on request. **Nearby** Restaurants (8km), 18-hole golf course, tennis, riding. **Credit cards** Not accepted. **Spoken** English, German. **Open** All year. 2 nights min. Nov 15 – Mar 15. **How to get there** (Map 26): 7km west of Villefranche-sur-Saône. Follow dir. Roanne, then D31 towards Chervinges.

Bois-Franc is in the countryside not far from villages constructed of golden stone from the Beaujolais region. The interior still has all its traditional old charm. Ask for the Suite Jaune, which is the most expensive but it is truly magnificent and very well furnished. The Suite Mireille is less comfortable but it has three bedrooms. Breakfast is served in a pretty dining room. There is an immense park.

672 - Les Pasquiers

69220 Lancié / Belleville
(Rhône)
Tel. 04 74 69 86 33
Fax 04 74 69 86 57
M. and Mme Gandilhon-Adelé
E-mail: ganpasq@aol.com

Rooms 4 with bath or shower and WC (TV on request). **Price** 400F/60,97€ (2 pers.), +100F/15,24€ (extra bed). **Meals** Breakfast incl. Evening meals at separate tables 120F/18,29€ (wine not incl.). **Facilities** Sitting room, swimming pool, tennis, bicycles. **Pets** Dogs allowed in 1 room. **Nearby** Fishing (Saône), riding, 18-hole golf course; the wine country of Beaujolais, Romanesque churches (Bourgogne), La Roche-de-Solutré, Cluny. **Spoken** English, German. **Open** All year. **How to get there** (Map 26): 15km south of Mâcon. From north, A6, exit Mâcon-Sud - from south, A6, exit Belleville -, then RN6 to Maison Blanche and Lancié (2km), then Les Pasquiers, on the Place. **No smoking** in bedrooms.

Set in a hamlet surrounded by Beaujolais vineyards, Les Pasquiers is a perfect B&B for families: The Céladon bedroom forms a small suite with a game room where the children can sleep and play to their heart's desire. The verger (orchard) room opening on the garden, has the advantage of being farther away. In good weather, everyone lives around the swimming pool behind the house. In the evening, you can enjoy delicious meals served by candlelight on a covered terrace.

673 - Saint-Colomban Lodge

7, rue du Hêtre-Pourpre
69130 Lyon-Ecully
(Rhône)
Tel. 04 78 33 05 57
Fax 04 72 18 90 80
Annick and Michaël Altuna

Rooms 6 with bath, WC, tel. and TV. **Price** 390-450F/59,46-68,60€ (1 pers.), 490-650F/74,70-99,09€ (2 pers.). **Meals** Breakfast incl. Evening meals on request 160F/24,39€ (wine not incl.). **Facilities** Sitting room, locked parking lot. **Pets** Dogs not allowed. **Nearby** Restaurants (200m), 18-hole golf course (5km), tennis in village, all entertainment in Lyon (5km); visit of Old Lyon, Dombes National Park, Lyon Mountains; gastronomy. **Credit cards** Not accepted. **Spoken** English. **Open** All year. **How to get there** (Map 26): 5km west of Lyon. Autoroute exit Ecully, then Ecully-Centre; after church, go towards Tassin (straight ahead), 2nd street on left (fire station). **No smoking** in bedrooms.

The Saint-Colomban Lodge is a very special place to stay in a residential suburb just outside Lyon. The house is protected by a garden which is very pleasant in good weather. The beautiful bedrooms have ultra-modern conveniences like a direct telephone and satellite television, and lovely bathrooms. There is a tasteful combination of fabrics, eiderdowns and honey-colored English pine furniture. Excellent breakfasts are served at a beautiful table in the salon or outdoors in sunny weather.

674 - La Javernière

69910 Villié-Morgon
(Rhône-Alpes)
Tel. 04 74 04 22 71
Fax 04 74 69 14 44
Mme Roux

Rooms 9 (2 of them can be converted into a suite) with bath or shower and WC. **Price** 470F/71,65€ (1 pers.), 590F/89,94€ (2 pers.), +150F/22,86€ (extra bed after 10 year); suite 1000F/152,44€ (4 pers.), +150F/22,86€ (extra pers.). **Meals** Breakfast 60F/9,14€ (served all morning). No communal meal. **Facilities** Sitting rooms. **Nearby** Restaurants(1km), tennis free (1.5km), hunting, fishing (25km), 2 18-hole golf courses; vineyards of Beaujolais, Romanesque churches, Cluny, music in summer. **Spoken** English. **Closed** Dec 15 – Jan 15, by reservation and confirmation by fax. **How to get there** (Map 26): 7km north of Belleville. Autoroute A6 dir. Belleville, then dir. Beaujeu. In Cercié, at the traffic light, on right dir. Morgon for 4km. Cross Morgon, go 600m, then turn on right and follow signs.

Situated in the middle of the Morgon vineyards, this elegant family home offers nine lovely bedooms adorned with antique furniture and beautiful fabrics. All of them are extremely comfortable and afford a breathtaking view over the open countryside. The grand salon and the terraced garden are added assets to this lovely mansion, which is almost like a hotel. For a stopover that is both refined and relaxing.

675 - Chalet Le Paradou

Prébérard
La Côte-d'Aime
73210 Aime
(Savoie)
Tel. 04 79 55 67 79
Élisabeth and Bernard Hanrard

Rooms 5 with shower and WC. **Price** In half-board: 255F/38,87€ pers. in double room. Weekly package rate, per pers. in double room, from Dec – beg May (full board, ski lifts, ski instructor) 4350F/663,15€. In summer (half board, escorted hiking) 2800F/426,85€. **Meals** Breakfast incl. Communal meals in evening. Cold meal at lunch 35F/5,33€. **Facilities** Sitting room, piano, metered telephone. **Nearby** Mountain biking, skiing. **Spoken** English, German, Italian, Spanish. **Closed** May 1 – Jun 20; and Aug 31 – Dec 1. **How to get there** (Map 27): 18km northeast of Moutiers, then N90 towards Bourg-Saint-Maurice. Exit at Aime, go through town toward the Versant du Soleil for 5km; then just after La Côte-d'Aime, 1st chalet on right on leaving village. **No smoking** in bedrooms.

Perched on a southern Alpine slope, this is an entirely wood-covered chalet of recent construction. Facing it on the other side of the valley are the ski resorts of La Plagne, Les Arcs, Montchavin and others. Bathed in sunshine, redolent of pine, the interior is simple and very pleasant. Bernard, a ski instructor, and Elisabeth organize ski trips to all the sites around and delight their guests with delicious meals in the evening. This is a convivial place, impeccably kept and comfortable.

676 - Le Selué

Le Cernix
73590 Crest-Voland
(Savoie)
Tel. 04 79 31 70 74
Anne-Marie Gressier

Rooms 1 with shower, WC; 2 with washroom and closet, shared bath, shower and WC. **Price** 150F/22,86€ (1 pers.), 260-300F/39,63-45,73€ (2 pers., 1 night), 240-280F/36,58-42,68€ (2 pers., from 3 nights). **Meals** Breakfast incl. No communal meal. **Restaurants** In the village (20m). **Facilities** Sitting room, tel. **Pets** Dogs not allowed. **Nearby** Alpine skiing (ski lift 100 m away) and cross-country skiing, bike rentals, hiking, mountain biking, climbing, riding, hang-gliding (summer and winter); Albertville (25km). **Credit cards** Not accepted. **Open** All year, by reservation. **How to get there** (Map 27): 16km southwest of Mégève via N212. 25km of Albertville.

Located in a quiet village of the Savoy region, this modern chalet has three very comfortable guestrooms which are especially well kept and prettily decorated with beautiful furniture, charming engravings and antique mirrors. The bathrooms also are charming. In the lovely salon, breakfast is served with homemade preserves.

677 - Les Châtaigniers

Rue Maurice-Franck
73110 La Rochette
(Savoie)
Tel. 04 79 25 50 21
Fax 04 79 25 79 97
Anne-Charlotte Rey

Rooms 2, 1 suite and 1 apartment with bath, WC and tel. **Price** Rooms 520F/79,27€ (2 pers.); suite 730F/111,28€ (2 pers.); apart. 930F/141,77€ (2 pers.), 1015F/154,73€ (3 pers.). **Meals** Breakfast incl. served 8:00AM-10:00AM. Dinner obligatory, at separate tables 160-300F/24,39-45,73€ (wine not incl.); theme dinners on request. Half board on request (3 days min.). **Facilities** Sitting room, piano, swimming pool. **Pets** Animals not allowed. **Credit card** Visa. **Spoken** English, German, Italian, Swedish. **Closed** (excep Public Holidays, group or 5 nights) Sept – Jul, from Sun evening to Wed incl.; Jul and Aug every days except Sat noon and Wed noon; 15 days in autumn and 15 days in Jan, by reservation. **How to get there** (Map 27): Autoroute A41, Chambéry/Grenoble, exit Pontcharra, then D925. In La Rochette in front of "Hôtel de Ville" towards Arvillard, 200m on left.

A beautiful, exquisitely decorated family house, a captivating hostess, and a poet-cook combine to make Les Châtaigniers a very special place. On the ground floor there is a ravishingly romantic salon full of lovely objects and curios and next to it, two cozy rooms that form the restaurant where you will have your dinner. The bedrooms are retro, charmingly outmoded but a pleasure to be in. Both breakfasts and dinners are tasty and refined.

678 - Yellow Stone Chalet

Bonconseil
73640 Sainte-Foy-Tarentaise
(Savoie)
Tel. 04 79 06 96 06
Fax 04 79 06 96 05
Nancy Tabardel
E-mail: yellowstone@wanadoo.fr
Web: www.yellowstone@limelab.com

Rooms 3 and 2 suites (4 pers.) with bath or shower, WC and TV. **Price** 550-850F/83,84-129,58€ (2 pers., depending on season), +100-150F/15,24-22,86€ (extra bed). **Meals** Breakfast incl. Evening meals at communal table, except Tues and Fri 185F/28,20€ (all incl.), 75F/11,43€ (child). **Credit Card** Visa. **Facilities** Sitting room, tel., whirlpool bath, sauna. **Nearby** Restaurant (150m), mountain biking, rafting, golf, skiing. **Spoken** English. **Closed** May, Jun, Oct and Nov. **How to get there** (Map 27): 5km southeast of Sainte-Foy-Tarentaise.In Sainte-Foy, towards Val d'Isère. In La Thuile, on left to the station, then follow signs.

This spacious chalet towers above the valley facing impressive Mount Pourri. Imaginatively designed as a bed and breakfast, it offers facilities and amenities of admirable quality. The guest rooms are spacious and elegant, the bathrooms beautiful, the cathedral-like living room is surrounded by a breathtaking terrace, the jacuzzi commands a panoramic view, and the excellent breakfasts and dinners are served in dining room that also has a wonderful view of the mountains. Hospitable owners add a lovely finishing touch.

679 - La Girandole

46, chemin de la Persévérance
74400 Chamonix-Mont-Blanc
(Haute-Savoie)
Tel. 04 50 53 37 58
Fax 04 50 55 81 77
M. and Mme Pierre Gazagnes

Rooms 3 (ground floor on garden with private entrance) which share 2 baths and 2 WCs. Rooms cleaned every day. **Price** 300F/45,73€ (1 pers.), 350F/53,35€ (2 pers.). **Meals** Breakfast incl. No communal meal. **Facilities** Sitting room (TV), library, games, garden, parking. **Nearby** Restaurants, winter and summer sports; walking, excursions to the Aiguille du Midi and the Mer de Glace; musical weeks (summer). **Credit cards** Not accepted. **Open** All year. **How to get there** (Map 27): In Chamonix, take towards Les Moussoux, then Montée des Moëntieux and Persévérance road (5mn by car from town center). **No smoking** in bedrooms.

Clinging to a mountainside at an altitude of 1150 meters, facing the Aiguille du Midi, Mont Blanc, and the Bossons Glacier. From the dining room, entirely glass walled on one side, you can enjoy this breathtaking view. The breakfasts (always excellent) are served facing this wonderful panorama. The bedrooms are small but very pleasant, as is the hospitality offered by Madame and Monsieur Gazagnes. They have an intimate knowledge of the area and will be delighted to help you to explore it.

680 - Les Bruyères

Mercy
74540 Saint-Félix
(Haute-Savoie)
Tel. 04 50 60 96 53
Fax 04 50 60 94 65
Denyse and Bernard L. Betts

Rooms 3 suites (2 pers.) with sitting room area, bath or shower, WC and TV. Small house for rent by week. **Price** 650F/99,09€ (2 pers.), +100F/15,24€ (extra bed). **Meals** Breakfast incl. Communal meals, by reservation 200F/30,48€ (wine incl.) **Facilities** Sitting room, tel., tennis. **Pets** Dogs not allowed. **Nearby** Riding, fishing, paragliding, canoeing, 18-hole golf course (15km), skiing; lakes, Montrottier Château, Hautecombe Abbey. **Credit card** Visa. **Spoken** English. **Open** All year. 2 nights min. **How to get there** (Map 27): 20km south of Annecy via RN201. In Saint-Félix, turn right and follow signs "Chambres d'hôtes". **No smoking.**

Monsieur and Madame Betts left Canada to make their home in this vast house where they have given full reign to their decorative talent and their sense of hospitality. Classic, cheerful, very cozy, verging on romantic, the suites are more than beautiful. All have luxurious bathrooms. Depending on the season, brunches are served in the sitting room or on the terrace, where you will enjoy a panoramic view over the valley and Mont Revard. This is an exceptional bed and breakfast.

681 - La Ferme sur les Bois

Le Biolley
74150 Vaulx
(Haute Savoie)
Tel. 04 50 60 54 50
Fax 04 50 60 52 34
Marie-Christine Skinazy
Web: perso.wanadoo.fr/annecy-attelage

Rooms 2 with shower and WC, 2 with private basins, shared shower and 2 WC. **Price** 220-280F/33,53-42,68€ (2 pers.), +110F/16,76€ (extra bed), +70F/10,67€ (extra child's bed). **Meals** Breakfast incl. Evening meals at communal table 90F/13,72€ (wine incl.), 50F/7,62€/day (children under 10). **Facilities** Sitting room, rides in horse-drawn carriage (supplement), hiking, harnessing lessons (price on request). **Nearby** Sailing (lakes of Annecy), skiing (45km). **Spoken** English. **Closed** Nov 11 – Easter. **How to get there** (Map 27): 15km northwest of Annecy. Autoroute A40 exit Eloise, then N508 towards Annecy. At the exit of La Balme-de-Sillingy D4 to Sillingy then Vaulx (2km).

Commanding a beautiful view from its position on the flank of a hill, this totally renovated Savoyard farmhouse is particularly suitable for families on a sports holiday. Marie-Chritine Skinazy will welcome you enthusiastically and cheerfully. Her guest rooms are well kept and simple (our favorites are Ouest and Sud), with a mountain atmosphere created by pine paneling on most walls. Delicious dinners are served in a spacious living room with a fireplace.

INDEX

HUNTER RIVAGES
4TH EDITION

HOTELS AND
COUNTRY INNS
of Character and Charm
IN FRANCE

• WITH COLOR MAPS AND PHOTOS •

HUNTER RIVAGES
4TH EDITION

HOTELS AND COUNTRY INNS
of Character and Charm
IN ITALY

• WITH COLOR MAPS AND PHOTOS •

HUNTER RIVAGES
3RD EDITION

HOTELS AND COUNTRY INNS
of Character and Charm
IN SPAIN

• WITH COLOR MAPS AND PHOTOS •

HUNTER RIVAGES GUIDES

The Guides Europeans Use.

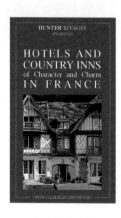

US $ 22.95
ISBN 1–55650–899–9

US $ 19.95
ISBN 1–55650–902–2

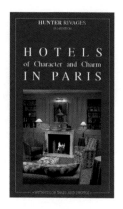

US $ 16.95
ISBN 1–55650–901–4

US $ 22.95
ISBN 1-55650-900-6

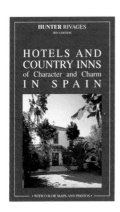

US $ 18.95
ISBN 1-55650-903-0

US $ 16.95
ISBN 1-55650-904-9

Notes

Notes

Printed in Italy
Litho Service (Verona)